Merriam-Webster's
Rhyming
Dictionary

Merriam-Webster, Incorporated
Springfield, Massachusetts

A GENUINE MERRIAM-WEBSTER

The name *Webster* alone is no guarantee of excellence. It is used by a number of publishers and may serve mainly to mislead an unwary buyer.

Merriam-Webster™ is the name you should look for when you consider the purchase of dictionaries or other fine reference books. It carries the reputation of a company that has been publishing since 1831 and is your assurance of quality and authority.

Library of Congress Cataloging-in-Publication Data

Merriam-Webster's rhyming dictionary.
    p. cm.
  ISBN 0-87779-632-7
    1. English language–Rhyme–Dictionaries. I. Title: Rhyming dictionary. II.
  Merriam-Webster, Inc.

PE1519 .M47 2002
423'.1–dc21

2001052192

Printed and bound in the United States of America
1234RRD/H05040302

Explanatory Notes

MERRIAM-WEBSTER'S RHYMING DICTIONARY is a listing of words grouped according to the way they rhyme. The words are drawn from *Merriam-Webster's Collegiate Dictionary.* Though many uncommon words can be found here, many highly technical or obscure words have been omitted, as have words whose only meanings are vulgar or offensive.

Rhyming sound Words in this book are gathered into entries on the basis of their rhyming sound. The rhyming sound is the last part of the word, from the vowel sound in the last stressed syllable to the end of the word. This last stressed syllable may receive either primary or secondary stress. That is, a word may be listed at a given entry either because (1) the rhyming sound begins with the word's most strongly accented syllable or (2) the rhyming sound begins with a following syllable that is only somewhat accented. In this book, the rhyming sound may have one, two, or three syllables.

One-syllable rhyming sounds are found in one-syllable words, as in *wide* \\'wīd\\ (rhyming sound \\īd\\), and in words in which the primary or secondary stress falls on the final syllable, as in *Dundee* \\ˌdən-'dē\\ or *passkey* \\'pas-ˌkē\\, both with rhyming sounds \\ē\\. Other words with one-syllable rhyming sounds are *appeal* \\ə-'pēl\\ (rhyming sound \\ēl\\), *mongoose* \\'män-ˌgüs\\ (rhyming sound \\üs\\), and *undergrad* \\'ən-dər-ˌgrad\\ (rhyming sound \\ad\\).

Two-syllable rhyming sounds are found in words in which the last syllable with primary or secondary stress is the next-to-last syllable in the word. For example, *cola* \\'kō-lə\\ and *remover* \\ri-'mü-vər\\ have two-syllable rhyming sounds. For *cola,* the rhyming sound is \\ō-lə\\, as in *granola* and *Gorgonzola;* for *remover,* it is \\ü-vər\\, as in *louver* and *maneuver.*

Three-syllable rhyming sounds are found in words in which the third syllable from the end carries the stress. *Mutable* \\'myüt-ə-bəl\\ and *frivolity* \\friv-'äl-ət-ē\\ have three-syllable rhyming sounds. For *mutable,* it is \\üt-ə-bəl\\ as in *suitable* and *inscrutable;* for *frivolity,* it is \\äl-ət-ē\\ as in *jollity* and *equality.*

Main entries Main entries in this dictionary consist of an entry form (in boldface type), a pronunciation, and a list of words that rhyme, separated into syllable groupings. The entry form is the most common spelling of the rhyming sound shown in the pronunciation. To find a rhyme for a given word, then, you need to know only the spelling of the word and its rhyming sound. If, for instance, you wanted to find a word to rhyme with *deep,* you would look up **eep,** because that is the way the rhyming sound is spelled. At **eep,** you will find the following entry:

> **eep** \ēp\ beep, bleep, cheap, cheep,
> clepe, creep, deep, heap, jeep, . . .

If the word you wanted to find a rhyme for had been *cheap,* you might have
looked up **eap**, and found the following cross-reference entry:

> **eap** \ēp\ see **eep**

When the same spelling is used for more than one rhyming sound,
superscript numbers are used to alert users to all identically spelled entries.
The user searching for a rhyme for *give,* for example, would look up **ive** and
find the following entries:

> **ive**[1] \īv\ chive, dive, drive, five,
> gyve, hive, I've, jive, . . .
>
> **ive**[2] \iv\ give, live, sheave, shiv,
> sieve, spiv
> forgive, . . .
>
> **ive**[3] \ēv\ see **eave**[1]

The rhyming sound in *give* is pronounced \iv\, so the second entry is the
appropriate one.

Since many words have more than one standard pronunciation, some
words appear in more than one list, and not every word on every list will
rhyme for every person.

An explanation of the pronunciation symbols is found on page ix.

Order of rhyming words The words that follow the boldface entry form
and the pronunciation are separated into groups by number of syllables, from
those with the fewest to those with the most, as shown in the following
example.

> **arten** \ärt-ᵊn\ Barton, carton,
> hearten, marten, martin, Martin,
> smarten, Spartan, tartan
> baum marten, dishearten,
> Dumbarton, freemartin, Saint Martin,
> Sint Maarten
> kindergarten

Cross-reference entries Main entries in this book are supplemented by
cross-reference entries. Like main entries, cross-reference entries have an
entry form and a pronunciation, but in place of a list of rhyming words,
cross-reference entries provide a note that directs the user to a main entry
where the list of rhyming words can be found. The pronunciation in the
cross-reference entry matches the pronunciation shown at the main entry.

The following cross-reference entries, for instance, send the reader to the entry **arten** shown above:

artin \ärt-ᵊn\ see arten

aarten \ärt-ᵊn\ see arten

If a cross-reference entry directs users to an entry that is one of several spelled identically, the superscript identification number ensures that users will find the correct entry:

ieve[1] \iv\ see ive[2]

ieve[2] \ēv\ see eave[1]

Unlisted rhyming words   In order to save space, inflected forms of words have not been listed as entries or included in the lists of rhymes. Inflected forms are those forms that are created by adding grammatical endings to the base word. For instance, the base word *arm,* a noun, is made plural by adding *-s* to form *arms,* and the base word *walk,* a verb, forms its past tense by adding *-ed* to form *walked.* Users must go to entries for the base word in such cases.

In some cases, both inflected and noninflected forms share the same rhyming sounds. For example, the uninflected forms *lox* and *paradox* share the same rhyming sound with the inflected forms *docks* and *socks.* In such cases, only the rhyming uninflected forms are listed, but an italicized note at the end of the entry indicates where the base words of the rhyming inflected forms can be found:

> **ox** \äks\ box, cox, fox, . . .
> —*also* -s, -'s, *and* -s' *forms of
> nouns, and* -s *forms of verbs, listed
> at* ock[1]

Such notes have been added whenever two or more rhyming words could be created by adding endings to the base words at the entry. (If only one such rhyme could be created, it has simply been added to the list.)

Other rhyming words that may not be listed are derived words. Like an inflected word, a derived word is one to which an ending has been added; however, a derived word generally represents a different part of speech from its base word. For instance, when *-ly* is added to the adjective *quick,* the derived word, *quickly,* is an adverb; likewise, when *-ness* is added to the adjective *glad,* the derived word, *gladness,* is a noun.

There is no entry for a rhyming sound if all the words that would be on the list are regular derived words formed by adding a suffix to words drawn from another list. For instance, there is no entry for **arkly**, because the only rhyming words, *darkly* and *starkly,* are adverbs formed by adding *-ly* to the adjectives found at the entry **ark**. If, however, any of the rhyming words are not derived forms, a complete list is given. The entry **eanly**[1], for instance, is included because among the adverbs at the entry there is also the adjective *queenly,* and, for the purposes of this book, adjectives ending in *-ly* are not treated as regular derived forms.

Editorial acknowledgments *Merriam-Webster's Rhyming Dictionary* is based on *Merriam-Webster's Pocket Rhyming Dictionary* and *Webster's Compact Rhyming Dictionary,* and thus on work done by the editors of those books. It was adapted by Jocelyn White Franklin, with assistance from Robert D. Copeland and Francesca M. Forrest.

Pronunciation Symbols

ə   b*a*n*a*n*a*, c*o*llide, *a*b*u*t

ᵊ   preceding \l\ and \n\, as in batt*le*, mitt*en*, and eat*en*; following \l\, \m\, \r\, as in French tab*le*, pris*me*, tit*re*

ər   f*ur*th*er*, m*er*g*er*, b*ir*d

a   m*a*t, g*a*g, s*a*p

ā   d*ay*, f*a*de, *a*orta

ä   b*o*ther, c*o*t, f*a*ther

aù   n*ow*, l*ou*d, F*au*st

b   *b*a*b*y, ri*b*

ch   *ch*in, na*t*ure \ˈnā-chər\

d   *d*i*d*, a*dd*er

e   b*e*t, p*e*ck, h*e*lp

ē   f*ee*, *ea*sy, med*i*a

f   *f*i*f*ty, *ph*one, rou*gh*

g   *g*o, bi*g*

h   *h*at, a*h*ead

i   t*i*p, ban*i*sh, act*i*ve

ī   s*i*te, b*uy*, den*y*

j   *j*ob, *g*em, ju*dg*e

k   *k*in, coo*k*, a*ch*e

k̲   German i*ch*, Bu*ch*

l   *l*i*l*y, poo*l*

m   *m*ur*m*ur, di*m*

n   *n*o, ow*n*

ⁿ   preceding vowel or diphthong is pronounced with the nasal passages open, as in French

un bon vin blanc \œⁿ-bōⁿ-vaⁿ-bläⁿ\

ŋ   si*ng* \ˈsiŋ\, fi*ng*er \ˈfiŋ-gər\, i*n*k \ˈiŋk\

ō   b*o*ne, kn*ow*, b*eau*

ȯ   s*aw*, *a*ll, c*au*ght

ȯi   c*oi*n, destr*oy*

p   *p*e*pp*er, li*p*

r   *r*ed, ca*r*, *r*a*r*ity

s   *s*ource, le*ss*

sh   *sh*y, mi*ss*ion, ma*ch*ine, spe*ci*al

t   *t*ie, a*tt*ack, la*t*e

th   *th*in, e*th*er

t̲h̲   *th*en, ei*th*er

ü   r*u*le, f*oo*l, *u*nion \ˈyün-yən\, f*ew* \ˈfyü\

ù   p*u*ll, w*ou*ld, b*oo*k

v   *v*i*v*id, gi*v*e

w   *w*e, a*w*ay

y   *y*ard, c*u*e \ˈkyü\, m*u*te \ˈmyüt\

z   *z*one, rai*s*e

zh   vi*si*on, a*z*ure \ˈa-zhər\

\   slant line used in pairs to mark off pronunciations

ˈ   precedes a syllable with primary (strongest) stress

ˌ   precedes a syllable with secondary (medium) stress

-    mark of syllable division

A

a¹ \ä\ aah, ah, baa, bah, blah, bra,
dah, droit, fa, Fra, ha, Jah, Kwa, la,
ma, na, nah, pa, pas, qua, Ra, rah,
schwa, shah, ska, spa
à bas, aba, Accra, aha, Allah,
Armagh, blah-blah, Borgia, bourgeois,
brava, Casbah, chamois, Chang-sha,
Chita, Degas, Dumas, éclat, fa la, faux
pas, fellah, fetah, foie gras, gaga,
galah, Galois, grandma, grandpa, ha-
ha, halvah, Hama, hoo-ha, hoopla,
Hsia, hurrah, huzzah, isba, Issa, Luda,
Marat, markka, mudra, Oita, opah,
orgeat, Oujda, quinoa, pai-hua, paisa,
Para, pasha, patois, pooh-bah, prutah,
pya, San'a, sangfroid, selah, Shema,
sola, supra, tola, Tonghua, Ufa, Utah,
Valois, Vaudois, viva, voilà, whoopla
abaca, Adana, agora, ahimsa, Akita,
aloha, assignat, Aymara, baccarat,
baklava, Bogotá, brouhaha, cervelat,
Chippewa, coup d'état, Cumanà,
Delacroix, entrechat, feria, habdalah,
haftarah, haniwa, Kashiwa, koruna,
Kostroma, la-di-da, Libera, ma-and-
pa, Machida, Malinois, Mardi Gras,
Modena, moussaka, Omaha, Oshawa,
Ottawa, pakeha, panama, Panama,
Paraná, parashah, pas de trois,
persona, picara, pietà, podesta,
polenta, polynya, port de bras,
Quebecois, reseda, rufiyaa, Shangri-la,
tempura, ulema, usquebaugh
Ahvenanmaa, Alma-Ata, ayatollah,
Baha' Allah, caracara, con anima,
coureur de bois, hispanidad, hors de
combat, je ne sais quoi, Karaganda,
Makhachkala, ménage à trois,
phenomena, res publica, sursum
corda, tamandua
Alto Paraná, Haleakala,
Katharevusa, mousseline de soie,
Nishinomiya, pâté de foie gras,
Tokorozawa, Utsunomiya
Afars and the Isas, exempli gratia,
Isthmus of Panama, Novaya Zemlya

a² \ā\ see ay¹

a³ \ȯ\ see aw¹

aa¹ \a\ see ah³

aa² \ä\ see a¹

aachen \ä-kən\ Aachen, lochan

aag \äg\ see og¹

aal¹ \āl\ see ail

aal² \ȯl\ see all

aal³ \äl\ see al¹

aam \äm\ see om¹

aan \an\ see an⁵

aans¹ \äns\ see ance²

aans² \änz\ see onze

aard \ärd\ see ard¹

aari \är-ē\ see ari¹

aaron \ar-ən\ see aron²

aarten \ärt-ᵊn\ see arten

aas \äs\ see os¹

aatz \ätz\ see ots

ab¹ \äb\ see ob¹

ab² \äv\ see olve²

ab³ \ab\ blab, cab, crab, dab, drab,
flab, gab, grab, jab, lab, Lab, Mab,
nab, scab, slab, stab, tab

Ahab, baobab, Cantab, confab,
Moab, prefab, Rajab, rehab, smack-
dab
astrolabe, minilab, pedicab, taxicab

aba \äb-ə\ Kaaba, Labe, PABA,
Saba, Sabah
casaba, djellaba, indaba
Ali Baba, Orizaba, Sorocaba
jaboticaba
Pico de Orizaba

abah \äb-ə\ see aba

abala \ab-ə-lə\ cabala, cabbalah
parabola

abalist \ab-ə-ləst\ cabalist
diabolist

abard \ab-ərd\ clapboard, scabbard,
tabard
—*also* -ed *forms of verbs listed at*
abber[2]

abatis \ab-ət-əs\ abatis, habitus

abbalah \ab-ələ\ see abala

abbard \ab-ərd\ see abard

abbas \ab-əs\ see abbess

abbat \ab-ət\ see abit

abbed[1] \ab-əd\ crabbed, rabid

abbed[2] \abd\ blabbed, stabbed
—*also* -ed *forms of verbs listed at*
ab[3]

abber[1] \äb-ər\ see obber

abber[2] \ab-ər\ blabber, clabber,
crabber, dabber, drabber, gabber,
grabber, jabber, slabber, stabber,
yabber
rehabber
bonnyclabber

abbess \ab-əs\ abbess
Barabbas

abbet \ab-ət\ see abit

abbey \ab-ē\ see abby

abbie[1] \äb-ē\ see obby

abbie[2] \ab-ē\ see abby

abbin \ab-ən\ see abin

abbit \ab-ət\ see abit

abbitry \ab-ə-trē\ see abbittry

abbitt \ab-ət\ see abit

abbittry \ab-ə-trē\ Babbittry,
rabbitry

abble[1] \äb-əl\ bauble, bobble,
cobble, gobble, hobble, Kabul, nobble,
obol, squabble, wabble, wobble

abble[2] \ab-əl\ Babel, babble,
brabble, dabble, drabble, gabble,
grabble, habile, rabble, scrabble
bedabble, hardscrabble
psychobabble, technobabble

abblement \ab-əl-mənt\
babblement, rabblement

abbler \ab-lər\ babbler, dabbler,
gabbler, grabbler, rabbler, scrabbler

abbly \ab-lē\ see ably

abbot \ab-ət\ see abit

abby \ab-ē\ abbey, Abby, blabby,
cabbie, crabby, flabby, gabby, grabby,
scabby, shabby, tabby
kohlrabi, Panjabi, Punjabi

abe[1] \āb\ babe, mabe, nabe
astrolabe

abe[2] \ab\ see ab

abe[3] \ä-bə\ see aba

abel \ā-bəl\ see able

aben \äb-ən\ see obin

aber[1] \ā-bər\ see abor

aber[2] \äb-ər\ see obber

abes \ā-bēz\ see abies

abi[1] \äb-ē\ see obby

abi[2] \əb-ē\ see ubby

abi[3] \ab-ē\ see abby

abia \ā-bē-ə\ labia, Swabia
Arabia
Bessarabia
Saudi Arabia

abian \ā-bē-ən\ Fabian, gabion
Arabian
Bessarabian

abid \ab-əd\ see abbed

abies \ā-bēz\ rabies, scabies, tabes
—*also* -s, -'s, *and* -s' *forms of nouns
listed at* aby

abile \ab-əl\ see abble²

abilis \äb-ə-ləs\ obelus
annus mirabilis

abin \ab-ən\ cabin, rabbin

abion \ā-bē-ən\ see abian

abit \ab-ət\ abbot, babbitt, Babbitt,
Cabot, habit, rabbet, rabbit, sabbat
cohabit, inhabit, jackrabbit

abitant \ab-ət-ənt\ habitant
cohabitant, inhabitant

abitus \ab-ət-əs\ see abatis

able \ā-bəl\ Abel, able, Babel, cable,
fable, Froebel, gable, label, Mabel,
sable, stable, table
disable, enable, instable, pin-table,
retable, round table, timetable,
turntable, unable, unstable, worktable

abled \ā-bəld\ fabled, gabled
—*also* -ed *forms of verbs listed at*
able

ablis \ab-lē\ see ably

ably \ab-lē\ chablis, drably, scrabbly

abola \ab-ə-lə\ see abala

abolist \ab-ə-ləst\ see abalist

abor \ā-bər\ caber, labor, neighbor,
saber, tabor
belabor, von Weber, zeitgeber

aborer \ā-bər-ər\ laborer, taborer

abot \ab-ət\ see abit

abra \äb-rə\ sabra, Sabra
candelabra

abre \äb\ see ob¹

abul \äb-əl\ see abble¹

abular \ab-yə-lər\ fabular, tabular
vocabular
acetabular

abulous \ab-yə-ləs\ fabulous
fantabulous

abulum \ab-yə-ləm\ pabulum
acetabulum, incunabulum

aby \ā-bē\ baby, gaby, maybe
crybaby, grandbaby

ac¹ \ak\ see ack²

ac² \äk\ see ock¹

ac³ \o\ see aw¹

aca¹ \äk-ə\ see aka¹

aca² \ak-ə\ Dacca, Dhaka, paca
alpaca, malacca, Malacca, sifaka
portulaca
Strait of Malacca

acable \ak-ə-bəl\ see ackable

acao \ō-kō\ see oco

acas \ak-əs\ Bacchus, fracas,
Gracchus
Caracas

acca¹ \ak-ə\ see aca

acca² \äk-ə\ see aka¹

accent \ak-sənt\ accent
relaxant

acchanal \ak-ən-ᵊl\ see aconal

acchic \ak-ik\ bacchic
halakic, stomachic, tribrachic
amphibrachic

acchus \ak-əs\ see acas

accid \as-əd\ see acid

accio \ä-chē-ō\ bocaccio, Bocaccio, carpaccio

acco¹ \ak-ə\ see aca

acco² \ak-ō\ see ako²

acculus \ak-yə-ləs\ sacculus
miraculous

ace¹ \ās\ ace, base, bass, brace, case, chase, dace, face, grace, Grace, lace, mace, Mace, pace, place, plaice, prase, race, res, space, Thrace, trace, vase
abase, airspace, Alsace, ambsace, apace, backspace, best-case, biface, birthplace, blackface, boldface, bookcase, bootlace, braincase, briefcase, crankcase, debase, deface, disgrace, displace, dogface, doughface, efface, embrace, emplace, encase, enchase, enlace, erase, firebase, fireplace, footpace, footrace, foreface, gyrase, half-space, hard case, headspace, Jerez, lightface, manes, millrace, milreis, misplace, notecase, null-space, outface, outpace, outrace, paleface, postface, Quilmes, replace, retrace, scapegrace, shoelace, showcase, showplace, slipcase, smearcase, someplace, staircase, subbase, subspace, suitcase, surbase, tailrace, tenace, typeface, ukase, unbrace, unlace, watchcase, wheelbase, whey-face, whiteface, workplace, worst-case
about-face, aerospace, anyplace, boniface, bouillabaisse, carapace, commonplace, contrabass, double-space, everyplace, interface, interlace, kilobase, lemures, lowercase, marketplace, pillowcase, Samothrace, single-space, steeplechase, thoroughbass, thoroughbrace, triple-space, uppercase
rarae aves
beta-lactamase, in medias res
Aguascalientes
Goya y Lucientes, superoxide dismutase
litterae humaniores

ace² \ā-sē\ see acy

ace³ \äs\ see os¹

ace⁴ \as\ see ass³

ace⁵ \äch-ē\ see otchy

ace⁶ \äs-ə\ see asa¹

aceable \ā-sə-bəl\ placeable, traceable
displaceable, effaceable, embraceable, erasable, persuasible, replaceable
ineffaceable, irreplaceable

acean \ā-shən\ see ation¹

aced \āst\ based, baste, chaste, faced, geest, haste, laced, mayest, paste, taste, waist, waste
bald-faced, barefaced, bold-faced, distaste, dough-faced, foretaste, impaste, lambaste, lightfaced, moonfaced, pie-faced, po-faced, posthaste, rad waste, self-paced, shamefaced, shirtwaist, snail-paced, slipcased, stone-faced, straight-faced, straitlaced, toothpaste, two-faced, unchaste, unplaced, white-faced
aftertaste, brazen-faced, double-faced, Janus-faced, hatchet-faced, pantywaist, poker-faced, thorough-paced
—also -ed forms of verbs listed at ace¹

aceless \ā-sləs\ baseless, faceless, graceless, laceless, placeless, spaceless, traceless

aceman \ā-smən\ baseman, placeman, spaceman

acement \ā-smənt\ basement, casement, placement
abasement, debasement, defacement, displacement, effacement, embracement, emplacement, encasement, enlacement, misplacement, outplacement, replacement
self-effacement

acence \ās-ᵊns\ see ascence¹

acency \ās-ᵊn-sē\ adjacency, complacency, subjacency

acent \ās-ᵊnt\ nascent
adjacent, complacent, complaisant, subjacent
circumjacent, superjacent

aceor \ā-sər\ see acer[1]

aceous \ā-shəs\ see acious

acer[1] \ā-sər\ baser, bracer, chaser, facer, pacer, placer, racer, spacer, tracer
defacer, disgracer, effacer, embraceor, embracer, eraser, replacer, subchaser
steeplechaser

acer[2] \as-ər\ see asser

acery \ās-rē\ tracery
embracery

acet[1] \ā-sət\ hic jacet, non placet

acet[2] \as-ət\ asset, facet, tacet, tacit

acewalking \ās-wȯ-kiŋ\ racewalking, spacewalking

acey \ā-sē\ see acy

ach[1] \äk\ Bach, saugh
Pesach, pibroch
Offenbach
Mönchengladbach

ach[2] \äk\ see ock[1]

ach[3] \ak\ see ack[2]

ach[4] \ach\ see atch[4]

acha \äch-ə\ cha-cha, dacha, kwacha
viscacha

achary \ak-ə-r-ē\ see ackery[2]

ache[1] \āk\ see ake[1]

ache[2] \ash\ see ash[3]

ache[3] \äch-ē\ see otchy

ache[4] \ach-ē\ see atchy

acheal \ā-kē-əl\ brachial, tracheal

ached \acht\ attached, detached
unattached
semidetached
—also -ed forms of verbs listed at atch[4]

acher \ā-kər\ see aker[1]

achet \ach-ət\ see atchet

achi \äch-ē\ see otchy

achial \ā-kē-əl\ see acheal

achian \ā-shən\ see ation[1]

achic \ak-ik\ see acchic

aching \ā-kiŋ\ see aking[1]

achio[1] \ash-ō\ mustachio, pistachio

achio[2] \ash-ē-ō\ mustachio, pistachio

achm \am\ see am[2]

achment \ach-mənt\ see atchment

achne \ak-nē\ see acne

acho \äch-ō\ muchacho, quebracho

achou \ash-ü\ see ashew

achsen \äk-sən\ see oxen

acht \ät\ see ot[1]

achtsman \ät-smən\ see otsman

achy \ā-kē\ see aky

acia \ā-shə\ Dacia, fascia, geisha
acacia, Croatia, Dalmatia, ex gratia, Galatia
prima facie
exempli gratia

acial \ā-shəl\ facial, glacial, racial, spatial
abbatial, bifacial, biracial, englacial, palatial, primatial, subglacial
interfacial, interglacial, interracial, multiracial

acian \ā-shən\ see ation[1]

acias \ā-shəs\ see acious

acid \as-əd\ acid, Chasid, flaccid, Hasid, jassid, placid
Abbasid, antacid

acie \ā-shə\ see acia

acient \ā-shənt\ see atient

acier¹ \ā-shər\ see asure¹

acier² \ā-zhər\ see azier

acile \as-əl\ see assel²

acing \ā-siŋ\ bracing, casing, facing, lacing, racing, spacing, tracing
catfacing, effacing
all-embracing, interfacing, letterspacing, self-effacing
—*also* -ing *forms of verbs listed at* ace¹

acious \ā-shəs\ gracious, spacious
audacious, bodacious, capacious, ceraceous, cretaceous, crustaceous, curvaceous, edacious, fallacious, flirtatious, fugacious, herbaceous, Horatius, Ignatius, loquacious, mendacious, mordacious, pomaceous, predaceous, pugnacious, rapacious, sagacious, salacious, sebaceous, sequacious, setaceous, tenacious, testaceous, ungracious, veracious, vexacious, vinaceous, vivacious, voracious
alliaceous, arenaceous, argillaceous, carbonaceous, contumacious, coriaceous, disputatious, efficacious, farinaceous, fieri facias, foliaceous, ostentatious, pectinaceous, perspicacious, pertinacious, saponaceous, scire facias, stercoraceous, violaceous
inefficacious

acis \as-ē\ see assy

acist \ā-səst\ see assist

acit \as-ət\ see acet²

acity¹ \as-tē\ see asty²

acity² \as-ət-ē\ audacity, capacity, fugacity, loquacity, mendacity,
opacity, rapacity, sagacity, tenacity, veracity, vivacity, voracity
efficacity, incapacity
overcapacity

acive \ā-siv\ see asive

ack¹ \äk\ see ock¹

ack² \ak\ back, black, clack, claque, crack, flack, flak, hack, jack, Jack, knack, lac, lack, mac, Mac, Mack, pack, plaque, quack, rack, sac, Sac, sack, sacque, shack, slack, smack, snack, stack, tach, tack, thwack, track, Wac, whack, wrack, yak
aback, ack-ack, alack, amtrac, Anzac, Arak, attack, backpack, backtrack, Balzac, bareback, blackjack, blue-black, bootblack, bootjack, brushback, bushwhack, buyback, callback, calpac, champac, cheapjack, Coalsack, coatrack, cognac, come back, comeback, cookshack, cossack, crackback, crookback, cut back, cutback, Dayak, dieback, draw back, drawback, fall back, fallback, fastback, fast-track, fatback, feedback, finback, fireback, flapjack, flareback, flashback, fullback, gimcrack, graywacke, greenback, gripsack, guaiac, halfback, half-track, hardback, hardhack, hardtack, hatchback, hayrack, haystack, hijack, hogback, hold back, holdback, hopsack, horseback, humpback, hunchback, Iraq, jam-pack, jet-black, kayak, Kazak, kickback, knapsack, knickknack, Kodak, kulak, kyack, laid-back, lampblack, leaseback, linac, macaque, man jack, manpack, Micmac, mossback, muntjac, Muzak, notchback, offtrack, outback, packsack, payback, pitch-black, play back, playback, plow back, plowback, pullback, quillback, racetrack, ransack, rickrack, roll back, rollback, roorback, rucksack, runback, scatback, serac, set back, setback, shellac, shellback, shoeblack, shoepac, sidetrack, six-pack, skewback,

skipjack, skyjack, slapjack, slotback, Slovak, smokejack, smokestack, snap back, snapback, snowpack, softback, sumac, swayback, sweepback, swept-back, switchback, tailback, tarmac, thornback, throw back, throwback, thumbtack, ticktack, tieback, tie tack, tombac, touchback, tow sack, trictrac, tripack, unpack, Welsbach, wetback, whaleback, wingback, wisecrack, woolpack, woolsack, yashmak, Yurak, zwieback
 almanac, amberjack, anorak, antiblack, applejack, Arawak, Armagnac, birdyback, bivouac, bric-a-brac, camelback, canvasback, cardiac, carryback, celiac, coeliac, cornerback, Cousin Jack, crackerjack, cul-de-sac, diamondback, fiddleback, fishyback, Frontenac, gunnysack, hackmatack, haversack, high-low-jack, huckaback, hydrocrack, iliac, ipecac, Kodiak, ladder-back, leatherback, lumberjack, maniac, medevac, minitrack, moneyback, nunatak, otomac, paperback, Pasternak, pickaback, piggyback, Pontiac, portapak, quarterback, razorback, retropack, running back, sandarac, Sarawak, Sazerac, silverback, single-track, Skaggerak, snapper-back, solonchak, steeplejack, stickleback, supplejack, Syriac, tamarack, tenure-track, theriac, tokamak, turtleback, umiak, zodiac
 Adirondack, ammoniac, amnesiac, Aniakchak, biofeedback, celeriac, counterattack, demoniac, elegiac, insomniac, Monterey Jack, paranoiac, simoniac, tacamahac
 aphrodisiac, coprophiliac, Dionysiac, dipsomaniac, egomaniac, hemophiliac, hypochondriac, intracardiac, kleptomaniac, melancholiac, monomaniac, mythomaniac, necrophiliac, neophiliac, nymphomaniac, pedophiliac, pyromaniac, Rhodesian Ridgeback, sacroiliac, sal ammoniac
 megalomaniac
 Cyrano de Bergerac

ackable \ak-ə-bəl\ packable, placable, stackable
 implacable

ackage \ak-ij\ package, trackage prepackage, repackage

ackal \ak-əl\ see ackle

acked \akt\ see act

acken \ak-ən\ blacken, bracken, flacon, slacken
 Arawakan

ackened \ak-ənd\ blackened
 —also -ed forms of verbs listed at acken

acker \ak-ər\ backer, clacker, cracker, hacker, jacker, knacker, lacquer, packer, sacker, slacker, smacker, stacker, tacker, tracker, whacker
 attacker, backpacker, bushwhacker, firecracker, hijacker, kayaker, linebacker, nutcracker, racetracker, ransacker, safecracker, shellcracker, skyjacker, unpacker, wisecracker
 simulacre
 counterattacker

ackeray \ak-ə-rē\ see ackery

ackerel \ak-rəl\ see acral

ackery \ak-ə-rē\ flackery, quackery, Thackeray, Zachary
 gimcrackery

acket \ak-ət\ bracket, jacket, packet, placket, racket
 bluejacket, straitjacket
 yellowjacket

ackey \ak-ē\ see acky

ackguard \ag-ərd\ see aggard

ackie \ak-ē\ see acky

acking \ak-iŋ\ backing, blacking, cracking, packing, sacking, smacking, tracking, whacking
 bushwhacking, kayaking, linebacking, meatpacking,

nerve-racking, nerve-wracking, safecracking, skyjacking
—*also* -ing *forms of verbs listed at* ack²

ackish \ak-ish\ blackish, brackish, quackish

ackle \ak-əl\ cackle, crackle, grackle, hackle, jackal, macle, rackle, shackle, spackle, tackle
debacle, gang-tackle, ramshackle, unshackle
tabernacle

ackly \ak-lē\ blackly, crackly, hackly
abstractly, compactly, exactly
inexactly

ackman \ak-mən\ hackman, packman, trackman

ackney \ak-nē\ see acne

ackneyed \ak-nēd\ see acned

acko \ak-ō\ see ako²

acksman \ak-smən\ see axman

ackson \ak-sən\ see axon

acky \ak-ē\ hackie, Jackie, Jacky, khaki, lackey, tacky, wacky
ticky-tacky

acle¹ \ik-əl\ see ickle

acle² \äk\ see ock¹

acle³ \äk-əl\ see ockle

acle⁴ \ak-əl\ see ackle

acne \ak-nē\ acne, hackney, Hackney
Arachne

acned \ak-nēd\ acned, hackneyed

aco \äk-ō\ see occo

acon¹ \ā-kən\ see aken¹

acon² \ak-ən\ see acken

aconal \ak-ən-əl\ bacchanal
diaconal
archidiaconal

acque¹ \ak\ see ack²

acque² \äk\ see ock¹

acquer \ak-ər\ see acker

acques \äk\ see ock¹

acral \ak-rəl\ mackerel, sacral

acre¹ \ā-kər\ see aker¹

acre² \ak-ər\ see acker

acrum \ak-rəm\ sacrum
simulacrum

act \akt\ act, backed, bract, cracked, fact, packed, pact, stacked, tact, tracked, tract
abstract, attract, coact, compact, contact, contract, crookbacked, detract, didact, diffract, distract, enact, entr'acte, epact, exact, extract, half-tracked, humpbacked, hunchbacked, impact, infract, intact, mossbacked, playact, protract, react, redact, refract, subtract, swaybacked, transact, unbacked
abreact, artifact, cataract, chain-react, counteract, cross-react, inexact, interact, overact, paperbacked, precontact, razor-backed, reenact, subcompact, subcontract, underact, vacuum-packed, ventifact
autodidact, matter-of-fact, overreact, semiabstract, underreact
— *also* -ed *forms of verbs listed at* ack²

actable \ak-tə-bəl\ actable, tractable
abstractable, attractable, compactible, contractible, distractable, extractable, intractable

actance \ak-təns\ attractance, reactance

actant \ak-tənt\ attractant, reactant, surfactant
interactant

acte¹ \äkt\ see ocked

acte² \akt\ see act

acted \ak-təd\ fracted
abstracted, impacted
—*also* -ed *forms of verbs listed at* act

acter \ak-tər\ see actor

actery \ak-trē\ see actory

actible \ak-tə-bəl\ see actable

actic \ak-tik\ lactic, tactic
atactic, climactic, didactic, galactic, syntactic
ataractic, chiropractic, parallactic, paratactic, prophylactic
anaphylactic, anticlimactic, autodidactic, extragalactic, intergalactic, intragalactic, stereotactic

actical \ak-ti-kəl\ practical, tactical
didactical, impractical, syntactical

actice \ak-təs\ cactus, practice
malpractice
cataractous

actics \ak-tiks\ tactics
didactics, syntactics
phonotactics
—*also* -s, -'s, *and* -s' *forms of nouns listed at* actic

actile \ak-t³l\ dactyl, tactile
contractile, protractile, refractile, retractile
polydactyl, pterodactyl

acting \ak-tiŋ\ acting
exacting, self-acting
—*also* -ing *forms of verbs listed at* act

action \ak-shən\ action, faction, fraction, taction, traction
abstraction, attraction, bolt-action, coaction, compaction, contraction, detraction, diffraction, distraction, exaction, extraction, impaction, inaction, infraction, olfaction, protraction, reaction, redaction, refraction, retraction, subtraction, transaction
benefaction, counteraction, interaction, liquefaction, malefaction,
overaction, petrifaction, putrefaction, rarefaction, retroaction, satisfaction, single-action, stupefaction, tumefaction
dissatisfaction, photoreaction, self-satisfaction

actional \ak-shnəl\ factional, fractional, tractional
abstractional, contractional, redactional, transactional
interactional, rarefactional

actious \ak-shəs\ factious, fractious

active \ak-tiv\ active, tractive
abstractive, attractive, coactive, contractive, detractive, distractive, extractive, impactive, inactive, proactive, reactive, refractive, subtractive
bioactive, counteractive, hyperactive, interactive, overactive, psychoactive, putrefactive, retroactive, unattractive
radioactive

actly \ak-lē\ see ackly

actor \ak-tər\ actor, factor, tractor
abstractor, attractor, cofactor, compactor, contractor, detractor, enactor, exactor, extractor, g-factor, impactor, infractor, protractor, reactor, redactor, refractor, retractor, subtracter, transactor
benefactor, chiropractor, malefactor, subcontractor
bioreactor, campylobacter

actory \ak-trē\ factory
olfactory, phylactery, refractory
calefactory, manufactory, satisfactory
dissatisfactory, unsatisfactory

actous \ak-təs\ see actice

actress \ak-trəs\ actress
benefactress

actual \ak-chəl\ actual, factual, tactual
artifactual, counterfactual

acture \ak-chər\ facture, fracture
contracture

actus   10

manufacture
remanufacture

actus \ak-təs\ see actice

actyl \ak-tᵊl\ see actile

acular \ak-yə-lər\ macular
oracular, spectacular, spiracular,
tentacular, vernacular
tabernacular

aculate \ak-yə-lət\ maculate
ejaculate, immaculate

aculous \ak-yə-ləs\ see acculus

acy \ā-sē\ Basie, lacy, pace, précis,
racy, spacey, Stacey, Stacy, Tracey,
Tracy
O'Casey
prima facie, Sulawesi, Veronese

acyl \as-əl\ see assel²

ad¹ \ä\ see a¹

ad² \äd\ see od¹

ad³ \ad\ ad, add, bad, bade, brad,
cad, chad, Chad, clad, dad, fad, gad,
Gad, glad, grad, had, lad, mad, pad,
plaid, rad, sad, scad, shad, tad, Thad,
trad
Akkad, aoudad, Baghdad, Belgrade,
Carlsbad, caudad, comrade, Conrad,
crawdad, doodad, dorsad, dryad, dyad,
egad, farad, footpad, forbade, gonad,
granddad, heptad, hexad, horn-mad,
ironclad, keypad, launchpad, maenad,
Mashad, monad, naiad, nicad, nomad,
notepad, pentad, pleiad, Sinbad,
Sindbad, tetrad, thinclad, triad, triclad,
Troad
armor-clad, Ashkhabad, cephalad,
chiliad, ennead, Galahad, hebdomad,
helipad, Hyderabad, laterad, mediad,
oread, overplaid, Pythiad, superadd,
Trinidad, undergrad, Volgograd
Allahabad, bromeliad, gesneriad,
hamadryad, hispanidad, Kaliningrad,
Kirovograd, olympiad, seminomad,
Upanishad
Voroshilovgrad

ada¹ \äd-ä\ Dada
aficionada

ada² \äd-ə\ nada, sadhe, tsade
Agada, Agade, Aggada, armada,
cicada, gelada, Granada, Haggadah,
Jumada, Nevada, panada, posada,
tostada
autostrada, empanada, enchilada,
Ensenada, Theravada
aficionada, Ponta Delgada,
Vijayawada
cascara sagrada, Sierra Nevada

ada³ \ād-ə\ Ada, Veda
armada, cicada, Grenada
alameda
Avellaneda

adable \ād-ə-bəl\ gradable, tradable,
wadable
abradable, degradable, evadable,
persuadable
biodegradable

a'dah \äd-ä\ see ada¹

adah \äd-ə\ see ada²

adal \ad-ᵊl\ see addle

adam \ad-əm\ Adam, madam
macadam
tarmacadam

adams \ad-əmz\ Adams
—also -s, -'s, and -s' forms of nouns
listed at adam

adan¹ \ad-n\ see adden

adan² \äd-n\ see odden

adant \ād-ᵊnt\ cadent
abradant, decadent

add \ad\ see ad³

adden \ad-ᵊn\ gladden, madden,
sadden
Aladdin, Ibadan

adder \ad-ər\ adder, bladder, ladder,
madder
stepladder
—also -er forms of adjectives listed
at ad³

addie \ad-ē\ see addy

addik \äd-ik\ see odic

addin \ad-ᵊn\ see adden

adding \ad-iŋ\ cladding, madding, padding
—*also* -ing *forms of verbs listed at* ad³

addish¹ \äd-ish\ see oddish

addish² \ad-ish\ see adish

addison \ad-ə-sən\ Addison, Madison

addle \ad-ᵊl\ addle, paddle, raddle, saddle, staddle, straddle
astraddle, foresaddle, gonadal, packsaddle, sidesaddle, skedaddle, unsaddle
fiddle-faddle

addler¹ \äd-lər\ see oddler

addler² \ad-lər\ saddler, paddler, straddler
skedaddler

addo \ad-ō\ see adow

addock¹ \ad-ik\ see adic²

addock² \ad-ək\ haddock, paddock, shaddock

addy¹ \ad-ē\ baddie, caddie, caddy, daddy, faddy, laddie, paddy
forecaddie, granddaddy
finnan haddie

addy² \äd-ē\ see ody¹

ade¹ \ād\ aid, aide, bade, blade, braid, cade, clade, fade, glade, grade, jade, lade, laid, made, maid, paid, raid, rayed, shade, spade, stade, staid, suede, they'd, trade, wade, Wade
abrade, afraid, aggrade, arcade, Band-Aid, barmaid, Belgrade, blockade, bondmaid, bridesmaid, brigade, brocade, cascade, Cascade, charade, clichéd, cockade, corrade, cross-trade, crusade, decade, degrade, dissuade, downgrade, evade, eyeshade, fair-trade, forebade, gainsaid, glissade, grenade, handmade, handmaid,

homemade, housemaid, inlaid, invade, limeade, low-grade, man-made, mermaid, milkmaid, navaid, nightshade, nursemaid, outlaid, parade, persuade, pervade, plain-laid, pomade, postpaid, repaid, sacheted, scalade, sea-maid, self-made, shroud-laid, souffléed, stockade, sunshade, switchblade, tirade, torsade, twayblade, twice-laid, unbraid, unlade, unmade, unpaid, upbraid, upgrade, waylaid
accolade, Adelaide, ambuscade, aquacade, autocade, balustrade, barricade, bastinade, cable-laid, cannonade, carronade, cavalcade, centigrade, chambermaid, chiffonade, colonnade, countertrade, custom-made, dairymaid, defilade, enfilade, escalade, escapade, esplanade, everglade, fusillade, gallopade, gasconade, grant-in-aid, hawser-laid, intergrade, lemonade, marinade, marmalade, masquerade, medicaid, motorcade, orangeade, orthograde, overtrade, palisade, pasquinade, plantigrade, promenade, ready-made, renegade, retrograde, serenade, stock-in-trade, tailor-made, underlaid
fanfaronade, harlequinade, overpersuade, rodomontade

ade² \äd\ see od¹

ade³ \ad\ see ad³

ade⁴ \äd-ə\ see ada²

aded \ād-əd\ bladed
arcaded, brocaded, cockaded
colonnaded
—*also* -ed *forms of verbs listed at* ade¹

adeless \ād-ləs\ fadeless, gradeless, shadeless

adely \ad-lē\ see adly

aden¹ \ād-ᵊn\ Aden, laden, maiden
handmaiden, menhaden

aden² \äd-ən\ Aden
Wiesbaden

adent \ād-ᵊnt\ see adant

ader \ād-ər\ aider, braider, cheder, fader, grader, heder, nadir, raider, seder, shader, spader, trader, wader
  blockader, crusader, degrader, dissuader, evader, invader, persuader
  masquerader, serenader

ades[1] \ād-ēz\ ladies, Hades
  quaker-ladies

ades[2] \ādz\ AIDS, Glades
  Cascades
  antitrades, Everglades
  jack-of-all-trades
  —also -s, -'s, and -s' forms of nouns, and -s forms of verbs, listed at ade[1]

adge \aj\ badge, cadge, hajj, Madge

adger \aj-ər\ badger, cadger

adh \äd\ see od[1]

adhe[1] \äd-ə\ see ada[2]

adhe[2] \äd-ē\ see ody[1]

adia \ād-ē-ə\ stadia
  Acadia, arcadia, Arcadia, palladia

adial \ād-ē-əl\ radial
  biradial
  interstadial

adian \ād-ē-ən\ Acadian, Akkadian, arcadian, Arcadian, Barbadian, Canadian, circadian, Orcadian, Palladian

adiant \ād-ē-ənt\ gradient, radiant

adic[1] \ād-ik\ Vedic
  tornadic

adic[2] \ad-ik\ Braddock, haddock, paddock
  balladic, dyadic, faradic, haggadic, hexadic, maenadic, monadic, nomadic, sporadic, tetradic, tornadic, triadic
  Iliadic
  seminomadic

adie \ād-ē\ see ady

adient \ād-ē-ənt\ see adiant

adies \ād-ēz\ see ades[1]

ading \ād-iŋ\ braiding, lading, shading
  arcading, degrading, downgrading, unfading
  —also -ing forms of verbs listed at ade[1]

adir \ād-ər\ see ader

adish \ad-ish\ caddish, faddish, radish
  horseradish

adison \ad-ə-sən\ see addison

adist[1] \ȯd-əst\ broadest, sawdust
  haggadist

adist[2] \äd-əst\ see odest

adium \ād-ē-əm\ radium, stadium
  caladium, palladium, vanadium

adle \ād-ᵊl\ cradle, dreidel, ladle, wedel

adley \ad-lē\ see adly

adly \ad-lē\ badly, Bradley, gladly, madly, sadly
  comradely

adness \ad-nəs\ badness, gladness, madness, sadness

ado[1] \äd-ō\ bravado, camisado, carbonado, cruzado, Manado, mikado, passado, stoccado, strappado
  avocado, bastinado, Colorado, Coronado, desperado, El Dorado, hacendado
  amontillado, zapateado
  aficionado, incommunicado, Llano Estacado

ado[2] \ād-ō\ dado, credo
  crusado, gambado, strappado, teredo, tornado
  barricado, bastinado, camisado, carbonado, desperado, El Dorado
  fettuccine Alfredo

ados \ā-dəs\ see adus

adow \ad-ō\ Caddo, shadow
foreshadow
overshadow

adrate \äd-rət\ see oderate

adre \ad-rē\ see adery

adrian \ā-drē-ən\ Adrian, Adrienne, Hadrian

adrienne \ā-drē-ən\ see adrian

adt \ät\ see ot¹

adual \aj-əl\ see agile

adus \ā-dəs\ Padus
Barbados
—also -s, -'s, and -s' *forms of nouns listed at* ada³

ady \ād-ē\ cedi, glady, lady, Sadie, shady
forelady, landlady, milady, saleslady

ae¹ \ā\ see ay¹

ae² \ē\ see ee¹

ae³ \ī\ see y¹

aea \ē-ə\ see ia¹

aean \ē-ən\ see ean¹

aedal \ēd-ᵊl\ see eedle

aedile \ēd-ᵊl\ see eedle

aedra \ē-drə\ see edra

aegis¹ \ā-jəs\ see ageous

aegis² \ē-jəs\ see egis

ael \āl\ see ail

aeli \ā-lē\ see aily

aelic¹ \äl-ik\ see olic¹

aelic² \al-ik\ see allic

aemon \ē-mon\ see emon¹

aen \äⁿ\ see ant¹

aena¹ \ā-nä\ scena
faena

aena² \ē-nə\ see ina²

aenia¹ \ē-nē-ə\ see enia¹

aenia² \ē-nyə\ see enia²

aens \äⁿs\ see ance¹

aeon \ē-ən\ see ean¹

aera \ir-ə\ see era²

aere¹ \er-ē\ see ary¹

aere² \ir-ē\ see eary

aerial¹ \er-ē-əl\ see arial

aerial² \ir-ē-əl\ see erial

aerie¹ \ā-rē\ aerie, aery, faerie, fairy

aerie² \er-ē\ see ary¹

aerie³ \ir-ē\ see eary

aero¹ \er-ō\ see ero²

aero² \ar-ō\ see arrow²

aeroe¹ \ar-ō\ see arrow²

aeroe² \er-ō\ see ero²

aery¹ \ā-rē\ see aerie¹

aery² \er-ē\ see ary¹

aesar \ē-zər\ see easer²

aese \ā-zə\ see esa²

aestor \ē-stər\ see easter

aestus \es-təs\ see estis

aet \āt\ see ate¹

aetor \ēt-ər\ see eater¹

aeum \ē-əm\ see eum¹

aeus \ē-əs\ see eus¹

af \af\ see aph

afe¹ \āf\ chafe, safe, strafe, waif
fail-safe, vouchsafe
bathyscaphe

afe² \af\ see aph

afel 14

afel \äf-əl\ offal, waffle
falafel, pantofle, rijsttafel

afer \ā-fər\ chafer, safer, strafer,
wafer
cockchafer

aff \af\ see aph

affable \af-ə-bəl\ affable, laughable

affe \af\ see aph

affed \aft\ see aft²

affer¹ \äf-ər\ see offer¹

affer² \af-ər\ chaffer, gaffer, Kaffir,
kafir, Kafir, laugher, staffer, zaffer
paragrapher, polygrapher

affia \af-ē-ə\ raffia
agraphia

affic \af-ik\ see aphic

affick \af-ik\ see aphic

affir \af-ər\ see affer²

affish \af-ish\ raffish
giraffish

affle¹ \äf-əl\ see afel

affle² \af-əl\ baffle, raffle, snaffle

affron \af-rən\ saffron
Biafran

affy \af-ē\ chaffy, daffy, taffy

afic \af-ik\ see aphic

afir \af-ər\ see affer²

afran \af-rən\ see affron

aft¹ \äft\ toft, waft
gemeinschaft, gesellschaft
— also -ed forms of verbs listed at
off¹

aft² \aft\ aft, craft, daft, draft, graft,
haft, kraft, raft, shaft, Taft, waft
abaft, aircraft, campcraft, camshaft,
crankshaft, engraft, handcraft, indraft,
kingcraft, rockshaft, scoutcraft,
seacraft, spacecraft, stagecraft,

statecraft, updraft, witchcraft,
woodcraft
countershaft, fore-and-aft,
handicraft, Hovercraft, overdraft,
rotorcraft, turboshaft, understaffed,
watercraft
antiaircraft

aftage \af-tij\ graftage, waftage

after \af-tər\ after, dafter, drafter,
grafter, laughter, rafter
hereafter, thereafter
fore-and-after, handicrafter,
hereinafter, thereinafter

aftness \af-nəs\ daftness, Daphnis,
halfness

aftsman \af-smən\ craftsman,
draftsman, raftsman
handcraftsman
handicraftsman

afty \af-tē\ crafty, drafty

ag \ag\ bag, brag, crag, dag, drag,
fag, flag, gag, hag, jag, lag, mag, nag,
quag, rag, sag, scag, scrag, shag, slag,
snag, sprag, stag, swag, tag, wag,
YAG, zag
beanbag, black-flag, chin-wag,
dirtbag, dishrag, fleabag, gasbag,
greylag, handbag, hangtag, mailbag,
postbag, ragbag, ragtag, ratbag,
sandbag, schoolbag, scumbag, seabag,
sleazebag, washrag, wigwag,
windbag, workbag, zigzag
ballyrag, bullyrag, carpetbag,
litterbag, lollygag, saddlebag,
scalawag, tucker-bag

aga¹ \äg-ə\ quagga, raga, saga
anlage, vorlage
's Gravenhage

aga² \ā-gə\ Vega
bodega, omega
rutabaga

aga³ \eg-ə\ see ega¹

aga⁴ \ȯ-gə\ see auga

agan \ā-gən\ see agin

agar¹ \ā-gər\ Hagar, jaeger

agar² \äg-ər\ see ogger¹

agar³ \əg-ər\ see ugger¹

agary \ag-ə-rē\ see aggery

agate \ag-ət\ see aggot

age¹ \āj\ dodge, lodge, raj, stodge, wodge
barrage, collage, corsage, dislodge, garage, hodgepodge, Karaj, massage, swaraj
camouflage
espionage
counterespionage

age² \äzh\ plage
assuage, barrage, collage, corsage, dressage, frottage, gavage, lavage, massage, ménage, mirage, montage, moulage, portage, potage, treillage, triage
arbitrage, assemblage, badinage, bon voyage, bricolage, cabotage, camouflage, colportage, curettage, decoupage, empennage, enfleurage, entourage, fuselage, Hermitage, maquillage, persiflage, repechage, sabotage, vernissage
décolletage, espionage, photomontage, rite de passage
counterespionage

age³ \āj\ age, cage, gage, Gage, gauge, mage, page, rage, sage, stage, swage, wage
assuage, backstage, birdcage, broad-gauge, downstage, encage, engage, enrage, forestage, front-page, greengage, offstage, onstage, Osage, outrage, presage, rampage, restage, soundstage, space-age, substage, teenage, uncage, upstage
disengage, multistage, ossifrage, overage, saxifrage, underage

age⁴ \āg\ see eg¹

age⁵ \äzh\ see eige¹

age⁶ \äg-ə\ see aga¹

ageable \ā-jə-bəl\ gaugeable, stageable
unassuageable

aged \ājd\ aged, gauged
broad-gauged, engaged, unpaged
middle-aged
—also -ed forms of verbs listed at age³

agel \ā-gəl\ bagel, Hegel, plagal
finagle, inveigle
wallydraigle

ageless \āj-ləs\ ageless, wageless

agen¹ \ā-gən\ see agin

agen² \ä-gən\ see oggin

agenous \aj-ə-nəs\ see aginous

ageous \ā-jəs\ aegis
ambagious, courageous, contagious, outrageous, rampageous, umbrageous
advantageous
disadvantageous

ager¹ \ā-jər\ gauger, major, Major, pager, stager, wager
teenager
Canis Major, golden-ager, middle-ager, Ursa Major

ager² \äg-ər\ see ogger¹

agey \ā-jē\ see agy

agga \äg-ə\ see aga¹

aggar \äg-ər\ see ogger¹

aggard \ag-ərd\ blackguard, haggard, laggard

agged \ag-əd\ cragged, jagged, ragged

agger \ag-ər\ bagger, bragger, dagger, dragger, gagger, jagger, lagger, nagger, sagger, stagger, swagger, wagger
foot dragger, four-bagger, one-bagger, sandbagger, three-bagger, two-bagger
carpetbagger

aggery \ag-ə-rē\ jaggery, staggery, vagary, waggery
carpetbaggery

aggie \ag-ē\ see aggy²

agging \ag-iŋ\ bagging, flagging, lagging, nagging
brown bagging, foot-dragging, unflagging
carpetbagging
—also -ing forms of verbs listed at ag

aggish \ag-ish\ haggish, waggish

aggle \ag-əl\ draggle, gaggle, haggle, raggle, straggle, waggle
bedraggle
raggle-taggle

aggly \ag-lē\ scraggly, straggly, waggly

aggot \ag-ət\ agate, faggot, fagot, maggot

aggy¹ \äg-ē\ see oggy¹

aggy² \ag-ē\ aggie, baggy, braggy, craggy, draggy, jaggy, quaggy, ragi, scraggy, shaggy, snaggy, staggy, swaggy

agh \ä\ see a¹

agi¹ \äg-ē\ see oggy¹

agi² \ag-ē\ see aggy²

agian \ā-jən\ see ajun

agic \aj-ik\ magic, tragic
choragic, pelagic

agile \aj-əl\ agile, fragile, gradual, vagile

agin \ā-gən\ fagin, pagan, Reagan
Copenhagen

aginal \aj-ən-ᵊl\ paginal, vaginal
imaginal

aging \ā-jiŋ\ aging, raging, staging
unaging
—also -ing forms of verbs listed at age³

aginous \aj-ə-nəs\ collagenous, farraginous, plumbaginous, viraginous
cartilaginous, mucilaginous, oleaginous

agion \ā-jən\ see ajun

agious \ā-jəs\ see ageous

aglia¹ \äl-yə\ see ahlia¹

aglia² \al-yə\ see alue

aglio \al-yō\ intaglio, seraglio

agm \am\ see am²

agma \ag-mə\ magma
syntagma

agman \ag-mən\ bagman, flagman, swagman

agna \än-yə\ see ania¹

agne \ān\ see ane¹

agnes \ag-nəs\ Agnes
Albertus Magnus

agnum \ag-nəm\ magnum, sphagnum

agnus \ag-nəs\ see agnes

ago¹ \äg-ō\ lago
Chicago, farrago, galago, virago
Asiago, Calinago, Santiago, solidago

ago² \ā-gō\ sago
farrago, galago, imago, lumbago, plumbago, sapsago, Tobago, virago
solidago, San Diego
Tierra del Fuego

ago³ \äŋ-gō\ see ongo

agon \ag-ən\ dragon, flagon, lagan, wagon
bandwagon, jolt-wagon, Pendragon, snapdragon
battlewagon

agonal \ag-ən-ᵊl\ agonal
diagonal, heptagonal, hexagonal, octagonal, pentagonal, tetragonal

agora \ag-ə-rə\ agora
mandragora

agoras \ag-ə-rəs\ Protagoras,
Pythagoras

agot \ag-ət\ see aggot

agrance \ā-grəns\ flagrance,
fragrance

agrancy \ā-grən-sē\ flagrancy,
fragrancy, vagrancy

agrant \ā-grənt\ flagrant, fragrant,
vagrant
conflagrant

agster \ag-stər\ dragster, gagster

agua \äg-wə\ majagua, Managua,
piragua
Aconcagua, Nicaragua

ague¹ \āg\ see eg¹

ague² \äg\ see og¹

aguey \eg-ē\ see eggy

agus \ā-gəs\ magus, Tagus
choragus, Las Vegas
Simon Magus

agy \ā-jē\ cagey, Meiji, stagy

ah¹ \ä\ see a¹

ah² \o̊\ see aw¹

ah³ \a\ baa, nah
pas de chat

aha \ä-hä\ Baja, Naha, Praha

aham \ā-əm\ see ahum

ahd \äd\ see od¹

ahdi \äd-ē\ see ody¹

ahdom \äd-əm\ see odom

ahib \äb\ see ob¹

ahl \äl\ see al¹

ahler \äl-ər\ see ollar

ahlia¹ \äl-yə\ dahlia
passacaglia

ahlia² \al-yə\ see alue

ahlia³ \ā-lē-ə\ see alia¹

ahma¹ \ā-mə\ see ama³

ahma² \äm-ə\ see ama¹

ahma³ \am-ə\ see ama²

ahman¹ \äm-ən\ see ommon

ahman² \am-ən\ see ammon

ahn \än\ see on¹

ahms \ämz\ see alms

ahnda \än-də\ see onda

ahr \är\ see ar³

ahru \ä-rü\ see aru

aht \ät\ see ot¹

ahua \ä-wə\ see awa¹

ahum \ā-əm\ Graham, mayhem,
Nahum
Te Deum

ahveh \ä-vā\ see ave¹

ai¹ \ā\ see ay¹

ai² \ē\ see ee¹

ai³ \ī\ see y¹

ai⁴ \o̊i\ see oy

ai⁵ \ā-ē\ see aii

a'i \ī\ see y¹

aia¹ \ā-ə\ Freya
Aglaia, cattleya, Hosea, Isaiah,
Nouméa
Himalaya, Kilauea, Mauna Kea,
Meghalaya

aia² \ī-ə\ see iah¹

aiad¹ \ā-əd\ naiad, pleiad

aiad² \ī-əd\ see yad

aiah \ā-ə\ see aia

aias \ā-əs\ see ais[1]

aic \ā-ik\ laic
alcaic, Altaic, archaic, Chaldaic,
deltaic, Hebraic, Incaic, Judaic,
Mishnaic, Mithraic, mosaic, Mosaic,
prosaic, Romaic, spondaic, stanzaic,
trochaic, voltaic
algebraic, Aramaic, Cyrenaic,
faradaic, formulaic, pharisaic,
Ptolemaic
apotropaic, paradisaic, photomosaic,
Ural-Altaic

aica \ā-ə-k-ə\ Judaica
Cyrenaica

aical \ā-ə-kəl\ laical
pharisaical
paradisaical

aice \ās\ see ace[1]

aich \āk̲\ see aigh

aiche \esh\ see esh[1]

aicos \ā-kəs\ see ecas

aid[1] \ād\ see ade[1]

aid[2] \ed\ see ead[1]

aid[3] \ad\ see ad[3]

aida \ī-də\ see ida[2]

aide[1] \ād\ see ade[1]

aide[2] \īd-ē\ see iday

aiden \ād-ᵊn\ see aden

aider \ād-ər\ see ader

aiding \ād-iŋ\ see ading

aido \ī-dō\ see ido[1]

aids \ādz\ see ades[2]

aiety \ā-ət-ē\ see aity

aif \āf\ see afe[1]

aig \āg\ see eg[1]

aiga \ī-gə\ taiga
Auriga

aigh \āk̲\ laigh, quaich

aight \āt\ see ate[1]

aighten \āt-ᵊn\ see aten[1]

aightly \āt-lē\ see ately[1]

aign \ān\ see ane[1]

aigne \ān\ see ane[1]

aignment \ān-mənt\ see ainment

aii \ä-ē\ Hawaii, Tubuai

aiian \ä-yən\ zayin
Hawaiian

aijin \ī-jēn\ gaijin, hygiene

aik \īk\ see ike[2]

aika \ī-kə\ see ica[1]

ail \āl\ ail, ale, baal, bail, bale, brail,
braille, Braille, dale, Dale, drail, fail,
flail, frail, Gael, gale, Gale, Gayle,
grail, hail, hale, Hale, jail, kale, mail,
male, nail, pail, pale, quail, Quayle,
rail, sail, sale, scale, shale, snail, stale,
swale, tael, tail, taille, tale, they'll,
trail, vail, vale, veil, wail, wale, whale,
Yale
abseil, airmail, assail, avail, bangtail,
bewail, blackmail, blacktail, bobtail,
broadscale, broadtail, bucktail,
canaille, cattail, Clydesdale, coattail,
cocktail, contrail, curtail, derail, detail,
doornail, dovetail, downscale,
ducktail, E-mail, entail, exhale, fantail,
female, fishtail, folktale, foresail,
foxtail, full-scale, Glendale,
greenmail, guardrail, Hallel, handrail,
hangnail, headsail, hightail, hobnail,
horntail, horsetail, impale, inhale,
Longueuil, lugsail, mainsail, oxtail,
pass-fail, percale, pigtail, pintail,
pinwale, portrayal, prevail, rattail,
regale, resale, rescale, retail, ringtail,
Sangreal, sei whale, shavetail,
shirttail, skysail, small-scale,
springtail, spritsail, staysail, surveil,

swordtail, taffrail, telltale, thumbnail,
timescale, toenail, topsail, travail,
treenail, trysail, unnail, unveil,
upscale, ventail, wagtail, wassail,
whitetail, wholesale
  abigail, Abigail, aventail, betrayal,
bristletail, Chippendale, Corriedale,
cottontail, countervail, defrayal,
disentail, draggle-tail, farthingale,
fingernail, flickertail, forestaysail,
gaff-topsail, galingale, martingale,
monorail, montadale, nightingale,
Nightingale, overscale, ponytail,
romeldale, scissortail, swallowtail,
tattletale, tripletail, trundle-tail,
yellowtail
  self-betrayal, Fort Lauderdale,
Oregon Trail, Santa Fe Trail

ailable \ā-lə-bəl\ bailable, mailable,
sailable, salable, scalable
  assailable, available, resalable
  unassailable

ailand \ī-lənd\ see ighland

ailant \ā-lənt\ see alant

aile \ī-lē\ see yly

ailed \āld\ mailed, nailed, sailed,
scaled, tailed, veiled
  detailed, engrailed, hobnailed,
pigtailed, ring-tailed, unveiled
  ponytailed, swallow-tailed
  —also -ed forms of verbs listed at ail

ailer \ā-lər\ alar, bailer, bailor, baler,
hailer, jailer, mailer, malar, nailer,
sailer, sailor, scalar, scaler, tailer,
tailor, Taylor, trailer, wailer, waler,
whaler
  blackmailer, curtailer, derailleur,
detailer, entailer, inhaler, loud-haler,
retailer, wassailer, wholesaler
  semitrailer
  —also -er forms of adjectives listed
at ail

ailey \ā-lē\ see aily

ailful \āl-fəl\ see aleful

ailie \ā-lē\ see aily

ailiff \ā-ləf\ bailiff, caliph

ailing \ā-liŋ\ failing, grayling,
mailing, paling, railing, sailing,
tailing, veiling, whaling
  boardsailing, prevailing, retailing,
self-mailing, unfailing
  parasailing, unavailing
  —also -ing forms of verbs listed at
ail

aille[1] \āl\ see ail

aille[2] \ī\ see y[1]

aille[3] \īl\ see ile[1]

aille[4] \ä-yə\ see aya[1]

ailles \ī\ see y[1]

ailleur \ā-lər\ see ailer

ailment \āl-mənt\ ailment, bailment
  curtailment, derailment, entailment,
impalement

ailor \ā-lər\ see ailer

ails \ālz\ see ales

ailsman \ālz-mən\ see alesman

aily \ā-lē\ bailey, Bailey, bailie,
daily, gaily, grayly, paly, scaly, shaley,
wally
  Bareilly, Bareli, Disraeli, Israeli,
shillelagh
  triticale, ukulele

aim \ām\ see ame[1]

aima \ī-mə\ see yma

aimable \ā-mə-bəl\ see amable

aiman \ā-mən\ see amen[1]

aimant \ā-mənt\ see ayment

aiment \ā-mənt\ see ayment

aimer \ā-mər\ blamer, claimer,
flamer, framer, gamer, tamer
  declaimer, defamer, disclaimer,
exclaimer
  —also -er forms of adjectives listed
at ame[1]

aimless \ām-ləs\ see ameless

ain¹ \ā-ən\ see ayan¹

ain² \ān\ see ane¹

ain³ \en\ see en¹

ain⁴ \in\ see in¹

ain⁵ \īn\ see ine¹

ain⁶ \aⁿ\ see in⁴

aina \ī-nə\ see ina¹

ainable \ā-nə-bəl\ stainable, trainable
attainable, containable, explainable, maintainable, restrainable, retrainable, sustainable
inexplainable

ainder \ān-dər\ attainder, remainder

aine¹ \ān\ see ane¹

aine² \en\ see en¹

ained \ānd\ brained, caned, craned, drained, grained, maned, pained, paned, stained, strained, vaned, veined
birdbrained, bloodstained, close-grained, coarse-grained, crackbrained, cross-grained, edge-grained, harebrained, ingrained, lamebrained, mad-brained, membraned, restrained, tearstained, unfeigned
featherbrained, rattlebrained, scatterbrained, self-contained, unrestrained
—also -ed forms of verbs listed at ane¹

ainer \ā-nər\ caner, drainer, feigner, gainer, planar, planer, seiner, stainer, strainer, trainer, veiner
campaigner, complainer, container, coplanar, cordwainer, detainer, lupanar, maintainer, ordainer, profaner, restrainer, retainer, sustainer, Trakehner
entertainer
—also -er forms of adjectives listed at ane¹

ainful \ān-fəl\ baneful, gainful, painful
disdainful

aininess \ā-nē-nəs\ braininess, graininess

aining \ā-niŋ\ veining
complaining, sustaining
self-sustaining, uncomplaining
—also -ing forms of verbs listed at ane¹

ainish \ā-nish\ brainish, Danish, swainish

ainless \ān-ləs\ brainless, painless, stainless

ainly \ān-lē\ mainly, plainly, thegnly, vainly
humanely, insanely, profanely, ungainly
inhumanely

ainment \ān-mənt\ arraignment, attainment, containment, detainment, detrainment, enchainment, entrainment, ordainment, refrainment
entertainment, preordainment, self-containment

aino \ī-nō\ see ino¹

ains \ānz\ Keynes, reins
cremains, Great Plains, Mains Plains, remains
—also -s, -'s, and -s' forms of nouns, and -s forms of verbs, listed at ane¹

ainsman \ānz-mən\ plainsman, reinsman

aint \ānt\ ain't, faint, feint, mayn't, paint, plaint, quaint, saint, taint, 'tain't
acquaint, attaint, bepaint, complaint, constraint, distraint, greasepaint, impaint, restraint
unconstraint, unrestraint

ain't \ānt\ see aint

ainting \ān-tiŋ\ underpainting
—also -ing forms of verbs listed at aint

aintly \ānt-lē\ faintly, quaintly, saintly

ainy \ā-nē\ brainy, grainy, meiny, rainy, veiny, zany
Allegheny

ainz \īnz\ see ines[3]

aipse \āps\ see apes

air[1] \er\ see are[4]

air[2] \īr\ see ire[1]

aira \ī-rə\ see yra

aird \erd\ see aired

aire[1] \er\ see are[4]

aire[2] \ir\ see eer[2]

aire[3] \īr\ see ire[1]

aired \ard\ caird, haired, laird
fair-haired, impaired, long-haired, misleared, prepared, shorthaired, unpaired
wirehaired
multilayered, underprepared, unimpaired
—also -ed forms of verbs listed at are[4]

airer \er-ər\ see earer[1]

aires[1] \er\ see are[4]

aires[2] \ar-ēs\ see ares[2]

airess[1] \er-əs\ see errous

airess[2] \ar-əs\ see aris[2]

airie \er-ē\ see ary[1]

airing \er-iŋ\ see aring[1]

airish \er-ish\ see arish[1]

airist \er-əst\ see arist

airly \er-lē\ fairly, ferlie, rarely, squarely

airn \ern\ see ern[1]

airo \ī-rō\ see yro[1]

airs \erz\ theirs
backstairs, downstairs, nowheres, somewheres, upstairs

unawares
—also -s, -'s, and -s' forms of nouns, and -s forms of verbs, listed at are[4]

airy[1] \er-ē\ see ary[1]

airy[2] \ā-rē\ see aerie[1]

ais[1] \ā-əs\ dais, Laius
Isaias
Menelaus

ais[2] \ā\ see ay[1]

aisal[1] \ā-zəl\ see asal[2]

aisal[2] \ī-səl\ see isal[1]

aisance \ās-ᵊns\ see ascence[1]

aisant \ās-ᵊnt\ see acent

aise[1] \āz\ see aze[1]

aise[2] \ez\ see ays[1]

aisement \āz-mənt\ see azement

aiser[1] \ā-zər\ see azer

aiser[2] \ī-zər\ see izer

aisian \ā-zhən\ see asion

aisin \āz-ᵊn\ see azon

aising \ā-ziŋ\ braising, glazing, hazing, phrasing
appraising, fund-raising, hair-raising, hell-raising, house-raising, stargazing, trailblazing
—also -ing forms of verbs listed at aze[1]

aisle \īl\ see ile[1]

aisley \āz-lē\ paisley
nasally

aisne \ān\ see ane[1]

aisse \ās\ see ace[1]

aisson \ās-ᵊn\ see ason[1]

aist[1] \ā-əst\ see ayest

aist[2] \āst\ see aced

aist[3] \äst\ see ost[1]

aisy \ā-zē\ see azy

ait¹ \ā\ see ay¹

ait² \āt\ see ate¹

ait³ \īt\ see ite¹

ait⁴ \at\ see at⁵

aite \īt\ see ite¹

aited \āt-əd\ see ated

aiten \āt-ᵊn\ see aten¹

aiter \āt-ər\ see ator

aith \āth\ eighth, faith, Faith, saithe, scathe, wraith
  unfaith
  interfaith

aithe \āth\ see aith

aithless \āth-ləs\ faithless, natheless

aiti \āt-ē\ see aty

aitian \ā-shən\ see ation¹

aiting \āt-iŋ\ see ating

aitly \āt-lē\ see ately¹

aitor \āt-ər\ see ator

aitorous \āt-ə-rəs\ see ateress

aitour \āt-ər\ see ator

aitress \ā-trəs\ traitress, waitress
  aviatress

aity \ā-ət-ē\ deity, gaiety, laity
  corporeity, spontaneity, synchroneity
  diaphaneity
  contemporaneity, extemporaneity

aius¹ \ā-əs\ see ais¹

aius² \ī-əs\ see ias¹

aiva \ī-və\ see iva¹

aive \āv\ see ave²

aix \ā\ see ay¹

aize \āz\ see aze¹

aj \äj\ see age¹

aja¹ \ä-hä\ see aha

aja² \ī-ə\ see iah¹

ajan \ā-jən\ see ajun

ajj \aj\ see adge

ajor \ā-jər\ see ager¹

ajos \ā-əs\ see ais¹

ajun \ā-jən\ Cajun, Trajan
  contagion, Pelagian, reagin

ak¹ \äk\ see ock¹

ak² \ak\ see ack²

aka¹ \äk-ə\ Dacca, Dhaka, kaka, paca, taka
  Lusaka, maraca, medaka, Oaxaca, Osaka, pataca
  Mbandaka, saltimbocca, Toyonaka
  Lake Titicaca
  Higashiosaka

aka² \ak-ə\ see aca²

akable \ā-kə-bəl\ breakable, makable, shakable
  mistakable, unslakable
  unmistakable

akan¹ \äk-ən\ see aken²

akan² \ak-ən\ see acken

akar \äk-ər\ see ocker

ake¹ \āk\ ache, bake, Blake, brake, break, cake, crake, drake, Drake, fake, flake, hake, jake, Jake, lake, make, quake, rake, sake, shake, sheikh, slake, snake, spake, stake, steak, strake, take, wake, Wake
  awake, backache, beefcake, beefsteak, betake, blacksnake, canebrake, caretake, cheesecake, clambake, corncrake, cupcake, daybreak, earache, earthquake, firebreak, firedrake, forsake, friedcake, fruitcake, grubstake, handshake, headache, heartache, heartbreak, hoecake, hotcake, housebreak, intake,

jailbreak, keepsake, lapstrake,
mandrake, Marsquake, mistake,
moonquake, muckrake, namesake,
newsbreak, oatcake, opaque, outbreak,
outtake, Pan-Cake, pancake, partake,
remake, retake, rewake, seaquake,
seedcake, sheldrake, shortcake,
snowflake, sweepstake, toothache,
unmake, uptake, windbreak,
youthquake
  bellyache, give-and-take,
halterbreak, johnnycake, kittiwake,
make-or-break, microquake, overtake,
pat-a-cake, patty-cake, put-and-take,
rattlesnake, stomachache, undertake,
wapentake, wideawake
  semiopaque

ake² \ak\ see ack²

ake³ \äk-ē\ see ocky

aked \ākt\ awaked, half-baked,
ringstraked, sunbaked
  —*also* -ed *forms of verbs listed at*
ake¹

akeless \ā-kləs\ brakeless, wakeless

aken¹ \ā-kən\ bacon, Bacon,
Macon, shaken, taken, waken
  awaken, betaken, forsaken, mistaken,
partaken, retaken, rewaken, well-taken
  godforsaken, overtaken, undertaken

aken² \äk-ən\ kraken
  Arawakan

aker¹ \ā-kər\ acre, baker, breaker,
faker, laker, maker, nacre, quaker,
Quaker, raker, saker, shaker, taker,
waker
  backbreaker, bookmaker, caretaker,
carmaker, comaker, dressmaker,
drugmaker, earthshaker, filmmaker,
glassmaker, groundbreaker,
grubstaker, hatmaker, haymaker,
heartbreaker, homemaker,
housebreaker, icebreaker, jawbreaker,
kingmaker, lawbreaker, lawmaker,
mapmaker, matchmaker, mistaker,
muckraker, mythmaker, noisemaker,
oddsmaker, pacemaker, peacemaker,

phrasemaker, platemaker, playmaker,
printmaker, rainmaker, saltshaker,
shirtmaker, shoemaker, snowmaker,
stavesacre, steelmaker, strikebreaker,
tastemaker, tiebreaker, toolmaker,
trailbreaker, watchmaker,
windbreaker, wiseacre
  automaker, bellyacher, boilermaker,
merrymaker, moneymaker,
moviemaker, papermaker, simulacre,
troublemaker, undertaker
  cabinetmaker, holidaymaker,
policymaker

aker² \ak-ər\ see acker

akery \ā-krē\ bakery, fakery

akes \āks\ jakes
  cornflakes, Great Lakes, sweepstakes
  —*also* -s, -'s *and* -s' *forms of nouns,
and* -s *forms of verbs, listed at* ake¹

ake-up \ā-kəp\ break-up, breakup,
make-up, makeup, shake-up, shakeup,
take-up, wake-up

akey \ā-kē\ see aky

akh¹ \äk\ see ock¹

akh² \ak\ see ack²

aki¹ \äk-ē\ see ocky

aki² \ak-ē\ see acky

akian \äk-ē-ən\ see ockian

akic \ak-ik\ see acchic

aking¹ \ā-kiŋ\ aching, making,
waking
  bookmaking, breathtaking,
caretaking, dressmaking,
earthshaking, filmmaking,
glassmaking, groundbreaking,
heartbreaking, housebreaking,
lawbreaking, lawmaking, leave-taking,
lovemaking, mapmaking,
matchmaking, mythmaking,
noisemaking, pacemaking,
painstaking, pathbreaking,
peacemaking, phrasemaking,
printmaking, rainmaking,

snowmaking, stocktaking,
strikebreaking, toolmaking,
watchmaking, world-shaking
merrymaking, moneymaking,
moviemaking, papermaking,
undertaking
cabinetmaking, policymaking
—*also* -ing *forms of verbs listed at*
ake¹

aking² \ak-iŋ\ see acking

ako¹ \äk-ō\ see occo

ako² \ak-ō\ shako, wacko
tobacco

aku \äk-ü\ Bunraku, gagaku,
nunchaku

akum \ā-kəm\ vade mecum
shalom aleichem

aky \ā-kē\ achy, braky, cakey, flaky,
laky, shaky, snaky
headachy

al¹ \äl\ Bâle, col, dahl, dal, doll, loll,
moll, nal, pol, sol, Sol, Taal, toile
Algol, atoll, austral, Baikal, Bhopal,
cabal, Chagall, chorale, grand mal,
gun moll, hamal, jacal, mistral,
narwhal, Natal, nopal, Pascal, petrol,
quetzal, real, rial, riyal, Shawwal,
tical, timbale, Transvaal
à cheval, aerosol, Emmenthal,
falderal, femme fatale, folderol,
Heyerdahl, parasol, pastoral,
pastorale, protocol, Provençal,
Simmental, urial, Wuppertal
entente cordiale, Neanderthal,
procès-verbal, sublittoral
succès de scandale

al² \el\ see el¹

al³ \ȯl\ see all

al⁴ \al\ Al, gal, Hal, pal, rale, sal, Val
banal, cabal, canal, Chagall, chorale,
copal, corral, decal, fal-lal, grand mal,
joual, La Salle, Laval, locale, mescal,
moral, morale, nopal, pall-mall,
pascal, percale, quetzal, salal, serval,
vinal

bacchanal, caracal, chaparral, femme
fatale, musicale, pastoral, pastorale,
pedocal, rationale, retinal, Seconal
Guadalcanal, kilopascal, sublittoral

ala¹ \äl-ä\ à la, Allah, gala

ala² \äl-ə\ Allah, olla, tala, wallah
cabala, cantala, Chapala,
chuckwalla, cicala, corolla, Douala,
halala, Kampala, koala, Lingala,
marsala, nyala, tambala, Tlaxcala,
Valhalla, Walhalla
ayotollah, Guatemala, Gujranwala

ala³ \ā-lə\ ala, gala
Venezuela, zarzuela

ala⁴ \al-ə\ see allow

alaam \ā-ləm\ Balaam, golem,
Salem
Winston-Salem

alable \ā-lə-bəl\ see ailable

alace \al-əs\ see alis²

alad \al-əd\ see alid²

alam \äl-əm\ see olumn

alamine \al-ə-mən\ allemande,
calamine

alan \al-ən\ see allon

alance \al-əns\ balance, valance
imbalance, outbalance, unbalance
counterbalance, overbalance

alant \ā-lənt\ assailant, bivalent,
covalent, exhalent, inhalant,
surveillant, trivalent
multivalent, pentavalent,
quadrivalent, tetravalent, univalent

alap \al-əp\ see allop²

alar \ā-lər\ see ailer

alary¹ \al-rē\ see allery

alary² \al-ə-rē\ calorie, gallery,
Mallory, Malory, salary, Valerie,
Valery
kilocalorie

alas \al-əs\ see alis²

alate \al-ət\ see allet²

alcon¹ \ȯ-kən\ see alkin¹

alcon² \al-kən\ falcon, gyrfalcon, grimalkin

ald¹ \ȯld\ bald, scald, skald, walled
close-hauled, keelhauled, kobold,
piebald, ribald, skewbald, so-called,
sunscald
Archibald, coveralled, overalled
—*also* -ed *forms of verbs listed at* all

ald² \ȯlt\ see alt

alder \ȯl-dər\ alder, balder, Balder

aldi \ȯl-dē\ Bartholdi, Vivaldi
Garibaldi

aldron \ȯl-drən\ aldron, caldron,
cauldron, chaldron

ale¹ \ā-lē\ see aily

ale² \āl\ see ail

ale³ \äl\ see al¹

ale⁴ \al\ see al⁴

ale⁵ \äl-ē\ see olly¹

ale⁶ \al-ē\ see ally⁴

alea \ā-lē-ə\ see alia¹

aleck¹ \el-ik\ see elic²

aleck² \al-ik\ see allic

aled \āld\ see ailed

aleful \āl-fəl\ baleful, wailful

aleigh¹ \äl-ē\ see olly¹

aleigh² \ȯl-ē\ see awly

alem \ā-ləm\ see alaam

alement \āl-mənt\ see ailment

alen \ä-lən\ see ollen⁵

alence \ā-ləns\ valence
surveillance

alends \al-ənz\ see allans

alent¹ \al-ənt\ see allant

alent² \ā-lənt\ see alant

alep \al-əp\ see allop²

aler¹ \ā-lər\ see ailer

aler² \äl-ər\ see ollar

alerie \al-ə-rē\ see alary²

alery \al-ə-rē\ see alary²

ales¹ \ālz\ sales, Wales
entrails, Marseilles
New South Wales, Prince of Wales
cat-o'-nine-tails
—*also* -s, -'s, *and* -s' *forms of nouns,
and* -s *forms of verbs, listed at* ail

ales² \äl-əs\ see olis

alesman \ālz-mən\ bailsman,
dalesman, salesman, talesman

alet \al-ət\ see allet²

alette \al-ət\ see allet²

aley \ā-lē\ see aily

alf \af\ see aph

alfa \al-fə\ see alpha

alfness \af-nəs\ see aftness

algia \al-jə\ neuralgia, nostalgia

ali¹ \äl-ē\ see olly¹

ali² \al-ē\ see ally⁴

ali³ \ȯ-lē\ see awly

ali⁴ \ā-lē\ see aily

alia¹ \ā-lē-ə\ dahlia
Australia, azalea, battalia, realia,
regalia, vedalia, Westphalia
bacchanalia, genitalia, glossolalia,
inter alia, Lupercalia, marginalia,
penetralia, saturnalia
Orientalia, paraphernalia

alia² \al-yə\ dahlia
  battalia, et alia
  passacaglia

alian¹ \ā-lē-ən\ alien
  Australian, Daedalian, Deucalion,
  Hegelian, mammalian, Pygmalion,
  Uralian
  bacchanalian, Lupercalian,
  saturnalian
  Episcopalian, sesquipedalian,
  tatterdemalion

alian² \al-yən\ see allion

alic \al-ik\ see allic

alice \al-əs\ see alis²

alid¹ \äl-əd\ see olid

alid² \al-əd\ ballad, pallid, salad,
valid
  invalid

alie \äl-yə\ see ahlia¹

alien \ā-lē-ən\ see alian¹

aling \ā-liŋ\ see ailing

alinist \äl-ə-nəst\ see olonist

alinn \al-ən\ see allon

alion¹ \ā-lē-ən\ see alian¹

alion² \al-yən\ see allion

aliph \ā-ləf\ see ailiff

alis¹ \ā-ləs\ see ayless

alis² \al-əs\ Alice, balas, callous,
callus, chalice, Dallas, gallus, malice,
palace, Pallas, phallus, talus, thallous,
thallus
  oxalis
  digitalis
  hemerocallis
  aurora borealis, Corona Borealis

alist \al-əst\ ballast, callused,
gallused
  cabalist, sodalist

ality¹ \äl-ət-ē\ jollity, polity, quality
  equality, frivolity
  coequality, inequality

ality² \al-ət-ē\ anality, banality,
brutality, carnality, causality,
centrality, duality, extrality, fatality,
feudality, finality, formality, frontality,
frugality, legality, locality, mentality,
modality, morality, mortality, nasality,
natality, neutrality, nodality, orality,
plurality, primality, rascality, reality,
regality, rurality, sodality, tonality,
totality, venality, vitality, vocality
  abnormality, actuality, amorality,
animality, atonality, axiality, bestiality,
bimodality, bipedality, cardinality,
classicality, coevality, comicality,
commonality, communality,
conjugality, cordiality, corporality,
criminality, criticality, ethicality,
externality, factuality, farcicality,
fictionality, functionality, generality,
geniality, hospitality, ideality,
illegality, immorality, immortality,
informality, integrality, internality,
irreality, lexicality, liberality, lineality,
literality, logicality, musicality,
mutuality, nationality, notionality,
nuptiality, optimality, partiality,
personality, physicality, principality,
punctuality, rationality, seasonality,
sexuality, sociality, spaciality,
speciality, subnormality, technicality,
temporality, topicality, triviality,
unmorality, unreality, verticality,
virtuality, whimsicality
  asexuality, atypicality, bisexuality,
collaterality, collegiality, colloquiality,
commerciality, conceptuality,
conditionality, congeniality,
connaturality, conventionality,
conviviality, corporeality,
dimensionality, directionality,
effectuality, emotionality,
ephemerality, equivocality,
essentiality, ethereality, eventuality,
exceptionality, extensionality,
fantasticality, grammaticality,
illiberality, illogicality, impersonality,
impracticality, inhospitality,
instrumentality, irrationality,
materiality, microtonality,
monumentality, municipality,
originality, orthogonality,

pansexuality, paranormality,
polytonality, potentiality, provinciality,
self-partiality, sentimentality,
spirituality, substantiality, theatricality,
transexuality, triaxiality, universality,
veridicality
    ambisexuality, artificiality,
circumstantiality, confidentiality,
consequentiality, constitutionality,
homosexuality, hypersexuality,
immateriality, individuality,
ineffectuality, insubstantiality,
intellectuality, internationality,
intersexuality, paradoxicality,
psychosexuality, referentiality,
superficiality, supranationality,
territoriality, tridimensionality, two-
dimensionality, uncongeniality,
unconventionality, ungrammaticality,
unisexuality, unsubstantiality
    exterritoriality, heterosexuality,
inconsequentiality, unconstitutionality,
unidimensionality
    extraterritoriality

alium \al-ē-əm\ see allium

alius \ā-lē-əs\ alius
Sibelius

alk \ȯk\ auk, balk, calk, caulk, chalk,
gawk, hawk, Koch, Salk, Sauk,
squawk, stalk, talk, walk
    Bartok, Black Hawk, bemock,
boardwalk, cakewalk, catwalk,
chalktalk, cornstalk, crosswalk,
duckwalk, eyestalk, fast-talk,
goshawk, jaywalk, langue d'oc,
leafstalk, Mohawk, nighthawk,
Norfolk, outtalk, ropewalk, shoptalk,
sidewalk, skywalk, sleepwalk, Suffolk,
sweet-talk
    belle epoque, catafalque, double-
talk, Swainson's hawk, tomahawk

alkan \ȯl-kən\ see alkin[1]

alker \ȯ-kər\ balker, caulker, gawker,
hawker, squawker, stalker, walker
    cakewalker, deerstalker, floorwalker,
jayhawker, jaywalker, nightwalker,
ropewalker, sleepwalker, spacewalker,
streetwalker, trackwalker
    double-talker

alkie \ȯ-kē\ balky, chalky, gawky,
gnocchi, pawky, stalky, talkie, talky
    Milwaukee
    Handie-Talkie, walkie-talkie
    Winnipesaukee

alkin[1] \ȯ-kən\ Balkan, falcon,
malkin
    grimalkin, gyrfalcon

alkin[2] \al-kən\ see alcon[2]

alking \ȯ-kiŋ\ caulking, walking
    racewalking, spacewalking,
streetwalking
    —also -ing forms of verbs listed at
alk

alkland \ȯk-lənd\ see auckland

alky \ȯ-kē\ see alkie

all[1] \ȯl\ all, awl, ball, bawl, brawl,
call, caul, crawl, doll, drawl, fall, Gall,
Gaul, hall, Hall, haul, kraal, mall,
maul, moll, pall, Paul, pawl, Saul,
scall, scrawl, shawl, small, Sol, spall,
sprawl, squall, stall, tall, thrall, trawl,
wall, y'all, yauld, yawl
    Algol, ALGOL, appall, argol, air
ball, ashfall, at all, atoll, AWOL,
baseball, Baikal, beanball, befall,
Bengal, best-ball, birdcall, blackball,
Bokmål, bookstall, boxhaul, bradawl,
broomball, catcall, catchall, COBOL,
cornball, Cornwall, cure-all, curveball,
deadfall, de Gaulle, dewfall,
dodgeball, downfall, downhaul,
drywall, enthrall, eyeball, fastball,
fireball, floodwall, football, footfall,
footstall, footwall, forestall, forkball,
four-ball, free-fall, gadwall, goofball,
googol, grease ball, guildhall, hair
ball, handball, hardball, headstall,
heelball, highball, holdall, icefall,
install, keelhaul, know-all, landfall,
Landsmål, line-haul, lowball,
meatball, menthol, Metol, miscall,
mothball, naphthol, Nepal, nightfall,
nutgall, oddball, outfall, outhaul,
pitfall, plimsoll, pratfall, pub-crawl,
puffball, punchball, pushball, rainfall,
rainsquall, recall, rial, Riksmål, riyal,

rockfall, rorqual, Saint Paul, save-all,
screwball, seawall, short-haul,
shortfall, sidewall, sleazeball,
slimeball, snowball, snowfall, softball,
speedball, spitball, Stendhal, stickball,
stonewall, stoopball, T-ball, tell-all,
three-ball, trackball, Tyrol, Walsall,
what all, Whitehall, whitewall,
windfall, windgall, withal, withdrawal,
you-all
  aerosol, alcohol, barbital, basketball,
bucky ball, butterball, buttonball,
cannonball, carryall, caterwaul, coverall, coverall, Demerol, disenthrall,
Donegal, entresol, evenfall, free-for-
all, gasohol, girasole, Grand Guignol,
haute école, know-it-all, knuckleball,
Komsomol, methanol, minié ball,
Montreal, Nembutal, overall, overcall,
overhaul, paddleball, parasol, Parsifal,
Pentothal, protocol, racquetball,
Seconal, Senegal, superball, tattersall,
tetherball, therewithal, timolol,
volleyball, waterfall, wherewithal
  cholesterol, Costa del Sol, Mariupol,
Massif Central, Neanderthal,
Sevastopol, Transalpine Gaul, Vincent
de Paul
  be-all and end-all

all² \äl\ see al¹

all³ \al\ see al⁴

alla¹ \äl-ə\ see ala²

alla² \al-ə\ see allow⁴

allable \ȯ-lə-bəl\ callable, spallable

allace \äl-əs\ see olis

allacy \al-ə-sē\ fallacy, jalousie

allad \al-əd\ see alid²

allage \al-ə-jē\ see alogy²

allah¹ \äl-ä\ see ala¹

allah² \äl-ə\ see ala²

allah³ \al-ə\ see allow⁴

allan \al-ən\ see allon

allans \al-ənz\ calends, Lallans
  —also -s, -'s, and -s' forms of nouns
  listed at allon

allant \al-ənt\ callant, gallant, talent
  topgallant
  fore-topgallant

allas \al-əs\ see alis²

allasey \äl-ə-sē\ see olicy

allast \al-əst\ see alist

alle¹ \al\ see al⁴

alle² \al-ē\ see ally⁴

alle³ \äl-ē\ see olly

alled \ȯld\ see ald

allee \al-ē\ see ally⁴

allemande \al-ə-mən\ see alamine

allen¹ \ȯ-lən\ fallen, stollen
  befallen, chapfallen, chopfallen,
  crestfallen, downfallen, tarpaulin
  unfallen

allen² \al-ən\ see allon

aller¹ \ȯ-lər\ bawler, brawler, caller,
  drawler, faller, hauler, mauler,
  scrawler, squaller, trawler
  fireballer, footballer, forestaller,
  installer, stonewaller
  knuckleballer

aller² \al-ər\ caller, pallor, valor

alles \ī-əs\ see ias¹

allet¹ \äl-ət\ see ollet

allet² \al-ət\ ballot, callet, mallet,
  palate, palette, pallet, sallet, shallot,
  valet

alley \al-ē\ see ally⁴

alli \al-ē\ see ally⁴

alliard \al-yərd\ galliard, halyard

allic \al-ik\ Gaelic, Gallic, malic,
  phallic, salic, Salic, thallic

cephalic, italic, mandalic, medallic, metallic, smart aleck, Uralic, Vandalic, vocalic
genitalic, intervallic, ithyphallic, nonmetallic, postvocalic, prevocalic
intervocalic

allid \al-əd\ see alid²

allie \al-ē\ see ally⁴

alling \ȯ-liŋ\ balling, calling, drawling, falling, galling, hauling, mauling, Pauling, stalling
infalling, name-calling
—also -ing forms of verbs listed at all¹

allion \al-yən\ scallion, stallion
battalion, Italian, medallion, rapscallion
tatterdemalion

allis¹ \al-əs\ see alis²

allis² \al-ē\ see ally⁴

allis³ \äl-əs\ see olis

allish \ȯ-lish\ Gaulish, smallish, tallish

allit \ä-lət\ see ollet

allith¹ \äl-əs\ see olis

allith² \äl-ət\ see ollet

allium \al-ē-əm\ allium, gallium, pallium, thallium, Valium

allment \ȯl-mənt\ enthrallment, forestallment, installment

allo \äl-ō\ see ollow¹

allon \al-ən\ Alan, Allan, Allen, Allyn, gallon, lallan, Talinn, talon

allop¹ \äl-əp\ see ollop

allop² \al-əp\ gallop, galop, jalap, salep, Salop, scallop, shallop
escallop

allor \al-ər\ see aller²

allory¹ \al-re\ see allery

allory² \al-ə-rē\ see alary²

allot \al-ət\ see allet²

allous \al-əs\ see alis²

allow¹ \el-ō\ see ello

allow² \äl-ə\ see ala²

allow³ \äl-ō\ see ollow¹

allow⁴ \al-ə\ Allah, gala, Galla
cavalla, impala, Valhalla

allow⁵ \al-ō\ aloe, callow, fallow, hallow, mallow, sallow, shallow, tallow
unhallow

allowed \al-ōd\ hallowed
unhallowed

allows \al-ōz\ gallows
Allhallows
—also -s, -'s, and -s' forms of nouns listed at allow⁵

alls \ȯlz\ Angel Falls
Niagara Falls
—also -s, -'s, and -s' forms of nouns, and -s forms of verbs, listed at all

allsy \ȯl-zē\ see alsy

allus \al-əs\ see alis²

allused \al-əst\ see alist

ally¹ \ā-lē\ see aily

ally² \äl-ē\ see olly¹

ally³ \ȯ-lē\ see awly

ally⁴ \al-ē\ alley, bally, challis, dally, galley, gally, mallee, pally, rally, sallie, sally, Sally, tally, valley
Aunt Sally, bialy, crevalle, Death Valley, finale, Nepali, tomalley
dillydally, Great Rift Valley, Mexicali, shilly-shally, teocalli,

allyn \al-ən\ see allon

alm \äm\ see om¹

alma \al-mə\ Alma, halma

almar \äm-ər\ see omber¹

almer \äm-ər\ see omber¹

almily \äm-ə-lē\ see omaly

almish \äm-ish\ see amish¹

almist \äm-əst\ palmist, psalmist
Islamist

almody \äm-əd-ē\ see omedy

almon \am-ən\ see ammon

almoner \äm-ə-nər\ see ommoner

alms \ämz\ alms, Brahms, Psalms
—*also* -s, -'s, *and* -s' *forms of nouns,
and* -s *forms of verbs, listed at* om¹

almy \äm-ē\ see ami¹

alo \äl-ō\ see ollow¹

aloe \al-ō\ see allow⁵

alogist¹ \äl-ə-jəst\ see ologist

alogist² \al-ə-jəst\ analogist,
dialogist, mammalogist
genealogist

alogy¹ \äl-ə-jē\ see ology

alogy² \al-ə-jē\ analogy, hypallage,
mammalogy, tetralogy
mineralogy

alom \äl-əm\ see olumn

alon \al-ən\ see allon

alop \al-əp\ see allop²

alor¹ \äl-ər\ see ollar

alor² \al-ər\ see aller²

alorie¹ \al-rē\ see allery¹

alorie² \al-ə-rē\ see alary²

alory¹ \al-rē\ see allery

alory² \al-ə-rē\ see alary²

alousie \al-ə-sē\ see allacy

alp \alp\ alp, salp, scalp

alpa \al-pə\ salpa
catalpa
Tegucigalpa

alpal \al-pəl\ palpal, scalpel

alpel \al-pəl\ see alpal

alpha \al-fə\ alpha
alfalfa

alque¹ \ok\ see alk

alque² \alk\ calque, talc
catafalque

als \älz\ see ols

alsa \ol-sə\ balsa, salsa

alse \ols\ false, waltz

alsey \ol-zē\ see alsy

alsy \ol-zē\ ballsy, Halsey, palsy

alt \olt\ fault, gault, halt, malt, salt,
smalt, vault, volt, Walt
asphalt, assault, basalt, cobalt,
default, desalt, exalt, footfault, gestalt,
Great Salt, Schwarzwald, stringhalt
double-fault, somersault
pepper-and-salt

alta \äl-tə\ Malta, Salta, Volta, Yalta

altar \ol-tər\ see alter

alter \ol-tər\ altar, alter, falter, halter,
palter, Psalter, salter, vaulter, Walter
defaulter, desalter, exalter, Gibraltar,
pole-vaulter

altery \ol-trē\ see altry

alti¹ \əl-tē\ Balti
difficulty

alti² \ol-tē\ see alty

altic \ol-tik\ Baltic
asphaltic, cobaltic, systaltic
peristaltic

alting \ol-tiŋ\ halting, salting,
vaulting
—*also* -ing *forms of verbs listed at*
alt

altless \olt-ləs\ faultless, saltless

alto \al-tō\ alto
contralto, rialto

alton \ȯlt-ᵊn\ Alton, dalton, Dalton,
Walton

altry \ȯl-trē\ paltry, psaltery, psaltry

alty \ȯl-tē\ Balti, faulty, malty, salty,
vaulty

altz \ȯls\ see alse

alu \äl-ü\ Yalu
Tuvalu

alue \al-yü\ value
devalue, disvalue, misvalue, revalue,
transvalue
overvalue, undervalue

alus¹ \ā-ləs\ see ayless

alus² \al-əs\ see alis²

alve¹ \äv\ see olve²

alve² \alv\ salve, valve
bivalve
univalve
inequivalve

alve³ \av\ calve, halve, have, salve

alver \al-vər\ salver, salvor
quacksalver

alvin \al-vən\ Alvin, Calvin

alvor \al-vər\ see alver

aly \al-ē\ see ally⁴

alyard \al-yərd\ see alliard

alysis \al-ə-səs\ analysis
dialysis, paralysis
cryptanalysis, metanalysis, self-
analysis

am¹ \äm\ see om¹

am² \am\ am, cam, cham, clam,
cram, dam, damn, damned, drachm,
dram, DRAM, flam, gam, Graham,
gram, ham, Ham, jam, jamb, lam,
lamb, Lamb, ma'am, Pam, pram, ram,
RAM, Sam, SAM, scam, scram, sham,
slam, swam, tam, tram, wham, yam

Annam, ashram, Assam, dirham,
Edam, ngram, exam, flimflam,
goddamn, grandam, iamb, logjam,
madame, mailgram, milldam, nizam,
Priam, program, quondam, tam-tam,
thiram, trigram, whim-wham,
ziram
Abraham, aerogram, Amsterdam,
anagram, Birmingham, Boulder Dam,
cablegram, centigram, Christogram,
chronogram, cofferdam, cryptogram,
decagram, deprogram, diagram,
diaphragm, dithyramb, epigram, fluid
dram, hexagram, histogram,
Hohokam, hologram, Hoover Dam,
kilogram, logogram, mammogram,
milligram, Minicam, monogram,
nomogram, oriflamme, pentagram,
phonogram, pictogram, reprogram,
Rotterdam, scattergram, skiagram,
Smithfield ham, sonogram,
subprogram, Surinam, telegram,
tetradrachm, thank-you-ma'am, Uncle
Sam
ad nauseam, cardiogram, heliogram,
ideogram, in personam,
microprogram, New Amsterdam,
Omar Khayyam
parallelogram

ama¹ \äm-ə\ Brahma, comma,
drama, Kama, lama, llama, mama,
momma, squama, Rama
Bahama, pajama, Toyama
Atacama, cyclorama, Dalai Lama,
diorama, docudrama, Fujiyama,
Fukuyama, Matsuyama, melodrama,
monodrama, Mount Mazama,
Okayama, panorama, photodrama,
psychodrama, Suriname, Wakayama,
Yokohama
Fuji-no-Yama
Puna de Atacama

ama² \am-ə\ Brahma, drama,
gamma, grama, mamma
da Gama, Manama, Miami, pajama
Alabama, anadama, cyclorama,
diorama, docudrama, melodrama,
monodrama, panorama, photodrama,
psychodrama

amable \ā-mə-bəl\ blamable,
claimable, framable, nameable,
tamable
  irreclaimable

amah \äm-ä\ see ama[1]

aman[1] \ā-mən\ see amen[1]

aman[2] \äm-ən\ see ommon

amant[1] \ā-mənt\ see ayment

amant[2] \am-ənt\ see ament[2]

amas \am-əs\ see amice

amash \äm-ish\ see amish[1]

amateur \am-ət-ər\ see ameter

amatist \am-ət-əst\ dramatist
  epigrammatist, melodramatist

amba \äm-bə\ gamba, mamba,
samba, Zomba
  Cochabamba
  viola da gamba

ambar[1] \äm-bər\ see omber[2]

ambar[2] \am-bər\ amber, Amber,
camber, sambar, timbre
  liquidambar

ambe \am-bē\ see amby

ambeau \am-bō\ see ambo

amber[1] \am-bər\ see ambar[2]

amber[2] \am-ər\ see ammer

ambia \am-bē-ə\ Gambia, Zambia

ambit \am-bət\ ambit, gambit

amble[1] \äm-bəl\ see emble[1]

amble[2] \am-bəl\ amble, bramble,
gamble, gambol, ramble, scramble,
shamble
  preamble, unscramble
  skimble-skamble

ambler \am-blər\ ambler, gambler,
rambler, scrambler
  unscrambler

ambo \am-bō\ crambo, jambeau,
sambo
  Ovambo

ambol \am-bəl\ see amble[2]

ambray \am-brē\ see ambry

ambry \am-brē\ ambry, chambray

ambulant \am-byə-lənt\ ambulant
  somnambulant

amby \am-bē\ crambe
  Dushanbe
  namby-pamby

ame[1] \ām\ aim, blame, came, claim,
dame, fame, flame, frame, game,
hame, kame, lame, maim, name, same,
shame, tame, wame
  A-frame, acclaim, aflame, airframe,
became, byname, cross-claim,
declaim, defame, disclaim, endgame,
enframe, exclaim, forename, freeze-
frame, grandame, inflame, mainframe,
misname, nickname, place-name,
prename, proclaim, quitclaim, reclaim,
selfsame, surname
  counterclaim, Niflheim, overcame

ame[2] \äm\ see om[1]

ame[3] \am\ see am[2]

ame[4] \äm-ə\ see ama[1]

ameable \ā-mə-bəl\ see amable

amed \āmd\ famed, named
  ashamed, forenamed
  unashamed
  —also -ed *forms of verbs listed at*
ame[1]

ameful \ām-fəl\ blameful, shameful

amel \am-əl\ see ammel

ameless \ām-ləs\ aimless,
blameless, nameless, shameless,
tameless

amely \ām-lē\ gamely, lamely,
namely, tamely

amen[1] \ā-mən\ bayman, Bremen, caiman, Cayman, Damon, drayman, flamen, Haman, layman, shaman, stamen, Yemen
examen, gravamen, highwayman

amen[2] \äm-ən\ see ommon

ameness \ām-nəs\ gameness, lameness, sameness, tameness

ament[1] \ā-mənt\ see ayment

ament[2] \am-ənt\ ament, clamant

amer \ā-mər\ see aimer

ames \āmz\ James
—*also* -s, -'s, *and* -s' *forms of nouns, and* -s *forms of verbs, listed at* ame[1]

ameter \am-ət-ər\ amateur
decameter, diameter, heptameter, hexameter, octameter, parameter, pentameter, tetrameter

amfer[1] \am-pər\ see amper[2]

amfer[2] \am-fər\ camphor, chamfer

ami[1] \äm-ē\ balmy, commie, mommy, palmy, qualmy, swami, Tommy
gourami, pastrami, Sagami, salami, tatami, tsunami
origami

ami[2] \am-ə\ see ama[4]

ami[3] \am-ē\ see ammy

amia \ā-mē-ə\ lamia, zamia
Mesopotamia

amic[1] \ō-mik\ see omic[2]

amic[2] \am-ik\ gamic
Adamic, agamic, balsamic, ceramic, dynamic
adynamic, cleistogamic, cryptogrammic, cycloramic, dioramic, exogamic, panoramic, phonogrammic, polygamic
aerodynamic, biodynamic, hydrodynamic, hypothalamic, ideogramic, thermodynamic
magnetodynamic

amice \am-əs\ amice, camas, chlamys, Lammas

amics \äm-iks\ see omics

amie[1] \ā-mē\ Amy, Jamie, Mamie, ramie
cockamamie, cockamamy

amie[2] \am-ē\ see ammy

amil[1] \äm-əl\ see ommel[1]

amil[2] \am-əl\ see ammel

amily \am-lē\ family
profamily, stepfamily

amin \am-ən\ see ammon

amina \am-ə-nə\ lamina, stamina

aminal \am-ən-ᵊl\ laminal
foraminal

aminant \am-ə-nənt\ contaminant, examinant

aminar \am-ə-nər\ see aminer[2]

amine \am-ən\ see ammon

aminer[1] \äm-ə-nər\ see ommoner

aminer[2] \am-ə-nər\ laminar
gewurztraminer

aming \ā-miŋ\ flaming, framing, gaming
—*also* -ing *forms of verbs listed at* ame[1]

amish[1] \äm-ish\ Amish, qualmish, quamash
schoolmarmish

amish[2] \am-ish\ Amish, famish

amist \äm-əst\ see almist

amity \am-ət-ē\ amity
calamity

amlet \am-lət\ camlet, hamlet, Hamlet, samlet

amlets \am-ləts\ Tower Hamlets
—*also* -s, -'s, *and* -s' *forms of nouns listed at* amlet

amma \am-ə\ see ama[4]

ammable \am-ə-bəl\ flammable
programmable
diagrammable

ammal \am-əl\ see ammel

ammany \am-ə-nē\ see ammony

ammar \am-ər\ see ammer

ammas \am-əs\ see amice

ammatist \am-ət-əst\ see amatist

amme \am\ see am[2]

ammel \am-əl\ camel, mammal,
stammel, Tamil, trammel
enamel

ammer \am-ər\ clamber, clammer,
clamor, clamour, crammer, dammar,
gammer, glamour, grammar, hammer,
jammer, lamber, rammer, shammer,
slammer, stammer, yammer
clawhammer, enamor, flimflammer,
jackhammer, programmer,
sledgehammer, trip-hammer,
windjammer
katzenjammer, monogrammer,
ninnyhammer, yellowhammer

ammes \äm-əs\ see omise

ammie \am-ē\ see ammy

ammies \am-ēz\ jammies
—also -s, -'s, and -s' forms of nouns
listed at ammy

amming \am-iŋ\ damning
programming
—also -ing forms of verbs listed at
am[2]

ammock \am-ək\ drammock,
hammock, mammock

ammon \am-ən\ Brahman, famine,
gamin, gammon, mammon, salmon
backgammon, examine
cross-examine

ammony \am-ə-nē\ scammony,
Tammany

ammy \am-ē\ chamois, clammy,
gammy, Grammy, hammy, mammy,
ramie, Sammie, Sammy, shammy,
whammy
Miami

amn \am\ see am[2]

amned \am\ see am[2]

amning \am-iŋ\ see amming

amois \am-ē\ see ammy

amon[1] \ā-mən\ see amen[1]

amon[2] \äm-ən\ see ommon

amor \am-ər\ see ammer

amorous \am-rəs\ amorous,
clamorous, glamorous

amos \ā-məs\ see amous

amour \am-ər\ see ammer

amous \ā-məs\ Amos, famous,
shamus, squamous
biramous, mandamus
ignoramus, Nostradamus

amp[1] \ämp\ see omp[1]

amp[2] \ä[n]\ see ant[1]

amp[3] \amp\ amp, camp, champ,
clamp, cramp, damp, gamp, gramp,
guimpe, lamp, ramp, samp, scamp,
stamp, tamp, tramp, vamp
blackdamp, C-clamp, chokedamp,
decamp, encamp, firedamp, headlamp,
off-ramp, on-ramp, preamp, revamp,
sunlamp, unclamp
afterdamp, aide-de-camp, minicamp

ampean[1] \äm-pē-ən\ pampean,
tampion

ampean[2] \am-pē-ən\ see ampion[2]

amper[1] \äm-pər\ see omper

amper[2] \am-pər\ camper, chamfer,
damper, hamper, pamper, scamper,
stamper, tamper

amphor \am-fər\ see amfer[2]

ampi[1] \äm-pē\ see ompy

ampi[2] \am-pē\ see ampy

ampian \am-pē-ən\ see ampion[2]

ampion[1] \äm-pē-ən\ see ampean[1]

ampion[2] \am-pē-ən\ campion, champion, Grampian, pampean, rampion, tampion

ample \am-pəl\ ample, sample, trample
ensample, example, subsample
counterexample

ampler \am-plər\ sampler, trampler

ampo \äm-pō\ see ompo

ampos \am-pəs\ see ampus

ampsia \am(p)-sē-ə\ eclampsia
preeclampsia

ampton \am-tən\ Hampton
Easthampton, Northampton,
Southampton
Wolverhampton

ampus \am-pəs\ Campos, campus, grampus
hippocampus

ampy \am-pē\ campy, scampi

ams \amz\ Jams
—also -s, -'s, and -s' forms of nouns,
and -s forms of verbs, listed at am[2]

amson \am-sən\ damson, Samson

amster \am-stər\ hamster, lamster

amsun \äm-sən\ Hamsun,
Thompson

amulus \am-yə-ləs\ famulus,
hamulus

amus[1] \ā-məs\ see amous

amus[2] \äm-əs\ see omise

amy \ā-mē\ see amie[1]

amys \am-əs\ see amice

an[1] \än\ see ant[1]

an[2] \än\ see on[1]

an[3] \ən\ see un

an[4] \aŋ\ see ang[2]

an[5] \an\ an, Ann, Anne, ban, bran, can, clan, Dan, fan, Fan, flan, Jan, Klan, man, Mann, nan, Nan, pan, Pan, panne, plan, ran, scan, San, Shan, span, Stan, tan, van, Van
adman, Afghan, aidman, ape-man, ashcan, Bataan, bedpan, began, Bhutan, birdman, boardman, brainpan, brogan, caftan, caiman, cancan, capstan, captan, caveman, Cayman, Cèzanne, chessman, Cheyenne, chlordan, Chopin, claypan, clubman, Cohan, cooncan, corban, cowman, Cruzan, cyan, deadpan, deskman, Dian, Diane, Diann, Dianne, dishpan, divan, doorman, dustpan, fan-tan, fibranne, flyman, foreran, FORTRAN, freedman, freeman, frogman, G-man, gagman, Georgeann, glucan, Gosplan, hardpan, he-man, iceman, inspan, Iran, japan, Japan, jazzman, Joann, Joanne, Kazan, kneepan, Koran, Kurgan, leadman, Leanne, legman, liftman, loran, Luanne, madman, Mandan, Marfan, mailman, merman, Milan, milkman, newsman, oilcan, oilman, outran, pavane, pecan, plowman, postman, preman, pressman, propman, Queen Anne, Qur'an, ragman, rattan, reedman, reman, rodman, Roseanne, routeman, Roxanne, Ruthann, Saipan, sampan, sandman, Saran, saucepan, scalepan, schoolman, sedan, sideman, snowman, soundman, soutane, spaceman, Spokane, stewpan, stickman, stockman, strongman, stuntman, Sudan, suntan, Susanne, Suzanne, T-man, TACAN, taipan, Tarzan, tisane, toucan, trainman, trashman, trepan, Tristan, unman, vegan, Walkman, wingspan, yardman, yes-man
Alcoran, allemande, also-ran, Ameslan, anchorman, Andaman, astrakhan, Astrakhan, ataman, Athelstan, attackman, automan,

balmacaan, Bantustan, bartizan, Belmopan, black-and-tan, bogeyman, boogeyman, businessman, Caliban, cameraman, caravan, catalan, cattleman, Civitan, colorman, cornerman, counterman, counterplan, countryman, courtesan, dairyman, defenseman, everyman, exciseman, expressman, fancy-dan, fellowman, funnyman, gamelan, garageman, garbageman, Hamadan, handyman, harmattan, Hindustan, hotelman, Isle of Man, jerrican, Juliann, Julianne, Kazakhstan, Ku Klux Klan, Kurdistan, Kyrgyzstan, man-for-man, man-to-man, Marianne, Maryann, Maryanne, middleman, minuteman, Monaghan, moneyman, Occitan, ombudsman, Omdurman, overman, overran, Pakistan, Parmesan, partisan, pattypan, Peter Pan, pivotman, plainclothesman, Port Sudan, Powhatan, Ramadan, repairman, rewrite man, Ryazan, safetyman, selectman, serviceman, shandrydan, Shantyman, shovelman, signalman, spick-and-span, superman, tallyman, tamarin, Teheran, teleman, teleran, triggerman, trimaran, turbofan, weatherman, workingman, yataghan, Yucatan
   Afghanistan, arrière-ban, Baluchistan, bipartisan, catamaran, catch-as-catch-can, cavalryman, committeeman, deliveryman, Kalimantan, newspaperman, orangutan, radioman, salary man, Tajikistan, Turkmenistan, Uzbekistan

an⁶ \än-yə\ see ania¹

an⁷ \äng\ see ong¹

an⁸ \änt\ see ant²

ana¹ \än-ə\ ana, anna, Anna, bwana, Dona, donna, Donna, fauna, Ghana, Kana, Lana, Lonna, mana
   Botswana, chicana, gymkhana, iguana, jacana, lantana, liana, Madonna, mañana, nagana, nirvana, piranha, Purana, ruana, Tijuana, Tirane, Toscana, zenana

Africana, belladonna, epifauna, French Guiana, Guadiana, Haryana, Hinayana, hiragana, ikebana, Ludhiana, Mahayana, marijuana, parmigiana, pozzolana, prima donna, Rajputana, Rosh Hashanah, Tatiana
   Americana, fata morgana, Lincolniana, Ljubljana, nicotiana, Shakespeareana, Victoriana
   Ciudad Guyana

ana² \ā-nə\ ana, Dana, Lana
Africana, cantilena, Cartagena
nicotiana, Shakespeareana

ana³ \an-ə\ ana, Anna, canna, manna, Ghana, Hannah, Lana, nana
banana, bandanna, cabana, Deanna, Diana, Dianna, Fermanagh, goanna, Guiana, Guyana, gymkhana, Havana, hosanna, Joanna, Johanna, Montana, savanna, Savannah, sultana, Susanna, Susannah
   Africana, Indiana, Juliana, Mariana, Marianna, poinciana, Pollyanna, Santa Ana
   Americana, fata morgana, Louisiana, nicotiana, Shakespeareana, Victoriana

aña \än-yə\ see ania¹

anacle \an-i-kəl\ see anical

anage \an-ij\ manage, tannage
stage-manage
micromanage

anagh \an-ə\ see ana³

anah¹ \ō-nə\ see ona¹

anah² \än-ə\ see ana¹

anal \ān-ᵊl\ anal, banal

analyst \an-ᵊl-əst\ analyst, annalist, panelist
cryptanalyst
psychoanalyst

anan \an-ən\ see annon

anape \an-ə-pē\ see anopy

anary¹ \än-rē\ see anery

anary² \an-rē\ see annery²

anate \an-ət\ see annet

anative \an-ət-iv\ sanative
explanative

anbe \am-bē\ see amby

anc[1] \a^n\ see ant[1]

anc[2] \aŋ\ see ang[2]

anc[3] \aŋk\ see ank

anca \aŋ-kə\ Kanka
barranca
Casablanca, lingua franca,
Salamanca

ance[1] \ä^{n}s\ nuance, outrance,
Provence, Saint-Saëns, séance
à outrance, diligence, Fort-de-
France, ordonnance, renaissance
mésalliance, par excellence
concours d'elegance
pièce de résistance

ance[2] \äns\ Hans, nonce, sconce
brisance, ensconce, faience, nuance,
response
Afrikaans, complaisance, fer-de-
lance, nonchalance, provenance,
renaissance
pièce de résistance

ance[3] \ans\ chance, dance, France,
glance, lance, Lance, manse, prance,
stance, trance, trans, Vance
advance, askance, bechance,
enhance, entrance, expanse, finance,
mischance, perchance, romance,
Romance, side-glance, sweatpants
circumstance, complaisance,
contredanse, country-dance, fer-de-
lance, happenchance, happenstance,
Liederkranz, Port-au-Prince,
refinance, smarty-pants, underpants
— also -s, -'s, and -s' forms of
nouns, and -s forms of verbs, listed at
ant[5]

anceable \an-sə-bəl\ see ansible

anced \anst\ canst
circumstanced
underfinanced

—also -ed forms of verbs listed at
ance[3]

ancel \an-səl\ cancel, chancel,
handsel
expansile, precancel

anceler \an-slər\ canceler,
chancellor
vice-chancellor

ancellor \an-slər\ see anceler

ancement \an-smənt\ advancement,
enhancement

ancer \an-sər\ answer, cancer,
dancer, glancer, lancer, prancer
advancer, enhancer, free-lancer,
merganser, romancer, ropedancer
anticancer, geomancer, necromancer,
rhabdomancer

ances \an(t)-səs\ see ancis

ancet \an-sət\ lancet
Narragansett

anch[1] \änch\ see aunch[1]

anch[2] \ȯnch\ see aunch[2]

anch[3] \anch\ blanch, Blanche,
branch, ranch
rebranch
avalanche

anche[1] \ä^{n}sh\ tranche
carte blanche, revanche

anche[2] \anch\ see anch[3]

anche[3] \an-chē\ see anchy

ancher[1] \ȯn-chər\ see auncher

ancher[2] \an-chər\ ceinture, rancher

anchi \an-chē\ see anchy

anchion \an-chən\ see ansion

anchor \aŋ-kər\ see anker

anchoress \aŋ-krəs\ see ankerous

anchy \an-chē\ branchy, Ranchi
Comanche

ancial \an-chəl\ see antial

ancis \an(t)-səs\ Frances, Francis Aransas
—*also* -s, -'s, *and* -s' *forms of nouns, and* -s *forms of verbs, listed at* ance³

anck \änk\ see onk¹

anco \äŋ-kō\ see onco

ancolin \aŋ-klən\ see anklin

ancor \aŋ-kər\ see anker

ancorous \aŋ-krəs\ see ankerous

ancre \aŋ-kər\ see anker

ancrous \aŋ-krəs\ see ankerous

anct \aŋt\ see anked

ancy \an-sē\ chancy, fancy, Nancy
unchancy
chiromancy, geomancy, hydromancy, necromancy, pyromancy, rhabdomancy, sycophancy
oneiromancy

and¹ \äⁿ\ see ant¹

and² \änd\ see ond¹

and³ \and\ and, band, bland, brand, canned, gland, grand, hand, land, manned, NAND, rand, Rand, sand, Sand, stand strand
armband, backhand, backland, badland, bandstand, benchland, blackland, broadband, brushland, bushland, cabstand, cloudland, coastland, command, cowhand, crash-land, cropland, deckhand, demand, disband, dockhand, dockland, downland, dreamland, dryland, duneland, expand, farmhand, farmland, fenland, filmland, firebrand, firsthand, flatland, forehand, four-hand, free hand, freehand, gangland, glad-hand, Gotland, grandstand, grassland, handstand, hardstand, hatband, headband, headstand, heartland, heathland, homeland,

Iceland, inkstand, inland, Inland, kickstand, Kokand, Lapland, left-hand, longhand, mainland, marshland, misbrand, newsstand, nightstand, northland, noseband, offhand, outland, outstand, parkland, pineland, playland, proband, Queensland, quicksand, rangeland, remand, repand, Rheinland, Rhineland, ribband, right-hand, rimland, roband, Saarland, scabland, screenland, scrubland, seastrand, shorthand, sideband, softland, southland, spaceband, stagehand, summand, swampland, sweatband, Thailand, thirdhand, tideland, trainband, unhand, unmanned, waistband, washstand, wasteland, watchband, wetland, wildland, withstand, wristband
ampersand, beforehand, behindhand, bellyband, belly-land, borderland, bottomland, confirmand, contraband, countermand, Damavand, Dixieland, fairyland, fatherland, Ferdinand, forestland, four-in-hand, graduand, hand-to-hand, hand to hand, hinterland, Krugerrand, lotusland, meadowland, motherland, Nagaland, narrowband, no-man's-land, operand, ordinand, overhand, overland, pastureland, reprimand, Rio Grande, Samarkand, saraband, secondhand, Swaziland, tableland, Talleyrand, timberland, Togoland, underhand, undermanned, understand, wonderland, Zululand
analysand, Bechuanaland, cloud-cuckoo-land, fantasyland, misunderstand, multiplicand, Prince Rupert's Land, Somaliland, Sudetenland, vacationland, videoland, Witwatersrand
Matabeleland
Alice-in-Wonderland
—*also* -ed *forms of verbs listed at* an⁵

and⁴ \än\ see on¹

and⁵ \änt\ see ant²

anda¹ \an-də\ Ganda, panda

Amanda, Luanda, Luganda,
Miranda, Uganda, veranda
jacaranda, memoranda, propaganda
nomina conservanda

anda² \än-də\ see onda

andable \an-də-bəl\ mandible
commandable, demandable,
expandable
understandable

andaed \an-dəd\ see anded

andal \an-dᵊl\ see andle

andaled \an-dᵊld\ handled, sandaled
well-handled
—*also* -ed *forms of verbs listed at*
andle

andall \an-dᵊl\ see andle

andalous \an-dləs\ see andless²

andam \an-dəm\ see andum

andant \an-dənt\ see andent

andar \ənd-ər\ see under

andarin \an-drən\ mandarin
alexandrine, salamandrine

ande¹ \ən\ see un

ande² \an\ see an⁵

ande³ \an-dē\ see andy

ande⁴ \and\ see and³

ande⁵ \än-də\ see onda

anded \an-dəd\ banded, branded,
candid, handed, landed, stranded
backhanded, bare-handed,
cleanhanded, forehanded, four-
handed, freehanded, ham-handed,
hardhanded, high-handed, ironhanded,
left-handed, light-handed, offhanded,
one-handed, red-handed, right-handed,
shorthanded, sure-handed, three-
handed, two-handed, unbranded,
verandaed
empty-handed, evenhanded, heavy-
handed, openhanded, overhanded,
singlehanded, underhanded

—*also* -ed *forms of verbs listed at*
and³

andel \an-dᵊl\ see andle

andem \an-dəm\ see andum

andent \an-dənt\ candent, scandent
demandant

ander¹ \en-dər\ see ender

ander² \än-dər\ see onder¹

ander³ \an-dər\ bander, brander,
candor, dander, gander, grandeur,
lander, pander, sander, slander,
strander, zander
auslander, backhander, blackhander,
bystander, commander, demander,
expander, flatlander, germander, glad-
hander, goosander, grandstander,
inlander, Leander, left-hander,
mainlander, meander, outlander,
philander, pomander, right-hander,
scrimshander, soft-lander, Uitlander
Africander, alexander, Alexander,
calamander, coriander, gerrymander,
oleander, salamander, single-hander
—*also* -er *forms of adjectives listed*
at and³

anderous \an-drəs\ see androus

anders \an-dərz\ Flanders
Bouvier des Flandres, golden
alexanders
—*also* -s, -'s, *and* -s' *forms of nouns,*
and -s *forms of verbs, listed at* ander³

andery \an-drē\ see andry

andes \an-dēz\ Andes
—*also* -s, -'s, *and* -s' *forms of nouns,*
and -s *forms of verbs, listed at* andy

andeur¹ \an-dər\ see ander³

andeur² \an-jər\ see anger⁴

andhi \an-dē\ see andy

andi \an-dē\ see andy

andible \an-də-bəl\ see andable

andid \an-dəd\ see anded

anding \an-diŋ\ standing
commanding, crossbanding,
freestanding, hardstanding, long-
standing, outstanding, upstanding
mind-expanding, notwithstanding,
understanding
—*also* -ing *forms of verbs listed at*
and³

andish \an-dish\ blandish, brandish,
standish, Standish
outlandish

andist \an-dəst\ contrabandist,
propagandist
—*also* -est *forms of adjectives listed
at* and³

andit \an-dət\ bandit, pandit

andle \an-dᵊl\ candle, dandle,
Handel, handle, Randall, sandal,
scandal, vandal
footcandle, manhandle, mishandle,
panhandle, stickhandle
coromandel, Coromandel

andled \an-dᵊl\ see andaled

andler \an-lər\ candler, chandler,
handler
panhandler, stickhandler

andless \an-ləs\ see anless

andly \an-lē\ see anly²

andment \an-mənt\ commandment,
disbandment

ando \an-dō\ Fernando, Orlando

andom \an-dəm\ see andum

andor \an-dər\ see ander³

andra \an-drə\ Sandra
Cassandra
Alexandra, pachysandra

andrea \an-drē-ə\ see andria

andrel \an-drəl\ mandrel, mandrill,
spandrel

andres \an-dərz\ see anders

andria \an-drē-ə\ Andrea
Alexandria

andrill \an-drəl\ see andrel

andrine \an-drən\ see andarin

andros \an-drəs\ see androus

androus \an-drəs\ Andros
slanderous
gynandrous, meandrous
polyandrous

andry \an-drē\ commandery,
monandry
polyandry

ands \anz\ Badlands, Lowlands
Canyonlands

andsel \an-səl\ see ancel

andsman \anz-mən\ bandsman,
clansman, Klansman, landsman

andsome \an-səm\ see ansom

andum \an-dəm\ fandom, grandam,
random, tandem
memorandum
nomen conservandum
subpoena ad testificandum

andy \an-dē\ Andy, bandy, brandy,
Brandy, candy, dandy, handy, Handy,
pandy, randy, Randy, sandhi, sandy,
Sandy, shandy
jim-dandy, unhandy
Rio Grande
modus operandi

ane¹ \ān\ ain, Aisne, ane, bane,
blain, Blaine, brain, Cain, cane, chain,
crane, Crane, Dane, deign, drain,
Duane, Dwain, Dwayne, fain, fane,
feign, gain, grain, Jane, Jayne, lane,
Lane, main, Maine, mane, pain, Paine,
pane, plain, plane, quean, rain, reign,
rein, sain, sane, seine, Seine, skein,
slain, Spain, sprain, stain, stane, strain,
swain, thane, thegn, train, twain,
Twain, vain, vane, vein, wain, wane,
Wayne, Zane

abstain, again, airplane, amain,
arcane, arraign, attain, Bahrain,
Bassein, Beltane, biplane, birdbrain,
Biscayne, bloodstain, bugbane,
campaign, champagne, champaign,
Champlain, checkrein, chicane,
chilblain, chow mein, cinquain,
cocaine, Cockaigne, coxswain,
complain, constrain, contain,
cordwain, cowbane, crackbrain,
demesne, deplane, destain, detain,
detrain, devein, disdain, distain,
distrain, dogbane, domain, drivetrain,
Duane, dumbcane, edge-grain, Elaine,
emplane, enchain, engrain, enplane,
entrain, explain, eyestrain, fleabane,
floatplane, floodplain, Fort Wayne,
Gawain, germane, grosgrain, Helaine,
Helene, henbane, house-train,
humane, Hussein, Igraine, immane,
inane, ingrain, insane, lamebrain,
lightplane, lo mein, Loraine, Lorraine,
maintain, marchpane, membrane,
migraine, Montaigne, montane,
moraine, mortmain, Moulmein,
mundane, neck-rein, obtain, octane,
ordain, pertain, plain-Jane, profane,
ptomaine, purslane, quatrain, refrain,
remain, restrain, retain, retrain,
romaine, sailplane, sea-lane, seaplane,
seatrain, sustain, tearstain, terrain,
terrane, triplane, Touraine, Ukraine,
unchain, urbane, vervain, vicereine,
villein, volplane, warplane, wolfsbane
 aeroplane, appertain, aquaplane,
Aquitaine, ascertain, avellane,
Bloemfontein, cellophane,
Charlemagne, Charles's Wain,
chatelain, chatelaine, counterpane, de
Montaigne, entertain, featherbrain,
foreordain, frangipane, gyroplane,
hurricane, hydroplane, hyperplane,
inhumane, Kwajalein, La Fontaine,
marocain, Mary Jane, mise-en-scène,
monoplane, Novocain, neutercane,
novocaine, overlain, paravane, paper-
train, peneplain, Port of Spain, port-
wine stain, preordain, rattlebrain,
scatterbrain, shaggymane, Spanish
Main, sugarcane, suzerain,

Tamburlaine, Tamerlane, terreplein,
tramontane, transmontane,
windowpane
 Alsace-Lorraine, auf Wiedersehen,
balletomane, convertiplane,
demimondaine, elecampane,
extramundane, intermontane, Lake
Pontchartraine, legerdemain,
ultramontane
 trichalomethane

ane² \an\ see an⁵

ane³ \än-ə\ see ana¹

ane⁴ \än\ see on¹

anea \ā-nē-ə\ see ania²

anean \ā-nē-ən\ see anian²

aned \ānd\ see ained

anee \an-ē\ see anny

aneful \ān-fəl\ see ainful

anel \an-ᵊl\ see annel

anelist \an-ᵊl-əst\ see analyst

aneous \ā-nē-əs\ cutaneous,
extraneous, spontaneous
 coetaneous, consentaneous,
instantaneous, miscellaneous,
porcelaneous, simultaneous,
succedaneous
 contemporaneous, extemporaneous

aner¹ \ā-nər\ see ainer

aner² \än-ər\ see onor¹

anery \ān-rē\ granary
chicanery

anet \an-ət\ see annet

aneum \ā-nē-əm\ see anium

aney \o̅-nē\ see awny¹

anford \an-fərd\ Sanford, Stanford

ang¹ \äŋ\ see ong¹

ang² \aŋ\ bang, bhang, clang, dang,
fang, Fang, gang, gangue, hang, pang,

prang, rang, sang, slang, spang, sprang,
stang, tang, twang, whang, yang
  cliff-hang, defang, ginseng,
harangue, linsang, meringue, mustang,
orang, parang, Pinang, press-gang,
probang, shebang, slam-bang,
straphang, trepang, whizbang
  boomerang, charabanc, overhang,
parasang, siamang
    interrobang, orangutan

ang³ \ȯŋ\ see ong²

anga \äŋ-gə\ see onga

angar \aŋ-ər\ see anger²

ange¹ \äⁿzh\ blancmange, mélange

ange² \ānj\ change, grange, mange,
range, strange
  arrange, derange, downrange,
estrange, exchange, free-range,
gearchange, long-range, outrange,
short-range, shortchange
    counterchange, disarrange,
interchange, omnirange
      Great Dividing Range

ange³ \anj\ flange
phalange

angel \aŋ-gəl\ see angle

angell \aŋ-gəl\ see angle

angement \ānj-mənt\ arrangement,
derangement, estrangement
  disarrangement

angency \an-jən-sē\ plangency,
tangency

angent \an-jənt\ plangent, tangent

anger¹ \ān-jər\ changer, danger,
granger, manger, ranger, stranger
  bushranger, endanger, estranger,
exchanger, shortchanger
    interchanger

anger² \aŋ-ər\ banger, clanger,
clangor, clangour, ganger, hangar,
hanger, languor, Sanger, twanger
  cliff-hanger, haranguer, straphanger
    paperhanger

anger³ \aŋ-gər\ anger, clangor

anger⁴ \an-jər\ flanger, grandeur
phalanger

angi \aŋ-ē\ see angy²

angible \an-jə-bəl\ frangible,
tangible
  infrangible, intangible, refrangible

angie \aŋ-ē\ see angy²

anging¹ \ān-jiŋ\ bushranging,
unchanging, wide-ranging
  —also -ing forms of verbs listed at
ange²

anging² \aŋ-iŋ\ hanging
cliff-hanging
paperhanging
  —also -ing forms of verbs listed at
ang²

angle \aŋ-gəl\ angle, bangle, dangle,
jangle, mangel, mangle, spangle,
strangle, tangle, wangle,
wrangle
  embrangle, entangle, Mount
Wrangell, pentangle, quadrangle,
rectangle, triangle, untangle, wide-
angle
    disentangle

angled \aŋ-gəld\ angled, tangled
  newfangled, oldfangled, right-
angled, star-spangled
    —also -ed forms of verbs listed at
angle

anglement \aŋ-gəl-mənt\
tanglement
  embranglement, entanglement
    disentanglement

angler \aŋ-glər\ angler, dangler,
jangler, mangler, strangler, wangler,
wrangler
  entangler

angles \aŋ-gəlz\ Angles, strangles
  —also -s, -'s, and -s' forms of nouns,
and -s forms of verbs, listed at angle

anglian \aŋ-glē-ən\ Anglian,
ganglion

angling \aŋ-gliŋ\ angling, gangling
—also -ing forms of verbs listed at angle

anglion \aŋ-glē-ən\ see anglian

angly \aŋ-glē\ gangly, jangly, tangly

ango \aŋ-gō\ mango, tango
Durango, fandango

angor¹ \aŋ-ər\ see anger²

angor² \aŋ-gər\ see anger³

angorous \aŋ-ə-rəs\ clangorous, languorous

angour \aŋ-ər\ see anger²

angster \aŋ-stər\ gangster, prankster

anguage \aŋ-gwij\ language, slanguage
metalanguage, paralanguage, protolanguage

angue \aŋ\ see ang²

anguer \aŋ-ər\ see anger²

anguish \aŋ-gwish\ anguish, languish

anguor \aŋ-ər\ see anger²

anguorous \aŋ-ə-rəs\ see angorous

angus \aŋ-gəs\ Angus, Brangus

angy¹ \ān-jē\ mangy, rangy

angy² \aŋ-ē\ tangy, twangy
Ubangi
collieshangie

anha \än-ə\ see ana¹

anhope \an-əp\ see annup

ani¹ \än-ē\ Bonnie, bonny, Connie, Donnie, fawny, johnny, Ronnie, tawny
afghani, Fulani
chalcedony, Kisangani, maharani, Nuristani, quadriphony, Rajasthani
mulligatawny

ani² \an-ē\ see anny

ania¹ \än-yə\ Agana, España, lasagna, Titania
Emilia-Romagna

ania² \ā-nē-ə\ mania, titania, Titania, Urania
Acarnania, Anglomania, Aquitania, collectanea, dipsomania, egomania, hypomania, kleptomania, Lithuania, Mauretania, Mauritania, miscellanea, monomania, mythomania, nymphomania, Oceania, Pennsylvania, Pomerania, pyromania, Transylvania
balletomania, bibliomania, decalcomania, megalomania

ania³ \än-yə\ Campania, Catania, Hispania, Titania
Aquitania, malaguena
Tripolitania
—also words listed at ania²

anian¹ \än-ē-ən\ Kiwanian, Turanian
Araucanian

anian² \ā-nē-ən\ Albanian, Dardanian, Iranian, Romanian, Rumanian, Sassanian, Turanian, Ukrainian, Uranian, vulcanian
Lithuanian, Pennsylvanian, Pomeranian, Ruritanian, subterranean
Indo-Iranian, Mediterranean

aniard \an-yərd\ lanyard, Spaniard

anic \an-ik\ manic, panic, tannic
Brahmanic, Britannic, cyanic, firemanic, galvanic, Germanic, Hispanic, Koranic, mechanic, melanic, organic, Romanic, satanic, shamanic, Sudanic, titanic, tympanic, volcanic
aldermanic, Alemannic, councilmanic, epiphanic, inorganic, messianic, oceanic, Ossianic, pre-Hispanic, talismanic, theophanic
Indo-Germanic, megalomanic, Rhaeto-Romanic, suboceanic, transoceanic

anical \an-i-kəl\ manacle, panicle, sanicle
botanical, mechanical, tyrannical
puritanical

anice \an-əs\ see anise

anicle \an-i-kəl\ see anical

anics \an-iks\ annex
mechanics
—*also* -s, -'s, *and* -s' *forms of nouns,
and* -s *forms of verbs, listed at* anic

anid¹ \ā-nəd\ ranid
tabanid

anid² \an-əd\ canid, ranid
Sassanid

aniel¹ \an-ᵊl\ see annel

aniel² \an-yəl\ see anual

anigan \an-i-gən\ see annigan

anikin \an-i-kən\ see annikin

animous \an-ə-məs\ animus
magnanimous, unanimous
pusillanimous

animus \an-ə-məs\ see animous

anion¹ \än-yən\ see onyon¹

anion² \an-yən\ banyan, canon,
canyon, fanion
companion, Grand Canyon, Hells
Canyon

anis \an-əs\ see anise

anise \an-əs\ anise, Janice, Janis,
stannous
johannes, Johnannes, pandanus,
titanous
Scipio Africanus

anish¹ \ā-nish\ see ainish

anish² \an-ish\ banish, clannish,
mannish, planish, Spanish, tannish,
vanish
Pollyannish, Judeo-Spanish

anist \än-əst\ see onest

anister \an-ə-stər\ banister, canister,
ganister

anite \an-ət\ see annet

anity \an-ət-ē\ sanity, vanity

humanity, inanity, insanity, profanity,
urbanity
Christianity, churchianity,
inhumanity
superhumanity

anium \ā-nē-əm\ cranium
geranium, uranium
succedaneum

ank \aŋk\ bank, blank, brank, clank,
crank, dank, drank, flank, franc, frank,
Frank, hank, lank, plank, prank, rank,
sank, shank, shrank, spank, stank,
swank, tank, thank, yank, Yank
Burbank, claybank, embank,
foreshank, gangplank, greenshank,
nonbank, outflank, outrank, pickthank,
point-blank, redshank, sandbank,
sheepshank, snowbank
mountebank, riverbank
clinkety-clank

anka¹ \äŋ-kə\ concha, tanka
Sri Lanka

anka² \aŋ-kə\ see anca

ankable \aŋ-kə-bəl\ bankable,
frankable

anked \aŋt\ shanked, tanked
spindle-shanked, sacrosanct
—*also* -ed *forms of verbs listed at*
ank

ankee \aŋ-kē\ see anky

anken \aŋ-kən\ flanken, Rankine

anker \aŋ-kər\ anchor, banker,
canker, chancre, flanker, franker,
hanker, rancor, ranker, spanker, tanker,
thanker
co-anchor, unanchor
—*also* -er *forms of adjectives listed
at* ank

ankerous \aŋ-krəs\ anchoress,
cankerous, chancrous, rancorous
cantankerous

ankh \äŋk\ see onk¹

ankie \aŋ-kē\ see anky

ankine \aŋ-kən\ see anken

ankish \aŋ-kish\ Frankish, prankish

ankle \aŋ-kəl\ ankle, crankle, rankle

ankly \aŋ-klē\ blankly, dankly, frankly

anks \aŋs\ see anx

ankster \aŋ-stər\ see angster

anky \aŋ-kē\ cranky, hankie, lanky, swanky, Yankee
hanky-panky

anless \an-ləs\ handless, manless, planless

anley \an-lē\ see anly²

anli \an-lē\ see anly²

anly¹ \än-lē\ fondly, thrawnly, wanly

anly² \an-lē\ blandly, grandly, manly, Stanley
Osmanli, unmanly

ann¹ \an\ see an⁵

ann² \än\ see on¹

anna¹ \än-ə\ see ana¹

anna² \an-ə\ see ana³

annage \an-ij\ see anage

annah \an-ə\ see ana³

annalist \an-ᵊl-əst\ see analyst

annan \an-ən\ see annon

anne \an\ see an⁵

anned \and\ see and³

annel \an-ᵊl\ channel, Channel, Daniel, flannel, panel, scrannel, spaniel
impanel
English Channel

annequin \an-i-kən\ see annikin

anner \an-ər\ banner, canner, fanner, lanner, manner, manor, planner, scanner, spanner, tanner, vanner
deadpanner, japanner
caravanner

annery¹ \än-rē\ ornery, swannery

annery² \an-rē\ cannery, granary, tannery

annes \an-əs\ see anise

anness \än-nəs\ fondness, wanness

annet \an-ət\ gannet, granite, Janet, planet
pomegranate

annexe \an-iks\ see anics

annibal \an-ə-bəl\ cannibal, Hannibal

annic \an-ik\ see anic

annie \an-ē\ see anny

annigan \an-i-gən\ brannigan
shenanigan

annikin \an-i-kən\ cannikin, manikin, mannequin, pannikin

annin \an-ən\ see annon

annish \an-ish\ see anish²

annon \an-ən\ cannon, canon, Shannon, tannin
Buchanan, Clackmannan, colcannon

annous \an-əs\ see anise

anns \anz\ see ans⁴

annual \an-yəl\ see anual

annular \an-yə-lər\ annular, cannular, granular

annulate \an-yə-lət\ annulate, annulet
campanulate

annulet \an-yə-lət\ see annulate

annum \an-əm\ see anum²

annup \an-əp\ sannup, stanhope

anny \an-ē\ Annie, canny, cranny, Danny, fanny, granny, Lanny, nanny
afghani, ca'canny, kokanee, uncanny
frangipani, Hindustani, hootenanny

ano¹ \än-ō\ guano, Kano, llano, mano, mono
Chicano, Marrano, Nagano, piano, Romano, Serrano, soprano
altiplano
boliviano, fortepiano, mezzo piano, mezzo-soprano
Città del Vaticano

ano² \ā-nō\ ripieno, volcano

ano³ \an-ō\ Hispano, piano, soprano fortepiano, mezzo-soprano

anon¹ \an-ən\ see annon

anon² \an-yən\ see anion²

anopy \an-ə-pē\ canape, canopy

anor \an-ər\ see anner

anous \an-əs\ see anise

anqui \äŋ-kē\ see onky

ans¹ \äns\ see ance²

ans² \änz\ see onze

ans³ \ans\ see ance³

ans⁴ \anz\ banns, Hans, sans, trans
Sextans
—also -s, -'s, and -s' forms of nouns, and -s forms of verbs, listed at an⁵

ans⁵ \aⁿ\ see ant¹

ansard \an-sərd\ see answered

ansas¹ \an(t)-səs\ see ancis

ansas² \an-zəs\ Kansas
Arkansas

anse \ans\ see ance³

ansea \än-zē\ see anzy

anser \an-sər\ see ancer

anset \an-sət\ see ancet

ansett \an-sət\ see ancet

ansible \an-sə-bəl\ danceable
expansible

ansile \an-səl\ see ancel

ansing \an-siŋ\ Lansing

—also -ing forms of verbs listed at ance³

ansion \an-chən\ mansion, scansion, stanchion
expansion

ansk \änsk\ Bryansk, Gdansk, Murmansk, Saransk

ansman \anz-mən\ see andsman

ansom \an-səm\ handsome, hansom, ransom, transom
unhandsome

anst \anst\ see anced

answer \an-sər\ see ancer

answered \an-sərd\ answered, mansard
unanswered

ansy \an-zē\ pansy, tansy
chimpanzee

ant¹ \äⁿ\ Caen, Gant
arpent, beurre blanc, croissant, en banc, Mont Blanc, riant, roman, Rouen, savant, versant
accouchement, aide-de-camp, au courant, battement, ci-devant, contretemps, debridement, denouement, en passant, Maupassant, Mitterand, Orléans, Perpignan, rapprochement, revenant, se tenant, soi-disant, vol-au-vent
arrondissement, chateaubriand, Chateaubriand, Clermont-Ferrand, de Maupassant, idiot savant, ressentiment, sauvignon blanc

ant² \änt\ aunt, can't, daunt, flaunt, font, fount, gaunt, taunt, vaunt, want, wont
avant, avaunt, bacchant, bacchante, Balante, Beaumont, bouffant, brisant, courante, détente, entente, Fremont, gallant, grandaunt, piedmont, Piedmont, piquant, romaunt, Rostand, savant, sirvente, Vermont
bon vivant, commandant, complaisant, confidant, debridement, debutant, debutante, dilettante, John of

Gaunt, intrigant, nonchalant, poste
restante, restaurant, symbiont
dicynodont, subdebutante
Montcalm de Saint Veran
sinfonia concertante

ant³ \ənt\ see ont¹

ant⁴ \ȯnt\ see aunt¹

ant⁵ \ant\ ant, aunt, brant, cant,
can't, chant, grant, Grant, hant, Kant,
pant, plant, rant, scant, shan't,
slant
  aslant, bacchant, bacchante, bezant,
courante, decant, descant, discant,
displant, eggplant, enceinte, enchant,
explant, extant, formant, gallant,
grandaunt, houseplant, implant,
incant, leadplant, levant, Levant,
pieplant, pissant, plainchant,
pourpoint, preplant, rampant, recant,
replant, savant, supplant, transplant
  adamant, commandant, complaisant,
confidant, cormorant, corposant,
Corybant, covenant, demipointe,
dilettante, disenchant, gallivant,
hierophant, interplant, sycophant

anta \ant-ə\ anta, manta
Atlanta, infanta, vedanta
Atalanta

antage \ant-ij\ vantage
advantage
coign of vantage, disadvantage

antain \ant-ᵊn\ see anton²

antal¹ \änt-ᵊl\ see ontal¹

antal² \ant-ᵊl\ see antle

antam \ant-əm\ bantam, phantom

antar \ant-ər\ see anter²

antasist \ant-ə-səst\ see anticist

ante¹ \än-tä\ Brontë, Dante
andante, Asante, volante
Belo Horizonte

ante² \änt\ see ant²

ante³ \ant\ see ant⁵

ante⁴ \änt-ē\ see anti¹

ante⁵ \ant-ē\ ante, canty, chantey,
pantie, scanty, shanty, slanty
andanti, Asante, Ashanti, Chianti,
infante
non obstante, penny-ante, vigilante
pococurante, status quo ante

antean \ant-ē-ən\ Dantean
Atlantean, post-Kantian

anteau \an-tō\ see anto²

anted \an-təd\ disenchanted
  —also -ed forms of verbs listed at
ant⁵

antel \ant-ᵊl\ see antle

antelet \ant-lət\ mantelet, plantlet

anter¹ \änt-ər\ see aunter¹

anter² \ant-ər\ antre, banter, canter,
cantor, chanter, granter, grantor,
plantar, planter, ranter, scanter
  decanter, implanter, instanter,
levanter, transplanter, trochanter
  covenanter, covenantor,
disenchanter

antes \an-tēz\ Cervantes
  —also -s, -'s, and -s' forms of nouns,
  and -s forms of verbs, listed at ante⁵

antey \ant-ē\ see ante⁵

anth \anth\ amaranth, coelacanth,
perianth, tragacanth

antha \an-thə\ Samantha
polyantha, pyracantha

anthemum \an-thə-məm\
chrysanthemum
mesembryanthemum

anther \an-thər\ anther, panther

anthropy \an-thrə-pē\ lycanthropy,
misanthropy, philanthropy

anthus \an-thəs\ acanthus,
ailanthus, dianthus
agapanthus, amianthus, polyanthus,
Rhadamanthus

anti¹ \änt-ē\ Brontë, jaunty, monte,
Monte, Monty, vaunty
andante, Asante, Ashanti, Chianti

anti² \ant-ē\ see ante⁵

antial \an-chəl\ financial, substantial
circumstantial, consubstantial,
insubstantial, transsubstantial,
unsubstantial
supersubstantial

antian¹ \änt-ē-ən\ see ontian

antian² \ant-ē-ən\ see antean

antic¹ \änt-ik\ see ontic

antic² \ant-ik\ antic, frantic, mantic
Atlantic, bacchantic, gigantic,
pedantic, romantic, semantic, Vedantic
corybantic, geomantic, hierophantic,
necromantic, sycophantic,
transatlantic

anticist \ant-ə-səst\ fantasist
Atlanticist, romanticist, semanticist

antid \ant-əd\ mantid
Quadrantid
—also -ed forms of verbs listed at
ant⁵

antie \ant-ē\ see ante⁵

antine \ant-ᵊn\ see anton²

anting¹ \ant-iŋ\ anting, canting
disenchanting
—also -ing forms of verbs listed at
ant⁵

anting² \ənt-iŋ\ see unting

antis \ant-əs\ cantus, mantis, Santos
Atlantis

antish \ant-ish\ dilettantish,
sycophantish

antle \ant-ᵊl\ cantle, mantel, mantle,
quintal
dismantle, quadrantal
consonantal, covenantal, overmantel
determinantal

antlet \ant-lət\ see antelet

antling \ant-liŋ\ bantling, scantling
dismantling

anto¹ \än-tō\ Squanto
bel canto, Toronto
Esperanto

anto² \an-tō\ canto, panto
coranto, Otranto, portmanteau
Esperanto
Strait of Otranto

antom \ant-əm\ see antam

anton¹ \änt-ᵊn\ see onton

anton² \ant-ᵊn\ Anton, canton,
Canton, plantain, Scranton, Stanton
adamantine

antor \ant-ər\ see anter²

antos¹ \an-təs\ see antis

antos² \än-təs\ Santos
Propontis

antra \ən-trə\ tantra, yantra

antre \ant-ər\ see anter²

antry \an-trē\ chantry, gantry, pantry

ants \ans\ see ance³

antua \anch-wə\ mantua
Gargantua

antus \ant-əs\ see antis

anty \ant-ē\ see ante⁵

anual¹ \an-yəl\ Daniel, spaniel
Nathaniel

anual² \an-yə-wəl\ annual, manual,
Manuel
biannual, bimanual, Emanuel,
Emmanuel, Immanuel
semi-annual
Victor Emmanuel

anuel \an-yəl\ see anual²

anular \an-yə-lər\ see annular

anulate \an-yə-lət\ see annulate

anum¹ \ā-nəm\ paynim
arcanum

anum² \an-əm\ per annum, solanum

anus¹ \ā-nəs\ see ayness

anus² \an-əs\ see anise

anx \aŋs\ Manx, thanks
Grand Banks, phalanx
—also -s, -'s, and -s' forms of nouns,
and -s forms of verbs, listed at ank

any¹ \ā-nē\ see ainy

any² \en-ē\ see enny

anyan \an-yən\ see anion²

anyard \an-yərd\ see aniard

anyon \an-yən\ see anion²

anz \ans\ see ance³

anza¹ \än-zə\ kwanza, Kwanza,
Kwanzaa
Sancho Panza

anza² \an-zə\ stanza, zanza
bonanza, organza
Sancho Panza
extravaganza

anzaa \än-zə\ see anza¹

anzee \an-zē\ see ansy

anzer \än-sər\ see onsor

anzo \än-zō\ gonzo
garbanzo

anzy \än-zē\ bronzy, Ponzi, Swansea

ao¹ \ā-ō\ see eo¹

ao² \ō\ see ow¹

ao³ \aù\ see ow²

ao⁴ \ä-ō\ Caliao
Mindanao

aoedic \ēd-ik\ see edic¹

aoighis \äsh\ see eche¹

aole \aù-lē\ see owly²

aône \ōn\ see one¹

aori \aùr-ē\ see owery

aos¹ \aùs\ see ouse²

aos² \ä-äs\ chaos, Laos

aotian \ō-shən\ see otion

aow \aù\ see ow²

ap¹ \äp\ see op¹

ap² \əp\ see up

ap³ \ap\ cap, chap, clap, crap, flap,
frap, gap, gape, hap, knap, lap, Lapp,
map, nap, nape, nappe, pap, rap, sap,
scrap, slap, snap, strap, tap, trap, wrap,
yap, Yap, zap
backslap, backwrap, blackcap,
bootstrap, burlap, catnap, claptrap,
dewlap, dognap, earflap, entrap,
enwrap, firetrap, flatcap, foolscap,
giddap, heeltap, hubcap, jockstrap,
kidnap, kneecap, lagniappe, livetrap,
madcap, mantrap, mayhap, mishap,
mobcap, mousetrap, nightcap,
pinesap, rattrap, recap, redcap, remap,
riprap, satrap, shiplap, shrink-wrap,
skullcap, skycap, snowcap, steel-trap,
stopgap, unsnap, unstrap, unwrap,
verb sap, whitecap, wiretap
afterclap, gingersnap, handicap,
overlap, rattletrap, thunderclap,
verbum sap, wentletrap
Venus's-flytrap

apa¹ \äp-ə\ grappa, Joppa, papa,
poppa, tapa
Jalapa
jipijapa

apa² \ap-ə\ kappa, tapa
Phi Beta Kappa

apable \ā-pə-bəl\ capable, drapable,
shapable
escapable, incapable
inescapable

apal \ā-pəl\ see aple

apas \äp-əs\ Chiapas
—also -s, -'s, and -s' forms of nouns
listed at apa¹

apboard \ab-ərd\ see abard

ape¹ \āp\ ape, cape, chape, crape, crepe, drape, gape, grape, jape, nape, rape, scape, scrape, shape, tape
agape, broomrape, cloudscape, duct tape, escape, landscape, moonscape, North Cape, reshape, seascape, shipshape, snowscape, streetscape, townscape, transshape, undrape, waveshape
cityscape, masking tape, waterscape, Xeriscape
audiotape, stereotape, videotape

ape² \ap\ see ap³

ape³ \äp-ē\ see oppy

ape⁴ \ap-ē\ see appy

aped \āpt\ bell-shaped
—*also* -ed *forms of verbs listed at* ape¹

apel \ap-əl\ see apple

apelin \ap-lən\ see aplain

apen \ā-pən\ capon, shapen
unshapen

aper \ā-pər\ caper, draper, gaper, paper, scraper, shaper, taper, tapir, vapor, vapour
curlpaper, endpaper, flypaper, glasspaper, landscaper, newspaper, notepaper, sandpaper, skyscraper, wallpaper, wastepaper
run-of-paper

aperer \ā-pər-ər\ paperer, taperer, vaporer

apery \ā-prē\ drapery, japery, napery, papery, vapory
sandpapery

apes \āps\ traipse
jackanapes
— *also* -s, -'s, *and* -s' *forms of nouns, and* -s *forms of verbs, listed at* ape¹

apey \ā-pē\ crepey, drapy, grapey, grapy, kepi, scrapie

aph \af\ caff, calf, chaff, daff, gaff, gaffe, graph, half, laugh, quaff, raff, sclaff, staff, staph, Waf, waff
agrafe, behalf, carafe, chiffchaff, cowlstaff, digraph, distaff, Falstaff, flagstaff, giraffe, half-staff, horselaugh, kenaf, mooncalf, paraph, pikestaff, riffraff, tipstaff
autograph, barograph, bathyscaphe, cenotaph, chronograph, cryptograph, epigraph, epitaph, half-and-half, hectograph, holograph, homograph, hygrograph, kymograph, lithograph, logograph, micrograph, monograph, pantograph, paragraph, phonograph, photograph, pictograph, polygraph, quarterstaff, seismograph, serigraph, shadowgraph, shandygaff, spectrograph, sphygmograph, telegraph, thermograph, typograph, understaff
cardiograph, choreograph, heliograph, ideograph, mimeograph, oscillograph, pseudepigraph, radiograph
chromolithograph, cinematograph, encephalograph, photomicrograph
radiotelegraph
electrocardiograph
electroencephalograph

aphael \af-ē-əl\ see aphial

aphe¹ \āf\ see afe¹

aphe² \af\ see aph

apher \af-ər\ see affer²

aphia \af-ē-ə\ see affia

aphial \af-ē-əl\ Raphael
epitaphial

aphic \af-ik\ graphic, maffick, sapphic, traffic
digraphic, edaphic, serafic, triaphic
allographic, autographic, barographic, biographic, calligraphic, cartographic, cosmographic, cryptographic, demographic, epigraphic, epitaphic, ethnographic,

geographic, hectographic,
homographic, hydrographic,
lithographic, logographic,
mammographic, monographic,
orthographic, pantographic,
paragraphic, petrographic,
phonographic, photographic,
pictographic, polygraphic,
pornographic, reprographic,
stenographic, stratigraphic,
telegraphic, tomographic, topographic,
typographic, xerographic
   bibliographic, choreographic,
   crystallographic, hagiographic,
   homolographic, iconographic,
   ideographic, lexicographic,
   oceanographic, stereographic
      autobiographic, cinematographic,
      historiographic
         echocardiographic
         electroencephalographic

aphical \af-i-kəl\ graphical
   biographical, cartographical,
   cosmographical, cryptographical,
   epigraphical, ethnographical,
   geographical, orthographical,
   petrographical, topographical,
   typographical
      bibliographical, choreographical,
      hagiographical, iconographical,
      lexicographical, oceanographical
         autobiographical, historiographical

aphics \af-iks\ graphics
   demographics, micrographics,
   supergraphics

aphnis \af-nəs\ see aftness

aphora \a-fə-rə\ anaphora,
cataphora

api \äp-ē\ see oppy

apid \ap-əd\ rapid, sapid, vapid

apie \ā-pē\ see apey

apin \ap-ən\ see appen

apine \ap-ən\ see appen

apir \ā-pər\ see aper

apis \ā-pəs\ Apis
   Priapus, Serapis

apist \ā-pəst\ rapist
   escapist, landscapist

aplain \ap-lən\ capelin, chaplain,
chaplin, sapling

aple \ā-pəl\ maple, papal, staple

aples \ā-pəlz\ Naples
   —also -s, -'s, and -s' forms of nouns,
   and -s forms of verbs, listed at aple

apless \ap-ləs\ hapless, napless,
sapless, strapless

aplin \ap-lə-n\ see aplain

aply \ap-lē\ see aptly

apnel \ap-nᵊl\ grapnel, shrapnel

apo \äp-ō\ capo
   da capo, gestapo, Mount Apo

apolis \ap-ə-ləs\ Annapolis
   Minneapolis
   Indianapolis

apon \ā-pən\ see apen

apor \ā-pər\ see aper

aporer \ā-pər-ər\ see aperer

apory \ā-pre\ see apery

apour \ā-pər\ see aper

app \ap\ see ap³

appa¹ \äp-ə\ see apa¹

appa² \ap-ə\ see apa²

appable \ap-ə-bəl\ flappable,
mappable
   recappable, unflappable

appalli \äp-ə-lē\ see opoly

appe \ap\ see ap³

apped \apt\ see apt

appen \ap-ən\ happen, lapin, rapine

apper¹ \äp-ər\ see opper

apper² \ap-ər\ capper, clapper, dapper, flapper, knapper, rapper, sapper, scrapper, snapper, strapper, tapper, wrapper, zapper
backslapper, catnapper, didapper, kidnapper, knee-slapper, petnapper, wiretapper
handicapper, snippersnapper, understrapper, whippersnapper

appet \ap-ət\ lappet, tappet

apphic \af-ik\ see aphic

appie \äp-ē\ see oppy

appily \ap-ə-lē\ happily, scrappily, snappily
unhappily

appiness \ap-ē-nəs\ happiness, sappiness, scrappiness, snappiness
unhappiness

apping \ap-iŋ\ capping, mapping, strapping, trapping, wrapping
kneecapping, petnapping
—also -ing forms of verbs listed at ap³

apple \ap-əl\ apple, chapel, dapple, grapple, scrapple
mayapple, pineapple
antechapel

apps \aps\ see apse

appy \ap-ē\ crappy, flappy, gappy, happy, nappy, pappy, sappy, scrappy, snappy, zappy
satrapy, serape, slaphappy, unhappy
triggerhappy

aps \aps\ see apse

apse \aps\ apse, chaps, craps, lapse, schnapps, taps, traps
collapse, elapse, perhaps, prolapse, relapse, synapse, time-lapse
—also -s, -'s, and -s' forms of nouns, and -s forms of verbs, listed at ap³

apt \apt\ apt, napped, rapt

adapt, black-capped, coapt, dewlapped, enrapt, inapt, snowcapped, unapt, untapped
periapt
—also -ed forms of verbs listed at ap³

apter \ap-tər\ captor, chapter, raptor
adapter

aption \ap-shən\ caption
adaption, contraption

aptive \ap-tiv\ captive
adaptive
maladaptive, preadaptive

aptly \ap-lē\ aptly, haply, raptly
inaptly, unaptly

aptor \ap-tər\ see apter

apture \ap-chər\ rapture
enrapture, recapture

apular \ap-yə-lər\ papular, scapular

apus \ā-pəs\ see apis

apy¹ \ā-pē\ see apey

apy² \ap-ē\ see appy

aq¹ \äk\ see ock¹

aq² \ak\ see ack²

aqi \äk-ē\ see ocky

aque¹ \āk\ see ake¹

aque² \ak\ see ack²

aqui \äk-ē\ see ocky

ar¹ \er\ see are⁴

ar² \or\ see or¹

ar³ \är\ ar, are, bar, barre, car, carr, char, charr, czar, far, gar, gnar, guar, jar, Lar, mar, moire, noir, our, par, parr, R, quare, Saar, scar, spar, SPAR, star, tar, tahr, Thar, tsar, tzar, yare
Adar, afar, ajar, all-star, armoire, attar, bazaar, beaux arts, bete noire, beurre noir, Bihar, bizarre, boudoir, boxcar, boyar, briard, bulbar, Bulgar,

bursar, canard, catarrh, Cathar, chukar, cigar, clochard, cougar, couloir, crossbar, crowbar, Dakar, daystar, debar, decare, devoir, dinar, disbar, drawbar, Dunbar, durbar, earthstar, Elgar, eschar, eyebar, feldspar, five-star, flatcar, four-star, fulmar, gazar, guitar, Gunnar, Hagar, handcar, Hoggar, horsecar, hussar, Invar, Ishtar, Kolar, Loire, Iyar, jack-tar, jowar, Khowar, lahar, Lamar, lekvar, lodestar, Magyar, memoir, Mizar, Mylar, Navarre, nightjar, paillard, peignoir, petard, Pindar, pissoir, planar, plantar, polestar, pourboire, pulsar, qintar, quasar, radar, railcar, rebar, Renoir, Safar, Samar, sandbar, scalar, shikar, shofar, sidebar, sidecar, sirdar, sitar, sofar, solar, sonar, streetcar, Svalbard, tramcar, trocar, unbar, volar, voussoir, Weimar

abattoir, acinar, Ahaggar, Aligarh, aide-memoire, au revoir, avatar, bolivar, Bolivar, café noir, caviar, cinnabar, commissar, communard, coplanar, Côte d'Ivoire, cultivar, deciare, deodar, Dreyfusard, escolar, escritoire, exemplar, fluorspar, handlebar, insofar, isobar, Issachar, jacamar, jaguar, Kandahar, Kashgar, kilobar, Krasnodar, Malabar, megabar, megastar, millibar, minicar, montagnard, motorcar, Mudejar, muscle car, Myanmar, Nicobar, objet d'art, pinot noir, Qiqihar, registrar, rent-a-car, repertoire, reservoir, ricercar, samovar, scimitar, seminar, simular, steak tartare, subahdar, superstar, tutelar, turbocar, VCR, Veadar, zamindar, Zanzibar

budgerigar, conservatoire, Gulf of Mannar, Hubli-Dharwar, kala-azar, Kathiawar, proseminar

ara¹ \är-ə\ Kara, Laura, Mara, Nara, para, vara

Asmara, Bambara, begorra, Bukhara, Camorra, Ferrara, Gomorrah, saguaro, Samara, samsara, tantara, tiara

capybara, carbonara, Connemara, deodara, Gemarara, Guanabara, solfatara, tuatara

Guadalajara, Ogasawara, Sagamihara, Tarahumara, Timisoara

ara² \er-ə\ see era¹

ara³ \ar-ə\ see arrow¹

ara⁴ \òr-ə\ see ora

arab \ar-əb\ Arab, Carib, carob, scarab

Shatt al Arab

arable \ar-ə-bəl\ arable, bearable, parable, shareable, spareable, wearable

declarable, unbearable

inenarrable

aracen \ar-ə-sən\ see arison

aracin \ar-ə-sən\ see arison

arad \ar-əd\ see arid

araday \ar-əd-ē\ faraday, parody

arage \ar-ij\ see arriage

aragon \ar-ə-gən\ paragon, tarragon

arah¹ \er-ə\ see era¹

arah² \ar-ə\ see arrow¹

aral¹ \ar-əl\ see arrel²

aral² \ər-əl\ see erral

aralee¹ \ar-ə-lē\ Marilee, Saralee

aralee² \er-ə-lē\ see arily

aran¹ \er-ən\ see aron¹

aran² \ar-ən\ see aron²

arant¹ \er-ənt\ see arent¹

arant² \ar-ənt\ see arent²

araoh¹ \er-ō\ see ero²

araoh² \ar-ō\ see arrow²

araph \ar-əf\ see ariff

aras \är-əs\ see orris¹

arass \ar-əs\ see aris²

arat \ar-ət\ Barrett, carat, caret, carrot, claret, garret, Garrett, karat, parrot
disparate

arate \ar-ət\ see arat

arative¹ \er-ət-iv\ declarative, imperative

arative² \ar-ət-iv\ narrative
comparative, declarative, preparative, reparative

arator \ar-ət-ər\ barrator
apparitor, comparator, preparator

arb \ärb\ barb, barbe, carb, darb, garb
bicarb, rhubarb

arbel \är-bəl\ see arble¹

arber \är-bər\ see arbor

arbered \är-bərd\ see arboard

arbin \är-bən\ see arbon

arble¹ \är-bəl\ barbel, garble, marble

arble² \òr-bəl\ see orbel

arboard \är-bərd\ barbered, larboard, starboard
astarboard, unbarbered

arbon \är-bən\ carbon, Harbin

arbor \är-bər\ arbor, barber, harbor
Pearl Harbor

arc¹ \äk\ see ock¹

arc² \ärk\ see ark¹

arca \är-kə\ see arka¹

arce¹ \ers\ scarce
Nez Percé

arce² \ärs\ see arse¹

arcel \är-səl\ see arsal

arcener \ärs-nər\ larcener, parcener
coparcener

arch \ärch\ arch, larch, march, March, parch, starch
cornstarch, frog-march
countermarch

archal \är-kəl\ darkle, sparkle
exarchal, monarchal
hierarchal, matriarchal, patriarchal

archate \är-kət\ see arket

arche \ärsh\ see arsh

arched \ärcht\ arched, parched
—also -ed forms of verbs listed at arch

archer \är-chər\ archer, marcher
departure

arches \är-chəz\ Arches, Marches

archic \är-kik\ anarchic, autarchic, autarkic, monarchic, tetrarchic
hierarchic, oligarchic

archical \är-ki-kəl\ autarchical, autarkical, monarchical
oligarchical

archon \är-kən\ see arken

archy \är-kē\ barky, charqui, larky, snarky
anarchy, autarchy, autarky, dyarchy, eparchy, exarchy, heptarchy, malarkey, menarche, monarchy, pentarchy, squirearchy, tetrarchy, triarchy, trierarchy
hierarchy, matriarchy, patriarchy, oligarchy

arck \ärk\ see ark¹

arco \är-kō\ arco, narco

arct \ärkt\ see arked

arctic¹ \ärk-tik\ arctic, Arctic
antarctic, Antarctic, Holarctic, Nearctic, subarctic
Palearctic, subantarctic

arctic² \ärt-ik\ see artic¹

arcy \är-sē\ farcy, Parsi

ard¹ \ärd\ bard, barred, card, chard, Dard, fard, guard, hard, lard, nard, pard, sard, shard, yard
Asgard, backyard, bankcard, barnyard, Bernard, blackguard, blowhard, boatyard, bombard, boneyard, brassard, brickyard, canard, churchyard, courtyard, deeryard, die-hard, diehard, discard, dockyard, dooryard, farmyard, filmcard, fireguard, foreyard, foulard, Gerard, graveyard, ill-starred, jacquard, junkyard, lifeguard, Lombard, mansard, Midgard, milliard, mudguard, noseguard, petard, placard, postcard, poularde, rear guard, rearguard, regard, retard, ritard, safeguard, scorecard, shipyard, spikenard, steelyard, stockyard, switchyard, tabard, tanyard, tiltyard, unbarred, unguard, vanguard, vizard
avant-garde, Beauregard, bodyguard, boulevard, disregard, goliard, Hildegard, interlard, Kierkegaard, Langobard, leotard, Longobard, no-holds-barred, lumberyard, Saint Bernard, Savoyard, Scotland Yard, self-regard, undercard, unitard
camelopard
—also -ed forms of verbs listed at ar³

ard² \är\ see ar³

ard³ \órd\ see oard

ardant \ärd-ᵊnt\ ardent, guardant regardant, retardant

arde \ärd\ see ard¹

arded¹ \ärd-əd\ guarded mansarded, retarded, unguarded
—also -ed forms of verbs listed at ard¹

arded² \órd-əd\ corded, sordid, swarded, warded
—also -ed forms of verbs listed at oard

ardee \órd-ē\ see ordy¹

arden¹ \ärd-ᵊn\ Arden, Dardan, garden, harden, pardon
bombardon, case-harden, Kincardine

arden² \órd-ᵊn\ cordon, Gordon, Jordan, warden
churchwarden

ardener \ärd-nər\ gardener, hardener, pardner, pardoner, partner

ardent \ärd-ᵊnt\ see ardant

arder¹ \ärd-ər\ ardor, carder, guarder, harder, larder
discarder, green-carder

arder² \órd-ər\ see order

ardi \ärd-ē\ see ardy

ardian¹ \ärd-ē-ən\ guardian Edwardian, Lombardian

ardian² \órd-ē-ən\ see ordion

ardic \ärd-ik\ bardic, Dardic Lombardic, Sephardic
goliardic, Longobardic

ardine \ärd-ⁿ\ see arden¹

arding \órd-iŋ\ see ording¹

ardingly \órd-iŋ-lē\ see ordingly

ardom \ärd-əm\ czardom, stardom superstardom

ardon \ärd-ᵊn\ see arden¹

ardoner \ärd-nər\ see ardener

ardor \ärd-ər\ see arder¹

ardy \ärd-ē\ hardy, Hardy, lardy, tardy
foolhardy, Lombardy, Sephardi

are¹ \er-ē\ see ary¹

are² \är\ see ar³

are³ \är-ē\ see ari¹

are⁴ \er\ air, Ayr, bare, bear, Blair, blare, chair, chare, Claire, Clare, dare, Dare, e'er, ere, err, eyre, fair, fare,

flair, flare, glair, glare, hair, hare, Herr,
heir, lair, mare, ne'er, pair, pare, pear,
prayer, quare, rare, rear, scare, share,
snare, spare, square, stair, stare, swear,
tare, tear, their, there, they're, vair,
ware, wear, weir, where, yare
  affair, aglare, airfare, Ajmer, Altair,
armchair, au pair, aware, barware,
Basseterre, Baudelaire, beachwear,
beware, bricklayer, bugbear, caneware,
carfare, clayware, cochair, coheir,
compare, compere, confrere,
cookware, corsair, courseware,
creamware, cudbear, day-care,
daymare, decare, declare, delftware,
despair, dishware, éclair, elsewhere,
enclair, ensnare, eyewear, fanfare,
fieldfare, firmware, flatware, Flaubert,
footwear, forbear, forebear, forswear,
foursquare, funfair, galère, giftware,
glassware, Great Bear, Gruyère,
hardware, hectare, horsehair, impair,
infare, Khmer, Kildare, knitwear, Lake
Eyre, life-care, longhair, loungewear,
menswear, meunière, midair, mohair,
Molière, neckwear, nightmare,
outstare, outwear, Pierre, playwear,
plein air, plowshare, Poor Clare,
portiere, premiere, prepare, pushchair,
rainwear, redware, repair, Saint Pierre,
Sancerre, shorthair, skiwear,
sleepwear, slipware, software,
somewhere, spongeware, sportswear,
stemware, stoneware, swimwear,
threadbare, tinware, torchère, trouvère,
tuyere, unfair, unhair, unswear,
Voltaire, warfare, welfare, wheelchair,
wirehair, workfare
  aftercare, air-to-air, antiair,
anywhere, bayadere, bêche-de-mer,
billionaire, boutonniere, Camembert,
chinaware, crackleware, Croix de
Guerre, cultivar, debonair, deciare, de
la Mare, Delaware, derriere,
dinnerware, disrepair, doctrinaire,
earthenware, étagère, everywhere,
fourragère, Frigidaire, graniteware,
hollowware, ironware, jasperware,
kitchenware, laissez-faire, Lake Saint
Clair, laquerware, legionnaire,
luminaire, lusterware, maidenhair, mal

de mer, medicare, metalware,
millionaire, minaudière, Mon-Khmer,
Mousquetaire, nom de guerre,
otherwhere, outerwear, overbear,
overwear, potty-chair, porte cochere,
questionnaire, rivière, Robespierre,
Santander, savoir faire, self-aware,
self-despair, silverware, solitaire,
tableware, thoroughfare, unaware,
underwear, vaporware, Venushair,
vivandière, willowware, woodenware,
yellowware, zillionaire
  Cape Finisterre, chargé d'affaires,
chemin de fer, commissionaire,
concessionaire, couturiere, devil-may-
care, enamelware, memoriter, pied-à-
terre, ready-to-wear, son et lumière,
vin ordinaire
  cordon sanitaire

area \er-ē-ə\ see aria

areable¹ \er-ə-bəl\ see earable¹

areable² \ar-ə-bəl\ see arable

areal \er-ē-əl\ see arial

arean¹ \er-ē-ən\ see arian¹

arean² \ar-ē-ən\ see arian²

ared \erd\ see aired

aredness \ar-əd-nəs\ see aridness

arel \ar-əl\ see arrel²

arely¹ \er-lē\ see airly

arely² \är-lē\ see arlie

arem \er-əm\ see arum²

arence¹ \er-əns\ clarence, Clarence,
Terence, Terrance, Terrence
  forbearance, transparence

arence² \ar-ən(ts)\ see arents

arent¹ \er-ənt\ daren't, errant, parent
  aberrant, afferent, apparent,
declarant, deferent, efferent,
godparent, grandparent, inerrant,
knight-errant, sederunt, stepparent,
transparent

inapparent
semitransparent

arent² \ar-ənt\ arrant, daren't,
parent
apparent, declarant, godparent,
grandparent, stepparent, transparent
inapparent
semitransparent

aren't¹ \er-ənt\ see arent¹

aren't² \ar-ənt\ see arent²

arents \ar-ən(t)s\ Barents, Clarence
—*also -s, -'s, and -s' forms of nouns
listed at* arent²

arer \er-ər\ see earer¹

ares¹ \erz\ see airs

ares² \ar-ēz\ Ares, caries, nares
Antares
Buenos Aires
primus inter pares
—*also -s, -'s, and -s' forms of nouns,
and -s forms of verbs, listed at* arry³

ares³ \är-əs\ see orris¹

aret \ar-ət\ see arat

areve \är-və\ see arva

arey¹ \ar-ē\ see arry³

arey² \er-ē\ see ary¹

arez \är-əs\ see orris¹

arf¹ \ärf\ barf, scarf

arf² \orf\ see orph

arfarin \or-fə-rən\ warfarin
hematoporphyrin

argain \är-gən\ bargain, jargon
plea-bargain

arge \ärj\ barge, charge, large,
marge, Marge, parge, sarge, sparge,
targe
discharge, enlarge, litharge,
recharge, surcharge, take-charge,
uncharge
by and large, hypercharge,
overcharge, supercharge, undercharge

argent \är-jənt\ argent, margent,
sargent, sergeant

arger \är-jər\ charger
discharger, enlarger, recharger
supercharger, turbocharger
turbosupercharger

arget \är-gət\ argot, garget, target
nontarget

argle \är-gəl\ gargle
argle-bargle

argo \är-gō\ Argo, argot, cargo,
Fargo, largo, Margo, Margot
embargo
supercargo

argon \är-gən\ see argain

argot¹ \är-gət\ see arget

argot² \är-gō\ see argo

arh \är\ see ar³

ari¹ \är-ē\ Bari, gharry, laari, sari,
scarry, sorry, starry
Bihari, curare, Imari, safari, scalare,
shikari, tamari
calamari, certiorari, cheboksary,
Kalahari, Stradivari, zamindari

ari² \er-ē\ see ary¹

ari³ \ar-ē\ see arry³

aria \er-ē-ə\ area, Beria, feria, kerria,
varia
Bavaria, Bulgaria, hysteria, malaria,
planaria, Samaria
adularia, Carpentaria, cineraria,
fritillaria, laminaria, luminaria,
militaria, sanguinaria
calceolaria, opera seria
acetabularia

arial \er-ē-əl\ aerial, areal, Ariel,
burial, gharial
glossarial, notarial, subaerial,
vicarial
actuarial, adversarial, estuarial,
secretarial
prothonotarial

arian¹ \er-ē-ən\ Arian, Aryan,
Carian, Marian, Marion, parian, Parian

agrarian, Aquarian, barbarian,
Bavarian, Bulgarian, Cancerian,
cesarean, Caesarian, cnidarian,
frutarian, grammarian, Hungarian,
Khymerian, librarian, Maid Marian,
ovarian, Pierian, riparian, rosarian,
Rotarian, sectarian, Sumerian,
Tartarean, Tartarian, Tocharian,
Tractarian, Vulgarian, Wagnerian
   antiquarian, apiarian, centenarian,
culinarian, Indo-Aryan, jubilarian,
lapidarian, libertarian, millenarian,
nonsectarian, postlapsarian,
prelapsarian, Presbyterian, proletarian,
Rastafarian, Ripuarian, Sabbatarian,
Sagittarian, sanitarian, seminarian,
trinitarian, Trinitarian, unitarian,
Unitarian, vegetarian, zoantharian
   abecedarian, Austro-Hungarian,
authoritarian, communitarian,
disciplinarian, documentarian,
egalitarian, equalitarian, futilitarian,
hereditarian, humanitarian,
majoritarian, necessitarian,
nonagenarian, octogenarian,
parliamentarian, postmillinarian,
premillinarian, predestinarian,
radiolarian, Sacramentarian,
sexagenarian, totalitarian, utilitarian,
veterinarian
   establishmentarian, inegalitarian,
latitudinarian, platitudinarian,
septuagenarian, solitudinarian,
uniformitarian, valetudinarian
   disestablishmentarian

arian² \ar-ē-ən\ Arian, Aryan,
carrion, clarion, Marian, Marion,
parian, Parian
   agrarian, Aquarian, barbarian,
Bavarian, Bulgarian, caesarean,
Caesarian, cesarean, contrarian,
Hungarian, Megarian, ovarian,
rosarian, Tartarean, Tartarian,
Tocharian, vulgarian
   Indo-Aryan, Rastafarian
   Austro-Hungarian

ariance \ar-ē-əns\ tarriance,
variance
   covariance, vicariance

ariant \ar-ē-ənt\ variant
vicariant

ariat¹ \er-ē-ət\ heriot, lariat, variate
bivariate, salariat, vicariate
commissariat, multivariate,
proletariat, secretariat
undersecretariat

ariat² \är-ē-ət\ see aureate¹

ariat³ \ar-ē-ət\ chariot, lariat
bivariate, salariat
commissariat, proletariat
Judas Iscariot

ariate \er-ē-ət\ see ariat¹

arib \ar-əb\ see arab

aric \ar-ik\ barrack, carrack
Amharic, barbaric, Dinaric, Megaric,
Pindaric
isobaric, Balearic

arice \ar-əs\ see aris²

aricide \ar-ə-sīd\ see arricide

arid \ar-əd\ arid, farad, semiarid

aridin \ar-ə-dᵊn\ see arridan

aridness \ar-əd-nəs\ aridness,
preparedness

aried¹ \er-ēd\ see erried

aried² \ar-ēd\ see arried

ariel \er-ē-əl\ see arial

arier¹ \er-ē-ər\ see errier

arier² \ar-ē-ər\ see arrier²

aries \ar-ēz\ see ares²

ariff \ar-əf\ paraph, tariff

aril \ar-əl\ see arrel²

arilee¹ \ar-ə-lē\ see aralee

arilee² \er-ə-lē\ see arily

arily \er-ə-lē\ Marilee, merrily,
Merrily, Saralee, scarily, sterily, verily
contrarily, primarily

arbitrarily, customarily, dietarily, exemplarily, fragmentarily, honorarily, literarily, mercenarily, militarily, momentarily, necessarily, salutarily, sanguinarily, sanitarily, secondarily, temporarily, unitarily, voluntarily
contemporarily, documentarily, elementarily, extemporarily, extraordinarily, hereditarily, imaginarily, involuntarily, preliminarily, rudimentarily, subsidiarily, unnecessarily
evolutionarily, revolutionarily

arin \är-ən\ florin, foreign, Lauren, Orrin, sarin, sporran, warren, Warren
Gagarin

arinate \ar-ə-nət\ see aronet

arinet \ar-ə-nət\ see aronet

aring¹ \er-iŋ\ airing, Bering, fairing, flaring, glaring, herring, paring, raring, sparing, tearing, wearing
cheeseparing, childbearing, seafaring, time-sharing, unerring, unsparing, wayfaring
—also -ing *forms of verbs listed at* are⁴

aring² \er-ən\ see aron¹

ario \er-ē-ō\ stereo
Ontario

arion¹ \ar-ē-ən\ see arian²

arion² \er-ē-ən\ see arian¹

ariot \ar-ē-ət\ see ariat³

arious \ar-ē-əs\ Arius, carious, Darious, scarious, various
Aquarius, burglarious, calcareous, contrarious, denarius, gregarious, guarnerius, hilarious, nefarious, precarious, senarius, vagarious, vicarious
multifarious, omnifarious, septenarius, Stradivarius, Sagittarius, temerarious

aris¹ \är-əs\ see orris¹

aris² \ar-əs\ arras, arris, Clarice, harass, Harris, heiress, Paris, parous, varus
coheiress, embarrass, Polaris
disembarrass, millionairess
Lewis with Harris, plaster of paris

arish¹ \er-ish\ bearish, cherish, fairish, garish, perish, squarish
nightmarish

arish² \ar-ish\ garish, marish, parish

arison \ar-ə-sən\ characin, garrison, Garrison, Harrison, Saracen, warison
caparison, comparison

arist \er-əst\ Marist, querist
aquarist, pleinairist, scenarist
apiarist
—also -est *forms of adjectives listed at* are⁴

aritan \er-ət-ᵊn\ see eratin

aritor \ar-ət-ər\ see arator

arity¹ \er-ət-ē\ see erity

arity² \ar-ət-ē\ carroty, charity, clarity, parity, rarity
barbarity, disparity, hilarity, imparity, polarity, unclarity, vulgarity
angularity, familiarity, insularity, peculiarity, popularity, regularity, similarity, singularity, solidarity
complementarity, dissimilarity, irregularity, particularity, unfamiliarity, unpopularity

arium \er-ē-əm\ barium
aquarium, herbarium, sacrarium, samarium, solarium, terrarium, velarium, vivarium
cinerarium, columbarium, honorarium, leprosarium, oceanarium, planetarium, sanitarium, syllabarium, termitarium
armamentarium

arius \er-ē-əs\ see arious

ark¹ \ärk\ arc, ark, hark, Clark, Clarke, dark, hark, lark, marc, Marc,

mark, Mark, marque, narc, nark, park,
Park, quark, sark, shark, spark, stark
 aardvark, airpark, anarch, ballpark,
birchbark, birthmark, Bismarck,
bookmark, debark, demark, Denmark,
earmark, embark, endarch, exarch,
footmark, futhark, Graustark,
hallmark, ironbark, landmark, Lake
Clark, Lamarck, monarch, ostmark,
Ozark, Petrarch, pitch-dark, Plutarch,
pockmark, postmark, pressmark,
pugmark, reichsmark, remark,
remarque, Remarque, ringbark,
seamark, shagbark, sitzmark, skylark,
soapbark, tanbark, tetrarch, tidemark,
titlark, touchmark, trademark
 acritarch, cutty sark, deutsche mark,
disembark, double-park, hierarch,
Joan of Arc, matriarch, meadowlark,
metalmark, minipark, oligarch,
patriarch, stringybark, telemark,
trierarch, watermark
 heresiarch, symposiarch

ark² \órk\ see ork²

ark³ \ərk\ see ork¹

arka¹ \är-kə\ charka, parka
 anasarca
 Hamilcar Barca

arka² \ər-kə\ see urka¹

arke \ärk\ see ark¹

arked \ärkt\ marked
 chop-marked, infarct
 ripple-marked, unremarked
 —also -ed forms of verbs listed at
ark¹

arken \är-kən\ darken, hearken

arker \är-kər\ barker, larker, marker,
parker, Parker, sparker
 bookmarker, skylarker
 nosey parker
 —also -er forms of adjectives listed
at ark¹

arket \är-kət\ market
 down-market, mass-market,
newmarket, test-market, upmarket

 aftermarket, hypermarket,
matriarchate, patriarchate,
supermarket

arkey \är-kē\ see archy

arkian \är-kē-ən\ Graustarkian,
Lamarckian, Monarchian

arkic \är-kik\ see archic

arking \är-kiŋ\ barking, Barking,
carking, parking
 loan-sharking
 —also -ing forms of verbs listed at
ark¹

arkle \är-kəl\ see archal

arks \ärks\ Marks, parks
 —also -s, -'s, and -s' forms of nouns,
and -s forms of verbs, listed at ark¹

arky \är-kē\ see archy

arl \ärl\ carl, Carl, farl, gnarl, jarl,
Karl, marl, parle, quarrel, snarl
 ensnarl, housecarl, unsnarl
 Albemarle

arla \är-lə\ Carla, Darla, Karla,
Marla

arlan \ä-lən\ see arline

arland \är-lənd\ garland, Garland,
Harland

arlatan \är-lət-ᵊn\ charlatan, tarlatan

arlay \är-lē\ see arlie

arle \ärl\ see arl

arlen \är-lən\ see arline

arler \är-lər\ see arlor

arless \är-ləs\ Carlos, parlous,
scarless, starless

arlet \är-lət\ charlotte, Charlotte,
harlot, scarlet, starlet, varlet

arley \är-lē\ see arlie

arlic \är-lik\ garlic
 pilgarlic

arlie \är-lē\ barley, charlie, Charlie, gnarly, Harley, marly, parlay, parley, snarly, yarely
  bizarrely

arlin \är-lən\ see arline

arline \är-lən\ Arlen, carline, Harlan, marlin, Marlin, marline, Marlyn

arling \är-liŋ\ carling, darling, Darling, starling
  —also -ing forms of verbs listed at arl

arlor \är-lər\ parlor, quarreler, snarler

arlos \är-ləs\ see arless

arlot \är-lət\ see arlet

arlotte \är-lət\ see arlet

arlous \är-ləs\ see arless

arlow \är-lō\ Barlow, Harlow

arly \är-lē\ see arlie

arlyn \ä-lən\ see arline

arm[1] \ärm\ arm, barm, charm, farm, harm, smarm
  alarm, disarm, firearm, forearm, gendarme, gisarme, poor farm, rearm, sidearm, stiff-arm, straight-arm, strong-arm, tonearm, unarm, yardarm
  overarm, underarm

arm[2] \äm\ see om[1]

arm[3] \orm\ see orm[2]

arma[1] \är-mə\ dharma, karma, Parma

arma[2] \ər-mə\ see erma

arman \är-mən\ barman, Carmen, carmine, Harmon

armed \ärmd\ armed, charmed
  unarmed
  —also -ed forms of verbs listed at arm[1]

armen \är-mən\ see arman

arment \är-mənt\ garment, varmint
  debarment, disbarment
  undergarment, overgarment

armer[1] \är-mər\ armor, charmer, farmer, harmer
  disarmer

armer[2] \or-mər\ see ormer[1]

armic \ər-mik\ see ermic

armine \är-mən\ see arman

arming[1] \är-miŋ\ charming, farming
  alarming, disarming
  —also -ing forms of verbs listed at arm[1]

arming[2] \or-miŋ\ see orming

armint \är-mənt\ see arment

armless \ärm-ləs\ armless, charmless, harmless

armoir \är-mər\ see armer[1]

armon \är-mən\ see arman

army \är-mē\ army, barmy, smarmy

arn[1] \ärn\ Arne, barn, darn, Marne, tarn, yarn
  carbarn, lucarne

arn[2] \orn\ see orn[1]

arna \ər-nə\ see erna

arnal \ärn-əl\ see arnel

arnate \är-nət\ Barnet, garnet
  discarnate, incarnate

arne[1] \ärn\ see arn[1]

arne[2] \är-nē\ see arny

arnel \ärn-əl\ carnal, charnel, darnel

arner[1] \är-nər\ darner, garner, yarner

arner[2] \or-nər\ see orner

arness \är-nəs\ harness
  bizarreness

arnet \är-nət\ see arnate

arney \är-nē\ see arny

arnhem \är-nəm\ see arnum

arning \or-niŋ\ see orning

arnish \är-nish\ garnish, tarnish, varnish

arnum \är-nəm\ Arnhem, Barnum

arny \är-nē\ Barney, barny, blarney, carny
Killarney
chili con carne

aro¹ \er-ō\ see ero²

aro² \ar-ō\ see arrow²

aro³ \är-ə\ see ara¹

aro⁴ \är-ō\ see orrow¹

arob \ar-əb\ see arab

arody \ar-əd-ē\ see araday

aroe¹ \ar-ō\ see arrow²

aroe² \er-ō\ see ero²

arol \ar-əl\ see arrel²

arold¹ \ar-əld\ Darold, Harold

arold² \er-əld\ see erald

arole \ar-əl\ see arrel²

arom \er-əm\ see arum²

aron¹ \er-ən\ Aaron, Charon, Erin, garron, heron, perron, raring, Sharon, Sharron
sierran
rose of Sharon, sub-Saharan

aron² \ar-ən\ Aaron, baron, barren, Charon, garron, Sharon, Sharron
rose of Sharon, sub-Saharan

aronet \ar-ə-nət\ baronet, carinate, clarinet

arous¹ \er-əs\ see errous

arous² \ar-əs\ see aris²

arp¹ \ärp\ carp, harp, scarp, sharp, tarp
cardsharp, Jew's harp
Autoharp, vibraharp

arp² \orp\ see orp

arpen \är-pən\ sharpen, tarpon

arper \är-pər\ carper, harper, scarper, sharper
cardsharper

arpie \är-pē\ see arpy

arpon \är-pən\ see arpen

arpy \är-pē\ harpy, sharpie

arque \ärk\ see ark¹

arquetry \är-kə-trē\ marquetry, parquetry

arqui \är-kē\ see archy

arrable \ar-ə-bəl\ see arable

arrack¹ \ar-ik\ see aric

arrack² \ar-ək\ arrack, barrack, carrack

arrage \är-ij\ see ¹orage

arragon \ar-ə-gən\ see aragon

arral \ar-əl\ see arrel²

arram \ar-əm\ see arum²

arrant¹ \ar-ənt\ see arent²

arrant² \or-ənt\ see orrent

arras \ar-əs\ see aris²

arrass \ar-əs\ see aris²

arrative \ar-ət-iv\ see arative²

arrator \ar-ət-ər\ see arator

arre \är\ see ar³

arred \ärd\ see ard¹

arrel¹ \orl\ see orl²

arrel² \ar-əl\ Aral, aril, barrel, carol, Carol, Carole, Caryl, carrel, Carroll,

Darrel, Darrell, Darryl, Daryl, Karol,
parol, parral, parrel
  apparel
  cracker-barrel, double-barrel

arrel³ \ȯr-əl\ see oral¹

arreler \är-lər\ see arlor

arrell \ar-əl\ see arrel²

arrely \är-lē\ see arlie

arren¹ \ar-ən\ see aron²

arren² \ȯr-ən\ see orin¹

arren³ \är-ən\ see arin

arrener \ȯr-ə-nər\ see oroner

arreness \är-nəs\ see arness

arret \ar-ət\ see arat

arrett \ar-ət\ see arat

arrh \är\ see ar³

arriage \ar-ij\ carriage, marriage
disparage, miscarriage
intermarriage, undercarriage

arriance \ar-ē-əns\ see ariance

arricide \ar-ə-sīd\ parricide
acaricide

arridan \ar-ə-dᵊn\ harridan
cantharidin

arrie \ar-ē\ see arry³

arried \ar-ēd\ harried, married,
varied
unmarried

arrier¹ \ȯr-ē-ər\ see arrior

arrier² \ar-ē-ər\ barrier, carrier,
farrier, harrier, varier
ballcarrier, spear-carrier

arrion \ar-ē-ən\ see arian²

arrior \ȯr-ē-ər\ quarrier, sorrier,
warrior

arris \ar-əs\ see aris²

arrison \ar-ə-sən\ see arison

arro \är-ō\ see orrow¹

arroll \ar-əl\ see arrel²

arron \ar-ən\ see aron²

arrot \ar-ət\ see arat

arroty \ar-ət-ē\ see arity²

arrow¹ \ar-ə\ Clara, jarrah, Kara,
Sara, Sarah, Tara
Bukhara, cascara, mascara, Sahara,
samara, Tamara, tantara, tiara
capybara, caracara, marinara, Santa
Clara

arrow² \ar-ō\ aero, arrow, barrow,
Darrow, Faeroe, faro, Faroe, farrow,
harrow, Harrow, marrow, narrow,
pharaoh, sparrow, taro, tarot, yarrow
handbarrow, Point Barrow,
wheelbarrow

arrowy \ar-ə-wē\ arrowy, marrowy

arry¹ \är-ē\ see ari¹

arry² \ȯr-ē\ see ory

arry³ \ar-ē\ Barrie, Barry, Carey,
Carrie, carry, Cary, chary, Gary, Garry,
gharry, harry, Harry, Larry, marry,
nary, parry, Shari, tarry
glengarry, miscarry, safari, shikari
cash-and-carry, hari-kari, intermarry,
Stradivari
Tom, Dick, and Harry

arryl \ar-əl\ see arrel²

ars \ärz\ Lars, Mars, ours
— also -s, -'s, and -s' forms of
nouns, and -s forms of verbs, listed at
ar³

arsal \är-səl\ parcel, versal, tarsal
metatarsal

arse¹ \ärs\ arse, farce, marse, parse,
sparse

arse² \ärz\ see ars

arsh \ärsh\ harsh, marsh
demarche

arshal \är-shəl\ see artial

arshall \är-shəl\ see artial

arshen \är-shən\ harshen, martian

arsi \är-sē\ see arcy

arsis \är-səs\ see arsus

arsle \äs-əl\ see ossal

arson \ärs-ᵊn\ arson, Carson, parson

arsus \är-səs\ arsis, tarsus, Tarsus
catharsis
metatarsus

art¹ \ärt\ art, Art, Bart, cart, chart,
Chartres, dart, fart, hart, Harte, heart,
kart, mart, part, Sartre, scart, smart,
start, tart
apart, blackheart, compart, depart,
Descartes, dispart, dogcart, Earhart,
flowchart, forepart, go-cart,
greenheart, handcart, Hobart, impart,
jump-start, Mozart, mouthpart,
outsmart, oxcart, oxheart, pushcart,
rampart, redstart, restart, street-smart,
Stuttgart, sweetheart, tipcart, upstart
à la carte, anti-art, applecart,
Bonaparte, counterpart, heart-to-heart,
purpleheart, underpart, upperpart

art² \ȯrt\ see ort¹

arta \är-tə\ Marta, Sparta
Jakarta
Magna Carta, Santa Marta,
Surakarta, yogyakarta

artable \ärt-ə-bəl\ see artible

artan¹ \ärt-ᵊn\ see arten

artan² \ȯrt-ᵊn\ see orten

artar \ärt-ər\ see arter¹

arte¹ \ärt-ē\ see arty¹

arte² \ärt\ see art¹

arted¹ \ärt-əd\ see earted

arted² \ȯrt-əd\ see orted

arten \ärt-ᵊn\ Barton, carton,
hearten, marten, martin, Martin,
smarten, Spartan, tartan
baum marten, dishearten,
Dumbarton, freemartin, Saint Martin,
Sint Maarten
kindergarten

arter¹ \ärt-ər\ barter, carter, Carter,
charter, darter, garter, martyr, starter,
tartar
nonstarter, self-starter
protomartyr
—also -er forms of adjectives listed
at art¹

arter² \ȯt-ər\ see ater¹

arter³ \ȯrt-ər\ see orter

artern \ȯt-ərn\ see auterne

artery \ärt-ə-rē\ artery, martyry

artes \ärt\ see art¹

artford \ärt-fərd\ Hartford, Hertford

arth \ärth\ garth, Garth, hearth
Hogarth

arti \ärt-ē\ see arty¹

artial \är-shəl\ marshal, Marshal,
Marshall, martial, Martial, partial
court-martial, impartial

artian \är-shən\ see arshen

artible \ärt-ə-bəl\ partible, startable
impartible, restartable

artic¹ \ärt-ik\ arctic, Arctic
antarctic, Antarctic, cathartic,
Nearctic
Palearctic

artic² \ȯrt-ik\ quartic
aortic

article \ärt-i-kəl\ article, particle
microparticle

artile \ȯrt-ᵊl\ see ortal

artily \ärt-ᵊl-ē\ artily, heartily

artin \ärt-ᵊn\ see arten

arting \ärt-iŋ\ carting, charting, karting, parting, starting flowcharting, self-starting
—*also* -ing *forms of verbs listed at* art[1]

artisan \ärt-ə-zən\ artisan, bartizan, partisan
bipartisan, nonpartisan

artist \ärt-əst\ artist, chartist, Chartist
Bonapartist

artizan \ärt-ə-zən\ see artisan

artless \ärt-ləs\ artless, heartless

artlet \ärt-lət\ martlet, partlet, tartlet

artly[1] \ärt-lē\ partly, smartly, tartly

artly[2] \ȯrt-lē\ see ortly

artment \ärt-mənt\ apartment, compartment, department

artner \ärt-nər\ partner
kindergartner

arton[1] \ȯrt-ᵊn\ see orton

arton[2] \ärt-ᵊn\ see arten

artre \ärt\ see art[1]

artres \ärt\ see art[1]

artridge \är-trij\ cartridge, partridge

arts[1] \är\ see ar[3]

arts[2] \ärts\ Hartz
—*also* -s, '*s, and* -s' *forms of nouns, and* -s *forms of verbs, listed at* art[1]

arture \är-chər\ see archer

arty[1] \ärt-ē\ arty, hearty, party, smarty, tarty
Astarte, ex parte, Havarti
Buonaparte
commedia dell'arte

arty[2] \ȯrt-ē\ see orty

artyr \ärt-ər\ see arter[1]

artyry \ärt-ə-rē\ see artery

artz[1] \ȯrts\ see orts

artz[2] \ärts\ see arts[2]

aru \ä-rü\ Bukaru
Pakanbaru
Johor Baharu

arum[1] \är-əm\ larum
alarum

arum[2] \er-əm\ arum, carom, harem, Sarum
Muharram
harum-scarum
arbiter elegantiarum

arus \ar-əs\ see aris[2]

arva \är-və\ larva, Marva, parve, pareve

arval \är-vəl\ see arvel

arve[1] \ärv\ carve, starve, varve

arve[2] \är-və\ see arva

arvel \är-vəl\ carvel, larval, marvel

arven \är-vən\ carven, Marvin
Caernarvon

arvin \är-vən\ see arven

arvon \är-vən\ see arven

ary[1] \er-ē\ aerie, aery, airy, berry, bury, Carey, Cary, Cherie, cherry, Cherry, chary, clary, dairy, Derry, faerie, fairy, ferry, Gary, Garry, Gerry, glairy, glary, hairy, Jere, Jeri, Jerrie, Jerry, kerry, Kerry, Mary, marry, merry, Merry, nary, perry, Perry, prairie, quaere, query, scary, serry, Shari, Sheri, Sherrie, sherry, Sherry, skerry, terry, Terry, vary, very, wary, wherry
baneberry, barberry, bayberry, bearberry, bilberry, blackberry, blaeberry, blueberry, Bradbury, bunchberry, Burberry, canary, Canary, chokeberry, chokecherry, cloudberry, contrary, costmary, cowberry, cranberry, crowberry, deerberry, dewberry, equerry, gooseberry, ground-cherry, hackberry, hegari, inkberry, Juneberry, knobkerrie, library, mulberry, nondairy, pokeberry,

primary, raspberry, rosemary,
Rosemary, scalare, shadberry,
sheepberry, snowberry, soapberry,
strawberry, summary, teaberry, tilbury,
twinberry, unwary, vagary, wolfberry,
youngberry
  actuary, adversary, airy-fairy,
ancillary, antiquary, apiary, arbitrary,
aviary, axillary, beriberi, bestiary,
biliary, boysenberry, breviary,
budgetary, calamari, calamary,
candleberry, Canterbury, capillary,
cartulary, cassowary, catenary,
cautionary, cavitary, cemetery,
centenary, certiorari, chartulary,
checkerberry, chinaberry, ciliary,
cinerary, cometary, commentary,
commissary, condottiere, coralberry,
corollary, coronary, culinary,
customary, dictionary, dietary,
dignitary, dingleberry, dromedary,
dysentery, elderberry, emissary,
estuary, farkleberry, February,
formicary, formulary, fragmentary,
fritillary, functionary, funerary,
honorary, huckleberry, intermarry,
janissary, January, lamasery, lapidary,
lectionary, legendary, legionary,
limitary, lingonberry, literary,
loganberry, luminary, mammillary,
mandatary, maxillary, medullary,
mercenary, miliary, military,
millenary, milliary, millinery,
miserere, missionary, momentary,
monastery, monetary, mortuary,
necessary, ordinary, ossuary, papillary,
parcenary, partridgeberry, pensionary,
phalanstery, pigmentary, plagiary,
planetary, Pondicherry, prebendary,
presbytery, pulmonary, pupillary,
quaternary, questionary, reliquary,
rowanberry, salivary, salmonberry,
salutary, sanctuary, sanguinary,
sanitary, secondary, secretary,
sedentary, seminary, serviceberry,
silverberry, solitary, stationary,
stationery, statuary, Stradivari,
subcontrary, sublunary, sugarberry,
sumptuary, syllabary, temporary,
termitary, tertiary, textuary,
thimbleberry, Tipperary, Tom and

Jerry, topiary, tributary, tutelary,
unitary, urinary, vestiary, visionary,
voluntary, vulnerary, Waterbury,
whortleberry, winterberry
  ablutionary, accretionary,
antiphonary, apothecary, bicentenary,
bilmillenary, concessionary,
conclusionary, concretionary,
confectionary, confectionery,
consigliere, constabulary,
contemporary, convulsionary,
coparcenary, deflationary, delusionary,
depositary, digressionary, disciplinary,
discretionary, distributary,
diversionary, electuary, epistolary,
exclusionary, expansionary,
extemporary, extortionary,
extraordinary, fiduciary, hereditary,
illusionary, imaginary, incendiary,
inflationary, insanitary, intercalary,
involuntary, itinerary, judiciary,
libationary, obituary, officiary,
pecuniary, petitionary, precautionary,
preliminary, presidiary, previsionary,
probationary, proprietary,
provisionary, reactionary,
recessionary, reflationary, residuary,
reversionary, revisionary,
stagflationary, stipendiary, subliterary,
subsidiary, subversionary,
tercentenary, traditionary, tumultuary,
unnecessary, veterinary, vocabulary,
voluptuary
  abolitionary, beneficiary,
consuetudinary, devolutionary,
disinflationary, domiciliary,
eleemosynary, elocutionary,
evidentiary, evolutionary,
expeditionary, extraliterary,
intermediary, paramilitary,
penitentiary, quatercentenary,
revolutionary, semicentenary,
semilegendary, sesquicentenary,
superciliary, supernumerary,
tintinnabulary, transdisciplinary,
usufructuary, valetudinary
  interdisciplinary, plenipotentiary
  counterrevolutionary

ary² \ar-ē\ see **arry³**

ary³ \är-ē\ see **ari¹**

aryan[1] \er-ē-ən\ see arian[1]

aryan[2] \ar-ē-ən\ see arian[2]

aryl \ar-əl\ see arrel[2]

as[1] \ash\ see ash[3]

as[2] \as\ see ass[3]

as[3] \az\ see azz

as[4] \ä\ see a[1]

as[5] \äsh\ see ash[1]

as[6] \äz\ see oise[1]

as[7] \əz\ see euse[1]

as[8] \äs\ see os[1]

as[9] \ȯ\ see aw[1]

asa[1] \äs-ə\ casa, fossa, glossa, Lhasa, Ossa
kielbasa, Kinshasa, Landrace, Mombasa
tabula rasa

asa[2] \äz-ə\ see aza[1]

asa[3] \as-ə\ see assa

asable[1] \ā-zə-bəl\ grazeable
persuasible
paraphrasable

asable[2] \ā-sə-bəl\ see aceable

asal[1] \ā-səl\ basal, Basil, staysail
forestaysail

asal[2] \ā-zəl\ basal, Basil, hazel, Hazel, nasal, phrasal
appraisal, Azazel

asally \āz-lē\ see aisley

asca \as-kə\ see aska

ascal \as-kəl\ paschal, rascal

ascan \as-kən\ see askin

ascar \as-kər\ see asker

ascence[1] \ās-ᵊns\ nascence
complacence, complaisance, renascence

ascence[2] \as-ᵊns\ nascence
renascence

ascent[1] \as-ᵊnt\ nascent, passant
renascent

ascent[2] \ās-ᵊnt\ see acent

asch[1] \ask\ see ask

asch[2] \äsh\ see ash[1]

asch[3] \ȯsh\ see ash[2]

aschal \as-kəl\ see ascal

ascia[1] \ā-shə\ see acia

ascia[2] \ash-ə\ see asha[2]

ascible \as-ə-bəl\ see assable

ascicle \as-i-kəl\ see assical

asco[1] \äs-kō\ see oscoe

asco[2] \as-kō\ fiasco, Tabasco

ascon \as-kən\ see askin

ascot \as-kət\ see asket

ascus \as-kəs\ Damascus, Velazquez

ase[1] \ās\ see ace[1]

ase[2] \āz\ see aze[1]

ase[3] \äz\ see oise[1]

asel \äz-əl\ see ozzle

ased \āst\ see aced

aseless \ā-sləs\ see aceless

aseman \ā-smən\ see aceman

asement \ās-mənt\ basement, casement
debasement
bargain-basement

aser[1] \ā-sər\ see acer[1]

aser[2] \ā-zər\ see azer

asey \ā-sē\ see acy

ash[1] \äsh\ bosh, cosh, Fosh, frosh, gosh, gouache, josh, Mâche, nosh,

posh, quash, slosh, squash, swash, tosh, wash
  awash, backwash, blackwash, cohosh, czardas, Dias, downwash, eyewash, galosh, ganache, goulash, kibosh, midrash, mishmash, mouthwash, musquash, panache, rainwash, Siwash, whitewash, wish-wash
  hamantasch, mackintosh, McIntosh

ash² \ȯsh\ Bosch, Foch, gosh, grosz, quash, slosh, squash, swash, wash
  awash, backwash, Balkhash, blackwash, brainwash, brioche, Bydgoszcz, downwash, eyewash, hogwash, mouthwash, outwash, rainwash, Siwash, whitewash, wish-wash
  hamantasch

ash³ \ash\ ash, bash, brash, cache, cash, clash, crash, dash, fash, flash, gash, gnash, hash, lash, mash, pash, plash, rash, sash, slash, smash, splash, stash, thrash, thresh, trash
  abash, backlash, backsplash, Balkhash, calash, Chumash, czardas, encash, eyelash, goulash, mishmash, moustache, mustache, panache, potash, rehash, slapdash, soutache, stramash, tongue-lash, unlash, whiplash
  balderdash, calabash, succotash

asha¹ \äsh-ə\ kasha, pasha, quassia
  Falasha

asha² \ash-ə\ cassia, fascia, pasha

ashan \ash-ən\ see assion

ashed¹ \ȯsht\ sloshed
  stonewashed, unwashed
  —also -ed forms of verbs listed at ash²

ashed² \asht\ dashed, Rasht, smashed
  unabashed
  —also -ed forms of verbs listed at ash³

ashen \ash-ən\ see assion

asher¹ \äsh-ər\ josher, nosher, squasher, swasher, washer
  dishwasher

asher² \ȯsh-ər\ swasher, washer
  brainwasher, dishwasher, whitewasher

asher³ \ash-ər\ Asher, basher, brasher, clasher, crasher, dasher, flasher, masher, rasher, slasher, smasher, splasher, thrasher
  gate-crasher
  haberdasher

ashew \ash-ü\ cachou, cashew

ashi¹ \äsh-ē\ see ashy¹

ashi² \ash-ē\ see ashy²

ashing \ash-iŋ\ crashing, dashing, flashing, mashing, slashing, smashing
  —also -ing forms of verbs listed at ash³

ashion \ash-ən\ see assion

asht \asht\ see ashed²

ashy¹ \äsh-ē\ dashi, Iasi, Kashi, squashy, washy
  Funabashi, Lubumbashi, Toyohashi, wishy-washy

ashy² \ash-ē\ ashy, flashy, Kashi, splashy, trashy

asi¹ \äs-ē\ see ossy¹

asi² \äz-ē\ see azi¹

asi³ \äsh-ē\ see ashy¹

asia \ā-zhə\ Asia
  aphasia, Eurasia, fantasia, Malaysia
  Anastasia, Australasia, euthanasia
  antonomasia

asian¹ \ā-shən\ see ation¹

asian² \ā-zhən\ see asion

asible \ā-zə-bəl\ see asable¹

asic \ā-zik\ basic, phasic
  biphasic, diphasic
  multiphasic, polyphasic

asid \as-əd\ see acid

asie \ā-sē\ see acy

asil[1] \as-əl\ see assel[2]

asil[2] \az-əl\ see azzle

asil[3] \ās-əl\ see asal[1]

asil[4] \āz-əl\ see asal[2]

asil[5] \äz-əl\ see ozzle

asin \ās-ᵊn\ see ason[1]

asing[1] \ā-siŋ\ see acing

asing[2] \ā-ziŋ\ see aising

asion \ā-zhən\ Asian, suasion
abrasion, Caucasian, corrasion,
dissuasion, equation, Eurasian,
evasion, invasion, occasion,
persuasion, pervasion
Amerasian, Athanasian,
dermabrasion, Rabelaisian
overpersuasion

asional \āzh-nəl\ equational,
occasional

asis[1] \ā-səs\ basis, stasis
oasis

asis[2] \as-əs\ see assis[2]

asium \ā-zē-əm\ dichasium,
gymnasium

asive \ā-siv\ suasive
abrasive, assuasive, corrasive,
dissuasive, embracive, evasive,
invasive, persuasive, pervasive
noninvasive

ask \ask\ ask, bask, Basque, cask,
casque, flask, mask, masque, Pasch,
task
unmask
photomask

aska \as-kə\ Alaska, Itasca,
Nebraska
Athabaska

askan \as-kən\ see askin

asked \ast\ see ast[2]

asker \as-kər\ lascar, masker,
masquer
Madagascar

asket \as-kət\ ascot, basket, casket,
gasket
breadbasket, handbasket,
wastebasket, workbasket

askin \as-kən\ gascon, gaskin
Alaskan, Tarascan
Athapaskan

asking \as-kiŋ\ multitasking
—*also* -ing *forms of verbs listed at*
ask

asm \az-əm\ chasm, plasm, spasm
chiasm, orgasm, phantasm, sarcasm
chiliasm, ectoplasm, pleonasm
blepharospasm, enthusiasm,
iconoclasm

asma \az-mə\ asthma, plasma
chiasma, miasma, phantasma

asman \az-mən\ see asmine

asmine \az-mən\ jasmine, Tasman

asn't \əz-ᵊnt\ doesn't, wasn't

aso[1] \as-ō\ see asso[1]

aso[2] \äs-ō\ see asso[2]

ason[1] \ās-ᵊn\ basin, caisson,
chasten, hasten, Jason, mason, Mason
Foxe Basin, Freemason, Great Basin,
stonemason, washbasin
diapason, Donets Basin

ason[2] \āz-ᵊn\ see azon

asp \asp\ asp, clasp, gasp, grasp,
hasp, rasp
enclasp, handclasp, last-gasp,
unclasp

asper \as-pər\ clasper, jasper, Jasper

asperate \as-prət\ aspirate
exasperate

aspirate \as-prət\ see asperate

asque \ask\ see ask

asquer \as-kər\ see asker

ass¹ \ās\ see ace¹

ass² \äs\ see os¹

ass³ \as\ as, ass, bass, Bass, brass, class, crass, frass, gas, glass, grass, has, lass, mass, pass, sass, strass, tace, tasse, trass, vas, wrasse
admass, alas, Alsace, amass, avgas, bagasse, band-pass, bluegrass, bromegrass, bunchgrass, bypass, cordgrass, crabgrass, crevasse, cuirass, cut-grass, declass, degas, Donbas, Drygas, eelgrass, en masse, eyeglass, first-class, groundmass, harass, high-class, hourglass, impasse, jackass, knotgrass, Kuzbass, landmass, Madras, morass, outclass, outgas, palliasse, Petras, plateglass, repass, ribgrass, rubasse, ryegrass, sandglass, shortgrass, spyglass, subclass, sunglass, surpass, switchgrass, tallgrass, teargas, trespass, Troas, wineglass, wiseass, witchgrass
biogas, biomass, demiglace, demitasse, fiberglass, gallowglass, gravitas, Hallowmas, hardinggrass, hippocras, isinglass, Kiribati, lemongrass, lower-class, middle-class, overpass, pampas grass, peppergrass, Plexiglas, sassafras, superclass, underclass, underpass, upper-class, weatherglass

assa \as-ə\ massa
Manasseh
Lake Nyasa

assable \as-ə-bəl\ chasuble, passable, passible
impassable, impassible, irascible

assail \äs-əl\ see ossal

assailer \äs-ə-lər\ see ossular

assal \as-əl\ see assel²

assant \as-ᵊnt\ see ascent¹

assar \as-ər\ see asser

asse¹ \as\ see ass³

asse² \äs\ see os¹

assed \ast\ see ast²

assee \as-ē\ see assy

asseh \as-ə\ see assa

assel¹ \äs-əl\ see ossal

assel² \as-əl\ acyl, basil, castle, facile, gracile, hassle, Kassel, passel, tassel, vassal, wrestle
forecastle, Newcastle

asser \as-ər\ crasser, gasser, Nasser, placer
harasser
antimacassar

asset \as-ət\ see acet²

assia¹ \ash-ə\ see asha²

assia² \äsh-ə\ see asha¹

assian \ash-ən\ see assion

assible \as-ə-bəl\ see assable

assic \as-ik\ classic
Jurassic, Liassic, thalassic, Triassic
neoclassic, pseudoclassic, semiclassic

assical \as-i-kəl\ classical, fascicle
postclassical, unclassical
semiclassical

assid \as-əd\ see acid

assie¹ \as-ē\ see assy

assie² \äs-ē\ see ossy¹

assim¹ \äs-əm\ see ossum

assim² \as-əm\ passim
sargassum

assin \as-ᵊn\ see asten²

assion \ash-ən\ ashen, fashion, passion, ration
Circassian, compassion, dispassion, impassion, refashion, Wakashan

assional \ash-nəl\ see ational[3]

assis[1] \as-ē\ see assy

assis[2] \as-əs\ classis, stasis
Parnassus
Halicarnassus

assist \ā-səst\ bassist, racist
contrabassist

assive \as-iv\ massive, passive
impassive

assle \as-əl\ see assel[2]

assless \as-ləs\ classless, glassless,
massless

assment \as-mənt\ blastment
amassment, harassment

assness \as-nəs\ see astness

asso[1] \as-ō\ basso, lasso
El Paso, Picasso, sargasso, Sargasso
Bobo-Dioulasso

asso[2] \äs-ō\ Campo Basso
Burkina Faso

assock \as-ək\ cassock, hassock

assum \as-əm\ see assim[2]

assus \as-əs\ see assis

assy \as-ē\ brassy, chassis, classy,
gassy, glacis, glassie, glassy, grassy,
lassie, massy, sassy
Malagasy, Tallahassee
Haile Salassie

ast[1] \əst\ see ust[1]

ast[2] \ast\ bast, blast, cast, caste,
clast, fast, gast, ghast, hast, last, mast,
past, vast
aghast, avast, bedfast, Belfast,
bombast, broadcast, bypast, contrast,
dicast, dismast, downcast, dynast,
fantast, flypast, forecast, foremast,
forepassed, gymnast, half-caste, half-
mast, handfast, holdfast, lightfast,
mainmast, makefast, march-past,
miscast, newscast, oblast, offcast,
outcast, outcaste, precast, recast,

repast, roughcast, sandblast, sand-cast,
shamefast, soothfast, sportscast,
steadfast, sunfast, topmast, trade-last,
typecast, unasked, upcast, windblast
acid-fast, chiliast, cineast, colorcast,
colorfast, flabbergast, fore-topmast,
hard-and-fast, main-topmast,
mizzenmast, narrowcast, opencast,
overcast, pederast, rebroadcast,
scholiast, simulcast, telecast,
weathercast
ecdysiast, encomiast, enthusiast,
iconoclast, radiocast, symposiast
radiobroadcast
—also -ed *forms of verbs listed at*
ass[3]

asta[1] \äs-tə\ see osta

asta[2] \as-tə\ Rasta
canasta, Jocasta, Mount Shasta

astable \at-ə-bəl\ see atible

astard \as-tərd\ bastard, dastard,
mastered, plastered

aste[1] \āst\ see aced

aste[2] \ast\ see ast[2]

asted \as-təd\ blasted, masted,
plastid
—also -ed *forms of verbs listed at*
ast[2]

asteful \āst-fəl\ tasteful, wasteful
distasteful

asten[1] \ās-ᵊn\ see ason[1]

asten[2] \as-ᵊn\ fasten
assassin, unfasten

aster[1] \ā-stər\ taster, waster

aster[2] \as-tər\ aster, Astor, caster,
castor, Castor, faster, gaster, master,
pastor, plaster, raster
bandmaster, broadcaster, bushmaster,
cadastre, choirmaster, disaster,
drillmaster, headmaster, linecaster,
loadmaster, paymaster, piaster,
pilaster, postmaster, quizmaster,
remaster, ringmaster, schoolmaster,
scoutmaster, shinplaster, shipmaster,

sportscaster, spymaster, taskmaster, three-master, toastmaster, truckmaster, wharfmaster, whoremaster, yardmaster
  alabaster, burgomaster, concertmaster, criticaster, ironmaster, oleaster, overmaster, poetaster, quartermaster, rallymaster, stationmaster, weathercaster, Zoroaster
  cotoneaster

astered \as-tərd\ see astard

astering \as-tə-riŋ\ overmastering
—*also* -ing *forms of verbs listed at* aster

astes \as-tēz\ cerastes
  Ecclesiastes
  —*also* -s, -'s, *and* -s' *forms of nouns listed at* asty²

asthma \az-mə\ see asma

astian \as-chən\ see astion

astic \as-tik\ drastic, mastic, plastic, spastic
  bombastic, dynastic, elastic, fantastic, gymnastic, monastic, sarcastic, scholastic, stochastic
  anelastic, Hudibrastic, inelastic, onomastic, orgiastic, paraphrastic, pederastic, periphrastic, superplastic
  ecclesiastic, enthusiastic, iconoclastic, interscholastic, semimonastic

astics \as-tiks\ gymnastics, slimnastics

astid \as-təd\ see asted

astie \as-tē\ see asty²

astiness \ā-stē-nəs\ hastiness, pastiness

asting¹ \ā-stiŋ\ basting, wasting
—*also* -ing *forms of verbs listed at* aced

asting² \as-tiŋ\ typecasting
  everlasting, narrowcasting, overcasting

—*also* -ing *forms of verbs listed at* ast²

astion \as-chən\ bastion
  Erastian

astle \as-əl\ see assel²

astly \ast-lē\ ghastly, lastly

astment \as-mənt\ see assment

astness \as-nəs\ crassness, fastness, gastness, pastness

asto \as-tō\ impasto
  antipasto

astor \as-tər\ see aster²

astoral \as-trəl\ see astral

astral \as-trəl\ astral, gastral, pastoral, plastral
  cadastral

astre \as-tər\ see aster²

astric \as-trik\ gastric
  nasogastric

astrophe \as-trə-fē\ anastrophe, catastrophe

asty¹ \ā-stē\ hasty, pasty, tasty

asty² \as-tē\ blastie, nasty, pasty, vasty
  capacity, contrasty
  pederasty
  angioplasty, bepharoplasty, osteoplasty, overcapacity

asuble \as-ə-bəl\ see assable

asure¹ \ā-shər\ glacier, Glacier, rasure
  erasure

asure² \ā-zhər\ see azier

asy \as-ē\ see assy

at¹ \ä\ see a¹

at² \ät\ see ot¹

at³ \ət\ see ut¹

at⁴ \ȯt\ see ought¹

at⁵ \at\ bat, batt, blat, brat, cat, Cat, chat, chert, drat, fat, flat, frat, gat, gnat, hat, mat, matt, Matt, matte, pat, Pat, plait, plat, rat, Rat, sat, scat, scatt, skat, slat, spat, splat, sprat, stat, tat, that, vat
  all that, at bat, backchat, begat, bobcat, brickbat, bullbat, Cassatt, chitchat, combat, comsat, cowpat, cravat, Croat, defat, dingbat, doormat, expat, fiat, firebrat, format, Hallstatt, hellcat, hepcat, high-hat, jurat, meerkat, muscat, Muscat, muskrat, nonfat, polecat, Sadat, savate, Sno-Cat, stand pat, standpat, stonechat, strawhat, Surat, thereat, tipcat, tomcat, whereat, whinchat, wildcat, wombat
  acrobat, apparat, Ararat, assignat, autocrat, Automat, bureaucrat, butterfat, caveat, cervelat, concordat, copycat, democrat, diplomat, Dixiecrat, Eurocrat, habitat, Kattegat, Laundromat, marrowfat, mobocrat, monocrat, Montserrat, ochlocrat, pas de quatre, photostat, pit-a-pat, plutocrat, pussycat, rat-a-tat, scaredy-cat, semimatte, technocrat, theocrat, thermostat, tit for tat, Uniate, ziggurat
  aristocrat, gerontocrat, heliostat, Jehoshaphat, magnificat, meritocrat, Physiocrat, requiescat, thalassocrat
  proletariat, professoriat, secretariat

at⁶ \a\ see ah³

ata¹ \ät-ə\ cotta, data, kata
  balata, cantata, Carlotta, errata, fermata, frittata, La Plata, Maratha, Niigata, non grata, pinata, pro rata, reata, riata, regatta, sonata, Sorata, toccata
  caponata, Hirakata, Mar del Plata, serenata, terracotta, Uspallata
  Basilicata, desiderata, inamorata, missa cantata, persona grata, res judicata
  persona non grata, res adjudicata, Rio de la Plata
  medulla oblongata

ata² \āt-ə\ beta, data, eta, strata, theta, zeta

muleta, peseta, potato, pro rata, substrata, tomato, viewdata
  corona radiata

ata³ \at-ə\ data
  errata, mulatto, non grata, pro rata, reata, regatta, riata, viewdata
  paramatta, Paramatta
  persona grata
  persona non grata

atable¹ \āt-ə-bəl\ datable, ratable, statable
  debatable, dilatable, inflatable, locatable, rotatable, translatable
  allocatable, circulatable, confiscatable, correlatable, detonatable, undebatable

atable² \at-ə-bəl\ see atible

atal \āt-ᵊl\ fatal, natal, ratel, shtetl
  hiatal, postnatal, prenatal
  antenatal, neonatal, perinatal

atalie \at-ᵊl-ē\ see attily

atally \āt-ᵊl-ē\ fatally, natally
  postnatally, prenatally
  antenatally, neonatally, perinatally

atalyst \at-ᵊl-əst\ catalyst
  philatelist

atan¹ \āt-ən\ see aten¹

atan² \at-ᵊn\ see atin²

atancy \āt-ᵊn-sē\ blatancy, latency
  dilatancy

atant¹ \āt-ᵊnt\ blatant, latent, natant, patent, statant

atant² \at-ᵊnt\ patent
  combatant
  noncombatant

atany \at-ᵊn-ē\ atony, rhatany

atar \ät-ər\ see otter

atary \ät-ə-rē\ see ottery

atch¹ \cch\ see etch

atch² \äch\ see otch

atch³ \òch\ see auch¹

atch⁴ \ach\ bach, batch, catch, cratch, hatch, klatch, latch, match, natch, patch, ratch, scratch, snatch, thatch
attach, book-match, crosshatch, crosspatch, despatch, detach, dispatch, nuthatch, outmatch, potlatch, rematch, Sasquatch, throatlatch, unlatch, Wasatch
coffee klatch, kaffeeklatsch, overmatch

atcher¹ \äch-ər\ botcher, watcher
bird-watcher, clock-watcher, debaucher, topnotcher

atcher² \ach-ər\ batcher, catcher, hatcher, matcher, scratcher, stature, thatcher
cowcatcher, dispatcher, dogcatcher, eye-catcher, flycatcher, gnatcatcher
oyster catcher

atchet \ach-ət\ hatchet, latchet, rachet, ratchet

atchily \ach-ə-lē\ patchily, patchouli

atching \ach-iŋ\ back-scratching, cross-hatching, eye-catching, nonmatching
—also -ing forms of verbs listed at atch⁴

atchman \äch-mən\ see otchman

atchment \ach-mənt\ catchment, hatchment
attachment, detachment

atchouli \ach-ə-lē\ see atchily

atchy \ach-ē\ catchy, patchy, scratchy
Apache

ate¹ \āt\ ait, ate, bait, bate, blate, cate, Cate, crate, date, eight, fate, fete, freight, gait, gate, grate, great, haet, hate, Kate, late, mate, pate, plait, plate, prate, quoit, rate, sate, skate, slate, spate, state, straight, strait, teth, trait, wait, weight

abate, ablate, adnate, aerate, agemate, agnate, airdate, airfreight, alate, arête, await, backdate, baldpate, bedmate, bedplate, berate, birthrate, bistate, bookplate, breastplate, casemate, castrate, caudate, cerate, cheapskate, checkmate, chordate, classmate, clavate, cognate, collate, comate, conflate, connate, cordate, create, cremate, crenate, curate, cutrate, deadweight, debate, deflate, delate, dentate, derate, dictate, dilate, disrate, donate, doorplate, downstate, drawplate, elate, equate, estate, faceplate, falcate, fellate, filtrate, firstrate, fishplate, fixate, flatmate, floodgate, flyweight, formate, frustrate, gelate, gestate, gyrate, hamate, hastate, headgate, helpmate, housemate, hydrate, ice-skate, inflate, ingrate, inmate, innate, instate, irate, jailbait, jugate, khanate, Kuwait, lactate, legate, liftgate, ligate, lightweight, liquate, lobate, locate, lunate, lustrate, lych-gate, lyrate, magnate, makebate, makeweight, mandate, messmate, migrate, misstate, mutate, nameplate, narrate, negate, Newgate, nitrate, notate, nutate, oblate, orate, ornate, ovate, palmate, palpate, peltate, phonate, pinnate, placate, playmate, plicate, portrait, postdate, predate, primate, probate, prolate, prorate, prostate, prostrate, pulsate, punctate, pupate, quadrate, ramate, rebate, red-bait, relate, restate, roommate, rostrate, rotate, saccate, schoolmate, seatmate, sedate, sensate, septate, serrate, shipmate, short weight, soleplate, spectate, spicate, squamate, stagnate, stalemate, stellate, striate, sublate, substrate, sulcate, summate, tailgate, teammate, Tebet, tenth-rate, ternate, terneplate, testate, third-rate, tinplate, toeplate, tollgate, tractate, translate, tristate, truncate, unweight, update, uprate, upstate, V-8, vacate, vallate, valvate, vibrate, virgate, vulgate, whitebait, workmate, zonate abdicate, abnegate, abrogate, absorbate, acclimate, acerbate, acetate, activate, actuate, acylate, adsorbate, advocate, adulate, adumbrate, aggravate, aggregate, agitate, allocate, altercate, alternate, ambulate, amputate, animate, annotate, annulate, antedate, antiquate, apartheid, apostate, approbate, arbitrate, arcuate, arrogate, aspirate, automate, aviate, bantamweight, bifurcate, billingsgate, bipinnate, boilerplate, bombinate, brachiate, cachinnate, calculate, calibrate, caliphate, candidate, cantillate, capitate, captivate, carbonate, carbon-date, carinate, castigate, catenate, cavitate, celebrate, cerebrate, circinate, circulate, city-state, cogitate, collimate, collocate, commentate, commutate, compensate, complicate, concentrate, condensate, confiscate, conglobate, conjugate, consecrate, constellate, consternate, constipate, consummate, contemplate, copperplate, copulate, coronate, correlate, corrugate, coruscate, counterweight, crenulate, crepitate, criminate, cruciate, cucullate, culminate, cultivate, cumulate, cuneate, cupulate, cuspidate, cyclamate, deaerate, decimate, decollate, decorate, decussate, dedicate, defalcate, defecate, delegate, demarcate, demonstrate, denigrate, deviate, deprecate, depredate, derivate, derogate, desecrate, desiccate, designate, desolate, detonate, devastate, deviate, digitate, diplomate, discarnate, dislocate, dissertate, dissipate, distillate, divagate, dominate, duplicate, edentate, educate, elevate, elongate, eluate, emanate, emigrate, emirate, emulate, enervate, ephorate, escalate, estimate, estivate, excavate, exculpate, excecrate, expiate, explicate, expurgate, exsiccate, extirpate, extricate, exudate, fabricate, fascinate, featherweight, fecundate, federate, fenestrate, festinate, fibrillate, flabellate, flagellate, flocculate, fluctuate, fluoridate, foliate,

formulate, fornicate, fractionate, fragmentate, fulminate, fumigate, fustigate, geminate, generate, germinate, glaciate, Golden Gate, graduate, granulate, gratulate, gravitate, heavyweight, hebetate, herniate, hesitate, hibernate, hundredweight, hyphenate, ideate, illustrate, imamate, imbricate, imitate, immigrate, immolate, impetrate, implicate, imprecate, impregnate, incarnate, increate, incubate, inculcate, inculpate, incurvate, indagate, indicate, indurate, infiltrate, innervate, innovate, insensate, insolate, inspissate, instigate, insulate, interstate, intestate, intimate, intonate, intraplate, inundate, invocate, iodate, irrigate, irritate, isolate, iterate, jubilate, juniorate, lacerate, laminate, Latinate, laureate, legislate, levigate, levitate, liberate, liquidate, litigate, littermate, lubricate, macerate, machinate, magistrate, marginate, margravate, marinate, masticate, masturbate, maturate, mediate, medicate, meditate, meliorate, menstruate, microstate, micturate, middleweight, militate, ministrate, miscreate, mithridate, mitigate, moderate, modulate, motivate, multistate, mutilate, nation-state, nauseate, navigate, neonate, nictitate, niobate, nominate, numerate, obfuscate, objurgate, obligate, obovate, obviate, operate, opiate, orchestrate, ordinate, oscillate, osculate, out-of-date, overstate, overweight, ovulate, paginate, palliate, palpitate, paperweight, patinate, peculate, penetrate, pennyweight, percolate, perennate, perforate, permeate, perorate, perpetrate, personate, pollinate, populate, postulate, potentate, predicate, procreate, profligate, promulgate, propagate, prorogate, pullulate, pulmonate, punctuate, quantitate, rabbinate, radiate, re-create, reclinate, recreate, regulate, reinstate, relegate, relocate, reluctate, remonstrate,

renovate, replicate, reprobate,
resonate, retardate, retranslate,
roseate, rubricate, ruminate, runagate,
rusticate, sagittate, salivate, sanitate,
satiate, saturate, scintillate, second-
rate, segregate, self-portrait, separate,
sequestrate, seriate, sibilate, simulate,
sinuate, situate, speculate, spoliate,
stablemate, stimulate, stipulate,
strangulate, stridulate, stylobate,
subjugate, sublimate, subrogate,
subulate, suffocate, sultanate,
supplicate, surrogate, syncopate,
syndicate, tablemate, tabulate,
terminate, tessellate, tête-à-tête, thirty-
eight, titillate, titivate, tolerate,
transmigrate, transudate, tribulate,
tribunate, trifurcate, trilobate,
tripinnate, triplicate, tunicate,
turbinate, ulcerate, ululate, umbellate,
uncinate, underrate, understate,
underweight, undulate, ungulate,
urinate, vaccinate, vacillate, validate,
valuate, variate, vaticinate, vegetate,
venerate, ventilate, vertebrate,
vicarate, vindicate, violate, vitiate,
Watergate, welterweight
    abbreviate, abominate, accelerate,
accentuate, accommodate, acculturate,
accumulate, acidulate, adjudicate,
administrate, adulterate, affiliate,
agglomerate, agglutinate, alienate,
alleviate, alliterate, amalgamate,
ameliorate, annihilate, annunciate,
anticipate, apostolate, appreciate,
appropriate, approximate, articulate,
asphyxiate, assassinate, asseverate,
assimilate, associate, attenuate,
authenticate, barbiturate, bicarbonate,
calumniate, campanulate, capacitate,
capitulate, catholicate, certificate,
circumvallate, coagulate, coelenterate,
collaborate, commemorate,
commiserate, communicate,
compassionate, concatenate,
concelebrate, conciliate, confabulate,
confederate, conglomerate,
congratulate, consociate, consolidate,
contaminate, cooperate, coordinate,
corroborate, de-escalate, debilitate,
decapitate, decerebrate, deconcentrate,

deconsecrate, decrepitate, defibrinate,
defibrillate, degenerate, deliberate,
delineate, demodulate, denominate,
depopulate, depreciate, deregulate,
desegregate, desiderate, devaluate,
diaconate, dilapidate, discriminate,
disintegrate, disseminate, dissimilate,
dissimulate, dissociate, divaricate,
domesticate, edulcorate, effectuate,
ejaculate, elaborate, electroplate,
eliminate, elucidate, elucubrate,
elutriate, emaciate, emancipate,
emarginate, emasculate, encapsulate,
enumerate, enunciate, episcopate,
equilibrate, equivocate, eradicate,
etiolate, evacuate, evaluate, evaporate,
eventuate, eviscerate, exacerbate,
exaggerate, exasperate, excogitate,
excoriate, excruciate, exfoliate,
exhilarate, exonerate, expatiate,
expatriate, expectorate, expostulate,
expropriate, extenuate, exterminate,
extrapolate, extravagate, exuberate,
facilitate, fantasticate, felicitate,
gesticulate, habilitate, habituate,
hallucinate, homologate, humiliate,
hypothecate, illuminate, impersonate,
inactivate, inaugurate, incarcerate,
incinerate, incorporate, incriminate,
indoctrinate, inebriate, infatuate,
infuriate, ingratiate, ingurgitate,
initiate, inoculate, inosculate,
inseminate, insinuate, instantiate,
intenerate, intercalate, interpellate,
interpolate, interrelate, interrogate,
intimidate, intoxicate, invaginate,
invalidate, investigate, invigilate,
invigorate, irradiate, italianate,
itinerate, lanceolate, legitimate,
luxuriate, machicolate, mandarinate,
manipulate, matriarchate, matriculate,
Merthiolate, necessitate, negotiate,
noncandidate, obliterate, obnubilate,
officiate, orientate, originate,
oxygenate, participate, particulate,
patriarchate, patriciate, penicillate,
perambulate, peregrinate, perpetuate,
pontificate, potentiate, precipitate,
predestinate, predominate,
prefabricate, premeditate,
prenominate, preponderate,

prevaricate, procrastinate,
prognosticate, proliferate, propitiate,
proportionate, quadruplicate,
quintuplicate, reciprocate,
recriminate, recuperate, redecorate,
redintegrate, reduplicate, reeducate,
refrigerate, regenerate, regurgitate,
reincarnate, reintegrate, reiterate,
rejuvenate, remunerate, renominate,
repatriate, repristinate, repudiate,
resupinate, resuscitate, retaliate,
reticulate, revaluate, revegetate,
reverberate, scholasticate,
seventy-eight, sextuplicate,
somnambulate, sophisticate,
stereobate, subordinate, substantiate,
syllabicate, tergiversate, transliterate,
transvaluate, triangulate, variegate,
vituperate, vociferate
  beneficiate, circumambulate,
circumnavigate, circumstantiate,
contraindicate, decontaminate,
deteriorate, differentiate, disaffiliate,
disambiguate, disarticulate,
disassociate, discombobulate,
disintoxicate, disorientate,
disproportionate, domiciliate,
excommunicate, free-associate,
hyperventilate, incapacitate,
individuate, intermediate,
interpenetrate, misappropriate,
multivariate, ratiocinate, recapitulate,
rehabilitate, renegotiate, supcrannuate,
superelevate, superheavyweight,
superordinate, supersaturate,
transilluminate, transubstantiate,
underestimate
  microencapsulate,
intercommunicate, lithium niobate
  diammonium phosphate,
phosphoenolpyruvate
  peroxyacetyl nitrate

ate² \at\ see at⁵

ate³ \ät\ see ot¹

ate⁴ \ät-ē\ see ati

ate⁵ \ət\ see ut¹

ated \āt-əd\ gaited, lated, pated,
stated

  belated, ill-fated, outdated, related,
striated, three-gaited, truncated,
unbated, X-rated
  aberrated, addlepated, animated,
calculated, capsulated, carbonated,
carburated, castellated, complicated,
crenellated, disrelated, elevated,
fenestrated, fimbriated, floriated,
foliated, inspissated, laminated,
marginated, mentholated, perforated,
pileated, pixilated, pustulated,
saturated, tessellated, trabeated,
unabated, uncreated, understated,
variegated
  affiliated, asteriated, configurated,
coordinated, decaffeinated,
domesticated, incorporated,
inebriated, interrelated, intoxicated,
opinionated, sophisticated,
uncalculated, uncelebrated,
uncomplicated, underinflated,
unmediated, unmitigated, unsaturated,
unsegregated
  unadulterated, unanticipated,
unarticulated, unconsolidated,
undereducated, underpopulated,
undissociated, unsophisticated
  polyunsaturated, underappreciated
  —also -ed forms of verbs listed at
ate¹

ateful \āt-fəl\ fateful, grateful,
hateful
  ungrateful

atel¹ \ət-ᵊl\ see ottle

atel² \āt-ᵊl\ see atal

ateless \āt-ləs\ dateless, stateless,
weightless

atelist \at-ᵊl-əst\ see atalyst

ately¹ \āt-lē\ greatly, lately, stately,
straightly, straitly
  innately, irately, ornately
  up-to-dately
  Johnny-come-lately

ately² \at-ᵊl-ē\ see attily

atem \ät-əm\ see atum¹

atement

atement \āt-mənt\ statement
abatement, debatement,
misstatement, restatement
overstatement, reinstatement,
understatement

aten¹ \āt-ᵊn\ greaten, laten, Satan,
straighten, straiten
Keewatin

aten² \at-ᵊn\ see atin²

aten³ \ät-ᵊn\ see otten

atent¹ \āt-ᵊnt\ see atant¹

atent² \at-ᵊnt\ see atant²

ater¹ \ȯt-ər\ daughter, slaughter,
tauter, water
backwater, bathwater, blackwater,
breakwater, cutwater, dewater,
deepwater, dishwater, firewater,
floodwater, forequarter, freshwater,
goddaughter, granddaughter,
groundwater, headwater, hindquarter,
jerkwater, limewater, manslaughter,
meltwater, rainwater, rosewater,
saltwater, seawater, self-slaughter,
shearwater, springwater, stepdaughter,
tailwater, tidewater, wastewater
milk-and-water, polywater,
underwater

ater² \āt-ər\ see ator

ateral \at-ə-rəl\ lateral
bilateral, collateral, trilateral
contralateral, dorsolateral,
equilateral, ipsilateral, multilateral,
quadrilateral, unilateral, ventrolateral
posterolateral

aterer \ȯt-ər-ər\ slaughterer, waterer
dewaterer

ateress \āt-ə-rəs\ cateress,
traitorous

atering \ȯt-ə-riŋ\ mouth-watering
—also -ing forms of verbs listed at
ater¹

atery¹ \ät-ə-rē\ see ottery

atery² \ȯt-ə-rē\ cautery, watery

ates¹ \āts\ Yeats
Gulf States
Papal States
Persian Gulf States, United States
Federated Malay States
United Arab Emirates
—also -s, -'s, and -s' forms of nouns,
and -s forms of verbs, listed at ate¹

ates² \āt-ēz\ nates
Achates, Euphrates, Penates
—also -s, -'s, and -s' forms of nouns
listed at aty

atest \āt-əst\ latest, statist
—also -est forms of adjectives listed
at ate¹

atey \āt-ē\ see aty

ath¹ \äth\ see oth¹

ath² \ȯth\ see oth²

ath³ \ath\ bath, hath, lath, math,
path, rathe, snath, strath, wrath
birdbath, bloodbath, bypath,
footbath, footpath, sunbath, towpath,
warpath
aftermath, polymath, psychopath,
telepath
naturopath, osteopath, sociopath

atha \ät-ə\ see ata¹

athe¹ \āt͟h\ swathe
enswathe, unswathe

athe² \āt͟h\ bathe, lathe, rathe,
saithe, scathe, spathe, swathe
sunbathe, unswathe

athe³ \ath\ see ath³

atheless \āth-ləs\ see aithless

ather¹ \ät͟h-ər\ bother, father, pother,
rather
forefather, godfather, grandfather,
housefather, stepfather

ather² \ət͟h-ər\ see other¹

ather³ \at͟h-ər\ blather, Cather,
gather, lather, Mather, rather, slather
forgather, ingather, wool-gather

athering \a<u>th</u>-riŋ\ ingathering,
woolgathering
—*also* -ing *forms of verbs listed at*
ather³

athi \ät-ē\ see ati

athic \ath-ik\ empathic
amphipathic, psychopathic,
telepathic
homeopathic, idiopathic, sociopathic

athlon \ath-lən\ biathlon, decathlon,
pentathlon, triathlon

athy \ath-ē\ Cathie, Cathy, Kathie,
Kathy, wrathy
allelopathy

ati¹ \ät-ē\ Ate, Dottie, dotty, Dotty,
grotty, knotty, naughty, plotty, potty,
Scottie, Scotty, snotty, spotty, squatty
Amati, basmati, chapati, coati,
flokati, karate, Marathi, metate,
Scarlatti, Tol'yatti
glitterati, Gujarati, Hakodate, literati,
manicotti
illuminati

ati² \atē\ see atty

ati³ \äts\ see ots

ati⁴ \as\ see ass³

atia \ā-shə\ see acia

atial \ā-shəl\ see acial

atian \ā-shən\ see ation¹

atians \ā-shənz\ see ations

atible \at-ə-bəl\ compatible,
getatable
incompatible, self-compatible
biocompatible, self-incompatible

atic¹ \ät-ik\ see otic¹

atic² \at-ik\ attic, Attic, batik, phatic,
static, vatic
agnatic, aquatic, astatic, asthmatic,
chromatic, climatic, comatic,
dalmatic, dogmatic, dramatic, ecstatic,
emphatic, erratic, fanatic, hepatic,
judgmatic, komatik, lymphatic,

magmatic, neumatic, phlegmatic,
plasmatic, pneumatic, pragmatic,
prismatic, protatic, quadratic,
rheumatic, schematic, schismatic,
sciatic, sematic, Socratic, somatic,
spermatic, stigmatic, sylvatic,
thematic, traumatic, villatic
achromatic, acrobatic, Adriatic,
aerobatic, anabatic, antistatic,
aromatic, astigmatic, autocratic,
automatic, bureaucratic, charismatic,
cinematic, democratic, dilemmatic,
diplomatic, Dixiecratic, Eleatic,
emblematic, enigmatic, enzymatic,
fungistatic, Hanseatic, hieratic,
Hippocratic, kerygmatic, leviratic,
melismatic, miasmatic, mobocratic,
monocratic, morganatic, numismatic,
ochlocratic, operatic, phonematic,
plutocratic, pre-Socratic, problematic,
programmatic, symptomatic,
syntagmatic, systematic, technocratic,
theocratic, timocratic, undogmatic,
undramatic
anagrammatic, apothegmatic,
aristocratic, asymptomatic, axiomatic,
conglomeratic, diagrammatic,
diaphragmatic, epigrammatic,
gerontocratic, gynecocratic,
homeostatic, idiomatic,
logogrammatic, melodramatic,
meritocratic, monochromatic,
monodramatic, monogrammatic,
pantisocratic, paradigmatic,
physiocratic, psychodramatic,
psychosomatic, semiaquatic,
theorematic, undemocratic,
undiplomatic
antidemocratic, Austroasiatic,
biosystematic, ideogrammatic,
semiautomatic

atica \at-i-kə\ Attica
hepatica, sciatica, viatica

atical \at-i-kəl\ statical
dogmatical, erratical, fanatical,
grammatical, piratical, pragmatical,
sabbatical, schismatical
autocratical, emblematical,
enigmatical, magistratical,
mathematical, ochlocratical,

problematical, systematical,
theocratical, timocratical,
ungrammatical
 anagrammatical, diagrammatical,
epigrammatical, pantisocratical

atics \at-iks\ statics
 chromatics, dogmatics, dramatics,
pneumatics, pragmatics
 acrobatics, informatics, mathematics,
numismatics, systematics
 melodramatics, psychosomatics
 —*also* -s, -s, *and* -s' *forms of nouns
listed at* atic²

atie \āt-ē\ see aty

atiens \ā-shənz\ see ations

atient \ā-shənt\ patient
 impatient, inpatient, outpatient
 rubefacient, somnifacient
 abortifacient

atik \at-ik\ see atic²

atile \at-ᵊl-ē\ see attily

atim \āt-əm\ see atum²

atin¹ \ät-ᵊn\ see otten

atin² \at-ᵊn\ batten, fatten, flatten,
gratin, Latin, latten, matin, paten,
patten, Patton, platan, platen, ratton,
satin
 cisplatin, manhattan, Manhattan,
Powhatan
 lovastatin, Neo-Latin

atin³ \āt-ᵊn\ see aten¹

atinate \at-ᵊn-ət\ concatenate,
Palatinate
 Rhineland-Palatinate

ating \āt-iŋ\ bating, grating, plating,
rating, skating, slating
 abating, bearbaiting, bullbaiting,
frustrating, self-rating
 calculating, lancinating, maid-in-
waiting, nauseating, operating,
titillating
 humiliating, lady-in-waiting,
nonterminating, self-liquidating, self-

regulating, self-replicating,
subordinating, uncalculating,
undeviating, unhesitating
 indiscriminating, self-incriminating
 —*also* -ing *forms of verbs listed at*
ate¹

atinous \at-nəs\ see atness

ation¹ \ā-shən\ Asian, Haitian,
nation, Nation, ration, station,
Thracian
 ablation, agnation, Alsatian,
carnation, castration, causation,
cessation, cetacean, chrismation,
citation, cognation, collation,
conation, conflation, creation,
cremation, crenation, Croatian,
crustacean, cunctation, dalmatian,
damnation, deflation, dictation,
dilation, donation, duration, elation,
enation, equation, Eurasian, filtration,
fixation, flotation, formation,
foundation, frustration, furcation,
gestation, gradation, gustation,
gyration, hydration, illation, inflation,
lactation, laudation, lavation, legation,
libation, libration, ligation, location,
lustration, mentation, migration,
mutation, narration, natation,
negation, nitration, notation, novation,
nutation, oblation, oration, outstation,
ovation, phonation, planation,
plantation, plication, potation,
predation, privation, probation,
pronation, proration, prostration,
pulsation, purgation, quotation,
reflation, relation, rogation, rotation,
saltation, salvation, sedation,
sensation, serration, slumpflation,
squamation, stagflation, stagnation,
starvation, striation, stylization,
sublation, substation, summation,
tarnation, taxation, temptation,
translation, truncation, vacation,
venation, vexation, vibration,
vocation, workstation, zonation
 abdication, aberration, abjuration,
abnegation, acceptation, acclamation,
acclimation, accusation, activation,
actuation, adaptation, adjuration,
admiration, adoration, adulation,

adumbration, advocation, affectation, affirmation, aggravation, aggregation, allegation, allocation, amputation, alteration, altercation, alternation, Amerasian, angulation, animation, annexation, annotation, annulation, antiquation, Appalachian, appellation, application, approbation, arbitration, aspiration, assentation, assignation, attestation, augmentation, Aurignacian, automation, aviation, avocation, blaxploitation, botheration, brachiation, cachinnation, calculation, calibration, cancellation, capitation, captivation, carbonation, carburation, castigation, celebration, cementation, cerebration, circulation, claudication, cogitation, collocation, coloration, combination, commendation, commination, commutation, compellation, compensation, compilation, complication, compurgation, computation, concentration, condemnation, condensation, condonation, confirmation, confiscation, conflagration, conformation, confrontation, confutation, congelation, congregation, conjugation, conjuration, connotation, consecration, conservation, consolation, conspiration, constellation, consternation, constipation, consultation, consummation, contemplation, contestation, conurbation, conversation, convocation, copulation, coronation, corporation, correlation, corrugation, coruscation, crenellation, culmination, cupellation, cuspidation, cybernation, decimation, declamation, declaration, declination, decoration, dedication, defalcation, defamation, defecation, defloration, deformation, degradation, degustation, dehydration, delectation, delegation, demarcation, demonstration, denegation, denigration, denotation, depilation, deportation, depravation, depredation, deprivation, deputation, derivation, derogation, desecration, desiccation,

designation, desolation, desperation, destination, detestation, detonation, devastation, deviation, dilatation, disclamation, disinflation, dislocation, dispensation, disputation, disrelation, dissertation, dissipation, distillation, divination, domination, dubitation, duplication, education, elevation, elongation, emanation, embarkation, embrocation, emendation, emigration, emulation, encrustation, enervation, epilation, equitation, eructation, escalation, estimation, estivation, evocation, exaltation, excavation, excitation, exclamation, exculpation, execration, exhalation, exhortation, expectation, expiation, expiration, explanation, explication, exploitation, exploration, exportation, expurgation, extirpation, extrication, exudation, exultation, fabrication, fascination, federation, fenestration, fermentation, fibrillation, figuration, filiation, flagellation, fluoridation, fluctuation, foliation, fomentation, formulation, fornication, fragmentation, fulguration, fulmination, fumigation, gemination, generation, germination, glaciation, graduation, granulation, gravitation, habitation, hesitation, hibernation, hyphenation, ideation, illustration, imbrication, imitation, immigration, immolation, implantation, implication, importation, imprecation, imputation, incantation, incarnation, incitation, inclination, incrustation, incubation, inculcation, indentation, indexation, indication, indignation, induration, infestation, infiltration, inflammation, information, inhalation, innovation, insolation, inspiration, installation, instauration, insufflation, insulation, intonation, inundation, invitation, invocation, irrigation, irritation, isolation, iteration, jactitation, jubilation, laceration, lacrimation, lamentation, lamination, legislation, levitation, liberation, limitation, lineation, liquidation, literation, litigation, lubrication, lucubration, maceration, machination, maculation, malformation, malversation, margination, mastication, masturbation, maturation, mediation, medication, meditation, melioration, menstruation, mensuration, metrication, ministration, moderation, modulation, molestation, motivation, navigation, nomination, numeration, obfuscation, objurgation, obligation, observation, obturation, occultation, occupation, operation, orchestration, ordination, oscillation, osculation, ostentation, ovulation, oxidation, ozonation, pagination, palliation, palpitation, patination, penetration, perforation, permeation, permutation, peroration, perpetration, perspiration, perturbation, pigmentation, pixilation, pollination, population, postulation, predication, preformation, prelibation, preparation, presentation, proclamation, procreation, procuration, profanation, prolongation, propagation, prorogation, protestation, provocation, publication, punctuation, radiation, recitation, reclamation, recordation, re-creation, recreation, reformation, refutation, registration, regulation, relaxation, relocation, reparation, replantation, replication, reprobation, reputation, reservation, resignation, respiration, restoration, retardation, revelation, revocation, ruination, salivation, salutation, sanitation, satiation, saturation, scatteration, scintillation, segmentation, segregation, separation, sequestration, sexploitation, simulation, situation, solmization, speciation, speculation, spoliation, sternutation, stimulation, stipulation, strangulation, structuration, subjugation, sublimation, subrogation, suffocation, suspiration, susurration, sustentation, syncopation, syndication, tabulation, termination, tessellation, titillation, titivation, toleration, transformation, translocation, transmigration, transmutation, transpiration,

transplantation, transportation, trepidation, tribulation, trituration, ulceration, ululation, undulation, urination, usurpation, vaccination, vacillation, validation, valuation, variation, vegetation, veneration, ventilation, vindication, violation, visitation

   abbreviation, abomination, acceleration, accentuation, accommodation, accreditation, acculturation, accumulation, actualization, adjudication, administration, adulteration, affiliation, afforestation, agglomeration, agglutination, alienation, alleviation, alliteration, amalgamation, amelioration, amortization, amplification, analyzation, anglicization, annihilation, annunciation, anticipation, appreciation, appropriation, approximation, argumentation, articulation, asphyxiation, assassination, asseveration, assimilation, association, attenuation, authorization, autoxidation, barbarization, bastardization, beautification, bowdlerization, brutalization, canalization, canonization, capacitation, capitulation, carbonylation, centralization, certification, cicatrization, civilization, clarification, classification, coagulation, coeducation, cohabitation, colonization, collaboration, columniation, commemoration, commiseration, communication, communization, compartmentation, complementation, concatenation, conciliation, confabulation, confederation, configuration, conglomeration, congratulation, consideration, consociation, consolidation, contamination, continuation, cooperation, coordination, corroboration, crustification, crystallization, deactivation, debilitation, decapitation, decompensation, defenestration, deforestation, degeneration, deglaciation, deification, deliberation, delineation, denomination, denunciation, depopulation, depreciation, deregulation, desegregation, despoliation, determination, devaluation, dilapidation, diphthongization, disapprobation, discoloration, discrimination, disembarkation, disinclination, disinformation, disintegration, dissemination, dissimilation, dissimulation, dissociation, divarication, documentation, domestication, dramatization, echolocation, edification, ejaculation, elaboration, elicitation, elimination, elucidation, emaciation, emancipation, emasculation, enumeration, enunciation, epoxidation, equalization, equivocation, eradication, evacuation, evagination, evaluation, evaporation, evisceration, exacerbation, exaggeration, examination, exasperation, excoriation, excruciation, exercitation, exhilaration, exoneration, expostulation, expropriation, extenuation, extermination, extrapolation, facilitation, factorization, falsification, fantastication, feminization, fertilization, Finlandization, formalization, formulization, fortification, fossilization, fructification, gasification, gentrification, gesticulation, glamorization, globalization, glorification, glycosylation, gratification, habituation, hallucination, harmonization, haruspication, hellenization, humanization, hyperinflation, idolization, illumination, imagination, immunization, impersonation, implementation, improvisation, inauguration, incarceration, incardination, incineration, incorporation, incrimination,

indoctrination, inebriation, infatuation, ingratiation, inhabitation, initiation, inoculation, insemination, insinuation, instrumentation, internalization, interpretation, interrelation, intimidation, intoxication, invagination, investigation, invigoration, irradiation, itemization, jollification, justification, labanotation, laicization, latinization, legalization, lionization, localization, machicolation, magnetization, magnification, maladaptation, manifestation, masculinization, matriculation, maximization, mechanization, miscegenation, mobilization, modernization, modification, mollification, mongrelization, monopolization, moralization, mortification, multiplication, mystification, nationalization, naturalization, necessitation, negotiation, neutralization, normalization, notarization, notification, novelization, nullification, optimization, organization, orientation, ornamentation, ossification, pacification, paralyzation, participation, pasteurization, patronization, penalization, perambulation, perpetuation, perseveration, personalization, plasticization, pluralization, petrification, polarization, pontification, preadaptation, precipitation, predestination, prefiguration, premeditation, preoccupation, preregistration, prettification, procrastination, prognostication, proliferation, pronunciation, propitiation, pulverization, purification, qualification, quantification, ramification, randomization, ratification, ratiocination, realization, reciprocation, recombination, recommendation, recrimination, recuperation, redecoration, reduplication, reforestation, refrigeration, regeneration,

regimentation, regurgitation,
reification, reincarnation,
reintegration, remediation,
remuneration, renunciation,
representation, republication,
repudiation, reticulation,
retrogradation, reverberation,
robotization, romanization,
sanctification, sanitization,
scarification, sedimentation,
sensitization, Serbo-Croatian,
signification, simplification,
socialization, solemnization,
solicitation, sophistication,
specialization, specification,
stabilization, standardization,
sterilization, stratification,
stultification, subalternation,
subinfeudation, subordination,
subpopulation, subsidization,
summarization, supplementation,
syllabication, symbolization,
synchronization, systemization,
teleportation, tergiversation,
terrorization, theorization,
transfiguration, transliteration,
transvaluation, traumatization,
triangulation, trivialization,
uglification, unification, unionization,
urbanization, vandalization,
vaporization, variegation, vaticination,
velarization, verbalization,
verification, versification,
victimization, vilification, vinification,
vitalization, vituperation, vocalization,
vociferation, vulgarization,
westernization, x-radiation
  acclimatization, allegorization,
alphabetization, autocorrelation,
automatization, beneficiation,
capitalization, characterization,
circumnavigation, codetermination,
commercialization, conceptualization,
consubstantiation, containerization,
counterreformation, criminalization,
cross-examination, cryopreservation,
decarboxylation, decimilization, de-
Stalinization, decasualization,
decentralization, declassification,
decontamination, dehumanization,
dehydrogenation, delegitimation,

demystification, derealization,
derivitization, desulfurization,
deterioration, differentiation,
disassociation, discombobulation,
disorientation, disorganization,
disproportionation, disqualification,
diversification, dolomitization,
electrification, excommunication,
exemplification, experimentation,
extemporization, externalization,
familiarization, federalization,
generalization, homogenization,
hospitalization, hyperventilation,
idealization, identification,
immobilization, immortalization,
incapacitation, inconsideration,
incoordination, indemnification,
indetermination, indiscrimination,
individuation, institutionalization,
insubordination, intensification,
intermediation, intermodulation,
intrapopulation, italicization,
legitimization, lexicalization,
maladministration, mathematization,
megacorporation, militarization,
miniaturization, misappropriation,
miscommunication, misinterpretation,
mispronunciation, misrepresentation,
noncooperation, nonproliferation,
overcompensation, overpopulation,
palatalization, periodization,
personification, photoduplication,
photoexcitation, popularization,
predetermination, prestidigitation,
proselytization, radicalization,
ratiocination, rationalization,
reafforestation, recapitulation,
reconciliation, reconsideration,
rehabilitation, reinterpretation,
renegotiation, reorganization,
revitalization, ritualization,
Schrödinger equation, secularization,
solidification, subvocalization,
supererogation, syllabification,
tintinnabulation, transubstantiation,
unappreciation, underestimation,
undervaluation, unsophistication,
visualization
  Americanization, automanipulation,
decriminalization, depersonalization,
electrodesiccation,

intercommunication, industrialization, internationalization, materialization, oversimplification, particularization, pictorialization, photointerpretation, pseudosophistication, recapitalization, spiritualization, telecommunication, universalization
  biodeterioration, deindustrialization, intellectualization, reindustrialization
  deinstitutionalization

ation² \ā-zhən\ see asion

ation³ \ash-ən\ see assion

ational¹ \ā-shnəl\ stational
citational, formational, gestational, gradational, migrational, narrational, notational, relational, sensational, vocational
  aberrational, adaptational, avocational, compensational, computational, conformational, confrontational, congregational, conjugational, connotational, conservational, conversational, convocational, derivational, educational, fluctuational, generational, gravitational, ideational, informational, innovational, inspirational, invitational, irrotational, limitational, navigational, observational, operational, orchestrational, postranslational, prevocational, progestational, recreational, reformational, situational, transformational
  communicational, coeducational, denominational, improvisational, interpretational, investigational, organizational, representational
  nonrepresentational, reorganizational
  interdenominational

ational² \āzh-nəl\ see asional

ational³ \ash-nəl\ national, passional, rational
  binational, cross-national, irrational, transnational
  international, multinational, supranational, suprarational

ationist \ā-shnəst\ salvationist, vacationist
  annexationist, confrontationist, conservationist, educationist, integrationist, isolationist, liberationist, operationist, preservationist, recreationist, segregationist, separationist, preservationist
  accomodationist, administrationist, assimilationist, associationist, collaborationist, emancipationist

ations \ā-shənz\ Galatians, impatiens, relations
  Lamentations, Revelations
  United Nations
  Rhode Island and Providence Plantations

atious \ā-shəs\ see acious

atis¹ \at-əs\ see atus³

atis² \ät-əs\ see ottis

atist \āt-əst\ see atest

atitude \at-ə-tüd\ see attitude

atium \ā-shē-əm\ Latium
pancratium, solatium

atius \ā-shəs\ see acious

ative \āt-iv\ dative, native, stative
ablative, constative, creative, dilative, mutative, rotative, summative, translative
  aggregative, agitative, alterative, applicative, carminative, cogitative, combinative, commutative, connotative, consecrative, consultative, contemplative, copulative, corporative, cumulative, decorative, denotative, dissipative, educative, explicative, facultative, federative, generative, germinative, imitative, implicative, innovative, integrative, irritative, iterative, legislative, limitative, meditative, meliorative, motivative, nominative, nuncupative, operative, palliative, pejorative, penetrative, procreative,

propagative, qualitative, quantitative,
recreative, regulative, replicative,
separative, speculative, terminative,
vegetative
  accelerative, accumulative,
administrative, agglutinative,
alliterative, appreciative, assimilative,
associative, authoritative,
collaborative, commemorative,
commiserative, communicative,
contaminative, continuative,
cooperative, corroborative,
degenerative, deliberative, delineative,
determinative, discriminative,
evaporative, exhilarative, exonerative,
illuminative, interpretative,
investigative, justificative,
multiplicative, obliterative,
opinionative, originative,
postoperative, premeditative,
preoperative, proliferative,
reciprocative, recuperative,
regenerative, remunerative,
reverberative, significative,
vituperative
  excommunicative, incommunicative,
noncooperative, quasi-legislative,
semiquantitative, uncommunicative

atl \ät-ᵊl\ see ottle

atlas \at-ləs\ atlas, Atlas, hatless

atless \at-ləs\ see atlas

atli \ät-lē\ see otly

atling \at-liŋ\ fatling, flatling,
rattling
  —also -ing forms of verbs listed at
attle

atly \at-lē\ flatly, rattly

atnam \ət-nəm\ Machilipatnam,
Vishakhapatnam

atness \at-nəs\ fatness, flatness
  platinous
  gelatinous

ato¹ \ät-ō\ auto, blotto, grotto, lotto,
motto, otto, Otto, potto

annatto, castrato, legato, marcato,
mulatto, rabato, rebato, ridotto, rubato,
sfumato, spiccato, staccato
  agitato, animato, ben trovato,
Guanajuato, moderato, obbligato,
ostinato, pizzicato

ato² \āt-ō\ Cato, Plato
  Orvieto, potato, tomato
  Barquisimeto

atomist \at-ə-məst\ atomist
  anatomist

atomy \at-ə-mē\ atomy
  anatomy

aton \at-ᵊn\ see atin²

atony \at-ᵊn-ē\ see atany

ator \āt-ər\ baiter, cater, crater,
Crater, dater, faitour, freighter, gaiter,
gator, grater, hater, krater, later, mater,
plater, rater, satyr, skater, slater, stater,
stator, tater, traitor, waiter
  aerator, collator, Bay Stater, creator,
curator, debater, Decatur, dictator,
donator, dumbwaiter, equator, first-
rater, glossator, headwaiter, levator,
locator, mandator, Mercator, narrator,
pronator, pulsator, rotator, spectator,
tailgater, testator, theater, third-rater,
translator, upstater, vibrator
  actuator, abdicator, activator,
adulator, advocator, agitator, alligator,
allocator, alternator, animator,
annotator, applicator, arbitrator,
aspirator, aviator, buccinator,
calculator, captivator, carburetor,
celebrator, circulator, commentator,
commutator, compensator,
compurgator, concentrator,
confiscator, congregator, consecrator,
consummator, contemplator,
corporator, correlator, depredator,
desecrater, desecrator, designator,
cultivator, decorator, delegator,
demonstrator, detonator, deviator,
dissipater, dominator, duplicator, dura
mater, educator, elevator, emulator,
escalator, estimator, excavator,

explicator, expurgator, extirpator, fascinator, formulator, fornicator, generator, gladiator, hibernator, illustrator, incubator, indicator, infiltrator, innovator, inhalator, inspirator, insulator, integrator, lacrimator, liquidator, literator, mediator, moderator, motivator, navigator, nomenclator, nominator, numerator, obturator, operator, orchestrator, oscillator, percolator, perpetrator, pia mater, pollinator, postulator, procreator, procurator, propagator, radiator, regulator, resonator, respirator, revelator, second-rater, selling-plater, separator, simulator, subjugator, syndicator, tabulator, terminator, valuator, ventilator, violator

    accelerator, accommodator, accumulator, administrator, adulterator, alienator, alleviator, annihilator, annunciator, anticipator, appreciator, appropriator, assassinator, attenuator, continuator, calumniator, collaborator, commemorator, communicator, conciliator, congratulator, consolidator, contaminator, cooperator, coordinator, corroborator, defibrillator, delineator, denominator, depreciator, determinator, discriminator, disseminator, dissimulator, ejaculator, eliminator, emancipator, enumerator, equivocator, eradicator, evaluator, evaporator, exterminator, extrapolator, impersonator, improvisator, incinerator, inseminator, interrogator, intimidator, investigator, negotiator, oxygenator, pacificator, perambulator, predestinator, procrastinator, purificator, redecorator, refrigerator, regenerator, resuscitator, subordinator, totalizator

    excommunicator, rehabilitator, turbogenerator

    immunomodulator

    —*also* -er *forms of adjectives listed at* ate¹

atre¹ \ätrᵊ\ pas de quatre
    coup de theatre

atre² \at\ see at⁵

atric \a-trik\ Patrick
    sympatric, theatric
    allopatric, geriatric, pediatric, podiatric, psychiatric

atrick \a-trik\ see atric

atrics \a-triks\ theatrics
    pediatrics

atrist \a-trəst\ geriatrist, physiatrist

atrix \ā-triks\ matrix
    cicatrix, testatrix
    aviatrix, dominatrix, mediatrix
    administratrix

atron \ā-trən\ matron, natron, patron

ats¹ \äts\ see ots

ats² \ats\ bats, rats
    ersatz
    —*also* -s, -'s, *and* -s' *forms of nouns, and* -s *forms of verbs, listed at* at⁵

atsa \ät-sə\ see atzo¹

atsch \ach\ see atch⁴

atsk \ätsk\ Bratsk
    Okhotsk
    Petrozavodsk

atsu \ät-sü\ shiatsu, shiatzu
    Hamamatsu, Takamatsu

atsy \at-sē\ see azi³

att¹ \at\ see at⁵

att² \ät\ see ot¹

atta \ät-ə\ see ata¹

attage \ät-ij\ see ottage

attan \at-ᵊn\ see atin²

atte \at\ see at⁵

atted \a-təd\ superfatted
    —*also* -ed *forms of verbs listed at* at⁵

attel \at-ᵊl\ see attle

atten \at-ᵊn\ see atin²

atter \at-ər\ attar, batter, blatter, chatter, clatter, fatter, flatter, hatter, latter, matter, natter, patter, plaiter, platter, ratter, satyr, scatter, shatter, smatter, spatter, splatter, tatter
backscatter, bespatter, flat-hatter, standpatter, wildcatter
antimatter, pitter-patter

attering \at-ə-riŋ\ nattering, smattering
backscattering, earth-shattering, self-flattering, unflattering
Rayleigh scattering
—also -ing forms of verbs listed at atter

attern \at-ərn\ pattern, Saturn, slattern

attery \at-ə-rē\ battery, cattery, clattery, flattery, mattery
Cape Flattery, self-flattery

atti¹ \ät-ē\ see ati¹

atti² \at-ē\ see atty

attic \at-ik\ see atic²

attica \at-i-kə\ see atica

attice¹ \at-əs\ see atus³

attice² \at-ish\ see attish

attie \at-ē\ see atty

attily \at-ᵊl-ē\ cattily, chattily, Natalie, Nathalie, nattily, rattly
philately
sal volatile

atting \at-iŋ\ batting, matting, tatting
—also -ing forms of verbs listed at at⁵

attish \at-ish\ brattish, fattish, flattish

attitude \at-ə-tüd\ attitude, latitude

attle \at-ᵊl\ battle, brattle, cattle, chattel, prattle, rattle, tattle
embattle, Seattle
tittle-tattle

attler \at-lər\ battler, prattler, rattler, tattler

attling \at-liŋ\ see atling

attly¹ \at-ᵊl-ē\ see attily

attly² \at-lē\ see atly

atto¹ \at-ə\ see ata³

atto² \ät-ō\ see ato¹

atton \at-ᵊn\ see atin²

atty \at-ē\ batty, catty, bratty, chatty, fatty, Hattie, natty, Patti, Pattie, patty, Patty, platy, ratty, scatty, tattie, tatty
Cincinnati

atum¹ \ät-əm\ bottom, datum, satem
erratum, pomatum
desideratum

atum² \āt-əm\ datum
pomatum, substratum, verbatim
ageratum, literatim, seriatim, ultimatum
corpus allatum, corpus striatum, desideratum

atum³ \at-əm\ atom, datum
erratum, substratum
seriatim

atuous \ach-wəs\ fatuous
ignis fatuus

atur \āt-ər\ see ator

atural \ach-rəl\ natural
connatural, transnatural, unnatural
preternatural, seminatural, supernatural

ature¹ \ā-chər\ nature
denature, 4-H'er
magistrature, nomenclature, supernature

ature² \ach-ər\ see atcher²

aturn \at-ərn\ see attern

atus[1] \āt-əs\ flatus, gratis, status,
stratus
afflatus, hiatus, meatus
apparatus
coitus reservatus

atus[2] \ät-əs\ see ottis

atus[3] \at-əs\ brattice, gratis, lattice,
status, stratus
clematis
altostratus, apparatus, cirrostratus,
nimbostratus

atute \ach-ət\ see atchet

atuus \ach-wəs\ see atuous

aty \āt-ē\ eighty, Haiti, Katie, Katy,
Leyte, matey, platy, slaty, weighty, yeti
1080, Papeete

atyr \āt-ər\ see ator

atz[1] \ats\ see ats[2]

atz[2] \äts\ see ots

atzo[1] \ät-sə\ matzo, tazza
Hidatsa, piazza

atzo[2] \ät-sō\ see azzo[1]

atzu \ät-sü\ see atsu

au[1] \ō\ see ow[1]

au[2] \ü\ see ew[1]

au[3] \au̇\ see ow[2]

au[4] \o̅\ see aw[1]

aub \äb\ see ob[1]

auba \o̅-bə\ carnauba, Catawba

aube \ōb\ see obe[1]

auber \o̅b-ər\ dauber
Micawber

auble \äb-əl\ see abble[1]

auce \o̅s\ see oss[1]

aucer \o̅-sər\ see osser

aucet \äs-ət\ see osset

auch[1] \o̅ch\ nautch, watch
debauch

auch[2] \äch\ see otch

auche \ōsh\ see oche[2]

auchely \ōsh-lē\ see ocially

auckland \o̅k-lənd\ Auckland,
Falkland

aucous \o̅-kəs\ caucus, glaucous,
raucous

aucus \o̅-kəs\ see aucous

aud[1] \o̅d\ awed, baud, bawd, broad,
Claud, Claude, clawed, fraud, gaud,
god, jawed, laud, Maud, Maude, yod
abroad, applaud, belaud, defraud,
dewclawed, maraud, whipsawed
eisteddfod, lantern-jawed,
quartersawed
— also -ed forms of verbs listed at
aw[1]

aud[2] \äd\ see od[1]

audable \o̅d-ə-bəl\ audible, laudable
applaudable, illaudable, inaudible

audal \o̅d-ᵊl\ caudal, caudle, dawdle

audative \o̅d-ət-iv\ see auditive

aude[1] \au̇d-ē\ see owdy

aude[2] \o̅d-ē\ see awdy

aude[3] \au̇d-ə\ howdah
cum laude
magna cum laude, summa cum laude

aude[4] \o̅d\ see aud[1]

audible \o̅d-ə-bəl\ see audable

auding \o̅d-iŋ\ auding
applauding
self-applauding
—also -ing forms of verbs listed at
aud[1]

audit \o̅d-ət\ audit, plaudit

auditive \o̅d-ət-iv\ auditive,
laudative

audle \ȯd-ᵊl\ see audal

audy¹ \äd-ē\ see ody¹

audy² \ȯd-ē\ see awdy

auer \au̇r\ see ower²

auf \au̇f\ see owff

auffeur \ō-fər\ see ofer

auga \ȯ-gə\ massasauga, Mississauga, Onondaga

auge \āj\ see age³

augeable \ā-jə-bəl\ see ageable

auged \ājd\ see aged

auger¹ \ȯ-gər\ see ogger²

auger² \ā-jər\ see ager¹

augh¹ \af\ see aph

augh² \ä\ see a¹

augh³ \äk̲\ see ach¹

augh⁴ \ȯ\ see aw¹

aughable \af-ə-bəl\ see affable

augham \ȯm\ see aum¹

aughn¹ \än\ see on¹

aughn² \ȯn\ see on³

aught¹ \ät\ see ot¹

aught² \ȯt\ see ought¹

aughter¹ \af-tər\ see after

aughter² \ȯt-ər\ see ater¹

aughterer \ȯt-ər-ər\ see aterer

aughty¹ \ȯt-ē\ haughty, naughty, zloty
  Michelangelo Buonarroti

aughty² \ät-ē\ see ati

augre \ȯg-ər\ see ogger²

augur \ȯg-ər\ see ogger²

augury \ȯ-gə-rē\ see oggery²

aui \au̇-ē\ see owie

auk \ȯk\ see alk

aukee \ȯ-kē\ see alkie

aul \ȯl\ see all

aulay \ȯ-lē\ see awly

auld¹ \ȯl\ see all

auld² \ō\ see ow¹

auldron \ȯl-drən\ see aldron

auled \ȯld\ see ald

auler \ȯ-lər\ see aller¹

aulin \ȯ-lən\ see allen

auling \ȯ-liŋ\ see alling

aulish \ȯ-lish\ see allish

aulk \ȯk\ see alk

aulker \ȯ-kər\ see alker

aulking \ȯ-kiŋ\ see alking

aulle \ȯl\ see all¹

aulm \ȯm\ see aum¹

ault¹ \ȯlt\ see alt

ault² \ō\ see ow¹

aulter \ȯl-tər\ see alter

aulting \ȯl-tiŋ\ see alting

aultless \ȯlt-ləs\ see altless

aulty \ȯl-tē\ see alty

aum¹ \ȯm\ gaum, haulm, Maugham, qualm, shawm
  meerschaum, Radom

aum² \äm\ see om¹

aun¹ \än\ see on¹

aun² \ən\ see un

aun³ \ȯn\ see on³

aun⁴ \au̇n\ see own²

auna¹ \än-ə\ see ana¹

auna² \ȯn-ə\ see onna¹

aunce \ȯns\ jaunce, launce

aunch¹ \änch\ conch, cranch, craunch, paunch, raunch, stanch Romansh

aunch² \ȯnch\ craunch, haunch, launch, paunch, raunch, stanch, staunch

auncher \ȯn-chər\ launcher, stancher, stauncher

aunchy \ȯn-chē\ paunchy, raunchy

aund \ȯnd\ awned, maund
—also -ed forms of verbs listed at on³

aunder¹ \ȯn-dər\ launder, maunder

aunder² \än-dər\ see onder¹

aunish \än-ish\ see onish

aunt¹ \ȯnt\ daunt, flaunt, gaunt, haunt, jaunt, taunt, vaunt, want, wont avant, avaunt, keeshond, romaunt John of Gaunt

aunt² \ant\ see ant⁵

aunt³ \änt\ see ant²

aunted \ȯnt-əd\ see onted

aunter¹ \änt-ər\ saunter, taunter mishanter, rencontre

aunter² \ȯnt-ər\ gaunter, haunter, saunter, taunter

aunty¹ \ȯnt-ē\ flaunty, jaunty, vaunty

aunty² \änt-ē\ see anti¹

aunus \än-əs\ see onus¹

aup \ȯp\ gawp, scaup, whaup, yawp

aupe \ōp\ see ope

auphin \ȯ-fən\ see offin

aur¹ \au̇r\ see ower²

aur² \ȯr\ see or¹

aura¹ \ȯr-ə\ see ora

aura² \är-ə\ see ara¹

aural \ȯr-əl\ see oral¹

aure \ȯr\ see or¹

aurea \ȯr-ē-ə\ see oria

aurean \ȯr-ē-ən\ see orian

aureate¹ \är-ē-ət\ baccalaureate, commisariat

aureate² \ȯr-ē-ət\ aureate, laureate baccalaureate, professoriat

aurel \ȯr-əl\ see oral¹

auren¹ \är-ən\ see arin

auren² \ȯr-ən\ see orin¹

aurence \ȯr-ən(t)s\ see awrence

aureus \ȯr-ē-əs\ see orious

auri \au̇r-ē\ see owery

aurian \ȯr-ē-ən\ see orian

auric \ȯr-ik\ see oric

aurice¹ \är-əs\ see orris¹

aurice² \ȯr-əs\ see aurus

auricle \ȯr-i-kəl\ see orical

aurie¹ \ȯr-ē\ see ory

aurie² \är-ē\ see ari

aurous \ȯr-əs\ see aurus

aurus \ȯr-əs\ aurous, Boris, chorus, Doris, Flores, Horace, Horus, loris, Maurice, morris, Morris, Norris, orris, porous, sorus, Taurus, Torres, torus canorous, Centaurus, clitoris, decorous, Delores, Dolores, pelorus, phosphorous, sonorous, thesaurus allosaurus, brontosaurus, deoch an doris, doch-an-dorris, stegosaurus apatosaurus, tyrannosaurus

aury \ȯr-ē\ see ory

aus¹ \ā-əs\ see ais¹

aus² \aủs\ see ouse²

aus³ \ȯz\ see ause¹

ausal \ȯ-zəl\ causal, clausal
menopausal
postmenopausal

ause¹ \ȯz\ Broz, cause, clause,
gauze, hawse, pause, tawse, yaws
applause, because, kolkhoz, sovkhoz
aeropause, diapause, menopause,
Santa Claus
— *also -s, -'s, and -s' forms of*
nouns, and -s forms of verbs, listed at
aw¹

ause² \əz\ see euse¹

auseous \ȯ-shəs\ see autious

auser \ȯ-zər\ causer, hawser

ausey \ȯ-zē\ causey, gauzy

auss \aủs\ see ouse¹

aussie¹ \äs-ē\ see ossy¹

aussie² \ȯ-sē\ see ossy²

aust¹ \aủst\ see oust

aust² \ȯst\ see ost³

austen \ȯs-tən\ see oston

austin \ȯs-tən\ see oston

austless \ȯst-ləs\ costless
exhaustless

austral¹ \äs-trəl\ see ostrel

austral² \ȯs-trəl\ see ostral¹

aut¹ \ō\ see ow¹

aut² \aủt\ see out³

aut³ \ät\ see ot¹

aut⁴ \ȯt\ see ought¹

autch \ȯch\ see auch¹

aute \ōt\ see oat

auten \ȯt-ᵊn\ boughten, tauten

auterne \ȯt-ərn\ quartern, sauterne,
sauternes

auternes \ȯt-ərn\ see auterne

autery \ȯt-ə-rē\ see atery

autic \ȯt-ik\ orthotic
aeronautic, astronautic

autical \ȯt-i-kəl\ nautical
aeronautical, astronautical

autics \ät-iks\ see otics

aution \ȯ-shən\ caution, groschen
incaution, precaution

autious \ȯ-shəs\ cautious, nauseous
incautious

auto¹ \ȯt-ō\ auto, Giotto
risotto

auto² \ät-ō\ see ato¹

auve \ōv\ see ove²

auze \ȯz\ see ause¹

auzer \aủ-zər\ see ouser

auzy \ȯ-zē\ see ausey

av¹ \äv\ see olve²

av² \av\ see alve²

ava¹ \äv-ə\ brava, fava, guava, java,
Java, kava, lava
baklava, cassava, ottava, Warszawa
balaclava, Bratislava, Costa Brava,
lavalava, piassava

ava² \av-ə\ java
Ungava
balaclava

avage \av-ij\ ravage, savage

avan \ā-vən\ see aven¹

avant \av-ənt\ haven't, savant

avarice \av-rəs\ see averous

ave¹ \äv-ä\ ave, clave, grave, Jahveh,
soave

ave² \āv\ brave, clave, cave, crave, Dave, fave, gave, glaive, grave, knave, lave, nave, pave, rave, save, shave, slave, stave, they've, trave, waive, wave, Wave
airwave, behave, concave, conclave, deprave, dissave, drawshave, enclave, engrave, enslave, exclave, forgave, Great Slave, margrave, octave, outbrave, p-wave, palsgrave, shortwave, spokeshave
after-shave, architrave, biconcave, microwave
contraoctave, photoengrave

ave³ \av\ see alve³

ave⁴ \äv\ see olve²

aved \āvd\ waved
depraved, unsaved
—*also* -ed *forms of verbs listed at* ave²

avel \av-əl\ cavil, gavel, gravel, ravel, travel
unravel

aveless \āv-ləs\ graveless, waveless

aveling \av-liŋ\ raveling, traveling
—*also* -ing *forms of verbs listed at* avel

avement \āv-mənt\ pavement
depravement, enslavement

aven¹ \ā-vən\ Avon, Cavan, craven, graven, haven, maven, raven, shaven
New Haven
riboflavin
Stratford-upon-Avon

aven² \av-ən\ see avin

aven't \av-ənt\ see avant

aver¹ \äv-ər\ slaver
palaver, windhover

aver² \ā-vər\ caver, claver, favor, flavor, graver, haver, laver, quaver, raver, saver, savor, shaver, slaver, waiver, waver
disfavor, enslaver, face-saver, flag-waver, lifesaver

semiquaver
demisemiquaver
hemidemisemiquaver
—*also* -er *forms of adjectives listed at* ave²

aver³ \av-ər\ slaver
cadaver, palaver

avern \av-ərn\ cavern, klavern, tavern

averous \av-rəs\ avarice
cadaverous

avery \āv-rē\ bravery, knavery, quavery, savory, slavery, wavery
unsavory

avey \ā-vē\ see avy

avia \ā-vē-ə\ Moldavia, Moravia
Scandinavia

avial \ā-vē-əl\ gavial
margravial

avian \ā-vē-ən\ avian, Shavian
Moravian
Scandinavian

avid \av-əd\ avid, gravid, pavid

avie \ā-vē\ see avy

avil \av-əl\ see avel

avin \av-ən\ Avon, raven, ravin, savin, spavin

aving \ā-viŋ\ caving, craving, paving, raving, saving, shaving
flagwaving, lifesaving, timesaving
laborsaving
—*also* -ing *forms of verbs listed at* ave²

avis \ā-vəs\ Davis, favus, mavis, Mavis
rara avis

avish¹ \ā-vish\ knavish, slavish

avish² \av-ish\ lavish, ravish

avist \äv-əst\ Slavist, suavest
Pan-Slavist

avity \av-ət-ē\ cavity, gravity
concavity, depravity

antigravity, microgravity, supergravity

avl \äv-əl\ see ovel[1]

avo[1] \äv-ō\ bravo, Bravo
centavo, octavo

avo[2] \ä-vō\ octavo, relievo
mezzo relievo

avon[1] \ä-vən\ see aven[1]

avon[2] \a-vən\ see avin

avor \ä-vər\ see aver[2]

avored \ä-vərd\ favored, flavored
ill-favored, well-favored
—also -ed *forms of verbs listed at*
aver[2]

avory \āv-rē\ see avery

avus \ā-vəs\ see avis

avvy \av-ē\ navvy, savvy

avy \ā-vē\ cavy, Davey, Davy, gravy,
navy, shavie, slavey, wavy

aw[1] \o\ aw, awe, blaw, braw, ca, caw,
chaw, claw, craw, daw, draw, faugh,
flaw, gnaw, haugh, haw, jaw, la, law,
maw, pa, paw, pshaw, Ra, rah, raw,
saw, shah, shaw, Shaw, slaw, spa,
squaw, straw, tau, taw, thaw, yaw
backsaw, bashaw, bedstraw,
bucksaw, bylaw, catclaw, cat's-paw,
coleslaw, cumshaw, cushaw, Danelaw,
declaw, dewclaw, Esau, forepaw,
fretsaw, grandma, grandpa, guffaw,
hacksaw, handsaw, hawkshaw, hee-
haw, hurrah, in-law, jackdaw,
jackstraw, jigsaw, kickshaw, lockjaw,
macaw, Nassau, old-squaw, outdraw,
outlaw, pasha, pooh-bah, ricksha,
rickshaw, ringtaw, ripsaw, scofflaw,
scrimshaw, seesaw, southpaw, trishaw,
tussah, undraw, Utah, vizsla, Warsaw,
whipsaw, windflaw, wiredraw,
withdraw
Arkansas, Chickasaw, Chippewa,
clapperclaw, decree-law, foofaraw,
jinrikisha, Kiowa, Mackinac,

mackinaw, Omaha, Ottawa, overawe,
overdraw, oversaw, overslaugh,
padishah, panama, son-in-law,
usquebaugh, Wichita, williwaw,
windlestraw, Yakima
brother-in-law, daughter-in-law,
father-in-law, mother-in-law,
pipsissewa, serjeant-at-law, sister-in-
law
Straits of Mackinac

aw[2] \äv\ see olve[2]

aw[3] \òf\ see off[2]

aw[4] \äf\ see off[1]

awa[1] \ä-wə\ Chihuahua, Tarawa,
Urawa
Fujisawa, Ichikawa, Kanazawa,
Okinawa
Ahashikawa

awa[2] \ä-və\ see ava[1]

awain \au̇-ən\ see owan[2]

awan \au̇-ən\ see owan[2]

awar \au̇r\ see ower[2]

awba \ò-bə\ see auba

awber[1] \äb-ər\ see obber

awber[2] \òb-ər\ see auber

awd \òd\ see aud[1]

awddle \äd-ᵊl\ see oddle

awdle \òd-ᵊl\ see audal

awdry \ò-drē\ Audrey, tawdry

awdust \òd-əst\ see adist[1]

awdy \òd-ē\ bawdy, gaudy
summa cum laude

awe \ò\ see aw[1]

awed \òd\ see aud[1]

aweless \ò-ləs\ see awless

awer \òr\ see or[1]

awers \òrz\ see oors

awful \ȯ-fəl\ awful, coffle, lawful, offal
god-awful, unlawful

awfully \ȯf-ə-lē\ awfully, lawfully, offaly
unlawfully

awing \ȯiŋ\ cloying, drawing wappenschawing
—*also* -ing *forms of verbs listed at* aw[1]

awk \ȯk\ see alk

awker \ȯ-kər\ see alker

awkes \ȯks\ Fawkes
—*also* -s, -'s, *and* -s' *forms of nouns, and* -s *forms of verbs, listed at* alk

awkish \ȯ-kish\ gawkish, hawkish, mawkish

awky \ȯ-kē\ see alkie

awl \ȯl\ see all

awler \ȯ-lər\ see aller[1]

awless \ȯ-ləs\ aweless, flawless, lawless

awling \ȯ-liŋ\ see alling

awly \ȯ-lē\ brawly, crawly, dolly, drawly, Raleigh, scrawly, squally
Bengali, Macaulay

awm \ȯm\ see aum[1]

awn¹ \än\ see on[1]

awn² \ȯn\ see on[3]

awned \ȯnd\ see aund

awner¹ \ȯn-ər\ fawner, goner, pawner, prawner, spawner

awner² \än-ər\ see onor[1]

awney \ȯ-nē\ see awny[1]

awning \än-iŋ\ see oning[1]

awnly \än-lē\ see anly[1]

awny¹ \ȯ-nē\ brawny, fawny, lawny, sawney, scrawny, Taney, tawny
mulligatawny

awny² \än-ē\ see ani[1]

awp \ȯp\ see aup

awrence \ȯr-ən(t)s\ Florence, Laurence, Lawrence, Torrence
abhorrence, Saint Lawrence
—*also* -s, -'s, *and* -s' *forms of nouns, and* -s *forms of verbs, listed at* orrent

awry \ȯr-ē\ see ory

aws \ȯz\ see ause[1]

awse \ȯz\ see ause[1]

awser \ȯ-zər\ see auser

awsi \aù-sē\ see ousy[2]

awy \ȯi\ see oy

awyer \ȯ-yər\ lawyer, sawyer

ax¹ \äks\ see ox

ax² \aks\ ax, fax, flax, lax, max, Max, pax, rax, sax, tax, wax
addax, Ajax, anthrax, banjax, beeswax, borax, broadax, climax, coax, earwax, galax, gravlax, hyrax, meat-ax, panchax, pickax, poleax, pretax, relax, smilax, storax, styrax, surtax, syntax, thorax, toadflax
aftertax, battle-ax, Halifax, minimax, overtax, parallax, supertax
anticlimax, Astyanax
—*also* -s, -'s, *and* -s' *forms of nouns, and* -s *forms of verbs, listed at* ack[2]

axant \ak-sənt\ see accent

axen \ak-sən\ see axon

axi \ak-sē\ see axy

axic \ak-sik\ ataraxic
stereotaxic

axis \ak-səs\ axis, Naxos, praxis

axman \ak-smən\ axman, cracksman

axon \ak-sən\ flaxen, Jackson,
Klaxon, Saxon, waxen
  Port Jackson
  Anglo-Saxon

axos \ak-səs\ see axis

axy \ak-sē\ flaxy, maxi, taxi, waxy

ay¹ \ā\ a , ae, aye, bay, bey, blae,
brae, bray, chez, clay, Clay, day, dey,
dray, eh, fay, Fay, Faye, fey, flay, fley,
frae, fray, Frey, gay, Gay, gey, gley,
gray, Gray, Grey, hae, hay, he, hey,
Hue, j, jay, Jay, Jaye, k, kay, Kay,
Kaye, lay, lei, may, May, nay, né, née,
neigh, pay, pe, play, pray, prey, qua,
quai, quay, Rae, ray, Ray, re, say, sei,
shay, slay, sleigh, spae, spay, splay,
spray, stay, stray, sway, they, tray, trey,
way, weigh, whey, yea
  abbé, affray, agley, airplay, airway,
all-day, allay, allée, Angers, Anhui,
Anhwei, archway, array, ashtray,
assay, astray, Augier, away, aweigh,
backstay, ballet, beignet, belay,
beltway, benday, Benet, beret, betray,
bewray, bidet, bikeway, birthday,
Biscay, Bizet, blasé, bobstay, Bombay,
bombe, bouchée, bouclé, boule,
bouquet, bourrée, breezeway,
Broadway, buffet, byplay, byway,
cachet, café, cahier, Cambay, Cape
May, Cartier, Cathay, causeway,
chaîné, chalet, chambray, chassé, ciré,
cliché, cloqué, congé, convey, corvée,
coudé, coupé, crawlway, crochet,
croquet, crossway, cube, curé, cy pres,
DA, daresay, decay, deejay, defray,
delay, dengue, dismay, display,
distrait, DJ, donnée, doomsday,
doorway, dossier, downplay, dragée,
driveway, duvet, embay, entrée, épée,
essay, estray, Ewe, fairway, filé, filet,
fillet, fireclay, fishway, flambé,
floodway, flyway, folkway, footway,
foray, forebay, foreplay, forestay,
formée, forte, fouetté, four-way,
fourchée, foyer, franglais, frappé,
freeway, frieze, frisé, fumet, gainsay,
Galway, gamay, gangway, Gaspé,
gateway, gelée, glacé, godet, gourmet,

Green Bay, greenway, guideway,
gunplay, halfway, hallway, hatchway,
headway, hearsay, Hebei, Hefei,
heyday, highway, homestay, hooray,
horseplay, Hubei, in re, inlay, inveigh,
issei, jackstay, jeté, keyway, Kobe,
koine, kouprey, lamé, laneway,
leeway, lifeway, Lomé, Lough Neagh,
lwei, lycée, M-day, maguey, mainstay,
Malay, malgré, man-day, Mande,
Manet, manqué, margay, Marseilles,
massé, maté, May Day, Mayday,
melee, metier, meze, midday, Midway,
Millay, Millet, mislay, misplay, moiré,
Monet, moray, nevé, Niamey, nisei,
noonday, Norway, nosegay, obey, OK,
olé, ombré, osprey, outlay, outré,
outstay, outweigh, oyez, PA, parfait,
parkway, parlay, parquet, partway,
passé, pâté, pathway, pavé, payday,
per se, pince-nez, piqué, piquet, PK,
plié, plissé, pommée, Pompeii,
portray, prepay, projet, pulque, puree,
purvey, quale, raceway, railway,
rappee, relay, Rene, Renee, repay,
replay, risqué, roadway, role-play,
ropeway, rosé, rosebay, Roubaix, roué,
routeway, runway, sachet, Salé, sansei,
sashay, sauté, screenplay, seaway,
semé, shar-pei, shipway, short-day,
sideway, Skopje, skyway, slideway,
slipway, sluiceway, soigné, soiree,
someday, someway, soothsay, soufflé,
speedway, spillway, stairway,
sternway, stingray, straightway,
strathspey, subway, survey, swordplay,
Taipei, tempeh, thoughtway, three-
way, thruway, tideway, Tigré, today,
Tokay, tollway, Torbay, touché,
toupee, trackway, tramway, unlay,
unsay, valet, V-day, veejay, vide, visé,
Vouvray, walkway, waylay, weekday,
windway, wireway, wordplay,
workday, X ray, x-ray, Yaoundé
  Adige, Agnus Dei, A-OK, alleyway,
anyway, appliqué, arrivé, atelier,
attaché, ballonet, Beaujolais, beurre
manié, BHA, botonée, braciole,
breakaway, bustier, cabaret, cableway,
Camagüey, canapé, cap-a-pie,
caraway, carriageway, Cartier,

cassoulet, castaway, champlevé, chansonnier, chardonnay, Charolais, chevalier, Chippewa, cloisonné, consommé, coryphée, croupier, crudités, cutaway, day-to-day, debauchee, déclassé, dégagé, degree-day, démodé, devotee, disarray, disobey, distingué, divorcé, divorcée, DNA, émigré, engagé, entranceway, entremets, entryway, espalier, etoufée, everyday, exposé, expressway, fadeaway, fallaway, faraday, Faraday, faraway, fiancé, fiancée, flageolet, flyaway, foldaway, Galloway, garde-manger, Georgian Bay, getaway, giveaway, gratiné, gratinée, guillemet, Harare, haulageway, Hemingway, hereaway, hideaway, HLA, Hogmanay, holiday, Hugh Capet, IgA, inter se, interplay, intraday, IPA, IRA, Joliet, Kootenay, Kutenai, kyrie, lackaday, latter-day, layaway, lingerie, macramé, Mandalay, Massenet, matinee, MIA, Molise, Monterrey, motorway, muscadet, negligee, overlay, overplay, overstay, overweigh, Paraguay, passageway, patissier, Petare, photoplay, pikake, piolet, pis aller, play-by-play, poly (A), Ponape, popinjay, pourparler, pousse-café, present-day, protégé, protégée, Rabelais, rambouillet, ratiné, recamier, rechauffé, recherché, reconvey, repartee, repoussé, résumé, retroussé, ricochet, right-of-way, rockaway, rondelet, roundelay, RNA, runaway, Saguenay, San Jose, San José, Santa Fe, São Tomé, semplice, sobriquet, sommelier, steerageway, standaway, stowaway, straightaway, Table Bay, taboret, take-away, tarsier, taxiway, tearaway, teleplay, Tempere, Tenebrae, thataway, throwaway, Thunder Bay, Udine, underlay, underpay, underplay, underway, Uruguay, velouté, Venite, vérité, vertebra, virelay, walkaway, waterway, wellaway, Whitsunday, workaday, Yenisey, Zuider Zee
   areaway, auto-da-fé, bichon frisé, boulevardier, cabriolet, café au lait, cantabile, cDNA, communiqué,

costumier, couturier, décolleté, diamanté, Dies Irae, eglomisé, felo-de-se, Fiesole, habitué, Jubilate, laissez-passer, Lavoisier, marrons glacé, mezzo forte, Morgan le Fay, objet trouvé, out-of-the-way, papier collé, papier-mâché, pas de bourrée, photo-essay, Port Philip Bay, pouilly-fuissé, Pouilly-Fumé, prêt-à-porter, roche moutonnée, roman à clef, roturier, sine die, sub judice, superhighway, ukiyo-e, Ulan-Ude, yerba maté
   Alto Adige, arrière pensée, Guanabara Bay, lettre de cachet catalogue raisonné, cinema verité, Dumfries and Galloway, vers de société, video verité
   sinfonia concertante, Trentino-Alto Adige

ay² \ē\ see ee¹

ay³ \ī\ see y¹

aya¹ \ä-yə\ ayah, maya, taille
Malaya
Koshigaya

aya² \ī-ə\ see iah¹

aya³ \ä-ə\ see aia¹

ayable \ā-ə-bəl\ payable, playable, sayable
defrayable, displayable, unsayable

ayah \ī-ə\ see iah¹

ayal \āl\ see ail

ayan¹ \ā-ən\ crayon
Chilean, Malayan, ouabain, papain, Pompeian, Pompeiian
Galilean, Himalayan

ayan² \ī-ən\ see ion¹

aybe¹ \ā-bē\ see aby

aybe² \eb-ē\ see ebby

ayday \ā-dā\ Ede, Mayday, May Day

ayden \ī-dᵊn\ see iden

aye¹ \ā\ see ay¹

aye² \ī\ see y¹

ayed \ād\ see ade¹

ayer \ā-ər\ brayer, layer, mayor, payer, player, prayer, preyer, sayer, sprayer, stayer, strayer
ballplayer, betrayer, bilayer, bricklayer, cardplayer, conveyer, crocheter, decayer, delayer, doomsayer, doomsdayer, essayer, forayer, gainsayer, horseplayer, inlayer, inveigher, obeyer, manslayer, minelayer, portrayer, purveyor, ratepayer, soothsayer, swordplayer, surveyor, taxpayer, tracklayer, yea-sayer
disobeyer, holidayer
— *also* -er *forms of adjectives listed at* ay¹

ayered \erd\ see aired

ayest \ā-əst\ mayest, sayest
épéeist, essayist, fideist, Hebraist, Mithraist
—*also* -est *forms of adjectives listed at* ay¹

ayin¹ \ī-ən\ see ion¹

ayin² \īn\ see ine¹

ayin³ \ä-yən\ see aiian

aying \ā-iŋ\ gleying, maying, playing, saying
bricklaying, long-playing, soothsaying, surveying, taxpaying, tracklaying
—*also* -ing *forms of verbs listed at* ay¹

ayish \ā-ish\ clayish, grayish

ayist \ā-əst\ see ayest

ayle \āl\ see ail

ayless \ā-ləs\ rayless, talus, wayless
Morelos
aurora australis, Corona Australis

ayling \ā-liŋ\ see ailing

aylor \ā-lər\ see ailer

ayly \ā-lē\ see aily

ayman \ā-mən\ see amen¹

ayment \ā-mənt\ ament, claimant, clamant, payment, raiment
co-payment, embayment, prepayment
underlayment, underpayment

ayne \ān\ see ane¹

ayness \ā-nəs\ anus, feyness, gayness, grayness, heinous, Janus, manus
awayness, uranous, Uranus
everydayness

aynim \ā-nəm\ see anum¹

ayn't \ā-ənt\ see eyant

ayo¹ \ā-ō\ see eo¹

ayo² \ī-ō\ see io¹

ayon \ā-ən\ see ayan¹

ayor \ā-ər\ see ayer¹

ayou¹ \ī-ə\ see iah¹

ayou² \ī-ō\ see io¹

ayr \er\ see are⁴

ays¹ \ez\ fez, Fez, Geez, prez, says
Cortez, gainsays, Inez, Suez, unsays
crème anglaise, Louis Seize, Louis Treize
Isthmus of Suez, Vincente López

ays² \āz\ see aze¹

aysia \ā-zhə\ see asia

ay-so \ā-sō\ see eso¹

ayton \āt-ᵊn\ Clayton, Dayton, Layton

ayyid¹ \ī-əd\ see yad

ayyid² \ēd-ē\ see eedy

az¹ \az\ see azz

az² \äz\ see oise¹

az³ \äts\ see ots

aza¹ \äz-ə\ Gaza, plaza
piazza
tabula rasa

aza² \az-ə\ plaza
piazza

azar¹ \äz-ər\ see ozzer

azar² \az-ər\ lazar
alcazar, Belshazzar

azard \az-ərd\ hazard, mazard,
mazzard
haphazard

aze¹ \āz\ baize, blaze, braise, braze,
chaise, craze, days, daze, Draize, faze,
feaze, fraise, gaze, glaze, graze, Hays,
haze, lase, laze, maize, maze, phase,
phrase, praise, raise, rase, raze, smaze,
vase, ways
ablaze, agaze, amaze, appraise,
breadthways, catchphrase, crossways,
deglaze, dispraise, edgeways,
emblaze, endways, flatways,
foodways, gainsays, hereways,
leastways, lengthways, liaise, malaise,
mores, pj's, sideways, slantways,
stargaze, ukase, upraise, weekdays
anyways, chrysoprase, cornerways,
crème anglaise, holidays, Louis Seize,
Louis Treize, lyonnaise, mayonnaise,
metaphrase, multiphase, nowadays,
overglaze, overgraze, paraphrase,
polonaise, polyphase, single-phase,
underglaze
—also -s, -'s, and -s' forms of nouns,
and -s forms of verbs, listed at ay¹

aze² \äz\ see oise¹

aze³ \äz-ē\ see azi¹

azeable \ā-zə-bəl\ see asable¹

azed \āzd\ unfazed
—also -ed forms of verbs listed at
aze¹

azel \ā-zəl\ see asal²

azement \āz-mənt\ amazement,
appraisement

azen \āz-ᵊn\ see azon

azer \ā-zər\ blazer, brazer, Fraser,
gazer, glazer, grazer, hazer, laser,
maser, mazer, praiser, razer, razor
appraiser, fund-raiser, hair-raiser,
hell-raiser, stargazer, trailblazer
paraphraser
free-electron laser

azi¹ \äz-ē\ quasi, Swazi
Benghazi
Anasazi, kamikaze

azi² \az-ē\ see azzy

azi³ \at-sē\ Nazi, patsy, Patsy
neo-Nazi

azi⁴ \ät-sē\ Nazi
neo-Nazi

azier \ā-zhər\ brazier, Frasier,
glacier, glazier, grazier, leisure,
measure, pleasure, rasure, treasure
admeasure, embrasure, erasure

azing \ā-ziŋ\ see aising

azo \az-ō\ diazo, terrazzo

azon \āz-ᵊn\ blazon, brazen, raisin
emblazon, Marquesan
diapason, hexenbesen

azor \ā-zər\ see azer

azquez \as-kəs\ see ascus

azy \ā-zē\ crazy, daisy, Daisy, hazy,
lazy, mazy
stir-crazy
witch of Agnesi

azz \az\ as, has, jazz, razz
Hejaz, La Paz, pizzazz, topaz,
whenas, whereas
razzmatazz

azza¹ \az-ə\ see aza²

azza² \äz-ə\ see aza¹

azza³ \ät-sə\ see atzo¹

azzar \az-ər\ see azar[2]

azzard \az-ərd\ see azard

azzle \az-əl\ basil, Basil, dazzle, frazzle
  bedazzle
  razzle-dazzle

azzo[1] \ät-sō\ matzo
  palazzo, terrazzo
  paparazzo

azzo[2] \az-ō\ see azo

azzy \az-ē\ jazzy, snazzy
  Ashkenazi

E

e¹ \ā\ see ay¹

e² \ē\ see ee¹

e³ \ə\ see u³

é \ā\ see ay¹

ea¹ \ā\ see ay¹

ea² \ā-ə\ see aia¹

ea³ \ē\ see ee¹

ea⁴ \ē-ə\ see ia¹

eabee \ē-bē\ see ebe¹

eace \ēs\ see iece

eaceable \ē-sə-bəl\ see easable¹

each \ēch\ beach, beech, bleach,
breach, breech, each, fleech, leach,
leech, peach, pleach, preach, reach,
screech, speech, teach
  beseech, forereach, impeach, Long
Beach, outreach, unteach
  overreach, practice-teach
  Huntington Beach

eachable \ē-chə-bəl\ bleachable,
leachable, reachable, teachable
  impeachable
  unimpeachable

eacher \ē-chər\ bleacher, creature,
feature, leacher, preacher, reacher,
screecher, teacher
  defeature, disfeature, schoolteacher

eacherous \ech-rəs\ see echerous

eachery \ech-rē\ see echery

eaching \ē-chiŋ\ see eeching

eachment \ēch-mənt\ preachment
  impeachment

eachy \ē-chē\ beachy, chichi,
Nietzsche, peachy, preachy, screechy
  caliche, Campeche

eacle \ē-kəl\ see ecal¹

eacly \ē-klē\ see eekly

eacon \ē-kən\ beacon, deacon,
sleeken, weaken
  archdeacon, Mohican, subdeacon
  Neorican

ead¹ \ed\ bed, bled, bread, bred,
dead, dread, ed, Ed, fed, fled, Fred,
head, Jed, lead, led, med, Ned, ped,
pled, read, red, Red, redd, said, shed,
shred, sled, sped, spread, stead, ted,
Ted, thread, tread, wed, zed
  abed, ahead, airhead, baldhead,
beachhead, bedspread, bedstead,
beebread, behead, bestead, bighead,
biped, blackhead, blockhead,
bloodred, bloodshed, bobsled,
bonehead, bridgehead, brown bread,
bulkhead, bullhead, cathead, childbed,
coed, cokehead, corn-fed, cowshed,
crispbread, crossbred, crosshead,
daybed, deadhead, death's-head,
deathbed, dispread, dogsled,
dopehead, drophead, drumhead,
dumbhead, egghead, embed, far-red,
farmstead, fathead, flatbed, forehead,
foresaid, gainsaid, Gateshead,
godhead, green-head, half-bred,
hardhead, highbred, hogshead,
homebred, homestead, hophead,
hotbed, hothead, ill-bred, inbred,
instead, jarhead, juicehead, lamed,
light bread, longhead, lowbred,
lunkhead, masthead, meathead,
misled, misread, moped, naled,
nonsked, outsped, outspread,
packthread, phys ed, pinhead, pithead,

pothead, premed, printhead, purebred, railhead, redhead, re-tread, retread, roadbed, roadstead, Roundhead, saphead, scarehead, seabed, seedbed, sheep ked, sheepshead, sheetfed, shewbread, shortbread, sickbed, skinhead, snowshed, softhead, sorehead, spearhead, springhead, steelhead, straightbred, streambed, subhead, sweetbread, swellhead, thickhead, toolhead, toolshed, towhead, trailhead, unbred, undead, unread, unsaid, unthread, untread, warhead, webfed, well-bred, well-read, wellhead, white-bread, whitehead, widespread, wingspread, woodshed, woolshed
 acidhead, aforesaid, arrowhead, barrelhead, Birkenhead, bubblehead, bufflehead, chowderhead, chucklehead, colorbred, copperhead, dragonhead, dunderhead, featherbed, featherhead, fiddlehead, figurehead, fountainhead, gingerbread, go-ahead, hammerhead, infrared, interbred, knucklehead, letterhead, loggerhead, lowlihead, maidenhead, newlywed, overhead, overspread, pinniped, pointy-head, poppyhead, quadruped, riverbed, saddlebred, Saint John's bread, Samoyed, showerhead, sleepyhead, slugabed, standardbred, straight-ahead, timberhead, thoroughbred, thunderhead, underbred, underfed, watershed, woodenhead
 far-infrared, fire-engine red, near-infrared, West Quoddy Head
 parallelepiped

ead² \ēd\ see eed

ead³ \əd\ see ud¹

eadable¹ \ēd-ə-bəl\ kneadable, pleadable, readable

eadable² \ed-ə-bəl\ see edible

eaded¹ \ed-əd\ bedded, headed
 bareheaded, bigheaded, bullheaded, clearheaded, coolheaded, eggheaded, embedded, fatheaded, hardheaded,
hotheaded, light-headed, longheaded, lunkheaded, pigheaded, pinheaded, roundheaded, sapheaded, softheaded, soreheaded, swelled-headed, swellheaded, thickheaded, towheaded, unleaded, white-headed
 bubbleheaded, chowderheaded, chuckleheaded, dunderheaded, empty-headed, featherheaded, hydra-headed, knuckleheaded, levelheaded, muddleheaded, pointy-headed, puzzleheaded, woodenheaded, woolly-headed

eaded² \ē-dəd\ see eeded

eaden \ed-ᵊn\ deaden, leaden, redden, steading
 Armageddon

eader¹ \ēd-ər\ bleeder, breeder, cedar, ceder, feeder, kneader, leader, pleader, reader, seeder, speeder, weeder
 bandleader, cheerleader, conceder, impeder, lip-reader, newsreader, nonreader, proofreader, repleader, ringleader, seceder, stampeder, stockbreeder, succeeder
 copyreader, interpleader

eader² \ed-ər\ bedder, cheddar, chedar, header, shedder, shredder, sledder, spreader, tedder, threader, treader, wedder
 homesteader
 doubleheader, triple-header

eadily \ed-ᵊl-ē\ headily, readily
 unsteadily

eading¹ \ed-iŋ\ bedding, heading, Reading, steading, wedding
 bobsledding, farmsteading, subheading, wide-spreading
 —also -ing forms of verbs listed at ead¹

eading² \ed-ᵊn\ see eaden

eading³ \ēd-ᵊn\ see edon

eading⁴ \ēd-iŋ\ see eeding¹

eadle¹ \ed-ᵊl\ see edal¹

eadle² \ēd-ᵊl\ see eedle

eadly \ed-lē\ see edley

eadsman¹ \edz-mən\ headsman, leadsman

eadsman² \ēdz-mən\ see eedsman

eady¹ \ed-ē\ Eddie, eddy, Eddy, Freddie, heady, leady, ready, steady, Teddie, teddy, Teddy, thready
already, makeready, unsteady
gingerbready, rough-and-ready

eady² \ēd-ē\ see eedy

eaf¹ \ef\ see ef¹

eaf² \ēf\ see ief¹

eafless \ē-fləs\ see iefless

eafy \ē-fē\ see eefy

eag \ēg\ see igue

eagan \ā-gən\ see agin

eager \ē-gər\ eager, leaguer, meager
beleaguer, intriguer
Xinjiang Uygur

eagh \ā\ see ay¹

eagle \ē-gəl\ see egal

eague \ēg\ see igue

eaguer \ē-gər\ see eager

eah \ē-ə\ see ia¹

eak¹ \ēk\ beak, bleak, cheek, chic, cleek, clique, creak, creek, Creek, eke, flic, freak, geek, gleek, Greek, keek, leak, leek, meek, peak, peek, peke, pic, pique, reek, screak, seek, sheik, sheikh, shriek, sic, Sikh, sleek, sneak, speak, squeak, steek, streak, streek, teak, tweak, weak, week, wreak
antique, apeak, batik, Belgique, Belleek, bespeak, bezique, boutique, cacique, caique, critique, debeak, forepeak, forespeak, grosbeak, hairstreak, halfbeak, houseleek, misspeak, muzhik, mystique, newspeak, nonpeak, oblique, off-peak,

outspeak, perique, physique, Pikes Peak, pip-squeak, pratique, relique, technic, technique, Tajik, unique, unspeak, workweek
biunique, Bolshevik, Chesapeake, dominique, doublespeak, ecofreak, fenugreek, hide-and-seek, Lassen Peak, Martinique, Menshevik, Mozambique, verd antique, Veronique
electroweak, semi-antique
opéra comique, realpolitik

eak² \āk\ see ake¹

eak³ \ek\ see eck

eakable \ā-kə-bəl\ see akable

eake \ēk\ see eak¹

eaked¹ \ē-kəd\ peaked, streaked

eaked² \ēkt\ beaked, freaked, peaked, streaked
apple-cheeked
—also -ed forms of verbs listed at eak¹

eaked³ \ik-əd\ see icked¹

eaken \ē-kən\ see eacon

eaker¹ \ē-kər\ beaker, leaker, reeker, seeker, sneaker, speaker, squeaker
loudspeaker, self-seeker, sunseeker
doublespeaker
—also -er forms of adjectives listed at eak¹

eaker² \ā-kər\ see aker¹

eaking¹ \ē-kiŋ\ freaking, sneaking, speaking, streaking
heat-seeking, self-seeking
—also -ing forms of verbs listed at eak¹

eaking² \ā-kiŋ\ see aking¹

eakish \ē-kish\ bleakish, cliquish, freakish, weakish

eakly \ē-klē\ see eekly

eaky \ē-kē\ cheeky, cliquey, creaky, freaky, leaky, piki, reeky, sneaky, screaky, squeaky, streaky, tiki

daishiki, dashiki, Tajiki
cock-a-leekie, Kurashiki, Manihiki

eal¹ \ē-əl\ empyreal, hymeneal,
laryngeal
  apophyseal, pharmacopeial

eal² \ēl\ ceil, chiel, creel, deal, deil,
eel, feel, heal, heel, he'll, keel, Kiel,
kneel, leal, meal, Neal, Neil, peal,
peel, real, reel, seal, seel, she'll, shiel,
speel, spiel, squeal, steal, steel, Steele,
Streel, teal, tuille, veal, weal, we'll,
wheal, wheel, zeal
  aiguille, allheal, anneal, appeal,
Arbil, bastille, Bastille, bonemeal,
bonspiel, Camille, Castile, cartwheel,
Cecile, chainwheel, chenille,
cogwheel, conceal, congeal, cornmeal,
enwheel, Erbil, flywheel, forefeel,
four-wheel, freewheel, genteel,
handwheel, ideal, inchmeal, Irbil,
irreal, Kuril, Lucille, misdeal, mobile,
Mobile, newsreel, nosewheel, oatmeal,
O'Neill, ordeal, pastille, piecemeal,
pinwheel, repeal, reveal, schlemiel,
self-heal, side-wheel, singspiel,
somedeal, stabile, surreal, tahsil,
Tarheel, thumbwheel, unreal, unreel,
unseal
  acetyl, airmobile, Ardabil,
bidonville, beau ideal, blastocoel,
bloodmobile, Bogomil, bookmobile,
campanile, chamomile, cochineal,
cockatiel, commonweal, difficile,
dishabille, down-at-heel, glockenspiel,
goldenseal, Guayaquil, manchineel,
megadeal, mercantile, pimpmobile,
skimobile, snowmobile, thunderpeal,
waterwheel
  automobile, Solomon's seal,
varicocele

eal³ \āl\ see ail

eal⁴ \il\ see ill

ealable \ē-lə-bəl\ peelable, reelable,
stealable
  appealable, concealable, revealable,
repealable
  irrepealable, unappealable

ealand \ē-lənd\ see eland

eald \ēld\ see ield

ealed \ēld\ see ield

ealer \ē-lər\ dealer, feeler, healer,
heeler, kneeler, peeler, reeler, sealer,
spieler, squealer, stealer, stelar, vealer,
velar, wheeler
  appealer, concealer, four-wheeler,
freewheeler, newsdealer, repealer,
revealer, scene-stealer, side-wheeler,
stern-wheeler, three-wheeler, two-
wheeler
  double-dealer, eighteen-wheeler, 18-
wheeler, snowmobiler, wheeler-dealer

ealie \ē-lē\ see eely

ealing \ē-liŋ\ see eeling

eally¹ \ē-ə-lē\ leally
ideally
hymeneally, industrially

eally² \il-ē\ see illy¹

eally³ \ē-lē\ see eely

ealm \elm\ see elm

ealment \ēl-mənt\ concealment,
congealment, revealment

ealot \el-ət\ see ellate

ealotry \el-ə-trē\ see elotry

ealous \el-əs\ Ellis, Hellas, jealous,
trellis, zealous
  cancellous, ocellus

ealousy \el-ə-sē\ see elacy

ealth \elth\ health, stealth, wealth
commonwealth

ealthy \el-thē\ healthy, stealthy,
wealthy
unhealthy

ealty \ēl-tē\ fealty, realty

eam¹ \ēm\ beam, bream, cream,
deem, deme, dream, gleam, mime,
neem, Nîmes, ream, scheme, scream,

seam, seem, seme, steam, stream,
team, teem, theme
 abeam, agleam, airstream, berseem,
beseem, bireme, blaspheme,
bloodstream, centime, daydream,
downstream, esteem, extreme,
grapheme, Gulf Stream, hakim,
headstream, hornbeam, ice cream,
inseam, kilim, lexeme, mainstream,
midstream, millime, millstream,
moonbeam, morpheme, onstream,
phoneme, redeem, regime, sememe,
sidestream, slipstream, sunbeam,
supreme, Tarim, taxeme, toneme,
trireme, unseam, upstream
 academe, disesteem, double-team,
enthymeme, misesteem, monotreme,
self-esteem, treponeme
 succès d'estime

eam² \im\ see im¹

eaman \ē-mən\ see emon¹

eamed¹ \emt\ see empt

eamed² \emd\ beamed, steamed,
teamed
 —also -ed forms of verbs listed at
eam¹

eamer \ē-mər\ creamer, dreamer,
femur, lemur, reamer, schemer,
screamer, seamer, steamer, streamer
 blasphemer, daydreamer, redeemer
 —also -er forms of adjectives listed
at eam¹

eaming \ē-miŋ\ see eeming

eamish \ē-mish\ beamish,
squeamish

eamless \ēm-ləs\ dreamless,
seamless

eamon \ē-mən\ see emon¹

eamster \ēm-stər\ seamster,
teamster

eamy \ē-mē\ beamy, creamy,
dreamy, gleamy, preemie, seamy,
steamy
 polysemy

ean¹ \ē-ən\ aeon, eon, Ian, Leon,
paean, peon, paeon, zein
 Achaean, Actaeon, Aegean, Antaean,
Archean, Augean, Chaldean, Chilean,
Fijian, Korean, Kuchean, Linnaean,
Mandaean, Matthean, pampean,
plebeian, protean, pygmaean, Tupian
 apogean, Aramaean, Atlantean,
Caribbean, Cerberean, circadian,
cyclopean, Clytherean, Damoclean,
empyrean, epigean, European,
Galilean, Hasmonaean, Herculean,
Jacobean, kallikrein, Maccabean,
Manichaean, Mycenaean, Odyssean,
panacean, perigean, Sadducean,
Sisyphean, Typhoean, Tyrolean
 antipodean, epicurean, Laodicean,
Ponce de Leon, proboscidean,
Pythagorean, terpsichorean, un-
European
 epithalamion, Indo-European, Tupi-
Guaranian

ean² \ēn\ see ine³

ean³ \ȯn\ see on³

ean⁴ \ā-ən\ see ayan¹

eane \ēn\ see ine³

eaner \ē-nər\ cleaner, gleaner,
keener, meaner, preener, teener,
weaner, weiner, wiener
 congener, convener, demeanor,
fourteener
 carabiner, contravener, intervenor,
misdemeanor, submariner, trampoliner

eanery \ēn-rē\ beanery, deanery,
greenery, scenery
 machinery
 turbomachinery

eanid \ē-ə-nəd\ Leonid
 Oceanid

eanie \ē-nē\ see ini¹

eaning \ē-niŋ\ greening, leaning,
meaning, screening
 housecleaning, spring-cleaning,
sunscreening, unmeaning, well-
meaning

overweening
—also -ing *forms of verbs listed at*
ine³

eanist¹ \ē-nəst\ see inist²

eanist² \ē-ə-nist\ see ianist

eanliness \en-lē-nəs\ see endliness

eanling \ēn-liŋ\ greenling,
weanling, yeanling

eanly¹ \ēn-lē\ cleanly, greenly,
leanly, meanly, queenly
pristinely, routinely, uncleanly
serpentinely

eanly² \en-lē\ see endly

eanne \ēn\ see ine³

eanness \ēn-nəs\ cleanness,
greenness, meanness
betweenness, uncleanness

eannie \ē-nē\ see ini¹

eano \ē-nō\ see ino²

eanor \ē-nər\ see eaner

eanse \enz\ see ens¹

eant \ent\ see ent¹

eany \ē-nē\ see ini¹

eap \ēp\ see eep

eapen \ē-pən\ see eepen

eaper \ē-pər\ see eeper

eapie \ē-pē\ see eepy

eapish \ē-pish\ see eepish

eapo \ē-pō\ see epot

ear¹ \er\ see are⁴

ear² \ir\ see eer²

earable¹ \er-ə-bəl\ bearable,
shareable, terrible, wearable
unbearable, unwearable

earable² \ar-ə-bəl\ see arable

earage \ir-ij\ see eerage

earance¹ \ir-əns\ see erence¹

earance² \er-əns\ see arence

earch \ərch\ see urch

earchist \ər-chəst\ see urchless

eard¹ \ird\ beard, eared, tiered,
weird
afeard, bat-eared, bluebeard, crop-
eared, dog-eared, graybeard, lop-
eared, misleared, whitebeard
chandeliered, engineered
pre-engineered
—also -ed *forms of verbs listed at*
eer²

eard² \ərd\ see ird

eare \ir\ see eer²

earean \ir-ē-ən\ see erian¹

eared¹ \erd\ see aired

eared² \ird\ see eard¹

earer¹ \er-ər\ airer, bearer, carer,
error, sharer, terror
casebearer, crossbearer, cupbearer,
declarer, furbearer, live-bearer,
pallbearer, seafarer, talebearer,
torchbearer, trainbearer, wayfarer
color-bearer, standard-bearer,
stretcher-bearer
—also -er *forms of adjectives listed
at* are⁴

earer² \ir-ər\ cheerer, clearer, fearer,
hearer, mirror, shearer, smearer
coherer, sheepshearer, veneerer
electioneerer
—also -er *forms of adjectives listed
at* eer²

earful \ir-fəl\ cheerful, earful,
fearful, tearful

earies \ir-ēz\ see eries

earing¹ \ir-iŋ\ clearing, earing,
earring, gearing
God-fearing, sheepshearing
fictioneering, hard-of-hearing
orienteering

—*also* -ing *forms of verbs listed at* eer²

earing² \er-iŋ\ see aring¹

earish \er-ish\ see arish¹

earl \ərl\ see irl¹

earle \irl\ see irl¹

earler \ər-lər\ see irler

earless \ir-ləs\ cheerless, fearless, gearless, peerless, tearless

earling¹ \ir-liŋ\ shearling, yearling

earling² \ər-lən\ see erlin

early¹ \ir-lē\ clearly, dearly, merely, nearly, queerly, yearly
    austerely, biyearly, severely, sincerely
    cavalierly, insincerely, semiyearly

early² \ər-lē\ see urly

earn \ərn\ see urn

earned \ərnd\ see urned

earner \ər-nər\ see urner

earnist \ər-nəst\ see ernist

earnt \ərnt\ burnt, learnt, weren't

earring \ir-iŋ\ see earing¹

earsal \ər-səl\ see ersal¹

earse \ərs\ see erse

earser \ər-sər\ see ursor

earst \ərst\ see urst

eart \ärt\ see art¹

earted \ärt-əd\ hearted, parted
    bighearted, coldhearted, downhearted, fainthearted, freehearted, good-hearted, greathearted, halfhearted, hardhearted, kindhearted, largehearted, lighthearted, proudhearted, softhearted, stouthearted, truehearted, uncharted, warmhearted, weakhearted, wholehearted

brokenhearted, chickenhearted, heavyhearted, ironhearted, lionhearted, openhearted, singlehearted, stonyhearted, tenderhearted
    —*also* -ed *forms of verbs listed at* art¹

earth¹ \ärth\ see arth

earth² \ərth\ see irth

eartha \ər-thə\ see ertha

earthen \ər-thən\ see urthen

earthy \ər-thē\ see orthy

eartily \ärt-ᵊl-ē\ see artily

eartless \ärt-ləs\ see artless

earty \ärt-ē\ see arty¹

eary \ir-ē\ aerie, beery, bleary, cheery, dreary, eerie, Erie, leery, Peary, peri, quaere, query, smeary, sphery, teary, veery, weary
    aweary, Kashmiri, Lake Erie, Valkyrie, world-weary
    hara-kiri, miserere, overweary, whigmaleerie
    Mount Dhaulagiri

eas \ē-əs\ see eus¹

easable¹ \ē-sə-bəl\ peaceable
    increasable

easable² \ē-zə-bəl\ see easible

easand¹ \iz-ᵊn\ see ison²

easand² \ēz-ᵊnd\ see easoned

ease¹ \ēs\ see iece

ease² \ēz\ see eze

eased¹ \ēzd\ pleased
    diseased
    —*also* -ed *forms of verbs listed at* eze

eased² \ēst\ see east¹

easel \ē-zəl\ bezel, deasil, diesel, easel, measle, teasel, weasel

easeless \ē-sləs\ ceaseless, creaseless, greaseless

easelly \ē-zlē\ see easly

easement \ēz-mənt\ easement appeasement

easer¹ \ē-sər\ creaser, greaser, piecer
degreaser, increaser, one-piecer, releaser, two-piecer

easer² \ē-zər\ Caesar, freezer, geezer, greaser, pleaser, seizer, sneezer, squeezer, teaser, tweezer
appeaser, brainteaser, crowd-pleaser, degreaser, misfeasor, stripteaser, timepleaser

eash \ēsh\ see iche²

easible \ē-zə-bəl\ feasible, squeezable
appeasable, defeasible, infeasible inappeasable, indefeasible, unappeasable

easil \ē-zəl\ see easel

easily \ēz-lē\ see easly

easing¹ \ē-siŋ\ leasing
unceasing
—also -ing forms of verbs listed at iece

easing² \ē-ziŋ\ pleasing
subfreezing
—also -ing forms of verbs listed at eze

easingly \ē-siŋ-lē\ decreasingly, increasingly, unceasingly

easle \ē-zəl\ see easel

easly \ēz-ə-lē\ easily, measly, weaselly

eason \ēz-ᵊn\ reason, season, seisin, treason
disseisin, off-season, unreason
diocesan

easonable \ēz-nə-bəl\ reasonable, seasonable, treasonable
unreasonable, unseasonable

easoned \ēz-ᵊnd\ weasand
unreasoned
—also -ed forms of verbs listed at eason

easoning \ēz-niŋ\ reasoning, seasoning
unreasoning

easonless \ēz-ᵊn-ləs\ reasonless, seasonless

easor \ē-zər\ see easer²

east¹ \ēst\ beast, east, East, feast, fleeced, geest, least, piste, priest, reest, triste, yeast
archpriest, artiste, batiste, deceased, Far East, modiste, Near East, northeast, southeast, tachiste
arriviste, dirigiste, hartebeest, Middle East, north-northeast, pointillist, wildebeest
—also -ed forms of verbs listed at iece

east² \est\ see est

easted \es-təd\ see ested

easter \ē-stər\ Dniester, Easter, keister, leister, quaestor
down-easter, northeaster, southeaster

eastie \ē-stē\ see easty

eastly \ēst-lē\ beastly, Priestley, priestly

easty \ē-stē\ beastie, yeasty

easurable \ezh-rə-bəl\ pleasurable, treasurable
immeasurable

easure¹ \ezh-ər\ leisure, measure, pleasure, treasure
admeasure, displeasure
countermeasure

easure² \ā-zhər\ see azier

easurer \ezh-ər-ər\ measurer, treasurer

easy¹ \ē-zē\ breezy, cheesy, easy, greasy, queasy, sleazy, sneezy, wheezy pachisi, Parcheesi, speakeasy, uneasy, Zambezi

easy² \ē-sē\ see eecy

eat¹ \ēt\ beat, beet, bleat, cheat, cleat, Crete, deet, eat, feat, fleet, Geat, gleet, greet, heat, keet, lied, meat, meet, mete, neat, peat, Pete, pleat, seat, sheet, skeet, sleet, street, suite, sweet, teat, treat, tweet, weet, wheat
accrete, aesthete, afreet, athlete, backbeat, backseat, backstreet, bedsheet, bolete, Bradstreet, broadsheet, browbeat, buckwheat, bystreet, clipsheet, compete, compleat, complete, conceit, concrete, crabmeat, deadbeat, deceit, defeat, delete, deplete, discreet, discrete, disseat, downbeat, drumbeat, effete, elite, en suite, entreat, escheat, esthete, excrete, facete, forcemeat, foresheet, groundsheet, heartbeat, heat-treat, helpmeet, hoofbeat, ill-treat, mainsheet, maltreat, mesquite, mincemeat, mistreat, offbeat, petite, preheat, receipt, recheat, regreet, repeat, replete, retreat, secrete, slip-sheet, sweetmeat, terete, unmeet, unseat, upbeat, vegete, volkslied, zizith
aquavit, biathlete, bittersweet, cellulite, corps d'elite, countryseat, decathlete, exegete, incomplete, indiscreet, indiscrete, lorikeet, marguerite, Marguerite, Masorete, meadowsweet, Nayarit, obsolete, overeat, overheat, Paraclete, parakeet, pentathlete, plebiscite, polychaete, progamete, self-conceit, semisweet, superheat, triathlete, winding-sheet

eat² \āt\ see ate¹

eat³ \et\ see et¹

eat⁴ \it\ see it¹

eatable \ēt-ə-bəl\ eatable, heatable, treatable
depletable, escheatable, repeatable, unbeatable

eated¹ \ēt-əd\ heated, pleated

conceited, deep-seated, repeated overheated, superheated
—*also* -ed *forms of verbs listed at* eat¹

eated² \et-əd\ see etid

eated³ \it-əd\ see itted

eaten¹ \ēt-ᵊn\ eaten, beaten, Cretan, cretin, Eaton, Eton, neaten, sweeten, wheaten
browbeaten, moth-eaten, secretin, unbeaten, worm-eaten
overeaten, weather-beaten

eaten² \āt-ᵊn\ see aten¹

eater¹ \ēt-ər\ beater, bleater, cheater, eater, fetor, greeter, heater, liter, meter, peter, Peter, pleater, praetor, rhetor, seater, sheeter, skeeter, teeter, treater, tweeter
anteater, beefeater, blue peter, Demeter, drumbeater, eggbeater, excreter, fire-eater, flowmeter, man-eater, Main Streeter, maltreater, preheater, propraetor, repeater, saltpeter, secretor, seedeater, toadeater, Wall Streeter, windcheater, world-beater
altimeter, centiliter, centimeter, deciliter, decimeter, lotus-eater, milliliter, millimeter, overeater, taximeter
—*also* -er *forms of adjectives listed at* eat¹

eater² \et-ər\ see etter

eatery \ēt-ə-rē\ see etory

eath¹ \ēth\ eath, heath, Keith, Meath, neath, sheath, wreath
beneath, bequeath, hadith, monteith, underneath

eath² \ēṯẖ\ see eathe

eathe \ēṯẖ\ breathe, Meath, seethe, sheathe, teethe, wreathe
bequeath, ensheathe, enwreathe, inbreathe, unsheathe, unwreathe, Westmeath

eathean \ē-thē-ən\ lethean
Promethean

eather[1] \eth-ər\ see ether[1]

eather[2] \ē-thər\ see either

eathern \eth-ərn\ see ethern

eathery \eth-rē\ feathery, heathery,
leathery

eathing \ē-thiŋ\ breathing,
sheathing, teething
firebreathing
—also -ing forms of verbs listed at
eathe

eathless \eth-ləs\ breathless,
deathless

eathy \ē-thē\ heathy, lethe, wreathy

eating \ēt-iŋ\ beating, eating,
fleeting, meeting, seating, sheeting,
sweeting
breast-beating, drumbeating, fire-
eating, man-eating, unweeting
Sunday-go-to-meeting
—also -ing forms of verbs listed at
eat[1]

eatise \ēt-əs\ see etus

eatly[1] \āt-lē\ see ately[1]

eatly[2] \ēt-lē\ see eetly

eaton \ēt-ᵊn\ see eaten[1]

eats[1] \ēts\ Keats
—also -s, -'s, and -s' forms of nouns,
and -s forms of verbs, listed at eat[1]

eats[2] \āts\ see ates[1]

eature \ē-chər\ see eacher

eaty \ēt-ē\ meaty, peaty, sleety,
sweetie, treaty, ziti
entreaty, Tahiti
Dolomiti, spermaceti

eau \ō\ see ow[1]

eaucracy \äk-rə-sē\ see ocracy

eauteous \üt-ē-əs\ see uteous

eautiful \üt-i-fəl\ see utiful

eauty \üt-ē\ see ooty[1]

eaux \ō\ see ow[1]

eavable \ē-və-bəl\ see eivable

eaval \ē-vəl\ see ieval

eave[1] \ēv\ breve, cleave, eve, Eve,
greave, grieve, heave, leave, lief,
peeve, reave, reeve, reive, scrieve,
sheave, shrieve, sleave, sleeve, steeve,
Steve, thieve, weave, weve
Abib, achieve, aggrieve, believe,
bereave, conceive, deceive, inweave,
khedive, Maldive, motive, naive,
perceive, qui vive, receive, relieve,
reprieve, retrieve, shirtsleeve, unreeve,
unweave, upheave
apperceive, by-your-leave,
disbelieve, Genevieve, interleave,
interweave, Laccadive, make-believe,
misbelieve, misconceive, preconceive,
semibreve, Tel Aviv, undeceive
adam-and-eve, recitative, ticket-of-
leave, underachieve
Saint Agnes' Eve

eave[2] \iv\ see ive[2]

eaved \ēvd\ leaved, sleeved
aggrieved, bereaved, relieved
—also -ed forms of verbs listed at
eave[1]

eavement \ēv-mənt\ see evement

eaven \ev-ən\ devon, Devon, Evan,
heaven, Kevin, leaven, levin, Nevin,
seven, Sevin, sweven
eleven, replevin, South Devon

eaver \ē-vər\ see iever

eavers \ē-vərz\ cleavers, vivers

eaves \ēvz\ eaves, Treves
shirtsleeves

eavey \ē-vē\ peavey
divi-divi

eaward \ē-wərd\ see eeward

eaze[1] \ēz\ see eze

eaze² \āz\ see aze¹

eazo \ē-zō\ see izo¹

eazy \ē-zē\ see easy¹

eb \eb\ bleb, deb, ebb, neb, pleb, reb, Reb, web
ardeb, celeb, cobweb, cubeb, Deneb, Horeb, subdeb, Zagreb, zineb
cause célèbre, Johnny Reb, spiderweb

eba \ē-bə\ Chiba, Reba, Sheba
amoeba, zareba
Curitiba

ebate \ab-ət\ see abit

ebb \eb\ see eb

ebbie \eb-ē\ see ebby

ebble \eb-əl\ pebble, rebel, treble

ebbuck \eb-ək\ kebbuck, rebec

ebby \eb-ē\ blebby, Debbie, Debby, maybe, webby
cobwebby

ebe¹ \ē-bē\ BB, freebie, Hebe, phoebe, Phoebe, Seabee
caribe, Galibi

ebe² \ēb\ glebe, grebe, plebe
ephebe, sahib

ebec \eb-ək\ see ebbuck

ebel \eb-əl\ see ebble

eber \ā-bər\ see abor

ebes \ēbz\ Thebes
—also -s, -'s, and -s' forms of nouns listed at ebe²

eble \eb-əl\ see ebble

ebo \ē-bō\ see ibo

ebral \ē-brəl\ cerebral, palpebral, vertebral

ebrity \eb-rət-ē\ celebrity
muliebrity

ebs¹ \eps\ see eps

ebs² \ebz\ Debs
—also -s, -'s, and -s' forms of nouns, and -s forms of verbs, listed at eb

ebt \et\ see et¹

ebted \et-əd\ see etid

ebtor \et-ər\ see etter

ebus \ē-bəs\ Phoebus, rebus
ephebus

ec¹ \ek\ see eck

ec² \ets\ see ets

eca \ē-kə\ see ika¹

ecal \ē-kəl\ cecal, fecal, meikle, treacle
intrathecal
bibliothecal

ecan \ek-ən\ see eckon

ecant \ē-kənt\ piquant, secant

ecas \ā-kəs\ Turks and Caicos, Zacatecas

ecca \ek-ə\ Decca, mecca, Mecca, weka
Rebecca, Rebekah, Rijeka

eccable \ek-ə-bəl\ see eckable

eccan \ek-ən\ see eckon

ecce \ek-ē\ see ecky

ecco \ek-ō\ see echo

ecency \ēs-ᵊn-sē\ decency, recency
indecency

ecent \ēs-ᵊnt\ decent, recent
indecent, obeisant

eces \ē-sēz\ see ecies

ech¹ \ek\ see eck

ech² \ək\ see uck

ech³ \esh\ see esh¹

eche¹ \āsh\ crèche, flèche, Laoighis, Leix, resh, seiche
bobeche, tête-bêche

Bangladesh
Andhra Pradesh, Madhya Pradesh,
Uttar Pradesh
Himadral Pradesh
Arunachal Pradesh

eche² \esh\ see esh¹

eche³ \ē-chē\ see eachy

êche \esh\ see esh¹

èche \esh\ see esh¹

eched \echt\ see etched

echerous \ech-rəs\ lecherous,
treacherous

echery \ech-rē\ lechery, treachery

echie \ek-ē\ see ecky

echin \ek-ən\ see eckon

echo \ek-ō\ deco, echo, gecko,
secco
El Greco, reecho

echnical \ek-ni-kəl\ technical
biotechnical, geotechnical

echt \ekt\ see ect

ecia \ē-shə\ see esia¹

ecially \esh-lē\ see eshly

ecian \ē-shən\ see etion¹

ecibel \es-ə-bəl\ see essible

ecie¹ \ē-sē\ see eecy

ecie² \ē-shē\ see ishi

ecies \ē-sēz\ feces, species, theses
prostheses, subspecies
exegeses

ecil¹ \ē-səl\ Cecil, diesel

ecil² \es-əl\ see estle¹

ecile \es-əl\ see estle¹

ecily \es-ə-lē\ see essaly

ecimal \es-ə-məl\ see esimal

eciman \es-mən\ see essman

ecious \ē-shəs\ specious
capricious, facetious, Lucretius

ecium \ē-shē-əm\ aecium
lutecium, technetium, zoecium
androecium, apothecium,
gynoecium, paramecium, perithecium

eck \ek\ beck, check, cheque, Czech,
deck, dreck, fleck, heck, lek, neck,
pec, peck, reck, sec, sneck, spec,
speck, trek, wreak, wreck
Aztec, Baalbek, backcheck, bedeck,
breakneck, Capek, cromlech,
crookneck, cross-check, cusec, ewe-
neck, exec, flyspeck, fore-check,
foredeck, gooseneck, haček, hatcheck,
henpeck, high tech, kopeck, limbeck,
low-tech, Lubeck, Mixtec, paycheck,
pinchbeck, Quebec, rebec, ringneck,
roll-neck, roughneck, samekh,
shipwreck, spot-check, Steinbeck,
tenrec, Toltec, Uzbek, wryneck, xebec
afterdeck, à la grecque, Aquidneck,
biotech, bodycheck, bottleneck,
Chiang Kai-shek, countercheck, demi-
sec, discotheque, double-check,
double-deck, hunt-and-peck,
leatherneck, littleneck, Pont l'évêque,
quarterdeck, rubberneck, triple sec,
turtleneck, Yucatec, Zapotec
cinematheque, Melchizedek,
Toulouse-Lautrec

eckable \ek-ə-bəl\ checkable
impeccable

ecked \ekt\ see ect

ecker \ek-ər\ checker, chequer,
decker, pecker, trekker, wrecker
exchequer, three-decker, woodpecker
dominicker, double-decker,
rubbernecker, triple-decker

ecking \ek-iŋ\ decking, necking
—also -ing forms of verbs listed at
eck

ecklace \ek-ləs\ see eckless

eckle \ek-əl\ deckle, freckle, heckle,
shekel, speckle
kenspeckle

eckless \ek-ləs\ feckless, checkless, necklace, reckless
affectless

ecko \ek-ō\ see echo

eckon \ek-ən\ beckon, Brecon, Deccan, reckon, zechin
Aztecan, misreckon, Toltecan
Yucatecan

ecks \ecks\ eks\ see ex

ecky \ek-ē\ Becky, recce, techie
Shimonoseki

econ \ek-ən\ see eckon

econd¹ \ek-ənd\ see ecund

econd² \ek-ənt\ see eccant

ecque \ek\ see eck

ecs \eks\ see ex

ect \ekt\ necked, sect, specked
abject, affect, aspect, bisect, cathect, collect, confect, connect, convect, correct, defect, deflect, deject, detect, direct, dissect, effect, eject, elect, erect, ewe-necked, expect, goosenecked, infect, inflect, inject, insect, inspect, neglect, object, pandect, perfect, porrect, prefect, prelect, project, prospect, protect, rednecked, refect, reflect, reject, resect, respect, ring-necked, select, stiff-necked, subject, suspect, traject, transect, trisect, Utrecht, V-necked
acrolect, architect, circumspect, deselect, dialect, disaffect, disconnect, disinfect, disrespect, double-decked, genuflect, gapholect, incorrect, indirect, intellect, interject, intersect, introject, introspect, misdirect, preselect, re-collect, recollect, redirect, reelect, resurrect, retrospect, self-respect, turtlenecked, vivisect
aftereffect, hypercorrect, idiolect, interconnect, megaproject, semierect
semi-indirect
—also -ed forms of verbs listed at eck

ecta \ek-tə\ dejecta, ejecta, perfecta, trifecta

ectable \ek-tə-bəl\ affectable, collectible, correctable, deflectable, delectable, detectable, ejectable, electable, erectable, expectable, inflectable, injectable, perfectible, projectable, respectable
disrespectable, indefectible

ectacle \ek-ti-kəl\ see ectical

ectal \ek-tᵊl\ see ectile

ectance \ek-təns\ expectance, reflectance

ectant \ek-tənt\ expectant, humectant, injectant, protectant
disinfectant

ectar \ek-tər\ see ector

ectarous \ek-trəs\ see ectress

ectary \ek-tə-rē\ sectary
insectary

ected \ek-təd\ affected, collected, complected, dejected
recollected, self-affected, self-collected, self-elected, self-selected, unaffected, undirected, unexpected, unselected
inner-directed, other-directed
—also -ed forms of verbs listed at ect

ecten \ek-tən\ nekton, pecten, pectin
fibronectin, ivermectin

ecter \ek-tər\ see ector

ectible \ek-tə-bəl\ see ectable

ectic \ek-tik\ hectic, pectic
cathectic, eclectic, synectic
anorectic, apoplectic, catalectic, dialectic

ectical \ek-ti-kəl\ spectacle
dialectical

ectile \ek-tᵊl\ sectile
erectile, insectile, projectile
colorectal, dialectal

ectin **114**

ectin \ek-tən\ see ecten

ecting \ek-tiŋ\ affecting
self-correcting, self-respecting
—also -ing forms of verbs listed at
ect

ection \ek-shən\ flexion, lection,
section
abjection, advection, affection,
bisection, collection, complexion,
confection, connection, connexion,
convection, correction, C-section,
defection, deflection, dejection,
detection, direction, dissection,
ejection, election, erection, evection,
infection, inflection, injection,
inspection, midsection, objection,
perfection, prelection, projection,
protection, refection, reflection,
rejection, resection, selection,
subjection, subsection, trajection,
transection, trisection
by-election, circumspection,
disaffection, disconnection,
disinfection, genuflection,
imperfection, indirection, introjection,
introspection, insurrection,
intellection, interjection, intersection,
misdirection, predilection,
preselection, recollection,
redirection, reelection, reinfection,
resurrection, retroflexion,
retrospection, vivisection
antirejection, hypercorrection,
interconnection
Cesarean section

ectional \ek-shnəl\ sectional
affectional, bisectional,
complexional, connectional,
convectional, correctional, cross-
sectional, directional, inflectional,
projectional, reflectional
bidirectional, introspectional,
interjectional, resurrectional,
vivisectional
omnidirectional, unidirectional

ectionist \ek-shə-nəst\
perfectionist, projectionist,
protectionist, selectionist

introspectionist, resurrectionist,
vivisectionist

ective \ek-tiv\ advective, affective,
adjective, bijective, collective,
connective, convective, corrective,
defective, deflective, detective,
directive, effective, elective, ejective,
infective, inflective, injective,
invective, objective, perfective,
perspective, projective, prospective,
reflective, respective, selective,
subjective
cost-effective, imperfective,
ineffective, intellective, introspective,
nondirective, nonobjective,
retrospective
cryoprotective, intersubjective

ectless \ek-ləs\ see eckless

ectly \ekt-lē\ abjectly, correctly,
directly, erectly
incorrectly, indirectly

ectness \ekt-nəs\ abjectness,
correctness, directness, erectness,
selectness
incorrectness, indirectness
hypercorrectness

ecto \ek-tō\ recto
perfecto

ectomy \ek-tə-mē\ mastectomy,
vasectomy
appendectomy, hysterectomy,
tonsillectomy
clitoridectomy

ector \ek-tər\ hector, Hector, lector,
nectar, rector, sector, specter, vector
bisector, collector, convector,
corrector, defector, deflector, detector,
director, dissector, effector, ejector,
elector, erector, infector, injector,
inspector, neglecter, objector,
perfecter, projector, prospector,
protector, reflector, selector, trisector
vivisector

ectoral \ek-trəl\ spectral, pectoral
electoral, protectoral
multispectral

ectorate \ek-tə-rət\ rectorate
directorate, electorate, inspectorate,
protectorate

ectory \ek-tə-rē\ rectory
directory, protectory, refectory,
trajectory
ex-directory

ectral \ek-trəl\ see ectoral

ectress \ek-trəs\ nectarous
directress, electress, protectress

ectrix \ek-triks\ rectrix
directrix

ectrum \ek-trəm\ plectrum,
spectrum
electrum

ectual¹ \ek-chə-wəl\ effectual
ineffectual, intellectual
anti-intellectual

ectual² \eksh-wəl\ see exual

ectually \ek-chə-lē\ effectually
ineffectually, intellectually

ectural¹ \ek-chə-rəl\ conjectural,
prefectural
architectural

ectural² \ek-shrəl\ flexural
conjectural
architectural

ecture \ek-chər\ lecture
conjecture, prefecture
architecture

ectus \ek-təs\ conspectus,
prospectus

ecular \ek-yə-lər\ secular, specular
molecular

ecum \ē-kəm\ vade mecum
subpoena duces tecum

ecund \ek-ənd\ fecund, second
femtosecond, microsecond,
millisecond, nanosecond
—also -ed forms of verbs listed at
eckon

ecutive \ek-ət-iv\ consecutive,
executive
inconsecutive

ed \ed\ see ead¹

e'd \ēd\ see eed

eda¹ \ēd-ə\ Freda, Frieda, Leda,
Vida
Machida
alameda
olla podrida

eda² \ād-ə\ see ada³

edal¹ \ed-ᵊl\ heddle, medal, meddle,
pedal, peddle, treadle
backpedal, bipedal, soft-pedal
intermeddle

edal² \ēd-ᵊl\ see eedle

edance \ēd-ᵊns\ see edence

edar¹ \ed-ər\ see eader²

edar² \ēd-ər\ see eader¹

edator \ed-ət-ər\ see editor

edd \ed\ see ead¹

edda \ed-ə\ Jedda, Vedda

eddar \ed-ər\ see eader²

edded \ed-əd\ see eaded

edden \ed-ᵊn\ see eaden

edder \ed-ər\ see eader²

eddie \ed-ē\ see eady¹

edding \ed-iŋ\ see eading¹

eddle \ed-ᵊl\ see edal¹

eddler \ed-lər\ meddler, medlar,
peddler
intermeddler

eddon \ed-ᵊn\ see eaden

eddy \ed-ē\ see eady¹

ede¹ \ād\ see ade¹

ede² \ēd\ see eed

ede³ \ā-dā\ see ayday

edeas \ēd-ē-əs\ see edious¹

eded \ē-dəd\ see eeded

edel \ād-əl\ see adle

eden \ēd-ᵊn\ Eden, Sweden
Dunedin

edence \ēd-ᵊns\ credence
impedance, precedence
antecedence

edent \ēd-ᵊnt\ credent, needn't
decedent, precedent, succedent
antecedent

eder¹ \ād-ər\ see ader

eder² \ ēd-ər\ see eader¹

edes \ē-dēz\ Archimedes, Diomedes

edge \ej\ dredge, edge, fledge,
hedge, kedge, ledge, pledge, sedge,
sledge, veg, wedge
allege, frankpledge, gilt-edge, two-
edged, hard-edge, knife-edge,
nutsedge, straightedge
featheredge, sortilege

edged \ejd\ edged, wedged
alleged, full-fledged, gilt-edged, two-
edged, unfledged
deckle-edged, double-edged
—also -ed forms of verbs listed at
edge

edger \ej-ər\ dredger, edger, hedger,
ledger, leger, pledger

edgie \ej-ē\ see edgy

edgy \ej-ē\ edgy, ledgy, Reggie,
sedgy, veggie, wedgie, wedgy
Himeji

edi \ād-ē\ see ady

edia \ēd-ē-ə\ media, Media
acedia
cyclopedia, via media
encyclopedia

edial \ēd-ē-əl\ medial, predial
remedial

edian \ēd-ē-ən\ median
comedian, tragedian

ediant \ēd-ē-ənt\ see edient

edible \ed-ə-bəl\ credible, edible,
spreadable
incredible, inedible

edic¹ \ēd-ik\ comedic
cyclopedic, logaoedic, orthopedic
encyclopedic

edic² \ed-ik\ Eddic, medic
comedic
paramedic, samoyedic

edic³ \ād-ik\ see adic¹

edicable \ed-i-kə-bəl\ medicable,
predicable
immedicable

edical \ed-i-kəl\ medical, pedicle
premedical
biomedical, paramedical

edicate \ed-i-kət\ dedicate,
predicate

edicle \ed-i-kəl\ see edical

edience \ēd-ē-əns\ expedience,
obedience
disobedience, inexpedience

edient \ēd-ē-ənt\ mediant
expedient, ingredient, obedient,
submediant
disobedient, inexpedient

ediment \ed-ə-mənt\ pediment,
sediment
impediment

edin \ēd-ᵊn\ see eden

eding \ēd-iŋ\ see eeding¹

edious¹ \ēd-ē-əs\ tedious
supersedeas

edious² \ē-jəs\ see egis

edist \ēd-əst\ orthopedist
encyclopedist

edit \ed-ət\ credit, edit

accredit, coedit, discredit, noncredit,
reedit, subedit
copyedit

editor \ed-ət-ər\ creditor, editor,
predator
coeditor, subeditor

edium \ēd-ē-əm\ medium, tedium
cypripedium

edlar \ed-lər\ see eddler

edley \ed-lē\ deadly, medley, redly
chance-medley

edly \ed-lē\ see edley

edo[1] \ēd-ō\ credo, lido, Lido, speedo
aikido, libido, Toledo, torpedo,
tuxedo

edo[2] \ād-ō\ see ado[2]

edo[3] \ēd-ə\ see eda[1]

edo[4] \e-dō\ Edo, meadow, Yedo

edom \ēd-əm\ see edum

edon \ēd-ᵊn\ bleeding, Eden,
steading, Sarpedon
boustrophedon

edouin \ed-wən\ see edwin

edra \ē-drə\ Phaedra
cathedra

edral \ē-drəl\ cathedral, dihedral,
trihedral
hemihedral, holohedral, octahedral,
pentahedral, polyhedral, procathedral,
tetrahedral
dodecahedral, icosahedral,
tetartohedral

edro \ā-drō\ Pedro
Murviedro

edulous \ej-ə-ləs\ credulous,
sedulous
incredulous

edum \ēd-əm\ Edam, Edom,
freedom, sedum

edure \ē-jər\ besieger, procedure
supersedure

edwin \ed-wən\ Edwin
bedouin

ee[1] \ē\ b, be, bee, Brie, c, cay, cee,
Cree, d, dee, Dee, dree, e, fee, flea,
flee, free, g, gee, ghee, gie, glee, gree,
he, key, Key, Klee, knee, lea, lee, Lee,
Leigh, li, me, mi, p, pea, plea, pree,
quay, re, scree, sea, see, she, shri, si,
ski, spree, sri, t, tea, tee, the, thee,
three, ti, tree, Ts, Tshi, twee, Twi, v,
vee, we, wee, whee, ye, z, zee
agley, aiguille, agree, alee, ani,
Bacchae, bailee, Bangui, banshee,
bargee, bawbee, Belgae, Black Sea,
bohea, bootee, bougie, buckshee,
bungee, burgee, Bt, Capri, carefree,
Castries, CB, CD, Chablis, Chaldee,
chick-pea, Chi-li, chili, confit, cowpea,
croquis, curie, Curie, Dead Sea,
debris, decree, deep-sea, degree,
Denis, donee, DP, draftee, drawee,
Dundee, emcee, ennui, esprit, etui,
farci, feoffee, foresee, fusee, GB,
germfree, glacis, goatee, grand prix,
grandee, grantee, GT, heart-free,
he/she, Horae, IC, IV, Jaycee, jaygee,
jayvee, Jiangxi, knock-knee, KP,
latchkey, lessee, look-see, low-key, LP,
mame, maquis, Marie, marquee, MC,
métis, Midi, mille-feuille, muggee,
must-see, Nancy, ngwee, OD, off-key,
ogee, Osee, Parcae, pardie, passkey,
Pawnee, payee, PC, perdie, per se, PG,
pledgee, pongee, post-free, précis,
puree, puttee, qt, raki, rani, razee,
rooftree, rupee, rushee, RV, sati,
scotfree, settee, Shaanxi, Shanxi,
Shawnee, s/he, sightsee, signee, sirree,
spadille, spahi, spondee, squeegee,
squilgee, standee, strophe, suttee,
sycee, T-3, TB, testee, 3-D, titi, to-be,
topee, towhee, townee, trainee, trustee,
trusty, Tupi, turfski, turnkey, tutee,
Tutsi, tutti, TV, unbe, vendee, vestee,
Volsci, vouchee, whangee, whoopee,
would-be, Yang-Tze, yen-shee
abatis, ABC, ABD, absentee,
addressee, adoptee, advisee, alienee,
allottee, ambergris, AMP, amputee,
appellee, appointee, après-ski,

arrestee, assignee, attendee, BVD,
Bahai, barley-bree, batterie, billi-bi,
bonhomie, booboisie, bourgeoisie,
brasserie, brusquerie, bumblebee,
camporee, cap-a-pie, causerie, CCD,
chickaree, chimpanzee, coati, Coligny,
committee, conferee, consignee,
counselee, context-free, counterplea,
Danae, DDD, Debussy, departee,
DDT, debauchee, DDE, deportee,
dernier cri, deshabille, designee,
detainee, devisee, devotee, diploe,
disagree, dischargee, dishabille,
divorcé, divorcée, DME, DMT,
dungaree, duty-free, eau-de-vie,
employee, endorsee, enlistee, enrollee,
epopee, escadrille, escapee, ESP,
evictee, expellee, FAD, fancy-free,
fantasie, fantasy, fedayee, filigree,
fleur-de-lis, formulae, franchisee,
fricassee, galilee, Galilee, garnishee,
gaucherie, Gemini, GTP, guarani,
guarantee, Hawaii, HIV, honeybee,
honoree, humble-bee, hydro-ski, IgE,
IgG, inductee, internee, invitee, IUD,
jacquerie, jamboree, jus soli, Kayseri,
kidnappee, LCD, LED, legatee,
libelee, licensee, LSD, maître d',
manatee, Medici, millidegree,
murderee, NAD, nominee, obligee,
oversea, oversee, parolee, parti pris,
patentee, pedigree, peppertree,
picotee, piroshki, point d'appui,
potpourri, praecipe, presentee,
promisee, rapparee, referee, refugee,
rejectee, renminbi, repartee, retiree,
retrainee, returnee, Rosemarie, RPV,
saddletree, Sadducee, San Luis,
sangaree, Savaii, selectee, Semele,
shivaree, snickersnee, SST, STD,
Tenebrae, Tennessee, thirty-three,
TNT, toile de Jouy, torii, transferee,
undersea, Urümqi, vaccinee, value-
free, verdigris, VIP, vis-á-vis,
warrantee
   Adar Sheni, Agri Dagi, alienee,
biographee, bouquet garni, casus belli,
charcuterie, charivari, chincherinchee,
chinoiserie, covenantee, DBCP,
dedicatee, de Medici, delegatee,
distributee, ESOP, evacuee, examinee,

exuviae, facetiae, fait accompli, felo-
de-se, fortunately, Galilei, HTLV,
interrogee, interviewee, jaborandi,
Jiamusi, minutiae, Omega-3, Pasiphae,
patisserie, prima facie, reliquiae,
relocatee, Sargasso Sea, Simon
Legree, Sault Sainte Marie, Southend
on Sea
   communicatee, HTLV-III, taedium
vitae, Tupi-Guarani
   ignoratio elenchi, petitio principii

ee² \ā\ see ay[1]

ée \ā\ see ay[1]

eeable \ē-ə-bəl\ seeable, skiable
agreeable, foreseeable
disagreeable

eebie \ē-bē\ see ebe[1]

eece \ēs\ see iece

eeced \ēst\ see east[1]

eech \ēch\ see each

eecher \ē-chər\ see eacher

eeches \ich-əz\ see itches

eeching \ē-chiŋ\ breeching
far-reaching
—also -ing forms of verbs listed at
each

eechy \ē-chē\ see eachy

eecy \ē-sē\ fleecy, greasy, specie
Tbilisi
AC/DC

eed \ēd\ bead, Bede, bleed, brede,
breed, cede, creed, deed, feed, Gide,
glede, gleed, greed, he'd, heed, keyed,
knead, kneed, lead, mead, Mead,
Mede, meed, need, plead, read, rede,
reed, Reed, Reid, screed, seed, she'd,
speed, steed, swede, Swede, treed,
tweed, Tweed, we'd, weed
   accede, airspeed, allseed, bindweed,
birdseed, blueweed, bourride, breast-
feed, bugseed, burweed, cheerlead,
chickweed, concede, crossbreed,
cudweed, debride, degreed, duckweed,
exceed, fairlead, fireweed, flaxseed,

Godspeed, gulfweed, half-breed, hand-feed, hawkweed, hayseed, high-speed, horseweed, impede, implead, inbreed, indeed, ironweed, Jamshid, jetbead, knapweed, knotweed, Lake Mead, linseed, lip-read, milkweed, misdeed, mislead, misread, moonseed, nosebleed, off-speed, oilseed, pigweed, pinweed, pokeweed, pondweed, Port Said, precede, proceed, proofread, ragweed, rapeseed, recede, reseed, rockweed, seaweed, secede, self-feed, Siegfried, sight-read, silkweed, smartweed, snakeweed, sneezeweed, speed-read, spoon-feed, stall-feed, stampede, stickseed, stickweed, stinkweed, succeed, ten-speed, tickseed, weak-kneed, witchweed, wormseed
  aniseed, antecede, beggarweed, bitterweed, bottle-feed, bugleweed, butterweed, carpetweed, centipede, copyread, cottonseed, cottonweed, crazyweed, Ganymede, interbreed, intercede, interplead, jewelweed, jimsonweed, locoweed, millipede, overfeed, pedigreed, pickerelweed, pumpkinseed, retrocede, riverweed, rosinweed, Runnymede, silverweed, supersede, thimbleweed, tumbleweed, underfeed, waterweed
  velocipede

eedal \ēd-ªl\ see eedle

eeded \ē-dəd\ beaded, deeded, kneaded
  receded
  —also -ed forms of verbs listed at eed

eeder \ēd-ər\ see eader¹

eedful \ēd-fəl\ heedful, needful

eeding¹ \ēd-iŋ\ bleeding, breeding, leading, reading, reeding
  inbreeding, linebreeding, lipreading, outbreeding, preceding, speed-reading
  —also -ing forms of verbs listed at eed

eeding² \ēd-ªn\ see edon

eedle \ēd-ªl\ aedile, beadle, credal, creedal, daedal, needle, wheedle

eedless \ēd-ləs\ deedless, heedless, needless, seedless

eedn't \ēd-ªnt\ see edent

eedo \ēd-ō\ see edo¹

eedom \ēd-əm\ see edum

eeds \ēdz\ Leeds, needs
  Beskids, proceeds
  —also -s, -'s, and -s' forms of nouns, and -s forms of verbs, listed at eed

eedsman \ēdz-mən\ beadsman, seedsman

eedy \ēd-ē\ beady, deedy, greedy, needy, reedy, seedy, speedy, tweedy, weedy

eef \ēf\ see ief¹

eefe \ēf\ see ief¹

eefy \ē-fē\ beefy, leafy, reefy

eegee \ē-jē\ see iji

eeing \ē-iŋ\ seeing, skiing
  farseeing, ill-being, sight-seeing, turfskiing, well-being
  heli-skiing, waterskiing
  —also -ing forms of verbs listed at ee¹

eek¹ \ik\ see ick

eek² \ēk\ see eak¹

eeked \ēkt\ see eaked²

eeken \ē-kən\ see eacon

eeker \ē-kər\ see eaker¹

eekie \ē-kē\ see eaky

eeking \ē-kiŋ\ see eaking¹

eekly \ē-klē\ bleakly, chicly, sleekly, weakly, weekly, treacly
  biweekly, midweekly, newsweekly, triweekly
  semiweekly

eeks \ēks\ see ixe¹

eeky \ē-kē\ see eaky

eel \ēl\ see eal²

eelable \ē-lə-bəl\ see ealable

eele \ēl\ see eal²

eeled \ēld\ see ield

eeler \ē-lər\ see ealer

eeley \ē-lē\ see eely

eelie \ē-lē\ see eely

eelin \ē-lən\ see elin

eeling \ē-liŋ\ ceiling, dealing,
Ealing, feeling, peeling, shieling,
wheeling
  appealing, Darjeeling, freewheeling,
self-dealing, self-feeling, self-sealing,
unfeeling
  double-dealing, self-revealing,
snowmobiling, unappealing
  —also -ing forms of verbs listed at
eal²

eelson \el-sən\ see elson

eely \ē-lē\ Chi-li, dele, eely, Ely,
freely, Greeley, mealie, mealy, really,
seely, steelie, steely, stele, syli, vealy,
wheelie
  scungilli, surreally, Swahili
  campanile, contumely, Isle of Ely,
monostele, touchy-feely

eem \ēm\ see eam¹

eeman \ē-mən\ see emon¹

eemer \ē-mər\ see eamer

eemie \ē-mē\ see eamy

eeming \ē-miŋ\ seeming, streaming
redeeming
unbeseeming
  —also -ing forms of verbs listed at
eam¹

eemly \ēm-lē\ seemly
supremely, unseemly

een¹ \in\ see in¹

een² \ēn\ see ine³

e'en \ēn\ see ine³

eena \ē-nə\ see ina²

eene \ēn\ see ine³

eener \ē-nər\ see eaner

eenery \ēn-rē\ see eanery

eening \ē-niŋ\ see eaning

eenling \ēn-liŋ\ see eanling

eenly \ēn-lē\ see eanly¹

eenness \ēn-nəs\ see eanness

eens \ēnz\ Queens, teens
Grenadines, Philippines, smithereens

eenwich \in-ich\ see inach

eeny \ē-nē\ see ini¹

eep \ēp\ beep, bleep, cheap, cheep,
clepe, creep, deep, heap, jeep, Jeep,
keep, leap, neap, neep, peep, reap,
seep, sheep, sleep, sneap, steep,
sweep, threap, veep, weep
  asleep, barkeep, bopeep, dustheap,
housekeep, knee-deep, skin-deep,
upkeep, upsweep
  overleap, oversleep
  Lakshadweep
  Louis Philippe

eepage \ē-pij\ creepage, seepage

eepen \ē-pən\ cheapen, deepen,
steepen

eepence \əp-əns\ see uppance

eepenny \əp-nē\ see openny

eeper \ē-pər\ beeper, creeper,
keeper, leaper, Dnieper, peeper, reaper,
sleeper, sweeper, weeper
  barkeeper, beekeeper, bookkeeper,
crowkeeper, doorkeeper, gamekeeper,
gatekeeper, goalkeeper, greenkeeper,
groundskeeper, housekeeper,
innkeeper, lockkeeper, minesweeper,

peacekeeper, scorekeeper, shopkeeper,
stockkeeper, storekeeper, timekeeper,
zookeeper
  honeycreeper
    —*also* -er *forms of adjectives listed*
at eep

eepie \ē-pē\ see eepy

eeping \ē-piŋ\ creeping, keeping,
weeping
  beekeeping, bookkeeping,
gatekeeping, housekeeping,
minesweeping, peacekeeping,
safekeeping, timekeeping
    —*also* -ing *forms of verbs listed at*
eep

eepish \ē-pish\ cheapish, sheepish

eeple \ē-pəl\ see eople

eepy \ē-pē\ cheapie, creepy, seepy,
sleepy, sweepy, tepee, tipi, weepie,
weepy

eer[1] \ē-ər\ freer, seer, skier, we're
  CBer, decreer, foreseer, sightseer
overseer, water-skier

eer[2] \ir\ beer, bier, blear, cere, cheer,
clear, dear, deer, drear, ear, fear, fere,
fleer, gear, hear, here, jeer, Lear, leer,
mere, mir, near, peer, pier, Pierre,
queer, rear, schmear, sear, seer, sere,
shear, sheer, skirr, smear, sneer, spear,
speer, sphere, spier, steer, tear, tier,
Trier, Tyr, veer, we're, year
  adhere, Aesir, Ajmer, ambeer,
appear, arrear, Asir, austere, Ayrshire,
Berkshire, besmear, brassiere, Cape
Fear, career, cashier, cashmere,
Cheshire, chimere, clavier, cohere,
compeer, destrier, dog-ear, Ellesmere,
emir, Empire, endear, ensphere, eyrir,
Fafnir, Fifeshire, Flintshire, footgear,
frontier, gambier, Goodyear, haltere,
Hampshire, headgear, inhere, Izmir,
Kashmir, kefir, killdeer, laveer, light-
year, man-year, menhir, mishear,
monsieur, mouse-ear, nadir,
Nairnshire, out-year, Pamir,
Perthshire, pickeer, porticre, premier,
premiere, redear, rehear, reindeer,

revere, Revere, Robespierre, revers,
Saint Pierre, santir, severe,
Shakespeare, Shropshire, sincere,
slick-ear, tapir, uprear, Vanir, veneer,
vizier, voir dire, wheatear, Wiltshire,
Ymir, Yorkshire, zaire, Zaire
  atmosphere, auctioneer, balladeer,
bandolier, bayadere, Bedfordshire,
Bedivere, belvedere, biosphere, black-
tailed deer, bombardier, boutonniere,
brigadier, buccaneer, budgeteer,
Cambridgeshire, cameleer, cannoneer,
cassimere, cavalier, chandelier,
chanticleer, chevalier, chiffonier,
chocolatier, commandeer, corsetiere,
cuirassier, Denbighshire, Derbyshire,
diapir, disappear, domineer,
Dumfriesshire, ecosphere, Elzevir,
engineer, fictioneer, financier,
fourdrinier, fusilier, gadgeteer,
gasolier, gazetteer, Gloucestershire,
gondolier, grenadier, Guinevere,
halberdier, hemisphere, Herefordshire,
Hertfordshire, IJsselmere, insincere,
interfere, jardiniere, junketeer,
kerseymere, Lanarkshire, Lancashire,
lavaliere, leafleteer, marketeer,
Meyerbeer, missileer, Monmouthshire,
Morayshire, mountaineer, Mount
Ranier, muleteer, musketeer, mutineer,
Oxfordshire, overhear, overseer,
oversteer, pamphleteer,
Pembrokeshire, persevere, pioneer,
pistoleer, pontonier, privateer,
profiteer, puppeteer, racketeer,
Radnorshire, rocketeer, Rutlandshire,
scrutineer, Selkirkshire, sloganeer,
sonneteer, souvenir, Staffordshire,
stratosphere, summiteer, Tyne and
Wear, understeer, volunteer,
Warwickshire, white-tailed deer,
Windermere, Worcestershire,
yesteryear
  acyclovir, animalier, black
marketeer, Buckinghamshire,
Clackmannanshire, carabineer,
Caernarvonshire, Cardiganshire,
Carmarthenshire, charioteer,
conventioneer, Dunbartonshire,
electioneer, Eskisehir,
Glamorganshire, free-marketeer,

harquebusier, Huntingdonshire, Invernessshire, Kincardineshire, Montgomeryshire, Northamptonshire, Nottinghamshire
Merionethshire

e'er \er\ see are[4]

eerage \ir-ij\ peerage, steerage
arrearage

eered \ird\ see eard[1]

eerer \ir-ər\ see earer[2]

eeress \ir-əs\ see erous

eerful \ir-fəl\ see earful

eerie[1] \ir-ē\ see eary

eerie[2] \ē-rē\ see eirie

eering \ir-iŋ\ see earing[1]

eerist \ir-əst\ see erist[1]

eerless \ir-ləs\ see earless

eerly \ir-lē\ see early[1]

eersman \irz-mən\ steersman
frontiersman

eerut \ir-ət\ see irit

eery \ir-ē\ see eary

ees \ēz\ see eze

eese \ēz\ see eze

eesh \ēsh\ see iche[2]

eesi \ē-zē\ see easy[1]

eesia \ē-zhə\ see esia[2]

eesome \ē-səm\ gleesome,
threesome

eest[1] \āst\ see aced

eest[2] \ēst\ see east[1]

eesy \ē-zē\ see easy[1]

eet \ēt\ see eat[1]

eetah \ēt-ə\ see ita[2]

eete \āt-ē\ see aty

eeten \ēt-ᵊn\ see eaten[1]

eeter \ēt-ər\ see eater[1]

eethe \ēth\ see eathe

eether \ē-thər\ see either

eething \ē-thiŋ\ see eathing

eetie \ēt-ē\ see eaty

eeting \ēt-iŋ\ see eating

eetle \ēt-ᵊl\ see etal

eetly \ēt-lē\ featly, fleetly, neatly, sweetly
completely, concretely, discreetly, discretely, effetely
bittersweetly, incompletely, indiscreetly

eety \ēt-ē\ see eaty

ee-um \ē-əm\ see eum[1]

eeve \ēv\ see eave[1]

eeved \ēvd\ see eaved

eeves \ēvz\ see eaves

eevil \ē-vəl\ see ieval

eevish \ē-vish\ peevish, thievish

eeward \ē-wərd\ leeward, Leeward, seaward

eewee \ē-wē\ kiwi, peewee, pewee

eewit \ü-ət\ see uet

eez \ēz\ see eze

eezable \ē-zə-bəl\ see easible

eeze \ēz\ see eze

eezer \ē-zər\ see easer[2]

eezing \ē-ziŋ\ see easing[2]

eezy \ē-zē\ see easy[1]

ef[1] \ef\ chef, clef, deaf, ef, f, lev, ref, teff
aleph, Brezhnev, enfeoff, HF, Kiev, stone-deaf, tone-deaf
emf, Kishinev

ef² \ā\ see ay¹

ef³ \ēf\ see ief¹

efanie \ef-ə-nē\ see ephony

efany \ef-ə-nē\ see ephony

efe \ef-ē\ see effie

eferable \ef-rə-bəl\ preferable, referable

eference \ef-rəns\ deference, preference, reference
cross-reference

eferent \ef-rənt\ deferent, referent

eff \ef\ see ef¹

effer \ef-ər\ see ephor

efic \ef-ik\ Efik
benefic, malefic

eficence \ef-ə-səns\ beneficence, maleficence

efik \e-fik\ see efic

efsk \efsk\ Izhefsk
Prokopyevsk

eft \eft\ cleft, deft, eft, heft, klepht, left, theft, weft
bereft

efty \ef-tē\ hefty, lefty

eg¹ \āg\ Craig, plague, vague
stravage, The Hague

eg² \eg\ beg, Craig, dreg, egg, gleg, Greg, Gregg, keg, leg, peg, reg, skeg, yegg
blackleg, bootleg, bowleg, dogleg, foreleg, jackleg, jake leg, muskeg, nutmeg, redleg, renege, roughleg, Tuareg, unpeg
Winnipeg
mumblety-peg

eg³ \ej\ see edge

ega¹ \eg-ə\ omega
rutabaga

ega² \ā-gə\ see aga²

ega³ \ē-gə\ see iga¹

egal \ē-gəl\ beagle, eagle, egal, legal, regal
illegal, porbeagle, spread-eagle, viceregal
extralegal, paralegal
medicolegal

egan \ē-gən\ Megan, vegan
Mohegan

egas \ā-gəs\ see agus

ege¹ \ezh\ barege, cortege, Liège, manege, solfege

ege² \eg\ see eg²

ege³ \ej\ see edge

ege⁴ \ēg\ see igue

ege⁵ \ig\ see ig

eged \ejd\ see edged

egel \āgəl\ see agel

egent \ē-jənt\ regent, sejant
allegiant, vice-regent

eger \ej-ər\ see edger

egg \eg\ see eg²

eggar \eg-ər\ see egger

eggary \eg-ə-rē\ beggary, Gregory

egger \eg-ər\ beggar
bootlegger, Heidegger
thousand-legger

eggie \ej-ē\ see edgy

eggio \ej-ē-ō\ Reggio
arpeggio, solfeggio

eggs \egz\ see egs

eggy \eg-ē\ dreggy, eggy, leggy, Peggy, plaguey
Carnegie

egia \ē-jə\ Ouija
aqua regia, aquilegia, paraplegia, quadriplegia

egian \ē-jən\ see egion

egiant \ē-jənt\ see egent

egiate \ē-jət\ collegiate, elegit
intercollegiate

egic \ē-jik\ strategic
paraplegic, quadriplegic

egie \eg-ē\ see eggy

egion \ē-jən\ legion, region
collegian, Norwegian, subregion

egious \ē-jəs\ see egis

egis \ē-jəs\ aegis, egis, Regis,
tedious
egregious

egit \ē-jət\ see egiate

egm \em\ see em¹

egn \ān\ see ane¹

egnant \eg-nənt\ pregnant, regnant
impregnant, unpregnant

egnly \ān-lē\ see ainly

egno \ān-yō\ see eno¹

ego¹ \ē-gō\ chigoe, ego, Vigo
amigo
alter ego, impetigo, superego

ego² \ā-gō\ see ago²

egory \eg-ə-rē\ see eggary

egs \egz\ sheerlegs
yellowlegs
butter-and-eggs, daddy longlegs
—also -s, -'s, and -s' forms of nouns,
and -s forms of verbs, listed at eg²

egular \eg-lər\ see egler

eh¹ \ā\ see ay¹

eh² \a\ see ah³

ehen \ān\ see ane¹

ehner \ā-nər\ see ainer

ei¹ \ēk\ dreich, skeigh

ei² \ā\ see ay¹

ei³ \ī\ see y¹

eia¹ \ē-ə\ see ia¹

eia² \ī-ə\ see iah¹

eial \ē-əl\ see eal¹

eian¹ \ē-ən\ see ean¹

eian² \ā-ən\ see ayan¹

eic \ē-ik\ oleic
epigeic, logorrheic, mythopoeic
onomatopoeic

eich \ēk\ see ei¹

eiche \āsh\ see eche¹

eickel \ī-kəl\ see ycle

eid¹ \āt\ see ate¹

eid² \īt\ see ite¹

eid³ \ēd\ see eed

eidel¹ \ād-əl\ see adle

eidel² \īd-ᵊl\ see idal

eidi \īd-ē\ see iday

eidon \īd-ᵊn\ see iden

eier \īr\ see ire¹

eifer \ef-ər\ see ephor

eige \āzh\ beige
assuage

eiger \ī-gər\ see iger

eigh¹ \ā\ see ay¹

eigh² \ē\ see ee¹

eighbor \ā-bər\ see abor

eight¹ \āt\ see ate¹

eight² \īt\ see ite¹

eighter \āt-ər\ see ator

eightless \āt-ləs\ see ateless

eights \īts\ see ights

eighty \āt-ē\ see aty

eign \ān\ see ane[1]

eigner \ā-nər\ see ainer

eii \ā\ see ay[1]

eiian \ā-ən\ see ayan[1]

eiji \ā-jē\ see agy

eik \ēk\ see eak[1]

eikh \ēk\ see eak[1]

eikle \ē-kəl\ see ecal

eil[1] \āl\ see ail

eil[2] \el\ see el[1]

eil[3] \ēl\ see eal[2]

eil[4] \īl\ see ile[1]

eila \ē-lə\ see ela[1]

eiled \āld\ see ailed

eiler \ī-lər\ see ilar

eiling[1] \ā-liŋ\ see ailing

eiling[2] \ē-liŋ\ see eeling

eill \ēl\ see eal[2]

eillance \ā-ləns\ see alence

eillant \ā-lənt\ see alant

eilles[1] \ā\ see ay[1]

eilles[2] \ālz\ see ales

eilly \ā-lē\ see aily

eim[1] \ām\ see ame[1]

eim[2] \īm\ see ime[1]

eimer \ī-mər\ see imer[1]

eims[1] \äⁿs\ see ance[1]

eims[2] \ēmz\ Reims, Rheims
—*also* -s, -'s, *and* -s' *forms of nouns,
and* -s *forms of verbs, listed at* eam[1]

ein[1] \ān\ see ane[1]

ein[2] \ē-ən\ see ean[1]

ein[3] \ēn\ see ine[3]

ein[4] \īn\ see ine[1]

eine[1] \ān\ see ane[1]

eine[2] \ēn\ see ine[3]

eine[3] \ī-nə\ see ina[1]

eine[4] \en\ see en[1]

eined \ānd\ see ained

einer[1] \ā-nər\ see ainer

einer[2] \ē-nər\ see eaner

eing \ē-iŋ\ see eeing

einie \ī-nē\ see iny[1]

eining \ā-niŋ\ see aining

einous \ā-nəs\ see ayness

eins \ānz\ see ains

einsman \ānz-mən\ see ainsman

eint \ānt\ see aint

einte \ant\ see ant[5]

einture \an-chər\ see ancher[2]

einy \ā-nē\ see ainy

eipt \ēt\ see eat[1]

eir \er\ see are[4]

eira \ir-ə\ see era[2]

eird \ird\ see eard[1]

eiress \ar-əs\ see aris[2]

eiric \ī-rik\ see yric

eiro \er-ō\ see ero[2]

eirs \erz\ see airs

eis[1] \ās\ see ace[1]

eis[2] \ē-əs\ see eus[1]

eis[3] \īs\ see ice[1]

eisant \ēs-ᵊnt\ see ecent

eise \ēz\ see eze

eisel \ī-zəl\ see isal[2]

eisen \īz-ᵊn\ see izen[1]

eiser[1] \ī-sər\ see icer

eiser[2] \ī-zər\ see izer

eisha[1] \ā-shə\ see acia

eisha[2] \ē-shə\ see esia[1]

eisin \ēz-ᵊn\ see eason

eiss \īs\ see ice[1]

eissen \īs-ᵊn\ see ison[1]

eist[1] \ā-əst\ see ayest

eist[2] \īst\ see ist[1]

eister[1] \ī-stər\ shyster, tryster
concertmeister, kapellmeister

eister[2] \ē-stər\ see easter

eisure \ē-zhər\ see eizure

eit[1] \ē-ət\ fiat
albeit, howbeit

eit[2] \it\ see it[1]

eit[3] \ēt\ see eat[1]

eit[4] \īt\ see ite[1]

eited \ēt-əd\ see eated[1]

eiter[1] \it-ər\ see itter

eiter[2] \ī-tər\ see iter[1]

eith \ēth\ see eath[1]

either \ē-thər\ breather, either,
neither, teether

eitus \īt-əs\ see itis

eity \ē-ət-ē\ deity
velleity
corporeity, spontaneity, synchroneity
diaphaneity, homogeneity,
incorporeity, instantaneity
contemporaneity, extemporaneity,
heterogeneity, inhomogeneity

eivable \ē-və-bəl\ cleavable
achievable, believable, conceivable,
deceivable, perceivable, receivable,
relievable, retrievable

imperceivable, inconceivable,
irretrievable, unbelievable,
unconceivable

eive \ēv\ see eave[1]

eiver \ē-vər\ see iever

eix \āsh\ see eche[1]

eize[1] \āz\ see aze[1]

eize[2] \ēz\ see eze

eizure \ē-zhər\ leisure, seizure

ejant \ē-jənt\ see egent

eji \ej-ē\ see edgy

ejo \ā-ō\ see eo[1]

ek \ek\ see eck

eka[1] \ek-ə\ see ecca

eka[2] \ē-kə\ see ika[1]

ekah \ek-ə\ see ecca

eke \ēk\ see eak[1]

ekel \ek-əl\ see eckle

ekh \ek\ see eck

eki \ek-ē\ see ecky

ekker \ek-ər\ see ecker

ekoe \ē-kō\ see icot

ekton \ek-tən\ see ecten

el[1] \el\ bel, bell, Bell, belle, cel, cell,
dell, dwell, el, ell, fell, gel, Hel, hell,
jell, knell, l, mell, quell, sel, sell, shell,
smell, snell, spell, swell, tell, they'll,
well, yell
Adele, Ardell, artel, barbell, befell,
Blackwell, bluebell, boatel,
bombshell, Boswell, botel, bridewell,
cadelle, cartel, carvel, chandelle,
clamshell, compel, cormel, cornel,
corral, cowbell, Cromwell, cupel,
Danielle, diel, dispel, doorbell,
dumbbell, duxelles, echelle, eggshell,
Estelle, excel, expel, farewell, foretell,
gabelle, gazelle, Giselle, gromwell,

handbell, hard-shell, harebell, hotel,
impel, indwell, inkwell, jurel,
lampshell, lapel, marcel, maxwell,
Maxwell, micelle, Michele, Michelle,
misspell, morel, Moselle, motel,
nacelle, Nobel, noel, nouvelle,
nutshell, oat-cell, Orel, Orwell,
outsell, pall-mall, Parnell, pastel, pell-
mell, pixel, pointelle, presell, propel,
quenelle, rakehell, rappel, Ravel,
rebel, refel, repel, respell, retell, riel,
Rochelle, rondel, saurel, scalpel,
seashell, sequel, Seychelles, soft-shell,
solgel, speedwell, spinel, stairwell,
unsell, unwell, upwell, Weddell, wind-
bell
  Annabelle, APL, aquarelle, asphodel,
Azazel, bagatelle, BAL, barbicel,
bechamel, brocatelle, Camberwell,
caramel, caravel, carousel, cascabel,
chanterelle, chaparral, Charles Martel,
citadel, clientele, cockleshell,
Cozumel, damozel, decibel,
demoiselle, fare-thee-well, fontanel,
immortelle, Isabel, Isabelle, Jezebel,
kiss-and-tell, lenticel, mangonel,
muscatel, ne'er-do-well, Neufchatel,
nonpareil, organelle, oversell,
parallel, pedicel, pennoncel,
personnel, petronel, Philomel,
pimpernel, show-and-tell,
tortoiseshell, undersell, T4 cell,
villanelle, William Tell, zinfandel
  Aix-la-Chapelle, au naturel, crème
caramel, mademoiselle, maître
d'hôtel, matériel, Mont-Saint-Michel,
spirituel, T-helper cell, Thompson's
gazelle, VLDL
  antiparallel, antipersonnel, AWOL

el² \āl\ see ail

ela¹ \ē-lə\ Gila, Leila, Lela, selah,
sheila, Sheila, stela, Vila
  Braila, candela, tequila, weigela
  Coahuila, Philomela, sinsemilla,
Tutuila

ela² \ā-lə\ see ala³

ela³ \el-ə\ see ella

elable \el-ə-bəl\ see ellable

elacy \el-ə-sē\ jealousy, prelacy

elagh \ā-lē\ see aily

elah \ē-lə\ see ela¹

eland \ē-lənd\ eland, Leland,
Zealand
  New Zealand

elanie \el-ə-nē\ see elony

elar \ē-lər\ see ealer

elate \el-ət\ see ellate

elatin \el-ət-ᵊn\ see eleton

elative \el-ət-iv\ relative
  appellative, correlative, irrelative

elba \el-bə\ Elba, Elbe, Melba

elbe \el-bə\ see elba

elbert \el-bərt\ Delbert, Elbert
  Mount Elbert

elch \elch\ belch, squelch, welch,
Welch

eld¹ \eld\ eld, geld, held, meld,
shelled, weld
  beheld, danegeld, handheld, hard-
shelled, upheld, withheld
  jet-propelled, self-propelled
  unparalleled
  —also -ed forms of verbs listed at
el¹

eld² \elt\ see elt

elda \el-də\ Zelda

eldam \el-dəm\ see eldom

elder \el-dər\ elder, welder

eldom \el-dəm\ beldam, seldom
hoteldom

eldon \el-dən\ Sheldon, Weldon

eldt \elt\ see elt

ele¹ \ā-lē\ see aily

ele² \el\ see el¹

ele³ \el-ē\ see elly

ele⁴ \ē-lē\ see eely

eled¹ \eld\ see eld¹

eled² \ēld\ see ield

elen \el-ən\ see elon

elena \el-ə-nə\ Elena, Helena

elens \el-ənz\ Saint Helens
Mount Saint Helens
—also -s, -'s, and -s' forms of nouns
listed at elon

eleon \ēl-yən\ see elian²

eletal \el-ət-ᵊl\ pelletal, skeletal

eleton \el-ət-ᵊn\ gelatin, skeleton

eleus \ē-lē-əs\ see elious

elf \elf\ elf, Guelf, pelf, self, shelf
bookshelf, herself, himself, itself,
myself, nonself, oneself, ourself, top-
shelf, thyself, yourself
mantelshelf
do-it-yourself

elfish \el-fish\ elfish, selfish
unselfish

elhi \el-ē\ see elly

eli \el-ē\ see elly

elia¹ \ēl-yə\ Delia, Lelia, Shelia
Amelia, camellia, Camellia, Cecilia,
Cornelia, Karelia, lobelia, obelia,
Ophelia, Rumelia, sedilia, stapelia
psychedelia, seguidilla

elia² \il-ē-ə\ see ilia¹

elial \ē-lē-əl\ Belial
epithelial

elian¹ \ē-lē-ən\ Melian, Pelion
abelian, Karelian, Mendelian

elian² \ēl-yən\ anthelion, aphelion,
carnelian, chameleon, cornelian,
Mendelian, parhelion
perihelion
Aristotelian, Mephistophelian

elian³ \el-ē-ən\ see ellian

elible \el-ə-bəl\ see ellable

elic¹ \ē-lik\ parhelic
autotelic

elic² \el-ik\ melic, relic, telic
angelic, Goidelic, smart aleck
archangelic, autotelic, philatelic,
psychedelic

elical \el-i-kəl\ helical, pellicle
angelical
double-helical, evangelical

elier \el-yer\ see elure

elin \ē-lən\ shieling, theelin

elion¹ \el-ē-ən\ see ellian

elion² \ēl-yən\ see elian²

elion³ \ēl-ē-ən\ see elian¹

elios \ē-lē-əs\ see elious

elious \ē-lē-əs\ Helios, Peleus
Cornelius
contumelious

elish \el-ish\ see ellish

elist \el-əst\ cellist, trellised
Nobelist, pastelist

elius¹ \ā-lē-əs\ see alius

elius² \ē-lē-əs\ see elious

elix \ē-liks\ Felix, helix
double helix

elk¹ \elk\ elk, whelk

elk² \ilk\ see ilk

ell \el\ see el¹

e'll \ēl\ see eal²

ella \el-ə\ Celle, Della, Ella, fella,
fellah, stella, Stella
Benguela, candela, Capella, Estella,
favela, Gisela, glabella, lamella,
Luella, Marcella, Mandela, novella,
paella, patella, prunella, quiniela,
rubella, sequela, umbrella, vanilla
a cappella, Cinderella, citronella,
columella, fraxinella, Isabella,

mortadella, mozzarella, panatela, salmonella, sarsaparilla, subumbrella, tarantella, villanella
  valpolicella

ellable \el-ə-bəl\ fellable, gelable
  compellable, expellable, indelible

ellah \el-ə\ see ella

ellan \el-ən\ see elon

ellant \el-ənt\ gellant
  appellant, flagellant, propellant, repellent
  water-repellent

ellar \el-ər\ see eller

ellas \el-əs\ see ealous

ellate \el-ət\ helot, pellet, prelate, zealot
  appellate, flagellate, haustellate, lamellate, scutellate

ellative \el-ət-iv\ see elative

elle¹ \el\ see el¹

elle² \el-ə\ see ella

ellean \el-ē-ən\ see ellian

elled \eld\ see eld¹

ellen \el-ən\ see elon

ellent \el-ənt\ see ellant

eller \el-ər\ cellar, dweller, feller, heller, Keller, seller, sheller, smeller, speller, stellar, teller, yeller
  best-seller, bookseller, compeller, expeller, foreteller, glabellar, impeller, indweller, lamellar, ocellar, patellar, propeller, rathskeller, repeller, rostellar, saltcellar, tale-teller
  cerebellar, circumstellar, columellar, fortune-teller, interstellar, Rockefeller, storyteller

elles¹ \el\ see el¹

elles² \elz\ see ells

ellet \el-ət\ see ellate

elletal \el-ət-ᵊl\ see eletal

elley \el-ē\ see elly

elli \el-ē\ see elly

ellia \ēl-yə\ see elia

ellian \el-ē-ən\ Chellean
  Boswellian, pre-Chellean, Sabellian, triskelion
  Machiavellian, Pantagruelian

ellicle \el-i-kəl\ see elical

ellie \el-ē\ see elly

elline \el-ən\ see elon

elling \el-iŋ\ belling, selling, spelling, swelling, telling
  bookselling, compelling, indwelling, misspelling, tale-telling, upwelling
  fortune-telling, self-propelling
  —also -ing forms of verbs listed at el¹

ellington \el-iŋ-tən\ Ellington, Wellington
  beef Wellington

ellion \el-yən\ hellion
  rebellion

ellis \el-əs\ see ealous

ellised \el-əst\ see elist

ellish \el-ish\ hellish, relish
  disrelish, embellish

ellist \el-əst\ see elist

ello \el-ō\ bellow, Bellow, cello, fellow, Jell-O, mellow, yellow, Yellow
  bargello, bedfellow, bordello, duello, hail-fellow, Longfellow, marshmallow, morello, niello, Othello, playfellow, schoolfellow, yokefellow
  Pirandello, punchinello, ritornello, saltarello
  Robin Goodfellow, violoncello

ell-o \el-ō\ see ello

ellous \el-əs\ see ealous

ellow¹ \el-ə\ see ella

ellow² \el-ō\ see ello

ells \elz\ Welles
Dardanelles
—*also* -s, -'s, *and* -s' *forms of nouns,
and* -s *forms of verbs, listed at* el¹

ellum \el-əm\ blellum, skellum,
vellum
postbellum, rostellum
antebellum, cerebellum

ellus \el-əs\ see ealous

elly \el-ē\ belly, Delhi, deli, felly,
jelly, Kellie, Kelly, Nellie, shelly,
Shelley, Shelly, smelly, tele, telly,
wellie
New Delhi, nice-nelly, potbelly,
rakehelly, sowbelly
Boticelli, nervous Nellie, underbelly,
vermicelli
Machiavelli
Dadra and Nagar Haveli

ellyn \el-ən\ see elon

elm \elm\ elm, helm, realm, whelm
overwhelm, underwhelm

elma \el-mə\ Selma, Velma

elmar \el-mər\ see elmer

elmer \el-mər\ Delmar, Delmer,
Elmer

elmet \el-mət\ helmet, Helmut,
pelmet

elmut \el-mət\ see elmet

elo \ē-lō\ see ilo²

elon \el-ən\ Ellen, Ellyn, felon,
Helen, melon
avellan, Magellan, McClellan,
muskmelon, vitelline
Mary Ellen, watermelon
Strait of Magellan

elony \el-ə-nē\ felony, Melanie

elop \el-əp\ develop, envelop
redevelop
overdevelop

elopment \el-əp-mənt\
development, envelopment
redevelopment
overdevelopment

elos \ā-ləs\ see ayless

elot \el-ət\ see ellate

elotry \el-ə-trē\ helotry, zealotry

elp \elp\ help, kelp, skelp, whelp,
yelp

elsea \el-sē\ see elsie

elsie \el-sē\ Chelsea, Elsie
Kensington and Chelsea

elson \el-sən\ keelson, nelson,
Nelson

elt \elt\ belt, celt, Celt, dealt, delt,
dwelt, felt, gelt, melt, pelt, Scheldt,
smelt, spelt, svelte, veld, welt
black belt, flybelt, forefelt, greenbelt,
heartfelt, hot-melt, jacksmelt, Krefeld,
self-belt, snowbelt, snowmelt, Sunbelt
Bielefeld, Roosevelt, shelterbelt

elte \elt\ see elt

elted \el-təd\ bias-belted
—*also* -ed *forms of verbs listed at* elt

elter \el-tər\ belter, melter, pelter,
shelter, skelter, smelter, spelter,
swelter, welter
helter-skelter

eltered \el-tərd\ earth-sheltered
—*also* -ed *forms of verbs listed at*
elter

elting \el-tiŋ\ belting, felting,
melting, pelting
—*also* -ing *forms of verbs listed at*
elt

elure \el-yər\ velure
hotelier

elve \elv\ delve, helve, shelve,
twelve

elves \elvz\ elves, ourselves,
themselves, yourselves

—also -s, -'s, *and* -s' *forms of nouns,*
and -s *forms of verbs, listed at* elve

elvin \el-vən\ Elvin, Kelvin, Melvin,
Melvyn

elvyn \el-vən\ see elvin

ely \ē-lē\ see eely

em¹ \em\ Clem, crème, em, femme,
gem, hem, m, mem, phlegm, REM,
Shem, stem, them
 ad rem, ahem, AM, Arnhem, Belem,
bluestem, condemn, contemn, FM,
idem, in rem, item, mayhem,
millieme, modem, poem, problem, pro
tem, proem, Shechem
 ABM, anadem, apothegm, apothem,
Bethlehem, diadem, exanthem,
ibidem, IgM, meristem, OEM, SAM,
stratagem
 ad hominem, carpe diem, crème de
la crème, ICBM
 post meridiem, star-of-Bethlehem,
terminus ad quem

em² \əm\ see um¹

ema \ē-mə\ bema, Lima, Pima,
schema
 Colima, eczema, edema
 diastema, emphysema, Hiroshima,
Iwo Jima, Kagoshima, Matsushima,
terza rima, Tokushima
 ottava rima

emacist \em-ə-səst\ see emicist

eman¹ \em-ən\ see emon²

eman² \ē-mən\ see emon¹

emane \em-ə-nē\ see emony

emanence \em-ə-nəns\ see
eminence

emanent \em-ə-nənt\ see eminent

ematis \em-ət-əs\ see emitus

ematist \em-ət-əst\ see emitist

ematous \em-ət-əs\ see emitus

ember \em-bər\ ember, member

December, dismember, November,
remember, September
 disremember

emble¹ \äm-bəl\ wamble
ensemble

emble² \em-bəl\ tremble
assemble, atremble, dissemble,
resemble
disassemble

embler \em-blər\ temblor, trembler
assembler, dissembler

emblor \em-blər\ see embler

embly \em-blē\ trembly
assembly
disassembly, self-assembly,
subassembly

eme¹ \em\ see em¹

eme² \ēm\ see eam¹

emel \ā-məl\ see emile

emely \ēm-lē\ see eemly

emen¹ \ē-mən\ see emon¹

emen² \em-ən\ see emon²

emen³ \ā-mən\ see amen¹

emer \ē-mər\ see eamer

emeral \em-rəl\ femoral
ephemeral

emery \em-rē\ emery, Emery,
Emory, memory

emesis \em-ə-səs\ emesis, nemesis

emi \em-ē\ see emmy

emia \ē-mē-ə\ anemia, bohemia,
Bohemia, leukemia, toxemia
academia, septicemia, thalassemia
hypoglycemia, hypokalemia
beta-thalassemia

emian \ē-mē-ən\ anthemion,
Bohemian

emic¹ \ē-mik\ emic
anemic, graphemic, morphemic,
lexemic, phonemic, taxemic, tonemic
epistemic

emic² \em-ik\ chemic
alchemic, endemic, pandemic,
polemic, sachemic, systemic, totemic
academic, epidemic, epistemic

emical \em-i-kəl\ chemical
alchemical, polemical
academical, biochemical,
epidemical, petrochemical
biogeochemical

emicist \em-ə-səst\ polemicist,
supremacist

emics \ē-miks\ graphemics,
morphemics, phonemics, proxemics

emile \ā-məl\ Emile, Memel

eminal \em-ən-ᵊl\ geminal, seminal

eminate \em-ə-nət\ geminate
effeminate

eminence \em-ə-nəns\ eminence,
remanence
preeminence

eminent \em-ə-nənt\ eminent,
remanent
preeminent

eming \em-iŋ\ Fleming, Heminge,
lemming
—*also* -ing *forms of verbs listed at*
em¹

eminge \em-iŋ\ see eming

emini \em-ə-nē\ see emony

eminy \em-ə-nē\ see emony

emion \ē-mē-ən\ see emian

emis \ē-məs\ see emus

emish \em-ish\ blemish, Flemish

emist \em-əst\ chemist
polemist
biochemist

emitist \em-ət-əst\ Semitist
systematist

emitus \em-ət-əs\ clematis, fremitus
edematous

emlin \em-lən\ gremlin, kremlin

emma \em-ə\ Emma, gemma,
lemma, stemma
dilemma

emme \em\ see em¹

emmer \em-ər\ emmer, hemmer,
stemmer, tremor
condemner, contemner

emming \em-iŋ\ see eming

emmy \em-ē\ Emmy, gemmy,
jemmy, phlegmy, semi, stemmy

emn \em\ see em¹

emner \em-ər\ see emmer

emnity \em-nət-ē\ indemnity,
solemnity

emo \em-ō\ demo, memo

emon¹ \ē-mən\ demon, freeman,
Freeman, gleeman, Piman, seaman,
semen
Lake Leman, pentstemon, Philemon
cacodemon, Lacedaemon

emon² \em-ən\ Bremen, leman,
lemon, Yemen

emone \em-ə-nē\ see emony

emony \em-ə-nē\ Gemini, lemony
anemone, bigeminy, Gethsemane,
hegemony

emor \em-ər\ see emmer

emoral \em-rəl\ see emeral

emory \em-rē\ see emery

emous \ē-məs\ see emus

emp \emp\ hemp, kemp, temp

emperer \em-pər-ər\ emperor,
temperer

emperor \em-pər-ər\ see emperer

emplar \em-plər\ Templar
exemplar

emple \em-pəl\ semple, temple

emps \äⁿ\ see ant[1]

empt \emt\ dreamt, kempt, tempt
attempt, contempt, exempt, preempt,
undreamed, unkempt
tax-exempt

emptable \em-tə-bəl\ attemptable,
contemptible

emptible \em-tə-bəl\ see emptable

emption \em-shən\ exemption,
preemption, redemption

emptive \em-tiv\ preemptive,
redemptive

emptor \em-tər\ tempter
preemptor
caveat emptor

emptory \em-trē\ peremptory,
redemptory

emulous \em-yə-ləs\ emulous,
tremulous

emur \ē-mər\ see eamer

emus \ē-məs\ Remus
in extremis, Polyphemus,
polysemous

emy \ē-mē\ see eamy

en¹ \en\ ben, Ben, den, en, fen, gen,
glen, Glen, Glenn, Gwen, hen, ken,
Ken, Len, men, n, pen, Penn, Rennes,
Seine, sen, Sten, ten, then, wen, when,
wren, Wren, yen, Zen
again, amen, Ardennes, Big Ben,
Cayenne, Cevennes, Cheyenne,
Chosen, Dairen, doyen, doyenne,
Duchenne, hapten, hymen, Karen, La
Tène, moorhen, peahen, pigpen,

Phnom Penh, playpen, RN, Touraine,
Tynmen, somewhen
Adrienne, Debrecen, DPN, five-and-
ten, FMN, julienne, Kerguelen, La
Fontaine, LPN, madrilene, mise-en-
scène, samisen, Sun Yat-sen, TPN
carcinogen, comedienne,
equestrienne, tamoxifen, tragedienne,
Valenciennes

en² \ēn\ see ine[3]

en³ \aⁿ\ see in[4]

en⁴ \ən\ see un

en⁵ \äⁿ\ see ant[1]

ena¹ \ā-nä\ see aena[1]

ena² \ā-nə\ see ana[2]

ena³ \än-yə\ see ania[3]

ena⁴ \ē-nə\ see ina[2]

enable \en-ə-bəl\ tenable
amenable, untenable

enace \en-əs\ see enis[1]

enacle \en-i-kəl\ see enical

enae \e-nē\ see ini[1]

enal \ēn-ᵊl\ penal, renal, venal
adrenal, vaccinal
duodenal

enancy \en-ən-sē\ tenancy
lieutenancy, subtenancy

enant \en-ənt\ pennant, tenant
lieutenant, se tenant, subtenant
sublieutenant, undertenant

enary \en-ə-rē\ hennery, plenary,
senary, venery
centenary, millenary
bicentenary, bimillenary,
quincentenary, tercentenary
quatercentenary, semicentenary,
sesquicentenary

enas \ē-nəs\ see enus[1]

enate \en-ət\ see ennet

enator \en-ət-ər\ see enitor

ençal \en-səl\ see encil

ence¹ \ens\ see ense

ence² \än̄s\ see ance¹

ence³ \äns\ see ance²

encel \en-səl\ see encil

enceless \en-sləs\ see enseless

encer \en-sər\ see ensor

ench \ench\ bench, blench, clench, drench, french, French, mensch, quench, stench, tench, trench, wench, wrench
entrench, luftmensch, retrench, unclench, workbench
Anglo-French
Mariana Trench

enchant \en-chənt\ see entient

enched \encht\ trenched
unblenched
—also -ed forms of verbs listed at ench

encher \en-chər\ see enture

enchman \ench-mən\ Frenchman, henchman

encia \en-chə\ see entia

encil \en-səl\ mensal, pencel, pencil, stencil, tensile
blue-pencil, commensal, extensile, Provençal, prehensile, red-pencil, utensil
intercensal

ençon \en-sən\ see ensign

ency \en-sē\ Montmorency, residency
nonresidency

end \end\ bend, blend, blende, end, fend, friend, lend, mend, rend, scend, send, shend, spend, tend, trend, vend, wend, Wend

addend, amend, append, ascend, attend, augend, befriend, Big Bend, bookend, boyfriend, closed-end, commend, compend, contend, dead end, dead-end, defend, depend, descend, distend, downtrend, emend, expend, extend, forfend, girlfriend, godsend, hornblende, impend, intend, Land's End, low-end, missend, misspend, offend, outspend, perpend, pitchblende, portend, pretend, propend, protend, rear-end, resend, South Bend, stipend, subtend, suspend, transcend, unbend, unkenned, upend, uptrend, weekend, year-end
adherend, apprehend, bitter end, comprehend, condescend, Damavend, discommend, dividend, minuend, overspend, recommend, repetend, reprehend, subtrahend, vilipend
hyperextend, misapprehend, overextend, superintend
—also -ed forms of verbs listed at en¹

enda \en-də\ Brenda, Glenda, Venda
addenda, agenda, pudenda
corrigenda, hacienda, referenda
definienda

endable \en-də-bəl\ lendable, mendable, spendable, vendible
amendable, ascendable, commendable, defendable, dependable, descendible, expendable, extendable, unbendable
comprehendable, recommendable

endal \en-dᵊl\ Grendel, Kendall, Mendel, Wendell
prebendal, pudendal

endall \en-dᵊl\ see endal

endance \en-dəns\ see endence

endancy \en-dən-sē\ see endency

endant \en-dənt\ see endent

ende¹ \end\ see end

ende² \en-dē\ see endi

ended \en-dəd\ ended, splendid
befriended, unfriended
double-ended, open-ended,
undescended
—*also* -ed *forms of verbs listed at*
end

endel \en-dᵊl\ see endal

endell \en-dᵊl\ see endal

endence \en-dəns\ tendance
ascendance, attendance, intendance,
resplendence, transcendence
condescendence, independence,
Independence
superintendence

endency \en-dən-sē\ pendency,
tendency
ascendancy, dependency,
resplendency, transcendency
independency
superintendency

endent \en-dənt\ pendant, pendent,
splendent
appendant, ascendant, attendant,
defendant, dependent, descendant,
impendent, intendant, respendent,
transcendent
independent
superintendent
semi-independent

ender \en-dər\ bender, blender,
fender, gender, lender, mender, render,
sender, slender, spender, splendor,
tender, vendor
amender, ascender, attender,
auslander, bartender, commender,
contender, defender, descender,
emender, engender, expender,
extender, fork-tender, goaltender,
hellbender, intender, offender,
pretender, surrender, suspender,
tailender, weekender
double-ender, moneylender, over-
spender, self-surrender

endi \en-dē\ bendy, Mende, trendy,
Wendy
effendi
modus vivendi

endible \en-də-bəl\ see endable

endid \en-dəd\ see ended

ending \en-diŋ\ bending, ending,
pending, sending
ascending, attending, fence-
mending, goaltending, heartrending,
mind-bending, unbending, unending
unpretending
uncomprehending
—*also* -ing *forms of verbs listed at*
end

endium \en-dē-əm\ compendium
antependium

endless \end-ləs\ endless, friendless

endliness \en-lē-nəs\ cleanliness,
friendliness
uncleanliness, unfriendliness

endly \en-lē\ cleanly, friendly
uncleanly, unfriendly
loop of Henle

endment \en-mənt\ amendment,
intendment

endo \en-dō\ kendo
crescendo, stringendo
decrescendo, innuendo
diminuendo

endor \en-dər\ see ender

endous \en-dəs\ horrendous,
stupendous, tremendous

endron \en-drən\ philodendron,
rhododendron

ends \enz\ see ens¹

endum \en-dəm\ addendum,
agendum, pudendum
corrigendum, referendum
definiendum

endy \en-dē\ see endi

ene¹ \ā-nā\ nene, sene

ene² \en\ see en¹

ene³ \en-ē\ see enny

ene⁴ \ē-nē\ see ini¹

ene⁵ \ēn\ see ine³

ene⁶ \ān\ see ane¹

enel \en-ᵊl\ see ennel

eneous \ē-nē-əs\ genius
homogeneous
heterogeneous

ener \ē-nər\ see eaner

enerable \en-rə-bəl\ generable,
venerable
regenerable

eneracy \en-rə-sē\ degeneracy,
regeneracy

enerate \en-rət\ degenerate,
regenerate
unregenerate

enerative \en-rət-iv\ generative
degenerative, regenerative
neurodegenerative

eneris \en-ə-rəs\ mons veneris
sui generis

enery¹ \en-ə-rē\ see enary²

enery² \ēn-rē\ see eanery

enet¹ \en-ət\ see ennet

enet² \ē-nət\ see eanut

eng¹ \aŋ\ see ang²

eng² \əŋ\ see ung¹

enge \enj\ venge
avenge, revenge, Stonehenge

engi \eŋ-gē\ dengue, sengi

english \iŋ-glish\ English, Yinglish

engo \eŋ-gō\ marengo
camerlengo

ength¹ \eŋth\ length, strength
full-length, half-length, wavelength
understrength
industrial-strength

ength² \enth\ see enth

engthen \eŋ-thən\ lengthen,
strengthen

engue \eŋ-gē\ see engi

enh \en\ see en¹

enia¹ \ē-nē-ə\ taenia
Slovenia
sarracenia, schizophrenia

enia² \ē-nyə\ Armenia, Encaenia,
Eugenia, gardenia, Ruthenia, Tigrinya

enial \ē-nē-əl\ genial, menial, venial
congenial

enian \ē-nē-ən\ Fenian
Armenian, Essenian, Icenian,
sirenian, Slovenian, Tyrrhenian
Achaemenian, Magdalenian

enic¹ \ēn-ik\ genic, scenic

enic² \en-ik\ fennec, pfennig,
phrenic, splenic, sthenic
arsenic, asthenic, Edenic, Essenic,
eugenic, Hellenic, hygienic, irenic,
transgenic
allergenic, androgenic, autogenic,
calisthenic, chromogenic, cryogenic,
cryptogenic, hygienic, mutagenic,
Panhellenic, pathogenic, photogenic,
Saracenic, schizophrenic, telegenic
carcinogenic, cariogenic
hallucinogenic, hypoallergenic

enical \en-i-kəl\ cenacle
arsenical, galenical
ecumenical

enice \en-əs\ see enis¹

enicist \en-ə-səst\ eugenicist
ecumenicist

enics \en-iks\ eugenics, euphenics,
euthenics, hygienics
calisthenics, cryogenics
—also -s, -'s, and -s' forms of nouns
listed at enic²

enie¹ \en-ē\ see enny

enie² \ē-nē\ see ini¹

enience \ē-nyəns\ lenience
convenience, provenience
inconvenience

enient \ēn-yənt\ convenient,
prevenient

enim \en-əm\ see enom

enin \en-ən\ see ennon

enior \ē-nyər\ senior
monsignor

enis¹ \en-əs\ Denis, Dennis, Denys,
genus, menace, tenace, tennis, Venice
summum genus

enis² \ē-nəs\ see enus¹

enison¹ \en-ə-sən\ benison,
Tennyson, venison

enison² \en-ə-zən\ benison,
denizen, venison

enist \en-əst\ tennist
euthenist

enitive \en-ət-iv\ genitive, lenitive
philoprogenitive
polyphiloprogenitive

enitor \en-ət-ər\ senator
progenitor
primogenitor

enity \en-ət-ē\ see entity

enium \ē-nē-əm\ hymenium,
proscenium

enius \ē-nē-əs\ see eneous

enizen \en-ə-zən\ see enison²

enn \en\ see en¹

enna \en-ə\ Glenna, henna, senna
antenna, duenna, Gehenna, sienna,
Vienna

ennae \en-ē\ see enny

ennant \en-ənt\ see enant

enne¹ \en\ see en¹

enne² \en-ē\ see enny

enne³ \an\ see an⁵

ennec \en-ik\ see enic²

enned \end\ see end

ennel \en-ᵊl\ crenel, fennel, kennel
unkennel

enner \en-ər\ see enor¹

ennery \en-ə-rē\ see enary²

ennes \en\ see en¹

ennet \en-ət\ Bennett, genet, jennet,
rennet, senate, sennet, sennit, tenet

ennett \en-ət\ see ennet

enney \en-ē\ see enny

enni \en-ē\ see enny

ennial \en-ē-əl\ biennial, centennial,
decennial, millennial, perennial,
quadrennial, quinquennial, septennial,
triennial, vicennial
bicentennial, bimillennial,
postmillennial, premillennial,
quincentennial, tercentennial
semicentennial, sesquicentennial,
quadricentennial

ennies \en-ēz\ tennies
—also -s, -'s, and -s' forms of nouns
listed at enny

ennig \en-ik\ see enic²

ennin \en-ən\ see ennon

ennis \en-əs\ see enis¹

ennist \en-əst\ see enist

ennit \en-ət\ see ennet

ennium \en-ē-əm\ biennium,
decennium, millennium, quadrennium,
quinquennium, triennium

ennon \en-ən\ Lenin, pennon,
rennin, tenon
antivenin

enny \en-ē\ any, benne, benny,
Benny, blenney, Dene, Denny, fenny,

genie, Jennie, jenny, Jenny, many,
penni, penny, Penny
antennae, catchpenny, halfpenny,
Kilkenny, Na-dene, pinchpenny,
sixpenny, tenpenny, threepenny,
truepenny, twopenny
lilangeni, spinning jenny

ennyson \en-ə-sən\ see enison[1]

eno[1] \ān-yō\ segno
dal segno
jalapeño

eno[2] \en-ō\ steno
ripieno

eno[3] \ā-nō\ see ano[2]

enoch \ē-nik\ see inic[1]

enom \en-əm\ denim, plenum,
venom
envenom

enon \en-ən\ see ennon

enor[1] \en-ər\ Brenner, Jenner,
tenner, tenor, tenour
countertenor, heldentenor

enor[2] \ē-nər\ see eaner

enour \en-ər\ see enor[1]

enous \ē-nəs\ see enus[1]

ens[1] \enz\ cleanse, gens, lens
amends, beam-ends, weekends
sapiens
definiens, locum tenens
—*also* -s, -'s, *and* -s' *forms of nouns,
and* -s *forms of verbs, listed at* en[1]

ens[2] \ens\ see ense

ensable \en-sə-bəl\ see ensible

ensal \en-səl\ see encil

ensary \ens-rē\ see ensory

ensch \ench\ see ench

ense \ens\ cense, dense, fence,
flense, gens, hence, mense, pence,
sense, spence, tense, thence, whence
commence, condense, defense,
dispense, expense, immense, incense,

intense, missense, nonsense, offense,
prepense, pretense, propense,
sequence, sixpence, suspense,
twopence
accidence, antisense, commonsense,
confidence, consequence, diffidence,
evidence, frankincense, multisense,
nondefense, providence, Providence,
recompense, residence, self-defense,
subsequence
coincidence, ego-defense,
inconsequence, New Providence,
nonresidence, self-confidence, self-
evidence

enseful \ens-fəl\ menseful, senseful
suspenseful

enseless \en-sləs\ fenceless,
senseless
defenseless, offenseless

ensem \en-səm\ see ensum

enser \en-sər\ see ensor

ensian \en-chən\ see ension

ensible \en-sə-bəl\ sensible
compensable, condensable,
defensible, dispensable, distensible,
extensible, insensible, ostensible
apprehensible, commonsensible,
comprehensible, incondensable,
indefensible, indispensable,
reprehensible, supersensible
incomprehensible

ensign \en-sən\ ensign
alençon

ensil \en-səl\ see encil

ensile \en-səl\ see encil

ension \en-chən\ gentian, mention,
pension, tension
abstention, ascension, attention,
contention, convention, declension,
descension, detention, dimension,
dissension, distension, extension,
indention, intension, intention,
invention, Laurentian, low-tension,
posttension, prehension, pretension,
prevention, recension, retention,

subvention, suspension, sustention,
Vincentian, Waldensian
  Albigensian, apprehension,
circumvention, comprehension,
condescension, contravention,
hypertension, hypotension,
inattention, reinvention, reprehension,
salientian
  incomprehension, misapprehension,
nonintervention, overextension,
Premonstratensian

ensional \ench-nəl\ tensional
ascensional, attentional,
conventional, declensional,
dimensional, extensional, intensional,
intentional
  unconventional, tridimensional,
unidimensional

ensioner \ench-nər\ see entioner

ensis \en-səs\ see ensus

ensitive \en-sət-iv\ sensitive
insensitive
  hypersensitive, oversensitive,
photosensitive, supersensitive

ensity \en-sət-ē\ density, tensity
extensity, immensity, intensity,
propensity

ensive \cn-siv\ pensive, tensive
ascensive, defensive, expensive,
extensive, intensive, offensive,
ostensive, protensive, suspensive
  apprehensive, coextensive,
comprehensive, hypertensive,
hypotensive, inexpensive,
inoffensive, reprehensive, self-
defensive
  counteroffensive, labor-intensive

ensor \en-sər\ censer, censor,
fencer, sensor, spencer, Spencer,
Spenser, tensor
  commencer, condenser, dispenser,
extensor, precensor, sequencer,
suspensor
  biosensor
  —also -er forms of adjectives listed
at ense

ensory \ens-rē\ sensory
dispensary, suspensory
  extrasensory, multisensory,
supersensory

ensual[1] \en-chəl\ see ential

ensual[2] \ench-wəl\ see entual[1]

ensum \en-səm\ sensum
per mensem

ensurable \ens-rə-bəl\ censurable,
mensurable
  commensurable, immensurable
incommensurable

ensure \en-chər\ see enture

ensus \en-səs\ census
consensus, dissensus
amanuensis

ent[1] \ent\ bent, Brent, cent, dent,
gent, Ghent, Gwent, hent, Kent, leant,
lent, Lent, meant, pent, rent, scent,
sent, sklent, spent, sprent, tent, Trent,
vent, went
  absent, accent, Advent, anent, ascent,
assent, augment, besprent, cement,
chimkent, comment, concent, consent,
content, convent, descent, detent,
dissent, docent, event, extent, ferment,
foment, forewent, forspent, fragment,
frequent, hell-bent, indent, intent,
invent, lament, loment, low-rent,
mordent, outspent, outwent, percent,
pigment, portent, present, prevent,
quitrent, relent, repent, resent,
segment, Tashkent, torment, unbent,
well-meant, wisent
  accident, aliment, argument,
circumvent, compartment,
complement, compliment, confident,
devilment, diffident, discontent,
document, evident, heaven-sent,
implement, instrument, Jack-a-Lent,
malcontent, nonevent, Occident,
ornament, orient, president, provident,
regiment, reinvent, represent, represent, resident, sediment, self-
content, Stoke on Trent, subsequent,
supplement, underwent

coincident, disorient, experiment,
ferro-cement, inconsequent,
misrepresent, nonresident,
privatdocent, self-evident

ent² \änt\ see ant²

ent³ \äⁿ\ see ant¹

enta \ent-ə\ menta, yenta
magenta, momenta, placenta,
polenta, tegmenta, tomenta
irredenta
impedimenta

entable \ent-ə-bəl\ fermentable,
presentable, preventable
documentable, representable,
sedimentable

entacle \ent-i-kəl\ see entical

entage \ent-ij\ tentage, ventage
percentage

ental \ent-ᵊl\ cental, dental, dentil,
gentle, lentil, mental, rental
cliental, fragmental, judgmental,
parental, placental, segmental
accidental, adjustmental,
apartmental, biparental,
compartmental, complemental,
condimental, continental,
departmental, detrimental,
documental, excremental, elemental,
firmamental, fundamental,
governmental, grandparental,
incidental, incremental, instrumental,
managemental, monumental,
nonjudgmental, occidental, oriental,
ornamental, regimental, rudimental,
sacramental, sentimental,
supplemental, temperamental,
transcendental, vestamental
coincidental, developmental,
environmental, experimental,
presentimental, subcontinental,
transcontinental, uniparental
intercontinental, interdepartmental,
intergovernmental, semigovernmental

entalist \ent-ᵊl-əst\ gentlest,
mentalist

documentalist, fundamentalist,
governmentalist, incrementalist,
instrumentalist, orientalist,
sacramentalist, sentimentalist,
transcendentalist
environmentalist, experimentalist

entalness \ent-ᵊl-nəs\ see
entleness

entance \ent-ᵊns\ see entence

entary \en-trē\ gentry, sentry
passementerie, reentry, subentry
alimentary, complementary,
complimentary, documentary,
elementary, filamentary,
parliamentary, rudimentary,
sedimentary, supplementary,
tenementary, testamentary
integumentary, uncomplimentary,
unparliamentary
semidocumentary

entative \ent-ət-iv\ tentative
augmentative, fermentative,
frequentative, presentative,
preventative
argumentative, representative
misrepresentative

ente¹ \en-tā\ al dente
lentamente

ente² \ent-ē\ see enty

ente³ \änt\ see ant²

ented \ent-əd\ tented
augmented, contented, demented,
lamented, segmented, untented
battlemented, malcontented,
oriented, self-contented, unfrequented
unprecedented
overrepresented, underrepresented
—also -ed forms of verbs listed at
ent¹

enten \ent-ᵊn\ Benton, dentin,
Denton, Kenton, Lenten, Quentin,
Trenton

entence \ent-ᵊns\ sentence
repentance

enter \ent-ər\ center, enter, mentor,
renter, stentor, tenter, venter
  assenter, augmentor, cementer,
concenter, consenter, dissenter,
fermenter, frequenter, incenter,
indenter, inventor, precentor,
preventer, rack-renter, reenter,
repenter, subcenter, tormentor
  documenter, epicenter, hypocenter,
metacenter, representer,
supplementer
    experimenter, hundred-percenter

entered \en-tərd\ centered
  face-centered, self-centered
  body-centered
  —*also* -ed *forms of verbs listed at*
enter

enterie \en-trē\ see **entary**

entful \ent-fəl\ eventful, resentful
uneventful

enth \enth\ nth, strength, tenth
crème de menthe

enthe \enth\ see **enth**

enthesis \en-thə-səs\ epenthesis,
parenthesis

enti \ent-ē\ see **enty**

entia \en-chə\ dementia, Florentia,
sententia, Valencia
  differentia, in absentia

ential \en-chəl\ cadential,
consensual, credential, demential,
essential, eventual, potential,
prudential, sciential, sentential,
sequential, tangential, torrential
  componential, conferential,
confidential, consequential,
deferential, differential, evidential,
existential, expedential, exponential,
inessential, inferential, influential,
nonessential, penitential, pestilential,
preferential, presidential, providential,
referential, residential, reverential,
transferential, unessential
    circumferential, equipotential,
experiential, inconsequential,

intelligential, interferential,
jurisprudential, multipotential,
reminiscential

entialist \en-chə-ləst\ essentialist
existentialist

entian \en-chən\ see **ension**

entiary \ench-rē\ century
penitentiary
plenipotentiary

entic \ent-ik\ lentic
  argentic, authentic, crescentic,
identic
  inauthentic

entical \ent-i-kəl\ denticle, pentacle,
tentacle
  conventicle, identical
  nonidentical, self-identical

entice \ent-əs\ see **entous**

enticle \ent-i-kəl\ see **entical**

entient \en-chənt\ penchant,
sentient, trenchant
  dissentient, insentient, presentient

entil \ent-ᵊl\ see **ental**

entin \ent-ᵊn\ see **enten**

enting \ent-iŋ\ dissenting
unrelenting
  —*also* -ing *forms of verbs listed at*
ent[1]

ention \en-chən\ see **ension**

entionable \ench-nə-bəl\
mentionable, pensionable
unmentionable

entional \ench- nəl\ see **ensional**

entioned \en-chənd\
aforementioned, well-intentioned
  —*also* -ed *forms of verbs listed at*
ension

entioner \ench-nər\ mentioner,
pensioner, tensioner

entious \en-chəs\ abstentious,
contentious, dissentious, licentious,
pretentious, sententious, tendentious
conscientious, unpretentious

entis \ent-əs\ see entous

entist \ent-əst\ dentist
cinquecentist, irredentist

entity \en-ət-ē\ entity, lenity
amenity, identity, nonentity,
obscenity, serenity
coidentity, self-identity

entium \ent-ē-əm\ jus gentium
unnilpentium

entive \ent-iv\ adventive, attentive,
incentive, inventive, pendentive,
preventive, retentive
argumentive, disincentive, inattentive

entle \ent-ᵊl\ see ental

entleness \ent-ᵊl-nəs\ gentleness
accidentalness

entment \ent-mənt\ contentment,
presentment, resentment
discontentment, self-contentment

ento \en-tō\ cento, lento, Trento
memento, pimento, pimiento,
seicento, trecento
cinquecento, Papiamento,
portamento, quatrocento, Sacramento
aggiornamento, divertimento,
risorgimento
pronunciamento

enton \ent-ᵊn\ see enten

entor \ent-ər\ see enter

entous \ent-əs\ prentice
apprentice, argentous, momentous,
portentous
compos mentis, filamentous,
ligamentous
non compos mentis
in loco parentis

entral \en-trəl\ central, ventral
subcentral
dorsiventral

entress \en-trəs\ gentrice
inventress

entric \en-trik\ centric
acentric, concentric, dicentric,
eccentric
acrocentric, androcentric,
Christocentric, egocentric,
ethnocentric, Eurocentric, geocentric,
phallocentric, polycentric, theocentric,
topocentric
anthropocentric, areocentric,
Europocentric, heliocentric,
selenocentric

entrice \en-trəs\ see entress

entry \en-trē\ see entary

ents \ents\ gents
events
dollars-and-cents
—also -s, -'s, and -s' forms of nouns,
and -s forms of verbs, listed at ent¹

entual¹ \en-chə-wəl\ sensual
accentual, consensual, conventual,
eventual

entual² \en-chəl\ see ential

entum \ent-əm\ centum, mentum
cementum, momentum, per centum,
tegmentum, tomentum
argumentum

enture \en-chər\ bencher, censure,
denture, drencher, trencher, venture,
wencher
adventure, backbencher, debenture,
front-bencher, indenture, misventure
misadventure, peradventure

enturer \ench-rər\ censurer,
venturer
adventurer

enturess \ench-rəs\ see enturous

enturous \ench-rəs\ venturous
adventuress, adventurous

entury \ench-rē\ see entiary

enty \ent-ē\ plenty, sente, senti,
tenty, twenty

aplenty, licente
cognoscente, twenty-twenty
Deo volente
dolce far niente

enuis \en-yə-wəs\ see enuous

enum \en-əm\ see enom

enuous \en-yə-wəs\ strenuous,
tenuis, tenuous
ingenuous
disingenuous

enus[1] \ē-nəs\ genus, lenis, penis,
venous, Venus
Campinas, Delphinus, Maecenas,
Quirinus, silenus
intravenous

enus[2] \en-əs\ see enis[1]

eny \ā-nē\ see ainy

enys \en-əs\ see enis[1]

enza[1] \en-zə\ Penza
cadenza, credenza
influenza

enza[2] \en-sə\ Polenza, Vicenza
Piacenza

eo[1] \ā-ō\ mayo, Mayo
cacao, paseo, rodeo
aparejo, Bulawayo, cicisbeo, zapateo
Montevideo

eo[2] \ē-ō\ see io[2]

eoff[1] \ef\ see ef[1]

eoff[2] \ēf\ see ief[1]

eoffor \ef-ər\ see ephor

eolate \ē-ə-lət\ triolet
alveolate, areolate, urceolate

eoman \ō-mən\ see oman

eon[1] \ē-ən\ see ean[1]

eon[2] \ē-än\ eon, freon, neon, prion

eonid \ē-ə-nəd\ see eanid

eopard \ep-ərd\ jeopard, leopard,
peppered, shepard, shepherd

eopardess \ep-ərd-əs\ leopardess,
shepherdess

eople \ē-pəl\ people, pipal, steeple
craftspeople, dispeople, laypeople,
newspeople, salespeople,
spokespeople, townspeople,
tradespeople, tribespeople, unpeople,
workpeople
anchorpeople, businesspeople,
congresspeople

eopled \ē-pəld\ unpeopled
—also -ed forms of verbs listed at
eople

eordie \ord-ē\ see ordy[1]

eorem \ir-əm\ see erum

eorge \orj\ see orge

eorgian \or-jən\ see orgian

eorist \ir-əst\ see erist[1]

eoul \ōl\ see ole[1]

eous \ē-əs\ see eus[1]

ep \ep\ hep, pep, prep, rep, schlepp,
skep, step, steppe, strep, yep
Alep, crowstep, doorstep, footstep,
goose-step, instep, lockstep, misstep,
one-step, quickstep, salep, sidestep,
two-step, unstep
corbiestep, demirep, overstep, step-
by-step
Gaziantep

eparable \ep-rə-bəl\ reparable,
separable
inseparable, irreparable

epard \ep-ərd\ see eopard

epe \āp\ see ape[1]

epee \ē-pē\ see eepy

eper \ep-ər\ see epper

eperous \ep-rəs\ leprous
obstreperous

epey \ā-pē\ see apey

eph \ef\ see ef[1]

epha \ē-fə\ ephah
synalepha, synaloepha

ephalin \ef-ə-lən\ cephalin
encephalon, enkephalin
acanthocephalan

ephaly \ef-ə-lē\ anencephaly,
brachycephaly, microcephaly

ephen \ē-vən\ see even

epherd \ep-ərd\ see eopard

epherdess \ep-ərd-əs\ see
eopardess

ephone \ef-ə-nē\ see ephony

ephony \ef-ə-nē\ Stefanie, Stefany
Persephone, telephony

ephor \ef-ər\ deafer, ephor, feoffor,
heifer, zephyr
hasenpfeffer

ephrine \ef-rən\ epinephrine
norepinephrine

epht \eft\ see eft

ephyr \ef-ər\ see ephor

epi \ā-pē\ see apey

epid \ep-əd\ tepid, trepid
intrepid

epo \ēp-ō\ see epot

epot \ēp-ō\ depot, Ipo, pepo
el cheapo

epp \ep\ see ep

eppe \ep\ see ep

epped \ept\ see ept

epper \ep-ər\ hepper, leper, pepper,
stepper
Colepeper, Culpeper, sidestepper

eppy \ep-ē\ peppy, preppy
orthoepy

eprous \ep-rəs\ see eperous

eps \eps\ biceps, forceps, triceps
quadriceps

editio princeps
—also -s, -'s, and -s' forms of nouns,
and -s forms of verbs, listed at ep

epsis \ep-səs\ skepsis
prolepsis, syllepsis
omphaloskepsis

epsy \ep-sē\ catalepsy, epilepsy,
narcolepsy, nympholepsy

ept \ept\ crept, kept, sept, slept,
stepped, swept, wept
accept, adept, backswept, concept,
except, incept, inept, percept, precept,
transept, upswept, windswept, yclept
high-concept, intercept, nympholept,
overslept, self-concept
—also -ed forms of verbs listed at ep

eptable \ep-tə-bəl\ see eptible

eptacle \ep-ti-kəl\ skeptical
conceptacle, receptacle

epter \ep-tər\ see eptor

eptible \ep-tə-bəl\ acceptable,
perceptible, susceptible
imperceptible, insusceptible,
unacceptable

eptic \ep-tik\ peptic, septic, skeptic
aseptic, dyspeptic, eupeptic,
proleptic, sylleptic
antiseptic, cataleptic, epileptic,
narcoleptic, nympholeptic

eptical \ep-ti-kəl\ see eptacle

eptile \ep-tᵊl\ see eptal

eption \ep-shən\ conception,
deception, exception, inception,
perception, reception, subreption
apperception, contraception,
interception, misconception,
preconception, self-conception, self-
perception

eptional \ep-shnəl\ conceptional,
deceptional, exceptional
unexceptional

eptive \ep-tiv\ acceptive,
conceptive, deceptive, exceptive,

inceptive, perceptive, preceptive,
receptive, susceptive
apperceptive, contraceptive,
imperceptive

eptor \ep-tər\ scepter
accepter, acceptor, inceptor,
preceptor, receptor
intercepter, interceptor

eptual \ep-chəl\ conceptual,
perceptual

eptus \ep-təs\ conceptus
textus receptus

epy \ep-ē\ see eppy

epys \ēps\ Pepys
—also -s, -'s, and -s' forms of nouns,
and -s forms of verbs, listed at eep

equal \ē-kwəl\ equal, prequel,
sequel
coequal, unequal

eque \ek\ see eck

equel \ē-kwəl\ see equal

equence \ē-kwəns\ frequence,
sequence
infrequence, subsequence

equency \ē-kwən-sē\ frequency,
sequency
infrequency

equent \ē-kwənt\ frequent, sequent
infrequent

equer \ek-ər\ see ecker

er¹ \ā\ see ay¹

er² \er\ see are⁴

er³ \ər\ see eur¹

er⁴ \ir\ see eer²

era¹ \er-ə\ era, Sara, Sarah, sclera,
terra
caldera, Rivera, sierra, tiara
aloe vera, ciguatera, cordillera,
guayabera, habanera, Halmahera,
riviera, Riviera, Santa Clara

era² \ir-ə\ era, gerah, Hera, lira,
Pyrrha, sera, sirrah, Vera, wirra

chimaera, chimera, hetaera, lempira,
Madeira, mbira
Altamira

erable \ər-ə-bəl\ thurible
conferrable, deferrable, deterrable,
inferable, preferable, transferable

erah \ir-ə\ see era²

eral¹ \ir-əl\ Cyril, feral, seral,
spheral, virile

eral² \er-əl\ see eril

eral³ \ər-əl\ see erral

erald \er-əld\ Gerald, Harold,
herald, Jerald, Jerold, Jerrold
Fitzgerald, FitzGerald

eraph \er-əf\ see erif

erapy \er-əld\ therapy
chemotherapy, chronotherapy
aromatherapy

eratin \er-ət-ᵊn\ keratin, Sheraton
Samaritan

erative \er-ət-iv\ see arative¹

eraton \er-ət-ᵊn\ see eratin

erb \ərb\ blurb, curb, herb, kerb,
Serb, verb
acerb, adverb, disturb, exurb,
perturb, potherb, pro-verb, proverb,
reverb, suburb, superb

erbal \ər-bəl\ burble, gerbil, herbal,
verbal
deverbal, nonverbal, preverbal

erbalist \ər-bə-ləst\ herbalist,
verbalist
hyperbolist

erbally \ər-bə-lē\ verbally
hyperbole, nonverbally

erber \ər-bər\ see urber

erberis \ər-bər-əs\ berberis,
Cerberus

erberus \ər-bər-əs\ see erberis

erbet \ər-bət\ see urbit

erbia \ər-bē-ə\ see urbia

erbial \ər-bē-əl\ adverbial, proverbial

erbid \ər-bəd\ see urbid

erbil \ər-bəl\ see erbal

erbium \ər-bē-əm\ erbium, terbium ytterbium

erbole \ər-bə-lē\ see erbally

erbolist \ər-bə-ləst\ see erbalist

erby \ər-bē\ derby, Derby, herby, Kirby

ercal \ər-kəl\ see ircle

erce \ərs\ see erse

ercé \ers\ see arce[1]

ercel \ər-səl\ see ersal[1]

ercement \ər-smənt\ amercement, disbursement reimbursement

ercer \ər-sər\ see ursor

ercery \ərs-rē\ see ursary

erch \ərch\ see urch

ercia \ər-shə\ see ertia

ercial \ər-shəl\ Herschel, Hershel commercial, inertial controversial, uncommercial semicommercial

ercian \ər-shən\ see ertian

ercible \ər-sə-bəl\ see ersible

ercion \ər-zhən\ see ersion[1]

ercis \ər-səs\ see ersus

ercive \ər-siv\ see ersive

ercular \ər-kyə-lər\ see ircular

ercy \ər-sē\ Circe, mercy, Percy, pursy gramercy controversy

erd \ərd\ see ird

erde[1] \erd\ see aired

erde[2] \ərd\ see ird

erde[3] \ərd-ē\ see urdy

erder \ərd-ər\ birder, girder, herder murder self-murder, sheepherder

erderer \ərd-ər-ər\ see urderer

erdi[1] \ər-dē\ see urdy

erdi[2] \er-dē\ Verdi Monteverdi

erdin \ərd-ᵊn\ see urden

erding \ərd-iŋ\ wording sheepherding —also -ing forms of verbs listed at ird

erdu \ər-dü\ perdu, perdue, Urdu

erdue \ər-dü\ see erdu

erdure \ər-jər\ see erger

ere[1] \er\ see are[4]

ere[2] \er-ē\ see ary[1]

ere[3] \ir\ see eer[2]

ere[4] \ir-ē\ see eary

ere[5] \ər\ see eur[1]

e're \ē-ər\ see eer[1]

ère \er\ see are[4]

ereal \ir-ē-əl\ see erial

ereid \ir-ē-əd\ see eriod

erek \erik\ see eric[1]

erely \ir-lē\ see early[1]

erement \er-ə-mənt\ see eriment

erence[1] \ir-əns\ clearance adherence, appearance, coherence, inherence incoherence, interference, perseverance erence² \ər-əns\ see urrence

erence³ \er-əns\ see arence

erency¹ \ir-ən-sē\ coherency,
vicegerency

erency² \er-ən-sē\ see errancy

erent¹ \ir-ənt\ gerent
adherent, coherent, inherent,
sederunt, vicegerent
incoherent

erent² \er-ənt\ see arent¹

eren't¹ \ərnt\ see earnt

eren't² \ər-ənt\ see urrent

ereo \er-ē-ō\ see ario

ereous \ir-ē-əs\ see erious

erer \ir-ər\ see earer²

eres¹ \erz\ see airs

eres² \ir-ēz\ see eries

eres³ \ərs\ see ers

eresy \er-ə-sē\ clerisy, heresy

ereth \er-ət\ see erit

ereus \ir-ē-əs\ see erious

erf \ərf\ see urf

erg \ərg\ berg, burg, erg
Augsburg, Boksburg, exergue,
hamburg, Hamburg, Hapsburg,
homburg, iceberg, Lemberg, Limburg,
Lindbergh, Newburg, Pittsburgh,
Salzburg, Sandburg, Strasbourg,
svedberg, Tilburg
Drakensberg, Gutenberg, Harrisburg,
Inselberg, Königsberg, Luxembourg,
Magdeburg, Nuremberg, Rube
Goldberg, Toggenburg, Venusberg,
Wallenberg, Württemberg
Johannesburg, St. Petersburg, von
Hindenburg
Baden-Württemberg,
Pietermaritzburg, Yekaterinburg
Roodepoort-Maraisburg

ergative \ər-gə-tir\ ergative,
purgative

erge \ərj\ see urge

ergeant \är-jənt\ see argent

ergen \ər-gən\ Bergen
Spitzbergen

ergence \ər-jəns\ convergence,
divergence, emergence, immergence,
insurgence, resurgence, submergence

ergency \ər-jən-sē\ urgency
convergency, detergency, divergency,
emergency, insurgency
counterinsurgency

ergent \ər-jənt\ see urgent

ergeon \ər-jin\ see urgeon

erger \ər-jər\ merger, perjure,
purger, scourger, urger, verdure, verger
deterger

ergh \ərg\ see erg

ergic \ər-jik\ allergic, synergic,
theurgic
demiurgic, dramaturgic,
thaumaturgic
alpha-adrenergic, beta-adrenergic

ergid \ər-jid\ see urgid

ergne¹ \ərn\ see urn

ergne² \ern\ see ern¹

ergo \ər-gō\ ergo, Virgo

ergue \ərg\ see erg

ergy \ər-jē\ see urgy

eri¹ \er-ē\ see ary¹

eri² \ir-ē\ see eary

eria¹ \ir-ē-ə\ feria, Styria, Syria
Algeria, Assyria, asteria, bacteria,
collyria, criteria, diphtheria, Egeria,
franseria, Illyria, Liberia, Nigeria,
plumeria, porphyria, Siberia, wisteria
cafeteria, cryptomeria, latimeria,
opera seria, sansevieria, washateria

eria² \er-ē-ə\ see aria

erial \ir-ē-əl\ aerial, cereal, ferial,
serial
arterial, bacterial, empyreal, ethereal,
funereal, imperial, material, sidereal,
venereal, vizierial
immaterial, magisterial, managerial,
ministerial, presbyterial

erian¹ \ir-ē-ən\ Adlerian, Assyrian,
Aterian, Cimmerian, criterion,
Hesperian, Hutterian, Hyperion,
Iberian, Illyrian, Mousterian,
Mullerian, Pierian, Shakespearean,
Spencerian, Spenglerian, Sumerian,
valerian, Valerian, Wagnerian
Hanoverian, Presbyterian
Thraco-Illyrian

erian² \er-ē-ən\ see arian¹

eric¹ \er-ik\ Berwick, cleric, Derek,
derrick, Eric, Erich, Erik, ferric,
Herrick, xeric
aspheric, chimeric, choleric,
entheric, generic, Homeric, mesmeric,
numeric
atmospheric, cholesteric, climacteric,
congeneric, dysenteric, esoteric
alphanumeric

eric² \ir-ik\ lyric, pyric, pyrrhic,
spheric, xeric
aspheric, chimeric, empiric, satiric,
satyric
atmospheric, hemispheric,
panegyric, stratospheric

erica \er-i-kə\ erica, Erica, Erika
America
esoterica, North America, South
America
Latin America

erical¹ \er-i-kəl\ clerical
chimerical, numerical
anticlerical

erical² \ir-i-kəl\ lyrical, miracle,
spherical, spiracle
empirical
hemispherical

erich \erik\ see eric¹

erics \er-iks\ sferics
hysterics
—also -s, -'s, and -s' forms of nouns
listed at eric¹

eried \ir-ē-əd\ see eriod

eries \ir-ēz\ Ceres, series
dundrearies
miniseries
—also -s, -'s, and -s' forms of nouns,
and -s forms of verbs, listed at eary

erif \er-əf\ seraph, serif, sheriff,
teraph
sans serif

eriff \er-əf\ see erif

erik \erik\ see eric¹

erika \er-i-kə\ see erica

eril \er-əl\ beryl, Beryl, Cheryl,
Errol, feral, ferrule, ferule, Merrill,
peril, Sherrill, Sheryl, sterile, Terrell,
Terrill
imperil
chrysoberyl

erilant \er-ə-lənt\ see erulent

erile \er-əl\ see eril

erilous \er-ə-ləs\ perilous, querulous
glomerulus

eriment \er-ə-mənt\ cerement
experiment
gedankenexperiment

erin \er-ən\ see aron¹

ering \ar-iŋ\ see aring¹

eriod \ir-ē-əd\ myriad, nereid,
Nereid, period
photoperiod

erion \ir-ē-ən\ see erian¹

erior \ir-ē-ər\ querier
anterior, exterior, inferior, interior,
posterior, superior, ulterior
Lake Superior
—also -er forms of adjectives listed
at eary

eriot \er-ē-ət\ see ariat¹

erious \ir-ē-əs\ cereus, Nereus, serious, Sirius
cinereous, delirious, Guarnerius, imperious, mysterious, Tiberius
deleterious

eris¹ \ir-əs\ see erous

eris² \er-əs\ see errous

erist¹ \ir-əst\ querist, theorist, verist
careerist
panegyrist
— *also* -est *forms of adjectives listed at* eer²

erist² \er-əst\ see arist

erisy \er-ə-sē\ see eresy

erit \er-ət\ ferret, merit, terret
demerit, inherit
disinherit
Shemini Atzereth

eritable \er-ət-ə-bəl\ heritable, veritable
inheritable

eritor \er-ət-ər\ ferreter, heritor
inheritor

erity \er-ət-ē\ ferity, ferrety, rarity, verity
asperity, celerity, dexterity, legerity, posterity, prosperity, severity, sincerity, temerity
insincerity
ambidexterity, subsidiarity

erium \ir-ē-əm\ Miriam
bacterium, collyrium, criterium, delirium, imperium, psalterium
atmospherium, magisterium
archaeobacterium

erius¹ \er-ē-əs\ see arious

erius² \ir-ē-əs\ see erious

erjure \ər-jər\ see erger

erjury \ərj-rē\ perjury, surgery
microsurgery, neurosurgery

erk \ərk\ see ork¹

erker \ər-kər\ see orker¹

erkin \ər-kən\ see irkin

erking \ər-kiŋ\ see orking

erkly \ər-klē\ clerkly
berserkly

erky \ər-kē\ birkie, jerky, murky, perky, smirky, turkey, Turkey, Turki
Albuquerque, herky-jerky

erle \ərl\ see irl¹

erlie \er-lē\ see airly

erlin \ər-lən\ merlin, Merlin, merlon, Merlyn, purlin, yearling

erling \ər-liŋ\ see urling

erlon \ər-lən\ see erlin

erlyn \ər-lən\ see erlin

erm \ərm\ see orm¹

erma \ər-mə\ dharma, Erma, herma, Irma
scleroderma, terra firma

ermal \ər-məl\ dermal, thermal
nonthermal, subdermal, transdermal
ectodermal, endothermal, epidermal, exothermal, hydrothermal, hypodermal, hypothermal

erman \ər-mən\ ermine, german, German, germen, Herman, Hermann, merman, sermon, Sherman, Thurman, vermin
determine, extermine, Mount Hermon
cousin-german, predetermine
Tibeto-Burman

ermanent \ərm-nənt\ permanent
determinant, impermanent
semipermanent

ermann \ər-mən\ see erman

ermary \ərm-rē\ see irmary

erment \ər-mənt\ averment, conferment, deferment, determent, interment, preferment
disinterment

ermer \ər-mər\ see urmur

ermes \ər-mēz\ Hermes, kermes

ermi \ər-mē\ see ermy

ermic \ər-mik\ dharmic, thermic
geothermic, hypodermic, taxidermic
electrothermic

ermin \ər-mən\ see erman

erminable \ərm-nə-bəl\ terminable
determinable, interminable
indeterminable

erminal \ərm-nəl\ germinal,
terminal
preterminal, subterminal

erminant \ərm-nənt\ see ermanent

ermine \ər-mən\ see erman

ermined \ər-mənd\ ermined
determined
self-determined
overdetermined

erminous \ər-mə-nəs\ terminus,
verminous
conterminous, coterminous

erminus \ər-mə-nəs\ see erminous

ermis \ər-məs\ dermis, kermis,
kirmess, thermos
endodermis, epidermis, exodermis

ermit \ər-mət\ hermit, Kermit,
Thermit

ermon \ər-mən\ see erman

ermos \ər-məs\ see ermis

ermy \ər-mē\ fermi, germy, squirmy,
wormy
diathermy, endothermy, taxidermy

ern[1] \ern\ bairn, Bern, cairn, hern,
Nairn
Auvergne, moderne, Pitcairn,
Sauternes, Ygerne
art moderne

ern[2] \ərn\ see urn

erna \ər-nə\ dharna, Myrna, sterna,
Verna
cisterna

ernal \ərn-ᵊl\ colonel, journal,
kernel, sternal, vernal
diurnal, eternal, external, fraternal,
hibernal, infernal, internal, maternal,
nocturnal, paternal, supernal
coeternal, sempiternal
semidiurnal

ernary \ər-nə-rē\ fernery, ternary,
turnery
quaternary

erne[1] \ern\ see ern[1]

erne[2] \ərn\ see urn

erned \ərnd\ see urned

ernel \ərn-ᵊl\ see ernal

erner \ər-nər\ see urner

ernes[1] \ern\ see ern[1]

ernes[2] \ərn\ see urn

ernest \ər-nəst\ see ernist

ernia \ər-ne-ə\ hernia
Hibernia

ernian \ər-nē-ən\ Hibernian,
quaternion, Saturnian

ernible \ər-nə-bəl\ see urnable

ernie \ər-nē\ see ourney[1]

ernier \ər-nē-ər\ see ourneyer

ernion \ər-nē-ən\ see ernian

ernist \ər-nəst\ earnest, Earnest,
Ernest
internist

ernity \ər-nət-ē\ eternity, fraternity,
maternity, modernity, paternity,
quaternity
coeternity, confraternity,
sempiternity

ernment \ərn-mənt\ adjournment,
attornment, concernment,
discernment, internment

ernum \ər-nəm\ see urnum

erny \ər-nē\ see ourney[1]

ero[1] \ē-rō\ giro, gyro, hero, Hero, Nero, zero
　subzero
　antihero, superhero

ero[2] \er-ō\ aero, cero, Duero, Faeroe, faro, Faroe, pharaoh, taro, tarot
　bolero, bracero, cruzeiro, Guerrero, Herero, Madero, montero, pampero, primero, ranchero, sombrero, torero, vaquero
　burladero, caballero, Mescalero, novillero
　banderillero, carabinero, embarcadero
　Rio de Janeiro

ero[3] \ir-ō\ giro, guiro, gyro, hero, zero
　primero

erod \er-əd\ Herod
　out-Herod, viverrid

erold \er-əld\ see erald

eron \er-ən\ see aron[1]

erous \ir-əs\ cerous, cirrus, Eris, peeress, Pyrrhus, scirrhous, seeress, serous

erp \ərp\ see urp

erpe \ər-pē\ see irpy

erque \ər-kē\ see erky

err[1] \er\ see are[4]

err[2] \ər\ see eur[1]

erra \er-ə\ see era[1]

errable \ər-ə-bəl\ see erable

errace \er-əs\ see errous

erral \ər-əl\ bharal, scurrile, squirrel
　conferral, deferral, demurral, referral, transferal

errance \er-əns\ see arence

errancy \er-ən-sē\ errancy
　aberrancy, coherency, inerrancy

errand \er-ənd\ errand, gerund

errant \er-ənt\ see arent[1]

erre \er\ see are[4]

errell \er-əl\ see eril

errence[1] \ər-əns\ see urrence

errence[2] \er-əns\ see arence

errent \ər-ənt\ see urrent

errer \ər-ər\ burrer, stirrer
　conferrer, deferrer, demurrer, deterrer, inferrer, preferrer, referrer, transferrer

erret \er-ət\ see erit

erreter \er-ət-ər\ see eritor

erria \er-ē-ə\ see aria

errible \er-ə-bəl\ see earable[1]

erric \er-ik\ see eric[1]

errick \er-ik\ see eric[1]

errid \er-əd\ see erod

errie \er-ē\ see ary[1]

erried \er-ēd\ berried, serried, varied
　—also -ed forms of verbs listed at ary[1]

errier \er-ē-ər\ burier, terrier, varier
　bullterrier
　—also -er forms of adjectives listed at ary[1]

errill \er-əl\ see eril

errily \er-ə-lē\ see arily

erring[1] \ar-iŋ\ see aring[1]

erring[2] \ər-iŋ\ see urring

erris \er-əs\ see errous

errol \er-əl\ see eril

errold \er-əld\ see erald

erron \er-ən\ see aron[1]

error \er-ər\ see earer[1]

errous \er-əs\ derris, Eris, ferrous, parous, terrace
nonferrous
millionairess

errule \er-əl\ see eril

erry \er-ē\ see ary[1]

ers[1] \ərz\ furze, hers
somewheres
Voyageurs
—*also* -s, -'s, *and* -s' *forms of nouns, and* -s *forms of verbs, listed at* eur[1]

ers[2] \ā\ see ay[1]

ersa \ər-sə\ bursa, Bursa
vice versa

ersable \ər-sə-bəl\ see ersible

ersal[1] \ər-səl\ bursal, tercel, versal
dispersal, rehearsal, reversal,
transversal, traversal
universal

ersal[2] \är-səl\ see arsal

ersant \ərs-ᵊnt\ versant
conversant

ersary \ərs-rē\ see ursary

erse \ərs\ birse, burse, curse, Erse,
hearse, nurse, perse, purse, terce,
terse, thyrse, verse, worse
adverse, amerce, asperse, averse,
coerce, commerce, converse, cutpurse,
disburse, disperse, diverse, immerse,
inverse, Nez Perce, obverse, perverse,
rehearse, reverse, sesterce, stress-
verse, submerse, transverse, traverse
intersperse, reimburse, universe

ersed \ərst\ see urst

erser \ər-sər\ see ursor

ersey \ər-zē\ furzy, jersey, Jersey,
kersey, Mersey
New Jersey

erschel \ər-shəl\ see ercial

ershel \ər-shəl\ see ercial

ersial \ər-shəl\ see ercial

ersian \ər-zhən\ see ersion[1]

ersible \ər-sə-bəl\ coercible,
conversable, dispersible, eversible,
immersible, reversible, submersible,
traversable
incoercible, irreversible
semisubmersible

ersion[1] \ər-zhən\ Persian, version
aspersion, aversion, coercion,
conversion, dispersion, diversion,
emersion, eversion, excursion,
immersion, incursion, inversion,
perversion, recursion, reversion,
submersion, subversion
ambiversion, extroversion,
interspersion, introversion,
reconversion, retroversion
animadversion, seroconversion

ersion[2] \ər-shən\ see ertian

ersional \ərzh-nəl\ versional
conversional, reversional

ersionist \ərzh-nəst\ diversionist,
excursionist

ersity[1] \ər-sət-ē\ adversity, diversity
multiversity, university
biodiversity

ersity[2] \ər-stē\ see irsty

ersive \ər-siv\ cursive
ambersive, aversive, coercive,
detersive, discursive, dispersive,
excursive, inversive, perversive,
recursive, subversive
extroversive, introversive

erson \ərs-ᵊn\ person, worsen
chairperson, craftsperson,
draftsperson, houseperson,
MacPherson, newsperson, nonperson,
salesperson, spokesperson, unperson
anchorperson, businessperson,
gentleperson, weatherperson

erst \ərst\ see urst

ersted \ər-stəd\ oersted, worsted
kilooersted

ersus \ər-səs\ cercis, thyrsus, versus
excursus

ersy \ər-sē\ see ercy

ert¹ \ərt\ Bert, blurt, Burt, chert,
curt, dirt, flirt, girt, hurt, Kurt, pert,
quirt, shirt, skirt, spurt, squirt, sturt,
vert, wert, wort
advert, alert, assert, avert, bellwort,
birthwort, Blackshirt, brownshirt,
Cape Vert, colewort, concert, convert,
covert, desert, dessert, dissert, divert,
evert, exert, expert, exsert, figwort,
fleawort, frankfurt, glasswort,
hoopskirt, hornwort, inert, insert,
invert, lousewort, lungwort, madwort,
milkwort, nightshirt, outskirt, overt,
pervert, pilewort, ragwort, redshirt,
revert, ribwort, saltwort, sandwort,
seagirt, Schubert, soapwort,
spearwort, spleenwort, stitchwort,
stonewort, subvert, sweatshirt,
toothwort, T-shirt, ungirt
ambivert, bladderwort, butterwort,
controvert, disconcert, extrovert,
feverwort, inexpert, introvert,
liverwort, malapert, miniskirt,
mitrewort, moneywort, overshirt,
overskirt, pennywort, pettiskirt,
preconcert, reconvert, Saint-John's-
wort, spiderwort, swallowwort,
thoroughwort, undershirt, underskirt
animadvert, interconvert

ert² \er\ see are⁴

ert³ \at\ see at⁵

erta \ərt-ə\ Gerta
Alberta, Roberta

ertain \ərt-ᵊn\ burton, Burton,
certain, curtain, Merton
uncertain

ertant \ərt-ᵊnt\ see ertent

erted \ərt-əd\ skirted
concerted, perverted, T-shirted
extroverted, miniskirted,
undershirted

— *also* -ed *forms of verbs listed at*
ert¹

ertedly \ərt-əd-lē\ assertedly,
concertedly, pervertedly

ertence \ərt-ᵊns\ advertence
inadvertence

ertent \ərt-ᵊnt\ advertent, revertant
inadvertent

erter \ərt-ər\ blurter, skirter,
squirter, stertor
converter, inverter, subverter
controverter
—*also* -er *forms of adjectives listed*
at ert¹

ertes¹ \ərt-ēz\ certes
Laertes

ertes² \ərts\ see erts

ertford \ärt-fərd\ see artford

erth \ərth\ see irth

ertha \ər-thə\ Bertha, Eartha

ertia \ər-shə\ Mercia, Murcia
inertia

ertial \ər-shəl\ see ercial

ertian \ər-shən\ Mercian, tertian
assertion, Cistercian, desertion,
exertion, insertion
self-assertion

ertible \ərt-ə-bəl\ convertible,
invertible
controvertible, inconvertible
incontrovertible, interconvertible

ertile \ərt-ᵊl\ curtal, fertile, hurtle,
kirtle, myrtle, Myrtle, spurtle, turtle
cross-fertile, exsertile, infertile
interfertile

ertinence \ərt-ᵊn-əns\ pertinence,
purtenance
appurtenance, impertinence

ertinent¹ \ərt-ᵊn-ənt\ pertinent
appurtentant, impertinent

ertinent² \ərt-nənt\ see irtinent

erting \ərt-iŋ\ shirting, skirting
disconcerting, self-asserting
—*also* -ing *forms of verbs listed at*
ert¹

ertion \ər-shən\ see ertian

ertisement \ərt-əs-mənt\
advertisement, divertissement

ertium \ər-shəm\ see urtium

ertive \ərt-iv\ furtive
assertive
self-assertive, unassertive

erton \ərt-n\ see ertain

ertor \ərt-ər\ see erter

erts \ərts\ certes, hertz, nerts
weltschmerz
gigahertz, kilohertz, megahertz
—*also* -s, -'s, *and* -s' *forms of nouns,*
and -s *forms of verbs, listed at* ert¹

erty \ər-tē\ see irty

ertz \ərts\ see erts

erule \er-əl\ see eril

erulent \er-ə-lənt\ sterilant
puberulent, pulverulent

erulous \er-ə-ləs\ see erilous

erum \ir-əm\ theorem, serum

erund \er-ənd\ see errand

erunt \er-ənt\ see arent¹

erval \ər-vəl\ see ervil

ervancy \ər-vən-sē\ see ervency

ervant \ər-vənt\ fervent, servant
maidservant, manservant, observant

ervative \ər-vət-iv\ conservative,
preservative
archconservative
neoconservative, semiconservative

ervator \ər-vət-ər\ see ervitor

erve \ərv\ curve, MIRV, nerve,
serve, swerve, verve
conserve, deserve, disserve, hors
d'oeuvre, incurve, observe, preserve,
reserve, self-serve, subserve, unnerve
unreserve

erved \ərvd\ nerved
decurved, deserved, recurved,
reserved
underserved, unreserved
— *also* -ed *forms of verbs listed at*
erve

ervency \ər-vən-sē\ fervency
conservancy

ervent \ər-vənt\ see ervant

erver \ər-vər\ fervor, server
deserver, observer, preserver,
timeserver

ervice \ər-vəs\ nervous, service
disservice, full-service, in-service,
self-service
interservice

ervil \ər-vəl\ chervil, serval, servile

ervile \ər-vəl\ see ervil

erviness \ər-vē-nəs\ nerviness
topsy-turviness

erving \ər-viŋ\ Irving, serving
deserving, self-serving, timeserving,
unswerving
—*also* -ing *forms of verbs listed at*
erve

ervitor \ər-vət-ər\ servitor
conservator

ervor \ər-vər\ see erver

ervous \ər-vəs\ see ervice

ervy \ər-vē\ see urvy

erwick \er-ik\ see eric¹

erwin \ər-wən\ Irwin, Sherwin

ery¹ \er-ē\ see ary¹

ery² \ir-ē\ see eary

eryl \er-əl\ see eril

erz \erts\ see ertz¹

es¹ \ā\ see ay¹

es² \ās\ see ace¹

es³ \āz\ see aze¹

es⁴ \es\ see ess

es⁵ \ēz\ see eze

e's \ēz\ see eze

esa¹ \ā-sə\ mesa, Mesa, presa
omasa, Teresa, Theresa

esa² \ā-zə\ presa
impresa, marchesa
Bel Paese
Maria Theresa

esage \es-ij\ see essage

esan¹ \āz-ᵊn\ see azon

esan² \ēz-ᵊn\ see eason

esant \ez-ᵊnt\ bezant, peasant,
pheasant, pleasant, present
unpleasant
omnipresent

esas \ā-zəs\ Marquesas
—also -s, -'s, and -s' forms of nouns
listed at esa²

esce \es\ see ess

escence \es-ᵊns\ essence
candescence, concrescence,
excrescence, florescence,
fluorescence, pearlescence,
pubescence, putrescence, quiescence,
quintessence, senescence, tumescence,
turgescence, virescence
acquiescence, adolescence,
arborescence, coalescence,
convalescence, decalescence,
defervescence, deliquescence,
detumescence, effervescence,
efflorescence, evanescence,
incandescence, inflorescence,
iridescence, juvenescence,

luminescence, obsolescence,
opalescence, prepubescence
preadolescence

escency \es-ᵊn-sē\ excrescency,
incessancy

escent \es-ᵊnt\ crescent, Crescent
candescent, canescent, concrescent,
decrescent, depressant, excrescent,
fluorescent, frutescent, incessant,
increscent, liquescent, pearlescent,
pubescent, putrescent, quiescent,
rufescent, senescent, suppressant,
tumescent, turgescent, virescent
acaulescent, acquiescent, adolescent,
arborescent, coalescent, convalescent,
detumescent, effervescent,
efflorescent, evanescent, incandescent,
inflorescent, intumescent, irridescent,
juvenescent, luminescent, opalescent,
phosphorescent, prepubescent,
recrudescent, viridescent
antidepressant, preadolescent

escible \es-ə-bəl\ see essible

escience \ēsh-əns\ nescience,
prescience

escive \es-iv\ see essive

esco \es-kō\ alfresco

escue \es-kyü\ fescue, rescue

ese¹ \ēs\ see iece

ese² \ēz\ see eze

ese³ \ā-sē\ see acy

esence \ez-ᵊns\ pleasance, presence
omnipresence

eseus \ē-sē-əs\ Theseus
Tiresias

esh¹ \esh\ crèche, flèche, flesh,
fresh, mesh, thresh
afresh, bobeche, calèche, crème
fraîche, enmesh, gooseflesh,
horseflesh, immesh, parfleche, refresh,
tête-bêche
Bangladesh, Gilgamesh, intermesh,
Marrakech

Andhra Pradesh, Madhya Pradesh,
Uttar Pradesh
Himachral Pradesh
Arunachal Pradesh

esh² \āsh\ see eche¹

esh³ \ash\ see ash³

eshed \esht\ fleshed, meshed
—also -ed forms of verbs listed at
esh¹

eshen \esh-ən\ see ession

eshener \esh-nər\ see essioner

esher \esh-ər\ see essure

eshly \esh-lē\ fleshly, freshly,
specially
especially

eshment \esh-mənt\ fleshment
enmeshment, refreshment

esi¹ \ā-zē\ see azy

esi² \ā-sē\ see acy

esia¹ \ē-shə\ geisha, Moesia
Letitia, Lucretia, Magnesia,
Phoenicia
alpoecia

esia² \ē-zhə\ freesia
amnesia, esthesia, frambesia,
magnesia, rafflesia, Silesia, Tunisia
analgesia, anesthesia, Austronesia,
Indonesia, Melanesia, Micronesia,
Polynesia, synesthesia

esial \ē-zē-əl\ mesial
ecclesial

esian¹ \ē-zhən\ Friesian, Frisian,
lesion
adhesion, Cartesian, cohesion,
etesian, Salesian
Austronesian, Holstein-Friesian,
Indonesian, Melanesian, Micronesian,
Polynesian

esian² \ē-shən\ see etion¹

esias \ē-sē-əs\ see eseus

esicant \es-i-kənt\ see esiccant

esiccant \es-i-kənt\ desiccant,
vesicant

esidency \ez-əd-ən-sē\ presidency,
residency
nonresidency, vice-presidency

esident \ez-əd-ənt\ president,
resident
nonresident, vice-president

esima \es-ə-mə\ Quinquagesima,
Sexagesima
Septuagesima

esimal \es-ə-məl\ centesimal,
millesimal, vigesimal
duodecimal, planetesimal,
sexagesimal
infinitesimal

esin \ez-ᵊn\ resin
muezzin
oleoresin

esion \ē-zhən\ see esian¹

esis \ē-səs\ Croesus, thesis, tmesis
ascesis, askesis, esthesis, mimesis,
prosthesis
anamnesis, catachresis, catechesis,
Dionysus, exegesis
hyperkinesis, Peloponnesus,
psychokinesis, telekinesis
amniocentesis

esium \ē-zē-əm\ see ezium

esive \ē-siv\ adhesive, cohesive
self-adhesive

esk \esk\ see esque

esley \es-lē\ see essly

eslie \es-lē\ see essly

esne \ēn\ see ine³

eso¹ \ā-sō\ peso, say-so

eso² \es-ō\ see esso

espass \es-pəs\ Thespis, trespass

espis \es-pəs\ see espass

espite \es-pət\ see espot

espot \es-pət\ despot, respite

ion

esque \esk\ desk
burlesque, grotesque, moresque
arabesque, Bunyanesque, copydesk,
gigantesque, humoresque, Junoesque,
Kafkaesque, picaresque, picturesque,
plateresque, Romanesque,
Rubenesque, sculpturesque, statuesque
churrigueresque

ess \es\ bless, cess, chess, cress,
dress, ess, fess, guess, Hesse, jess,
less, loess, mess, ness, press, s, stress,
tress, yes
abscess, access, address, aggress,
assess, caress, clothespress, coatdress,
compress, confess, CS, depress,
digress, distress, duress, egress,
excess, express, finesse, handpress,
headdress, housedress, impress,
ingress, largess, Meknes, nightdress,
noblesse, obsess, oppress, outguess,
pantdress, possess, precess, prestress,
princess, process, profess, progress,
recess, redress, regress, re-press,
repress, shirtdress, sidedress, SS,
success, sundress, suppress, top-dress,
transgress, undress, unless, winepress
ABS, acquiesce, baroness, coalesce,
convalesce, DES, decompress,
deliquesce, derepress, dispossess,
effervesce, effloresce, evanesce,
gentilesse, GR-S, IHS, in-process,
incandesce, intumesce, inverness,
Inverness, letterpress, luminesce,
Lyonnesse, minidress, nonetheless,
obsolesce, otherguess, overdress,
pennycress, phosphoresce, politesse,
prepossess, preprocess, recrudesce,
repossess, reprocess, retrogress,
second-guess, SOS, sweaterdress,
unsuccess, watercress, window-dress
another-guess, nevertheless

essa \es-ə\ see esse[3]

essable \es-ə-bəl\ see essible

essage \es-ij\ message, presage
expressage

essaly \es-ə-lē\ Cecily, Thessaly

essamine \es-mən\ see essman

essan \es-ᵊn\ see essen

essancy \es-ᵊn-sē\ see escency

essant \es-ᵊnt\ see escent

esse[1] \es\ see ess

esse[2] \es-ē\ see essy

esse[3] \es-ə\ Hesse
Odessa, Vanessa

essed \est\ see est

essedly \es-əd-lē\ blessedly,
confessedly, professedly, possessedly
self-possessedly

essel \es-əl\ see estle[1]

essen \es-ᵊn\ Essen, lessen, lesson,
messan
delicatessen

essence \es-ᵊns\ see escence

esser \es-ər\ see essor

essex \es-iks\ Essex, Wessex

essful \es-fəl\ stressful
distressful, successful
unsuccessful

essian \esh-ən\ see ession

essible \es-ə-bəl\ decibel
accessible, addressable,
compressible, confessable,
depressible, expressible, impressible,
processible, putrescible, suppressible
inaccessible, incompressible,
inexpressible, insuppressible,
irrepressible

essie \es-ē\ see essy

essile \es-əl\ see estle[1]

ession \esh-ən\ cession, freshen,
hessian, session
accession, aggression, compression,
concession, confession, depression,
digression, discretion, egression,
expression, impression, ingression,
obsession, oppression, possession,
precession, procession, profession,

progression, recession, refreshen,
regression, repression, secession,
succession, suppression, transgression
  decompression, dispossession,
indiscretion, intercession, intersession,
introgression, misimpression,
prepossession, reimpression,
repossession, retrogression, self-
confession, self-expression, self-
possession, supersession

essional \esh-nəl\ sessional
accessional, concessional,
congressional, diagressional,
expressional, obsessional,
possessional, precessional,
processional, professional,
progressional, recessional,
successional
  preprofessional, subprofessional
  paraprofessional, semiprofessional

essioner \esh-nər\ freshener
concessioner

essionist \esh-nəst\ expressionist,
impressionist, repressionist,
secessionist

essity \es-tē\ see esty

essive \es-iv\ crescive
aggressive, caressive, compressive,
concessive, degressive, depressive,
digressive, excessive, expressive,
impressive, ingressive, obsessive,
oppressive, possessive, progressive,
recessive, regressive, successive,
suppressive, transgressive
  inexpressive, retrogressive,
  unexpressive
  manic-depressive

essly \es-lē\ Leslie, Lesley, Wesley
expressly

essman \es-mən\ chessman,
pressman
  expressman, jessamine, specimen

essment \es-mənt\ see estment

esso \es-ō\ gesso
espresso

esson \es-ᵊn\ see essen

essor \es-ər\ dresser, guesser, lesser,
pressor, stressor
  addresser, aggressor, assessor,
caresser, compressor, confessor,
depressor, expressor, hairdresser,
oppressor, processor, professor,
regressor, repressor, successor,
suppressor, transgressor, vinedresser
  antecessor, dispossessor, intercessor,
predecessor, repossessor, second-
guesser
  microprocessor, multiprocessor

essory \es-ə-rē\ pessary
accessory, possessory
  intercessory

essure \esh-ər\ pressure
impressure, low-pressure, refresher
  acupressure, overpressure

essy \es-ē\ Bessie, dressy, Jesse,
Jessie, messy

est \est\ best, breast, Brest, chest,
crest, gest, geste, guest, hest, jessed,
jest, lest, nest, pest, prest, quest, rest,
test, tressed, vest, west, West, wrest,
zest
  abreast, appressed, armrest, arrest,
attest, backrest, beau geste, behest,
bequest, bird's-nest, celeste, Celeste,
compressed, congest, conquest,
contest, detest, devest, digest, divest,
egest, field-test, flight-test, footrest,
gabfest, hard-pressed, headrest,
hillcrest, houseguest, imprest, incest,
infest, ingest, inquest, interest, invest,
low-test, Mae West, Midwest, molest,
northwest, posttest, pretest, professed,
protest, redbreast, repressed, request,
retest, revest, slugfest, southwest,
suggest, trapnest, Trieste, t-test,
unblessed, undressed, unrest,
unstressed
  almagest, anapest, Bucharest,
Budapest, decongest, disinfest,
disinvest, empty-nest, galley-west,
manifest, north-northwest, palimpsest,
predigest, reinvest, rinderpest, second-
best, self-addressed, self-confessed,

self-interest, self-possessed,
sweatervest, uninterest, unprofessed
autosuggest, disinterest, robin
redbreast, supraprotest, underinvest
thirty-second rest
—*also* -ed *forms of verbs listed at*
ess

esta \es-tə\ cesta, cuesta, testa,
vesta, Vesta
Avesta, celesta, egesta, fiesta,
ingesta, siesta
Zend-Avesta

estable \es-tə-bəl\ see estible

estae \es-tē\ see esty

estal \es-tᵊl\ crestal, pestle, vestal

estan \es-tən\ see estine

estant \es-tənt\ arrestant,
contestant, infestant, protestant,
Protestant
decongestant, disinfestant,
manifestant

este \est\ see est

ested \es-təd\ bested, crested,
nested, tested, vested
time-tested
barrel-chested, double-breasted,
hairy-chested, indigested, single-
breasted
—*also* -ed *forms of verbs listed at*
est

ester \es-tər\ Chester, ester, Esther,
fester, Hester, jester, Leicester, Lester,
nester, Nestor, pester, quaestor,
quester, questor, nester, tester, wester,
yester, zester
ancestor, arrester, contester, detester,
digester, infester, investor,
Manchester, molester, northwester,
Rochester, semester, sequester,
southwester, sou'wester,
suggester, Sylvester, trimester,
Winchester
arbalester, empty-nester, monoester,
polyester

esti \es-tē\ see esty

estial \es-tē-əl\ celestial, forestial

estible \es-tə-bəl\ testable
comestible, detestable, digestible,
ingestible, investable, suggestible
incontestable, indigestible

estic \es-tik\ gestic
domestic, majestic
anapestic, catachrestic

estical \es-ti-kəl\ see esticle

esticle \es-ti-kəl\ testicle
catachrestical

estimate \es-tə-mət\ estimate,
guesstimate

estinate \es-tə-nət\ festinate
predestinate

estine \es-tən\ destine, Preston
Avestan, clandestine, intestine,
predestine

esting \es-tiŋ\ cresting, vesting,
westing
arresting
—*also* -ing *forms of verbs listed at*
est

estion \es-chən\ question
congestion, cross-question,
digestion, egestion, ingestion, self-
question, suggestion
decongestion, indigestion, self-
suggestion
autosuggestion

estis \es-təs\ cestus, testis
Alcestis, asbestos, Hephaestus

estival \es-tə-vəl\ estival, festival

estive \es-tiv\ festive, restive
congestive, digestive, egestive,
ingestive, suggestive
decongestive

estle¹ \es-əl\ Bessel, Cecil, decile,
nestle, pestle, sessile, trestle, vessel,
wrestle
Indian-wrestle

estle² \as-əl\ see assel²

estle³ \əs-əl\ see ustle

estless \est-ləs\ crestless, restless

estment \es-mənt\ vestment
arrestment, assessment, divestment,
impressment, investment
disinvestment, reinvestment

esto \es-tō\ pesto, presto
manifesto

eston \es-tən\ see estine

estor \es-tər\ see ester

estos \es-təs\ see estis

estra \es-trə\ fenestra, orchestra,
palaestra
Clytemnestra

estral \es-trəl\ estral, kestrel
ancestral, campestral, fenestral,
orchestral, semestral

estrel \es-trəl\ see estral

estress \es-trəs\ see estrus

estrial \es-trē-əl\ semestrial,
terrestrial
extraterrestrial

estrian \es-trē-ən\ equestrian,
pedestrian

estrous \es-trəs\ see estrus

estrum \es-trəm\ estrum
sequestrum

estrus \es-trəs\ estrous, estrus
ancestress

estry \es-trē\ vestry
ancestry

estuous \es-chə-wəs\ incestuous,
tempestuous

esture \es-chər\ gesture, vesture

estus \es-təs\ see estis

esty \es-tē\ chesty, pesty, testae,
testy, zesty
necessity, res gestae, Tibesti

esus \ē-səs\ see esis

et¹ \et\ bet, Bret, Brett, debt, et, fret,
get, jet, let, Lett, met, net, pet, ret, set,
stet, sweat, Tet, threat, vet, wet, whet,
yet
abet, aigrette, Annette, asset,
Babette, backset, baguette, banquette,
barbette, Barnet, Barnett, barquette,
barrette, beget, beset, blanquette,
boneset, brevet, briquette, brochette,
brunet, burette, burnet, cadet, cassette,
cermet, Claudette, Colette, coquet,
coquette, cornet, corselet, corvette,
coset, courgette, croquette, curette,
curvet, cuvette, daleth, dinette,
diskette, dragnet, duet, egret, fan-jet,
fishnet, flechette, forget, frisette,
gazette, georgette, Georgette, gillnet,
godet, grisette, handset, hard-set,
headset, ink-jet, inlet, inset, Janette,
Jeanette, Jeannette, Juliet, kismet,
layette, lorgnette, lunette, Lynette,
maquette, Marquette, mind-set,
moonset, moquette, motet, musette,
Nanette, Nannette, noisette, nonet,
nymphet, octet, offset, onset, Osset,
outlet, outset, paillette, palet, pallette,
palmette, Paulette, pipette, piquet,
planchette, poussette, preset, quartet,
quickset, quintet, raclette, ramet,
regret, reset, revet, rocket, roomette,
rosette, roulette, saw-whet, septet,
sestet, sextet, sharp-set, soubrette,
spinet, stylet, sublet, subset, sunset,
Syrette, tacet, thickset, Tibet, toilette,
tonette, trijet, twinset, typeset, unset,
upset, vedette, vignette, well-set,
Yvette
aiguillette, alphabet, anchoret,
andouilette, anisette, Antoinette,
avocet, banneret, basinet, bassinet,
bayonet, Bernadette, bobbinet,
briolette, burgonet, calumet, canzonet,
castanet, cellarette, chemisette,
cigarette, clarinet, consolette, coronet,
corselet, crepe suzette, dragonet,
electret, en brochette, epaulet, epithet,
etiquette, falconet, farmerette,
featurette, flageolet, flannelette,
guillemet, heavyset, jaconet, Juliett,
kitchenette, Lafayette, landaulet,
lanneret, launderette, Leatherette,

luncheonette, maisonette, majorette, marmoset, marquisette, martinet, mignonette, minaret, minuet, miquelet, novelette, Olivet, oubliette, parapet, paupiette, photoset, pirouette, quodlibet, rondelet, Samoset, satinet, scilicet, sermonette, serviette, silhouette, sobriquet, solleret, somerset, Somerset, soviet, spinneret, statuette, stockinette, suffragette, superjet, swimmeret, taboret, thermoset, towelette, trebuchet, tricolette, underlet, usherette, vinaigrette, wagonette
   analphabet, bachelorette, drum majorette, electrojet, Hospitalet, marionette, microcassette, micropipette, musique concrète, photo-offset, videlicet
   audiocassette, caulifloweret, hail-fellow-well-met, Marie Antoinette, videocassette

et² \ā\ see ay¹

et³ \āt\ see ate¹

et⁴ \es\ see ess

eta¹ \āt-ə\ see ata²

eta² \et-ə\ see etta

eta³ \ēt-ə\ see ita²

etable¹ \et-ə-bəl\ see ettable

etable² \ēt-ə-bəl\ see eatable

etal¹ \ēt-ᵊl\ beetle, betel, fetal
   decretal, excretal

etal² \et-ᵊl\ see ettle

etan¹ \et-ᵊn\ Breton, threaten
   Cape Breton, Tibetan

etan² \ēt-ᵊn\ see eaten¹

etch \ech\ catch, etch, fetch, fletch, ketch, kvetch, lech, letch, retch, sketch, stretch, vetch, wretch
   backstretch, homestretch, outstretch

etched \echt\ teched
   farfetched

—*also* -ed *forms of verbs listed at* etch

etcher \ech-ər\ etcher, catcher, fetcher, fletcher, Fletcher, lecher, sketcher, stretcher
   cowcatcher, dogcatcher, eye-catcher, flycatcher, gnatcatcher

etching \ech-iŋ\ etching, fletching
—*also* -ing *forms of verbs listed at* etch

etchy \ech-ē\ sketchy, stretchy, tetchy

ete¹ \āt\ see ate¹

ete² \et\ see et¹

ete³ \ēt\ see eat¹

ete⁴ \āt-ē\ see aty

ête \āt\ see ate¹

eted \ād\ see ade¹

etel \ēt-ᵊl\ see etal

etely \ēt-lē\ see eetly

eteor \ēt-ē-ə-ər\ meteor
   confiteor
—*also* -er *forms of adjectives listed at* eaty

eter \ēt-ər\ see eater¹

etera \e-trə\ see etra

eterate \et-ə-rət\ see eterit

eterit \et-ə-rət\ preterit
   inveterate

etes \ēt-əs\ see etus

eth¹ \eth\ Beth, breath, breadth, death, saith, Seth, snath
   daleth, handbreadth, hairbreadth, Macbeth
   Ashtoreth, isopleth, megadeath, shibboleth
   Elisabeth, Elizabeth

eth² \ās\ see ace¹

eth³ \āt\ see ate¹

eth⁴ \et\ see et¹

etha \ē-thə\ Aretha, Ibiza

ethane \e-thān\ ethane, methane
nitromethane
dichloroethane

ethe \ē-thē\ see eathy

ether¹ \e<u>th</u>-ər\ blether, feather,
heather, Heather, leather, nether,
tether, weather, wether, whether
aweather, bellwether, pinfeather,
together, untether
altogether, get-together

ether² \ə<u>th</u>-ər\ see other¹

ethic \eth-ik\ ethic
erethic

ethral \ē-thrəl\ urethral
bulbourethral

ethyl \eth-əl\ bethel, Ethel, ethyl,
methyl
triethyl

eti¹ \ēt-ē\ see eaty

eti² \āt-ē\ see aty

etia \ē-shə\ see esia¹

etian \ē-shən\ see etion¹

etic¹ \ēt-ik\ thetic
acetic, docetic

etic² \et-ik\ etic, thetic
aesthetic, ascetic, athletic, balletic,
bathetic, cosmetic, docetic, eidetic,
emetic, frenetic, gametic, genetic,
hermetic, kinetic, limnetic, magnetic,
mimetic, noetic, Ossetic, paretic,
pathetic, phenetic, phonetic, phrenetic,
phyletic, poetic, prophetic, prosthetic,
pyretic, splenetic, syncretic, syndetic,
synthetic, tonetic, Venetic
alphabetic, analgetic, anesthetic,
antithetic, apathetic, asyndetic,
copacetic, cybernetic, diabetic,
dietetic, digenetic, diphyletic, diuretic,
empathetic, energetic, epithetic,
geodetic, homiletic, Masoretic,

nomothetic, parenthetic, sympathetic,
synergetic, synesthetic
aeromagnetic, antimagnetic,
antipathetic, antipoetic, antipyretic,
apologetic, epexigetic, epigenetic,
ferrimagnetic, ferromagnetic,
geomagnetic, gyromagnetic,
homogametic, hydrokinetic,
hydromagnetic, hyperkinetic,
isomagnetic, monophyletic,
morphogenetic, ontogenetic,
optokinetic, palingenetic,
paramagnetic, pathogenetic,
peripatetic, phylogenetic,
polyphyletic, psychokinetic,
telekinetic, thermomagnetic
aposiopetic, cyanogenetic,
electrokinetic, electromagnetic,
heterogametic, parasympathetic,
parthenogenetic, psychotomimetic,
unapologetic
onomatopoetic

etical \et-i-kəl\ metical, reticle
aesthetical, genetical, heretical,
phonetical
antithetical, arithmetical,
catechetical, cybernetical, epithetical,
exegetical, geodetical, hypothetical,
parenthetical, theoretical
atheoretical, epexegetical

eticist \et-ə-səst\ geneticist,
kineticist
cyberneticist

etics \et-iks\ aesthetics, athletics,
genetics, kinetics, phonetics, poetics,
tonetics
cybernetics, dietetics, homiletics
apologetics, cytogenetics
immunogenetics
—also -s, -'s, and -s' forms of nouns
listed at etic

etid \et-əd\ fetid, fretted, sweated
indebted
parapeted
—also -ed forms of verbs listed at
et¹

etin \ēt-ᵊn\ see eaten¹

etion¹ \ē-shən\ Grecian
accretion, Capetian, completion,
concretion, deletion, depletion,
excretion, Ossetian, Phoenician,
repletion, secretion, suppletion,
Tahitian
Austronesian, Diocletian,
Melanesian, Polynesian
Taracahitian

etion² \esh-ən\ see ession

etious \ē-shəs\ see ecious

etis¹ \ēt-əs\ see etus

etis² \et-əs\ see ettuce

etist \et-əst\ cornetist, librettist,
vignettist
clarinetist, exegetist, operettist
—*also* -est *forms of adjectives listed
at* et¹

etitive \et-ət-iv\ competitive,
repetitive
uncompetitive
anticompetitive

etium \ē-shē-əm\ see ecium

etius \ē-shəs\ see ecious

etive \ēt-iv\ accretive, completive,
decretive, depletive, secretive,
suppletive

etl¹ \āt-ᵊl\ see atal

etl² \et-ᵊl\ see ettle

etland \et-lənd\ Shetland, wetland

etment \et-mənt\ abetment,
besetment, curettement, revetment

eto¹ \āt-ō\ see ato²

eto² \ēt-ō\ see ito¹

eton \ēt-ᵊn\ see eaten¹

etor¹ \et-ər\ see etter

etor² \ēt-ər\ see eater¹

etory \ēt-ə-rē\ eatery
decretory, secretory, suppletory

etous \ēt-əs\ see etus

etra¹ \e-trə\ Petra, tetra
etcetera

etra² \ē-trə\ Petra
Kenitra

etral¹ \ē-trəl\ petrel, retral

etral² \e-trəl\ see etrel¹

être \etr³\ fête champêtre, raison
d'être

etrel¹ \e-trəl\ petrel, petrol, retral

etrel² \ē-trəl\ see etral¹

etric \e-trik\ metric
obstetric, symmetric
asymmetric, barometric, decametric,
dekametric, diametric, dissymmetric,
geometric, hypsometric, isometric,
optometric, psychometric, telemetric,
volumetric
acidometric, amperometric,
sociometric

etrical \e-tri-kəl\ metrical
obstetrical, symmetrical
asymmetrical, barometrical,
diametrical, geometrical,
unsymmetrical

etrics \e-triks\ obstetrics
geometrics, isometrics, sabermetrics

etrist \e-trəst\ metrist
belletrist

etrol \e-trəl\ see etrel¹

ets \ets\ let's
Donets, rillettes, Steinmetz
pantalets, solonetz, Sosnowiec
—*also* -s, -'s, *and* -s' *forms of nouns,
and* -s *forms of verbs, listed at* et¹

etsk \etsk\ Donetsk, Kuznetsk,
Lipetsk
Novokuznetsk

ett \et\ see et¹

etta \et-ə\ betta, Etta, feta, geta,
Greta, Quetta

biretta, cabretta, galleta, Loretta,
mozzetta, pancetta, poinsettia,
Rosetta, Valletta, vendetta
anchoveta, arietta, cabaletta,
Henrietta, Marietta, operetta,
sinfonietta

ettable \et-ə-bəl\ retable, wettable
forgettable, regrettable
unforgettable

ette \et\ see et[1]

etter \et-ər\ better, bettor, debtor,
fetter, getter, letter, netter, rhetor,
setter, sweater, tetter, wetter, whetter
abettor, begetter, bonesetter, enfetter,
gill-netter, go-getter, jet-setter,
newsletter, pacesetter, pinsetter, red-
letter, regretter, trendsetter, typesetter,
unfetter, vignetter
carburettor
—also -er forms of adjectives listed
at et[1]

ettered \et-ərd\ fettered, lettered
unfettered, unlettered

ettes \ets\ see ets

ettia \et-ə\ see etta

ettie \et-ē\ see etty[1]

ettier \it-ē-ər\ see ittier

ettiness \it-ē-nəs\ see ittiness

etting \et-iŋ\ netting, setting
bed-wetting, bloodletting, go-
getting, onsetting, typesetting
thermosetting
phototypesetting
—also -ing forms of verbs listed at
et[1]

ettish \et-ish\ fetish, Lettish, pettish,
wettish
coquettish
novelettish

ettle \et-ᵊl\ fettle, kettle, metal,
mettle, nettle, petal, settle, shtetl
bimetal, gunmetal, nonmetal,
teakettle, unsettle

Citialtepetl
Popocatepetl

ettlesome \et-ᵊl-səm\ mettlesome,
nettlesome

ettling \et-liŋ\ fettling, settling
unsettling
—also -ing forms of verbs listed at
ettle

etto \et-ō\ ghetto, stretto
cavetto, falsetto, in petto, larghetto,
libretto, palmetto, stiletto, zucchetto
allegretto, amaretto, amoretto,
fianchetto, Kazan Retto, lazaretto,
Tintoretto, vaporetto

ettor \et-ər\ see etter

ettuce \et-əs\ lettuce, Thetis
Hymettus

ettus \et-əs\ see ettuce

etty[1] \et-ē\ Betty, jetty, Nettie, netty,
petit, petty, sweaty, yeti
brown Betty, cavetti, confetti,
libretti, machete, Rossetti, spaghetti
amoretti, cappelletti, cavalletti,
Donizetti, Serengeti, spermacetti,
vaporetti

etty[2] \it-ē\ see itty

etum \ēt-əm\ pinetum
arboretum, equisetum

etus \ēt-əs\ Cetus, fetus, Thetis,
treatise
acetous, Admetus, boletus, coitus,
quietus
diabetes

etzsche \ē-chē\ see eachy

euben \ü-bən\ Cuban, Reuben,
Ruben
von Steuben

euce \üs\ see use[1]

euced \ü-səd\ see ucid

eucey \ü-sē\ see uicy

euch \ük\ see uke

euchre \ü-kər\ see ucre

eucid \ü-səd\ see ucid

eud[1] \üd\ see ude

eud[2] \o͝id\ see oid[1]

eudal \üd-ᵊl\ see oodle

eudist \üd-əst\ see udist[1]

eudo \üd-ō\ see udo

eue \ü\ see ew[1]

euer \ü-ər\ see ewer[1]

euil \āl\ see ail

euille \ē\ see ee[1]

euk \ük\ see uke

eukin \ü-kən\ see ucan

eul[1] \əl\ see ull[1]

eul[2] \ərl\ see irl[1]

eulah \ü-lə\ see ula

eulean \ü-lē-ən\ see ulean

eum[1] \ē-əm\ geum
lyceum, museum, no-see-um,
odeum, per diem, Te Deum
athenaeum, coliseum, colosseum,
hypogcum, mausoleum

eum[2] \ā-əm\ see ahum

eum[3] \üm\ see oom[1]

euma \ü-mə\ see uma

eume \üm\ see oom[1]

eumon \ü-mən\ see uman

eumy \ü-mē\ see oomy

eunice \ü-nəs\ see ewness

eunt \u͝nt\ see unt[1]

eunuch \ü-nik\ see unic

eur[1] \ər\ birr, blur, buhr, burr, Burr,
chirr, churr, cur, curr, err, fir, for, fur,
her, knur, murre, myrrh, per, purr,
shirr, sir, skirr, slur, spur, stir, thir,
'twere, were, whir, your, you're
as per, astir, auteur, aver, bestir,
chasseur, chauffeur, claqueur, coiffeur,
concur, confer, danseur, defer, demur,
deter, douceur, du jour, farceur,
flaneur, friseur, frondeur, hauteur,
him/her, his/her, incur, infer, inter,
jongleur, larkspur, liqueur, longspur,
masseur, millefleur, occur, Pasteur,
poseur, prefer, recur, refer, sandbur,
sandspur, seigneur, transfer, voyeur
accoucheur, amateur, cocklebur,
colporteur, connoisseur, cri de coeur,
cross-refer, cubature, curvature, de
rigueur, disinter, force majeure, franc-
tireur, monseigneur, nonconcur,
pasticheur, prosateur, raconteur,
rapporteur, regisseur, saboteur,
secateur, underfur, voyageur
arbitrageur, carillonneur,
entrepreneur, litterateur, provocateur,
restaurateur
conglomerateur
agent provocateur

eur[2] \u͝r\ see ure[1]

eure \ər\ see eur[1]

eurial \u͝r-ē-əl\ see urial[1]

eurish \ər-ish\ see ourish

eurs \ərz\ see ers[1]

eury \u͝r-ē\ see ury[1]

eus[1] \ē-əs\ Aeneas, Aggeus,
Alpheus, Arius, Chryseis, Linnaeus,
Micheas, Piraeus, uraeus
coryphaeus, epigeous, scarabaeus
prelate nullius
Duque de Caxias, Judas Maccabaeus

eus[2] \üs\ see use[1]

euse[1] \əz\ buzz, 'cause, coz, does,
fuzz, 'twas, was
abuzz, because, outdoes, undoes
overdoes

euse[2] \üs\ see use[1]

euse[3] \üz\ see use[2]

eusel[1] \ü-səl\ see usal[1]

eusel[2] \ü-zəl\ see usal[2]

eut \üt\ see ute

euter \üt-ər\ see uter

euth \üth\ see ooth[2]

eutian \ü-shən\ see ution

eutic \üt-ik\ see utic

eutical \üt-i-kəl\ see utical

eutics \üt-iks\ toreutics
hermeneutics, therapeutics

eutist \üt-əst\ see utist

euton \üt-ᵊn\ see utan

eutonist \üt-ᵊn-əst\ see utenist

euve \əv\ see ove[1]

euver \ü-vər\ see over[3]

eux \ü\ see ew[1]

ev[1] \ef\ see ef[1]

ev[2] \ȯf\ see off[2]

eva \ē-və\ see iva[2]

eval \ē-vəl\ see ieval

evalent \ev-ə-lənt\ see evolent

evan[1] \ē-vən\ see even

evan[2] \ev-ən\ see eaven

eve[1] \ev\ breve, rev, Sevres
Negev
alla breve

eve[2] \ēv\ see eave[1]

evel \ev-əl\ bevel, devil, level,
Neville, revel
baselevel, bedevil, bi-level,
daredevil, dishevel, go-devil, split-
level
entry-level

eveler \ev-lər\ leveler, reveler

evelly \ev-ə-lē\ heavily, levelly,
reveille

evement \ēv-mənt\ achievement,
aggrievement, bereavement
underachievement

even \ē-vən\ even, Stephen, Steven
breakeven, break-even, Genevan,
Kesteven, uneven

eventh \ev-ənth\ seventh
eleventh

ever[1] \ev-ər\ clever, ever, lever,
never, sever, Trevor
dissever, endeavor, forever, however,
soever, whatever, whenever, wherever,
whichever, whoever, whomever
cantilever, howsoever, live-forever,
whatsoever, whencesoever,
whensoever, wheresoever,
whichsoever, whomsoever,
whosesoever, whosoever
whithersoever

ever[2] \ē-vər\ see iever

everage \ev-rij\ beverage, leverage

everence \ev-rəns\ reverence,
severance
disseverance, irreverence

every \ev-rē\ every, reverie

eves \ēvz\ see eaves

eviate \ē-vē-ət\ deviate, qiviut

evice \ev-əs\ clevis, crevice
Ben Nevis

evil \ē-vəl\ see ieval

eville \ev-əl\ see evel

evilry \ev-əl-rē\ devilry, revelry

evin \ev-ən\ see eaven

evious \ē-vē-əs\ devious, previous

evis[1] \ev-əs\ see evice

evis[2] \ē-vəs\ see evus

evity \ev-ət-ē\ brevity, levity
longevity

evo \ē-vō\ in vivo, relievo, ring-a-
lievo

alto-relievo, basso-relievo, mezzo-relievo, recitativo
Antananavivo

evocable \ev-ə-kə-bəl\ evocable,
revocable
irrevocable

evolence \ev-ə-ləns\ prevalence
benevolence, malevolence

evolent \ev-ə-lənt\ prevalent
benevolent, malevolent

evor \ev-ər\ see ever[1]

evous \ē-vəs\ grievous, Nevis, nevus
longevous
redivivus
Saint Kitts and Nevis

evsk \efsk\ see efsk

evus \ē-vəs\ see evous

evy \ev-ē\ bevy, heavy, levee, levy
replevy, top-heavy

ew[1] \ü\ blue, boo, brew, chew, clew,
clue, coo, coup, crew, cue, dew, do,
doux, drew, due, ewe, few, flew, flu,
flue, fou, glue, gnu, goo, hew, hue,
Hugh, Jew, knew, lieu, loo, Lou, mew,
moo, moue, mu, new, nu, ooh, pew,
phew, piu, pooh, prau, q, queue, roux,
rue, screw, shoe, shoo, shrew, Sioux,
skew, slew, slough, slue, smew, sou,
sous, spew, sprue, stew, strew, sue,
Sue, thew, threw, thro, through, to,
too, true, two, u, view, whew, who,
woo, Wu, xu, yew, you, zoo
accrue, adieu, ado, aircrew, airscrew,
anew, Anjou, askew, au jus, Baku,
bamboo, battu, battue, bedew,
beshrew, bestrew, bijou, boubou,
brand-new, breakthrough, burgoo,
cachou, can-do, canoe, caoutchouc,
Cebu, Cheng-du, Chongju, Chonju,
construe, Corfu, corkscrew, coypu,
CQ, debut, ecu, endue, ensue, eschew,
floor-through, fondue, fordo,
foreknew, Gansu, Gentoo, Gifu,
gumshoe, guru, hairdo, hereto, HQ,

Hutu, imbrue, imbue, IQ, jackscrew,
K2, Kansu, karoo, Karoo, kazoo,
Khufu, kung fu, Kwangju, leadscrew,
lean-to, make-do, Matthew, me-too,
mildew, milieu, miscue, misdo,
misknew, muumuu, Nehru, non-U,
old-shoe, one-two, outdo, outgrew,
perdu, Peru, poilu, preview, pursue,
purview, ragout, redo, renew, Ren
Crew, review, revue, rough-hew, run-through, sandshoe, see-through, set-to,
setscrew, shampoo, Shih Tzu, skiddoo,
snafu, snowshoe, soft-shoe, span-new,
subdue, surtout, taboo, Taegu, tattoo,
thank-you, thereto, thumbscrew, to-do,
too-too, undo, undue, unglue, unscrew,
untrue, vatu, vendue, venue, vertu,
virtu, wahoo, walk-through,
wherethrough, whereto, who's who,
withdrew, worldview
aperçu, avenue, babassu, ballyhoo,
barbecue, barley-broo, billet-doux,
black-and-blue, buckaroo, bugaboo,
callaloo, caribou, catechu, clerihew,
cockapoo, cockatoo, Cotonou,
counterview, déjá vu, derring-do,
detinue, feverfew, follow-through,
gardyloo, hitherto, honeydew, Ignaçu,
ingenue, interview, IOU, jabiru,
Jiangsu, kangaroo, Kathmandu,
kinkajou, loup-garou, Makalu,
manitou, marabou, Masaru,
Montague, Montesquieu, ormolu,
overdo, overdue, overflew, overgrew,
overshoe, overstrew, overthrough,
overview, parvenu, parvenue, pas de
deux, passe-partout, PDQ, peekaboo,
Port Salut, rendezvous, residue,
retinue, revenue, Richelieu, Ryukyu,
seppuku, Shikoku, succès fou,
switcheroo, talking-to, teleview,
Telugu, thereunto, thirty-two,
thitherto, Timbuktu, tinamou, trou-de-loup, twenty-two, view halloo,
vindaloo, w, wallaroo, waterloo, well-to-do, whoop-de-do, Xanadu
Aracaju, Brian Boru, didgeridoo,
Guangxi Zhuangzu, hullabaloo,
Ningxia Huizu, Ouagadougou,
pirarucu, Port du Salut, tu-whit
tu-whoo, Vanuatu

Daman and Diu, Kota Baharu, Nova Iguaçu

ew² \ō\ see ow¹

ewable¹ \ō-ə-bəl\ see owable¹

ewable² \ü-ə-bəl\ see uable

ewage \ü-ij\ brewage, sewage

ewal \ü-əl\ see uel¹

ewar \ü-ər\ see ewer¹

eward¹ \ùrd\ see ured¹

eward² \ü-ərd\ Seward, steward

ewd \üd\ see ude

ewdness \üd-nəs\ see udinous

ewe¹ \ō\ see ow¹

ewe² \ü\ see ew¹

ewed \üd\ see ude

ewee \ē-wē\ see eewee

ewel \ü-əl\ see uel¹

eweled \üld\ see ooled

ewell \ü-əl\ see uel¹

ewer¹ \ü-ər\ brewer, chewer, dewar, doer, ewer, fewer, hewer, queuer, screwer, sewer, skewer, spewer, suer, viewer, wooer, you're
   horseshoer, me-tooer, misdoer, previewer, renewer, reviewer, shampooer, snowshoer, tattooer, undoer, wrongdoer
   barbecuer, evildoer, interviewer, revenuer, televiewer
   —also -er *forms of adjectives listed at* ew¹

ewer² \ùr\ see ure¹

ewer³ \ō-ər\ see oer⁴

ewerage \ùr-ij\ see oorage¹

ewery \ùr-ē\ see ury¹

ewey \ü-ē\ see ewy

ewie \ü-ē\ see ewy

ewing¹ \ō-iŋ\ see oing¹

ewing² \ù-iŋ\ see oing²

ewis \ü-əs\ see ouis²

ewish \ü-ish\ bluish, Hewish Jewish, newish, shrewish
   aguish

ewl \ül\ see ool¹

ewless \ü-ləs\ clueless, crewless, dewless, shoeless, viewless

ewly \ü-lē\ see uly

ewman \ü-mən\ see uman

ewment \ü-mənt\ strewment accruement

ewn \ün\ see oon¹

ewness \ü-nəs\ blueness, dueness, Eunice, newness, skewness, Tunis
   askewness

ewpie \ü-pē\ see oopy

ewry \ùr-ē\ see ury¹

ews \üz\ see use²

ewsman \üz-mən\ bluesman, newsman

ewsy \ü-zē\ see oozy

ewt \üt\ see ute

ewter \üt-ər\ see uter

ewterer \üt-ər-ər\ see uiterer

ewton \üt-ᵊn\ see utan

ewy \ü-ē\ bluey, buoy, chewy, Dewey, dewy, flooey, gluey, gooey, hooey, Louie, Louis, newie, phooey, rouille, screwy, sloughy, viewy
   chop suey, mildewy, Port Louis ratatouille, waterzooi

ex \eks\ dex, ex, flex, hex, lex, rex, Rex, sex, specs, vex, x
   annex, apex, carex, codex, complex, convex, cortex, culex, desex, duplex, DX, fourplex, ibex, ilex, index,

Kleenex, Lastex, latex, mirex, murex, MX, narthex, perplex, Perspex, pollex, Pyrex, reflex, remex, Rx, scolex, silex, silvex, simplex, spandex, telex, Tex-Mex, triplex, unsex, vertex, vortex
analects, belowdecks, biconvex, circumflex, cross-index, googolplex, haruspex, intersex, Malcolm X, Middlesex, multiplex, PBX, pontifex, retroflex, spinifex, subindex, unisex
videotex
—*also* -s, -'s, *and* -s' *forms of nouns, and* -s *forms of verbs, listed at* eck

exas \ek-səs\ see exus

exed \ekst\ see ext

exedly \ek-səd-lē\ vexedly
perplexedly

exer \ek-sər\ flexor, hexer
duplexer, indexer
multiplexer
demultiplexer

exia \ek-sē-ə\ dyslexia
anorexia

exic \ek-sik\ dyslexic
anorexic

exical \ek-si-kəl\ lexical
indexical, nonlexical

exion \ek-shən\ see ection

exis \ek-səs\ see exus

exity \ek-sət-ē\ complexity,
convexity, perplexity

exor \ek-sər\ see exer

ext \ekst\ next, sexed, sext, text,
vexed
context, deflexed, inflexed, perplexed, plaintext, pretext, reflexed, subtext, urtext
ciphertext, oversexed, teletext, undersexed
—*also* -ed *forms of verbs listed at* ex

extant \ek-stənt\ extant, sextant

exterous \ek-strəs\ dexterous
ambidextrous

extrous \ek-strəs\ see exterous

extual \eks-chəl\ textual
contextual, subtextual

exual \eksh-wəl\ sexual
asexual, bisexual, effectual, pansexual, transsexual
ambisexual, homosexual, hypersexual, intersexual, parasexual, psychosexual, unisexual
heterosexual, sociosexual
anti-intellectual

exural \ek-shrəl\ see ectural[2]

exus \ek-səs\ lexis, nexus, plexus, texas, Texas
Alexis

exy \ek-sē\ prexy, sexy
apoplexy

ey[1] \ā\ see ay[1]

ey[2] \ē\ see ee[1]

ey[3] \ī\ see y[1]

eya[1] \ā-ə\ see aia[1]

eya[2] \ē-ə\ see ia[1]

eyance \ā-əns\ abeyance,
conveyance, purveyance, surveillance
reconveyance

eyant \ā-ənt\ mayn't
abeyant, surveillant

eyas \ī-əs\ see ias

ey'd \ād\ see ade[1]

eye \ī\ see y[1]

eyed[1] \ēd\ see eed

eyed[2] \īd\ see ide[1]

eyedness \īd-nəs\ eyedness,
snideness
cockeyedness

eyeless \ī-ləs\ see ilus

eyelet \ī-lət\ see ilot

eyen \īn\ see ine[1]

eyer¹ \ā-ər\ see ayer¹

eyer² \īr\ see ire¹

eyes \īz\ see ize

eying \ā-iŋ\ see aying

ey'll¹ \āl\ see ail

ey'll² \el\ see el¹

eyn \in\ see in¹

eynes \ānz\ see ains

eyness \ā-nəs\ see ayness

eyor \ā-ər\ see ayer¹

eyre \er\ see are⁴

ey're \er\ see are⁴

eyrie \īr-ē\ see iry¹

eys \ēz\ see eze

eyser \ī-zər\ see izer

eyte \ā-tē\ see aty

ey've \āv\ see ave²

ez¹ \ez\ see ays¹

ez² \ā\ see ay¹

ez³ \ās\ see ace¹

eza \ē-zə\ Giza, Lisa, Pisa, visa
mestiza
lespedeza

eze \ēz\ bise, breeze, cheese, ease,
feaze, feeze, freeze, frieze, he's, jeez,
lees, please, res, seize, she's, sleaze,
sneeze, squeeze, tease, tweeze,
wheeze
Andes, appease, Aries, Belize,
betise, Burmese, camise, Castries,
cerise, chemise, Chinese, deep-freeze,
Deep-freeze, degrease, Denise,
disease, displease, disseise, d.t.'s,
Elise, fasces, fauces, Ganges,
headcheese, heartsease, Hermes,
Kirghiz, Louise, Maltese, marquise,

menses, nates, Pisces, quick-freeze,
Ramses, reprise, sharp-freeze, soubise,
striptease, Tabriz, Thales, trapeze,
unease, unfreeze, Xerxes
Amboinese, Androcles, Annamese,
antifreeze, Assamese, Balinese,
Brooklynese, Cantonese, Cervantes,
Chersonese, Congolese, Cyclades.
Damocles, diocese, Eloise, Erinyes,
expertise, Faeroese, federalese,
genovese, gourmandise, Hebrides,
Heracles, Hercules, Hunanese,
Hyades, Japanese, Javanese,
Johnsonese, journalese, Kanarese,
Lake Louise, legalese, litotes,
manganese, Nipponese, overseas,
Pekinese, Pekingese, Pericles,
Pleiades, Portuguese, Pyrenees,
Siamese, Silures, Sinhalese, Socrates,
Sophocles, Sporades
Albigenses, antipodes, Aragonese,
archdiocese, Averroës, bona fides,
bureaucratese, cheval-de-frise,
computerese, Diogenes, Dodecanese,
Eumenides, Euripides, Florida Keys,
Gaucher's disease, governmentese,
Great Pyrenees, Hesperides,
Hippocrates, Hippomenes, Hodgkin's
disease, Indo-Chinese, nephritides,
officialese, pentagonese, Philoctetes,
Sammarinese, superficies,
telegraphese, Themistocles,
Thucydides, Vietnamese
Alcibiades, Aristophanes,
educationese, ferromanganese, Lou
Gehrig's disease, Mephistopheles,
sociologese, sword of Damocles
muscae volitantes, Pillars of
Hercules
—also -s, -'s, and -s' forms of nouns,
and -s forms of verbs, listed at ee¹

ezel \ē-zəl\ see easel

ezi \ē-zē\ see easy¹

ezium \ē-zē-əm\ cesium
magnesium, trapezium

ezzle \ez-əl\ bezel
embezzle

I

i¹ \ē\ see ee¹

i² \ī\ see y¹

i³ \ā\ see ay¹

ia¹ \ē-ə\ Gaea, kea, Leah, Mia, rhea, Rhea, rya, via
  Achaea, althaea, Apia, Bahia, Baile Atha Cliath, buddleia, cabrilla, cattleya, Chaldea, Crimea, Euboea, Hygeia, idea, Judea, Kaffiyeh, Korea, mantilla, Maria, Medea, mens rea, Morea, Nicaea, ohia, Omiya, Oriya, ouguiya, rupiah, sangria, Sofia, Sophia, spirea, tortilla
  Banranquilla, barathea, bougainvillea, camarilla, Caesarea, cascarilla, Cytherea, dulcinea, Eritrea, fantasia, Galatea, gonorrhea, granadilla, hamartia, Hialeah, Idumea, Ikaria, Jicarilla, Kampuchea, latakia, Latakia, logorrhea, Manzanilla, mausolea, mythopoeia, Nabatea, Nicosia, panacea, Parousia, pizzeria, ratafia, sabadilla, Santeria, sapodilla, seguidilla, sinfonia, Tanzania, trattoria
  alfilaria, Andalucia, Andalusia, Ave Maria, Cassiopeia, echeveria, Ismailia, peripeteia, pharmacopoeia, prosopopoeia
  Diego Garcia, onomatopoeia
  Joseph of Arimathea

ia² \ī-ə\ see iah¹

ia³ \ä\ see a¹

iable¹ \ī-ə-bəl\ dryable, dyeable, flyable, friable, liable, pliable, triable, viable
  deniable, inviable, reliable
  certifiable, classifiable, justifiable, liquefiable, notifiable, pacifiable, qualifiable, quantifiable, rectifiable, satisfiable, specifiable, undeniable, unifiable, verifiable
  emulsifiable, identifiable, unfalsifiable

iable² \ē-ə-bəl\ see eeable

iacal \ī-ə-kəl\ dandiacal, heliacal, maniacal, theriacal, zodiacal
  ammoniacal, elegiacal, simoniacal dipsomaniacal, egomaniacal, hypochondriacal, monomaniacal, nympomaniacal, pyromaniacal, paradisiacal
  bibliomaniacal, megalomaniacal

iad \ī-əd\ see yad

iah¹ \ī-ə\ ayah, maya, Maya, playa, Praia, stria, via
  Aglaia, Mariah, messiah, papaya, pariah, Thalia
  Hezekiah, jambalaya, Jeremiah, Nehemiah, Obadiah, Surabaja, Zechariah, Zephaniah
  Atchafalaya, Iphigenia, peripeteia

iah² \ē-ə\ see ia¹

ial¹ \ī-əl\ dial, diel, pial
  redial

ial² \īl\ see ile¹

ialer \ī-lər\ see ilar

ially \ē-ə-lē\ see eally¹

iam \ī-əm\ Priam
  per diem

ian¹ \ē-ən\ see ean¹

ian² \ī-ən\ see ion¹

iance \ī-əns\ science
affiance, alliance, appliance,
compliance, defiance, nonscience,
reliance
mesalliance, misalliance

iancy \ī-ən-sē\ pliancy
compliancy

ianist \ē-t-nist\ pianist
Indo-Europeanist

iant \ī-ənt\ Bryant, client, giant,
pliant, riant
affiant, compliant, defiant, reliant
incompliant, self-reliant, supergiant

iao \aù\ see ow²

iaour \aùr\ see ower²

iaper \ī-pər\ see iper

iar \īr\ see ire¹

iary¹ \ī-ə-rē\ diary, fiery, priory

iary² \īr-ē\ see iry¹

ias¹ \ī-əs\ Aias, bias, dais, eyas,
Laius, Lias, pious, Pius
Abdias, Elias, Messias, Tobias
Ananias, Jeremias, Malachias,
Nehemias, Roncesvalles, Sophonias,
Zacharias
Mount Saint Elias

ias² \ē-əs\ see eus¹

ias³ \äsh\ see ash¹

iasis \ī-ə-səs\ diesis, diocese
archdiocese, psoriasis
acariasis, amebiasis, ascariasis,
bilharziasis, helminthiasis,
leishmaniasis, satyriasis
elephantiasis, hypochondriasis,
schistosomiasis

iat¹ \ē-ət\ see eit¹

iat² \ī-ət\ see iet

iate \ī-ət\ see iet

iath¹ \ī-əth\ Wyeth
Goliath

iath² \ē-ə\ see ia¹

iatry \ī-ə-trē\ podiatry, psychiatry

iaus \aùs\ see ouse²

ib¹ \ib\ bib, bibb, crib, drib, fib, gib,
glib, jib, lib, nib, rib, sib, squib
ad-lib, corncrib, midrib, sahib
memsahib

ib² \ēb\ see ebe²

ib³ \ēv\ see eave¹

iba \ē-bə\ see eba

ibable \ī-bə-bəl\ bribable
ascribable, describable
indescribable

ibal \ī-bəl\ bible, Bible, libel, scribal,
tribal

ibb \ib\ see ib¹

ibband \ib-ən\ see ibbon

ibbed \ibd\ bibbed
rock-ribbed
—also -ed forms of verbs listed at
ib¹

ibber \ib-ər\ bibber, cribber, dibber,
fibber, gibber, glibber, jibber, ribber

ibbet \ib-ət\ gibbet
exhibit, inhibit, prohibit
flibbertigibbet

ibbing \ib-iŋ\ cribbing, ribbing
—also -ing forms of verbs listed at
ib¹

ibble \ib-əl\ dibble, dribble, fribble,
gribble, kibble, nibble, quibble,
scribble, sibyl, Sibyl

ibbler \ib-lər\ dribbler, nibbler,
quibbler, scribbler

ibbly \ib-lē\ dribbly, ghibli, glibly

ibbon \ib-ən\ gibbon, Gibbon,
ribbon
inhibin

ibby \ib-ē\ Libby, ribby

173 / ice

ibe¹ \īb\ bribe, gibe, gybe, jibe, kibe, scribe, tribe, vibe ascribe, conscribe, describe, imbibe, inscribe, prescribe, proscribe, subscribe, transcribe circumscribe, diatribe, redescribe, superscribe oversubscribe

ibe² \ē-bē\ see ebe¹

ibel \ī-bəl\ see ibal

iber \ī-bər\ briber, fiber, giber, Khyber, scriber, Tiber describer, inscriber, prescriber, proscriber, subscriber, transcriber

ibi \ē-bē\ see ebe¹

ibia \i-bē-ə\ Lybia, tibia Namibia

ibin \ib-ən\ see ibbon

ibit \ib-ət\ see ibbet

ibitive \ib-ət-iv\ exhibitive, prohibitive

ibitor \ib-ət-ər\ exhibitor, inhibitor ACE inhibitor

ible \ī-bəl\ see ibal

iblet \ib-lət\ driblet, giblet, riblet

ibli \ib-lē\ see ibbly

ibly \ib-lē\ see ibbly

ibo \ē-bō\ Ibo, Kibo gazebo

iboly \i-ə-lē\ see ybele

ibrous \ī-brəs\ fibrous, hybris

ibs \ibz\ dibs, nibs spareribs —also -s, -'s, and -s' forms of nouns, and -s forms of verbs, listed at ib¹

ibular \ib-yə-lər\ fibular mandibular, vestibular infundibular

ibute¹ \ib-yət\ tribute

attribute, contribute, distribute redistribute

ibute² \ib-ət\ see ibbet

ibutive \ib-yət-iv\ attributive, contributive, distributive, retributive redistributive

ibutor \ib-ət-ər\ see ibitor

ibyl \ib-əl\ see ibble

ic¹ \ik\ see ick

ic² \ēk\ see eak¹

ica¹ \ī-kə\ mica, Micah, pica, pika, plica, spica, Spica Formica, lorica balalaika

ica² \ē-kə\ see ika¹

icable \ik-ə-bəl\ despicable, explicable, extricable inexplicable, inextricable

icah \ī-kə\ see ica¹

ical \ik-əl\ see ickle

icament \ik-ə-mənt\ medicament, predicament

ican \ē-kən\ see eacon

icar \ik-ər\ see icker¹

icative \ik-ət-iv\ fricative, siccative affricative, explicative, indicative, vindicative multiplicative

iccative \ik-ət-iv\ see icative

iccio \ē-chō\ capriccio, pasticcio

ice¹ \īs\ Bryce, dice, fice, fyce, gneiss, ice, lice, lyse, mice, nice, pice, price, rice, rise, slice, spice, splice, syce, thrice, trice, twice, vice, vise advice, allspice, Brandeis, bride-price, concise, cut-price, deice, device, entice, excise, precise, suffice beggars-lice, cockatrice, edelweiss, imprecise, merchandise, overprice,

paradise, point-device, sacrifice, underprice
  imparadise, self-sacrifice

ice² \ē-chā\ see iche¹

ice³ \ēs\ see iece

ice⁴ \ī-sē\ see icy

ice⁵ \īz\ see ize

ice⁶ \ēt-zə\ see itza¹

iceless \ī-sləs\ iceless, priceless

icely \is-lē\ see istly

iceous \ish-əs\ see icious¹

icer \ī-sər\ dicer, Dreiser, nicer, pricer, ricer, slicer, splicer
  deicer, sufficer
  sacrificer
  self-sacrificer

ices \ī-sēz\ Pisces
  Anchises
  Polynices
  Coma Berenices

icety \ī-stē\ see eisty

icey \ī-sē\ see icy

ich¹ \ich\ see itch

ich² \ik\ see ick

ichael \ī-kəl\ see ycle¹

iche¹ \ē-chā\ ceviche, seviche
  Beatrice, cantatrice

iche² \ēsh\ fiche, leash, quiche, sneesh
  baksheesh, corniche, hashish, maxixe, pastiche, schottische, unleash
  microfiche, nouveau riche

iche³ \ish\ see ish¹

iche⁴ \ich\ see itch

iche⁵ \ē-chē\ see eachy

ichen¹ \ī-kən\ lichen, liken
  proteoglycan

ichen² \ich-ən\ see itchen

ichener \ich-nər\ see itchener

icher \ich-ər\ see itcher

iches \ich-əz\ see itches

ichi¹ \ē-chē\ see eachy

ichi² \ē-shē\ see ishi

ichment \ich-mənt\ see itchment

ichore \ik-rē\ see ickery

ichu \ish-ü\ see issue¹

icia¹ \ish-ə\ see itia

icia² \ēsh-ə\ see esia¹

icial \ish-əl\ altricial, comitial, initial, judicial, official, simplicial, solstitial, surficial
  artificial, beneficial, cicatricial, interstitial, prejudicial, sacrificial, superficial

ician \ē-shən\ see etion¹

icience \ish-əns\ omniscience
  insufficience

iciency \ish-ən-sē\ deficiency, efficiency, proficiency, sufficiency
  inefficiency
  immunodeficiency

icient \ish-ənt\ deficient, efficient, omniscient, proficient, sufficient
  coefficient, cost-efficient, inefficient, insufficient, self-sufficient

icinable \is-nə-bəl\ see istenable

icinal \is-ᵊn-əl\ vicinal
  medicinal, officinal, vaticinal

icing¹ \ī-siŋ\ icing, splicing
  self-sufficing
  —also -ing *forms of verbs listed at* ice¹

icing² \ī-ziŋ\ see izing

icious¹ \ish-əs\ vicious
  ambitious, auspicious, capricious, delicious, factitious, fictitious,

flagitious, judicious, lubricious,
malicious, Mauritius, nutritious,
officious, pernicious, propitious,
pumiceous, seditious, sericeous,
suspicious
  adscititious, adventitious, avaricious,
expeditious, inauspicious, injudicious,
meretricious, prejudicious,
subreptitious, superstitious,
suppositious, surreptitious
  excrementitious, supposititious

icious² \ē-shəs\ see ecious

icipal \is-ə-bəl\ see issible

icipant \is-ə-pənt\ anticipant,
participant

icit \is-ət\ licit
complicit, elicit, explicit, illicit,
implicit, solicit
  inexplicit

icitor¹ \is-ət-ər\ elicitor, solicitor

icitor² \is-tər\ see ister

icitous \is-ət-əs\ complicitous,
duplicitous, felicitous, solicitous
  infelicitous

icity¹ \is-ət-ē\ basicity, causticity,
centricity, chronicity, complicity,
conicity, cyclicity, duplicity, ethnicity,
felicity, lubricity, mendicity, plasticity,
publicity, rhythmicity, seismicity,
simplicity, spasticity, sphericity,
tonicity, toxicity, triplicity
  atomicity, authenticity, canonicity,
catholicity, concentricity, domesticity,
eccentricity, elasticity, electricity,
ellipticity, endemicity, ergodicity,
historicity, iconicity, impudicity,
infelicity, multiplicity, organicity,
pneumaticity, quadruplicity,
specificity, synchronicity, volcanicity
  aromaticity, automaticity,
ecumenicity, egocentricity,
epidemicity, ethnocentricity,
hydrophilicity, hydrophobicity,
inauthenticity, inelasticity,
pathogenicity, periodicity,
theocentricity

  aeroelasticity, anthropocentricity,
aperiodicity, carcinogenicity,
homoscedasticity
  quasiperiodicity

icity² \is-tē\ christie, Christie, misty,
twisty, wristy
  Corpus Christi, sacahuiste

ick \ik\ brick, chick, click, crick,
creek, Dick, flick, hick, kick, KWIC,
lick, mick, nick, Nick, pic, pick, prick,
quick, rick, shtick, sic, sick, slick,
snick, stick, strick, thick, tic, tick,
trick, wick
  airsick, bluetick, bootlick, boychick,
brainsick, broomstick, carsick,
chopstick, cowlick, crabstick,
dabchick, dead-stick, detick, dik-dik,
dipstick, drop-kick, drumstick,
firebrick, flagstick, goldbrick,
greensick, handpick, hayrick,
heartsick, homesick, joystick, lipstick,
lovesick, matchstick, moujik, muzhik,
nightstick, nitpick, nonstick, nutpick,
outslick, peacenik, pigstick, pinprick,
placekick, redbrick, rubric, seasick,
self-stick, shashlik, sidekick, slapstick,
slipstick, Tajik, toothpick, topkick,
unpick, unstick, uptick, yardstick
  bailiwick, biopic, Bolshevik,
candlestick, candlewick, Dominic,
dominick, Dominick, double-quick,
EBCDIC, fiddlestick, hemistich,
heretic, lunatic, Menshevik,
meterstick, overtrick, politic, politick,
polyptych, Reykjavik, singlestick,
taperstick, undertrick, Watson-Crick
  arithmetic, carrot-and-stick,
computernik, impolitic, kinnikinnick

icka \ē-kə\ see ika¹

icked¹ \ik-əd\ picked, wicked

icked² \ikt\ see ict¹

ickel \ik-əl\ see ickle

icken \ik-ən\ chicken, quicken,
sicken, stricken, thicken
  awestricken
  panic-stricken, planet-stricken
  poverty-stricken

ickens \ik-ənz\ dickens, Dickens, pickings
—*also* -s, -'s, *and* -s' *forms of nouns, and* -s *forms of verbs, listed at* icken

icker[1] \ik-ər\ bicker, dicker, flicker, icker, kicker, liquor, nicker, picker, pricker, sicker, slicker, snicker, sticker, ticker, tricker, vicar, whicker, wicker
billsticker, bootlicker, dropkicker, flea-flicker, nitpicker, pigsticker, placekicker, pot likker, ragpicker
dominicker, politicker
—*also* -er *forms of adjectives listed at* ick

icker[2] \ek-ər\ see ecker

ickery \ik-rē\ chicory, flickery, hickory, snickery, trickery
Terpsichore

icket \ik-ət\ cricket, picket, Pickett, pricket, spigot, stickit, thicket, ticket, wicket
Big Thicket, big-ticket

ickett \ik-ət\ see icket

ickety \ik-ət-ē\ rickety, thickety
pernickety, persnickety

ickey \ik-ē\ see icky

icki \ik-ē\ see icky

ickie \ik-ē\ see icky

icking \ik-iŋ\ ticking, wicking
brain-picking, flat-picking, high-sticking, nit-picking
cotton-picking, finger-picking
—*also* -ing *forms of verbs listed at* ick

ickings \ik-ənz\ see ickens

ickish \ik-ish\ hickish, sickish, trickish

ickit \ik-ət\ see icket

ickle \ik-əl\ brickle, chicle, fickle, mickle, nickel, pickle, prickle, sickle, stickle, strickle, tical, tickle, trickle

bicycle, icicle, obstacle, Popsicle, spectacle, tricycle, vehicle
pumpernickel

ickler \ik-lər\ stickler, tickler
bicycler, particular

ickly \ik-lē\ fickly, prickly, quickly, sickly, slickly
impoliticly

ickness \ik-nəs\ lychnis, quickness, sickness, slickness, thickness
airsickness, heartsickness, homesickness, lovesickness, seasickness

icksy \ik-sē\ see ixie

icky \ik-ē\ dickey, hickey, icky, kicky, Mickey, picky, quickie, rickey, sickie, sticky, tricky, Vicki, Vickie, Vicky
doohickey

icle \ik-əl\ see ickle

icly[1] \ik-lē\ see ickly

icly[2] \ē-klē\ see eekly

ico \ē-kō\ see icot

icope \ik-ə-pē\ see icopy

icopy \ik-ə-pē\ wicopy
pericope

icory \ik-rē\ see ickery

icot \ē-kō\ fico, pekoe, picot, tricot
Tampico
Puerto Rico

ics \iks\ see ix[1]

ict[1] \ikt\ picked, Pict, strict, ticked
addict, afflict, conflict, constrict, convict, delict, depict, edict, evict, inflict, lipsticked, predict, restrict, unlicked
benedict, Benedict, contradict, derelict, interdict, maledict, retrodict
eggs Benedict
—*also* -ed *forms of verbs listed at* ick

ict[2] \īt\ see ite[1]

ictable \īt-ə-bəl\ see itable[1]

ictal \ik-t°l\ fictile, rictal
edictal

icted \ik-təd\ conflicted, evicted,
restricted
—also -ed *forms of verbs listed at* ict

icter \ik-tər\ see ictor

ictic \ik-tik\ deictic, panmictic
amphimictic, apodictic

ictile \ik-t°l\ see ictal

ictim \ik-təm\ see ictum

iction \ik-shən\ diction, fiction,
friction, stiction
addiction, affliction, confliction,
constriction, conviction, depiction,
eviction, indiction, infliction,
nonfiction, prediction, reliction,
restriction, transfixion
benediction, contradiction,
crucifixion, dereliction, jurisdiction,
malediction, metafiction, valediction

ictional \ik-shnəl\ fictional,
frictional
nonfictional
jurisdictional

ictionist \ik-shnəst\ fictionist
restrictionist

ictive \ik-tiv\ fictive
addictive, afflictive, conflictive,
constrictive, inflictive, restrictive,
vindictive
nonrestrictive

ictment \īt-mənt\ see itement

ictor \ik-tər\ lictor, stricter, victor
constrictor, depicter, evictor, inflicter
contradictor
vasoconstrictor

ictory \ik-tə-rē\ victory
benedictory, contradictory,
maledictory, valedictory

ictual \it-°l\ see ittle

ictualler \it-°l-ər\ see italer

ictum \ik-təm\ dictum, victim
obiter dictum

icture \ik-chər\ picture, stricture

ictus \ik-təs\ ictus, rictus
Benedictus

icula \ik-yə-lə\ auricula, Canicula

iculant \ik-yə-lənt\ gesticulant,
matriculant

icular[1] \ik-yə-lər\ spicular
acicular, articular, auricular,
canicular, clavicular, curricular,
cuticular, fascicular, follicular,
funicular, lenticular, navicular,
orbicular, ossicular, particular,
radicular, reticular, testicular,
vehicular, ventricular, vermicular,
versicular, vesicular
appendicular, perpendicular
extracurricular, extravehicular, intra-
articular, supraventricular

icular[2] \ik-lər\ see ickler

iculate \ik-yə-lət\ articulate,
denticulate, geniculate, particulate,
reticulate, straticulate, vermiculate
inarticulate

iculous \ik-yə-ləs\ meticulous,
pediculous, ridiculous

iculum \ik-yə-ləm\ curriculum,
reticulum
diverticulum

icuous \ik-yə-wəs\ conspicuous,
perspicuous, transpicuous
inconspicuous

icy \ī-sē\ dicey, icy, pricey, spicy

id[1] \id\ bid, chid, Cid, did, fid, gid,
grid, hid, id, kid, Kidd, lid, mid, quid,
rid, skid, slid, squid, SQUID, whid
amid, backslid, bifid, El Cid, equid,
eyelid, forbid, grandkid, Madrid,
nonskid, outdid, resid, schoolkid,
trifid, undid
katydid, ootid, overbid, overdid,
pyramid, underbid
tertium quid, Valladolid

id² \ēd\ see eed

I'd \īd\ see ide¹

ida¹ \ēd-ə\ see eda¹

ida² \ī-də\ Haida, Ida, Vida

idable¹ \īd-ə-bəl\ guidable
decidable, dividable
subdividable

idable² \id-ə-bəl\ see iddable

idal \īd-ᵊl\ bridal, bridle, idle, idol,
idyll, seidel, sidle, tidal
unbridle
Barmecidal, fratricidal, fungicidal,
genocidal, germicidal, herbicidal,
homicidal, intertidal, lunitidal,
matricidal, parricidal, patricidal,
septicidal, spermicidal, suicidal,
viricidal, virucidal
bactericidal, infanticidal, insecticidal

idance \īd-ᵊns\ guidance, stridence
abidance, misguidance

idas \īd-əs\ Midas, nidus

iday \īd-ē\ Friday, Heidi, tidy, vide
alcaide, man Friday, untidy
mala fide

idays \īd-ēz\ see ides¹

idd \id\ see id¹

iddable \id-ə-bəl\ biddable
formidable

iddance \id-ᵊns\ riddance
forbiddance

idden \id-ᵊn\ bidden, chiden,
hidden, midden, ridden, stridden,
swidden
backslidden, bedridden, bestridden,
forbidden, outbidden, unbidden
overridden

idder \id-ər\ bidder, gridder, kidder,
siddur, skidder
consider, forbidder
reconsider, underbidder

iddie \id-ē\ see iddy

iddish \id-ish\ kiddish, Yiddish

iddity \id-ət-ē\ see idity

iddle \id-ᵊl\ diddle, fiddle, griddle,
middle, piddle, riddle, twiddle
unriddle
paradiddle, taradiddle

iddler \id-lər\ diddler, fiddler,
middler, riddler, tiddler

iddling \id-liŋ\ fiddling, middling,
piddling, riddling

iddly \id-le\ diddly, ridley, tiddly

iddock \id-ik\ see idic

iddur \id-ər\ see idder

iddy \id-ē\ biddy, giddy, kiddie,
middy, midi, skiddy, widdy

ide¹ \īd\ bide, bride, chide, Clyde,
eyed, fried, glide, guide, hide, I'd,
pied, plied, pride, ride, side, slide,
snide, stride, thighed, tide, tried, wide
abide, allied, applied, aside, astride,
backside, backslide, bankside,
beachside, bedside, beside, bestride,
betide, blear-eyed, blindside,
blowdried, blue-eyed, broadside,
bromide, bug-eyed, Burnside, clear-
eyed, cockeyed, cold-eyed, collide,
confide, courtside, cowhide, cross-
eyed, curbside, dayside, decide,
deride, divide, dockside, doe-eyed,
downside, downslide, dry-eyed, elide,
fireside, fluoride, foreside, four-eyed,
freeze-dried, glass-eyed, graveside,
green-eyed, hagride, hawkeyed,
hayride, hillside, horsehide, inside,
ironside, joyride, kingside, lakeside,
landslide, lynx-eyed, misguide, moon-
eyed, nearside, nightside, noontide,
offside, onside, outride, outside, pie-
eyed, poolside, pop-eyed, preside,
provide, quayside, queenside, rawhide,
reside, ringside, riptide, roadside,
seaside, sharp-eyed, shipside,
shoreside, Shrovetide, sloe-eyed,
snowslide, springtide, squint-eyed,
stateside, statewide, storewide,

Strathclyde, streamside, subside,
tailslide, Tayside, tongue-tied, topside,
trackside, trailside, untried, upside,
vat-dyed, walleyed, waveguide,
wayside, wide-eyed, wild-eyed,
worldwide, yuletide
  alkoxide, almond-eyed, alongside,
Argus-eyed, Barmecide, bleary-eyed,
bona fide, chicken-fried,
Christmastide, citified, citywide,
classified, coincide, countrified,
countryside, countrywide, cut-and-
dried, cyanide, deicide, demand-side,
dewy-eyed, dignified, double-wide,
Eastertide, eventide, feticide,
formamide, fratricide, fungicide,
genocide, germicide, gimlet-eyed,
glassy-eyed, goggle-eyed, googly-
eyed, harbor-side, herbicide,
homicide, Humberside, humified,
matricide, Merseyside, misty-eyed,
miticide, monoxide, mountainside,
nationwide, Naugahyde, open-eyed,
override, overstride, parricide,
Passiontide, patricide, pesticide,
planetwide, qualified, rarefied,
raticide, regicide, riverside, Riverside,
set-aside, silverside, sissified,
slickenside, spermicide, starry-eyed,
subdivide, suicide, supply-side,
trisulfide, underside, verbicide,
vermicide, viricide, waterside,
Whitsuntide, wintertide
  acrylamide, antimonide,
borohydride, dissatisfied,
formaldehyde, infanticide, insecticide,
interallied, Jekyll and Hyde,
preoccupied, rodenticide, self-
satisfied, thalidomide, Trinitytide,
tyrannicide, uxoricide
  monoglyceride, overqualified,
parasiticide
  —*also* -ed *forms of verbs listed at* y[1]

ide[2] \ēd\ see eed

idean \id-ē-ən\ see idian

ided \īd-əd\ sided
  lopsided, misguided, one-sided, slab-
sided, two-sided
  many-sided, sobersided

  —*also* -ed *forms of verbs listed at*
ide[1]

ideless \īd-ləs\ idlesse, tideless

iden \īd-ᵊn\ guidon, Haydn, widen
  Poseidon

idence \īd-ᵊns\ see idance

ideness \īd-nəs\ see eyedness

ident \īd-ᵊnt\ strident, trident

ideon \id-ē-ən\ see idian

ideous \id-ē-əs\ see idious

ider[1] \īd-ər\ bider, cider, eider,
glider, guider, hider, rider, slider,
spider, strider, stridor
  abider, backslider, confider, decider,
derider, divider, insider, joyrider,
misguider, outrider, outsider, presider,
provider, resider, rough rider, Top-
Sider
  subdivider, supply-sider
  supercollider
  —*also* -er *forms of adjectives listed
at* ide[1]

ider[2] \id-ər\ see idder

ides[1] \īd-ēz\ Fridays
  Aristides
  —*also* -s, -'s, *and* -s' *forms of nouns,
and* -s *forms of verbs, listed at* iday

ides[2] \īdz\ ides
  besides, burnsides
  silversides, sobersides
  —*also* -s, -'s, *and* -s' *forms of nouns,
and* -s *forms of verbs, listed at* ide[1]

idge \ij\ bridge, fidge, fridge, midge,
ridge
  abridge, Blue Ridge, browridge,
drawbridge, footbridge, Oxbridge,
teethridge

idged \ijd\ ridged
  unabridged
  —*also* -ed *forms of verbs listed at*
idge

idgen \ij-ən\ see ygian

idget \ij-ət\ Brigitte, digit, fidget,
midget, widget
   double-digit

idgin \ij-ən\ see ygian

idi \id-ē\ see iddy

idia \i-dē-ə\ Lydia
   basidia, chlamydia, clostridia,
coccidia, conidia, glochidia, nephridia,
Numidia, oidia, peridia, Pisidia,
presidia, pycnidia, pygidia
   antheridia, enchiridia, hesperidia,
miricidia, ommatidia

idian \id-ē-ən\ Gideon, Lydian,
Midian
   ascidian, Dravidian, euclidean,
Floridian, meridian, obsidian,
ophidian, quotidian, viridian
   enchiridion, non-euclidean

idic \id-ik\ piddock
   acidic, bromidic, Davidic, druidic,
fatidic, fluidic, Hasidic, nuclidic

idical \id-i-kəl\ druidical, fatidical,
juridical, veridical
   pyramidical

idice \id-ə-sē\ Chalcidice, Eurydice

idiem \id-ē-əm\ idiom
   iridium, presidium, rubidium
   post meridiem
   ante meridiem

iding \īd-iŋ\ riding, Riding, siding,
tiding
   abiding, confiding, East Riding,
joyriding, West Riding
   law-abiding, nondividing
   —also -ing forms of verbs listed at
ide[1]

idiom \id-ē-əm\ see idiem

idious \id-ē-əs\ hideous
   fastidious, insidious, invidious,
perfidious

idity \id-ət-ē\ quiddity
   acidity, aridity, avidity, cupidity,
fluidity, flaccidity, floridity, frigidity,

gelidity, gravidity, hispidity, humidity,
hybridity, limpidity, liquidity, lividity,
lucidity, morbidity, rabidity, rapidity,
rigidity, sapidity, solidity, stupidity,
tepidity, timidity, torridity, turbidity,
turgidity, validity, vapidity, viridity,
viscidity
   illiquidity, insipidity, intrepidity,
invalidity

idium \id-ē-əm\ see idiem

idle \īd-ᵊl\ see idal

idlesse \īd-ləs\ see ideless

idley \id-lē\ see iddly

idney \id-nē\ kidney, Sidney,
Sydney

ido[1] \īd-ō\ dido, Dido, fido
   Hokkaido

ido[2] \ēd-ō\ see edo[1]

idol \īd-ᵊl\ see idal

ids[1] \idz\ Beskids, rapids
   Grand Rapids
   —also -s, -'s, and -s' forms of nouns,
and -s forms of verbs, listed at id[1]

ids[2] \ēdz\ see eeds

idst \idst\ didst, midst
   amidst

idual[1] \ij-wəl\ residual
   individual

idual[2] \ij-əl\ see igil

idulent \ij-ə-lənt\ see igilant

idulous \ij-ə-ləs\ stridulous
   acidulous

idus \īd-əs\ see idas

iduum \ij-ə-wəm\ triduum
   residuum

idy \īd-ē\ see iday

idyll \īd-ᵊl\ see idal

ie[1] \ā\ see ay[1]

ie[2] \ē\ sec ee[1]

181
ieler

ie³ \ī\ see y¹

iece \ēs\ cease, crease, fleece, grease, Greece, kris, lease, Nice, niece, peace, piece
apiece, Bernice, Burmese, camise, caprice, cassis, cerise, chemise, Chinese, Clarice, Cochise, codpiece, coulisse, crosspiece, decease, decrease, degrease, Denise, Dumfries, earpiece, Elise, eyepiece, Felice, fieldpiece, grandniece, hairpiece, headpiece, heelpiece, increase, Janice, lend-lease, Matisse, Maurice, mouthpiece, nosepiece, obese, one-piece, pastis, pelisse, police, re-lease, release, seapiece, shankpiece, showpiece, sidepiece, stringpiece, sublease, surcease, tailpiece, Therese, timepiece, toepiece, two-piece, valise, workpiece
afterpiece, altarpiece, Amboinese, Annamese, Assamese, Balinese, Brooklynese, Cantonese, centerpiece, Chersonese, chimneypiece, diocese, directrice, ex libris, expertise, Faeroese, frontispiece, mantelpiece, masterpiece, Nipponese, Pekinese, Pekingese, Portugese, predecease, rerelease, S„o Luis, Siamese, Sinhalese, timed-release, verdigris
archdiocese, computerese, Dodecanese, officialese, telegraphese, Vietnamese
educationese

iecer \ē-sər\ see easer¹

ied¹ \ēd\ see eed

ied² \ēt\ see eat¹

ied³ \īd\ see ide¹

ieda \ēd-ə\ see eda¹

ief¹ \ēf\ beef, brief, chief, fief, grief, kef, leaf, lief, reef, sheaf, thief
belief, debrief, endleaf, enfeoff, flyleaf, loose-leaf, massif, motif, naif, O'Keefe, relief, sharif, sherif, shinleaf
bas-relief, cloverleaf, disbelief, handkerchief, leatherleaf, neckerchief,

leitmotiv, misbelief, overleaf, unbelief, waterleaf
aperitif, Capitol Reef, Vinson Massif
Great Barrier Reef
Santa Cruz de Tenerife

ief² \ēv\ see eave¹

iefless \ē-fləs\ briefless, leafless

iefly \ē-flē\ briefly, chiefly

ieg¹ \ēg\ see igue

ieg² \ig\ see ig

iege¹ \ēj\ liege, siege
besiege, prestige

iege² \ēzh\ see ige¹

ieger \ē-jər\ see edure

iek \ēk\ see eak¹

iel¹ \ēl\ see eal²

iel² \ī-əl\ see ial

iela \el-ə\ see ella

ield \ēld\ bield, field, keeled, shield, weald, wheeled, wield, yield
afield, airfield, backfield, brickfield, coalfield, cornfield, downfield, Enfield, four-wheeled, Garfield, goldfield, grainfield, infield, Masefield, midfield, minefield, outfield, playfield, Sheffield, Smithfield, snowfield, Springfield, subfield, unsealed, upfield, well-heeled, windshield, Winfield
battlefield, broken-field, chesterfield, Chesterfield, color-field, Huddersfield, track-and-field, unaneled
—also -ed forms of verbs listed at eal²

ielder \ēl-dər\ fielder, shielder, wielder, yielder
infielder, outfielder

ields \ēldz\ South Shields
—also -s, -'s, and -s' forms of nouns, and -s forms of verbs, listed at ield

ieler \ē-lər\ see ealer

ieless \ī-ləs\ see ilus

ieling[1] \ē-lən\ see elin

ieling[2] \ē-liŋ\ see eeling

iem[1] \ē-əm\ see eum[1]

iem[2] \ī-əm\ see iam

ien \ēn\ see ine[3]

ience \ī-əns\ see iance

iend \end\ see end

iendless \en-ləs\ see endless

iendliness \en-lē-nəs\ see
endliness

iendly \en-lē\ see endly

iene \ēn\ see ine[3]

iener[1] \ē-nər\ see eaner

iener[2] \ē-nē\ see ini[1]

ienic \en-ik\ see enic[2]

ienics \en-iks\ see enics

ienie \ē-nē\ see ini[1]

ienist \ē-nəst\ see inist[2]

iennes \en\ see en[1]

ient \ī-ənt\ see iant

ieper \ē-pər\ see eeper

ier[1] \ir\ see eer[2]

ier[2] \ē-ər\ see eer[1]

ier[3] \īr\ see ire[1]

ierate \ir-ət\ see irit

ierce \irs\ Bierce, birse, fierce,
pierce, Pierce, tierce
   transpierce

iere[1] \er\ see are[4]

iere[2] \ir\ see eer[2]

iered \ird\ see eard[1]

ieria \ir-ē-ə\ see eria[1]

ierial \ir-ē-əl\ see erial

ierian \ir-ē-ən\ see erian[1]

ierly \ir-lē\ see early[1]

ierre[1] \ir\ see eer[2]

ierre[2] \er\ see are[4]

iers \irz\ Algiers, Pamirs
   —also -s, -'s, and -s' forms of nouns,
   and -s forms of verbs, listed at eer[2]

iersman \irz-mən\ see eersman

iery \ī-ə-rē\ see iary[1]

ies[1] \ēz\ see eze

ies[2] \ē\ see ee[1]

ies[3] \ēs\ see iece

iesel[1] \ē-zəl\ see easel

iesel[2] \ē-səl\ see ecil[1]

ieseling \ēz-liŋ\ see esling

iesian \ē-zhən\ see esian[1]

iesis \ī-ə-səs\ see iasis

iesling \ēz-liŋ\ see esling

iest \ēst\ see east[1]

iester \ē-stər\ see easter

iestley \ēst-lē\ see eastly

iestly \ēst-lē\ see eastly

iet \ī-ət\ diet, fiat, quiet, riot, striate,
Wyatt
   disquiet, unquiet

ietal \ī-ət-ᵊl\ parietal, societal,
varietal

ieter \ī-ət-ər\ dieter, quieter, rioter
   proprietor

ietor \ī-ət-ər\ see ieter

iety \ī-ət-ē\ piety
   anxiety, dubiety, impiety, nimiety,
   propriety, satiety, sobriety, society,
   Society, variety

contrariety, impropriety, inebriety, insobriety, notoriety

ietzsche \ē-chē\ see eachy

ieu \ü\ see ew¹

ieur \ir\ see eer²

iev \ef\ see ef¹

ievable \ē-və-bəl\ see eivable

ieval \ē-vəl\ evil, shrieval, weevil
coeval, khedival, medieval, primeval,
reprieval, retrieval, upheaval

ieve¹ \iv\ see ive²

ieve² \ēv\ see eave¹

ieved \ēvd\ see eaved

ievement \ēv-mənt\ see evement

iever \ē-vər\ beaver, cleaver, fever,
griever, leaver, reaver, reiver, weaver
achiever, believer, conceiver,
deceiver, enfever, perceiver, receiver,
reliever, retriever, upheaver
school-leaver, transceiver
cantilever, disbeliever, misbeliever,
misconceiver, unbeliever
overachiever, underachiever

ievish \ē-vish\ see eevish

ievo \ē-vō\ see evo

ievous \ē-vəs\ see evous

ieze \ēz\ see eze

if¹ \if\ see iff

if² \ēf\ see ief¹

ife¹ \īf\ fife, Fife, knife, life, rife,
strife, wife
alewife, drawknife, fishwife, flick-
knife, goodwife, half-life, housewife,
jackknife, loosestrife, lowlife, midlife,
nightlife, oldwife, penknife, pro-life,
true-life, wakerife, whole-life, wildlife
afterlife, antilife, Duncan Phyfe,
nurse-midwife, pocketknife, right-to-
life, Yellowknife

ife² \ēf\ see ief¹

ifeless \ī-fləs\ lifeless, strifeless,
wifeless

ifer \ī-fər\ see ipher

iferous \if-ər-əs\ coniferous,
floriferous, lactiferous, luciferous,
pestiferous, somniferous,
splendiferous, vociferous
carboniferous, luminiferous,
odoriferous, salutiferous,
seminiferous, soporiferous,
sudoriferous

iff \if\ biff, cliff, glyph, if, iff, jiff,
kif, miff, quiff, riff, Riff, skiff, sniff,
spiff, spliff, stiff, syph, tiff, whiff
Er Rif, midriff, Plovdiv, triglyph,
what-if, Wycliffe
anaglyph, bindle stiff, hieroglyph,
hippogriff, logogriph, petroglyph

iffany \if-ə-nē\ see iphony

iffe \if\ see iff

iffed \ift\ see ift

iffen \if-ən\ see iffin

iffey \if-ē\ see iffy

iffian \if-ē-ən\ Riffian
Pecksniffian

iffin \if-ən\ griffin, griffon, stiffen,
tiffin

iffish \if-ish\ sniffish, stiffish

iffle \if-əl\ piffle, riffle, skiffle,
sniffle, whiffle, Wiffle

iffler \if-lər\ riffler, sniffler, whiffler

iffness \if-nəs\ stiffness, swiftness

iffon \if-ən\ see iffin

iffy \if-ē\ iffy, cliffy, jiffy, Liffey,
sniffy, spiffy

ific \if-ik\ glyphic
calcific, febrific, horrific, magnific,
pacific, Pacific, prolific, salvific,
specific, terrific, vivific

anaglyphic, beatific, calorific,
colorific, felicific, frigorific,
hieroglyphic, honorific, scientific,
soporific, sudorific, tenebrific
prescientific

ifical \if-i-kəl\ magnifical, pontifical

ificate \if-i-kət\ certificate,
pontificate

ificent \if-ə-sənt\ magnificent,
omnificent

ifle \ī-fəl\ rifle, stifle, trifle

ifling \ī-fliŋ\ rifling, stifling, trifling

ift \ift\ drift, gift, grift, lift, rift, shift,
shrift, sift, squiffed, swift, Swift, thrift
adrift, airlift, blueshift, downshift,
face-lift, festschrift, forklift,
frameshift, gearshift, Great Rift,
makeshift, redshift, shoplift,
snowdrift, spendthrift, spindrift,
spoondrift, unshift, uplift, upshift
—*also* -ed *forms of verbs listed at* iff

ifter \if-tər\ drifter, snifter, swifter
sceneshifter, shape-shifter, shoplifter

ifth \ith\ see ith²

iftness \if-nəs\ see iffness

ifty \if-tē\ drifty, fifty, nifty, shifty,
thrifty, wifty
fifty-fifty, LD₅₀

ig \ig\ big, brig, dig, fig, gig, Grieg,
grig, jig, pig, prig, rig, sprig, swig,
trig, twig, vig, Whig, wig, zig,
bagwig, bigwig, bushpig, earwig,
hedgepig, lime-twig, renege, shindig,
unrig
caprifig, infra dig, jury-rig, periwig,
thimblerig, whirligig, WYSIWYG,
Zagazig
thingamajig

iga¹ \ē-gə\ Riga, Vega, viga
Antigua, omega, quadriga

iga² \ī-gə\ see aiga

igamous \ig-ə-məs\ bigamous
polygamous

igamy \ig-ə-mē\ bigamy, digamy
polygamy

igan¹ \ī-gən\ ligan, tigon

igan² \ig-ən\ see iggin

igand \ig-ənd\ brigand, ligand

igas \ī-gəs\ see ygous

igate \ig-ət\ see igot¹

ige¹ \ēzh\ siege
prestige
noblesse oblige

ige² \ēj\ see iege¹

igel \ij-əl\ see igil

igenous \ij-ə-nəs\ see iginous

igeon \ij-ən\ see ygian

iger \ī-gər\ tiger
braunschweiger

igerent \ij-rənt\ belligerent,
refrigerant
cobelligerent

iggan \ig-ən\ see iggin

iggard \ig-ərd\ niggard, triggered
—*also* -ed *forms of verbs listed at*
igger

igged \igd\ twigged, wigged
bewigged, cat-rigged, square-rigged
periwigged
—*also* -ed *forms of verbs listed at* ig

igger \ig-ər\ bigger, chigger, digger,
jigger, rigger, rigor, snigger, swigger,
trigger, vigor, vigour
ditchdigger, outrigger, rejigger,
reneger, square-rigger
thimblerigger

iggered \ig-ərd\ see iggard

iggery \ig-ə-rē\ piggery, priggery,
Whiggery

iggie \ig-ē\ see iggy

iggin \ig-ən\ biggin, piggin, wigan
balbriggan

iggish \ig-ish\ biggish, piggish, priggish, Whiggish

iggle \ig-əl\ giggle, higgle, jiggle, niggle, sniggle, squiggle, wiggle, wriggle

iggler \ig-lər\ giggler, higgler, niggler, wiggler, wriggler

iggy \ig-ē\ biggie, piggy, twiggy

igh \ī\ see y[1]

ighed \īd\ see ide[1]

ighland \ī-lənd\ highland, Highland, island, Thailand
Long Island, Rhode Island
Staten Island
Prince Edward Island

ighlander \ī-lən-dər\ highlander, islander

ighlands \ī-lənz\ Highlands
Virgin Islands

ighly \ī-lē\ see yly

ighness \ī-nəs\ see inus[1]

ight \īt\ see ite[1]

ightable \īt-ə-bəl\ see itable[1]

ighted \īt-əd\ blighted, sighted, whited
attrited, benighted, clear-sighted, farsighted, foresighted, longsighted, nearsighted, sharp-sighted, shortsighted, skylighted, united
unrequited
—also -ed forms of verbs listed at ite[1]

ighten \īt-ᵊn\ brighten, Brighton, chitin, chiton, frighten, heighten, lighten, tighten, titan, Titan, triton, Triton, whiten
enlighten

ightener \īt-nər\ brightener, lightener, tightener, whitener

ightening \īt-niŋ\ see ightning

ighter \īt-ər\ see iter[1]

ightful \īt-fəl\ frightful, rightful, spiteful, sprightful
delightful, despiteful, foresightful, insightful

ightie \īt-ē\ see ite[2]

ightily \īt-ᵊl-ē\ flightily, mightily

ightiness \īt-ē-nəs\ flightiness, mightiness
almightiness

ighting \īt-iŋ\ see iting

ightless \īt-ləs\ flightless, lightless, sightless

ightly \īt-lē\ brightly, knightly, lightly, nightly, rightly, sightly, slightly, sprightly, tightly, tritely, whitely
contritely, finitely, forthrightly, fortnightly, midnightly, outrightly, politely, unsightly, uprightly
eruditely, impolitely, reconditely

ightment \īt-mənt\ see itement

ightning \īt-niŋ\ lightning, tightening
belt-tightening
—also -ing forms of verbs listed at ighten

ightn't \īt-ᵊnt\ see itant

ighton \īt-ən\ see ighten

ights \īts\ lights, nights, tights
footlights, houselights, weeknights
Dolomites, Golan Heights
—also -s, -'s, and -s' forms of nouns, and -s forms of verbs, listed at ite[1]

ightsome \īt-səm\ lightsome
delightsome

ighty \īt-ē\ see ite[2]

igian \ij-ən\ see ygian

igid \ij-əd\ Brigid, frigid, rigid

igil \ij-əl\ Rigel, sigil, strigil, vigil
residual

igilant \ij-ə-lənt\ vigilant
acidulent

igine \ij-ə-nē\ polygyny
aborigine

iginous \ij-ə-nəs\ caliginous,
fuliginous, indigenous, polygynous,
vertiginous

igion \ij-ən\ see ygian

igious \ij-əs\ litigious, prestigious,
prodigious, religious
irreligious

igit \ij-ət\ see idget

igitte \ij-ət\ see idget

iglet \ig-lət\ piglet, wiglet

igm¹ \im\ see im¹

igm² \īm\ see ime¹

igma \ig-mə\ sigma, stigma
enigma, kerygma

igment \ig-mənt\ figment, pigment

ign \īn\ see ine¹

ignable \ī-nə-bəl\ see inable

ignancy \ig-nən-sē\ benignancy,
malignancy

ignant \ig-nənt\ benignant,
indignant, malignant

igned \īnd\ see ind¹

igneous \ig-nē-əs\ igneous,
ligneous

igner \ī-nər\ see iner¹

igness \ig-nəs\ bigness, Cygnus

ignet \ig-nət\ see ygnet

igning \ī-niŋ\ see ining

ignity \ig-nət-ē\ dignity
indignity, malignity

ignly \īn-lē\ see inely¹

ignment \īn-mənt\ alignment,
assignment, confinement,
consignment, enshrinement,
refinement
nonalignment, realignment

ignon \in-yən\ see inion

ignor \ē-nyər\ see enior

igo¹ \ī-gō\ Sligo
prurigo
vitiligo

igo² \ē-gō\ see ego

igoe \ē-gō\ see ego

igon \ī-gən\ see igan¹

igor \ig-ər\ see igger

igorous \ig-rəs\ rigorous, vigorous

igot¹ \ig-ət\ bigot, frigate, gigot,
spigot

igot² \ik-ət\ see icket

igour \ig-ər\ see igger

igrapher \ig-rə-fər\ calligrapher,
epigrapher, polygrapher, serigrapher

igraphist \ig-rə-fəst\ calligraphist,
epigraphist, polygraphist

igraphy \ig-rə-fē\ calligraphy,
epigraphy
pseudepigraphy

igua \ē-gə\ see iga¹

igue \ēg\ gigue, Grieg, league
blitzkrieg, colleague, fatigue,
garigue, intrigue, squeteague
wampumpeag

iguer \ē-gər\ see eager

iguous \ig-yə-wəs\ ambiguous,
contiguous, exiguous
unambiguous

igured \ig-ərd\ see iggard

ii \ī\ see y¹

iing \ē-iŋ\ see eeing

ija \ē-jə\ see egia

ijah \ī-jə\ Elijah
steatopygia

iji \ē-jē\ Fiji, squeegee

ijl \īl\ see ile¹

ijn \īn\ see ine[1]

ijssel \ī-sə\ see isal

ik[1] \ik\ see ick

ik[2] \ēk\ see eak[1]

ika[1] \ē-kə\ pika, theca
areca, eureka, Frederica, Fredericka,
paprika, Topeka
Costa Rica, Dominica, oiticica,
Tanganyika
bibliotheca

ika[2] \ī-kə\ see ica[1]

ike[1] \ī-kē\ crikey, Nike, Psyche,
spiky

ike[2] \īk\ bike, caique, dike, fyke,
haik, hike, like, mike, Mike, pike,
psych, shrike, sike, spike, strike, trike,
tyke
alike, belike, catlike, childlike,
clocklike, dislike, fly-strike, garpike,
godlike, handspike, hitchhike,
homelike, Klondike, lifelike, mislike,
pealike, prooflike, push-bike, rampike,
restrike, scalelike, sheaflike, shunpike,
suchlike, ten-strike, turnpike, unlike,
Updike, Vandyke, warlike, wifelike,
winglike
berrylike, businesslike, fatherlike,
ladylike, look-alike, machinelike,
marlinespike, marlinspike, minibike,
motorbike, rubberlike, Scafell Pike,
soundalike, thunderstrike, womanlike,
workmanlike
unsportsmanlike

iked[1] \īkt\ liked, piked, spiked
vandyked
—also -ed forms of verbs listed at
ike[2]

iked[2] \ī-kəd\ see ycad

iken \ī-kən\ see ichen[1]

iker \ī-kər\ biker, diker, duiker,
hiker, piker, spiker, striker
disliker, hitchhiker, shunpiker
minibiker

ikes \īks\ yikes
—also -s, -'s, and -s' forms of nouns,
and -s forms of verbs, listed at ike[2]

ikey \ī-kē\ see ike[1]

ikh \ēk\ see eak[1]

iki[1] \ik-ē\ see icky

iki[2] \ē-kē\ see eaky

iking \ī-kiŋ\ liking, striking, Viking
shunpiking
—also -ing forms of verbs listed at
ike[2]

ikker \ik-ər\ see icker[1]

iky \ī-kē\ see ike[1]

il[1] \il\ see ill

il[2] \ēl\ see eal[2]

ila[1] \il-ə\ see illa[2]

ila[2] \ē-lə\ see ela[1]

ila[3] \ī-lə\ Lila
Delilah

ilae \ī-le\ see yly

ilage \ī-lij\ mileage, silage

ilah \ī-lə\ see ila[3]

ilament \il-ə-mənt\ filament
habiliment
monofilament

ilar \ī-lər\ dialer, filar, flier, hilar,
miler, smiler, stylar, styler, tiler, Tyler
beguiler, bifilar, compiler, defiler,
freestyler, profiler, rottweiler,
stockpiler

ilary \il-ə-rē\ see illary

ilate \ī-lət\ see ilot

ilbe \il-be\ see ilby

ilbert \il-bərt\ filbert, gilbert, Gilbert

ilby \il-bē\ trilby
astilbe

ilch[1] \ilk\ see ilk

ilch² \ilch\ filch, milch, zilch

ild¹ \īld\ mild, piled, wild, Wilde
brainchild, godchild, grandchild,
hog-wild, man-child, pantiled,
Rothschild, schoolchild, self-styled,
stepchild
—also -ed *forms of verbs listed at*
ile¹

ild² \il\ see ill

ild³ \ilt\ see ilt

ild⁴ \ild\ see illed

ilda \il-də\ Hilda, tilde, Wilda

ilde¹ \il-də\ see ilda

ilde² \īld\ see ild¹

ilder¹ \il-dər\ builder, gilder, guilder,
wilder
bewilder, boatbuilder, shipbuilder,
upbuilder
bodybuilder, jerry-builder

ilder² \īl-dər\ milder, wilder, Wilder

ilding \il-diŋ\ building, gilding,
hilding
abuilding, outbuilding, shipbuilding
bodybuilding
—also -ing *forms of verbs listed at*
illed

ildish \īl-dish\ childish, wildish

ildly \īld-lē\ childly, mildly, wildly

ile¹ \īl\ aisle, bile, dial, faille, file,
guile, I'll, isle, Kyle, lisle, Lyle, mile,
Nile, phial, pile, rile, roil, smile, spile,
stile, style, tile, trial, vial, vile, viol,
while, wile
abseil, aedile, agile, anile, argyle,
Argyll, audile, awhile, axile, beguile,
Blue Nile, Carlyle, compile, condyle,
cross-file, de Stijl, decile, defile,
denial, docile, ductile, enisle, ensile,
erewhile, erstwhile, espial, exile,
febrile, fictile, fissile, flexile, fragile,
freestyle, futile, genial, gentile,
gracile, habile, hairstyle, Kabyle,
labile, life-style, meanwhile, mistrial,
mobile, motile, nubile, pantile, penile,

pensile, profile, puerile, quartile,
quintile, redial, reptile, resile, retrial,
revile, sandpile, scissile, sectile,
senile, servile, sessile, stabile,
stockpile, sundial, tactile, tensile,
textile, turnstile, typestyle, unpile,
utile, vagile, virile, woodpile,
worthwhile
afebrile, airmobile, Anglophile,
chamomile, contractile, crocodile,
discophile, domicile, endostyle,
epistyle, erectile, extensile,
Francophile, Gallophile, halophile,
homophile, hypostyle, infantile,
interfile, juvenile, low-profile,
mercantile, oenophile, otherwhile,
pedophile, percentile, peristyle,
prehensile, projectile, protractile,
pulsatile, reconcile, refractile,
retractile, self-denial, Slavophile,
spermophile, technopile, thermopile,
turophile, urostyle, versatile, vibratile,
xenophile
ailurophile, amphiprostyle,
audiophile, bibliophile, electrophile,
fluviatile, Germanophile, heterophile,
Italophile, nucleophile

ile² \il\ see ill

ile³ \ē-lē\ see eely

ile⁴ \ēl\ see eal²

ile⁵ \il-ē\ see illy¹

ilead \il-ē-əd\ see iliad

ileage \ī-lij\ see ilage

ileal \il-ē-əl\ see ilial¹

ileless \īl-ləs\ guileless, pileless,
smileless

iler¹ \ē-lər\ see ealer

iler² \ī-lər\ see ilar

iles \īlz\ Giles, Miles, Niles
Wade-Giles
British Isles, Western Isles

ileum \il-ē-əm\ see ilium

iley \ī-lē\ see yly

ilford \il-fərd\ Milford, Wilford

ili¹ \il-ē\ see illy¹

ili² \ē-lē\ see eely

ilia¹ \il-ē-ə\ Celia, cilia
Cecelia, Cecilia, Massilia
Anglophilia, basophilia, coprophilia,
hemophilia, juvenilia, necrophilia,
neophilia, pedophilia, sensibilia
memorabilia

ilia² \il-yə\ Brasilia, sedilia
bougainvillea, sensibilia
memorabilia

ilia³ \ēl-yə\ see elia

iliad \il-ē-əd\ Gilead, Iliad
balm of Gilead

ilial \il-ē-əl\ filial, ileal
familial, unfilial

ilian¹ \il-ē-ən\ Gillian, Ilian, Lillian
Basilian, reptilian
Abbevillian, crocodilian, preexilian,
vespertilian

ilian² \il-yən\ see illion

ilias \il-ē-əs\ see ilious¹

iliate \il-ē-ət\ ciliate
affiliate

ilic \il-ik\ killick
acrylic, allylic, Cyrillic, dactylic,
exilic, idyllic, sibylic
amphiphilic, Anglophilic,
hemophilic, necrophilic, pedophilic,
postexilic, zoophilic
bibliophilic

ilica \il-i-kə\ silica
basilica

ilican \il-i-kən\ see ilicon

ilicon \il-i-kən\ Millikan, silicon,
spillikin
basilican
ferrosilicon

ilience \il-yəns\ see illiance

iliency \il-yən-sē\ see illiancy

ilient \il-yənt\ brilliant
resilient

iliment \il-ə-mənt\ see ilament

iling¹ \ī-liŋ\ filing, piling, spiling,
styling, tiling
hairstyling

iling² \ē-liŋ\ see eeling

ilion¹ \il-yən\ see illion

ilion² \il-ē-ən\ see ilian¹

ilious¹ \il-ē-əs\ punctilious
supercilious
materfamilias, paterfamilias

ilious² \il-yəs\ bilious
atrabilious, supercilious

ilip \il-əp\ see illip

ilitant \il-ə-tɔnt\ militant
rehabilitant

ility \il-ət-ē\ ability, agility, anility,
civility, debility, docility, ductility,
facility, fertility, fragility, futility,
gentility, gracility, hostility, humility,
lability, mobility, motility, nobility,
nubility, scurrility, sectility, senility,
stability, sterility, suability, tactility,
tranquility, utility, vagility, virility
actability, affability, arability,
audibility, bearability, biddability,
breathability, brushability, capability,
changeability, coilability, contractility,
countability, credibility, crossability,
culpability, curability, cutability,
disability, disutility, drapability,
drillability, drinkability, durability,
dyeability, edibility, equability,
erectility, fallibility, feasibility,
fishability, flammability, flexibility,
forgeability, formability, frangibility,
friability, gullibility, imbecility,
immobility, inability, incivility,
indocility, infantility, infertility,
instability, inutility, juvenility,
laudability, leachability, legibility,
liability, likability, livability,
mailability, meltability, miscibility,
movability, mutability, notability,
packability, placability, plausibility,
playability, portability, possibility,

potability, pregnability, prehensility, printability, probability, puerility, readability, risibility, roadability, salability, sensibility, sewability, shareability, sociability, solubility, solvability, spreadability, squeezability, stainability, stretchability, tenability, testability, traceability, treatability, tunability, usability, vendability, versatility, viability, visibility, volatility, washability, wearability, wettability, workability

absorbability, acceptability, accessibility, accountability, adaptability, adjustability, admirability, admissibility, adoptability, adorability, advisability, affectability, agreeability, alterability, amenability, amiability, amicability, appealability, applicability, approachability, assumability, attainability, automobility, availability, believability, collapsibility, combustability, comparability, compatibility, compensability, compressability, computability, conceivability, conductability, confirmability, contemptibility, contractibility, controllability, convertibility, corrigibility, corruptibility, cultivability, damageability, decidability, deductibility, defeasibility, defensibility, delectability, demonstrability, deniability, dependability, desirability, destructibility, detachability, detectability, deterrability, detonability, digestibility, dilatability, dispensability, disposability, dissociability, dissolubility, distensibility, distractibility, divisibility, educability, electability, eligibility, employability, enforceability, equitability, erasability, erodability, exchangeability, excitability, excludability, exhaustibility, expansibility, expendability, explosibility, exportability, extensibility,

extractibility, extrudability, fashionability, fatigability, filterability, fissionability, formidability, habitability, heritability, illegibility, immiscibility, immovability, immutability, impalpability, impassability, impassibility, impeccability, implacability, implausibility, impossibility, impregnability, impressibility, improbability, improvability, inaudibility, incapability, incredibility, indelibility, inductibility, ineffability, infallibility, infeasibility, inflammability, inflexibility, infrangibility, infusibility, insensibility, insolubility, insurability, intangibility, invincibility, invisibility, irascibility, irritability, knowledgeability, machinability, maintainability, manageability, marketability, merchantability, measurability, modulability, navigability, negligibility, nonflammability, openability, operability, opposability, palatability, penetrability, perceptibility, perdurability, perfectibility, performability, perishability, permeability, permissibility, pleasurability, practicability, preferability, presentability, preservability, preventability, processibility, programmability, punishability, reasonability, refundability, reliability, renewability, repeatability, reputability, resistibility, respectability, responsibility, retrievability, reusability, reversability, salvageability, separability, severability, serviceability, suggestability, supportability, suppressibility, survivability, susceptibility, sustainability, tolerability, trafficability, transferability, translatability, transmissibility, transplantability, transportability, unflappability, unthinkability, untouchability, variability, violability, vulnerability, weatherability

alienability, analyzability,
assimilability, codifiability,
commensurability, communicability,
comprehensibility, decomposability,
deliverability, discriminability,
disrespectability, distinguishability,
enumerability, exceptionability,
hypnotizability, illimitability,
impenetrability, imperishability,
impermeability, impermissibility,
imponderability, impracticability,
impressionability, inaccessibility,
inadmissibility, inadvisability,
inalterability, inapplicability,
incalculability, incombustibility,
incomparability, incompatibility,
incompressibility, inconceivability,
incontestability, inconvertibility,
incorrigibility, incorruptibility,
indefeasibility, indefensibility,
indefinability, indestructibility,
indigestibility, indispensability,
indissolubility, indivisibility,
indomitability, indubitability,
ineducability, ineffaceability,
ineligibility, ineluctability,
inevitability, inexhaustibility,
inexplicability, inexpressibility,
inextricability, inheritability,
insatiability, inseparability,
insociability, insusceptibility,
intelligibility, interchangeability,
intolerability, invariability,
invulnerability, irreducibility,
irreformability, irrefutability,
irremovability, irrepealability,
irreplaceability, irrepressibility,
irreproachability, irresistibility,
irresponsibility, irretrievability,
irreversibility, irrevocability,
maneuverability, manipulability,
negotiability, polarizability,
recognizability, recoverability,
rectifiability, reprehensibility,
reproducibility, substitutability,
unacceptability, unaccountability,
understandability, undesirability,
verifiability
  biocompatability, biodegradability,
differentiability, inalienability,
incommensurability,

incommunicability,
incomprehensibility,
incontrovertibility, indefatigability,
indistinguishability, ineradicability,
interoperability, irreconcilability,
irreproducibility

ilium \il-ē-əm\ cilium, ileum, ilium,
  Ilium, milium, trillium
  beryllium
  penicillium

ilk \ilk\ bilk, ilk, milch, milk, silk
  buttermilk, liebfraumilch

ilker \il-kər\ bilker, milker

ilky \il-kē\ milky, silky

ill \il\ bill, Bill, brill, chill, dill, drill,
  fill, frill, gill, grill, grille, hill, ill, Jill,
  kill, krill, mil, mill, mille, nil, nill, Phil,
  pill, prill, quill, rill, shill, shrill, sild,
  sill, skill, spill, squill, still, swill, thill,
  thrill, til, till, trill, twill, vill, will, Will
    anthill, backfill, bluegill, Brazil,
  Catskill, Churchill, cranesbill,
  crossbill, de Mille, dentil, deskill,
  distill, doorsill, downhill, duckbill,
  dullsville, dunghill, foothill, freewill,
  fulfill, goodwill, Granville, gristmill,
  handbill, hawksbill, hornbill,
  Huntsville, instill, Knoxville, lambkill,
  landfill, limekiln, manille, Melville,
  molehill, mudsill, Nashville, no-till,
  playbill, quadrille, refill, roadkill,
  sawmill, self-will, Seville, sheathbill,
  shoebill, sidehill, sigil, spadille,
  spoonbill, stabile, standstill, stockstill,
  storksbill, T-bill, treadmill, unreal,
  until, uphill, vaudeville, waxbill,
  waybill, windchill, windmill
    Brazzaville, chlorophyll, daffodil,
  deshabille, de Toqueville, dishabille,
  escadrille, espadrille, Evansville,
  fiberfill, Francophil, Hooverville,
  Jacksonville, Libreville, Louisville,
  minimill, overfill, overkill, overspill,
  razorbill, rototill, tormentil, verticil,
  windowsill, whippoorwill, winter-kill,
  Yggdrasil
    acidophil, ivorybill, minoxydil,
  Nizhni Togil, run-of-the-mill

I'll \īl\ see ile[1]

illa[1] \ē-yə\ barilla, cuadrilla
banderilla, quesadilla

illa[2] \il-ə\ scilla, Scylla, squilla, villa,
Willa
ancilla, Aquila, Attila, axilla,
Camilla, cedilla, chinchilla, flotilla,
gorilla, guerrilla, manila, Manila,
megillah, papilla, perilla, Priscilla,
scintilla, vanilla
camarilla, cascarilla, granadilla,
potentilla, sabadilla, sapodilla,
sarsaparilla

illa[3] \ē-ə\ see ia[1]

illa[4] \ēl-yə\ see elia

illa[5] \ē-lə\ see ela[1]

illable \il-ə-bəl\ billable, drillable,
fillable, spillable, syllable, tillable
disyllable, refillable, trisyllable
decasyllable, monosyllable,
octosyllable, polysyllable
hendecasyllable

illage \il-ij\ grillage, millage, pillage,
spillage, tillage, village
no-tillage, permillage
Greenwich Village

illah \il-ə\ see illa[2]

illain \il-ən\ see illon

illar \il-ər\ see iller

illary \il-ə-rē\ Hilary, Hillary,
phyllary
codicillary

illate \il-ət\ see illet

ille[1] \il\ see ill

ille[2] \ē\ see ee[1]

ille[3] \ēl\ see eal[2]

illea \il-yə\ see ilia[2]

illed \ild\ build, dilled, drilled, gild,
gilled, guild, skilled, twilled, willed

Brynhild, engild, gold-filled,
goodwilled, rebuild, self-willed,
spoonbilled, unbuild, unskilled,
upbuild, wergild
jerry-build, overbuild, semiskilled
—also -ed forms of verbs listed at ill

illedness \il-nəs\ see ilness

illein \il-ən\ see illon

iller \il-ər\ biller, chiller, driller,
filler, giller, griller, hiller, killer,
miller, Miller, pillar, schiller, spiller,
swiller, thriller, tiller, triller
axillar, distiller, fulfiller, painkiller,
pralltriller, von Schiller
caterpillar, lady-killer, Rototiller
—also -er forms of adjectives listed
at ill

illery \il-rē\ pillory
artillery, distillery

illes \il-ēz\ see illies

illet \il-ət\ billet, fillet, millet, rillet,
skillet, willet
distillate

illful \il-fəl\ skillful, willful
unskillful

illi[1] \il-ē\ see illy[1]

illi[2] \ē-lē\ see eely

illian[1] \il-ē-ən\ see ilian[1]

illian[2] \il-yən\ see illion

illiance \il-yəns\ brilliance
resilience

illiancy \il-yən-sē\ brilliancy
resiliency

illiant \il-yənt\ see ilient

illick \il-ik\ see ilic

illie \il-ē\ see illy[1]

illies \il-ēz\ willies
Achilles, Antilles
Greater Antilles, Lesser Antilles
Netherlands Antilles

—also -s, -'s, *and* -s' *forms of nouns listed at* illy¹

illikan \il-i-kən\ see ilicon

illikin \il-i-kən\ see ilicon

illin¹ \il-əm\ see illum

illin² \il-ən\ see illon

illing \il-iŋ\ billing, drilling, filling, killing, milling, schilling, shilling, skilling, twilling, willing
  fulfilling, spine-chilling, unwilling
  —also -ing *forms of verbs listed at* ill

illion \il-yən\ billion, jillion, Lillian, million, pillion, trillion, zillion
  caecilian, Castilian, centillion, civilian, cotillion, decillion, modillion, nonillion, octillion, pavilion, postilion, quadrillion, Quintilian, quintillion, reptilian, septillion, sextillion, toubillion, vaudevillian, vermilion
  crocodilian, Maximilian, preexilian, quindecillion, sexdecillion, tredecillion, undecillion, vespertilian, vigintillion
  duodecillion, novemdecillion, octodecillion, septendecillion
  quattuordecillion

illip \il-əp\ fillip, Philip

illis \il-əs\ see illus

illium \il-ē-əm\ see ilium

illness \il-nəs\ chillness, illness, shrillness, stillness

illo¹ \il-ō\ billow, pillow, willow
  Negrillo, tornillo
  Amarillo, armadillo, cigarillo, coyotillo, peccadillo, tamarillo

illo² \ē-ō\ see io²

illon \il-ən\ billon, Dylan, Uilleann, villain, villein
  tefillin
  penicillin
  amoxycillin

illory \il-rē\ see illery

illous \il-əs\ see illus

illow¹ \il-ə\ see illa²

illow² \il-ō\ see illo¹

illowy \il-ə-wē\ billowy, pillowy, willowy

ills \ilz\ Black Hills, no-frills
  Alban Hills
  —also -s, -'s, *and* -s' *forms of nouns, and* -s *forms of verbs, listed at* ill

illum \il-əm\ chillum
  vexillum

illus \il-əs\ Phyllis, villous, Willis
  bacillus, lapillus
  amaryllis
  toga virilis

illy¹ \il-ē\ Billie, billy, Chile, chili, chilly, dilly, filly, frilly, gillie, hilly, illy, Lillie, lily, Lily, Millie, really, Scilly, silly, stilly, Willie, Willy
  bacilli, Caerphilly, daylily, fusilli, guidwillie, hillbilly
  piccalilli, rockabilly, willy-nilly

illy² \il-lē\ shrilly, stilly

iln¹ \il\ see ill

iln² \iln\ kiln, Milne

ilne \iln\ see iln²

ilo¹ \ī-lō\ milo, Milo, phyllo, silo

ilo² \ē-lō\ helo, kilo, phyllo
  Iloilo

ilom \ī-ləm\ see ilum

iloquence \il-ə-kwəns\ grandiloquence, magniloquence

iloquent \il-ə-kwənt\ grandiloquent, magniloquent

iloquist \il-ə-kwəst\ soliloquist, ventriloquist

iloquy \il-ə-kwē\ soliloquy, ventriloquy

ilot \ī-lət\ eyelet, islet, Pilate, pilot, stylet
  copilot
  autopilot, Pontius Pilate

ils \ils\ fils, grilse, Nils

ilse \ils\ see ils

ilt \ilt\ built, gilt, guilt, hilt, jilt, kilt, lilt, milt, quilt, silt, stilt, tilt, wilt
  atilt, bloodguilt, Brunhild, homebuilt, inbuilt, rebuilt, unbuilt, uptilt
  carvel-built, clinker-built, custom-built, purpose-built

ilter \il-tər\ filter, kilter, milter, philter
  off-kilter

ilth \ilth\ filth, spilth, tilth

iltie \il-tē\ see ilty

ilton \ilt-ᵊn\ Hilton, Milton, Stilton, Wilton

ilty \il-tē\ guilty, kiltie, milty, silty
  bloodguilty

ilum \ī-ləm\ filum, hilum, phylum, whilom, xylem
  asylum

ilus \ī-ləs\ eyeless, pilus, stylus, tieless

ily¹ \ī-lē\ see yly

ily² \il-ē\ see illy¹

im¹ \im\ bream, brim, dim, glim, grim, Grimm, gym, him, hymn, Jim, Kim, limb, limn, mim, nim, prim, rim, scrim, shim, skim, slim, swim, Tim, trim, vim, whim
  bedim, dislimn, forelimb, passim, prelim, Purim, Sikkim, slim-jim, snap-brim
  acronym, anonym, antonym, eponym, homonym, metonym, paradigm, paronym, pseudonym, seraphim, synonym, tautonym, toponym, underbrim
  ad interim, heteronym

im² \ēm\ see eam¹

I'm \īm\ see ime¹

ima \ē-mə\ see ema

imable \ī-mə-bəl\ climable
  sublimable, unclimbable

imace \im-əs\ grimace, tzimmes

image \im-ij\ image, scrimmage
  self-image
  afterimage

iman \ē-mən\ see emon¹

imate \ī-mət\ climate, primate
  acclimate

imb¹ \im\ see im¹

imb² \īm\ see ime¹

imba \im-bə\ limba
  kalimba, marimba

imbable \ī-mə-bəl\ see imable

imbal \im-bəl\ see imble

imbale \im-bəl\ see imble

imbed \imd\ limbed, rimmed
  clean-limbed
  —also -ed forms of verbs listed at im¹

imber¹ \im-bər\ limber, timber
  sawtimber, unlimber

imber² \ī-mər\ see imer¹

imble \im-bəl\ cymbal, gimbal, nimble, symbol, thimble, timbal, timbale, wimble

imbo \im-bō\ bimbo, limbo
  akimbo
  gumbo-limbo

imbral \əm-brəl\ see ambrel

imbre \am-bər\ see ambar²

imbrel \im-brəl\ timbrel, whimbrel

imbus \im-bəs\ limbus, nimbus

ime¹ \īm\ chime, climb, clime, crime, dime, disme, grime, I'm, lime,

mime, prime, rhyme, rime, slime,
stime, thyme, time
 airtime, all-time, bedtime, begrime,
big time, birdlime, daytime,
downtime, dreamtime, enzyme,
flextime, foretime, halftime, lifetime,
longtime, lunchtime, Mannheim,
Maytime, mealtime, meantime,
nighttime, noontime, old-time,
onetime, part-time, pastime,
peacetime, playtime, quicklime,
ragtime, schooltime, seedtime, small-
time, sometime, space-time,
springtime, sublime, teatime, two-
time, uptime, wartime
 aftertime, Anaheim, anytime,
beforetime, Christmastime,
dinnertime, double-time, harvesttime,
Jotunheim, lysozyme, maritime,
monorhyme, overtime, pantomime,
paradigm, summertime, wintertime
 nickel-and-dime

ime² \ēm\ see eam¹

imel \im-əl\ gimel, gimmal, kümmel

imeless \īm-ləs\ rhymeless, timeless

imely \īm-lē\ primely, timely
 untimely

imen \ī-mən\ flyman, hymen,
Hymen, limen, Lyman, Simon

imeon \im-ē-ən\ see imian

imeous \ī-məs\ see imis

imer¹ \ī-mər\ chimer, climber,
dimer, mimer, primer, rhymer, timer,
trimer
 full-timer, old-timer, small-timer,
sublimer, two-timer
 wisenheimer

imer² \im-ər\ see immer

imerick \im-rik\ see ymric

imes¹ \īmz\ times
 betimes, daytimes, sometimes
 betweentimes, oftentimes
 —also -s, -'s, and -s' forms of nouns,
and -s forms of verbs, listed at ime¹

imes² \ēm\ see eam¹

imeter \im-ət-ər\ dimeter, limiter,
scimitar, trimeter
 altimeter, delimiter, perimeter,
tachymeter

imetry \im-ə-trē\ symmetry
 gravimetry
 polarimetry, sypersymmetry

imian \im-ē-ən\ Simeon, simian
 Endymion, prosimian

imic \im-ik\ see ymic²

imical \im-i-kəl\ inimical,
metonymical, synonymical,
toponymical

imicry \im-i-krē\ gimmickry,
mimicry

imilar \im-ə-lər\ similar
 dissimilar

imile \im-ə-lē\ simile, swimmily
 facsimile

iminal¹ \im-ən-ᵊl\ criminal, liminal
 subliminal
 supraliminal

iminal² \im-nəl\ see ymnal

iminy \im-ə-nē\ see imony

imis \ī-məs\ primus, thymus,
timeous
 imprimis, untimeous

imitable \im-ət-ə-bəl\ imitable
 illimitable, inimitable

imitar \im-ət-ər\ see imeter

imiter \im-ət-ər\ see imeter

imits \im-its\ limits, Nimitz

imity \im-ət-ē\ dimity
 proximity, sublimity
 anonymity, equanimity, longanimity,
magnanimity, pseudonymity,
synonymity, unanimity
 pusillanimity

imitz \im-its\ see imits

imm \im\ see im[1]

immable \im-ə-bəl\ dimmable, swimmable

immage \im-ij\ see image

immal \im-əl\ see imel

imme \i-mē\ see immy

immed \imd\ see imbed

immer \im-ər\ brimmer, dimmer, glimmer, krimmer, limmer, limner, primer, shimmer, simmer, skimmer, slimmer, swimmer, trimmer
—*also* -er *forms of adjectives listed at* im[1]

immes \im-əs\ see imace

immick \im-ik\ see ymic[2]

immickry \im-i-krē\ see imicry

immily \im-ə-lē\ see imile

immy \im-ē\ gimme, jimmy, limby, shimmy, swimmy

imn \im\ see im[1]

imner \im-ər\ see immer

imo \ē-mō\ primo
sentimo

imon \ī-mən\ see imen

imony \im-ə-nē\ simony
niminy-piminy

imothy \im-ə-thē\ timothy, Timothy
polymathy

imp \imp\ blimp, chimp, crimp, gimp, guimpe, imp, limp, pimp, primp, scrimp, shrimp, simp, skimp, wimp

impe \imp\ see imp

imper \im-pər\ limper, shrimper, simper, whimper

imping \im-pən\ see ympan

impish \im-pish\ blimpish, impish

imple \im-pəl\ dimple, pimple, simple, wimple
oversimple

imply \im-plē\ dimply, limply, pimply, simply

impy \im-pē\ crimpy, gimpy, scrimpy, shrimpy, skimpy, wimpy

imsy \im-zē\ flimsy, slimsy, whimsy

imulus \im-yə-ləs\ limulus, stimulus

imus \ī-məs\ see imis

imy \ī-mē\ grimy, limey, limy, rimy, slimy, stymie, thymy
old-timey

in[1] \in\ been, bin, blin, chin, din, fin, Finn, gin, grin, Gwyn, hin, in, inn, kin, linn, Lynn, Lynne, pin, shin, Shin, sin, skin, spin, thin, tin, twin, whin, win, wyn, yin, zin
again, agin, akin, all-in, backspin, bearskin, begin, Benin, Berlin, Boleyn, bowfin, break-in, buckskin, built-in, burn-in, calfskin, capeskin, cave-in, chagrin, check-in, Chongjin, close-in, clothespin, coonskin, Corinne, crankpin, cut-in, deerskin, doeskin, drive-in, drop-in, duckpin, dustbin, fade-in, fill-in, foreskin, goatskin, Guilin, hairpin, Harbin, has-been, headpin, herein, Jilin, Kerin, kidskin, kingpin, lambskin, lead-in, lie-in, linchpin, live-in, lived-in, lobe-fin, locked-in, look-in, love-in, moleskin, munchkin, Nankin, ninepin, no-win, oilskin, Pekin, phone-in, pigskin, pinyin, plug-in, pushpin, ruin, run-in, saimin, scarfpin, scarfskin, sealskin, set-in, sharkskin, sheepskin, shoo-in, shut-in, sidespin, sit-in, sleep-in, snakeskin, stand-in, step-in, stickpin, swanskin, tailspin, take-in, tap-in, teach-in, tenpin, therein, tholepin, threadfin, throw-in, tie-in, tiepin, tip-in, toe-in, trade-in, tuned-in, turn-in, unpin, walk-in, weigh-in, wherein, wineskin, within, woolskin, write-in

candlepin, catechin, Ha-erh-pin, Ho
Chi Minh, Lohengrin, lying-in,
mandolin, maximin, Mickey Finn,
onionskin, palanquin, Tianjin,
underpin, underspin, Vietminh, violin,
whipper-in
canthaxanthin

in² \ēn\ see ine³

in³ \an\ see an⁵

in⁴ \aⁿ\ Chopin, doyen, Gauguin,
moulin, Petain, Rodin, serin
coq au vin, coup de main, fleur de
coin, Mazarin

in⁵ \ən\ see un¹

ina¹ \ī-nə\ china, China, Dina,
Dinah, Heine, Ina, mina, mynah
Aegina, angina, Lucina, nandina,
piscina, Regina, salina, shechinah,
vagina
Cochin China, Carolina, Indochina,
kamaaina, Poland China
North Carolina, South Carolina

ina² \ē-nə\ Deena, Dena, kina, Lena,
Nina, plena, Shina, Tina, vena, vina
arena, Athena, cantina, catena,
Christina, coquina, corbina, corvina,
czarina, Edwina, euglena, farina,
fontina, Georgina, hyena, kachina,
Kristina, marina, Marina, medina,
Medina, Messina, nandina, novena,
patina, piscina, platina, Regina,
retsina, Rowena, salina, sestina,
Shechinah, subpoena, verbena
Agrippina, amberina, Angelina,
Argentina, ballerina, casuarina,
Carolina, Catalina, catilena, cavatina,
Chianina, concertina, Filipina,
javelina, Katerina, ocarina, Palestrina,
Pasadena, Saint Helena, semolina,
signorina, sonatina, Taormina,
Teresina, Wilhelmina
Herzegovina, Pallas Athena, Strait of
Messina

inable \ī-nə-bəl\ minable
consignable, declinable, definable,
inclinable
indeclinable, indefinable

inach \in-ich\ Greenwich, spinach

inah¹ \ē-nə\ see ina²

inah² \ī-nə\ see ina¹

inal¹ \īn-ᵊl\ clinal, final, rhinal,
spinal, trinal, vinyl
matutinal, officinal, quarterfinal,
semifinal, serotinal

inal² \ēn-ᵊl\ see enal

inally \īn-ᵊl-ē\ clinally, finally,
spinally
matutinally

inary \ī-nə-rē\ binary, trinary

inas¹ \ī-nəs\ see inus¹

inas² \ē-nəs\ see enus¹

inative \in-ət-iv\ see initive

inc \iŋk\ see ink

inca \iŋ-kə\ Dinka, Inca, vinca
Mandinka

incal \iŋ-kəl\ see inkle

incan \iŋ-kən\ Incan
Lincoln

ince¹ \ins\ blintz, chintz, mince,
prince, quince, rinse, since, wince
convince, evince, shinsplints
Port-au-Prince

ince² \ans\ see ance³

incely \in-slē\ princely, tinselly

incer \in-chər\ see incher

inch \inch\ chinch, cinch, clinch,
finch, flinch, grinch, inch, lynch,
pinch, squinch, winch
bullfinch, goldfinch, greenfinch,
hawfinch, unclinch

incher \in-chər\ clincher, flincher,
lyncher, pincer, pincher, wincher
affenpinscher, penny-pincher
Doberman pinscher

inching \in-chiŋ\ unflinching

penny-pinching
—*also* -ing *forms of verbs listed at*
inch

incible \in-sə-bəl\ principal,
principle, vincible
evincible, invincible
inconvincible

incing \in-siŋ\ ginseng, mincing
convincing
unconvincing
—*also* -ing *forms of verbs listed at*
ince[1]

incipal \in-sə-bəl\ see incible

inciple \in-sə-bəl\ see incible

inck \iŋk\ see ink

incky \iŋ-kē\ see inky

incoln \iŋ-kən\ see incan

inct \iŋt\ linked, kinked, tinct
distinct, extinct, instinct, precinct,
succinct, unlinked
indistinct

inction \iŋ-shən\ distinction,
extinction
contradistinction

inctive \iŋ-tiv\ distinctive,
extinctive, instinctive
indistinctive

incture \iŋ-chər\ cincture, tincture

ind[1] \īnd\ bind, blind, find, grind,
hind, kind, mind, rind, signed, spined,
tined, wind, wynd
affined, behind, confined, inclined,
in-kind, night-blind, purblind, refined,
remind, rewind, sand-blind, snow-
blind, spellbind, stone-blind,
streamlined, unbind, unkind, unwind
color-blind, double-blind, gavelkind,
gravel-blind, hoodman-blind,
humankind, mastermind, nonaligned,
single-blind, unaligned, undersigned,
well-defined, womankind
—*also* -ed *forms of verbs listed at*
ine[1]

ind[2] \ind\ finned, Ind, Sind, skinned,
wind
buckskinned, crosswind, downwind,
exscind, prescind, rescind, soft-finned,
thick-skinned, thin-skinned, upwind,
whirlwind, woodwind
Amerind, spiny-finned, tamarind
—*also* -ed *forms of verbs listed at*
in[1]

ind[3] \int\ see int

inda \in-də\ Linda
Lucinda, Melinda
Samarinda

indar \in-dər\ see inder[2]

inded[1] \īn-dəd\ minded, rinded
broad-minded, fair-minded, high-
minded, large-minded, like-minded,
low-minded, right-minded, small-
minded, strong-minded, tough-
minded, weak-minded
absentminded, bloody-minded, civic-
minded, evil-minded, feebleminded,
narrow-minded, open-minded,
simpleminded, single-minded, social-
minded, tender-minded
—*also* -ed *forms of verbs listed at*
ind[1]

inded[2] \in-dəd\ brinded,
long-winded, short-winded
broken-winded
—*also* -ed *forms of verbs listed at*
ind[2]

inder[1] \īn-dər\ binder, blinder,
finder, grinder, hinder, minder, winder
bookbinder, faultfinder, highbinder,
netminder, pathfinder, reminder, ring
binder, self-binder, sidewinder,
spellbinder, stem-winder, viewfinder
organ-grinder
—*also* -er *forms of adjectives listed
at* ind[1]

inder[2] \in-dər\ cinder, hinder,
Pindar, tinder

indful \īn-fəl\ mindful
remindful, unmindful

indhi \in-dē\ see **indy**

indi \in-dē\ see **indy**

indic \in-dik\ Indic, syndic

indie \in-dē\ see **indy**

inding \īn-diŋ\ binding, finding, winding
bookbinding, fact-finding, faultfinding, pathfinding, self-winding, spellbinding, stem-winding
—*also* -*ing forms of verbs listed at* ind¹

indlass \in-ləs\ see **inless**

indle \in-dᵊl\ brindle, dwindle, kindle, spindle, swindle
enkindle

indless \īn-ləs\ kindless, mindless, spineless

indling¹ \in-lən\ pindling, kindling

indling² \ind-liŋ\ dwindling, kindling, pindling, spindling
—*also* -*ing forms of verbs listed at* indle¹

indly¹ \in-lē\ see **inly**

indly² \īn-lē\ see **inely¹**

indness \īn-nəs\ blindness, fineness, kindness
purblindness, unkindness
loving-kindness

indowed \in-dəd\ see **inded²**

indus \in-dəs\ Indus, Pindus

indy \in-dē\ Cindy, Hindi, indie, lindy, shindy, Sindhi, windy
Rawalpindi

ine¹ \īn\ bine, brine, chine, cline, dine, dyne, eyen, fine, Jain, kine, line, Line, Main, mine, nine, pine, Rhein, Rhine, rind, shine, shrine, sign, spine, spline, stein, Stein, swine, syne, thine, tine, trine, twine, vine, whine, wine
A-line, affine, airline, align, alkyne, alpine, assign, balkline, baseline,

beeline, benign, Bernstein, bloodline, bovine, bowline, branchline, breadline, buntline, bustline, byline, canine, caprine, carbine, carmine, cervine, clothesline, coastline, combine, compline, condign, confine, consign, corvine, cutline, dateline, deadline, decline, define, design, divine, dragline, driveline, earthshine, Einstein, eiswein, enshrine, ensign, entwine, equine, ethyne, feline, ferine, fraulein, frontline, gantline, grapevine, guideline, hairline, hard-line, headline, hemline, hipline, Holbein, Holstein, incline, indign, in-line, jawline, landline, lang syne, lifeline, longline, lupine, mainline, malign, midline, moline, moonshine, off-line, old-line, opine, outline, outshine, ovine, Pauline, Pennine, Petrine, pipeline, piscine, plotline, pontine, Pontine, porcine, potline, propine, quinine, rapine, recline, redline, refine, reline, repine, resign, ridgeline, roofline, Sabine, saline, setline, shoreline, sideline, Sixtine, skyline, soft-line, straight-line, strandline, streamline, strychnine, subline, sunshine, supine, syncline, taurine, tie-line, time-line, topline, touchline, towline, tramline, trapline, trephine, trotline, truckline, tumpline, turbine, untwine, ursine, vespine, vulpine, waistline, woodbine, zayin, zebrine
aerodyne, alkaline, androgyne, Angeline, anodyne, anserine, anticline, aquiline, argentine, asinine, auld lang syne, borderline, bottomline, Byzantine, calamine, calcimine, Caroline, catarrhine, Catiline, celandine, centerline, cisalpine, Cisalpine, clandestine, colubrine, columbine, Columbine, concubine, Constantine, countermine, countersign, crystalline, cytokine, disincline, eglantine, endocrine, exocrine, falconine, fescennine, Frankenstein, gregarine, infantine, interline, intertwine, iodine, Johannine, leonine, Liechtenstein, monkeyshine, muscadine, opaline,

palatine, Palestine, passerine,
porcupine, psittacine, realign,
redefine, redesign, riverine,
Rubenstein, saccharine, sapphirine,
saturnine, serpentine, sibylline, sixty-
nine, subalpine, Theatine, timberline,
turnverein, turpentine, underline,
undermine, Ursuline, uterine,
valentine, vespertine, viperine,
vulturine, waterline, zibeline
  accipitrine, adamantine, adulterine,
alexandrine, amaranthine, Capitoline,
elephantine, Evangeline, Frankfurt am
Main, Rembrandt van Rijn,
Schleswig-Holstein
  nonoxynol-9

ine² \ē-nā\ fine
wahine

ine³ \ēn\ bean, clean, dean, Dean,
Deane, dene, e'en, gene, Gene, glean,
green, Green, greene, jean, Jean,
Jeanne, keen, lean, lien, mean, mesne,
mien, peen, preen, quean, queen,
scene, screen, seen, sheen, shin, sin,
skean, skene, spean, spleen, teen,
tween, wean, ween, wheen, yean
  Aileen, Arlene, baleen, beguine,
Beguine, Benin, Bernstein, between,
boreen, bovine, buckbean, caffeine,
canteen, carbine, careen, Carlene,
Cathleen, Charlene, chlorine, chopine,
chorine, Christine, citrine, Claudine,
codeine, colleen, Colleen, convene,
Coreen, cotquean, cuisine, Darlene,
dasheen, dauphine, demean, demesne,
dentine, Doreen, dry-clean, dudeen,
eighteen, Eileen, Essene, Eugene,
fanzine, fascine, fifteen, fluorine,
fourteen, Francine, gamine, gangrene,
glassine, gyrene, Helene, Hellene,
Hermine, hoatzin, holstein, Holstein,
horsebean, houseclean, hygiene, Ilene,
Irene, Jacqueline, Jeanine, Jeannine,
Jolene, Justine, Kathleen, khamsin,
Kristine, Ladin, lateen, latrine,
Lorene, Lublin, machine, malines,
marine, Marlene, Maureen, Maxine,
moline, moreen, morphine, Nadine,
nankeen, naphthene, Nicene, nineteen,
nongreen, Noreen, obscene, offscreen,

on-screen, patine, Pauline, piscine,
Pontine, poteen, praline, preteen,
pristine, propine, protein, quinine,
Rabin, Racine, ratteen, ravine, routine,
saline, saltine, Salween, sardine,
sateen, scalene, serene, shagreen,
Sharlene, shebeen, siren, Sistine,
sixteen, Slovene, soybean, spalpeen,
strychnine, subteen, sunscreen,
Szczecin, takin, taurine, terrene,
terrine, thirteen, Tolkien, tontine,
tureen, umpteen, unclean, undine,
unseen, vaccine, vitrine, windscreen,
yestreen, Yibin, zechin
  Aberdeen, almandine, Angeline,
argentine, Argentine, Augustine,
barkentine, bengaline, Bernadine,
bombazine, Borodin, brigandine,
brigantine, brilliantine, Byzantine,
carotene, carrageen, celandine,
clandestine, columbine, Constantine,
contravene, crepe de chine, crystalline,
damascene, Dexedrine, Dramamine,
duvetyn, eglantine, endocrine, Eocene,
epicene, Ernestine, estaurine,
evergreen, fescennine, figurine,
Florentine, fukerene, gabardine,
gaberdine, gadarene, galantine,
gasoline, Geraldine, Ghibelline, go-
between, grenadine, Gretna Green,
guillotine, Halloween, haute cuisine,
Hippocrene, histamine, Holocene,
Imogene, in-between, indigene,
intervene, Jeraldine, Josephine,
Kalinin, kerosene, langoustine,
legatine, libertine, limousine, M16,
magazine, mangosteen, margravine,
Medellín, melamine, messaline,
Methedrine, mezzanine, Miocene,
mousseline, Nazarene, nectarine,
nicotine, overseen, opaline, organzine,
palanquin, palatine, pelerine,
percaline, peregrine, philhellene,
Philistine, plasticene, plasticine,
Pleistocene, Pliocene, riverine,
quarantine, reserpine, saccharine,
Sakhalin, Saladin, San Joaquin, San
Martin, sapphirine, schizophrene,
serpentine, seventeen, silkaline,
Stelazine, submarine, subroutine,
supervene, tambourine, tangerine,

Theatine, tourmaline, trampoline, transmarine, travertine, Tridentine, Vaseline, velveteen, wintergreen, wolverine, Ursuline
adamantine, alexandrine, amphetamine, aquamarine, Benedictine, bromocriptine, carbon 13, doxycycline, elephantine, Evangeline, internecine, leukotirene, methylxanthene, mujahideen, niphedipine, nouvelle cuisine, Oligocene, Paleocene, pentamcdine, tricothecene, ultramarine
antihistamine, benzoapyrene, diphenhydramine, Mary Magdalene, NC-17, polybutadiene
alpha-fetaprotein, apolipoprotein, buckminsterfullerene, General San Martin, oleomargarine

ine⁴ \in-ē\ see inny

ine⁵ \ē-nē\ see ini¹

ine⁶ \ən\ see un

inea \in-ē\ see inny

ineal \in-ē-əl\ finial, lineal
matrilineal, patrilineal, unilineal

ined \īnd\ see ind¹

inee \ī-nē\ see iny¹

ineless \īn-ləs\ see indless

inely¹ \īn-lē\ blindly, finely, kindly
affinely, condignly, equinely, felinely, purblindly, unkindly

inely² \ēn-lē\ see eanly¹

inement \īn-mənt\ see ignment

ineness \īn-nəs\ see indness

ineous \in-ē-əs\ gramineous, sanguineous
consanguineous, ignominious

iner¹ \ī-nər\ briner, diner, finer, liner, miner, minor, shiner, Shriner, signer, twiner, whiner
airliner, aligner, baseliner, byliner, combiner, confiner, cosigner, definer,

designer, diviner, eyeliner, hardliner, headliner, incliner, jetliner, long-liner, moonshiner, one-liner, recliner, refiner, repiner, sideliner, soft-liner, streamliner
Asia Minor, Canis Minor, forty-niner, party-liner, superliner, Ursa Minor

iner² \ē-nər\ see eaner

inery¹ \īn-rē\ finery, pinery, vinery, winery
refinery

inery² \ēn-rē\ see eanery

ines¹ \ēn\ see ine³

ines² \ēnz\ see eens

ines³ \īnz\ Mainz
Appenines
—also -s, -'s, and -s' forms of nouns, and -s forms of verbs, listed at ine¹

inest \ī-nəst\ see inist¹

inet \in-ət\ see innet

inew \in-yü\ see inue

infield \in-fēld\ infield, Winfield

ing \iŋ\ bring, Ching, cling, ding, fling, king, King, ling, Ming, ping, ring, sing, sling, spring, sting, string, swing, thing, wing, wring, zing
backswing, Baoding, bedspring, Beijing, bi-swing, bitewing, bowstring, bullring, Chongqing, clearwing, downswing, drawstring, D ring, earring, first-string, forewing, G-string, greenwing, hairspring, hamstring, handspring, headspring, heartstring, Kunming, lacewing, lapwing, latchstring, mainspring, Nanjing, Nanning, O-ring, offspring, Paoting, plaything, redwing, shoestring, showring, unsling, unstring, upspring, upswing, wellspring, whitewing, wind-wing, wingding, Xining
à la king, anything, buck-and-wing, ding-a-ling, double-ring, everything,

innerspring, Liaoning, pigeonwing, superstring, underwing

inga \iŋ-gə\ anhinga, syringa

inge \inj\ binge, cringe, dinge, fringe, hinge, singe, springe, swinge, tinge, twinge, whinge
impinge, infringe, syringe, unhinge

inged \iŋd\ ringed, stringed, winged
net-winged
—*also* -ed *forms of verbs listed at* ing

ingement \inj-mənt\ impingement, infringement

ingency \in-jən-sē\ stringency
astringency, contingency

ingent \in-jənt\ stringent
astringent, constringent, contingent, refringent

inger¹ \iŋ-ər\ bringer, clinger, dinger, flinger, pinger, ringer, singer, springer, stinger, stringer, swinger, winger, wringer, zinger
folksinger, gunslinger, humdinger, left-winger, mudslinger, right-winger
mastersinger, Meistersinger, minnesinger

inger² \iŋ-gər\ finger, linger
five-finger, forefinger, malinger
ladyfinger

inger³ \in-jər\ ginger, Ginger, injure, singer, swinger

ingery \inj-rē\ gingery, injury

inghy \iŋ-ē\ see ingy¹

ingi \iŋ-ē\ see ingy¹

ingian \in-jən\ Thuringian
Carlovingian, Carolingian, Merovingian

inging \iŋ-iŋ\ ringing, springing, stringing, swinging
folksinging, free-swinging, gunslinging, handwringing, mudslinging, upbringing

—*also* -ing *forms of verbs listed at* ing

ingit \iŋ-kət\ see inket

ingle \iŋ-gəl\ cringle, dingle, jingle, mingle, shingle, single, tingle
atingle, commingle, immingle, Kriss Kringle, surcingle
intermingle

ingler \iŋ-glər\ jingler, shingler

inglet \iŋ-lət\ kinglet, ringlet, winglet

ingletree \iŋ-gəl-trē\ singletree, swingletree

ingli \iŋ-glē\ see ingly

inglish \iŋ-glish\ see english

ingly \iŋ-glē\ jingly, shingly, singly, tingly, Zwingli

ingo \iŋ-gō\ bingo, dingo, jingo, lingo, pingo
flamingo, Mandingo
Santo Domingo

ings \iŋz\ Kings, springs
eyestrings, Hot Springs
Colorado Springs
—*also* -s, -'s, *and* -s' *forms of nouns, and* -s *forms of verbs, listed at* ing

ingue \aŋ\ see ang²

inguish \iŋ-wish\ distinguish, extinguish

ingy¹ \iŋ-ē\ clingy, dinghy, springy, stringy, swingy, zingy
shilingi

ingy² \in-jē\ dingy, mingy, stingy

inh \in\ see in¹

ini¹ \ē-nē\ beanie, djinni, genie, greeny, Jeanie, Jeannie, meanie, meany, jinni, Meany, sheeny, spleeny, teeny, weanie, weeny, wienie
Alcmene, Athene, Bellini, Bernini, bikini, Bikini, Cabrini, Cellini, Eugenie, linguine, martini, Mazzini, Mbini, Mycenae, Puccini, rappini,

Rossini, Selene, tahini, wahine, zucchini
  fantoccini, fettucine, kundalini, malihini, Mussolini, Mytilene, nota bene, scaloppine, spaghettini, teeny-weeny, tetrazzini, tortellini

ini² \in-ē\ see inny

inia \in-ē-ə\ zinnia
  Bithynia, Gdynia, gloxinia, Lavinia, Sardinia, Virginia
  Abyssinia, West Virginia

inial \in-ē-əl\ see ineal

inian¹ \in-ē-ən\ Arminian, Darwinian, Latinian, Sardinian, Socinian
  Apollinian, Argentinian, Augustinian, Carolinian

inian² \in-yən\ see inion

inic¹ \ē-nik\ Enoch
  nicotinic

inic² \in-ik\ clinic, cynic, Finnic
  platinic, rabbinic
  Jacobinic, mandarinic, misogynic, muscarinic, nicotinic, parafinic

inical \in-i-kəl\ binnacle, clinical, cynical, finical, pinnacle
  dominical
  Jacobinical

inican \in-i-kən\ see inikin

inikin \in-i-kən\ minikin
  Dominican

inim \in-əm\ minim
  Houyhnhnm

ining \ī-niŋ\ lining, mining, shining
  declining, designing, inclining, long-lining
  interlining, undesigning
  —also -ing forms of verbs listed at ine

inion \in-yən\ minion, minyan, pinion, piñon

  champignon, dominion, Justinian, opinion, Sardinian
  Abyssinian

inis¹ \in-əs\ finis, pinnace
  Erinys

inis² \ī-nəs\ see inus¹

inish \in-ish\ finish, Finnish, thinnish
  diminish, refinish

inist¹ \ī-nəst\ dynast, finest

inist² \ē-nəst\ hygienist, machinist, Orleanist
  Byzantinist, magazinist, trampolinist

initive \in-ət-iv\ carminative, definitive, infinitive

inity \in-ət-ē\ trinity, Trinity
  affinity, bovinity, concinnity, divinity, felinity, feminity, infinity, latinity, salinity, sanguinity, vicinity, virginity
  alkalinity, aquitinity, clandestinity, consanguinity, crystallinity, femininity, inconcinnity, masculinity, saccharinity

inium \in-ē-əm\ delphinium, triclinium
  condominium

injure \in-jər\ see inger³

injury \inj-rē\ see ingery

ink \iŋk\ blink, brink, chink, clink, dink, drink, fink, gink, ink, jink, kink, link, mink, pink, plink, prink, rink, shrink, sink, skink, slink, stink, swink, sync, think, wink, zinc
  bethink, chewink, cross-link, eyewink, groupthink, hoodwink, iceblink, lip-synch, misthink, outthink, preshrink, rethink, snowblink, unkink
  bobolink, countersink, distelfink, doublethink, interlink, kitchen-sink, Maeterlinck, rinky-dink

inka \iŋ-kə\ see inca

inkable \iŋ-kə-bəl\ drinkable, sinkable, thinkable
undrinkable, unsinkable, unthinkable

inkage \iŋ-kij\ linkage, shrinkage, sinkage

inke \iŋ-kē\ see inky

inked \iŋt\ see inct

inker \iŋ-kər\ blinker, clinker, drinker, pinker, sinker, skinker, stinker, tinker, winker
diesinker, freethinker, headshrinker

inket \iŋ-kət\ Tlingit, trinket

inkey \iŋ-kē\ see inky

inkgo \iŋ-kō\ see inko

inki \iŋ-kē\ see inky

inkie \iŋ-kē\ see inky

inking \iŋ-kiŋ\ freethinking, unblinking, unthinking
—also -ing forms of verbs listed at ink

inkle \iŋ-kəl\ crinkle, inkle, sprinkle, tinkle, twinkle, winkle, wrinkle
besprinkle
periwinkle, Rip van Winkle

inkling \iŋ-kliŋ\ inkling, sprinkling, twinkling
—also -ing forms of verbs listed at inkle

inkly \iŋ-klē\ crinkly, pinkly, tinkly, twinkly, wrinkly

inko \iŋ-kō\ ginkgo, pinko

inks \iŋs\ see inx

inky \iŋ-kē\ dinkey, dinky, inky, kinky, pinkie, pinky, slinky, stinky, zincky
Helsinki, Malinke

inland \in-lənd\ Finland, inland, Vinland

inless \in-ləs\ chinless, sinless, skinless, spinless, windlass

inley \in-lē\ see inly

inly \in-lē\ inly, spindly, thinly
McKinley
Mount McKinley

inn \in\ see in¹

innace \in-əs\ see inis¹

innacle \in-i-kəl\ see inical

inned \ind\ see ind²

inner \in-ər\ dinner, ginner, grinner, inner, pinner, sinner, skinner, spinner, spinor, thinner, tinner, winner
beginner, breadwinner, prizewinner
money-spinner

innet \in-ət\ linnet, minute, spinet

inney \in-ē\ see inny

inni \ē-nē\ see ini¹

innia \in-ē-ə\ see inia

innic \in-ik\ see inic²

innie \in-ē\ see inny

inning \in-iŋ\ ginning, inning, spinning, winning
beginning, breadwinning, prizewinning
underpinning
—also -ing forms of verbs listed at in

innish \in-ish\ see inish

innity \in-ət-ē\ see inity

innow \in-ō\ minnow, winnow
topminnow

inny \in-ē\ cine, finny, ginny, guinea, Guinea, hinny, mini, Minnie, ninny, pinny, Pliny, shinny, skinny, spinney, squinny, tinny, whinny, Winnie
ignominy, micromini
Papua New Guinea
Equatorial Guinea

ino¹ \ī-nō\ lino, rhino, Taino, wino
albino

ino² \ē-nō\ beano, chino, fino, keno, leno, Pinot, vino, Zeno
bambino, casino, cioppino, ladino, merino, sordino, zecchino
andantino, Angeleno, Bardolino, campesino, cappuccino, concertino, Filipino, maraschino, palomino, San Marino, pecorino, sopranino
Cape Mendocino, San Bernardino

ino³ \ē-nə\ see ina²

iñon \in-yən\ see inion

inor¹ \in-ər\ see inner

inor² \ī-nər\ see iner¹

inos \ī-nəs\ see inns

inot \ē-nō\ see ino²

inous \ī-nəs\ see inus¹

inscher \in-chər\ see incher

inse \ins\ see ince

inselly \in-slē\ see incely

inseng \in-siŋ\ see incing

insk \insk\ Minsk
Dzerzhinsk
Semipalatinsk

insky \in-skē\ buttinsky, kolinsky, Nijinsky, Stravinsky

inster \in-stər\ minster, spinster
Axminster, Westminster
Kidderminster

int \int\ bint, Clint, dint, flint, Flint, glint, hint, lint, mint, print, quint, skint, splint, sprint, squint, stint, suint, tint
blueprint, catmint, footprint, forint, gunflint, handprint, hoofprint, horsemint, imprint, in-print, large-print, newsprint, offprint, preprint, remint, reprint, skinflint, spearmint, thumbprint, voiceprint
aquatint, calamint, cuckoopint, fingerprint, mezzotint, monotint, overprint, peppermint, photoprint, wunderkind
Septuagint

intage \int-ij\ mintage, vintage

intager \int-i-jər\ see integer

intain \int-ᵊn\ see inton

intal¹ \int-ᵊl\ lintel, pintle, quintal
Septuagintal

intal² \ant-ᵊl\ see antle

integer \int-i-jər\ integer, vintager

intel \int-ᵊl\ see intal¹

inter \int-ər\ hinter, linter, minter, printer, sinter, splinter, sprinter, squinter, tinter, winter
imprinter, midwinter, reprinter
overwinter, teleprinter

intery \int-ə-rē\ printery, splintery

inth \inth\ plinth, synt
helminth
colocynth, labyrinth, terebinth

inthia \in-thē-ə\ Cynthia
Carinthia

inthian \in-thē-ən\ Corinthian
labyrinthian

inthine \in-thən\ hyacinthine, labyrinthine

inting \int-iŋ\ imprinting, unstinting
—also -ing forms of verbs listed at int

intle \int-ᵊl\ see intal¹

into¹ \in-tō\ pinto, Shinto, spinto

into² \in-tü\ thereinto, whereinto

inton \int-ᵊn\ Clinton, quintain, Winton
badminton

ints \ins\ see ince

inty \int-ē\ flinty, linty, minty, squinty
pepperminty

intz \ins\ see ince

inue \in-yü\ sinew
continue
discontinue

inuous \in-yə-wəs\ sinuous
continuous
discontinuous

inus¹ \ī-nəs\ dryness, finis, highness,
Minas, Minos, minus, shyness, sinus,
slyness, spinous, vinous, wryness
Aquinas, Delphinus, echinus,
Quirinus
Antoninus
Pontus Euxinus

inus² \ē-nəs\ see enus¹

inute \in-ət\ see innet

inx \iŋs\ jinx, links, lynx, minx,
sphinx
hijinks, methinks
tiddledywinks

iny¹ \ī-nē\ briny, heinie, liny, piny,
shiny, spiny, tiny, twiny, viny, whiny,
winy
enshrinee, sunshiny

iny² \in-ē\ see inny

inya \ē-nyə\ see enia²

inyan \in-yən\ see inion

inyl \īn-ᵊl\ see inal¹

inys \in-əs\ see inis¹

io¹ \ī-ō\ bayou, bio, Clio, Io
Lucayo, Ohio

io² \ē-ō\ brio, Cleo, clio, guyot, Krio,
Leo, Rio, trio
caudillo, con brio, Negrillo, tornillo,
Trujillo
cigarillo, Hermosillo, Manzanillo,
ocotillo

iocese \ī-ə-səs\ see iasis

iolate \ī-ə-lət\ see iolet¹

iolet¹ \ī-ə-lət\ triolet, violate, violet,
Violet
inviolate
ultraviolet
near-ultraviolet

iolet² \ē-ə-lət\ see eolate

ion¹ \ī-ən\ ayin, Brian, Bryan, cyan,
ion, lion, Lyon, Mayan, Ryan, scion,
Sion, Zion
Amphion, anion, Bisayan, Ixion,
Orion, Visayan
counterion, dandelion, zwitterion

ion² \ē-ən\ see ean¹

ion³ \ē-än\ see eon²

ior \īr\ see ire¹

iory \ī-ə-rē\ see iary¹

iot \ī-ət\ see iet

ioter \ī-ət-ər\ see ieter

iouan \ü-ən\ see uan

ious \ī-əs\ see ias

ioux \ü\ see ew¹

ip \ip\ blip, chip, clip, dip, drip, flip,
grip, grippe, gyp, hip, kip, lip, nip,
pip, quip, rip, scrip, ship, sip, skip,
slip, snip, strip, tip, trip, whip, yip, zip
airship, airstrip, atrip, bullwhip,
catnip, chiefship, clerkship, courtship,
cowslip, deanship, equip, fieldstrip,
filmstrip, flagship, friendship,
guildship, gunship, half-slip, handgrip,
hardship, harelip, headship,
horsewhip, inclip, judgeship, kingship,
kinship, landslip, lightship, lordship,
nonslip, outstrip, oxlip, pip-pip,
princeship, Q-ship, queenship, reship,
round-trip, saintship, sheep-dip,
sideslip, spaceship, steamship,
thaneship, township, transship,
troopship, unship, unzip, wardship,
warship
airmanship, authorship, battleship,
biochip, brinkmanship, censorship,
chairmanship, chaplainship,
chieftainship, churchmanship,
coverslip, dealership, draftsmanship,
ego-trip, externship, fellowship,
fingertip, gamesmanship, Gaza Strip,
grantsmanship, helmsmanship,
horsemanship, internship, ladyship,

leadership, lectureship, listenership,
marksmanship, membership,
microchip, oarsmanship, overslip,
ownership, partnership, penmanship,
pogonip, premiership, readership,
ridership, rulership, salesmanship,
scholarship, seamanship,
showmanship, skinny-dip,
speakership, sponsorship,
sportsmanship, statesmanship,
stewardship, studentship,
swordsmanship, trusteeship, underlip,
upmanship, viewership, workmanship
  assistantship, attorneyship,
championship, chancellorship,
citizenship, companionship,
containership, cross-ownership,
dictatorship, directorship, good-
fellowship, guardianship,
instructorship, landownership,
laureateship, governorship,
musicianship, one-upmanship,
outdoorsmanship, professorship,
protectorship, receivership,
relationship, survivorship,
treasurership
  ambassadorship, associateship,
bipartisanship, entrepreneurship,
librarianship, nonpartisanship,
proprietorship, secretaryship,
solicitorship
  interrelationship

ipal \ē-pəl\ see eople

ipari \ip-rē\ see ippery

ipatus \ip-ət-əs\ see ipitous

ipe \īp\ Cuyp, gripe, hype, pipe, ripe,
slype, snipe, stipe, stripe, swipe, tripe,
type, wipe
  bagpipe, blowpipe, downpipe,
drainpipe, hornpipe, hosepipe, lead-
pipe, n-type, p-type, panpipe,
pinstripe, rareripe, sideswipe,
standpipe, stovepipe, tintype, touch-
type, unripe, windpipe
  archetype, calotype, Dutchman's-
pipe, guttersnipe, haplotype, Linotype,
liripipe, logotype, monotype, overripe,
prototype, stenotype, Teletype

daguerreotype, electrotype,
stereotype
  anti-idiotype

iped¹ \ī-ped\ biped
parallelepiped

iped² \īpt\ stiped, striped
pin-striped
  —also -ed forms of verbs listed at
ipe

ipend \ī-pənd\ ripened, stipend

iper \ī-pər\ diaper, griper, hyper,
piper, riper, sniper, striper, viper,
wiper
  bagpiper, sandpiper
  candy-striper
  stereotyper

iperous \ī-prəs\ see ypress

ipetal \ip-ət-ºl\ basipetal, bicipital,
centripetal, occipital

ipety \ip-ət-ē\ snippety
peripety
serendipity

iph \if\ see iff

iphany \if-ə-nē\ see iphony

ipher \ī-fər\ cipher, lifer, rifer
decipher, encipher, pro-lifer
right-to-lifer

iphery \if-rē\ see ifery

iphon \ī-fən\ see yphen

iphony \if-ə-nē\ tiffany, Tiffany
antiphony, epiphany, polyphony

ipi \ē-pē\ see eepy

ipid \ip-əd\ lipid
insipid

ipience \ip-ē-əns\ incipience,
percipience
impercipience

ipient \ip-ē-ənt\ excipient, incipient,
percipient, recipient
impercipient

iping \ī-piŋ\ piping, striping
blood-typing
—*also* -ing *forms of verbs listed at*
ipe

ipit \ip-ət\ see ippet

ipital \ip-ət-əl\ see ipetal

ipitance \ip-ət-əns\ see ipotence

ipitant \ip-ət-ənt\ see ipotent

ipitous \ip-ət-əs\ peripatus,
precipitous
serendipitous

ipity \ip-ət-ē\ see ipety

iple[1] \ip-əl\ see ipple

iple[2] \ī-pəl\ see ypal

ipless \ip-ləs\ dripless, lipless,
zipless

ipling \ip-liŋ\ Kipling, stripling
—*also* -ing *forms of verbs listed at*
ipple

ipment \ip-mənt\ shipment
equipment, transshipment

ipo \ēp-ō\ see epot

ipoli \ip-ə-lē\ see ippily

ipotence \ip-ət-əns\ omnipotence,
precipitance

ipotent \ip-ət-ənt\ omnipotent,
plenipotent, pluripotent, precipitant

ippe[1] \ip\ see ip

ippe[2] \ip-ē\ see ippy

ippe[3] \ēp\ see eep

ipped \ipt\ see ipt

ippee \ip-ē\ see ippy

ippen \ip-ən\ lippen, pippin

ipper \ip-ər\ chipper, clipper, dipper,
dripper, flipper, gripper, hipper, kipper,
nipper, ripper, shipper, sipper, skipper,
slipper, snipper, stripper, tipper,
tripper, whipper, zipper

blue-chipper, day-tripper,
mudskipper, Yom-Kippur
double-dipper, gallinipper, lady's
slipper, skinny-dipper

ippery \ip-rē\ frippery, Lipari,
slippery

ippet \ip-ət\ pipit, sippet, snippet,
tippet, trippet, whippet

ippety \ip-ət-ē\ see ipety

ippi \ip-ē\ see ippy

ippie \ip-ē\ see ippy

ippily \ip-ə-lē\ nippily, tripoli,
Tripoli
Gallipoli

ippin \ip-ən\ see ippen

ipping \ip-iŋ\ chipping, clipping,
dripping, lipping, nipping, ripping,
shipping
double-dipping, skinny-dipping
—*also* -ing *forms of verbs listed at*
ip

ippingly \ip-iŋ-lē\ grippingly,
nippingly, trippingly

ipple \ip-əl\ cripple, nipple, ripple,
stipple, tipple, triple
participle

ippur \ip-ər\ see ipper

ippy \ip-ē\ chippy, dippy, drippy,
flippy, grippy, hippie, hippy, Lippi,
lippy, nippy, slippy, snippy, tippy,
trippy, whippy, yippee, yippie, zippy
Xanthippe
Mississippi

ips \ips\ snips, thrips, yips
eclipse, ellipse, midships
amidships, athwartships, fish-and-
chips, tidytips, apocalypse
—*also* -s, -'s, *and* -s' *forms of nouns,*
and -s *forms of verbs, listed at* ip

ipse \ips\ see ips

ipso \ip-sō\ dipso
calypso, Calypso

ipster \ip-stər\ hipster, quipster, tipster

ipsy \ip-sē\ see ypsy

ipt \ipt\ crypt, hipped, lipped, ripped, script, tipped
conscript, decrypt, encrypt, harelipped, postscript, prescript, rescript, subscript, tight-lipped, transcript, typescript
eucalypt, filter-tipped, manuscript, nondescript, superscript, swivel-hipped
—also -ed *forms of verbs listed at* ip

ipter \ip-tər\ scripter
lithotripter

iptic \ip-tik\ see yptic

iption \ip-shən\ ascription, conniption, conscription, decryption, description, Egyptian, encryption, inscription, prescription, proscription, subscription, transcription
circumscription, nonprescription

iptive \ip-tiv\ ascriptive, descriptive, inscriptive, prescriptive, proscriptive

iptych \ip-tik\ see yptic

ipular \ip-yə-lər\ stipular
manipular

ipy \ī-pē\ stripy, typey
stenotypy
daguerrotypy, stereotypy

iquant \ē-kənt\ see ecant

ique \ēk\ see eak[1]

iquey \ē-kē\ see eaky

iquish \ē-kish\ see eakish

iquitous \ik-wət-əs\ iniquitous, ubiquitous

iquity \ik-wət-ē\ antiquity, iniquity, obliquity, ubiquity

iquor \ik-ər\ see icker[1]

ir[1] \ir\ see eer[2]

ir[2] \ər\ see eur[1]

ira[1] \ir-ə\ see era[2]

ira[2] \ī-rə\ see yra

irable \ī-rə-bəl\ wirable
acquirable, desirable, respirable
undesirable

iracle \ir-i-kəl\ see erical[2]

irae \īr-ē\ see iry[1]

iral \ī-rəl\ chiral, gyral, spiral, viral

irant \ī-rənt\ spirant, tyrant
aspirant, retirant

irate \ir-ət\ see irit

irby \ər-bē\ see erby

irca \ər-kə\ see urka[1]

irce \ər-sē\ see ercy

irch \ərch\ see urch

irchen[1] \ər-chən\ see urchin

irchen[2] \ər-kən\ see irkin

ircher \ər-chər\ Bircher, lurcher, nurture

irchist \ər-chəst\ Birchist
researchist

ircon \ər-kən\ see irkin

ircuit \ər-kət\ circuit
trifurcate
microcircuit

ircular \ər-kyə-lər\ circular
opercular, tubercular
semicircular

ird \ərd\ bird, burred, curd, furred, gird, heard, herd, nerd, spurred, surd, third, word
absurd, begird, bellbird, blackbird, bluebird, buzzword, byword, Cape Verde, catbird, catchword, cowbird, cowherd, crossword, cussword, engird, goatherd, headword, jailbird, jaybird, kingbird, loanword, lovebird, lyrebird, oilbird, password, potsherd,

railbird, rainbird, redbird, reword, ricebird, seabird, Sigurd, shorebird, snakebird, snowbird, songbird, sunbird, surfbird, swearword, swineherd, textured, ungird, unheard, watchword, yardbird
afterword, bowerbird, butcher-bird, cedarbird, dollybird, hummingbird, ladybird, mockingbird, ovenbird, overheard, riflebird, tailorbird, thunderbird, undergird, wattlebird, weaverbird, whirlybird
—*also* -ed *forms of verbs listed at* eur[1]

irder \ərd-ər\ see erder

irdie \ərd-ē\ see urdy

irdle \ərd-ᵊl\ see urdle

irdum \ərd-əm\ dirdum
reductio ad absurdum

ire[1] \īr\ briar, brier, byre, choir, dire, drier, fire, flier, friar, fryer, gyre, hire, ire, liar, lyre, mire, prier, prior, pyre, quire, shire, sire, Speyer, spier, spire, squire, tier, tire, trier, tyer, Tyre, wire, zaire
acquire, admire, afire, Altair, aspire, attire, backfire, balefire, barbed wire, barbwire, bemire, Blantyre, blow-dryer, bonfire, brushfire, bushfire, catbrier, cease-fire, complier, conspire, defier, denier, desire, drumfire, empire, Empire, entire, esquire, expire, flytier, grandsire, greenbrier, gunfire, haywire, hellfire, highflier, hot-wire, inquire, inspire, misfire, outlier, perspire, pismire, prior, quagmire, require, respire, retire, rimfire, samphire, sapphire, satire, Shropshire, spitfire, surefire, suspire, sweetbrier, tightwire, transpire, umpire, vampire, wildfire
amplifier, Biedermeier, butterflyer, classifier, fly-by-wire, fortifier, lammergeier, magnifier, modifier, multiplier, nitrifier, nullifier, pacifier, qualifier, quantifier, rapid-fire, rectifier, retrofire, sanctifier, signifier, testifier, versifier

down-to-the-wire, identifier, intensifier, Second Empire
—*also* -er *forms of adjectives listed at* y[1]

ire[2] \ir\ see eer[2]

ire[3] \ī-rē\ see iary[1]

ire[4] \īr-ē\ see iry[1]

ire[5] \ər\ see eur

ired \īrd\ fired, spired, tired, wired
hardwired, retired
—*also* -ed *forms of verbs listed at* ire[1]

ireless \īr-ləs\ tireless, wireless

ireman \īr-mən\ fireman, wireman

irement \īr-mənt\ environment, requirement, retirement

iren \ī-rən\ Byron, gyron, Myron, siren
environ
ribavirin

irge \ərj\ see urge

irgin \ər-jən\ see urgeon

irgo \ər-gō\ see ergo

iri \ir-ē\ see eary

iriam \ir-ē-əm\ see erium

iric \ir-ik\ see eric[2]

irile \ir-əl\ see eral[1]

irin \ī-rən\ see iren

irine \ī-rən\ see iren

iring \īr-iŋ\ firing, wiring
retiring
—*also* -ing *forms of verbs listed at* ire

irious \ir-ē-əs\ see erious

iris \ī-rəs\ see irus

irish \īr-ish\ Irish, squirish

irit \ir-ət\ Meerut, spirit
   dispirit, emirate, inspirit, vizierate

irium \ir-ē-əm\ see erium

irius \ir-ē-əs\ see erious

irk¹ \irk\ birk, skirk

irk² \ərk\ see ork¹

irker \ər-kər\ see orker¹

irkie \ər-kē\ see erky

irkin \ər-kən\ firkin, gherkin, jerkin, zircon
   Gelsenkirchen

irky \ər-kē\ see erky

irl¹ \ərl\ birl, burl, churl, curl, dirl, earl, Earl, Earle, furl, girl, hurl, knurl, merle, Merle, pearl, Pearl, purl, skirl, squirrel, swirl, thirl, thurl, tirl, twirl, virl, whirl, whorl
   aswirl, awhirl, cowgirl, impearl, pas seul, playgirl, salesgirl, schoolgirl, showgirl, uncurl, unfurl
   mother-of-pearl

irl² \irl\ dirl, skirl

irler \ər-lər\ birler, curler, pearler, twirler, whirler

irley \ər-lē\ see urly

irlie \ər-lē\ see urly

irling \ər-liŋ\ see urling

irlish \ər-lish\ see urlish

irly \ər-lē\ see urly

irm \ərm\ see orm¹

irma \ər-mə\ see erma

irmary \ərm-rē\ spermary
   infirmary

irmess \ər-məs\ see ermis

irmity \ər-mət-ē\ furmity
   infirmity

irmy \ər-mē\ see ermy

irn¹ \irn\ firn, girn, pirn

irn² \ərn\ see urn

iro¹ \ir-ō\ see ero³

iro² \ē-rō\ see ero¹

iro³ \ī-rō\ see yro¹

iron¹ \īrn\ iron
   andiron, environ, flatiron, gridiron

iron² \ī-rən\ see iren

ironment \īr-mənt\ see irement

irp \ərp\ see urp

irps \ərps\ stirps, turps
   —also -s, -'s, and -s' forms of nouns, and -s forms of verbs, listed at urp

irpy \ər-pē\ chirpy
   Euterpe

irque \ərk\ see ork¹

irr¹ \ir\ see eer²

irr² \ər\ see eur¹

irra \ir-ə\ see era²

irrah \ir-ə\ see era²

irrel¹ \ərl\ see irl¹

irrel² \ər-əl\ see erral

irrely \ər-lē\ see urly

irrer \ər-ər\ see errer

irrhous \ir-əs\ see erous

irring \ər-iŋ\ see urring

irror \ir-ər\ see earer²

irrup \ər-əp\ chirrup, stirrup, syrup

irrupy \ər-ə-pē\ chirrupy, syrupy

irrus \ir-əs\ see erous

irry \ər-ē\ see urry

irs \irz\ sce iers

irsch \irsh\ see irsh

irse¹ \irs\ see ierce

irse² \ərs\ see erse

irsh \irsh\ girsh, kirsch

irst \ərst\ seeurst

irsty \ər-stē\ thirsty
bloodthirsty

irt \ərt\ see ert¹

irted \ərt-əd\ see erted

irter \ərt-ər\ see erter

irth \ərth\ berth, birth, dearth, earth,
firth, girth, mirth, Perth, worth
childbirth, Fort Worth, rebirth, self-
worth, stillbirth, unearth, Wordsworth
afterbirth, down-to-earth,
pennyworth

irthful \ərth-fəl\ mirthful, worthful

irthless \ərth-ləs\ mirthless,
worthless

irtinent \ərt-nənt\ pertinent
appurtenant, impertinent

irting \ərt-iŋ\ see erting

irtle \ərt-ᵊl\ see ertiile

irtually \ərch-lē\ see urchly

irtue \ər-chə\ see ercha

irty \ərt-ē\ dirty, QWERTY, shirty,
thirty

irus \ī-rəs\ Cyrus, iris, Iris, Skyros,
virus
desirous, Epirus, Osiris, papyrus
lentivirus, parvovirus, rotavirus
papillomavirus

irv \ərv\ see erve

irving \ər-viŋ\ see erving

irwin \ər-wən\ see erwin

iry \īr-ē\ eyrie, friary, miry, spiry,
wiry
expiry, inquiry, venire
praemunire
anno hegirae

is¹ \is\ see iss¹

is² \iz\ see iz¹

is³ \ē\ see ee¹

is⁴ \ēs\ see iece

is⁵ \ish\ see ish¹

i's \īz\ see ize

isa¹ \ē-zə\ see eza

isa² \ī-zə\ Lisa, Liza
Elisa, Eliza

isabeth \iz-ə-bəth\ see izabeth

isable \ī-zə-bəl\ see izable

isal¹ \ī-səl\ Faisal, Ijssel, sisal,
skysail, trysail

isal² \ī-zəl\ Geisel
incisal, reprisal, revisal, surprisal
paradisal

isan \is-ᵊn\ see isten

isbane \iz-bən\ see isbon

isbe \iz-bē\ Frisbee, Thisbe

isbee \iz-bē\ see isbe

isbon \iz-bən\ Brisbane, Lisbon

isc \isk\ see isk

iscable \is-kə-bəl\ confiscable,
episcopal

iscan \is-kən\ see iskin

iscate \is-kət\ see isket

isce \is\ see iss¹

iscean¹ \ī-sē-ən\ Piscean
Dionysian

iscean² \is-kē-ən\ Piscean
saurischian
ornithischian

iscean³ \is-ē-ən\ see ysian¹

Iscence \is-ᵊns\ puissance
dehiscence, impuissance

indehiscence, reminiscence, reviviscence

iscent \is-ᵊnt\ puissant
dehiscent, impuissant
indehiscent, reminiscent, reviviscent

isces \ī-sēz\ see ices

ische \ēsh\ see iche²

ischian \is-kē-ən\ see iscean²

iscia \ish-ə\ see itia

iscible \is-ə-bəl\ see issible

iscience \ish-əns\ see icience

iscient \ish-ənt\ see icient

isco \is-kō\ cisco, disco
Francisco, Jalisco, Morisco
San Francisco

iscopal \is-kə-bəl\ see iscable

iscous \is-kəs\ see iscus

iscuit \is-kət\ see isket

iscus \is-kəs\ discus, viscous, viscus
hibiscus, meniscus

ise¹ \ēs\ see iece

ise² \ēz\ see eze

ise³ \īs\ see ice¹

ise⁴ \īz\ see ize

ised¹ \īst\ see ist¹

ised² \īzd\ see ized

isel \iz-əl\ see izzle

iseled \iz-əld\ see izzled

iseler \iz-lər\ see izzler

isement \īz-mənt\ advisement,
chastisement, despisement,
disguisement
advertisement, disfranchisement,
enfranchisement
disenfranchisement

iser \ī-zər\ see izer

ises \ī-sēz\ see ices

ish¹ \ish\ dish, fiche, fish, flysch,
Nis, pish, squish, swish, whish, wish
blackfish, blowfish, bluefish,
bonefish, catfish, codfish, crawfish,
crayfish, dogfish, filefish, finfish,
flatfish, garfish, globefish, goldfish,
goosefish, Irtysh, kingfish, knish,
lungfish, lumpfish, monkfish, pigfish,
pipefish, ratfish, redfish, rockfish,
sailfish, sawfish, shellfish, spearfish,
starfish, stonefish, sunfish, swordfish,
tilefish, unwish, weakfish, whitefish
angelfish, anglerfish, archerfish,
butterfish, candlefish, cuttlefish,
damselfish, devilfish, jellyfish, John
Bullish, ladyfish, lionfish, microfiche,
muttonfish, needlefish, overfish,
paddlefish, ribbonfish, silverfish,
surgeonfish, triggerfish

ish² \ēsh\ see iche²

isha \ish-ə\ see itia

ishable \ish-ə-bəl\ fishable
justiciable

ished \isht\ dished, whisht
—*also* -ed *forms of verbs listed at*
ish¹

isher \ish-ər\ fisher, fissure, swisher
ill-wisher, kingfisher, well-wisher

ishery \ish-rē\ fishery, Tishri
shellfishery

ishi \ē-shē\ chichi, specie
maharishi

ishing \ish-iŋ\ bonefishing, fly-
fishing, sportfishing, well-wishing
—*also* -ing *forms of verbs listed at*
ish¹

ishioner \ish-nər\ see itioner

ishna \ish-nə\ Krishna, Mishnah

ishnah \ish-nə\ see ishna

isht \isht\ see ished

ishu \ish-ü\ see issue[1]

ishy \ish-ē\ dishy, fishy, squishy, swishy

isi[1] \ē-zē\ see easy[1]

isi[2] \ē-sē\ see eecy

isia[1] \izh-ə\ baptisia
artemisia, Dionysia

isia[2] \ē-zhə\ see esia[2]

isian[1] \izh-ən\ see ision

isian[2] \ē-zhən\ see esian[1]

isible \iz-ə-bəl\ risible, visible
divisible, invisible
indivisible

isin \i-zən\ see ison[2]

ising \ī-ziŋ\ see izing

ision \izh-ən\ fission, Frisian,
scission, vision
abscission, collision, concision,
decision, derision, division, elision,
elysian, envision, excision, incision,
misprision, precisian, precision,
prevision, provision, recision,
rescission, revision
circumcision, Dionysian,
imprecision, indecision, subdivision,
supervision, television

isional \izh-nəl\ visional
collisional, decisional, divisional,
excisional, previsional, provisional

isis \ī-səs\ crisis, Isis, lysis, nisus
Dionysus
stare decisis

isit \iz-ət\ visit
exquisite, revisit

isite \iz-ət\ see isit

isitive \iz-ət-iv\ acquisitive,
inquisitive

isitor \iz-ət-ər\ visitor
acquisitor, inquisitor

isive[1] \ī-siv\ visive

decisive, derisive, divisive, incisive
indecisive

isive[2] \iz-iv\ visive
derisive, divisive

isk \isk\ bisque, brisk, disc, disk,
fisc, frisk, risk, whisk
lutefisk
asterisk, basilisk, blastodisc,
compact disc, laserdisc, obelisk,
odalisque, tamarisk
videodisc

isker \is-kər\ brisker, frisker, risker,
whisker

isket \is-kət\ biscuit, brisket, frisket

iskey \is-kē\ see isky

iskie \is-kē\ see isky

iskin \is-kən\ siskin
Franciscan

isky \is-kē\ frisky, pliskie, risky,
whiskey

island \ī-lənd\ see ighland

islander \ī-lən-dər\ see ighlander

islands \ī-lənz\ see ighlands

isle \īl\ see ile[1]

isles \īlz\ see iles

islet \ī-lət\ see ilot

isling \iz-liŋ\ brisling, quisling

isly \iz-lē\ see izzly

ism \iz-əm\ chrism, chrisom, ism,
prism, schism
abysm, autism, baalism, baptism,
Birchism, bossism, Buddhism,
casteism, centrism, charism, Chartism,
chemism, classism, cubism, cultism,
czarism, deism, dwarfism, faddism,
fascism, fauvism, Gaullism, Grecism,
Hobbism, holism, Jainism, Klanism,
leftism, lyrism, Mahdism, Maoism,
Marxism, monism, mutism, Nazism,
nudism, Orphism, priggism, purism,
racism, Ramism, rightism, sadism,

Saivism, sapphism, Scotism, sexism, Shaktism, Shiism, Sikhism, simplism, snobbism, sophism, statism, Sufism, tachism, Tantrism, Taoism, theism, Thomism, tourism, tropism, truism, Turkism, verism, Whiggism, Yahwism absurdism, activism, Adventism, alarmism, albinism, alpinism, altruism, amorphism, anarchism, aneurysm, anglicism, animism, aphorism, Arabism, archaism, asterism, atavism, atheism, atomism, atticism, Bahaism, barbarism, Benthamism, biblicism, blackguardism, bolshevism, boosterism, botulism, bourbonism, Brahmanism, Briticism, Byronism, cabalism, Caesarism, Calvinism, careerism, Castroism, cataclysm, catechism, Catharism, centralism, chauvinism, chimerism, classicism, colorism, communism, concretism, conformism, cretinism, criticism, cronyism, cynicism, dadaism, dandyism, Darwinism, defeatism, de Gaullism, despotism, die-hardism, dimorphism, dirigisme, Docetism, do-goodism, dogmatism, Donatism, Don Juanism, druidism, dualism, dynamism, egoism, egotism, elitism, embolism, endemism, erethism, ergotism, erotism, escapism, Essenism, etatism, eunuchism, euphemism, euphuism, exorcism, expertism, extremism, fairyism, familism, fatalism, feminism, feudalism, fideism, Fidelism, fogyism, foreignism, formalism, futurism, Galenism, gallicism, galvanism, gangsterism, genteelism, Germanism, giantism, gigantism, globalism, gnosticism, Gongorism, Gothicism, gourmandism, gradualism, grangerism, greenbackism, Hasidism, heathenism, Hebraism, hedonism, Hellenism, helotism, hermetism, hermitism, heroism, highbrowism, Hinduism, hipsterism, hirsutism, hispanism, Hitlerism, hoodlumism, hoodooism, huckstérism, humanism, Hussitism, hybridism, hypnotism,

Ibsenism, idealism, imagism, Irishism, Islamism, Jansenism, jingoism, journalism, John Bullism, Judaism, Junkerism, kaiserism, Krishnaism, Ku Kluxism, laconism, laicism, Lamaism, Lamarckism, landlordism, Latinism, legalism, Leninism, lobbyism, localism, locoism, Lollardism, luminism, lyricism, magnetism, mammonism, mannerism, Marcionism, masochism, mechanism, melanism, meliorism, Menshevism, Mendelism, mentalism, mesmerism, methodism, me-tooism, modernism, Mohockism, monachism, monadism, monarchism, mongolism, Montanism, moralism, Mormonism, morphinism, mullahism, mysticism, narcissism, nationalism, nativism, nepotism, neutralism, new dealism, nihilism, nomadism, occultism, onanism, optimism, oralism, Orangeism, organism, ostracism, pacifism, paganism, Pan-Slavism, pantheism, paroxysm, Parsiism, passivism, pauperism, pessimism, phallicism, pianism, pietism, plagiarism, Platonism, pleinairism, Plotinism, pluralism, pointillism, populism, pragmatism, presentism, privatism, prosaism, Prussianism, puerilism, pugilism, Puseyism, Pyrrhonism, Quakerism, quietism, rabbinism, racialism, rationalism, realism, reformism, rheumatism, rigorism, robotism, Romanism, Rousseauism, rowdyism, royalism, satanism, savagism, scapegoatism, schematism, scientism, sciolism, Scotticism, Semitism, Shakerism, Shamanism, Shintoism, skepticism, socialism, solecism, solipsism, Southernism, specialism, speciesism, Spartanism, Spinozism, spiritism, spoonerism, Stalinism, standpattism, stoicism, syllogism, symbolism, synchronism, syncretism, synergism, talmudism, tarantism, tectonism, tenebrism, terrorism, Teutonism, titanism, Titoism, tokenism, Toryism, totalism, totemism, transvestism, traumatism,

tribalism, tritheism, Trotskyism, ultraism, unionism, urbanism, utopism, Vaishnavism, vampirism, vandalism, vanguardism, Vedantism, veganism, verbalism, virilism, vitalism, vocalism, volcanism, voodooism, vorticism, voyeurism, vulcanism, vulgarism, Wahhabism, warlordism, welfarism, Wellerism, witticism, yahooism, Yankeeism, Yiddishism, Zionism, zombiism
absenteeism, absolutism, abstractionism, adoptionism, adventurism, aestheticism, Africanism, agnosticism, alcoholism, alienism, amateurism, amoralism, anabaptism, anachronism, Anglicanism, animalism, antagonism, Arianism, astigmatism, athleticism, asynchronism, Atlanticism, atonalism, Australianism, automatism, avant-gardism, behaviorism, Big Brotherism, bilingualism, biologism, bipedalism, biracialism, Bonapartism, bureaucratism, cannibalism, capitalism, Cartesianism, catastrophism, Catholicism, cavalierism, charlatanism, clericalism, collectivism, Colonel Blimpism, commensalism, commercialism, communalism, Confucianism, conservatism, constructivism, consumerism, corporatism, creationism, credentialism, determinism, diabolism, didacticism, diffusionism, dilettantism, doctrinairism, do-nothingism, eclecticism, ecumenism, egocentrism, Eleatism, empiricism, epicenism, epicurism, epigonism, eremitism, eroticism, erraticism, essentialism, ethnocentrism, eudaemonism, euhemerism, evangelism, exclusivism, exoticism, expansionism, expressionism, externalism, Fabianism, factionalism, factualism, fanaticism, favoritism, federalism, Fenianism, feuilletonism, fifth columnism, flagellantism, Fourierism, fraternalism, freneticism, Freudianism, funambulism,

functionalism, gallicanism, gutturalism, henotheism, hermeticism, Hispanicism, historicism, hooliganism, Huguenotism, hypocorism, idiotism, illiberalism, illuminism, illusionism, immanentism, immobilism, impressionism, indifferentism, Indianism, infantilism, inflationism, initialism, insularism, invalidism, iotacism, irredentism, Ishmaelitism, Italianism, Jacobinism, Jacobitism, jesuitism, Keynesianism, know-nothingism, legitimism, lesbianism, liberalism, libertinism, literalism, Lutheranism, Lysenkoism, Magianism, malapropism, mandarinism, McCarthyism, medievalism, mercantilism, messianism, metabolism, metamorphism, militarism, minimalism, misoneism, monasticism, monetarism, monotheism, mosaicism, mutualism, naturalism, Naziritism, necrophilism, negativism, neologism, neo-Nazism, neuroticism, nice-nellyism, nominalism, nonconformism, objectivism, obscurantism, obstructionism, officialism, opportunism, organicism, pacificism, Pantagruelism, parallelism, parasitism, pastoralism, paternalism, patriotism, Peeping Tomism, perfectionism, personalism, pharisaism, physicalism, plebeianism, poeticism, polyglotism, polytheism, positivism, postmodernism, pragmaticism, primitivism, probabilism, progressivism, proselytism, protectionism, Protestantism, provincialism, pseudomorphism, psychologism, puritanism, radicalism, rationalism, recidivism, reductionism, refugeeism, regionalism, relativism, restrictionism, revisionism, revivalism, ritualism, romanticism, ruffianism, Sadduceeism, salvationism, sanculottism, sardonicism, scholasticism, secessionism, sectionalism, secularism, sensualism, separatism, serialism, Slavophilism,

solidarism, somnambulism, sovietism, Stakhanovism, structuralism, subjectivism, suprematism, surrealism, Sybaritism, sycophantism, systematism, Tammanyism, teetotalism, theocentrism, triumphalism, Uncle Tomism, vagabondism, ventriloquism, vigilantism, voluntarism, volunteerism, Wesleyanism, workaholism, Zwinglianism
abolitionism, academicism, agrarianism, Americanism, analphabetism, anthropomorphism, anthropopathism, anti-Semitism, Arminianism, autoerotism, barbarianism, bibliophilism, bicameralism, biculturalism, biloquialism, bipartisanism, bohemianism, colloquialism, colonialism, conceptualism, confessionalism, constitutionalism, conventionalism, corporativism, cosmopolitism, deviationism, ecumenicism, emotionalism, esotericism, Europocentrism, evolutionism, exceptionalism, exhibitionism, existentialism, expatriatism, fundamentalism, governmentalism, Hegelianism, hermaphroditism, hypercriticism, hyperrealism, hyperurbanism, imperialism, incendiarism, incrementalism, indeterminism, industrialism, instrumentalism, interventionism, introspectionism, irrationalism, isolationism, Malthusianism, Manichaeanism, manorialism, materialism, millennialism, Monarchianism, mongolianism, Monophysitism, Muhammadanism, multilingualism, neoclassicism, Neoplatonism, neorealism, Nestorianism, Occidentalism, operationism, orientalism, Palladianism, parajournalism, parochialism, particularism, pedestrianism, Pelagianism, Pentecostalism, phenomenalism, photojournalism, pictorialism, pococurantism,

Postimpressionism, professionalism, pseudoclassicism, reconstructionism, republicanism, Rosicrucianism, sacerdotalism, sacramentalism, self-determinism, sadomasochism, sectarianism, sensationalism, sentimentalism, Socinianism, spiritualism, theatricalism, Tractarianism, traditionalism, transcendentalism, transsexualism, trilateralism, ultramontanism, universalism, utopianism, vernacularism, Victorianism, vocationalism, voluntaryism
Albigensianism, anticlericalism, antiquarianism, apocalypticism, assimilationism, associationism, Augustinianism, autoeroticism, ceremonialism, collaborationism, congregationalism, cosmopolitanism, ecclesiasticism, ecumenicalism, environmentalism, epicureanism, Evangelicalism, experimentalism, Hamiltonianism, homoeroticism, immaterialism, individualism, institutionalism, intellectualism, internationalism, libertarianism, middle-of-the-roadism, millenarianism, neo-conservatism, neo-impressionism, operationalism, Pan-Americanism, Peripateticism, photoperiodism, Pre-Raphaelitism, Presbyterianism, Pythegoreanism, Rastafarianism, reactionaryism, Sabbatarianism, supernaturalism, Swedenborgianism, territorialism, Trinitarianism, unitarianism, vegetarianism, Zoroastrianism
Aristotelianism, authoritarianism, egalitarianism, Episcopalianism, humanitarianism, Machiavellianism, neocolonialism, neo-Expressionism, predestinarianism, representationalism, utilitarianism
establishmentarianism, latitudinarianism

isma \iz-mə\ charisma, melisma

ismal \iz-məl\ see ysmal

isme[1] \īm\ see ime[1]

isme

218

isme² \iz-°m\ see ism

ismo \ēz-mō\ machismo, verismo
caudillismo

iso \ē-sō\ miso, piso

isom \iz-əm\ see ism

ison¹ \īs-°n\ bison, hyson, Meissen
streptomycin
Aureomycin, erythromycin

ison² \iz-°n\ dizen, mizzen, prison,
risen, weasand, wizen
arisen, imprison, Tok Pisin, uprisen

isor \ī-zər\ see izer

isored \ī-zərd\ guisard, visored

isory \īz-rē\ advisory, provisory,
revisory
supervisory

isp \isp\ crisp, lisp, LISP, wisp
will-o-the-wisp

isper \is-pər\ crisper, lisper, whisper

ispy \is-pē\ crispy, wispy

isque \isk\ see isk

iss \is\ bis, bliss, cis, Chris, cuisse,
Dis, hiss, kiss, miss, sis, Swiss, this,
vis, wis
abyss, amiss, coulisse, dehisce,
dismiss, iwis, koumiss, remiss,
submiss
ambergris, hit-and-miss, hit-or-miss,
reminisce, verdigris

issa \is-ə\ abscissa, mantissa,
Melissa, Orissa, vibrissa

issable \is-ə-bəl\ see issible

issal \is-əl\ see istle

issance \is-°ns\ see iscence

issant \is-°nt\ see iscent

isse¹ \is\ see iss

isse² \ēs\ see iece

issed \ist\ see ist²

issel \is-əl\ see istle

isser \is-ər\ hisser, kisser

issible \is-ə-bəl\ kissable, miscible
admissible, immiscible, municipal,
omissible, permissible, remissible,
transmissible
impermissible, inadmissible

issile \is-əl\ see istle

ission¹ \ish-ən\ see ition

ission² \izh-ən\ see ision

issionable \ish-nə-bəl\ fissionable
conditionable

issioner \ish-nər\ see itioner

issive \is-iv\ missive
admissive, derisive, dismissive,
emissive, permissive, submissive,
transmissive

issome \is-əm\ lissome
alyssum

issor \iz-ər\ scissor, whizzer

issue¹ \ish-ü\ fichu, issue, tissue
reissue
Mogadishu, overissue

issue² \ish-ə\ see itia

issure \ish-ər\ see isher

issus \is-əs\ byssus, missus, Mrs.
narcissus, Narcissus

issy \is-ē\ hissy, missy, prissy, sissy

ist¹ \īst\ Christ, feist, heist, hist, tryst
zeitgeist
Antichrist, black-a-vised, poltergeist
—*also* -ed *forms of verbs listed at*
ice¹

ist² \ist\ cist, cyst, fist, gist, grist,
kist, list, Liszt, mist, schist, tryst,
twist, whist, wist, wrist
assist, backlist, blacklist, checklist,
consist, delist, desist, encyst, enlist,
entwist, exist, handlist, insist, persist,
playlist, protist, Rehnquist, resist,
shortlist, subsist, untwist

catechist, coexist, dadaist, exorcist,
intertwist, preexist
love-in-a-mist
—*also* -ed *forms of verbs listed at*
iss

ist³ \ēst\ see east¹

ista¹ \ē-stə\ turista
camorrista, Fidelista

ista² \is-tə\ crista, vista
arista, ballista
sacahuiste

istaed \is-təd\ see isted

istal \is-tᵊl\ Bristol, crystal, Crystal,
distal, listel, pistil, pistol

istan \is-tən\ see iston

istance \is-təns\ see istence

istant \is-tənt\ see istent

iste¹ \is-tē\ see icity²

iste² \ēst\ see east¹

iste³ \is-tə\ see ista²

isted \is-təd\ twisted, vistaed
closefisted, enlisted, ham-fisted,
hardfisted, limp-wristed, tightfisted,
two-fisted, unlisted, untwisted, white-
listed
ironfisted, unassisted
—*also* -ed *forms of verbs listed at*
ist²

istel \is-tᵊl\ see ist²

isten \is-ᵊn\ christen, glisten, listen,
Nisan

istenable \is-nə-bəl\ listenable
medicinable

istence \is-təns\ distance
assistance, consistence, existence,
insistence, outdistance, persistence,
resistance, subsistence
coexistence, inconsistence,
inexistence, nonexistence,
nonresistance, preexistence

istency \is-tən-sē\ consistency,
insistency, persistency
inconsistency

istent \is-tənt\ distant
assistant, consistent, existent,
insistent, persistent, resistant,
subsistent
coexistent, equidistant, inconsistent,
inexistent, nonexistent, nonpersistent,
nonresistant, preexistent

ister \is-tər\ bister, blister, clyster,
glister, klister, lister, Lister, mister,
sister, twister
resister, resistor, solicitor, stepsister,
transistor

istery \is-trē\ see istory

istful \ist-fəl\ tristful, wistful

isthmus \is-məs\ see istmas

isti \is-tē\ see icity²

istic \is-tik\ cystic, distich, fistic,
mystic
artistic, autistic, ballistic, cladistic,
cubistic, eristic, fascistic, faunistic,
floristic, heuristic, holistic, hubristic,
juristic, linguistic, logistic, meristic,
monistic, patristic, phlogistic, puristic,
sadistic, simplistic, sophistic, statistic,
stylistic, Taoistic, theistic, Thomistic,
touristic, truistic, veristic, wholistic,
Yahwistic
activistic, agonistic, alchemistic,
altruistic, amoristic, anarchistic,
animistic, aphoristic, archaistic,
atavistic, atheistic, atomistic,
belletristic, cabalistic, Calvinistic,
casuistic, catechistic, Catharistic,
centralistic, chauvinistic,
communistic, crosslinguistic,
dadaistic, dualistic, dyslogistic,
egoistic, egotistic, essayistic,
eucharistic, eulogistic, euphemistic,
euphuistic, exorcistic, fabulistic,
familistic, fatalistic, feministic,
fetishistic, feudalistic, fideistic,
formalistic, futuristic, gongoristic,
haggadistic, Hebraistic, hedonistic,

Hellenistic, humanistic, humoristic, idealistic, imagistic, inartistic, Jansenistic, jingoistic, journalistic, Judaistic, Lamaistic, legalistic, masochistic, mechanistic, melanistic, mentalistic, methodistic, modernistic, moralistic, narcissistic, nationalistic, nativistic, nepotistic, nihilistic, novelistic, onanistic, optimistic, pantheistic, pessimistic, pianistic, pietistic, plagiaristic, Platonistic, pluralistic, pointillistic, populistic, pugilistic, quietistic, realistic, Romanistic, sciolistic, shamanistic, shintoistic, socialistic, solecistic, solipsistic, specialistic, surrealistic, syllogistic, symbolistic, synchronistic, syncretistic, synergistic, terroristic, totalistic, totemistic, ultraistic, unrealistic, urbanistic, utopistic, vandalistic, verbalistic, vitalistic, voodooistic, voyeuristic, Zionistic
  absolutistic, adventuristic, anachronistic, animalistic, anomalistic, antagonistic, behavioristic, cannibalistic, capitalistic, characteristic, collectivistic, commercialistic, contortionistic, deterministic, evangelistic, eudaemonistic, euhemeristic, expansionistic, expressionistic, extralinguistic, functionalistic, Hinayanistic, hypocoristic, immanentistic, impressionistic, liberalistic, literalistic, Mahayanistic, melioristic, mercantilistic, militaristic, mediumistic, metalinguistic, misogynistic, monopolistic, monotheistic, naturalistic, negativistic, neologistic, opportunistic, paternalistic, physicalistic, polytheistic, probabilistic, propagandistic, psycholinguistic, rationalistic, recidivistic, reductionistic, relativistic, revivalistic, ritualistic, secularistic, sensualistic, separatistic, sociolinguistic, somnambulistic, ventriloquistic, violinistic, voluntaristic

  colonialistic, Deuteronomistic, emotionalistic, exhibitionistic, fundamentalistic, existentialistic, imperialistic, indeterministic, introspectionistic, irrationalistic, materialistic, oligopolistic, Postimpressionistic, sadomasochistic, sensationalistic, sociolinguistic, spiritualistic, traditionalistic
  individualistic

istical \is-ti-kəl\ mystical
  deistical, eristical, linguistical, logistical, monistical, patristical, sophistical, statistical, theistical
  alchemistical, atheistical, casuistical, egoistical, egotistical, exorcistical, pantheistical
  anomalistical, hypocoristical, monotheistical, polytheistical

istich \is-tik\ see istic

istics \is-tiks\ ballistics, ekistics, linguistics, logistics, patristics, statistics, stylistics
  futuristics
  criminalistics
  —also -s, -'s, and -s' forms of nouns listed at istic

istie \is-tē\ see icity²

istil \is-t°l\ see istal

istin \is-tən\ see iston

istine \is-tən\ see iston

istle \is-əl\ bristle, fissile, gristle, missal, missile, scissile, thistle, whistle
  abyssal, dickcissel, dismissal, epistle
  pennywhistle

istler \is-lər\ whistler, Whistler
  epistler

istless \ist-ləs\ listless
  resistless

istly \is-lē\ bristly, gristly, thistly
  sweet cicely

istmas \is-məs\ Christmas, isthmus
  Kiritimati

isto \is-tō\ aristo, Callisto

istol \is-tᵊl\ see istal

iston \is-tən\ Kristin, piston, Tristan
Philistine, phlogiston
amethystine

istor \is-tər\ see ister

istory \is-trē\ blistery, history,
mystery
consistory, prehistory

istral \is-trəl\ mistral
sinistral

istress \is-trəs\ mistress
headmistress, postmistress,
schoolmistress, sinistrous,
taskmistress, toastmistress

istrophe \is-trə-fē\ antistrophe,
epistrophe

istrous \is-trəs\ see istress

isty \is-tē\ see icity²

isus \ī-səs\ see isis

iszt \ist\ see ist²

it¹ \it\ bit, bitt, brit, Brit, chit, dit, fit,
flit, frit, git, grit, hit, it, kit, knit, lit,
mitt, nit, pit, Pitt, quit, sit, skit, slit,
snit, spit, split, Split, sprit, teat, tit,
twit, whit, wit, writ, zit
acquit, admit, armpit, backbit,
backfit, befit, bowsprit, Brigitte,
bushtit, cesspit, close-knit, cockpit,
commit, culprit, demit, Dewitt,
dimwit, emit, fleapit, gaslit, godwit,
half-wit, henbit, house-sit, legit, lit
crit, misfit, mishit, moonlit, nitwit,
obit, omit, outfit, outwit, peewit,
permit, pinch-hit, Prakrit, pulpit, refit,
remit, sandpit, Sanskrit, snakebit,
starlit, submit, sunlit, switch-hit,
tidbit, tight-knit, titbit, tomtit,
transmit, turnspit, twilit, two-bit, unfit,
unknit, well-knit
baby-sit, benefit, candlelit,
counterfeit, hypocrite, intermit,

intromit, manumit, megahit,
recommit, retrofit
cost-benefit, lickety-split,
overcommit
jack-in-the-pulpit

it² \ē\ see ee¹

it³ \ēt\ see eat¹

ita¹ \īt-ə\ vita
baryta
amanita

ita² \ēt-ə\ cheetah, eta, Greta, Nita,
pita, Rita, theta, vita, zeta
Akita, Anita, Bonita, bonito, casita,
excreta, Granita, Juanita, Lolita,
partita, Suita
amanita, arboreta, feterita, incognita,
manzanita, margarita, senhorita,
senorita
Bhagavad Gita

itable¹ \īt-ə-bəl\ citable, writable
excitable, indictable
copyrightable, extraditable

itable² \it-ə-bəl\ see ittable

itae \īt-ē\ see ite²

itain \it-n\ see itten

ital¹ \īt-ᵊl\ title, vital
detrital, entitle, nontitle, recital,
requital, subtitle
disentitle, intravital, supravital

ital² \it-ᵊl\ see ittle

italer \it-ᵊl-ər\ whittler, victualler
belittler, Hospitaler

italist \īt-ᵊl-əst\ titlist, vitalist
recitalist

itan \īt-ᵊn\ see ighten

itant \īt-ᵊnt\ mightn't
excitant, incitant, renitent

itany \it-ᵊn-ē\ Brittany, dittany,
litany

itch \ich\ bitch, ditch, fitch, flitch,
glitch, hitch, itch, kitsch, niche, pitch,

quitch, rich, snitch, stitch, such,
switch, twitch, which, witch
  backstitch, bewitch, cross-stitch,
enrich, fast-twitch, hemstitch,
lockstitch, slow-pitch, slow-twitch,
topstitch, unhitch, whipstitch
czarevitch, featherstitch,
microswitch

itchen \ich-ən\ kitchen, richen

itchener \ich-nər\ Kitchener,
Michener

itcher \ich-ər\ hitcher, pitcher,
richer, snitcher, stitcher, switcher
  enricher, hemstitcher
  Lubavitcher, water witcher

itchery \ich-ə-rē\ bitchery, stitchery,
witchery
  bewitchery, obituary

itches \ich-əz\ britches, riches
  Dutchman's-breeches
  —*also* -s, -'s, *and* -s' *forms of nouns,
and* -s *forms of verbs, listed at* itch

itchman \ich-mən\ pitchman,
switchman

itchment \ich-mənt\ bewitchment,
enrichment

itchy \ich-ē\ bitchy, itchy, kitschy,
pitchy, twitchy, witchy

it'd \it-əd\ see itted

ite[1] \īt\ bight, bite, blight, bright,
byte, cite, dight, dite, Dwight, fight,
flight, fright, height, hight, kite,
knight, krait, kyte, light, lite, might,
mite, night, plight, quite, right, rite,
sight, site, sleight, slight, smite, spite,
sprite, tight, trite, white, White, wight,
Wight, wite, wright, Wright, write
  affright, airtight, albite, alight, all
right, all-night, aright, backbite,
backlight, bedight, Birchite, birthright,
bobwhite, bombsight, bullfight,
campsite, cockfight, contrite, Cushite,
daylight, deadlight, delight, despite,
dogfight, downright, droplight,
earthlight, excite, eyebright, eyesight,

fanlight, finite, firefight, firelight,
fistfight, flashlight, fleabite, floodlight,
foresight, forthright, fortnight,
frostbite, Gadite, gaslight, gastight,
ghostwrite, graphite, gunfight, Gunite,
half-light, Hamite, handwrite,
headlight, highlight, hindsight, Hittite,
homesite, hoplite, Hussite, ignite,
illite, infight, in-flight, incite, indict,
indite, insight, invite, jacklight,
jadeite, lamplight, Levite, lighttight,
lignite, limelight, lintwhite, lowlight,
Lucite, Luddite, lyddite, Melchite,
midnight, millwright, miswrite,
moonlight, night-light, off-site, off-
white, on-site, outright, outsight,
partite, penlight, playwright, polite,
prizefight, pyrite, recite, requite,
respite, rushlight, safelight,
searchlight, Semite, Servite, Shemite,
Shiite, shipwright, sidelight, skintight,
skylight, skywrite, smectite, snakebite,
snow-white, spaceflight, speedlight,
spotlight, starlight, sticktight,
stoplight, streetlight, sunlight, Sunnite,
taillight, termite, tonight, torchlight,
trothplight, twilight, twi-night,
typewrite, unite, unsight, upright,
uptight, wainwright, weeknight,
wheelwright
  acolyte, aconite, Ammonite,
Amorite, amosite, anchorite,
anthracite, antiwhite, apartheid,
appetite, Bakelite, Benthamite,
bipartite, black-and-white,
blatherskite, bleacherite, chalcocite,
Canaanite, Carmelite, castroite,
catamite, cellulite, copyright,
disinvite, disunite, dynamite, erudite,
expedite, extradite, Fahrenheit,
featherlight, fly-by-night, gelignite,
gesundheit, gigabyte, Hashemite,
Hepplewhite, Himyarite, Hitlerite,
hug-me-tight, impolite, Ishmaelite,
Israelite, Jacobite, Josephite,
Kimberlite, laborite, Leninite,
leukocyte, lily-white, localite,
malachite, manganite, Marcionite,
Masonite, Mennonite, Minorite,
Moabite, muscovite, Nazirite, out-of-
sight, overbite, overflight, overnight,

oversight, overwrite, parasite,
perovskite, plebiscite, proselyte,
Puseyite, pyrrhotite, recondite, reunite,
satellite, shergottite, socialite, sodalite,
sodomite, Stagirite, stalactite,
stalagmite, Sybarite, time-of-flight,
transfinite, transvestite, tripartite,
troglodyte, Trotskyite, ultralight,
underwrite, urbanite, Wahhabite,
watertight, Wycliffite, yesternight
  adipocyte, anthophyllite,
cosmopolite, exurbanite,
gem͵tlichkeit, hermaphrodite, Indo-
Hittite, McCarthyite, multipartite,
quadripartite, suburbanite, theodolite
  Areopagite, Pre-Raphaelite
  Great Australian Bight

ite² \īt-ē\ flighty, mighty, nightie,
righty, whity
  almighty, Almighty, Venite
  Aphrodite, aqua vitae, arborvitae,
lignum vitae

ite³ \īt\ see it¹

ite⁴ \ēt\ see eat¹

ited \īt-əd\ see ighted

iteful \īt-fəl\ see ightful

itely \īt-lē\ see ightly

item \īt-əm\ item
  ad infinitum

itement \īt-mənt\ alightment,
excitement, incitement, indictment

iten \īt-ᵊn\ see ighten

itener \īt-nər\ see ightener

itent \īt-ᵊnt\ see itant

iteor \ēt-ē-ər\ see eteor

iter¹ \īt-ər\ blighter, fighter, lighter,
miter, niter, titer, writer
  all-nighter, braillewriter, exciter,
first-nighter, lamplighter, nail-biter,
one-nighter, prizefighter, screenwriter,
scriptwriter, songwriter, speechwriter,
sportswriter, states righter, typewriter

copywriter, expediter, fly-by-nighter,
Gastarbeiter, underwriter
  teletypewriter
  —also -er *forms of adjectives listed
at* ite¹

iter² \it-ər\ see itter

iter³ \ēt-ər\ see eater¹

iteral \it-ə-rəl\ clitoral, literal,
littoral
  sublittoral, triliteral

iterally \it-ər-lē\ see itterly

iterate \it-ə-rət\ literate
  illiterate, nonliterate, postliterate,
preliterate, presbyterate, subliterate
  semiliterate

ites¹ \īt-ēz\ barytes, sorites,
Thersites
  —also -s, -'s, *and* -s' *forms of nouns
listed at* ite²

ites² \īts\ see ights

itey \īt-ē\ see ite²

ith \ith\ fifth, frith, grith, kith, myth,
pith, sith, smith, Smith, swith, with,
withe
  blacksmith, forthwith, goldsmith,
Goldsmith, gunsmith, herewith,
locksmith, songsmith, therewith,
tinsmith, tunesmith, wherewith,
whitesmith, wordsmith
  coppersmith, eolith, Granny Smith,
Hammersmith, megalith, metalsmith,
microlith, monolith, neolith,
silversmith
  paleolith

ith³ \ēt\ see eat¹

ith⁴ \ēth\ see eath¹

ithe¹ \īth\ blithe, kithe, lithe, scythe,
tithe, withe, writhe

ithe² \ith\ see ith²

ithe³ \ith\ see ith¹

ithee¹ \ith-ē\ see ithy²

ithee² \ith̠-ē\ see ithy¹

ither \ith̠-ər\ blither, cither, dither, hither, slither, swither, thither, whither, wither, zither
come-hither, nowhither, somewhither

itherward \ith̠-ər-wərd\
thitherward, whitherward

ithesome \īth̠-səm\ blithesome, lithesome

ithia \ith-ē-ə\ see ythia

ithic \ith-ik\ lithic
ornithic
batholithic, Eolithic, granolithic, megalithic, Mesolithic, monolithic, neolithic
Paleolithic

ithing \ī-th̠iŋ\ tithing, trithing
—also -ing forms of verbs listed at ithe¹

ithmic \ith̠-mik\ see ythmic

ithy¹ \ith̠-ē\ prithee, withy

ithy² \ith-ē\ mythy, pithy, prithee, smithy, withy

iti \ēt-ē\ see eaty

itia¹ \ish-ə\ Lycia, Mysia, wisha
Alicia, Cilicia, comitia, episcia, Galicia, indicia, Letitia, militia, Patricia, Phoenicia
Dionysia

itia² \ē-shə\ see esia¹

itial \ish-əl\ see icial

itian¹ \ish-ən\ see ition

itian² \ē-shən\ see etion¹

itiate \ish-ət\ initiate, novitiate
uninitiate

itic \it-ik\ clitic, critic
arthritic, bronchitic, dendritic, enclitic, granitic, graphitic, Hamitic, jaditic, mephitic, proclitic, pruritic, rachitic, Sanskritic, Semitic, Shemitic, Sinitic

anaclitic, analytic, anchoritic, catalytic, cenobitic, copralitic, crystallitic, diacritic, dialytic, dynamitic, eremitic, Himyaritic, hypercritic, jesuitic, paralytic, parasitic, sodomitic, stalactitic, stalagmitic, sybaritic, thallophytic, thrombolytic, troglodytic
cryptanalytic, electrolytic, hermaphroditic, meteoritic, Monophysitic
psychoanalytic

itical \it-i-kəl\ critical
Levitical, political
analytical, apolitical, cenobitical, diacritical, eremitical, hypercritical, hypocritical, impolitical, Jacobitical, jesuitical, parasitical, sodomitical, supercritical
geopolitical, meteoritical
sociopolitical

itics \it-iks\ Semitics
analytics
meteoritics
—also -s, -'s, and -s' forms of nouns listed at itic

itid \it-əd\ see itted

itimati \is-məs\ see istmas

itin \īt-ᵊn\ see ighten

iting \īt-iŋ\ biting, flyting, lighting, whiting, writing
backbiting, bullfighting, cockfighting, daylighting, exciting, freewriting, frostbiting, handwriting, infighting, inviting, newswriting, prewriting, prizefighting, skywriting, songwriting, sportswriting, typewriting
—also -ing forms of verbs listed at ite¹

ition \ish-ən\ fission, hycian, mission, titian, Titian
addition, admission, ambition, attrition, audition, beautician, clinician, cognition, coition, commission, condition, contrition, demission, dentition, dismission, Domitian, edition, emission, ethician,

fruition, ignition, lenition, logician,
magician, monition, mortician,
munition, musician, nutrition,
omission, optician, partition, patrician,
perdition, permission, petition,
Phoenician, physician, position,
punition, remission, rendition,
sedition, submission, suspicion,
tactician, technician, tradition,
transition, transmission, tuition,
volition
  abolition, acquisition, admonition,
aesthetician, air-condition,
ammunition, apparition, apposition,
coalition, competition, composition,
cosmetician, decommission,
decondition, definition, demolition,
deposition, dietitian, Dionysian,
disposition, disquisition, electrician,
erudition, exhibition, expedition,
exposition, extradition, imposition,
inhibition, inquisition, intermission,
intromission, intuition, linguistician,
logistician, malnutrition, malposition,
manumission, mathematician,
mechanician, micturition, obstetrician,
opposition, Ordovician, parturition,
phonetician, politician, precognition,
precondition, premonition,
preposition, prohibition, proposition,
recognition, recondition, repetition,
requisition, rhetorician, statistician,
submunition, superstition, supposition,
transposition
  academician, arithmetician,
decomposition, diagnostician,
dialectician, disinhibition,
geometrician, geriatrician,
indisposition, interposition,
juxtaposition, metaphysician,
onomastician, pediatrician,
presupposition, redefinition,
semiotician, theoretician
  superimposition

itionable \ish-nə-bəl\ see issionable

itional \ish-nəl\ additional,
attritional, cognitional, coitional,
conditional, nutritional, positional,
traditional, transitional, tuitional,
volitional

apparitional, appositional,
compositional, definitional,
depositional, expositional,
inquisitional, oppositional,
prepositional, propositional,
repetitional, suppositional,
transpositional, unconditional
  juxtapositional, presuppositional

itioner \i-shə-nər\ missioner
commissioner, conditioner,
parishioner, partitioner, petitioner,
practitioner
  exhibitioner, malpractitioner, nurse-
practitioner

itionist \i-shə-nəst\ nutritionist,
partitionist
  abolitionist, coalitionist,
demolitionist, exhibitionist,
intuitionist, oppositionist,
prohibitionist

itious \ish-əs\ see icious[1]

itis \īt-əs\ situs, Titus
  arthritis, botrytis, bronchitis, bursitis,
colitis, cystitis, detritus, gastritis, iritis,
mastitis, nephritis, neuritis, phlebitis
  dermatitis, enteritis, gingivitis,
hepatitis, Heracleitus, ileitis,
laryngitis, meningitis, pharyngitis,
pneumonitis, prostatitis, retinitis,
sinusitis, tonsillitis, spondylitis,
tendinitis, urethritis, vaginitis
  appendicitis, conjunctivitis,
encephalitis, endocarditis,
endometritus, folliculitis,
Hermaphroditus, peritonitis
  analysis situs, diverticulitis,
gastroenteritis, poliomyelitis

itish \it-ish\ British, skittish

itius \ish-əs\ see icious

itle \īt-əl\ see ital[1]

it'll \it-əl\ see ittle

itment \it-mənt\ fitment
commitment, remitment
  recommitment
  overcommitment

itness \it-nəs\ fitness, witness
earwitness, eyewitness, unfitness

itney \it-nē\ jitney, Whitney
Mount Whitney

ito[1] \ēt-ō\ keto, Leto, Quito, Tito,
veto
bonito, burrito, graffito, magneto,
Miskito, mosquito, Negrito
Hirohito, incognito, sanbenito

ito[2] \ēt-ə\ see ita[2]

iton[1] \it-ᵊn\ see itten

iton[2] \īt-ᵊn\ see ighten

itoral \it-ə-rəl\ see iteral

itra \ē-trə\ see etra[2]

itral \ī-trəl\ mitral, nitrile

itrile \ī-trəl\ see itral

its \its\ blitz, ditz, Fritz, glitz, grits,
its, it's, quits, spitz
Chemnitz, Saint Kitts
slivovitz
—also -s, -'s, and -s' forms of nouns,
and -s forms of verbs, listed at it[1]

it's \its\ see its

itsail \it-səl\ see itzel

itsch \ich\ see itch

itschy \ich-ē\ see itchy

itsy \it-sē\ see itzy

itt \it\ see it[1]

itta \it-ə\ shittah, vitta

ittable \it-ə-bəl\ committable,
habitable, hospitable, remittable,
transmittable
inhospitable

ittah \it-ə\ see itta

ittal \it-ᵊl\ see ittle

ittance \it-ᵊns\ pittance, quittance
acquittance, admittance, emittance,
immittance, remittance, transmittance
intermittence

ittany \it-ᵊn-ē\ see itany

itte \it\ see it[1]

itted \it-əd\ fitted, it'd, nitid, pitted,
teated, witted
committed, dim-witted, half-witted,
quick-witted, sharp-witted, slow-
witted, thick-witted, unbitted, unfitted
uncommitted
—also -ed forms of verbs listed at it[1]

ittee \it-ē\ see itty

itten \it-ᵊn\ bitten, Britain, Briton,
Britten, kitten, litten, Lytton, mitten,
smitten, witting, written
backbitten, flea-bitten, Great Britain,
hard-bitten, New Britain, rewritten,
snakebitten, unwritten

ittence \it-ᵊns\ see ittance

ittent \it-ᵊnt\ remittent
intermittent, intromittent

itter \it-ər\ bitter, chitter, critter,
fitter, flitter, fritter, glitter, hitter, jitter,
knitter, litter, quitter, quittor, sitter,
skitter, slitter, spitter, titter, twitter
aglitter, atwitter, bed-sitter, embitter,
emitter, hairsplitter, no-hitter, outfitter,
rail-splitter, remitter, shipfitter,
steamfitter, switch-hitter, transmitter
benefiter, counterfeiter, intromitter

itterer \it-ər-ər\ fritterer, litterer,
twitterer

itterly \it-ər-lē\ bitterly, literally

ittern \it-ərn\ bittern, cittern, gittern

ittery \it-ə-rē\ glittery, jittery, littery,
skittery, twittery

ittie \it-ē\ see itty

ittier \it-ē-ər\ grittier, prettier,
Whittier, wittier

ittiness \it-ē-nəs\ grittiness,
prettiness, wittiness

itting[1] \it-iŋ\ fitting, sitting, splitting,
witting

befitting, earsplitting, fence-sitting,
formfitting, hairsplitting, hard-hitting,
house-sitting, resitting, sidesplitting,
unfitting, unwitting, unremitting
—*also* -ing *forms of verbs listed at*
it[1]

itting[2] \it-ᵊn\ see itten

ittish \it-ish\ see itish

ittle \it-ᵊl\ brittle, it'll, kittle, little,
skittle, spital, spittle, tittle, victual,
whittle, wittol
  acquittal, belittle, committal,
  embrittle, hospital, lickspittle,
  remittal, transmittal
  noncommittal, recommittal

ittler \it-ᵊl-ər\ see italer

ittol \it-ᵊl\ see ittle

ittor \it-ər\ see itter

ittoral \it-ə-rəl\ see iteral

itts \its\ see its

itty \it-ē\ bitty, city, ditty, gritty,
kitty, Kitty, pity, pretty, tittie, witty
  committee, self-pity, itty-bitty,
  Kansas City, megacity, nitty-gritty,
  Salt Lake City, subcommittee,
  supercity, Walter Mitty
    Ho Chi Minh City

itual \ich-ə-wəl\ ritual
  habitual

ituary \ich-ə-rē\ see itchery[1]

itum \īt-əm\ see item

itus \īt-əs\ see itis

ity[1] \it-ē\ see itty

ity[2] \īt-ē\ see ite[2]

itz \its\ see its

itza[1] \ēt-sə\ pizza
  czaritza
    Chichén Itza, Katowice

itza[2] \it-sə\ czaritza
  tamburitza

itzel \it-səl\ schnitzel, spritsail
  Wiener schnitzel

itzi \it-sē\ see itzy

itzy \it-sē\ bitsy, glitzy, Mitzi, ritzy,
schizy

iu \ü\ see ew[1]

ius[1] \ē-əs\ see eus[1]

ius[2] \ī-əs\ see ias[1]

iv[1] \iv\ see ive[2]

iv[2] \ēf\ see ief[1]

iv[3] \if\ see iff

iv[4] \ēv\ scc eave

iva[1] \ī-və\ Saiva
  gingiva, Godiva, saliva

iva[2] \ē-və\ diva, Eva, kiva, Shiva,
siva, Siva, viva
  geneva, Geneva, yeshiva

iva[3] \iv-ə\ Shiva, Siva

ivable[1] \ī-və-bəl\ drivable
  derivable, revivable, survivable

ivable[2] \iv-ə-bəl\ livable
  forgivable

ival \ī-vəl\ rival
  archival, arrival, revival, survival
  adjectival, conjunctival, genitival,
  substantival
    infinitival

ivalent \iv-ə-lənt\ ambivalent,
equivalent
  unambivalent

ivan \iv-ən\ see iven

ivance \ī-vəns\ connivance,
contrivance, survivance

ivative \iv-ət-iv\ privative
  derivative

ive[1] \īv\ chive, dive, drive, five,
gyve, hive, I've, jive, live, rive, shrive,
skive, strive, thrive, wive

alive, archive, Argive, arrive,
beehive, connive, contrive, deprive,
derive, endive, nosedive, ogive, revive,
self-drive, skin-dive, survive, test-
drive
  forty-five, overdrive, power-dive

ive² \iv\ give, live, sheave, shiv,
sieve, spiv
  forgive, misgive, outlive, relive,
unlive
  underactive

ive³ \ēv\ see eave¹

ivel \iv-əl\ civil, drivel, frivol,
shrivel, snivel, swivel

iven \iv-ən\ driven, given, riven,
Sivan, striven, thriven
  forgiven
  menu-driven

iver¹ \ī-vər\ diver, driver, fiver
  arriver, cabdriver, conniver,
contriver, deriver, reviver, screwdriver,
survivor

iver² \iv-ər\ flivver, giver, liver,
quiver, river, shiver, sliver
  almsgiver, aquiver, deliver,
downriver, forgiver, lawgiver, upriver
  Guadalquivir

ivers¹ \ī-vərz\ divers, vivers
  —also -s, -'s, and -s' forms of nouns
listed at iver¹

ivers² \ē-vərz\ see eavers

ivery \iv-rē\ livery, shivery
  delivery

ives \īvz\ fives, hives, Ives
  —also -s, -'s, and -s' forms of nouns,
and -s forms of verbs, listed at ive¹

ivet \iv-ət\ civet, divot, pivot, privet,
rivet, swivet, trivet

ivi¹ \iv-ē\ see ivvy

ivi² \ē-vē\ see eavey

ivia \iv-ē-ə\ Bolivia, Olivia

ivial \iv-ē-əl\ trivial
  convivial, quadrivial

ivid \iv-əd\ livid, vivid

ivil \iv-əl\ see ivel

ivilly \iv-ə-lē\ civilly, privily
  uncivilly

ivily \iv-ə-lē\ see ivilly

iving \iv-iŋ\ giving, living
  almsgiving, forgiving, free-living,
misgiving, thanksgiving
  —also -ing forms of verbs listed at
ive²

ivion \iv-ē-ən\ Vivian
  oblivion

ivious \iv-ē-əs\ lascivious, oblivious

ivir \iv-ər\ see iver²

ivity \iv-ət-ē\ privity
  acclivity, activity, captivity, declivity,
festivity, motivity, nativity, proclivity
  absorptivity, adaptivity, additivity,
affectivity, aggressivity, coercivity,
cognitivity, collectivity, compulsivity,
conductivity, connectivity, creativity,
destructivity, diffusivity, directivity,
effectivity, emissivity, emotivity,
exclusivity, exhaustivity, expansivity,
expressivity, impassivity, inactivity,
infectivity, negativity, perceptivity,
perfectivity, permittivity, positivity,
primitivity, productivity, progressivity,
reactivity, receptivity, reflexivity,
relativity, resistivity, retentivity,
selectivity, sensitivity, subjectivity,
susceptivity, transitivity
  distributivity, hyperactivity,
insensitivity, overactivity, retroactivity
  hypersensitivity, radioactivity

ivium \iv-ē-əm\ trivium
  quadrivium

iviut \ē-vē-ət\ see eviate

ivo \ē-vō\ see evo

ivocal \iv-ə-kəl\ equivocal, univocal
  unequivocal

ivol \iv-əl\ see ivel

ivor \ī-vər\ see iver¹

ivorous \iv-rəs\ carnivorous, granivorous, omnivorous insectivorous

ivot \iv-ət\ see ivet

ivus \ē-vəs\ see evous

ivver \iv-ər\ see iver²

ivvy \iv-ē\ chivy, civvy, divvy, Livy, privy, skivvy
tantivy
divi-divi

ivy \iv-ē\ see ivvy

iwi \ē-wē\ see eewee

ix¹ \iks\ Brix, Dix, fix, mix, nix, pyx, six, Styx
admix, affix, blanc fixe, commix, deep-six, immix, infix, postfix, prefix, premix, prix fixe, prolix, subfix, suffix, transfix, unfix
antefix, cicatrix, crucifix, eighty-six, intermix, politics, six-o-six, superfix
geopolitics
RU 486
—*also* -s, -'s, *and* -s' *forms of nouns, and* -s *forms of verbs, listed at* ick

ix² \ē\ see ee¹

ixal \ik-səl\ pixel
affixal, prefixal, suffixal

ixe¹ \ēks\ breeks
prix fixe
idée fixe
Macgillicuddy's Reeks
—*also* -s, -'s, *and* -s' *forms of nouns, and* -s *forms of verbs, listed at* eak¹

ixe² \iks\ see ix¹

ixe³ \ēsh\ see iche²

ixed \ikst\ fixed, mixed, twixt
betwixt, well-fixed
—*also* -ed *forms of verbs listed at* ix¹

ixel \ik-səl\ see ixal

ixen \ik-sən\ vixen, Nixon
Mason-Dixon

ixer \ik-sər\ fixer, mixer
elixir

ixia \ik-sē-ə\ asphyxia, panmixia

ixie \ik-sē\ Dixie, nixie, Nixie, pixie, pyxie, tricksy

ixion \ik-shən\ see iction

ixir \ik-sər\ see ixer

ixit \ik-sət\ quixote
ipse dixit

ixon \ik-sən\ see ixen

ixote \ik-sət\ see ixit

ixt \ikst\ see ixed

ixture \iks-chər\ fixture, mixture
admixture, commixture
intermixture

iya \ē-ə\ see ia¹

iyeh \ē-ə\ see ia¹

iz¹ \iz\ biz, fizz, frizz, his, is, Ms., phiz, quiz, 'tis, whiz, wiz
gee-whiz, show biz

iz² \ēz\ see eze

iza¹ \ē-zə\ see eza

iza² \ē-thə\ see etha

izabeth \iz-ə-bəth\ Elisabeth, Elizabeth
Port Elizabeth

izable \ī-zə-bəl\ sizable
advisable, cognizable, devisable, excisable
amortizable, analyzable, criticizable, dramatizable, exercisable, fertilizable, hypnotizable, inadvisable, localizable, magnetizable, mechanizable, memorizable, pulverizable, recognizable, vaporizable
computerizable, generalizable, uncompromisable

izar \ī-zər\ see izer

izard \iz-ərd\ blizzard, gizzard, izzard, lizard, vizard, wizard

ize¹ \īz\ guise, prise, prize, rise, size, wise

abscise, advise, apprise, apprize, arise, assize, baptize, breadthwise, capsize, chastise, clockwise, cognize, comprise, crabwise, crosswise, demise, despise, devise, disguise, disprize, downsize, earthrise, edgewise, emprise, endwise, excise, fanwise, franchise, full-size, grecize, high-rise, incise, king-size, leastwise, lengthwise, Levi's, life-size, likewise, low-rise, man-size, midsize, misprize, moonrise, nowise, outsize, piecewise, pint-size, premise, quantize, remise, reprise, revise, slantwise, streetwise, stylize, suffice, sunrise, surmise, surprise, twin-size, uprise

advertise, aggrandize, agonize, alchemize, amortize, analyze, anglicize, anywise, aphorize, arabize, atomize, authorize, autolyze, balkanize, barbarize, bastardize, bestialize, bolshevize, botanize, bowdlerize, brutalize, burglarize, canalize, canonize, capsulize, caramelize, carbonize, cartelize, catalyze, catechize, cauterize, centralize, channelize, Christianize, cicatrize, circumcise, civilize, classicize, colonize, communize, compromise, concertize, concretize, creolize, criticize, crystalize, customize, demonize, deputize, dialyze, digitize, disfranchise, dogmatize, dramatize, elegize, empathize, emphasize, energize, enfranchise, enterprise, equalize, erotize, eternize, etherize, eulogize, euphemize, exercise, exorcise, factorize, fantasize, fascistize, feminize, fertilize, feudalize, fictionize, finalize, formalize, formulize, fossilize, fragmentize, fraternize, gallicize, galvanize, germanize, ghettoize, glamorize, globalize, gormandize, gothicize, gourmandize, grecianize, harmonize, heathenize, hebraize, hellenize, hierarchize, humanize, hybridize, hypnotize, idolize, immunize,

improvise, ionize, ironize, Islamize, itemize, jeopardize, journalize, Judaize, laicize, latinize, legalize, lionize, liquidize, localize, magnetize, marbleize, martyrize, maximize, mechanize, melanize, melodize, memorize, merchandise, mesmerize, methodize, metricize, minimize, mobilize, modernize, moisturize, monetize, mongrelize, moralize, motorize, mythicize, narcotize, nasalize, neutralize, normalize, notarize, novelize, obelize, odorize, optimize, organize, ostracize, otherwise, oversize, oxidize, paganize, paradise, paralyze, pasteurize, patronize, pauperize, penalize, penny-wise, pidginize, plagiarize, plasticize, Platonize, pluralize, pocket-size, poetize, polarize, polemize, pressurize, privatize, prussianize, publicize, pulverize, randomize, realize, recognize, rhapsodize, robotize, romanize, rubberize, sanitize, satirize, scandalize, schematize, schismatize, scrutinize, sensitize, sermonize, signalize, simonize, sinicize, slenderize, sloganize, socialize, sodomize, solarize, sonnetize, specialize, stabilize, Stalinize, standardize, sterilize, stigmatize, strategize, subsidize, summarize, supervise, syllogize, symbolize, sympathize, synchronize, syncretize, synopsize, synthesize, systemize, tantalize, televise, temporize, tenderize, terrorize, tetanize, teutonize, texturize, theorize, thermalize, totalize, tranquilize, traumatize, tyrannize, unionize, unitize, urbanize, utilize, valorize, vandalize, vaporize, verbalize, vernalize, victimize, vitalize, vocalize, vulcanize, vulgarize, weather-wise, weatherize, westernize, winterize, womanize, worldly-wise

accessorize, acclimatize, actualize, allegorize, alphabetize, analogize, anatomize, anesthetize, animalize, annualize, antagonize, anthologize, anticlockwise, apologize, apostatize,

apostrophize, arabicize, aromatize,
baby blue-eyes, bureaucratize,
cannibalize, capitalize, categorize,
catholicize, characterize,
commercialize, communalize,
computerize, conservatize,
containerize, contrariwise,
conveyorize, cosmeticize,
counterclockwise, criminalize,
cryptanalize, decentralize, decolonize,
de-emphasize, de-energize,
dehumanize, deionize, demagnetize,
demobilize, democratize, demoralize,
deodorize, depersonalize, depolarize,
desalinize, desensitize, destabilize,
digitalize, disenfranchise, disorganize,
economize, emotionalize, epitomize,
epoxidize, eroticize, eternalize,
euthanatize, evangelize, extemporize,
externalize, familiarize, fanaticize,
federalize, fictionalize, formularize,
gelatinize, generalize, geologize,
Hispanicize, homogenize, hospitalize,
hypothesize, idealize, illegalize,
immobilize, immortalize,
impersonalize, Indianize, indigenize,
initialize, internalize, italicize,
legitimize, liberalize, literalize,
lobotomize, lysogenize, macadamize,
metabolize, metastasize, militarize,
mineralize, monopolize, mythologize,
nationalize, naturalize, parenthesize,
philosophize, politicize, popularize,
proselytize, regularize, reorganize,
revitalize, romanticize, secularize,
sexualize, sovietize, subjectivize,
suburbanize, subvocalize, systematize,
temporalize, theologize, traditionalize,
transistorize, trivialize, ventriloquize,
visualize
    Americanize, apotheosize,
colonialize, compartmentalize,
conceptualize, contextualize,
decriminalize, demilitarize,
denaturalize, departmentalize,
depoliticize, desexualize,
Europeanize, exteriorize, ideologize,
immaterialize, individualize,
industrialize, internationalize,
legitimatize, materialize, miniaturize,
particularize, politicalize,

psychoanalyze, self-actualize,
sentimentalize, spiritualize,
underutilize, universalize
constitutionalize, dematerialize,
editorialize, intellectualize
deinstitutionalize
    —also -s, -'s, and -s' forms of nouns,
and -s forms of verbs, listed at y[1]

ize² \ēz\ see eze

ized \īzd\ sized
advised, outsized
ergotized, ill-advised, pearlized,
Sanforized, unadvised, undersized,
varisized, well-advised
elasticized, modularized,
unexercised
immunocompromised
    —also -ed forms of verbs listed at
ize[1]

izen¹ \īz-ᵊn\ bison, dizen, greisen
bedizen, horizon
spiegeleisen

izen² \iz-ᵊn\ see ison²

izer \ī-zər\ Dreiser, geyser, kaiser,
miser, prizer, riser, sizar, visor, wiser
adviser, divisor, incisor
appetizer, atomizer, energizer,
enterpriser, equalizer, exerciser,
fertilizer, organizer, oxidizer,
stabilizer, supervisor, synthesizer,
totalizer, tranquilizer, tyrannizer,
vaporizer
complementizer, deodorizer

izing \ī-ziŋ\ rising, sizing
uprising
appetizing, enterprising,
merchandising, self-sufficing,
unsurprising
self-sacrificing, uncompromising
    —also -ing forms of verbs listed at
ize[1]

izo¹ \ē-zō\ sleazo
chorizo, mestizo

izo² \ē-sō\ see iso

izon \īz-ᵊn\ see izen¹

izy \it-sē\ see itzy

izz \iz\ see iz[1]

izza \ēt-sə\ see itza[1]

izzard \iz-ərd\ see izard

izzen \iz-ᵊn\ see ison[2]

izzer \iz-ər\ see issor

izzical \iz-i-kəl\ see ysical

izzie \i-zē\ see izzy

izzle \iz-əl\ chisel, drizzle, fizzle, frizzle, grizzle, mizzle, pizzle, sizzle, swizzle

izzled \iz-əld\ chiseled, grizzled
—*also* -ed *forms of verbs listed at* izzle

izzler \iz-lər\ chiseler, sizzler, swizzler

izzly \iz-lē\ drizzly, grisly, grizzly, mizzly

izzy \iz-ē\ busy, dizzy, fizzy, frizzy, tizzy
  tin lizzie

O

o¹ \ü\ see ew¹

o² \ō\ see ow¹

oa¹ \ō-ə\ boa, Goa, koa, moa, Noah,
proa, stoa
aloha, balboa, Balboa, jerboa, Samoa
Krakatoa, Mauna Loa, Shenandoah,
Sinaloa
Guanabacoa, João Pessoa

oa² \ō\ see ow¹

oable \ü-ə-bəl\ see uable

oach \ōch\ broach, brooch, coach,
loach, poach, roach
abroach, approach, caroche,
cockroach, encroach, reproach,
stagecoach

oachable \ō-chə-bəl\ coachable
approachable
inapproachable, irreproachable,
unapproachable

oacher \ō-chər\ broacher, coacher,
cloture, poacher
encroacher

oad¹ \ōd\ see ode

oad² \od\ see aud¹

oader \ōd-ər\ see oder

oadie \ōd-ē\ see ody²

oady \ōd-ē\ see ody²

oaf \ōf\ loaf, oaf, qoph
meatloaf, witloof
sugarloaf

oafer \ō-fər\ see ofer

oagie \ō-gē\ see ogie

oah \ō-ə\ see oa¹

oak \ōk\ see oke

oaken \ō-kən\ see oken

oaker \ō-kər\ see oker

oakum \ō-kəm\ see okum

oaky \ō-kē\ see oky

oal \ōl\ see ole¹

oalie \ō-lē\ see oly¹

oam¹ \ō-əm\ see oem¹

oam² \ōm\ see ome¹

oamer \ō-mər\ see omer¹

oaming \ō-miŋ\ coaming, combing,
gloaming
Wyoming
—also -ing forms of verbs listed at
ome¹

oamy \ō-mē\ foamy, homey, loamy,
show-me
Dahomey, Naomi, Salome

oan¹ \ō-ən\ Owen, roan, rowan
Minoan, Samoan, waygoing
Eskimoan, protozoan

oan² \ōn\ see one¹

oaner \ō-nər\ see oner¹

oaning \ō-niŋ\ see oning²

oap \ōp\ see ope

oaper \ō-pər\ see oper

oapy \ō-pē\ see opi

oar \or\ see or¹

oard \ord\ board, bored, chord, cord,
cored, floored, ford, Ford, gourd,

hoard, horde, lord, Lord, oared, pored,
poured, sward, sword, toward, ward,
Ward
   aboard, accord, afford, award,
backboard, backsword, baseboard,
billboard, blackboard, breadboard,
broadsword, buckboard, cardboard,
chalkboard, chessboard, chipboard,
clapboard, clipboard, concord,
corkboard, dashboard, discord,
duckboard, fjord, flashboard,
floorboard, footboard, freeboard,
garbord, Gaylord, greensward,
hardboard, headboard, inboard,
keyboard, kickboard, landlord,
lapboard, leeboard, longsword,
matchboard, moldboard, onboard,
outboard, packboard, pasteboard,
patchboard, pegboard, pressboard,
punchboard, rearward, record, reward,
sailboard, scoreboard, seaboard,
shipboard, sideboard, signboard,
skateboard, slumlord, smallsword,
snowboard, soundboard, splashboard,
springboard, surfboard, switchboard,
tailboard, untoward, wallboard,
washboard, word-hoard, warlord,
whipcord
   aboveboard, bungee cord,
centerboard, checkerboard, clavichord,
disaccord, fiberboard, fingerboard,
harpsichord, mortarbord,
motherboard, overboard, overlord,
paddleboard, paperboard, pinafored,
plasterboard, pompadoured,
shuffleboard, smorgasbord,
storyboard, teeterboard, tetrachord,
untoward, weatherboard
   misericord, particleboard
   —also -ed forms of verbs listed at
or[1]

oarder \ȯrd-ər\ see order

oarding \ȯrd-iŋ\ see ording[1]

oared \ȯrd\ see oard

oarer \ȯr-ər\ see orer

oaring \ȯr-iŋ\ see oring

oarious \ȯr-ē-əs\ see orious

oarish \ȯr-ish\ see orish[1]

oarse \ȯrs\ see orse[1]

oarsen \ȯrs-ᵊn\ coarsen, hoarsen,
whoreson

oarsman \ȯrz-mən\ oarsman
outdoorsman

oart \ȯrt\ see ort[1]

oary \ȯr-ē\ see ory

oast \ōst\ see ost[2]

oastal \ōs-tᵊl\ see ostal[1]

oaster \ō-stər\ coaster, poster,
roaster, throwster, toaster
   billposter, four-poster
   roller-coaster, roller coaster

oasty \ō-stē\ see osty

oat \ōt\ bloat, boat, coat, cote, dote,
float, gloat, goat, groat, haute, moat,
mote, note, oat, quote, rote, shoat,
smote, stoat, throat, tote, vote, wrote
   afloat, airboat, bareboat, bluecoat,
bumboat, capote, catboat, compote,
connote, coyote, cutthroat, demote,
denote, devote, dovecote, eighth note,
emote, endnote, fireboat, fistnote,
flatboat, footnote, greatcoat, gunboat,
half note, headnote, Hohhot,
houseboat, housecoat, iceboat,
keelboat, keynote, lifeboat, longboat,
one-note, pigboat, promote, Q-boat,
raincoat, Rajkot, redcoat, remote,
rewrote, rowboat, sailboat, scapegoat,
sheepcote, showboat, speedboat,
steamboat, stoneboat, Sukkot,
Sukkoth, surfboat, tailcoat, topcoat,
towboat, tugboat, turncoat, U-boat,
unquote, wainscot, whaleboat,
whitethroat, whole note, woodnote,
workboat
   anecdote, antidote, asymptote,
creosote, entrecote, ferryboat,
Huhehot, motorboat, overcoat,
paddleboat, papillote, petticoat,
powerboat, quarter note, redingote,
riverboat, rubythroat, Shabuoth,

Sialkot, sugarcoat, symbiote, table
d'hôte, sixteenth note, undercoat,
yellowthroat
thirty-second note

oate \ō-ət\ see oet[1]

oated \ōt-əd\ coated, noted, throated
devoted, tailcoated
petticoated
—also -ed *forms of verbs listed at*
oat

oaten \ōt-ᵊn\ see oton

oater \ōt-ər\ bloater, boater, coater,
doter, floater, gloater, motor, noter,
oater, rotor, scoter, toter, voter
houseboater, iceboater, keynoter,
promoter, pulmotor, sailboater, tilt-
rotor, trimotor
locomotor, motorboater

oath \ōth\ see owth

oathe \ō<u>th</u>\ see othe

oathing \ō-<u>thi</u>ŋ\ see othing

oating \ōt-iŋ\ boating, coating,
floating
free-floating, sailboating,
scapegoating, speedboating,
wainscoting
motorboating, undercoating
—also -ing *forms of verbs listed at*
oat

oatswain \ōs-ᵊn\ see osin

oaty \ōt-ē\ see ote[1]

oax \ōks\ coax, hoax
—also -s, -'s, *and* -s' *forms of nouns,*
and -s *forms of verbs, listed at* oke

ob[1] \äb\ Ab, blob, bob, Bob, cob,
daub, fob, glob, gob, hob, job, knob,
lob, mob, nob, Ob, rob, slob, snob,
sob, squab, stob, swab, throb, yob
bedaub, corncob, demob, doorknob,
heartthrob, hobnob, kabob, macabre,
memsahib, nabob, nawab, Punjab,
skibob
shish kebab
thingamabob

ob[2] \ōb\ see obe[1]

oba \ō-bə\ arroba, jojoba
algaroba, Manitoba

obably \äb-lē\ see obbly

obal \ō-bəl\ see oble

obally \ō-bə-lē\ globally
primum mobile

obar \ō-bər\ see ober

obber \äb-ər\ bobber, caber,
clobber, cobber, jobber, robber,
slobber, swabber, throbber
hobnobber, Micawber, Skibobber,
stockjobber

obbery \äb-rē\ bobbery, jobbery,
robbery, slobbery, snobbery
corroboree

obbes \äbz\ Hobbes
—also -s, -'s, *and* -s' *forms of nouns,*
and -s *forms of verbs, listed at* ob[1]

obbet \äb-ət\ gobbet, probit

obbie \äb-ē\ see obby

obbin \äb-ən\ see obin

obbish \äb-ish\ slobbish, snobbish

obble \äb-əl\ see abble[1]

obbler \äb-lər\ cobbler, gobbler,
hobbler, nobbler, squabbler, wobbler

obbly \äb-lē\ knobbly, probably,
wobbly, Wobbly

obby \äb-ē\ Bobbie, bobby, Bobby,
cobby, dobby, globby, hobby, knobby,
lobby, nobby, snobby, swabbie
Mesabi, Punjabi, Wahhabi
Abu Dhabi, Hammurabi

obe[1] \ōb\ daube, globe, Job, lobe,
probe, robe, strobe
bathrobe, conglobe, disrobe, earlobe,
enrobe, microbe, wardrobe
Anglophobe, claustrophobe,
Francophobe, homophobe,
negrophobe, xenophobe
ailurophobe, computerphobe

obe² \ō-bē\ see oby

obeah \ō-bē-ə\ see obia

obee \ō-bē\ see oby

obelus \äb-ə-ləs\ see abilis

ober \ō-bər\ lobar, sober
October

obi \ō-bē\ see oby

obia \ō-bē-ə\ cobia, obeah, phobia
acrophobia, algophobia,
Anglophobia, claustrophobia,
homophobia, hydrophobia,
negrophobia, photophobia,
technophobia, xenophobia
agoraphobia
triskaidekaphobia

obic \ō-bik\ phobic
aerobic
anaerobic, claustrophobic,
homophobic, hydrophobic,
photophobic, xenophobic

obile¹ \ō-bə-lē\ see obally

obile² \ō-bəl\ see oble

obin \äb-ən\ bobbin, dobbin,
graben, robin, Robin, Robyn
round-robin

obit¹ \ō-bət\ obit, Tobit
post-obit

obit² \äb-ət\ see obbet

oble \ō-bəl\ coble, global, mobile,
noble
airmobile, ennoble, Grenoble,
ignoble, immobile
San Cristóbal

obo \ō-bō\ gobo, hobo, kobo, lobo,
oboe
adobo

oboe \ō-bō\ see obo

obol \äb-əl\ see abble¹

oboree \äb-ə-rē\ see obbery

obot \ō-bət\ see obit¹

obra \ō-brə\ cobra, dobra

obster \äb-stər\ lobster, mobster

obular \äb-yə-lər\ globular, lobular

obule \äb-yül\ globule, lobule

oby \ō-bē\ Gobi, goby, Kobe, obi,
Obie, toby, Toby
adobe, Nairobi
Okeechobee

obyn \äb-ən\ see obin

oc¹ \ōk\ see oke

oc² \äk\ see ock¹

oc³ \ȯk\ see alk

oca \ō-kə\ coca, mocha, oca
Asoka
carioca, Fukuoka, mandioca,
Shizuoka, tapioca

ocable \ō-kə-bəl\ smokable,
vocable
evocable

ocage \äk-ij\ see ockage

ocal \ō-kəl\ focal, local, socle,
vocal, yokel
bifocal, subvocal, trifocal, unvocal

ocally \ō-kə-lē\ locally, vocally

ocative \äk-ət-iv\ locative, vocative
evocative, provocative

occa \äk-ə\ see aka¹

occer \äk-ər\ see ocker

occie \äch-ē\ see otchy

occhi \ȯ-kē\ see alkie

occo \äk-ō\ socko, taco
cheechako, guanaco, morocco,
Morocco, scirocco, sirocco

occule \äk-yül\ floccule, locule

occulent \äk-yə-lənt\ flocculent
inoculant

occulus \äk-yə-ləs\ flocculus,
loculus, oculus

oce \ō-chē\ see oche[1]

ocean \ō-shən\ see otion

ocent \ōs-ᵊnt\ docent, nocent

ocess \äs-əs\ Knossos, process
colossus, proboscis

och[1] \äk\ see ock[1]

och[2] \ȯsh\ see ash[2]

och[3] \ȯk\ see alk

ocha \ō-kə\ see oca

ochal \äk-əl\ see ockle

ochan \ä-kən\ see achen

oche[1] \ō-chē\ Kochi, Sochi
penoche, veloce
mezza voce, sotto voce

oche[2] \ōsh\ cloche, gauche, skosh
brioche, caroche, guilloche

oche[3] \ō-kē\ see oky

oche[4] \ōch\ see oach

oche[5] \ȯsh\ see ash[2]

ochee \ō-kē\ see oky

ocher \ō-kər\ see oker

ochi \ō-chē\ see oche[1]

ochle \ək-əl\ see uckle

ochs \äks\ see ox

ochum \ō-kəm\ see okum

ocia \ō-shə\ see otia[1]

ociable \ō-shə-bəl\ sociable
associable, dissociable, insociable,
negotiable, unsociable
indissociable, renegotiable

ocial \ō-shəl\ social
asocial, dissocial, precocial, unsocial
antisocial

ocile \äs-əl\ see ossal

ocious \ō-shəs\ atrocious, ferocious,
precocious
Theodosius

ock[1] \äk\ Bach, bloc, block, bock,
brock, chock, clock, cock, croc, crock,
doc, dock, floc, flock, frock, hock,
Jacque, Jacques, jock, knock, lakh,
loch, lock, Locke, lough, Mach, moc,
mock, nock, pock, roc, rock, schlock,
shock, smock, sock, stock, wok, yak,
yock
acock, ad hoc, amok, Arak,
backblock, Balzac, bangkok,
Bangkok, baroque, Bartok, bawcock,
bedrock, bemock, bibcock, bitstock,
blackcock, blesbok, bloodstock, bois
d'arc, Brecknock, breechblock,
burdock, buttstock, caprock, coldcock,
Comstock, deadlock, debacle, defrock,
dry dock, duroc, Dvořák, earlock, en
bloc, epoch, fatstock, feedstock,
fetlock, firelock, flintlock, forelock,
foreshock, gamecock, gemsbok,
gridlock, gunlock, Hancock, havelock,
haycock, headlock, headstock,
hemlock, Hickock, Iraq, jazz-rock,
Kanak, Kazak, Kazakh, kapok,
kneesock, livestock, lovelock,
matchlock, Mohock, Nisroch, nostoc,
o'clock, oarlock, padlock, peacock,
penstock, petcock, pibroch, picklock,
pinchcock, post doc, post hoc, rhebok,
rimrock, roadblock, rootstock,
Rorschach, Rostock, rowlock,
shamrock, Sheetrock, sherlock,
shylock, Sirach, slick rock, Slovak,
springbok, steenbok, stopcock, Tarlak,
tarok, ticktock, traprock, van Gogh,
warlock, wedlock, woodcock,
wristlock, zwieback
aftershock, alpenstock, Anahuac,
antiknock, antilock, Antioch, Arawak,
Ayers Rock, billycock, chockablock,
hammerlock, hollyhock, interlock,
John Hancock, lady's-smock,
Languedoc, laughingstock, Little
Rock, manioc, mantlerock,
monadnock, Offenbach, Otomac,
poppycock, Ragnarok, Sarawak,
shuttlecock, spatterdock, turkey-cock,
weathercock
Czechoslovak, Bialystok,
electroshock, Inupiaq, Pontianak,
Vladivostok

ock² \ȯk\ see alk

ockage \äk-ij\ blockage, brockage, dockage, lockage, socage

ocke \äk\ see ock¹

ocked \äkt\ blocked, crocked
concoct, decoct, entr'acte, half-cocked, landlocked
entoproct
—*also* -ed *forms of verbs listed at* ock¹

ocker \äk-ər\ blocker, clocker, cocker, docker, hocker, knocker, locker, makar, mocker, rocker, shocker, soccer, stocker
footlocker
appleknocker, beta-blocker, knickerbocker

ockery \äk-rē\ crockery, mockery, rockery

ocket \äk-ət\ brocket, crocket, Crockett, docket, locket, pocket, rocket, socket, sprocket
pickpocket, skyrocket
out-of-pocket, retro-rocket

ockett \äk-ət\ see ocket

ockey \äk-ē\ see ocky

ockian \äk-ē-ən\ Comstockian, Slovakian
Czechoslovakian

ockiness \äk-ē-nəs\ cockiness, rockiness, stockiness

ocking \äk-iŋ\ flocking, shocking, smocking, stocking
bluestocking, silk-stocking
—*also* -ing *forms of verbs listed at* ock¹

ockish \äk-ish\ blockish, stockish

ockle \äk-əl\ coccal, cockle, socle
debacle, epochal

ockney \äk-nē\ cockney, Procne

ocko \äk-ō\ see occo

ocks \äks\ see ox

ocky \äk-ē\ blocky, cocky, hockey, jockey, pocky, rocky, Rocky, sake, schlocky, stocky, Yaqui
Abnaki, Iraqi, Ontake, peacocky, rumaki
jabberwocky, Kawasaki, Miyazaki, Nagasaki, Okazaki, sukiyaki, teriyaki
Amagasaki, enokidake

ocle \ō-kəl\ see ocal

ocne \äk-nē\ see ockney

oco \ō-kō\ coco, cocoa, loco, poco
Bioko, iroko, rococo
crème de cacao, Locofoco, Orinoco
poco a poco

ocoa \ō-kō\ see oco

ocracy \äk-rə-sē\ autocracy, bureaucracy, democracy, hypocrisy, mobocracy, plutocracy, slavocracy, technocracy, theocracy
aristocracy, gerontocracy, gynecocracy, meritocracy, thalassocracy

ocre \ō-kər\ see oker

ocrisy \äk-rə-sē\ see ocracy

ocsin \äk-sən\ see oxin

oct \äkt\ see ocked

oction \äk-shən\ concoction, decoction

octor \äk-tər\ doctor, proctor
concocter

oculant \äk-yə-lənt\ see occulent

ocular \äk-yə-lər\ jocular, locular, ocular
binocular, monocular
intraocular

ocule \äk-yül\ see occule

oculus \äk-yə-ləs\ see occulus

ocum \ō-kəm\ see okum

ocus \ō-kəs\ crocus, focus, hocus, locus

prefocus, refocus, soft-focus
hocus-pocus

ocused \ō-kəst\ see ocust

ocust \ō-kəst\ locust
unfocused

ocutor \äk-yət-ər\ prolocutor
interlocutor

od[1] \äd\ bod, clod, cod, fade, Fahd,
gaud, god, hod, mod, nod, od, odd,
plod, pod, prod, quad, quod, rod,
scrod, shod, sod, squad, tod, trod, wad
Akkad, Arad, aubade, ballade,
Belgrade, bipod, Cape Cod, couvade,
croustade, dry-shod, ephod, facade,
fantod, glissade, hot-rod, jihad,
lingcod, Nimrod, oeillade, pomade,
peasecod, ramrod, Riyadh, roughshod,
roulade, saccade, scalade, seedpod,
slipshod, synod, tie-rod, tightwad,
tomcod, torsade, tripod
  accolade, amphipod, arthropod,
Ashkhabad, Bacolod, Beograde,
bigarade, carbonnade, chiffonade,
defilade, demigod, enfilade, esculade,
esplanade, fusillade, gallopade,
gastropod, goldenrod, hexapod,
lycopod, monkeypod, Novgorod, Novi
Sad, octopod, promenade, pseudopod
  Ahmadabad, Allahabad, cephalopod,
dégringolade, Faisalabad, fanfaronade,
Islamabad, ornithopod, prosauropod,
rodomontade, Scheherazade,
Upanishad
  Nizhni Novgorod

od[2] \ō\ see ow[1]

od[3] \ōd\ see ode

od[4] \u̇d\ see ood[1]

od[5] \ȯd\ see aud[1]

o'd \üd\ see ude

oda \ōd-ə\ coda, Rhoda, soda
Baroda, pagoda, sal soda

odal \ōd-ᵊl\ Godel, modal, nodal,
yodel
cathodal
intermodal

odden \äd-ᵊn\ sodden, trodden
downtrodden, Ibadan

odder \äd-ər\ dodder, fodder,
khaddar, modder, nodder, odder,
plodder, prodder, solder, wadder
glissader, hot-rodder
promenader
  —also -er forms of adjectives listed
at od[1]

oddery \äd-rē\ see awdry

oddess \äd-əs\ bodice, goddess
demigoddess

oddish \äd-ish\ cloddish, kaddish

oddle \äd-ᵊl\ coddle, model, noddle,
swaddle, toddle, twaddle, waddle
remodel
mollycoddle

oddler \äd-lər\ coddler, modeler,
toddler, twaddler, waddler
mollycoddler

oddly \äd-lē\ see odly

oddy \äd-ē\ see ody[1]

ode \ōd\ bode, bowed, code, goad,
load, lode, mode, node, ode, road,
rode, Spode, strode, toad, toed, woad,
wood
  abode, bestrode, boatload, busload,
byroad, carload, cartload, caseload,
commode, corrode, crossroad, decode,
displode, embowed, encode, epode,
erode, explode, forebode, freeload,
geode, highroad, implode, inroad, no-
load, off-load, outmode, payload,
planeload, postcode, railroad,
rhapsode, sarod, shipload, square-
toed, threnode, trainload, truckload,
two-toed, unload, upload
  à la mode, antipode, Comstock
Lode, discommode, eigenmode,
electrode, episode, impastoed,
incommode, Kozhikode,
Nesselrode, overrode, palinode,
pigeon-toed
  —also -ed forms of verbs listed at
ow[1]

odeine \ōd-ē-ən\ see odian

odel \ōd-ᵊl\ see odal

odeler \äd-lər\ see oddler

oden \ōd-ᵊn\ loden, Odin, Woden

odeon \ōd-ē-ən\ see odian

oder \ōd-ər\ coder, loader, Oder, odor
breechloader, decoder, freeloader, malodor, railroader, unloader
middle-of-the-roader

oderate \äd-rət\ moderate, quadrate
immoderate

odes \ōdz\ Rhodes
—also -s, -'s, and -s' forms of nouns, and -s forms of verbs, listed at ode

odest \äd-əst\ Mahdist, modest
haggadist, immodest
—also -est forms of adjectives listed at od[1]

odesy \äd-ə-sē\ odyssey
geodesy, theodicy

odeum \ōd-ē-əm\ see odium

odge \äj\ see age[1]

odger \äj-ər\ codger, dodger, lodger, roger, Roger
Jolly Roger

odgy \äj-ē\ dodgy, podgy, stodgy
mystagogy, pedagogy

odian \ōd-ē-ən\ Cambodian, custodian, melodeon
nickelodeon

odic \äd-ik\ zaddik
cathodic, ergodic, melodic, methodic, monodic, prosodic, rhapsodic, spasmodic, synodic, threnodic
episodic, periodic
antispasmodic, aperiodic, upanishadic
quasiperiodic

odical \äd-i-kəl\ methodical, monodical, prosodical, synodical
episodical, immethodical, periodical

odice \äd-əs\ see oddess

odicy \äd-ə-sē\ see odesy

odie \ō-dē\ see ody[2]

odin \ōd-ᵊn\ see oden

odious \ōd-ē-əs\ odious
commodious, melodious, Methodius
incommodious

odity \äd-ət-ē\ oddity
commodity
incommodity

odium \ōd-ē-əm\ odeum, odium, podium, rhodium, sodium

odius \ō-dē-əs\ see odious

odless \äd-ləs\ godless, rodless

odling \äd-liŋ\ codling, godling
—also -ing forms of verbs listed at oddle

odly \äd-lē\ godly, oddly
ungodly

odo \ōd-ō\ dodo
Komodo
Quasimodo

odom \äd-əm\ shahdom, Sodom

odor \ōd-ər\ see oder

odsk \ätsk\ see atsk

odular \äj-ə-lər\ modular, nodular

odule \äj-ül\ module, nodule

ody[1] \äd-ē\ body, cloddy, gaudy, Mahdi, noddy, sadhe, shoddy, toddy, waddy, wadi
anybody, blackbody, dogsbody, embody, homebody, nobody, somebody, wide-body
antibody, busybody, disembody, everybody, Irrawaddy, underbody

ody² \ōd-ē\ Cody, Jodie, Jody, roadie, toady
  polypody

odyssey \äd-ə-sē\ see odesy

odz \üj\ see uge¹

oe¹ \ō\ see ow¹

oe² \ō-ē\ see owy

oe³ \ē\ see ee¹

oea¹ \ói-ə\ see oia

oea² \ē-ə\ see ia¹

oeba \ē-bə\ see eba

oebe \ē-bē\ see ebe¹

oebel \ā-bəl\ see able

oebus \ē-bəs\ see ebus

oed \ōd\ see ode

oehn \ən\ see un

oeia \ē-ə\ see ia¹

oeic \ē-ik\ see eic

oek \ùk\ see ook¹

oel \ō-əl\ Joel, Lowell, Noel
  bestowal
  Baden-Powell, protozoal

oeless¹ \ō-ləs\ see olus

oeless² \ü-ləs\ see ewless

oem¹ \ō-əm\ poem, proem
  jeroboam

oem² \ōm\ see ome¹

oeman \ō-mən\ see oman

oena \ē-nə\ see ina²

oentgen¹ \en-chən\ see ension

oentgen² \ən-chən\ see uncheon

oepha \ē-fə\ see epha

oer¹ \ór\ see or¹

oer² \ü-ər\ see ewer¹

oer³ \ùr\ see ure¹

oer⁴ \ō-ər\ blower, knower, lower, mower, sewer, shower, sower
  beachgoer, churchgoer, flamethrower, filmgoer, foregoer, forgoer, mindblower, snowblower, snowthrower, winegrower
  concertgoer, moviegoer, whistleblower,
  cinemagoer, operagoer, theatergoer

o'er \ór\ see or¹

oes¹ \əz\ see euse¹

oes² \ōz\ see ose²

oes³ \üz\ see use²

oesia \ē-shə\ see esia¹

oesn't \əz-³nt\ see asn't

oest \ü-əst\ see ooist

oesus \ē-səs\ see esis

oet \ō-ət\ poet
  inchoate, introit

oetess \ō-ət-əs\ coitus, poetess

oeuf \əf\ see uff

oeur \ər\ see eur¹

oeuvre \ərv\ see erve

oey \ō-ē\ see owy

of¹ \äv\ see olve²

of² \əv\ see ove¹

of³ \óf\ see off²

ofar \ō-fər\ see ofer

ofer \ō-fər\ chauffeur, gofer, gopher, loafer, Ophir, shofar

off¹ \äf\ boff, coif, doff, goif, kaph, prof, quaff, scoff, shroff, taw, toff
  carafe, cook-off, pilaf, Wroclaw
  Romanov

off² \ȯf\ cough, doff, off, scoff, taw, trough
  Azov, beg off, blast-off, brush-off, cast-off, castoff, checkoff, Chekhov, cook-off, cutoff, die-off, drop-off, face-off, falloff, far-off, goof-off, hands-off, jump-off, Khartov, kickoff, Kirov, knockoff, Khrushchev, layoff, leadoff, lift-off, Lvov, one-off, Pavlov, payoff, pick-off, pickoff, play-off, rake-off, rip-off, roll-off, Rostov, runoff, sawed-off, sell-off, send-off, setoff, show-off, shutoff, spin-off, standoff, takeoff, Tambov, tap-off, tip-off, trade-off, turnoff, well-off, Wolof, write-off
  better-off, cooling-off, damping-off, Gorbachev, Molotov, Nabokov, philosophe, Pribilof
  beef Stroganoff, Rachmaninoff
  Rimsky-Korsakov

offal¹ \äf-əl\ see afel

offal² \ȯ-fəl\ see awful

offaly \ȯf-ə-lē\ see awfully

offee \ȯ-fē\ coffee, toffee

offer¹ \äf-ər\ coffer, gauffer, goffer, offer, proffer, quaffer, scoffer, troffer
  reoffer

offer² \ȯf-ər\ goffer, offer, troffer
  reoffer

offin \ȯ-fən\ coffin, dauphin, soften
  uncoffin

offit \äf-ət\ see ofit

offle \ȯ-fəl\ see awful

ofit \äf-ət\ profit, prophet, soffit
  nonprofit
  not-for-profit

ofle \ü-fəl\ see ueful

oft¹ \ȯft\ croft, loft, oft, soft, toft
  aloft, hayloft
  undercroft
  —also -ed *forms of verbs listed at* off²

oft² \äft\ see aft¹

often \ȯ-fən\ see offin

ofty \ȯf-tē\ lofty, softy
  toplofty

og¹ \äg\ bog, clog, cog, flog, fog, frog, grog, hog, jog, log, nog, Prague, prog, quag, shog, slog, smog, tog
  agog, backlog, bullfrog, defog, eclogue, eggnog, footslog, groundhog, gulag, photog, prologue, putlog, quahog, Rolvaag, sandhog, stalag, warthog
  analog, analogue, antilog, apalogue, catalog, decalogue, demagogue, dialogue, golliwog, monologue, mummichog, mystagogue, nouvelle vague, pedagogue, pollywog, semilog, sinologue, synagogue, Taganrog, theologue, waterlog

og² \ȯg\ bog, clog, dog, fog, frog, hog, jog, log, smog
  backlog, bandog, befog, bird-dog, bulldog, bullfrog, coydog, defog, eclogue, firedog, groundhog, hangdog, hedgehog, hotdog, lapdog, leapfrog, prologue, quahog, sandhog, seadog, sheepdog, warthog, watchdog
  analog, analogue, apologue, catalog, decalogue, dialogue, dog-eat-dog, duologue, epilogue, homologue, monologue, mummichog, overdog, pettifog, pollywog, sinologue, Tagalog, theologue, travelogue, underdog, waterlog, yellow-dog ideologue

og³ \ōg\ see ogue¹

oga \ō-gə\ toga, yoga
  Conestoga

ogamous \äg-ə-məs\ endogamous, exogamous, monogamous
  heterogamous

ogamy \äg-ə-mē\ endogamy, exogamy, homogamy, misogamy, monogamy

ogan \ō-gən\ brogan, shogun, slogan
Mount Logan

ogany \äg-ə-nē\ see ogony

ogative \äg-ət-iv\ derogative, prerogative
interrogative

oge¹ \ōj\ doge
gamboge
horologe

oge² \ōzh\ loge
Limoges

oge³ \ō-jē\ see oji

oge⁴ \üzh\ see uge²

ogel \ō-gəl\ see ogle¹

ogenous \äj-ə-nəs\ androgynous, erogenous, homogenous, monogynous
heterogenous

ogeny \äj-ə-nē\ progeny
androgeny, autogeny, homogeny, misogyny, monogyny, ontogeny, phylogeny
heterogeny

oger¹ \äj-ər\ see odger

oger² \ȯg-ər\ see ogger²

oges \ōzh\ see oge²

ogey¹ \ō-gē\ see ogie

ogey² \ȯg-ē\ see oogie

oggan \äg-ən\ see oggin

oggar \äg-ər\ see ogger¹

ogger¹ \äg-ər\ agar, clogger, flogger, Hoggar, jogger, laager, lager, logger, slogger
Ahaggar, defogger, footslogger
agar-agar, cataloger, pettifogger

ogger² \ȯg-ər\ auger, augur, clogger, jogger, logger, maugre, sauger
dcfogger, hotdogger
cataloger, pettifogger

oggery¹ \äg-rē\ toggery
demagoguery

oggery² \ȯg-ə-rē\ augury, doggery

oggin \äg-ən\ noggin
toboggan
Copenhagen

oggle \äg-əl\ boggle, goggle, joggle, ogle, toggle
boondoggle, hornswoggle
synagogal

oggy¹ \äg-ē\ boggy, foggy, groggy, moggy, quaggy, smoggy, soggy, yagi
demagogy

oggy² \ȯg-ē\ foggy, soggy

ogh¹ \ōg\ see ogue¹

ogh² \ōk\ see oke

ogh³ \äk\ see ock¹

ogh⁴ \ō\ see ow

ogi \ō-gē\ see ogie

ogian \ō-jən\ see ojan

ogic \äj-ik\ logic
choplogic, illogic
anagogic, analogic, biologic, chronologic, cryptologic, cytologic, demagogic, dendrologic, dialogic, ecologic, ethnologic, geologic, histologic, horologic, hydrologic, mythologic, neurologic, nosologic, oncologic, pathologic, pedagogic, pedologic, petrologic, phonologic, proctologic, psychologic, serologic, technologic, theologic, virologic, zoologic
dermatologic, etiologic, gerontologic, gynecologic, hagiologic, hematologic, ideologic, immunologic, ophthalmologic, ornithologic, pharmacologic, physiologic, roentgenologic, sociologic, teleologic, teratologic, toxicologic, volcanologic
bacteriologic, endocrinologic, meteorologic, paleontologic,

parasitologic, sedimentologic,
symptomatologic
epidemiologic

ogical \äj-i-kəl\ logical
alogical, illogical
anagogical, analogical, biological,
Christological, chronological,
cosmological, cryptological,
cytological, dendrological, ecological,
enological, ethnological, ethological,
extralogical, gemological, geological,
graphological, histological,
horological, hydrological,
limnological, morphological,
mycological, mythological,
necrological, neurological,
nomological, oncological,
pathological, pedagogical,
pedological, penological, petrological,
philological, phonological,
phrenological, phycological,
proctological, psephological,
psychological, scatological,
seismological, serological, sinological,
tautological, technological,
theological, topological, typological,
ufological, virological, zoological
abiological, anthropological,
archaeological, cardiological,
climatological, criminological,
demonological, dermatological,
embryological, entomological,
eschatological, etiological,
etymological, futurological,
genealogical, gerontological,
gynecological, hagiological,
hematological, herpetological,
ichthyological, iconological,
ideological, immunological,
Mariological, methodological,
mineralogical, musicological,
numerological, ophthalmological,
ornithological, pharmacological,
phraseological, physiological,
primatological, roentgenological,
selenological, semiological,
sociological, teleological,
teratological, terminological,
thanatological, toxicological,
volcanological

bacteriological, characterological,
dialectological, ecclesiological,
endocrinological, epistemological,
geomorphological, meteorological,
paleontological, parasitological,
phenomenological, sedimentological,
symptomatological
epidemiological, gastroenterological

ogie \ō-gē\ bogey, bogie, dogie,
fogy, hoagie, logy, pogy, stogie, vogie,
yogi
pirogi

ogle¹ \ō-gəl\ Gogel, ogle

ogle² \äg-əl\ see **oggle**

oglio \ōl-yō\ see **ollo¹**

ogna¹ \ō-nə\ see **ona**

ogna² \ō-nē\ see **ony¹**

ogna³ \ōn-yə\ see **onia²**

ogne \ōn\ see **one¹**

ogned \ōnd\ see **oned¹**

ogo \ō-gō\ go-go, logo, Logo, Togo
a-go-go

ogony \äg-ə-nē\ cosmogony,
mahogany, theogony

ographer \äg-rə-fər\ biographer,
cartographer, chorographer,
cryptographer, demographer,
discographer, ethnographer,
geographer, lithographer,
mythographer, phonographer,
photographer, pornographer,
stenographer, typographer
bibliographer, choreographer,
chromatographer, hagiographer,
heliographer, iconographer,
lexicographer, oceanographer,
paleographer
autobiographer, biogeographer,
cinematographer, historiographer

ography \äg-rə-fē\ aerography,
autography, biography, cacography,
cartography, chorography,
chronography, cosmography,

cryptography, demography,
discography, ethnography,
filmography, geography, holography,
hydrography, hypsography,
lithography, lymphography,
mammography, mythography,
nomography, orthography,
phonography, photography,
pictography, planography,
pornography, reprography,
sonography, stenography,
thermography, tomography,
topography, typography, venography,
xerography, xylography
  angiography, aortography,
bibliography, cardiography,
choreography, chromatography,
crystallography, hagiography,
heliography, iconography,
lexicography, metallography,
oceanography, paleography,
physiography, radiography,
roentgenography, videography
  arteriography, autobiography,
cinematography, encephalography,
historiography, psychobiography
  electroencephalography

ogress \ō-grəs\ ogress, progress

ogrom \äg-rəm\ grogram, pogrom

ogue[1] \ōg\ brogue, drogue, rogue,
togue, vogue, yogh, collogue,
crannog, pirogue, prorogue
  disembogue

ogue[2] \äg\ see og[1]

ogue[3] \og\ see og[2]

oguery \äg-rē\ see oggery[1]

oguish \ō-gish\ roguish, voguish

ogun \ō-gən\ see ogan

ogynous \äj-ə-nəs\ see ogenous

ogyny \äj-ə-nē\ see ogeny

oh \ō\ see ow[1]

oha \ō-ə\ see oa[1]

ohl \ōl\ see ole[1]

ohm \ōm\ see ome[1]

ohn \än\ see on[1]

ohns \änz\ see onze

ohn's \onz\ see onze

ohnson \än-sən\ Johnson, Jonson
Wisconsin

ohr \or\ see or[1]

oi[1] \ä\ see a[1]

oi[2] \oi\ see oy

oia \oi-ə\ cholla, Goya, Hoya, olla,
toea
  Nagoya, sequoia, Sequoya
  atemoya, cherimoya, paranoia

oian \oi-ən\ see oyen

oic \ō-ik\ stoic
  azoic, bistroic, echoic, heroic
  anechoic, Cenozoic, Mesozoic,
mock-heroic, vetinoic
  antiheroic, Paleozoic

oice \ois\ choice, Joyce, Royce,
voice
  devoice, Du Bois, invoice, pro-
choice, rejoice, unvoice
  sailor's-choice

oiced \oist\ see oist

oicer \oi-sər\ choicer, voicer
  pro-choicer, rejoicer

oid[1] \oid\ Boyd, Floyd, Freud, void
  android, avoid, chancroid, colloid,
conoid, cuboid, cycloid, deltoid,
dendroid, devoid, discoid, factoid,
fungoid, globoid, hydroid, hypnoid,
keloid, mucoid, Negroid, ovoid,
percoid, prismoid, pygmoid, rhizoid,
rhomboid, schizoid, scombroid,
sigmoid, spheroid, steroid, styloid,
tabloid, thalloid, thyroid, toroid,
toxoid, trochoid, typhoid, Veddoid,
viroid
  adenoid, alkaloid, amoeboid,
aneroid, anthropoid, arachnoid,
asteroid, Australoid, carcinoid,

Caucasoid, celluloid, crystalloid, ellipsoid, embryoid, eunuchoid, helicoid, hemorrhoid, hominoid, humanoid, hysteroid, metalloid, Mongoloid, myeloid, nautiloid, nucleoid, obovoid, opioid, osteoid, overjoyed, paranoid, planetoid, Polaroid, retinoid, rheumatoid, solenoid, Stalinoid, trapezoid, unalloyed, unemployed
 cannabinoid, carotenoid, eicosanoid, meteoroid, philanthropoid, tuberculoid, underemployed
 Neanderthaloid
 —also -ed forms of verbs listed at oy

oid² \ä\ see a¹

oidal \òid-ᵊl\ chancroidal, choroidal, colloidal, conchoidal, cuboidal, cycloidal, discoidal, spheroidal, toroidal
 adenoidal, asteroidal, ellipsoidal, emulsoidal, hemorrhoidal, metalloidal, planetoidal, saccharoidal, trapezoidal
 paraboloidal

oider \òid-ər\ broider, voider
 avoider, embroider
 reembroider

oie \ä\ see a¹

oif \äf\ see off¹

oign \òin\ see oin¹

oil \òil\ boil, Boyle, broil, coil, Doyle, foil, hoyle, moil, loyal, noil, oil, roil, royal, Royal, soil, spoil, toil, voile
 aboil, airfoil, assoil, charbroil, cinquefoil, despoil, disloyal, embroil, entoil, garboil, gargoyle, gumboil, hard-boil, Isle Royal, langue d'oïl, milfoil, non-oil, parboil, recoil, rhyme royal, subsoil, surroyal, tinfoil, topsoil, trefoil, turmoil
 counterfoil, hydrofoil, quatrefoil, pennyroyal, supercoil

oilage \òi-lij\ soilage, spoilage

oile¹ \äl\ see al¹

oile² \òil\ see oil

oiled \òild\ foiled, oiled
 hard-boiled, soft-boiled, uncoiled, well-oiled
 —also -ed forms of verbs listed at oil

oiler \òi-lər\ boiler, broiler, moiler, oiler, spoiler, toiler
 charbroiler, despoiler, Free-Soiler, potboiler, subsoiler

oiling \òi-liŋ\ boiling, moiling
 —also -ing forms of verbs listed at oil

oilless \òil-ləs\ soilless
 recoilless

oilsman \òilz-mən\ foilsman, spoilsman

oilus \òi-ləs\ see oyless

oily \òi-lē\ doily, oily, roily

oin¹ \òin\ coin, foin, groin, groyne, join, loin, quoin
 adjoin, Burgoyne, conjoin, Des Moines, disjoin, eloign, enjoin, essoin, purloin, recoin, rejoin, sainfoin, sirloin, subjoin
 tenderloin
 Assiniboin

oin² \aⁿ\ see in⁴

oine \än\ see on¹

oined \òind\ conjoined, uncoined
 —also -ed forms of verbs listed at oin¹

oiner \òi-nər\ coiner, joiner

oines \òin\ see oin¹

oing¹ \ō-iŋ\ bowing, going, knowing, rowing, sewing, showing
 churchgoing, deep-going, foregoing, free-flowing, glassblowing, ingrowing, mind-blowing, ongoing, outgoing, seagoing, waygoing
 concertgoing, easygoing, moviegoing, oceangoing, operagoing, theatergoing, thoroughgoing, whistle-blowing

to-ing and fro-ing
—*also* -ing *forms of verbs listed at*
ow[1]

oing[2] \ü-iŋ\ bluing, doing, Ewing
misdoing, undoing, wrongdoing
evildoing
—*also* -ing *forms of verbs listed at*
ew[1]

oing[3] \ō-ən\ see oan[1]

o-ing \ō-iŋ\ see oing[1]

oings \ō-iŋz\ outgoings
—*also* -s, -'s, *and* -s' *forms of nouns,*
and -s *forms of verbs, listed at* oing[1]

oint[1] \óint\ joint, point
adjoint, anoint, appoint, aroint,
ballpoint, bluepoint, checkpoint,
conjoint, disjoint, drypoint, eyepoint,
gunpoint, knifepoint, midpoint,
nonpoint, outpoint, pinpoint,
pourpoint, standpoint, tuck-point,
viewpoint
counterpoint, disappoint,
needlepoint, petit point, silverpoint

oint[2] \ant\ see ant[5]

ointe \ant\ see ant[5]

ointed \óint-əd\ jointed, pointed
lap-jointed, loose-jointed
double-jointed, well-appointed
—*also* -ed *forms of verbs listed at*
oint[1]

ointer \óint-ər\ jointer, pointer
anointer

ointing \óin-tiŋ\ finger-pointing
—*also* -ing *forms of verbs listed at*
oint[1]

ointment \óint-mənt\ ointment
anointment, appointment
disappointment

oir[1] \īr\ see ire[1]

oir[2] \är\ see ar[3]

oir[3] \óir\ see oyer

oir[4] \ór\ see or[1]

oire[1] \är\ see ar[3]

oire[2] \óir\ see oyer

oire[3] \ór\ see or[1]

ois[1] \ä\ see a[1]

ois[2] \ói\ see oy

ois[3] \ō-əs\ Lois, Powys

ois[4] \óis\ see oice

oise[1] \äz\ poise, 'twas, vase, was
Ahwaz, bourgeoise, Lamaze, Shiraz
vichyssoise
Afars and the Issas
—*also* -s, -'s, *and* -s' *forms of nouns,*
and -s *forms of verbs, listed*
at a[1]

oise[2] \óiz\ hoise, noise, Noyes,
poise
turquoise
counterpoise, equipoise
avoirdupois
—*also* -s, -'s, *and* -s' *forms of nouns,*
and -s *forms of verbs, listed at* oy

oise[3] \ói-zē\ see oisy

oison \óiz-ᵊn\ foison, poison
empoison

oist \óist\ foist, hoist, joist, moist,
voiced
unvoiced
semimoist
—*also* -ed *forms of verbs listed at*
oice

oister \ói-stər\ cloister, moister,
oyster, roister

oisterous \ói-strəs\ see oistress

oistral \ói-strəl\ cloistral, coistrel

oistrel \ói-strəl\ see oistral

oistress \ói-strəs\ boisterous,
cloistress, roisterous

oisy \ói-zē\ Boise, noisy
cramoisie

oit 248

oit¹ \ȯit\ doit, droit, quoit
adroit, Detroit, exploit
maladroit, Massasoit

oit² \āt\ see ate¹

oit³ \ō-ət\ see oet¹

oit⁴ \ä\ see a¹

oite \ät\ see ot¹

oiter \ȯit-ər\ goiter, loiter
exploiter
reconnoiter

oitus \ō-ət-əs\ see oetess

oivre \äv\ see olve¹

oix¹ \ä\ see a¹

oix² \ȯi\ see oy

oiz \ȯis\ see oise²

ojan \ō-jən\ Trojan
theologian

oje \ō-jē\ see oji

oji \ō-jē\ Moji, shoji
anagoge, Hachioji

ok¹ \äk\ see ock¹

ok² \ək\ see uck

ok³ \ȯk\ see alk

oka \ō-kə\ see oca

okable \ō-kə-bəl\ see ocable

oke¹ \ōk\ bloke, broke, choke, cloak,
coke, Coke, croak, folk, hoke, joke,
moke, oak, oke, poke, Polk, roque,
smoke, soak, soke, spoke, stoke,
stroke, toke, toque, woke, yogh, yoke,
yolk
ad hoc, awoke, backstroke, baroque,
bespoke, breaststroke, chain-smoke,
convoke, cowpoke, downstroke,
evoke, heatstroke, housebroke, in-
joke, invoke, keystroke, kinfolk,
kinsfolk, menfolk, outspoke, presoak,
provoke, revoke, she-oak, sidestroke,
slowpoke, sunchoke, sunstroke,

townsfolk, uncloak, unyoke, upstroke,
workfolk
artichoke, equivoque, fisherfolk,
gentlefolk, herrenvolk, masterstroke,
okeydoke, Roanoke, thunderstroke,
womenfolk
Mount Revelstoke

oke² \ō-kē\ see oky

oke³ \ō\ see ow¹

oke⁴ \ùk\ see ook¹

oked \ōkt\ stoked, yolked

okee \ō-kē\ see oky

okel \ō-kəl\ see ocal

oken \ō-kən\ broken, oaken, spoken,
token, woken
awoken, bespoken, betoken, fair-
spoken, foretoken, free-spoken,
heartbroken, housebroken, outspoken,
plainspoken, short-spoken, soft-
spoken, unbroken, well-spoken, wind-
broken

oker \ō-kər\ broker, choker, croaker,
joker, ocher, poker, soaker, smoker,
stoker, stroker
chain-smoker, invoker, pawnbroker,
provoker, revoker, stockbroker
mediocre

okey \ō-kē\ see oky

oki \ō-kē\ see oky

oking \ō-kiŋ\ broking, choking
—also -ing forms of verbs listed at
oke¹

oko \ō-kō\ see oco

okum \ō-kəm\ Bochum, hokum,
locum, oakum

oky \ō-kē\ choky, croaky, folkie,
hokey, Loki, pokey, poky, smoky,
troche, trochee, yolky
enoki, Great Smoky
hokeypokey, karaoke
Okefenokee

ol¹ \ōl\ see ole¹

ol² \äl\ see al¹

ol³ \ȯl\ see all

ola \ō-lə\ bola, cola, Kola, Lola, tola, Zola
Angola, boffola, Canola, gondola, granola, mandola, payola, pergola, plugola, scagliola, Victrola, viola, Viola
acerola, ayatollah, braciola, Española, gladiola, Gorgonzola, hemiola, Hispaniola, moviola, Osceola, roseola
Savonarola

olable \ō-lə-bəl\ see ollable

olace \äl-əs\ see olis

olan \ō-lən\ see olon

oland \ō-lənd\ see owland

olander \əl-ən-dər\ colander, Jullundur

olar¹ \ō-lər\ see oller

olar² \äl-ər\ see ollar

olas \ō-ləs\ see olus

olater \äl-ət-ər\ bardolater, idolater bibliolater, Mariolater

olatrous \äl-ə-trəs\ idolatrous bibliolatrous, heliolatrous

olatry \äl-ə-trē\ bardolatry, idolatry, statolatry, zoolatry
bibliolatry, heliolatry, iconolatry, Mariolatry

old¹ \ōld\ bold, bowled, cold, fold, gold, hold, mold, mould, old, polled, scold, sold, soled, souled, told, wold
acold, age-old, ahold, behold, billfold, blindfold, controlled, Cotswold, cuckold, enfold, fanfold, foothold, foretold, freehold, gatefold, handhold, household, ice-cold, infold, leasehold, pinfold, potholed, roothold, scaffold, sheepfold, stone-cold, stronghold, threshold, toehold, twice-told, unfold, unmold, untold, uphold, whole-souled, withhold

centerfold, copyhold, fingerhold, manifold, manyfold, marigold, multifold, oversold, petioled, severalfold, stranglehold, throttlehold
—also -ed forms of verbs listed at ole¹

old² \ȯld\ see ald

oldan \ōl-dən\ see olden

olden \ōl-dən\ golden, holden, olden, soldan
beholden, embolden

older¹ \ōl-dər\ boulder, folder, holder, molder, polder, scolder, shoulder, smolder
beholder, bondholder, cardholder, householder, jobholder, landholder, placeholder, shareholder, slaveholder, stadtholder, stakeholder, stallholder, stockholder, toolholder
officeholder, titleholder
policyholder
—also -er forms of adjectives listed at old¹

older² \äd-ər\ see odder

oldi \ȯl-dē\ see aldi

oldie \ōl-dē\ see oldy

olding \ōl-diŋ\ folding, holding, molding
hand-holding, inholding, landholding, slaveholding
—also -ing forms of verbs listed at old¹

oldster \ōl-stər\ see olster

oldt \ōlt\ see olt¹

oldy \ōl-dē\ moldy, oldie

ole¹ \ōl\ bole, boll, bowl, coal, cole, Cole, dhole, dole, droll, foal, goal, hole, knoll, kohl, Kohl, mole, ole, pole, Pole, poll, prole, role, roll, scroll, Seoul, shoal, skoal, sol, sole, soul, stole, stroll, thole, tole, toll, troll, vole, whole
armhole, atoll, bankroll, beanpole, bedroll, blowhole, bolthole, borehole,

bunghole, cajole, catchpole, charcoal,
chuckhole, condole, console, control,
creole, Creole, drumroll, enroll,
ensoul, extol, eyehole, fishbowl,
flagpole, foxhole, frijol, hellhole,
Huichol, inscroll, insole, keyhole,
kneehole, knothole, logroll, loophole,
manhole, maypole, midsole, Mongol,
Nicole, outsole, parole, patrol, payroll,
peephole, pesthole, pinhole, pistole,
pitchpole, porthole, posthole, pothole,
redpoll, resole, ridgepole, Sheol,
sinkhole, sotol, stokehole, tadpole,
taphole, thumbhole, top-hole,
touchhole, turnsole, unroll, Walpole,
washbowl, wormhole
    amatol, aureole, banderole, bannerol,
barcarole, buttonhole, cabriole,
camisole, capriole, caracole,
carmagnole, casserole, croquignole,
cubbyhole, decontrol, Demerol,
escarole, farandole, fumarole,
girandole, grand guignol, innersole,
methanol, oriole, oversoul, petiole,
pick-and-roll, pigeonhole, protocol,
rigmarole, Seminole
    cholesterol, Costa del Sol

ole² \ō-lē\ see oly¹

ole³ \ȯl\ see all

olean \ō-lē-ən\ see olian¹

oled \ōld\ see old¹

oleful \ōl-fəl\ doleful, soulful

olely \ō-lē\ see oly¹

olem¹ \ō-ləm\ golem, solum

olem² \ā-ləm\ see alaam

olemn \äl-əm\ see olumn

oleon¹ \ō-lē-ən\ see olian¹

oleon² \ōl-yən\ see olian²

oler¹ \ō-lər\ see oller

oler² \äl-ər\ see ollar

olery \ōl-rē\ see ollery

olesome \ōl-səm\ dolesome,
Folsom, wholesome

oless \ō-ləs\ see olus

oleum \ō-lē-əm\ see olium

oleus \ō-lē-əs\ coleus, soleus

oley \ō-lē\ see oly¹

olf¹ \älf\ golf, Rolf
    Adolph, Randolph, Rudolph
    Lake Rudolf

olf² \əlf\ see ulf

olfing \ȯf-iŋ\ see offing

olga \äl-gə\ Olga, Volga

oli \ō-lē\ see oly¹

olia \ō-lē-ə\ Mongolia, pignolia
    Anatolia, melancholia
    Inner Mongolia, Outer Mongolia

olian \ō-lē-ən\ aeolian, Aeolian,
eolian, Mongolian, napoleon,
Napoleon, simoleon, Tyrolean
    Anatolian

olic¹ \äl-ik\ colic, frolic, Gaelic,
rollick
    Aeolic, bucolic, carbolic, embolic,
Mongolic, symbolic, systolic
    alcoholic, anabolic, apostolic,
catabolic, diabolic, hyperbolic,
melancholic, metabolic, parabolic,
vitriolic, workaholic

olic² \ō-lik\ colic
    fumarolic
    bibliopolic

olicking \ä-lik-iŋ\ frolicking,
rollicking

olicy \äl-ə-sē\ policy, Wallasey

olid \äl-əd\ solid, squalid, stolid

olin¹ \äl-ən\ see ollen⁵

olin² \ō-lən\ see olon

olis \äl-əs\ braless, Hollis, polis,
solace, tallith, Wallace, Wallis
    Cornwallis
    Manizales, torticollis

olish \äl-ish\ polish
abolish, demolish
apple-polish

olitan \äl-ət-ᵊn\ cosmopolitan, megapolitan, metropolitan, Neapolitan megalopolitan

olity \äl-ət-ē\ see ality[1]

olium \ō-lē-əm\ scholium
linoleum, petroleum, trifolium

olivar \äl-ə-vər\ see oliver

olk[1] \elk\ see elk[1]

olk[2] \ōk\ see oke

olk[3] \əlk\ see ulk

olk[4] \ȯk\ see alk

olked \ōkt\ see oked

olkie \ō-kē\ see oky

olky \ō-kē\ see oky

oll[1] \ōl\ see ole[1]

oll[2] \äl\ see al[1]

oll[3] \ȯl\ see all

olla[1] \äl-ə\ see ala[2]

olla[2] \ȯi-ə\ see oia

ollable \ō-lə-bəl\ controllable
inconsolable, uncontrollable

ollack \äl-ək\ see oloch

ollah[1] \ō-lə\ see ola

ollah[2] \äl-ə\ see ala[2]

ollah[3] \əl-ə\ see ullah[1]

ollands \äl-ənz\ see ollins

ollar \äl-ər\ choler, collar, dollar, dolor, haler, holler, loller, Mahler, scholar, squalor, taler, thaler
blue-collar, brass-collar, half-dollar, white-collar
Emmentaler, Eurodollar, petrodollar

ollard \äl-ərd\ bollard, collard, collered, hollered, Lollard, pollard

olled \ōld\ see old[1]

ollee \ō-lē\ see oly[1]

ollege \äl-ij\ see owledge

ollen[1] \ō-lən\ see olon

ollen[2] \əl-ə\ see ullah[1]

ollen[3] \əl-ən\ see ullen

ollen[4] \ȯ-lən\ see allen

ollen[5] \äl-ən\ Colin, pollen, Rollin
Nordrhein-Westfalen

oller \ō-lər\ bowler, choler, dolor, droller, molar, polar, poler, poller, roller, solar, stroller, troller
bankroller, cajoler, comptroller, controller, extoller, logroller, patroller, premolar, steamroller
antisolar, buttonholer, Maryknoller, pigeonholer

ollery \ōl-rē\ drollery
cajolery

ollet \äl-ət\ collet, Smollett, tallith, wallet
whatchamacallit

ollett \äl-ət\ see ollet

olley \äl-ē\ see olly[1]

ollick \äl-ik\ see olic[1]

ollicking \ä-lik-iŋ\ see olicking

ollie \äl-ē\ see olly[1]

ollin \äl-ən\ see ollen[5]

olling \ō-liŋ\ bowling
logrolling
—also -ing forms of verbs listed at ole[1]

ollins \äl-ənz\ collins, Hollands
Tom Collins

ollis \äl-əs\ see olis

ollity \äl-ət-ē\ see ality[1]

ollo[1] \ōl-yō\ imbroglio
arroz con pollo

ollo² \ō-yō\ yo-yo
criollo

ollo³ \äl-ō\ see ollow¹

ollop \äl-əp\ collop, dollop, lollop,
polyp, scallop, scollop, trollop, wallop
codswallop, escallop

ollow¹ \äl-ō\ follow, hollo, hollow,
swallow, wallow
Apollo, robalo
Leoncavallo

ollow² \äl-ə\ see ala²

ollower \äl-ə-wər\ follower,
swallower, wallower

ollster \ōl-stər\ see olster

olly¹ \äl-ē\ Bali, Cali, brolly, collie,
colly, dolly, folly, golly, Halle, holly,
Holly, jolly, Lally, lolly, Mali, Mollie,
molly, Molly, Ollie, Pali, poly, Polly,
quale, Raleigh, trolley, volley
Denali, finale, Kigali, loblolly,
Nepali, petrale, Somali, Svengali,
tamale
melancholy, pastorale, teocalli

olly² \ȯ-lē\ see awly

olm \ōm\ see ome¹

olman \ōl-mən\ dolman, dolmen
patrolman

olmen \ōl-mən\ see olman

olmes \ōmz\ Holmes
—also -s, -'s, and -s' forms of nouns,
and -s forms of verbs, listed at ome¹

olo \ō-lō\ bolo, kolo, nolo, polo, solo
Barolo
Marco Polo

oloch \äl-ək\ Moloch, pollack,
rowlock

ologer \äl-ə-jər\ astrologer,
chronologer, horologer, mythologer

ologist \äl-ə-jəst\ anthologist,
biologist, cetologist, conchologist,
cosmologist, cryptologist, cytologist,
dendrologist, ecologist, enologist,
ethnologist, ethologist, fetologist,
gemologist, geologist, graphologist,
histologist, horologist, hydrologist,
Indologist, limnologist, mixologist,
morphologist, mycologist,
mythologist, necrologist, nephrologist,
neurologist, oncologist, ontologist,
oologist, pathologist, pedologist,
penologist, petrologist, philologist,
phonologist, phrenologist,
phycologist, psychologist,
seismologist, serologist, sexologist,
sinologist, technologist, topologist,
typologist, ufologist, virologist,
zoologist
anthropologist, archaeologist,
audiologist, cardiologist,
climatologist, cosmetologist,
criminologist, dermatologist,
Egyptologist, embryologist,
entomologist, enzymologist,
escapologist, etymologist,
futurologist, genealogist,
gerontologist, gynecologist,
hematologist, herpetologist,
ichthyologist, ideologist,
immunologist, kremlinologist,
lexicologist, martyrologist,
methodologist, mineralogist,
musicologist, nematalogist,
numerologist, oceanologist,
ophthalmologist, ornithologist,
osteologist, papyrologist,
pharmacologist, phraseologist,
physiologist, planetologist,
primatologist, rheumatologist,
roentgenologist, semiologist,
sociologist, speleologist, teleologist,
teratologist, thanatologist,
toxicologist, urbanologist,
volcanologist
bacteriologist, diabetologist,
dialectologist, endocrinologist,
epistemologist, liturgiologist,
meteorologist, neonatologist,
paleontologist, parasitologist,
phenomenologist, sedimentologist
anesthesiologist, epidemiologist,
gastroenterologist, otolaryngologist

ologous \äl-ə-gəs\ homologous,
tautologous
heterologous

ology \äl-ə-jē\ anthology, apology,
astrology, biology, bryology, cetology,
Christology, chronology, conchology,
cosmology, cryptology, cytology,
dendrology, doxology, ecology,
enology, ethnology, ethology, fetology,
gemology, geology, graphology,
haplology, histology, homology,
horology, hydrology, hymnology,
Indology, limnology, lithology,
mixology, morphology, mycology,
myology, mythology, necrology,
nephrology, neurology, nosology,
oncology, ontology, oology, pathology,
pedology, penology, petrology,
philology, phlebology, phonology,
phrenology, phycology, proctology,
psychology, scatology, seismology,
serology, sexology, sinology,
symbology, tautology, technology,
tetralogy, theology, topology,
trichology, typology, ufology, urology,
virology, zoology
  angelology, anthropology,
archaeology, audiology, axiology,
cardiology, climatology, codicology,
cohomology, cosmetology, craniology,
criminology, dactylology,
demonology, deontology,
dermatology, Egyptology,
embryology, entomology,
enzymology, escapology, eschatology,
etiology, etymology, futurology,
genealogy, gerontology, gynecology,
hematology, herpetology, ichthyology,
iconology, ideology, immunology,
kremlinology, laryngology, lexicology,
lichenology, Mariology, martyrology,
methodology, mineralogy, museology,
musicology, narratology, nematology,
numerology, oceanology,
opthalmology, ornithology, osteology,
pharmacology, phraseology,
physiology, planetology, primatology,
radiology, reflexology, rheumatology,
roentgenology, semiology, sociology,
speleology, sumerology, teleology,

teratology, terminology, thanatology,
toxicology, urbanology, volcanology,
vulcanology
  bacteriology, chronobiology,
cryptozoology, dialectology,
ecclesiology, endocrinology,
epistemology, liturgiology,
metapsychology, meteorology,
microbiology, micromorphology,
neonatology, onomatology,
paleontology, parapsychology,
parasitology, phenomenology,
sedimentology, symptomatology
  anesthesiology, epidemiology,
ethnomusicology, gastroenterology,
otolaryngology, paleobiology,
paleopathology, periodontology
  otorhinolaryngology

olon \ō-lən\ bowline, Colin, colon,
Nolan, solon, stolen, stollen, stolon,
swollen
eidolon
semicolon

olonel \ərn-ᵊl\ see ernal

olonist \äl-ə-nəst\ colonist, Stalinist

olor¹ \əl-ər\ color, cruller, culler,
muller, sculler
bicolor, discolor, off-color, three-
color, tricolor
Technicolor, watercolor

olor² \ō-lər\ see oller

olor³ \äl-ər\ see ollar

olored \əl-ərd\ colored, dullard
bicolored, rose-colored
varicolored

olp \ōp\ see ope

olpen \ō-pən\ see open

olph \älf\ see olf

ols \älz\ hols, Casals

olsom \ōl-səm\ see olesome

olster \ōl-stər\ bolster, holster,
oldster, pollster
upholster

olt¹ \ōlt\ bolt, colt, dolt, holt, jolt, molt, poult, smolt, volt
eyebolt, Humboldt, kingbolt, revolt, ringbolt, unbolt
thunderbolt

olt² \ȯlt\ see alt

olta \äl-tə\ see alta

olter \ōl-tər\ bolter, coulter

oltish \ōl-tish\ coltish, doltish

oluble \äl-yə-bəl\ soluble, voluble, dissoluble, insoluble, resoluble
indissoluble, irresoluble

olum \ō-ləm\ see olem

olumn \äl-əm\ column, slalom, solemn
Malayalam

olus \ō-ləs\ bolas, bolus, solus, snowless, toeless
Coriolis, electroless, gladiolus, holus-bolus

olvable \äl-və-bəl\ solvable
dissolvable, evolvable, insolvable, resolvable, revolvable
irresolvable

olve¹ \älv\ salve, solve
absolve, au poivre, convolve, devolve, dissolve, evolve, involve, resolve, revolve
coevolve

olve² \äv\ grave, of, salve, Slav, suave, taw, waw
moshav, thereof, whereof, Zouave
Tishah-b'Ab, unheard-of, well-thought-of

olvement \älv-mənt\ evolvement, involvement
noninvolvement

olvent \äl-vənt\ solvent, dissolvent

olver \äl-vər\ solver
absolver, dissolver, involver, revolver

oly¹ \ō-lē\ goalie, holey, holy, lowly, mole, moly, pollee, slowly, solely
aioli, amole, anole, cannoli, frijole, pinole, unholy
guacamole, ravioli, roly-poly

oly² \äl-ē\ see olly¹

olyp \äl-əp\ see ollop

om¹ \äm\ balm, bomb, bombe, calm, from, gaum, Guam, glom, malm, mom, palm, Pom, pram, prom, psalm, qualm, rhomb, ROM, tom
A-bomb, aplomb, ashram, becalm, Ceram, cheongsam, coulomb, Coulomb, dive-bomb, embalm, EPROM, firebomb, grande dame, H-bomb, imam, Islam, Long Tom, napalm, nizam, noncom, phenom, pogrom, pom-pom, reclame, rhabdom, salaam, seram, sitcom, Songnam, tam-tam, therefrom, tom-tom, wherefrom, wigwam
cardamom, diatom, intercom, Peeping Tom, Uncle Tom, Vietnam
Dar es Salaam, Omar Khayyám

om² \ōm\ see ome¹

om³ \üm\ see oom¹

om⁴ \əm\ see um¹

om⁵ \ùm\ see um²

om⁶ \ȯm\ see aum¹

oma \ō-mə\ chroma, coma, Roma, soma
aroma, diploma, glaucoma, sarcoma, Tacoma
carcinoma, granuloma, melanoma, Oklahoma
glioblastoma, neurofibroma

omac \ō-mik\ see omic²

omace¹ \äm-əs\ see omise

omace² \əm-əs\ see ummous

omach \əm-ək\ see ummock

omache \äm-ə-kē\ see omachy

omachy \äm-ə-kē\ Andromache, logomachy

omal \ō-məl\ domal, stomal
prodromal
chromosomal

omaly \äm-ə-lē\ balmily, homily
anomaly

oman \ō-mən\ bowman, foeman,
gnomon, nomen, omen, Roman,
showman, snowman, yeoman
agnomen, cognomen, crossbowman,
longbowman, praenomen, Sertoman

omany \äm-ə-nē\ see ominy

omas \äm-əs\ see omise

omathy \äm-ə-thē\ chrestomathy,
stichomythy

omb¹ \ōm\ see ome¹

omb² \üm\ see oom¹

omb³ \äm\ see om¹

omb⁴ \əm\ see um¹

omba \äm-bə\ see amba

ombe¹ \ōm\ see ome¹

ombe² \üm\ see oom¹

ombe³ \äm\ see om¹

ombed \ümd\ see oomed

omber¹ \äm-ər\ bomber, calmer,
palmar, palmer, Palmer
dive-bomber, embalmer
fighter-bomber

omber² \äm-bər\ ombre, sambar,
somber

omber³ \ō-mər\ see omer¹

ombic \ō-mik\ see omic²

ombical \ō-mi-kəl\ see omical²

ombie \äm-bē\ zombie
Abercrombie

ombing \ō-miŋ\ see oaming

ombo¹ \äm-bō\ combo, mambo,
sambo

ombo² \əm-bō\ see umbo

ombre¹ \äm-brē\ hombre, ombre

ombre² \äm-bər\ see omber²

ombre³ \əm-brē\ see umbery

ombus \äm-bəs\ rhombus, thrombus

ome¹ \ōm\ brougham, chrome,
comb, combe, dome, foam, gloam,
gnome, holm, home, loam, mome,
nome, ogham, ohm, om, poem, pome,
roam, Rom, Rome, tome
airdrome, at-home, bichrome,
cockscomb, coulomb, coxcomb,
defoam, down-home, Jerome,
Nichrome, seadrome, shalom, sholom,
Stockholm, syndrome
aerodrome, astrodome, catacomb,
chromosome, currycomb, double-
dome, gastronome, halidrome,
hecatomb, hippodrome, honeycomb,
metronome, monochrome,
motordrome, palindrome, ribosome,
stay-at-home, Styrofoam

ome² \ō-mē\ see oamy

ome³ \əm\ see um¹

omedy \äm-əd-ē\ comedy,
psalmody
tragicomedy

omely \əm-lē\ see umbly²

omen \ō-mən\ see oman

omenal \äm-ən-ᵊl\ see ominal

omene \äm-ə-nē\ see ominy

omer¹ \ō-mər\ comber, foamer,
homer, Homer, omer, roamer, vomer
beachcomber, Reaumur, Lag
b'Omer, misnomer

omer² \əm-ər\ see ummer

omery \əm-ə-rē\ see ummery

omet \äm-ət\ comet, grommet,
vomit

ometer \äm-ət-ər\ barometer,
chronometer, cyclometer,

drunkometer, ergometer, gasometer,
geometer, hydrometer, hygrometer,
kilometer, manometer, micrometer,
odometer, pedometer, photometer,
pulsometer, pyrometer, rheometer,
seismometer, spectrometer,
speedometer, tachometer,
thermometer
anemometer, audiometer,
diffractometer, electrometer,
magnetometer
alcoholometer

ometry \äm-ə-trē\ astrometry,
barometry, chronometry, cytometry,
geometry, isometry, micrometry,
optometry, photometry, psychometry,
seismometry, thermometry
craniometry, sociometry,
trigonometry

omey \ō-mē\ see oamy

omi \ō-mē\ see oamy

omia \ō-mē-ä\ peperomia,
Utsunomia

omic¹ \äm-ik\ comic
anomic, atomic, coelomic, Islamic,
tsunamic
agronomic, anatomic, antinomic,
autonomic, economic, ergonomic,
gastronomic, metronomic, subatomic,
taxonomic, tragicomic
Deuteronomic, heroicomic,
physiognomic, polyatomic, seriocomic
macroeconomic, microeconomic
socioeconomic

omic² \ō-mik\ gnomic, oghamic
Potomac, rhizomic
catacombic, monochromic,
palindromic

omical¹ \äm-i-kəl\ comical, domical
agronomical, anatomical,
astronomical, economical,
gastronomical, metronomical,
tragicomical
heroicomical, physiognomical

omical² \ō-mi-kəl\ domical
coxcombical

omics \äm-iks\ atomics, Islamics,
tectonics
bionomics, economics, ergonomics
macroeconomics, microeconomics
—also -s, -'s, and -s' forms of nouns
listed at omic¹

omily \äm-ə-lē\ see omaly

ominal \äm-ən-ᵊl\ nominal
abdominal, cognominal, phenomenal
epiphenomenal

ominance \äm-nəns\ dominance,
prominence
predominance

ominant \äm-nənt\ dominant,
prominent
predominant, subdominant
semidominant, superdominant

ominate \äm-ə-nət\ innominate,
prenominate

omine \äm-ə-nē\ see ominy

ominence \äm-nəns\ see ominance

ominent \äm-nənt\ see ominant

oming¹ \əm-iŋ\ coming, plumbing
becoming, forthcoming,
homecoming, incoming, oncoming,
shortcoming, upcoming
unbecoming, up-and-coming
—also -ing forms of verbs listed at
um¹

oming² \ō-miŋ\ see oaming

omini \äm-ə-nē\ see ominy

ominous \äm-ə-nəs\ ominous
prolegomenous

ominy \äm-ə-nē\ hominy, Romany
Melpomene
anno Domini, eo nomine

omise \äm-əs\ pomace, promise,
shammes, shamus, Thomas
Saint Thomas
doubting Thomas

omit \äm-ət\ see omet

omium \ō-mē-əm\ chromium, holmium
encomium, prostomium

omma¹ \äm-ə\ see ama²

omma² \əm-ə\ see umma

ommel¹ \äm-əl\ pommel, Jamil, Rommel, trommel

ommel² \əm-əl\ pommel, pummel
Beau Brummell

ommet \äm-ət\ see omet

ommie \äm-ē\ see ami¹

ommon \äm-ən\ Amon, Brahman, common, shaman, yamen
Roscommon
Tutankhamen

ommoner \äm-ə-nər\ almoner, commoner
gewürztraminer

ommy¹ \äm-ē\ see ami¹

ommy² \əm-ē\ see ummy

omo \ō-mō\ bromo, Como, homo, Pomo, promo
Oromo
majordomo

omon \ō-mən\ see oman

omp¹ \ämp\ champ, chomp, clomp, comp, pomp, romp, stamp, stomp, swamp, tramp, tromp, whomp

omp² \əmp\ see ump

ompany \əmp-nē\ company
accompany
intracompany

ompass \əm-pəs\ compass, rumpus
encompass
gyrocompass

omper \äm-pər\ romper, stamper, stomper, swamper
wafflestomper

ompers \äm-pərz\ Gompers
—also -s, -'s, and -s' forms of nouns listed at omper

ompey \äm-pē\ see ompy

omplement \äm-plə-mənt\ complement, compliment

ompliment \äm-plə-mənt\ see omplement

ompo \äm-pō\ campo, compo

ompous \äm-pəs\ see ompass¹

ompson \äm-sən\ see amsun

ompt \aunt\ see ount²

ompy \äm-pē\ Pompey, swampy

omythy \äm-ə-thē\ see omathy

on¹ \än\ ban, Bonn, chon, con, conn, dawn, don, Don, Donn, drawn, Fan, faun, fawn, gone, guan, Han, John, Jon, khan, maun, mon, on, pan, pawn, phon, prawn, Ron, Shan, spawn, swan, Vaughn, wan, yawn, yon
aeon, add-on, agon, agone, Akan, alençon, Amman, ancon, anon, Anshan, Anton, archon, argon, Argonne, Aswan, atman, Avon, axon, barchan, baton, blouson, bon ton, bonbon, boron, boson, bouillon, Brython, bygone, caisson, Calgon, canton, capon, Ceylon, chaconne, chiffon, chignon, Chiron, chiton, chrismon, cistron, clip-on, codon, come-on, cordon, coupon, crampon, crayon, crepon, cretonne, crouton, Dacron, dead-on, Dear John, dewan, doggone, doggoned, Dogon, Don Juan, eon, exon, far-gone, flacon, foregone, Freon, fronton, Fujian, Garonne, Gibran, gluon, gnomon, Golan, Gosplan, guidon, hadron, Hainan, hazan, Henan, hogan, Huainan, Hunan, icon, Inchon, intron, Ivan, Jinan, Kanban, kaon, Kashan, Kazan, Kerman, Khoisan, Kirman, koan, krypton, kurgan, Kurgan, lauan, Leon, lepton, liman, log on, Luzon, macron, Massan, Medan, Memnon, meson, micron, Milan, mod con, moron, mouton, Multan, muon, natron, neon, nephron, neuron,

neutron, ninon, nylon, odds-on, Oman,
Oran, Orlon, outgone, pacon, parton,
Pathan, pavane, pecan, peon,
Phaëthon, photon, phyton, pion,
pinon, piton, plankton, pluton,
pompon, prion, proton, Pusan, put-on,
pylon, python, Qur'an, radon, rayon,
recon, rhyton, run-on, Saint John,
Saipan, salon, San Juan, Schumann,
Shaban, shaman, shaitan, Shingon,
Simplon, Sjoelland, slip-on, snap-on,
solon, soupçon, soutane, Stefan,
stolon, Suwon, Szechuan, Szechwan,
Tainan, Taiwan, taipan, tampon, taxon,
Teflon, teston, Tétouan, Tetuán,
thereon, tisane, torchon, toucan,
toyon, trigon, Tristan, triton, trogon,
Tucson, Typhon, tzigane, uhlan,
Ulsan, upon, walk-on, witan, whereon,
Wonsan, wonton, Wuhan, xenon,
Xi'an, yaupon, yuan, Yukon, Yunnan,
Yvonne, zircon
    Abadan, Abijan, Acheron, Ahriman,
aileron, amazon, Amazon, amnion,
Aragon, autobahn, Avalon, Babylon,
Bakhtaran, Balaton, balmacaan,
Bantustan, Barbizon, baryon, Basilan,
betatron, biathlon, cabochon, calutron,
carillon, carryon, celadon, chorion,
colophon, Culiacán, cyclotron,
decagon, decathlon, demijohn,
deuteron, dipteron, echelon, electron,
elevon, epsilon, etymon, fermion,
follow-on, Fujisan, Genghis Khan,
goings-on, gonfalon, Grand Teton,
graviton, harijan, helicon, heptagon,
hexagon, hopping John, Huascarán,
Ilion, Irian, Isfahan, Kazakhstan,
Kublai Khan, Kyrgyzstan, Lake
Huron, Lebanon, leprechaun, lexicon,
liaison, Lipizzan, logion, macédoine,
marathon, Marathon, marzipan,
mastodon, Mazatlán, Mbabane,
Mellotron, Miquelon, morion,
myrmidon, negatron, nonagon,
noumenon, nucleon, Oberon, octagon,
omicron, Oregon, organon, ostracon,
Pakistan, Palawan, pantheon, paragon,
Parmesan, parmigiana, Parthenon,
pentagon, Percheron, Phaethon,
Phlegethon, polygon, positron,

Procyon, put-upon, Rajasthan,
Ramadan, Rubicon, silicon, Suleiman,
tachyon, Taiyuan, talkathon, Teheran,
telamon, telethon, thereupon, Tian
Shan, Tucumán, undergone, upsilon,
virion, walkathon, whereupon,
woebegone, Yerevan, Xiangtan,
Zahedan
    abutilon, Agamemnon, archenteron,
arrière-ban, asyndeton, automaton,
Azerbaijan, Bellerophon,
bildungsroman, carrying-on,
Diazenon, dimetrodon, dodecagon,
encephalon, ephemeron, himation,
interferon, kakiemon, Laocoön,
mesenteron, Michoacán, millimicron,
oxymoron, phenomenon, protozoon,
pteranodon, Saskatchewan,
septentrion, sine qua non, t'ai chi
ch'uan, Taklimakan, Vientiane, West
Irian
    anacoluthon, diencephalon,
ferrosilicon, mesencephalon,
metencephalon, prolegomenon,
prothalamion, prosencephalon,
spermatozoon, telencephalon,
ultramarathon
    epiphenomenon, myelencephalon
    kyrie eleison, San Miguel de
Tucumán

on² \ōⁿ\ fond, ton
    ballon, baton, bouillon, Dijon,
flacon, fourgon, frisson, Gabon,
garçon, lorgnon, Lyons, maçon,
marron, Marron, mouflon, soupçon,
Toulon, Villon
    Aubusson, bourguignon, feuilleton,
Ganelon, gueridon, limaçon, papillon
    filet mignon
    Saint Emilion

on³ \ȯn\ awn, Bonn, bonne, brawn,
dawn, Dawn, drawn, faun, fawn, gone,
lawn, maun, on, pawn, prawn, Sean,
spawn, Vaughn, won, yawn
    add-on, agon, agone, begone,
bygone, chaconne, clip-on, come-on,
dead-on, doggone, far-gone, foregone,
hands-on, head-on, hereon, impawn,
indrawn, Kherson, odds-on, outgone,
Puchon, put-on, Quezon, run-on, slip-

on, snap-on, Taejon, thereon, turned-
on, upon, walk-on, whereon,
wiredrawn, withdrawn
  bourguignonne, carryon, follow-on,
goings-on, hanger-on, hereupon,
looker-on, put-upon, thereupon,
undergone, whereupon, woebegone
  carrying-on

on⁴ \ōn\ see one¹

on⁵ \ən\ see un

ona¹ \ō-nə\ dona, Dona, Jonah,
krone, Mona, Nona, Rhona, Rona,
Shona, trona
  Ancona, Bellona, bologna, Bologna,
cinchona, corona, kimono, Leona,
madrona, Pamplona, persona,
Ramona, Verona
  Arizona, Barcelona, Desdemona
  in propria persona

ona² \än-ə\ see ana¹

oña \ōn-yə\ see onia³

onachal \än-i-kəl\ see onical

onae \ō-nē\ see ony¹

onah \ō-nə\ see ona

onal¹ \ōn-ᵊl\ clonal, tonal, zonal
atonal, coronal, hormonal
  baritonal, microtonal, polyclonal,
polytonal, semitonal

onal² \än-ᵊl\ Donal, Ronal

onald \än-ᵊld\ Donald, Ronald
MacDonald

onant \ō-nənt\ see onent

onas \ō-nəs\ see onus²

onative \ō-nət-iv\ conative, donative

onc \äŋk\ see onk¹

once¹ \äns\ see ance²

once² \əns\ see unce

onch¹ \äŋk\ see onk¹

onch² \änch\ see aunch¹

oncha \äŋ-kə\ see anka

oncho \än-chō\ honcho, poncho,
rancho

onchus \äŋ-kəs\ bronchus,
rhonchus

onco \äŋ-kō\ bronco, Franco

ond¹ \änd\ blond, bond, fond, frond,
Gond, pond, rand, sonde, wand, yond
  abscond, Armand, beau monde,
beyond, despond, fishpond, Gironde,
gourmand, haut monde, millpond,
neoned, pair-bond, respond
  allemande, towmond, correspond,
demimonde, Eurobond, Trebizond,
Trobriand, vagabond
  radiosonde, slough of despond
  —also -ed forms of verbs listed at
on¹

ond² \ōⁿ\ see on²

ond³ \ȯnt\ see aunt¹

onda \än-də\ Lahnda, Rhonda,
Rhondda, Ronda, Wanda
  Golconda, Luganda, Ruanda,
Rwanda, Uganda
  anaconda, Campo Grande

ondam \än-dəm\ see ondom¹

ondant \än-dənt\ see ondent

onday \ən-dē\ see undi

ondays \ən-dēz\ see undays

ondda \än-də\ see onda

onde \änd\ see ond¹

ondeau \än-dō\ see ondo

ondel \än-dᵊl\ condyle, fondle,
rondel

ondence \än-dəns\ despondence
correspondence

ondency \än-dən-sē\ despondency
correspondency

ondent \än-dənt\ fondant
despondent, respondent
corespondent, correspondent

onder¹ \än-dər\ bonder, condor, maunder, ponder, squander, wander, yonder, zander
absconder, responder, transponder
—also -er *forms of adjectives listed at* ond¹

onder² \ən-dər\ see under

ondly \än-lē\ see anly¹

ondness \än-nəs\ see anness

ondo \än-dō\ condo, Hondo, rondeau, rondo, tondo
forzando, glissando, lentando, parlando, scherzando, secondo, sforzando
allargando, rallentando, ritardando
accelerando

ondom¹ \än-dəm\ condom, quondam

ondom² \ən-dəm\ see undum

ondor \än-dər\ see onder¹

ondrous \ən-drəs\ see underous

ondyle \än-dᵊl\ see ondel

one¹ \ōn\ blown, bone, clone, cone, crone, drone, flown, groan, grown, hone, Joan, known, loan, lone, moan, Mon, mown, none, own, phone, pone, prone, Rhône, roan, Saône, scone, sewn, shone, shoon, shown, sone, sown, stone, throne, thrown, tone, trone, won, zone
agon, aitchbone, alone, atone, backbone, bemoan, birthstone, Blackstone, breastbone, brimstone, brownstone, capstone, cheekbone, chinbone, cogon, cologne, Cologne, colon, Colón, condone, curbstone, cyclone, daimon, debone, depone, dethrone, disown, drystone, earphone, enthrone, fieldstone, flagstone, flyblown, freestone, full-blown, gallstone, gemstone, Gijón, Gladstone, gravestone, grindstone, hailstone, halftone, handblown, headphone, headstone, high-flown, hipbone, homegrown, hormone, impone,

ingrown, inkstone, intone, jawbone, keystone, León, leone, limestone, lodestone, milestone, millstone, misknown, moonstone, oilstone, outgrown, outshown, ozone, peon, pinbone, pinecone, pinon, pinyon, postpone, propone, Ramon, rezone, rhinestone, sandstone, shade-grown, shinbone, Shoshone, soapstone, T-bone, tailbone, thighbone, tombstone, touchstone, Touch-Tone, tritone, trombone, turnstone, twelve-tone, two-tone, Tyrone, unknown, unthrone, well-known, whalebone, wheel-thrown, whetstone, windblown, wishbone, Yangon
allophone, anglophone, anklebone, barbitone, Barbizon, barytone, Bayamon, bombardon, Canal Zone, chaperon, cherrystone, cobblestone, collarbone, cornerstone, cortisone, cuttlebone, diaphone, Dictaphone, epigone, francophone, free-fire zone, Gaborone, gramophone, herringbone, homophone, ironstone, knucklebone, marrowbone, megaphone, mellophone, methadone, microphone, microtone, minestrone, monotone, Mount Mayon, overblown, overflown, overgrown, overthrown, overtone, Picturephone, polyphone, rottenstone, sacaton, saxophone, semitone, shacklebone, silicone, sousaphone, speakerphone, stepping-stone, telephone, Toreón, undertone, vibraphone, xylophone, Yellowstone
anticyclone, Asunción, bred-in-the-bone, Concepción, Darby and Joan, eau de cologne, mesocyclone, norethindrone, Nuevo León, radiophone, sine qua non, testosterone, videophone
Ponce de León, Sierra Leone
radiotelephone

one² \ō-nē\ see ony¹

one³ \än\ see on¹

one⁴ \ən\ see un

one⁵ \ȯn\ see on³

onean \ō-nē-ən\ see onian[1]

oned[1] \ōnd\ boned, stoned, toned
cologned, high-toned, pre-owned,
rawboned, rhinestoned, two-toned
cobblestoned
—*also* -ed *forms of verbs listed at*
one[1]

oned[2] \än\ see on[1]

oneless \ōn-ləs\ boneless, toneless

onely \ōn-lē\ lonely, only, pronely

onement \ōn-mənt\ atonement,
cantonment, dethronement,
disownment, enthronement

oneness \ən-nəs\ dunness,
doneness, oneness
rotundness

onent \ō-nənt\ sonant
component, deponent, exponent,
opponent, proponent
bicomponent

oneous \ō-nē-əs\ see onious

oner[1] \ō-nər\ boner, donor, droner,
groaner, honer, loaner, loner, moaner,
stoner, toner, zoner
condoner, dethroner, intoner,
landowner, shipowner
telephoner

oner[2] \ȯn-ər\ see awner[1]

onerous \än-ə-rəs\ onerous,
sonorous

ones \ōnz\ Jones, nones
sawbones
Davy Jones, lazybones
skull and crossbones
—*also* -s, -'s, *and* -s' *forms of nouns,
and* -s *forms of verbs, listed at* one[1]

onest \än-əst\ honest
dishonest
Hinayanist, Mahayanist

oney[1] \ō-nē\ see ony[1]

oney[2] \ən-ē\ see unny

oney[3] \ü-nē\ see oony

ong[1] \äŋ\ Chang, Fang, gong, hong,
Huang, prong, Shang, Tang, tong,
yang
Anyang, barong, biltong, Da Nang,
dugong, Guiyang, Hanyang, Heng-
yang, Hong Kong, kiang, liang, Mah-
Jongg, Malang, Padang, satang,
Shenyang, Wuchang, Zhejiang,
Zhenjiang
billabong, Chittagong, Liaoyang,
Pyong-yang, Semarang, scuppernong,
Sturm und Drang, Vietcong,
Wollongong
Heilongjiang, Shijiazhuang, Ujung
Pandang, ylang-ylang

ong[2] \ȯŋ\ bong, dong, gong, long,
prong, song, strong, thong, throng,
tong, wrong
agelong, along, Armstrong, barong,
belong, biltong, birdsong, chaise
longue, daylong, dingdong, diphthong,
dugong, endlong, erelong, furlong,
Geelong, Haiphong, headlong,
headstrong, Kaesong, kampong,
lifelong, livelong, Mekong,
monthlong, Nanchang, nightlong,
oblong, oolong, part-song, ping-pong,
Ping-Pong, plainsong, prolong,
sarong, Shandong, sidelong, singsong,
so long, souchong, weeklong, yard-
long, yearlong
billabong, Chittagong, cradlesong,
evensong, Palembang, scuppernong,
sing-along, summerlong, tagalong,
Vietcong

ong[3] \əŋ\ see ung[1]

ong[4] \u̇ng\ see ung[2]

onga \äŋ-gə\ conga, panga, tonga,
Tonga
Kananga, mridanga
Alba Longa, Zamboanga
Bucaramanga

onge \ənj\ see unge

onged \ȯŋd\ pronged, thonged
multipronged
—*also* -ed *forms of verbs listed at*
ong[2]

onger¹ \əŋ-gər\ hunger, monger,
younger
fellmonger, fishmonger, ironmonger,
newsmonger, phrasemonger,
scaremonger, warmonger,
whoremonger, wordmonger
costermonger, fashionmonger,
gossipmonger, rumormonger,
scandalmonger

onger² \ən-jər\ see unger¹

ongery \əŋ-grē\ hungry
fellmongery, ironmongery

ongful \óŋ-fəl\ wrongful, songful

ongin \ən-jən\ see ungeon

ongish \óŋ-ish\ longish, strongish

ongo \äŋ-gō\ bongo, Congo,
congou, Kongo, mongo
Niger-Congo, Pago Pago

ongous \əŋ-gəs\ see ungous

ongue¹ \əŋ\ see ung¹

ongue² \óŋ\ see ong²

ongued \əŋd\ lunged, tongued

ongy \ən-jē\ see ungy

onhomous \än-ə-məs\ see
onymous

oni \ō-nē\ see ony¹

onia¹ \ō-nē-ə\ bignonia, clintonia,
Estonia, Laconia, Livonia, mahonia,
paulownia, Polonia, Slavonia,
Snowdonia, tithonia, valonia, zirconia
Amazonia, Caledonia, Catalonia,
Macedonia

onia² \ō-nyə\ Konya, Sonia, Sonja,
Sonya
ammonia, Bologna, pneumonia,
Polonia, tithonia, valonia
anhedonia, Caledonia, Macedonia,
Patagonia
New Caledonia

onia³ \ōn-yə\ doña
begonia

onial \ō-nē-əl\ baronial, colonial
ceremonial, matrimonial, testimonial

onian¹ \ō-nē-ən\ chthonian
aeonian, Antonian, Baconian,
Clactonian, demonian, Devonian,
draconian, Estonian, Etonian,
favonian, gorgonian, Ionian,
Jacksonian, Oxonian, plutonian,
Samsonian, Shoshonean, Slavonian
Amazonian, Apollonian, Arizonian,
Babylonian, calypsonian,
Chalcedonian, Hamiltonian,
parkinsonian

onian² \ō-nyən\ Zonian
Estonian
Amazonian, Babylonian,
Macedonian

onic \än-ik\ chronic, chthonic,
conic, dornick, phonic, sonic, tonic
Aaronic, agonic, atonic, benthonic,
bionic, Brittonic, Brythonic, bubonic,
Byronic, canonic, carbonic, cryonic,
cyclonic, daimonic, demonic,
draconic, euphonic, gnomonic,
harmonic, hedonic, ionic, Ionic,
ironic, laconic, Masonic, mnemonic,
planktonic, platonic, plutonic,
pneumonic, Puranic, Pythonic,
sardonic, Saronic, sermonic, Slavonic,
symphonic, synchronic, tectonic,
Teutonic, zirconic
catatonic, diachronic, diatonic,
disharmonic, electronic, embryonic,
hegemonic, histrionic, homophonic,
hydroponic, inharmonic, isotonic,
macaronic, megaphonic, microphonic,
monophonic, monotonic, nonionic,
pharaonic, Philharmonic, polyphonic,
quadraphonic, semitonic, Solomonic,
supersonic, supertonic, telephonic,
thermionic, ultrasonic
architectonic, chameleonic,
cardiotonic, electrotonic, geotectonic,
Neoplatonic, stereophonic
extraembryonic

onica \än-i-kə\ Monica
harmonica, japonica, Salonika,
veronica, Veronica
Thessalonica

onical \än-i-kəl\ chronicle, conical,
monachal, monocle
   canonical, demonical, ironical
   deuterocanonical

onicals \än-i-kəlz\ Chronicles
   canonicals

onicker \ä-ni-kər\ see onnicker

onicle \än-i-kəl\ see onical

onicles \än-i-kəlz\ see onicals

onics \än-iks\ onyx, phonics
   bionics, cryonics, mnemonics,
Ovonics, photonics, sardonyx,
tectonics
   avionics, electronics, histrionics,
hydroponics, microphonics,
nucleonics, quadriphonics, radionics,
supersonics, thermionics
   architectonics
   —also -s, -'s, *and* -s' *forms of nouns
listed at* onic

onika \än-i-kə\ see onica

oniker \ä-ni-kər\ see onnicker

oning[1] \än-iŋ\ awning
   couponing
   —also -ing *forms of verbs listed at*
on[1]

oning[2] \ō-niŋ\ loaning
   jawboning, landowning
   —also -ing *forms of verbs listed at*
one[1]

onion \ən-yən\ see union

onious \ō-nē-əs\ erroneous,
euphonious, felonious, harmonious,
Polonius, Suetonius, symphonious
   acrimonious, ceremonious,
disharmonious, inharmonious,
parsimonious, sanctimonious
   Marcus Antonius, unceremonious

onis[1] \ō-nəs\ see onus[2]

onis[2] \än-əs\ see onus[1]

onish \än-ish\ donnish, monish
   admonish, astonish, premonish
   leprechaunish

onishment \än-ish-mənt\
admonishment, astonishment

onium \ō-nē-əm\ euphonium,
harmonium, plutonium
   pandemonium, Pandemonium

onius \ō-nē-əs\ see onious

onja \ō-nyə\ see onia[2]

onjon \ən-jən\ see ungeon

onjure \än-jər\ conjure, rondure

onk[1] \äŋk\ ankh, bronc, clonk,
conch, conk, Franck, honk, Planck,
plonk, zonk
   honkytonk

onk[2] \əŋk\ see unk

onker \äŋ-kər\ conker, conquer,
honker

onkey[1] \äŋ-kē\ see onky

onkey[2] \əŋ-kē\ see unky

onkian \äŋ-kē-ən\ conquian
   Algonkian

onky \äŋ-kē\ conkey, donkey,
wonky, yanqui

onless \ən-ləs\ see unless

only \ōn-lē\ see onely

onment \ōn-mənt\ see onement

onn[1] \än\ see on[1]

onn[2] \òn\ see on[3]

onna[1] \òn-ə\ donna, Donna, fauna
   megafauna, prima donna

onna[2] \än-ə\ see ana[1]

onnage \ən-ij\ see unnage

onne[1] \än\ see on[1]

onne[2] \ən\ see un

onne[3] \òn\ see on[3]

onner \än-ər\ see onor[1]

onnet \än-ət\ bonnet, sonnet
   bluebonnet, sunbonnet, warbonnet

onnicker \ä-ni-kər\ donnicker, doniker, monicker, moniker

onnie \än-ē\ see ani¹

onnish \än-ish\ see onish

onnor \än-ər\ see onor¹

onny¹ \än-ē\ see ani¹

onny² \ən-ē\ see unny

ono¹ \ō-nō\ phono
cui bono, kimono, pro bono
kakemono, makimono

ono² \ō-nə\ see ona

ono³ \än-ō\ see ano¹

onocle \än-i-kəl\ see onical

onomer \än-ə-mər\ monomer
astronomer, comonomer

onomist \än-ə-məst\ agronomist, autonomist, economist, ergonomist, gastronomist, synonymist, taxonomist
Deuteronomist

onomous \än-ə-məs\ see onymous

onomy \än-ə-mē\ agronomy, antonymy, astronomy, autonomy, economy, eponymy, gastronomy, homonomy, metonymy, synonymy, taphonomy, taxonomy, toponymy
Deuteronomy, diseconomy, heteronomy, teleonomy

onor¹ \än-ər\ Bonner, fawner, goner, honor, pawner, pawnor, spawner, wanner, yawner
dishonor, O'Connor
Afrikaner, Lipizzaner, marathoner, weimaraner

onor² \ō-nər\ see oner¹

onorous \än-ə-rəs\ see onerous

onquer \äŋ-kər\ see onker

onquian \äŋ-kē-ən\ see onkian

ons¹ \änz\ see onze

ons² \ōⁿ\ see on²

onsil \än-səl\ see onsul

onsin \än-sən\ see ohnson

onson \än-sən\ see ohnson

onsor \än-sər\ panzer, sponsor

onsul \än-səl\ consul, tonsil

ont¹ \ənt\ blunt, brunt, bunt, front, grunt, hunt, lunt, punt, runt, shunt, strunt, stunt, want, wont
affront, beachfront, bowfront, breakfront, confront, forefront, housefront, lakefront, manhunt, outfront, seafront, shirtfront, shorefront, storefront, swell-front, up-front, witch-hunt
battlefront, oceanfront, riverfront, waterfront

ont² \änt\ see ant²

ont³ \ȯnt\ see aunt¹

on't \ōnt\ don't, won't

ontal¹ \änt-ᵊl\ pontil, fontal, quantal
horizontal
periodontal

ontal² \ənt-ᵊl\ see untle

ontan \änt-ⁿ\ see onton

ontas \änt-əs\ see ontus

onte¹ \änt-ē\ see anti¹

onte² \än-tā\ see ante¹

onted \ȯnt-əd\ vaunted, wonted
undaunted
—also -ed forms of verbs listed at aunt¹

onter \ənt-ər\ see unter

onth \ənth\ month
billionth, millionth, trillionth, twelvemonth

ontian \änt-ē-ən\ Zontian
post-Kantian

ontic \änt-ik\ ontic
deontic, Vedantic
orthodontic
anacreontic

ontil \änt-ᵊl\ see ontal[1]

ontinent \änt-ᵊn-ənt\ continent
incontinent, subcontinent
supercontinent

ontis \än-təs\ see antos[2]

ontist \änt-əst\ Vedantist
orthodontist, prosthodontist

onto \än-tō\ see anto[1]

onton \änt-ᵊn\ ponton, wanton
Lahontan

ontra \än-trə\ contra, mantra, tantra
per contra

ontre \änt-ər\ see aunter[1]

ontus \änt-əs\ Pontus
Pocahontas

onty \änt-ē\ see anti[1]

onus[1] \än-əs\ Cronus, Faunus
Adonis

onus[2] \ō-nəs\ bonus, Cronus, Jonas,
onus, slowness
Adonis, colonus

ony[1] \ō-nē\ bony, coney, crony,
phony, pony, stony, Toni, tony, Tony,
yoni
  baloney, Benoni, bologna, canzone,
Marconi, Moroni, Oenone, padrone,
spumoni, tortoni
  abalone, acrimony, agrimony,
alimony, antimony, cannelloni,
ceremony, chalcedony, colophony,
macaroni, mascarpone, matrimony,
minestrone, palimony, parsimony,
patrimony, pepperoni, provolone,
rigatoni, sanctimony, telephony,
testimony, zabaglione
  con espressione, conversazione,
dramatis personae

ony[2] \än-ē\ see ani[1]

onya \ō-nyə\ see onia[2]

onymist \än-ə-məst\ see onomist

onymous \än-ə-məs\ bonhomous

anonymous, antonymous,
autonomous, eponymous,
homonymous, pseudonymous,
synonymous
heteronomous

onymy \än-ə-mē\ see onomy

onyon[1] \än-yən\ ronyon, wanion

onyon[2] \ən-yən\ see union

onyx \än-iks\ see onics

onze \änz\ bonze, bronze, pons
long johns, Saint John's
Afrikaans, solitons
islet of Langerhans
  —also -s, -'s, and -s' forms of nouns,
and -s forms of verbs, listed at on[1]

onzi \än-zē\ see onzy

onzy \än-zē\ bronzy, Ponzi

oo[1] \ü\ see ew[1]

oo[2] \ō\ see ow[1]

oob \üb\ see ube

oober \ü-bər\ see uber

ooby \ü-bē\ booby, looby, ruby,
Ruby

ooch[1] \üch\ brooch, hooch, mooch,
pooch, smooch
  capuche
  scaramouch

ooch[2] \ōch\ see oach

oocher \ü-chər\ see uture

oochy \ü-chē\ smoochy
Baluchi, penuche, Vespucci
Kawaguchi

ood[1] \ud\ good, hood, pud, rudd,
should, stood, wood, would, yod
  basswood, bentwood, blackwood,
boxwood, brushwood, childhood,
cordwood, deadwood, do-good,
dogwood, driftwood, Ellwood,
Elwood, falsehood, fatwood, feel-
good, firewood, fruitwood, girlhood,
godhood, greasewood, greenwood,

groundwood, gumwood, hardwood,
ironwood, kingwood, knighthood,
maidhood, manhood, monkhood,
monkshood, Mount Hood, no-good,
pinewood, plywood, priesthood,
pulpwood, redwood, rosewood,
sainthood, selfhood, Sherwood,
softwood, sonhood, statehood,
stinkwood, Talmud, teakwood,
unhood, Wedgwood, wifehood,
withstood, wormwood
  arrowwood, bachelorhood,
brotherhood, buttonwood,
candlewood, cedarwood, cottonwood,
fatherhood, hardihood, Hollywood,
likelihood, livelihood, maidenhood,
motherhood, nationhood,
neighborhood, parenthood,
personhood, Robin Hood,
sandalwood, scattergood, servanthood,
sisterhood, spinsterhood, toddlerhood,
tulipwood, understood, widowhood,
womanhood
  misunderstood, unlikelihood,
widowerhood

ood² \ōd\ see **ode**

ood³ \üd\ see **ude**

ood⁴ \əd\ see **ud¹**

ooded¹ \əd-əd\ blooded
  cold-blooded, full-blooded, half-
blooded, hot-blooded, pure-blooded,
red-blooded, star-studded, warm-
blooded
  —also -ed *forms of verbs listed at*
ud¹

ooded² \ùd-əd\ hooded, wooded
  hard-wooded, soft-wooded

ooder¹ \üd-ər\ see **uder**

ooder² \əd-ər\ see **udder**

ooding \ùd-iŋ\ pudding
  do-gooding, unhooding

oodle \üd-ᵊl\ boodle, doodle, feudal,
noodle, poodle, strudel
  caboodle, flapdoodle, paludal
  Yankee-Doodle

oodman \ùd-mən\ goodman,
woodman

oodoo \üd-ü\ doo-doo, hoodoo,
kudu, voodoo

oods \ùdz\ backwoods, dry goods
  piney woods
  —*also* -s, -'s, *and* -s' *forms of nouns,
and* -s *forms of verbs, listed at* ood¹

oodsman \ùdz-mən\ woodsman
  backwoodsman, ombudsman

oody¹ \üd-ē\ broody, Judi, Judie,
Judy, moody, Rudy, Trudy

oody² \ùd-ē\ cuddy, goody, hoody,
woody
  goody-goody

oody³ \əd-ē\ see **uddy¹**

ooer \ü-ər\ see **ewer¹**

ooey \ü-ē\ see **ewy**

oof¹ \üf\ goof, kloof, poof, pouf,
proof, roof, spoof, woof
  aloof, behoof, disproof, fireproof,
foolproof, forehoof, rustproof,
shadoof, soundproof, sunroof,
Tartuffe, unroof
  bulletproof, opera bouffe,
shatterproof, waterproof, weatherproof

oof² \ùf\ hoof, poof, roof, woof
  forehoof, Tartuffe

oof³ \ōf\ see **oaf**

oof⁴ \üv\ see **ove³**

oofah \ü-fə\ see **ufa**

oofer¹ \ü-fər\ proofer, roofer, twofer
  waterproofer

oofer² \ùf-ər\ hoofer, woofer

oofy \ü-fē\ goofy, spoofy, Sufi

ooga \ü-gə\ see **uga**

ooge \üj\ see **uge¹**

ooger \ùg-ər\ see **ugur**

oogie \ùg-ē\ bogey, boogie
boogie-woogie

oo-goo \ü-gü\ see ugu

ooh \ü\ see ew¹

ooh-pooh \ü-pü\ hoopoe, pooh-
pooh

ooi \ü-ē\ see ewy

ooist \ü-əst\ doest
tattooist, voodooist
—also -est forms of adjectives listed
at ew¹

ook¹ \ùk\ book, brook, Brooke,
chook, cook, Cook, crook, gook,
hook, look, nook, rook, schnook,
shook, snook, stook, took
bankbook, betook, billhook,
caoutchouc, chapbook, checkbook,
Chinook, cookbook, forsook,
fishhook, guidebook, handbook,
hornbook, hymnbook, Innsbruck,
Kobuk, logbook, matchbook, mistook,
Mount Cook, notebook, outlook,
partook, passbook, Pembroke,
playbook, pothook, promptbook,
psalmbook, retook, schoolbook,
scrapbook, sketchbook, skyhook,
songbook, studbook, textbook,
unhook, Windhoek, workbook,
yearbook
buttonhook, copybook, donnybrook,
gerenuk, inglenook, Leeuwenhoek,
overbook, overlook, overtook,
pocketbook, storybook, tenterhook,
undertook, Volapuk
gobbledygook

ook² \ük\ see uke

ooka \ü-kə\ yuca
bazooka, felucca, palooka, Toluca,
verruca
Juan de Fuca

ookah \ùk-ə\ hookah, sukkah

ooke \ùk\ see ook¹

ooker \ùk-ər\ booker, cooker,
hooker, Hooker, looker, snooker
good-looker, onlooker

ookery \ùk-ə-rē\ crookery, rookery

ookie \ùk-ē\ bookie, brookie,
cookie, cooky, hooky, rookie, rooky
Takatsuki, walkie-lookie

ooking \ùk-iŋ\ booking, cooking
good-looking, onlooking
—also -ing forms of verbs listed at
ook¹

ooklet \ùk-lət\ booklet, brooklet,
hooklet

ooks¹ \üks\ deluxe, gadzooks
—also -s, -'s, and -s' forms of nouns,
and -s forms of verbs, listed at uke

ooks² \ùks\ Brooks, crux, luxe,
zooks
deluxe, gadzooks
—also -s, -'s, and -s' forms of nouns,
and -s forms of verbs, listed at ook¹

ooky¹ \ü-kē\ kooky, spooky
bouzouki, Kabuki, saluki, tanuki

ooky² \ùk-ē\ see ookie

ool¹ \ül\ boule, boulle, buhl, cool,
drool, fool, fuel, ghoul, gul, joule,
mewl, mule, pool, Poole, pul, pule,
rule, school, spool, stool, tool, tulle,
you'll, yule
air-cool, ampoule, babul, Banjul,
befool, Blackpool, carpool, cesspool,
curule, Elul, faldstool, footstool,
hangul, Kabul, Kurnool, misrule,
Mosul, preschool, retool, self-rule,
synfuel, toadstool, tomfool, uncool,
vanpool, whirlpool
Barnaul, fascicule, gallinule,
graticule, groupuscule, Hartlepool,
Istanbul, lenticule, Liverpool,
majuscule, minuscule, molecule,
monticule, overrule, reticule, ridicule,
vestibule, water-cool
biomolecule

ool² \ùl\ see ul¹

oola \ü-lə\ see ula

oole \ül\ see ool¹

oolean \ü-lē-ən\ see ulean

ooled \üld\ bejeweled, unschooled
vestibuled
—*also* -ed *forms of verbs listed at*
ool¹

ooler \ü-lər\ cooler, gular, puler,
ruler
carpooler, grade-schooler, high
schooler, preschooler
ridiculer, watercooler

oolie \ü-lē\ see uly

oolish \ü-lish\ coolish, foolish,
ghoulish, mulish
pound-foolish

oolly¹ \ü-lē\ see uly

oolly² \ul-ē\ see ully²

oom¹ \üm\ bloom, boom, broom,
brougham, brume, combe, cwm,
doom, flume, fume, gloom, glume,
groom, Hume, khoum, loom, neume,
plume, rheum, room, spume, tomb,
toom, vroom, whom, womb, zoom
abloom, assume, backroom,
ballroom, barroom, bathroom,
bedroom, boardroom, bridegroom,
broadloom, checkroom, classroom,
cloakroom, coatroom, consume,
costume, courtroom, darkroom,
dayroom, entomb, enwomb, exhume,
foredoom, greenroom, guardroom,
headroom, heirloom, homeroom,
houseroom, illume, inhume, jibboom,
Khartoum, legroom, legume,
lunchroom, mudroom, mushroom,
newsroom, perfume, playroom,
poolroom, pressroom, presume,
proofroom, relume, resume,
salesroom, schoolroom, showroom,
sickroom, simoom, stateroom,
stockroom, storeroom, subsume,
taproom, Targum, tearoom, toolroom,
wardroom, washroom, workroom
anteroom, checkerbloom, dyer's
broom, elbowroom, impostume,
locker-room, miniboom, nom de
plume, smoke-filled room, witches'-
broom

oom² \um\ see um²

oomed \ümd\ groomed, plumed,
wombed
well-groomed
—*also* -ed *forms of verbs listed at*
oom¹

oomer \ü-mər\ see umer

oomily \ü-mə-lē\ gloomily
contumely

ooming¹ \ü-mən\ see uman

ooming² \ü-miŋ\ see uming

oomlet \üm-lət\ boomlet, plumelet

oomy \ü-mē\ bloomy, boomy,
doomy, fumy, gloomy, plumy, rheumy,
roomy, spumy
costumey

oon¹ \ün\ boon, Boone, coon, croon,
dune, goon, hewn, June, loon, lune,
moon, noon, prune, rune, shoon, soon,
spoon, swoon, strewn, toon, tune
aswoon, attune, baboon, balloon,
bassoon, buffoon, Calhoun, cardoon,
cartoon, cocoon, commune, doubloon,
dragoon, festoon, fine-tune, forenoon,
gaboon, gadroon, galloon, Gudrun,
half-moon, harpoon, immune, impugn,
jargoon, jejune, Kowloon, Kunlun,
lagoon, lampoon, lardoon, maroon,
monsoon, Neptune, oppugn, Pashtun,
patroon, platoon, poltroon, pontoon,
premune, puccoon, quadroon,
raccoon, ratoon, repugn, rockoon,
rough-hewn, saloon, shalloon,
soupspoon, spittoon, spontoon,
teaspoon, Torun, tribune, triune,
tuchun, tycoon, typhoon, untune,
Walloon
afternoon, barracoon, Brigadoon,
Cameroon, demilune, dessertspoon,
honeymoon, importune, macaroon,
octoroon, opportune, pantaloon,
picaroon, picayune, rigadoon,
saskatoon, Saskatoon, tablespoon
contrabassoon, inopportune

oon² \ōn\ see one¹

oona \ü-nə\ see una

oonal \ün-ᵊl\ see unal

oone \ün\ see oon¹

ooner \ü-nər\ crooner, crowner, lunar, pruner, schooner, sooner, swooner, tuner
  harpooner, lacunar, lampooner, oppugner
  honeymooner, importuner, semilunar

oonery¹ \ün-rē\ buffoonery, lampoonery, poltroonery

oonery² \ü-nə-rē\ see unary

ooney \ü-nē\ see oony

oonie \ü-nē\ see oony

ooning \ü-niŋ\ nooning
  ballooning, cartooning, gadrooning
  —also -ing forms of verbs listed at oon¹

oonish \ü-nish\ moonish
  buffoonish, cartoonish
  picayunish

oonless \ün-ləs\ moonless, tuneless, woundless

oons \ünz\ lunes, zounds
  eftsoons
  afternoons
  —also -s, -'s, and -s' forms of nouns, and -s forms of verbs, listed at oon¹

oony \ü-nē\ gooney, loony, luny, Moonie, moony, muni, puisne, puny, spoony, Zuni
  Mulroney

oop \üp\ bloop, coop, croup, droop, drupe, dupe, goop, group, hoop, loop, loupe, poop, roup, scoop, sloop, snoop, soup, stoop, stoup, stupe, swoop, troop, troupe, whoop
  age-group, in-group, out-group, recoup, regroup, subgroup, T-group
  alley-oop, cock-a-hoop, Guadalupe, Guadeloupe, nincompoop, paratroop, supergroup

o-op \üp\ see oop¹

ooped \üpd\ looped
  —also -ed forms of verbs listed at oop

oopee \ü-pē\ see oopy

ooper \ü-pər\ blooper, cooper, Cooper, Cowper, duper, grouper, looper, scooper, snooper, stupor, swooper, super, trooper, trouper
  party pooper, paratrooper, pooper-scooper, super-duper

ooping \ü-piŋ\ grouping, trooping, trouping
  —also -ing forms of verbs listed at oop

oopoe \ü-pü\ see ooh-pooh

oops \ùps\ hoops, oops, whoops, woops

oopy \ü-pē\ croupy, droopy, groupie, Kewpie, loopy, snoopy, soupy, Tupi, whoopee

oor¹ \òr\ see or¹

oor² \ùr\ see ure¹

oorage¹ \ùr-ij\ moorage
  sewerage

oorage² \òr-ij\ see orage²

oore¹ \òr\ see or¹

oore² \ùr\ see ure¹

oored \òrd\ see oard

oorer \òr-ər\ see orer

oori \ùr-ē\ see ury¹

ooring¹ \òr-iŋ\ see oring

ooring² \ùr-iŋ\ see uring

oorish¹ \ùr-ish\ boorish, Moorish, poorish

oorish² \òr-ish\ see orish¹

oorly \ùr-lē\ see urely

oorman \òr-mən\ see orman

oors \órz\ Bors, drawers, yours
Azores, indoors, outdoors
underdrawers, withindoors,
withoutdoors
Louis Quatorze
—*also* -s, -'s, *and* -s' *forms of nouns,
and* -s *forms of verbs, listed at* or[1]

oorsman \órz-mən\ see oarsman

oort \órt\ see ort[1]

oosa \ü-sə\ see usa[1]

oose[1] \üs\ see use[1]

oose[2] \üz\ see use[2]

ooser[1] \ü-sər\ see ucer

ooser[2] \ü-zər\ see user

oosey \ü-sē\ see uicy

oosh[1] \üsh\ see ouche

oosh[2] \ush\ see ush[2]

oost \üst\ boost, juiced, Proust,
roost
langouste, produced
self-induced, Zlatoust
—*also* -ed *forms of verbs listed at*
use[1]

oosy \ü-zē\ see oozy

oot[1] \ut\ foot, put, root, Root, soot
afoot, barefoot, bigfoot, bird's-foot,
Blackfoot, clubfoot, crow's-foot,
enroot, flatfoot, forefoot, hotfoot,
input, kaput, outfoot, output, Rajput,
shot put, snakeroot, splayfoot, taproot,
throughput, uproot
acre-foot, arrowroot, bitterroot,
cajeput, candle-foot, gingerroot,
orrisroot, pussyfoot, tenderfoot,
underfoot

oot[2] \üt\ see ute

oot[3] \ət\ see ut[1]

ootage[1] \üt-ij\ fruitage, rootage,
scutage

ootage[2] \ut-ij\ footage, rootage

ooted[1] \üt-əd\ booted, fruited,
muted, suited
abluted, deep-rooted, jackbooted,
pantsuited, voluted
—*also* -ed *forms of verbs listed at*
ute

ooted[2] \ut-əd\ footed
barefooted, clubfooted, deep-rooted,
duckfooted, fleet-footed, four-footed,
light-footed, slow-footed, splayfooted,
surefooted, web-footed, wing-footed
cloven-footed
—*also* -ed *forms of verbs listed at*
oot[1]

ooter[1] \ut-ər\ footer, putter
shot-putter
pussyfooter

ooter[2] \üt-ər\ see uter

ooth[1] \üth\ smooth, soothe, tooth

ooth[2] \üth\ booth, Booth, couth,
crwth, routh, ruth, Ruth, scouth,
sleuth, sooth, tooth, truth, Truth, youth
bucktooth, Duluth, eyetooth,
forsooth, half-truth, sawtooth,
selcouth, tollbooth, uncouth, untruth,
vermouth
snaggletooth

oothe \üth\ see ooth[1]

oothed \ütht\ toothed
gap-toothed
snaggletoothed

oothless \üth-ləs\ see uthless

oothly \üth-lē\ soothly
uncouthly

oothy \ü-thē\ couthie, toothy

ootie \üt-ē\ see ooty[1]

ooting[1] \ut-iŋ\ footing
off-putting
—*also* -ing *forms of verbs listed at*
oot[1]

ooting[2] \üt-iŋ\ see uting

ootle \üt-ᵊl\ see utile

ootless \üt-ləs\ bootless, fruitless

ootlet \üt-lət\ fruitlet, rootlet

oots \üts\ boots
firstfruits, grassroots, slyboots, Vaduz
shoot-the-chutes
—also -s, -'s, and -s' forms of nouns, and -s forms of verbs, listed at ute

ootsie \üt-sē\ footsie, tootsie

ooty[1] \üt-ē\ beauty, booty, Clootie, cootie, cutie, duty, footy, fluty, fruity, hooty, rooty, snooty, sooty, tutti, zooty
agouti, Djibouti
Funafuti, heavy-duty, persecutee, tutti-frutti

ooty[2] \ùt-ē\ rooty, sooty, tutti

ooty[3] \ət-ē\ see utty

oove \üv\ see ove[3]

oover \ü-vər\ see over[3]

oovy \ü-vē\ groovy, movie

ooze \üz\ see use[2]

oozer \ü-zər\ see user

oozle \ü-zəl\ see usal[2]

oozy \ü-zē\ bluesy, boozy, choosy, floozy, newsy, oozy, Susie, woozy
Jacuzzi

op[1] \äp\ bop, chap, chop, clop, cop, crop, drop, flop, fop, glop, hop, knop, lop, mop, op, plop, pop, prop, scop, shop, slop, sop, stop, strop, swap, top, whop
Aesop, airdrop, atop, backdrop, backstop, bakeshop, barhop, bebop, bellhop, blacktop, bookshop, carhop, cartop, chop-chop, clip-clop, clop-clop, coin-op, cooktop, co-op, desktop, dewdrop, doorstop, dramshop, Dunlop, eardrop, eavesdrop, ESOP, estop, f-stop, firestop, flattop, flip-flop, foretop, grogshop, gumdrop, hardtop, hedgehop, high-top, hilltop, hip-hop,

hockshop, housetop, joypop, maintop, milksop, nonstop, one-stop, outcrop, pawnshop, pop-top, ragtop, raindrop, redtop, ripstop, rooftop, sharecrop, shortstop, skin-pop, slipslop, snowdrop, soursop, stonecrop, sweatshop, sweetshop, teardrop, tiptop, treetop, unstop, workshop
agitprop, barbershop, carrottop, countertop, double-crop, double-stop, Ethiop, island-hop, lollipop, malaprop, mom-and-pop, mountaintop, overtop, table-hop, tabletop, techno-pop, teenybop, turboprop, whistle-stop, window-shop
Babelthuap

op[2] \ō\ see ow[1]

opa \ō-pə\ opa, opah
Europa

opah \ō-pə\ see opa

opal \ō-pəl\ copal, nopal, opal, Opal
Simferopol
Constantinople

ope \ōp\ cope, coup, dope, grope, holp, hope, Hope, lope, mope, nope, ope, pope, Pope, rope, scop, scope, slope, soap, stope, taupe, tope, trope
aslope, borescope, downslope, elope, gantlope, gantelope, Good Hope, myope, nightscope, pyrope, sandsoap, soft-soap, tightrope, towrope
antelope, antipope, calliope, cantaloupe, chronoscope, envelope, epitope, Ethiope, gyroscope, horoscope, interlope, isotope, kinescope, microscope, misanthrope, periscope, phalarope, radarscope, sniperscope, snooperscope, stethoscope, telescope
heliotrope, kaleidoscope, stereoscope

opean \ō-pē-ən\ see opian

opee \ō-pē\ see opi

open \ō-pən\ holpen, open
reopen, wide-open

opence \əp-əns\ see uppance

openny \əp-nē\ threepenny, twopenny

oper \ō-pər\ coper, doper, groper, loper, moper, roper, soaper, toper
eloper, no-hoper, soft-soaper
interloper

opera \äp-rə\ see opra

opey \ō-pē\ see opi

oph \ōf\ see oaf

ophagous \äf-ə-gəs\ coprophagous, esophagus, necrophagous, sarcophagus, zoophagous
anthropophagous

ophagy \äf-ə-jē\ coprophagy, geophagy
anthropophagy

ophe¹ \ō-fē\ see ophy

ophe² \ȯf\ see off²

opher \ō-fər\ see ofer

ophet \äf-ət\ see ofit

ophic¹ \äf-ik\ strophic
antistrophic, apostrophic, catastrophic

ophic² \ō-fik\ strophic, trophic
atrophic

ophical \äf-i-kəl\ philosophical, theosophical

ophie \ō-fē\ see ophy

ophir \ō-fər\ see ofer

ophonous \äf-ə-nəs\ cacophonous, homophonous

ophony \äf-ə-nē\ cacophony, colophony, homophony, monophony, theophany
heterophony, stereophony

ophy \ō-fē\ Sophie, sophy, strophe, trophy

opi \ō-pē\ dopey, Hopi, mopey, ropy, soapy, topee, topi

opia \ō-pē-ə\ dystopia, myopia, sinopia, utopia
cornucopia, Ethiopia

opian \ō-pē-ən\ Aesopian, cyclopean, dystopian, utopian
cornucopian, Ethiopian

opic¹ \äp-ik\ topic, tropic
Aesopic, anthropic, ectopic, subtropic
Ethiopic, gyroscopic, hygroscopic, macroscopic, microscopic, misanthropic, periscopic, philanthropic, semitropic, stethoscopic, telescopic
kaleidoscopic, stereoscopic

opic² \ō-pik\ tropic
myopic
Ethiopic, psychotropic

opical \äp-i-kəl\ topical, tropical
anthropical, subtropical
microscopical, Neotropical, philanthropical, semitropical

oplar \äp-lər\ see oppler

ople \ō-pəl\ see opal

opol \ō-pəl\ see opal

opolis¹ \äp-ə-ləs\ propolis
acropolis, cosmopolis, metropolis, necropolis
Heliopolis, megalopolis
Florianopolis

opolis² \äp-ləs\ see opless

opolist \äp-ə-ləst\ monopolist
bibliopolist

opoly \äp-ə-lē\ choppily, floppily, sloppily
duopoly, monopoly, vox populi
oligopoly
Tiruchchirappalli

oppa \äp-ə\ see apa¹

opped \äpt\ see opt

oppel \äp-əl\ see opple

opper \äp-ər\ bopper, chopper, copper, cropper, dropper, flopper, hopper, lopper, mopper, popper, proper, shopper, stopper, swapper, topper, whopper, yapper
clodhopper, eavesdropper, eyedropper, eyepopper, grasshopper, hedgehopper, improper, job-hopper, joypopper, leafhopper, namedropper, rockhopper, sharecropper, showstopper, skin-popper, treehopper, woodchopper
table-hopper, teenybopper, window-shopper

oppery \äp-rē\ coppery, foppery

oppet \äp-ət\ moppet, poppet

oppily \äp-ə-lē\ see opoly

oppiness \äp-ē-nəs\ choppiness, floppiness, sloppiness

opping \äp-iŋ\ hopping, sopping, topping, whopping
clodhopping, eye-popping, job-hopping, name-dropping, outcropping
—*also* -ing *forms of verbs listed at* op¹

opple \äp-əl\ popple, stopple, topple
estoppel

oppler \äp-lər\ Doppler, poplar

oppy \äp-ē\ choppy, copy, crappie, floppy, gloppy, hoppy, kopje, poppy, sloppy, soppy, stroppy
jalopy, okapi, serape
microcopy, Nahuel Huapi, photocopy

opra \äp-rə\ copra, opera

ops \äps\ chops, copse, Ops, tops
beechdrops, cyclops, eyedrops, Pelops, pinedrops, sundrops
muttonchops
triceratops
—*also* -s, -'s, *and* -s' *forms of nouns, and* -s *forms of verbs, listed at* op¹

opse \äps\ see ops

opsy \äp-sē\ dropsy
autopsy, biopsy, necropsy

opt \äpt\ Copt, knopped, opt, topped
adopt, close-cropped, co-opt, end-stopped
—*also* -ed *forms of verbs listed at* op¹

opter \äp-tər\ copter
adopter
helicopter, ornithopter

optic \äp-tik\ Coptic, optic
panoptic, synoptic
electro-optic

optimist \äp-tə-məst\ optimist, Optimist
Soroptimist

option \äp-shən\ option
adoption, co-option

optric \äp-trik\ catoptric, dioptric

opula \äp-yə-lə\ copula, scopula

opulace \äp-yə-ləs\ populace, populous

opulate \äp-yə-lāt\ copulate, populate
overpopulate

opuli \äp-ə-lē\ see opoly

opulous \äp-yə-ləs\ see opulace

opus \ō-pəs\ opus
Canopus
magnum opus
pithecanthropus

opy¹ \ō-pē\ see opi

opy² \äp-ē\ see oppy

oque¹ \ōk\ see oke

oque² \äk\ see ock¹

oque³ \ȯk\ see alk

oquial \ō-kwē-əl\ colloquial
ventriloquial

or¹ \ȯr\ boar, Boer, Bohr, bore, chore, core, corps, crore, door, drawer, floor, for, fore, four, frore, gore, Gore,

hoar, hoer, kor, lore, Moore, mor,
more, More, nor, o'er, oar, or, ore,
poor, pore, pour, roar, score, shore,
snore, soar, sore, splore, spoor, spore,
store, swore, Thor, tor, tore, torr, war,
whore, wore, yore, your, you're
abhor, actor, adore, afore, and/or,
ashore, backdoor, bailor, bandore,
Beardmore, bedsore, before, bezoar,
bookstore, candor, captor, centaur,
claymore, closed-door, condor, decor,
deplore, dime-store, donor, downpour,
drugstore, encore, ephor, explore,
Exmoor, eyesore, feoffor, fetor,
Fillmore, folklore, footsore, forebore,
forswore, forscore, galore, hardcore,
ichor, ignore, implore, Indore, indoor,
inpour, inshore, Lahore, lakeshore,
Lenore, lessor, memoir, mentor,
Mysore, nearshore, Nestor, offshore,
onshore, outdoor, outpour, outsoar,
outwore, pastor, psywar, rancor,
rapport, raptor, Realtor, restore, rhetor,
savior, seafloor, seashore, sector,
seignior, senhor, señor, sensor, settlor,
Seymour, signor, smoothbore,
sophomore, stentor, stertor, stressor,
stridor, subfloor, temblor, tensor,
therefor, therefore, threescore, Timor,
trapdoor, turgor, uproar, vendor,
wherefore, woodlore
albacore, alongshore, anaphor,
anymore, archosaur, Baltimore,
Bangalore, Barrymore, brontosaur,
carnivore, CD4, Coimbatore,
commodore, comprador, confessor,
consignor, corridor, cuspidor, devisor,
dinosaur, door-to-door, Ecuador,
either-or, Eleanor, Eleanore, elector,
Elinor, en rapport, evermore,
franchisor, furthermore, guarantor,
Gwalior, hackamore, hadrosaur,
hellebore, herbivore, heretofore,
humidor, Labrador, louis d'or, man-of-
war, manticore, matador, metaphor,
meteor, millepore, Minotaur, mirador,
Mount Rushmore, nevermore,
omnivore, out-of-door, petit four,
picador, pinafore, pompadour,
predator, promisor, pterosaur,
reservoir, sagamore, Salvador,

Salvatore, semaphore, Singapore,
stegosaur, stevedore, superstore,
sycamore, Theodore, theretofore,
troubador, tug-of-war, two-by-four,
uncalled-for, underscore, vavasor,
warrantor
alienor, ambassador, ankylosaur,
conquistador, conservator, Corregidor,
de Pompadour, El Salvador, esprit de
corps, forevermore, hereinbefore,
ichthyosaur, insectivore, legislator,
plesiosaur, San Salvadore, toreador,
tyrannosaur, Ulan Bator
administrator, lobster thermidor
Talleyrand-Perigord

or² \ər\ see **eur¹**

ora \ȯr-ə\ aura, bora, Cora, Dora,
flora, Flora, hora, Laura, Lora, mora,
Nora, sora, Torah
Andorra, angora, aurora, Aurora,
begorra, camorra, fedora, gemara,
Gomorrah, Lenora, Masora, menorah,
pandora, Pandora, remora, senhora,
señora, signora, Sonora
grandiflora, Juiz de Fora, Leonora,
Simchas Torah, Tuscarora
Lomas de Zamora

orable \ȯr-ə-bəl\ horrible, pourable,
storable
adorable, deplorable, restorable

orace \ȯr-əs\ see **aurus**

oracle \ȯr-ə-kəl\ coracle, oracle

orage¹ \är-ij\ barrage, borage,
forage, porridge

orage² \ȯr-ij\ borage, floorage,
forage, porridge, storage

orah \ȯr-ə\ see **ora**

oral¹ \ȯr-əl\ aural, choral, coral,
Coral, floral, laurel, Laurel, moral,
oral, quarrel, sorrel
aboral, amoral, auroral, balmoral,
binaural, immoral, monaural, peroral,
restoral, sororal

oral² \ȯrl\ see **orl²**

oram \ȯr-əm\ see orum

orate \ȯr-ət\ see oret

orative \ȯr-ət-iv\ explorative, pejorative, restorative

oray \ə-rē\ see urry

orb \ȯrb\ forb, orb, sorb, Sorb absorb, adsorb, desorb, resorb

orbate \ȯr-bət\ see orbit

orbeil \ȯr-bəl\ see orbel

orbel \ȯr-bəl\ corbeil, corbel, warble

orbent \ȯr-bənt\ absorbent immunosorbent

orbet \ȯr-bət\ see orbit

orbit \ȯr-bət\ orbit, sorbet adsorbate

orc \ȯrk\ see ork²

orca \ȯr-ka\ orca Majorca, Minorca Palma de Mallorca

orcas \ȯr-kəs\ Dorcas, orchis

orce \ȯrs\ see orse¹

orced \ȯrst\ see orst¹

orceful \ȯrs-fəl\ see orseful

orcement \ȯr-smənt\ see orsement

orcer \ȯr-sər\ courser, forcer discourser, enforcer reinforcer
—also -er forms of adjectives listed at orse¹

orch \ȯrch\ porch, scorch, torch blowtorch, sunporch

orcher \ȯr-chər\ scorcher, torture

orchid \ȯr-kəd\ forked, orchid cryptorchid, monorchid

orchis \ȯr-kəs\ see orcas

ord¹ \ȯrd\ see oard

ord² \ərd\ see ird

ord³ \ȯr\ see or¹

ordan \ȯrd-ᵊn\ see arden²

ordancy \ȯrd-ᵊn-sē\ mordancy discordancy

ordant \ȯrd-ᵊnt\ mordant, mordent accordant, concordant, discordant

orde \ȯrd\ see oard

orded \ȯrd-əd\ see arded²

ordent \ȯrd-ᵊnt\ see ordant

order \ȯrd-ər\ boarder, border, corder, hoarder, order, warder awarder, disorder, keyboarder, recorder, reorder, rewarder, skateboarder, surfboarder made-to-order

ordered \ȯrd-ərd\ bordered, ordered
—also -ed forms of verbs listed at order

orders \ȯrd-ərz\ Borders
—also -s, -'s, and -s' forms of nouns, and -s forms of verbs, listed at order

ordial \ȯrd-ē-əl\ exordial, primordial

ordid \ȯrd-əd\ see arded²

ording¹ \ȯrd-iŋ\ boarding, hoarding, lording recording, rewarding, skateboarding weatherboarding
—also -ing forms of verbs listed at oard

ording² \ərd-iŋ\ see erding

ordingly \ȯrd-iŋ-lē\ accordingly, rewardingly

ordion \ȯrd-ē-ən\ accordion, Edwardian

ordist \ȯrd-əst\ recordist clavichordist, harpsichordist

ordon \ȯrd-ᵊn\ see arden²

ordure \ȯr-jər\ see orger

ordy¹ \órd-ē\ Geordie, Lordy
awardee

ordy² \ərd-ē\ see urdy

ore¹ \ór-ē\ see ory

ore² \ùr\ see ure¹

ore³ \ər-ə\ see orough¹

ore⁴ \ór\ see or¹

oreal \ór-ē-əl\ see orial

orean \ór-ē-ən\ see orian

oreas \ór-ē-əs\ see orious

ored \órd\ see oard

oredom \órd-əm\ boredom,
whoredom

orehead \ór-əd\ see orrid

oreign¹ \är-ən\ see arin

oreign² \ór-ən\ see orin¹

oreigner \ór-ə-nər\ see oroner

orem \ór-əm\ see orum

oreman \ór-mən\ see orman

orence \ór-ən(t)s\ see awrence

oreous \ór-ē-əs\ see orious

orer \ór-ər\ borer, corer, floorer,
horror, pourer, roarer, scorer,
schnorrer, snorer, soarer, sorer
abhorer, adorer, deplorer, explorer
—also -er forms of adjectives listed
at or¹

ores¹ \ór-əs\ see aurus

ores² \órz\ see oors

oreson \órs-ᵊn\ see oarsen

orest \ór-əst\ see orist

orester \ór-ə-stər\ see orister

oret \ór-ət\ floret, sororate

oreum \ór-ē-əm\ see orium

oreward \ór-wərd\ see orward

oreword \ór-wərd\ see orward

orey \ór-ē\ see ory

orf \órf\ see orph

org¹ \órg\ morgue
cyborg

org² \ór-ē\ see ory

organ \ór-gən\ gorgon, morgan,
Morgan, organ
Glamorgan
Demogorgon, Mid Glamorgan,
South Glamorgan, West Glamorgan

orge \órj\ forge, George, gorge,
scourge
disgorge, drop-forge, engorge, Lloyd
George, reforge
Olduvai Gorge

orger \ór-jər\ bordure, forger,
gorger, ordure

orgi \ór-gē\ see orgy

orgia \ór-jə\ Borgia, Georgia
Strait of Georgia

orgian \ór-jən\ Georgian
Swedenborgian

orgon \ór-gən\ see organ

orgue \órg\ see org

orgy \ór-gē\ corgi, porgy

ori \ór-ē\ see ory

oria \ór-ē-ə\ gloria, Gloria, noria,
scoria
centaurea, euphoria, Peoria, Pretoria,
victoria, Victoria, Vitoria
phantasmagoria

orial \ór-ē-əl\ boreal, oriel, oriole
arboreal, armorial, auctorial,
authorial, cantorial, censorial,
corporeal, cursorial, factorial,
fossorial, manorial, marmoreal,
memorial, pictorial, praetorial,
proctorial, raptorial, rectorial,
sartorial, seignorial, sensorial,
sponsorial, tonsorial, tutorial, uxorial,
vectorial

conductorial, consistorial, curatorial,
dictatorial, directorial, editorial,
equatorial, immemorial, incorporeal,
janitorial, monitorial, monsignorial,
natatorial, piscatorial, preceptorial,
professorial, purgatorial, reportorial,
senatorial, territorial
  ambassadorial, conservatorial,
combinatorial, conspiratorial,
extracorporeal, gladiatorial,
gubernatorial, imperatorial,
inquisitorial, legislatorial,
procuratorial, propriatorial,
prosecutorial
    extraterritorial, improvisatorial

oriam \ȯr-ē-əm\ see orium

orian \ȯr-ē-ən\ Dorian, saurian,
Taurean
  aurorean, Gregorian, historian,
Nestorian, praetorian, stentorian,
victorian
    dinosaurian, hyperborean, Oratorian,
prehistorian, senatorian, terpsichorean
      salutatorian, valedictorian

oriant \ȯr-ē-ənt\ see orient

oriat \ȯr-ē-ət\ see aureate[2]

oric \ȯr-ik\ auric, choric, Doric,
toric
  Armoric, caloric, clitoric, dysphoric,
euphoric, folkloric, historic,
phosphoric, plethoric, pyloric
    anaphoric, cataphoric, metaphoric,
meteoric, paregoric, prehistoric,
sophomoric
      aleatoric, phantasmagoric

orical \ȯr-i-kəl\ auricle
  historical, rhetorical
    ahistorical, allegorical, categorical,
metaphorical, oratorical,
transhistorical
      sociohistorical

orics \ȯr-iks\ see oryx

orid \ȯr-əd\ see orrid

oriel \ȯr-ē-əl\ see orial

orient \ȯr-ē-ənt\ orient, Orient
euphoriant

orin[1] \ȯr-ən\ chlorine, florin,
foreign, Lauren, Orrin, sporran,
warren, Warren
  cyclosporine
    cephalosporin

orin[2] \är-ən\ see arin

orine \ȯr-ən\ see orin[1]

oring \ȯr-iŋ\ boring, flooring,
roaring, shoring
  inpouring, longshoring, outpouring,
rip-roaring
  —also -ing forms of verbs listed at
or[1]

öring \ər-iŋ\ see urring

oriole \ȯr-ē-əl\ see orial

orious \ȯr-ē-əs\ aureus, Boreas,
glorious
  arboreous, censorious, inglorious,
laborious, notorious, sartorius,
uproarious, uxorious, vainglorious,
victorious
    meritorious

oris \ȯr-əs\ see aurus

orish[1] \ȯr-ish\ boarish, poorish,
whorish
  folklorish

orish[2] \u̇r-ish\ see oorish[1]

orist \ȯr-əst\ florist, forest, Forrest,
sorest
  afforest, Black Forest, deforest,
folklorist, reforest
    allegorist
    Petrified Forest
  —also -est forms of adjectives listed
at or[1]

orister \ȯr-ə-stər\ chorister, forester

ority \ȯr-ət-ē\ authority, majority,
minority, priority, seniority, sonority
  apriority
    exteriority, inferiority, interiority,
posteriority, superiority

orium \ȯr-ē-əm\ castoreum,
ciborium, emporium, pastorium,
scriptorium, sensorium

auditorium, crematorium, in memoriam, moratorium, natatorium, sanitorium, sudatorium

ork¹ \ərk\ burke, Burke, chirk, cirque, clerk, dirk, Dirk, irk, jerk, kirk, Kirk, lurk, murk, perk, quirk, shirk, smirk, stirk, Turk, work, yerk, zerk
artwork, berserk, breastwork, brickwork, bridgework, brightwork, brushwork, capework, casework, clockwork, coachwork, de Klerk, ductwork, Dunkirk, earthwork, falsework, fieldwork, firework, flatwork, footwork, formwork, framework, goldwork, groundwork, guesswork, hackwork, handwork, headwork, homework, housework, ironwork, knee-jerk, legwork, lifework, make-work, meshwork, millwork, network, outwork, paintwork, patchwork, piecework, presswork, quillwork, rework, roadwork, salesclerk, schoolwork, Selkirk, Southwark, spadework, steelwork, stickwork, stonework, teamwork, timework, topwork, waxwork, webwork, woodwork
basketwork, busywork, crewelwork, donkeywork, fancywork, handiwork, journeywork, laquerwork, masterwork, needlework, openwork, overwork, paperwork, plasterwork, soda jerk, wonderwork
cabinetwork

ork² \ȯrk\ cork, Cork, dork, fork, pork, quark, stork, torque, York
bulwark, Cape York, futhorc, hayfork, New York, North York, pitchfork, uncork

orked¹ \ȯrkt\ corked, forked
uncorked

orked² \ȯr-kəd\ see orchid

orker¹ \ər-kər\ jerker, lurker, shirker, worker
berserker, caseworker, dockworker, fieldworker, handworker, ironworker, outworker, pieceworker, steelworker, tearjerker, wageworker, woodworker

autoworker, metalworker, needleworker, wonderworker

orker² \ȯr-kər\ corker, forker, porker, torquer

orkie \ȯr-kē\ see orky

orking \ər-kiŋ\ hardworking, tearjerking, woodworking
wonder-working
—also -ing forms of verbs listed at ork¹

orky \ȯr-kē\ corky, dorky, forky, Gorky, porky, Yorkie

orl¹ \ərl\ see irl¹

orl² \ȯrl\ schorl, whorl
ceorl

orld \ərld\ burled, knurled, whorled, world
dreamworld, New World, old-world
demiworld, microworld, netherworld, otherworld, underworld
—also -ed forms of verbs listed at irl¹

orled \ərld\ see orld

orm¹ \ərm\ berm, firm, germ, herm, perm, Perm, sperm, squirm, term, therm, worm
affirm, bookworm, budworm, confirm, cutworm, deperm, deworm, earthworm, flatworm, glowworm, heartworm, hookworm, hornworm, inchworm, infirm, long-term, lugworm, lungworm, midterm, pinworm, ringworm, roundworm, sandworm, screwworm, short-term, silkworm, tapeworm, woodworm
angleworm, armyworm, caddis worm, disaffirm, disconfirm, gymnosperm, pachyderm, reconfirm
angiosperm, echinoderm

orm² \ȯrm\ corm, dorm, form, norm, storm, swarm, warm
aswarm, barnstorm, brainstorm, conform, deform, Delorme, firestorm, free-form, hailstorm, inform, L-form, landform, life-form, lukewarm, perform, planform, platform,

postform, preform, rainstorm, re-form,
reform, sandstorm, snowstorm,
transform, triform, windstorm
  chloroform, cruciform, dendriform,
dentiform, disciform, fungiform,
funnelform, fusiform, letterform,
microform, multiform, nonconform,
thunderstorm, uniform, vermiform

ormable \òr-mə-bəl\ formable
  conformable, performable,
transformable

ormal \òr-məl\ formal, normal
  abnormal, conformal, informal,
subnormal
  paranormal, semiformal,
supernormal

ormally \òr-mə-lē\ formally,
formerly, normally, stormily
  abnormally, informally, subnormally
paranormally, supernormally

orman \òr-mən\ corpsman,
doorman, foreman, Mormon, Norman
longshoreman
  Anglo-Norman

ormance \òr-məns\ conformance,
performance
  nonconformance

ormant \òr-mənt\ dormant, formant
informant

ormative \òr-mət-iv\ formative,
normative
  informative, performative,
reformative, transformative

orme \òrm\ see orm²

ormed \òrmd\ formed, normed
  informed, malformed, unformed
  —also -ed *forms of verbs listed at*
orm²

ormer¹ \òr-mər\ dormer, former,
swarmer, warmer
  barnstormer, benchwarmer,
brainstormer, conformer, heart-
warmer, informer, performer,
reformer, transformer

ormer² \ər-mər\ see urmur

ormerly \òr-mə-lē\ see ormally

ormie \òr-mē\ see ormy¹

ormily \òr-mə-lē\ see ormally

orming \òr-miŋ\ brainstorming,
heartwarming, housewarming
habit-forming, nonperforming
  —also -ing *forms of verbs listed at*
orm²

ormist \òr-məst\ warmest
  conformist, reformist
nonconformist

ormity \òr-mət-ē\ conformity,
deformity, enormity
  nonconformity, uniformity

ormless \òrm-ləs\ formless,
gormless

ormon \òr-mən\ see orman

ormy¹ \òr-mē\ dormie, stormy

ormy² \ər-mē\ see ermy

orn¹ \òrn\ born, borne, bourn, corn,
horn, lorn, morn, mourn, Norn, porn,
scorn, shorn, sworn, thorn, torn, warn,
worn
  acorn, adorn, airborne, alphorn,
althorn, baseborn, bicorne, bighorn,
blackthorn, boxthorn, broomcorn,
buckthorn, bullhorn, Cape Horn,
careworn, Christ's-thorn, Dearborn,
dehorn, earthborn, einkorn, firethorn,
firstborn, foghorn, foreborn,
foresworn, forewarn, forlorn, forworn,
freeborn, greenhorn, hartshorn,
hawthorn, Hawthorne, highborn,
inborn, inkhorn, krummhorn, leghorn,
longhorn, lovelorn, lowborn, newborn,
outworn, popcorn, pronghorn, reborn,
seaborne, shipborne, shoehorn,
shopworn, shorthorn, skyborne,
soilborne, staghorn, stillborn,
stinkhorn, suborn, timeworn, tinhorn,
tricorne, trueborn, twice-born, unborn,
unworn, wayworn, wellborn, well-
worn, wind-borne

alpenhorn, barleycorn, Capricorn, flügelhorn, foreign-born, Golden Horn, Matterhorn, peppercorn, unicorn, waterborne, waterworn, weatherworn, winterbourne

orn² \ərn\ see urn

ornament \ȯr-nə-mənt\ ornament, tournament

orne \ȯrn\ see orn¹

orned \ȯrnd\ horned, thorned
unadorned
—*also* -ed *forms of verbs listed at* orn¹

orner \ȯr-nər\ warner, Warner
Cape Horner, dehorner, suborner

ornery \än-rē\ see annery¹

orney \ər-nē\ see ourney¹

ornful \ȯrn-fəl\ mournful, scornful

ornice \ȯr-nəs\ cornice, ornice
notornis

orning \ȯr-niŋ\ morning, mourning, warning
aborning

ornis \ȯr-nəs\ see ornice

ornment \ərn-mənt\ see ernment

orny \ȯr-nē\ corny, horny, porny, thorny, tourney

oro¹ \ər-ə\ see orough¹

oro² \ȯ-rō\ Chamorro, Mindoro
Rio de Oro

oroner \ȯr-ə-nər\ coroner, foreigner, warrener

orough¹ \ər-ə\ borough, burgh, burro, burrow, curragh, furrow, ore, thorough
Gainsborough, Greensboro, Roxborough, Scarborough, Yarborough
Edinburgh, kookaburra, Peterborough
Soke of Peterborough
Huntingdon and Peterborough

orough² \ər-ō\ see urrow¹

orous \ȯr-əs\ see aurus

orp \ȯrp\ dorp, gorp, thorp, warp
Australorp, Krugersdorp, octothorp, Oglethorpe

orpe \ȯrp\ see orp

orper \ȯr-pər\ dorper, torpor

orph \ȯrf\ corf, dwarf, morph
Düsseldorf
anthropomorph

orphan \ȯr-fən\ orphan
endorphin
beta-endorphin

orpheus \ȯr-fē-əs\ Morpheus, Orpheus

orphic \ȯr-fik\ orphic
ectomorphic, endomorphic, mesomorphic, metamorphic, pseudomorphic
anthropomorphic

orphin \ȯr-fən\ see orphan

orphous \ȯr-fəs\ amorphous
isomorphous

orphrey \ȯr-frē\ orphrey, porphyry

orphyrin \ȯr-fə-rən\ see arfarin

orphyry \ȯr-frē\ see orphrey

orpoise \ȯr-pəs\ see orpus

orpor \ȯr-pər\ see orper

orps \ȯr\ see or¹

orpsman \ȯr-mən\ see orman

orpus \ȯr-pəs\ corpus, porpoise
habeas corpus

orque \ȯrk\ see ork²

orquer \ȯr-kər\ see orker²

orr \ȯr\ see or¹

orra¹ \är-ə\ see ara¹

orra² \ȯr-ə\ see ora

orrader \är-əd-ər\ see orridor

orrah¹ \ȯr-ə\ see ora

orrah² \är-ə\ see ara¹

orran¹ \är-ən\ see arin

orran² \ȯr-ən\ see orin¹

orrence \ȯr-əns\ see awrence

orrel \ȯr-əl\ see oral¹

orrent \ȯr-ənt\ horrent, torrent, warrant
abhorrent

orrer \ȯr-ər\ see orer

orres \ȯr-əs\ see aurus

orrest \ȯr-əst\ see orist

orrible \ȯr-ə-bəl\ see orable

orrid \ȯr-əd\ florid, horrid, torrid

orridge¹ \är-ij\ see orage¹

orridge² \ȯr-ij\ see orage²

orridor \är-əd-ər\ corridor, forrader

orrie¹ \är-ē\ see ari¹

orrie² \ȯr-ē\ see ory

orrier \ȯr-ē-ər\ see arrior

orrin¹ \är-en\ see arin

orrin² \ȯr-ən\ see orin¹

orris¹ \är-əs\ charas, Ju·rez, Maurice, morris, Morris, Norris, orris
Banaras, Benares, Polaris
Ciudad Juárez

orris² \ȯr-əs\ see aurus

orro \ȯ-rō\ see oro²

orror \ȯr-ər\ see orer

orrow¹ \är-ō\ borrow, claro, morrow, sorrow, taro
Pizarro, saguaro, tomorrow
Catanzaro
Kilimanjaro, Mohenjo-Daro

orrow² \är-ə\ see ara¹

orry¹ \är-ē\ see ari¹

orry² \ər-ē\ see urry

ors \ȯrz\ see oors

orsal \ȯr-səl\ see orsel

orse¹ \ȯrs\ coarse, corse, course, force, gorse, hoarse, horse, Morse, Norse, source
clotheshorse, concourse, deforce, discourse, divorce, endorse, enforce, extrorse, introrse, midcourse, packhorse, perforce, post-horse, racecourse, racehorse, recourse, remorse, resource, retrorse, sawhorse, stringcourse, unhorse, war-horse, Whitehorse, workhorse
charley horse, Crazy Horse, hobbyhorse, intercourse, nonrecourse, reinforce, stalking-horse, telecourse, tour de force, watercourse

orse² \ərs\ see erse

orseful \ȯrs-fəl\ forceful
remorseful, resourceful

orsel \ȯr-səl\ dorsal, morsel

orseman \ȯr-smən\ horseman, Norseman

orsement \ȯr-smənt\ deforcement, divorcement, endorsement, enforcement
reinforcement

orsen \ərs-ᵊn\ see erson

orser \ər-sər\ see ursor

orset \ȯr-sət\ corset, Dorset

orsey \ȯr-sē\ see orsy

orsion \ȯr-shən\ see ortion

orst¹ \ȯrst\ forced, horst
—also -ed forms of verbs listed at orse¹

orst² \ərst\ see urst

orsted \ər-stəd\ see ersted

orsum \òr-səm\ dorsum, foursome

orsy \òr-sē\ gorsy, horsey

ort¹ \òrt\ boart, bort, court, fort, forte, mort, Oort, ort, port, Porte, quart, short, snort, sort, sport, swart, thwart, tort, torte, wart, wort
  abort, airport, amort, aport, assort, athwart, backcourt, bellwort, birthwort, bistort, Bridgeport, cavort, cohort, colewort, comport, consort, contort, crosscourt, deport, disport, distort, downcourt, effort, escort, exhort, export, extort, forecourt, frontcourt, glasswort, gosport, half-court, homeport, milkwort, Newport, outport, passport, presort, purport, ragwort, report, re-sort, resort, retort, seaport, Shreveport, spaceport, spoilsport, Stockport, support, transport
    bladderwort, davenport, life-support, nonsupport, pennywort, Saint-John's wort, teleport, ultrashort, worrywart
      pianoforte, underreport

ort² \òr\ see or¹

ort³ \ərt\ see ert¹

ortable \òrt-ə-bəl\ portable
  deportable, exportable, importable, reportable, supportable, transportable
    insupportable

ortage \òrt-ij\ portage, shortage
  colportage

ortal \òrt-ᵊl\ chortle, mortal, portal, quartile
  immortal

ortar \òrt-ər\ see orter

ortative \òrt-ət-iv\ hortative, portative
  assortative, exhortative

orte¹ \òrt\ see ort¹

orte² \òrt-ē\ see orty

orted \òrt-əd\ warted
  assorted, ill-sorted
    —also -ed forms of verbs listed at ort¹

ortedly \òrt-əd-lē\ purportedly, reportedly

orten \òrt-ᵊn\ quartan, shorten
  foreshorten

orter \òrt-ər\ mortar, porter, Porter, quarter, snorter, sorter, thwarter
  aborter, colporteur, distorter, exhorter, exporter, extorter, headquarter, importer, lambs-quarter, reporter, resorter, ripsnorter, transporter
    —also -er forms of adjectives listed at ort¹

orteur \òrt-ər\ see orter

orth¹ \òrth\ forth, Forth, fourth, north, North
  thenceforth
    Firth of Forth

orth² \ərth\ see irth

orthful \ərth-fəl\ see irthful

orthless \ərth-ləs\ see irthless

orthy \ər-thē\ earthy, worthy
  airworthy, blameworthy, Galsworthy, newsworthy, noteworthy, praiseworthy, seaworthy, trustworthy
    creditworthy

ortic \òrt-ik\ see artic²

ortical \òrt-i-kəl\ cortical, vortical

ortie \òrt-ē\ see orty

orting \òrt-iŋ\ sporting
  self-supporting

ortion \òr-shən\ portion, torsion
  abortion, apportion, contortion, distortion, extorsion, extortion, proportion, retortion
    disproportion, proabortion, reapportion
      antiabortion

ortionate \òr-shnət\ extortionate, proportionate
  disproportionate

ortionist \òr-shnəst\ abortionist, contortionist, extortionist

ortis \òrt-əs\ fortis, mortise, tortoise
aquafortis, rigor mortis

ortise \òrt-əs\ see ortis

ortive \òrt-iv\ sportive
abortive, contortive, extortive

ortle \òrt-ᵊl\ see ortal

ortly \òrt-lē\ courtly, portly, shortly,
thwartly

ortment \òrt-mənt\ assortment,
comportment, deportment,
disportment

ortoise \òrt-əs\ see ortis

orton \òrt-ᵊn\ Morton, Norton,
Wharton

orts \òrts\ quartz, shorts, sports
undershorts
—*also* -s, -'s, *and* -s' *forms of nouns,
and* -s *forms of verbs, listed at* ort¹

ortunate \òrch-nət\ fortunate
importunate, unfortunate

orture \òr-chər\ see orcher

orty \òrt-ē\ forty, shorty, sortie,
sporty, warty
mezzo forte
pianoforte

orum \òr-əm\ foram, forum, jorum,
quorum
decorum, Mizoram
ad valorem, cockalorum, indecorum,
Karakoram, variorum
pons asinorum, sanctum sanctorum,
schola cantorum

orus \òr-əs\ see aurus

orward \òr-wərd\ forward,
foreward, shoreward
henceforward
carryforward

ory \òr-ē\ Corey, corrie, dory, glory,
gory, hoary, Laurie, Lori, lorry, lory,
nori, quarry, saury, sorry, story, Tory,
zori

centaury, clerestory, John Dory,
outlawry, satori, vainglory
a priori, allegory, amatory, auditory,
cacciatore, castratory, category, con
amore, crematory, damnatory,
decretory, desultory, dilatory,
dormitory, expletory, feudatory,
fumitory, Göteborg, gustatory,
gyratory, hortatory, hunky-dory,
inventory, Lake Maggiore, laudatory,
lavatory, mandatory, migratory,
minatory, monitory, Montessori,
nugatory, offertory, oratory, overstory,
predatory, prefatory, probatory,
promissory, promontory, purgatory,
repertory, Ruwenzori, signatory,
statutory, sudatory, territory, transitory,
understory, vibratory, vomitory,
yakitori
accusatory, admonitory, adulatory, a
fortiori, aleatory, ambulatory,
amendatory, applicatory, approbatory,
celebratory, circulatory, combinatory,
commendatory, compensatory,
condemnatory, confirmatory,
confiscatory, conservatory,
consolatory, contributory, copulatory,
cosignatory, declamatory, declaratory,
dedicatory, defamatory, denigratory,
depilatory, depository, derogatory,
designatory, dispensatory, divinatory,
escalatory, excitatory, exclamatory,
exculpatory, excusatory, exhibitory,
exhortatory, expiatory, expiratory,
explanatory, explicatory, exploratory,
expository, expurgatory, incantatory,
incubatory, indicatory, inflammatory,
informatory, innovatory, inspiratory,
inundatory, invitatory, judicatory,
laboratory, masticatory, masturbatory,
memento mori, millefiori, modulatory,
obfuscatory, obligatory, observatory,
performatory, persecutory, predicatory,
premonitory, preparatory, prohibitory,
reformatory, regulatory, repository,
retributory, revelatory, respiratory,
salutatory, stipulatory, supplicatory,
transmigratory, undulatory
adjudicatory, a posteriori,
annihilatory, annunciatory,
anticipatory, appreciatory,

assimilatory, circumlocutory,
classificatory, concilliatory,
confabulatory, congratulatory, de-
escalatory, denunciatory, depreciatory,
discriminatory, ejaculatory,
hallucinatory, improvisatore,
improvisatory, interrogatory,
intimidatory, investigatory,
participatory, propitiatory,
recommendatory, recriminatory,
renunciatory, reverberatory, viola
d'amore
 amelioratory, overcompensatory,
 reconciliatory, supererogatory
 immunoregulatory

oryx \òr-iks\ oryx
Armorics
combinatorics

orze \òrz\ see oors

os[1] \äs\ boss, doss, dross, floss,
fosse, gloss, joss, Maas, os, pross,
stoss, toss
Argos, bathos, benthos, bugloss,
chaos, Chios, cosmos, Delos, demos,
Ellás, emboss, Eos, epos, Eros, ethos,
Hyksos, kaross, kudos, kvass, Lagos,
Laplace, Lemnos, Lesbos, Logos,
Madras, Melos, mythos, nol-pros,
nonpros, Paros, pathos, peplos,
pharos, ringtoss, Samos, telos, topos,
tripos
 coup de grace, demitasse, extrados,
gravitas, intrados, isogloss, omphalos,
reredos, semigloss, Thanatos,
underboss, volte-face

os[2] \ō\ see ow[1]

os[3] \ōs\ see ose[1]

os[4] \òs\ see oss[1]

osa[1] \ō-sə\ Xhosa
Formosa, mimosa, Reynosa
curiosa, virtuosa
anorexia nervosa

osa[2] \ō-zə\ mimosa, mucosa, serosa,
Spinoza, sub rosa
curiosa, virtuosa, Zaragoza

osable[1] \ō-zə-bəl\ closable
disposable, erosible, explosible,
opposable, reclosable, supposable
decomposable, superposable
indecomposable, superimposable

osable[2] \ü-zə-bəl\ see usable

osal \ō-zəl\ hosel, losel
deposal, disposal, proposal, reposal,
supposal

osan \ōs-ᵊn\ see osin

osch \äsh\ see ash[2]

oschen[1] \ō-shən\ see otion

oschen[2] \ò-shən\ see aution

oscible \äs-ə-bəl\ see ossible

osco \äs-kō\ see oscoe

oscoe \äs-kō\ Bosco, roscoe,
Roscoe
fiasco

oscopy \äs-kə-pē\ arthroscopy,
microscopy, spectroscopy
sigmoidoscopy

ose[1] \ōs\ close, dose, gross, os
arkose, Carlos, cosmos, crustose,
cymose, dextrose, engross, erose,
fructose, globose, glucose, jocose,
lactose, maltose, mannose, morose,
mythos, nodose, pappose, pathos,
pentose, pilose, plumose, ramose,
rhamnose, ribose, rugose, scapose,
schistose, setose, spinose, strigose,
sucrose, Sukkoth, triose, vadose,
verbose, viscose
 adios, adipose, bellicose, calvados,
cellulose, comatose, diagnose,
grandiose, granulose, Helios,
lachrymose, megadose, otiose,
overdose, racemose, Shabuoth,
tuberose, varicose, ventricose
 inter vivos, metamorphose, religiose
 inter alios

ose[2] \ōz\ brose, Broz, chose, close,
clothes, cloze, doze, froze, gloze,
hose, nose, pose, prose, rose, Rose

Ambrose, appose, aros, bedclothes,
bluenose, brownnose, bulldoze,
Burroughs, compose, depose,
dextrose, disclose, dispose, enclose,
expose, foreclose, fructose, glucose,
hardnose, impose, nightclothes,
oppose, plainclothes, primrose,
propose, quickfroze, repose, rockrose,
suppose, transpose, tuberose, unclose,
uprose, viscose, wind rose
    Berlioz, counterpose, decompose,
diagnose, discompose, indispose,
interpose, juxtapose, letters close,
pettitoes, predispose, presuppose,
pussytoes, recompose, shovelnose,
superpose, underclothes
    anastomose, metamorphose,
overexpose, superimpose,
underexpose
    —also -s, -'s, and -s' forms of nouns,
and -s forms of verbs, listed at ow¹

ose³ \üz\ see use²

osed \ōzd\ closed, nosed
composed, exposed, hard-nosed,
opposed, pug-nosed, snub-nosed,
stenosed, supposed, unclosed
indisposed, shovel-nosed, toffee-
nosed, well-disposed
    —also -ed forms of verbs listed at
ose²

osee \ō-zē\ see osy

osel \ō-zəl\ see osal

osen \ōz-ᵊn\ chosen, frozen
quickfrozen
lederhosen

oser¹ \ō-zər\ closer, dozer, poser,
proser
brownnoser, bulldozer, composer,
discloser, disposer, exposer, imposer,
opposer, proposer
decomposer, interposer
photocomposer

oser² \ü-zər\ see user

oset¹ \ō-zət\ see osit²

oset² \äz-ət\ see osit¹

oset³ \äs-ət\ see osset

osey \ō-zē\ see osy

osh¹ \ȯsh\ see ash²

osh² \ōsh\ see oche²

oshed¹ \äsht\ sloshed
galoshed
    —also -ed forms of verbs listed at
ash¹

oshed² \ȯsht\ see ashed¹

oshen \ō-shən\ see otion

osher \äsh-ər\ see asher¹

osia \ō-shə\ see otia¹

osible \ō-zə-bəl\ see osable¹

osier \ō-zhər\ see osure

osily \ō-zə-lē\ cozily, nosily, rosily

osin \ōs-ᵊn\ boatswain, Mosan
pocosin

osing \ō-ziŋ\ closing, nosing
disclosing, imposing, supposing
    —also -ing forms of verbs listed at
ose²

osion \ō-zhən\ plosion
corrosion, displosion, erosion,
explosion, implosion

osis \ō-səs\ gnosis
hypnosis, narcosis, necrosis,
neurosis, orthosis, osmosis, prognosis,
psychosis, sclerosis, thrombosis
brucellosis, cyanosis, dermatosis,
diagnosis, halitosis, heterosis,
psittacosis, scoliosis, silicosis,
symbiosis
anaplasmosis, autohypnosis,
coccidiosis, hyperhidrosis,
pediculosis, psychoneurosis,
tuberculosis
mononucleosis
immunodiagnosis, neurofibromatosis

osit¹ \äz-ət\ closet, posit
composite, deposit, exposit

osit² \ō-zət\ prosit, roset

osite \äz-ət\ see osit¹

ositive \äz-ət-iv\ positive
appositive
seropositive

ositor \äz-ət-ər\ compositor,
depositor, expositor

osius \ō-shəs\ see ocious

osive \ō-siv\ plosive
corrosive, erosive, explosive,
implosive, purposive

osk \äsk\ mosque
kiosk
abelmosk

oso¹ \ō-sō\ proso
maestoso, rebozo
arioso, furioso, gracioso, grandioso,
mafioso, Mato Grosso, oloroso,
spiritoso, vigoroso, virtuoso
concerto grosso

oso² \ō-zō\ bozo
rebozo
furioso, gracioso, grandioso,
spiritoso, vigoroso

oso³ \ü-sō\ see usoe

osophy \äs-ə-fē\ philosophy,
theosophy
anthroposophy

osque \äsk\ see osk

oss¹ \òs\ boss, cross, crosse, floss,
gloss, loss, moss, Ross, sauce, toss
across, bugloss, crisscross, emboss,
Kinross, kouros, lacrosse, outcross,
pathos, ringtoss, topcross, uncross
albatross, applesauce, autocross,
double-cross, intercross, motocross,
semigloss

oss² \ōs\ see ose¹

oss³ \äs\ see os¹

ossa \äs-ə\ see asa¹

ossable \äs-ə-bəl\ see ossible

ossal \äs-əl\ docile, dossal, fossil,
glossal, jostle, tassel, throstle, warsle,
wassail
apostle, colossal, indocile
isoglossal

osse¹ \äs\ see os¹

osse² \äs-ē\ see ossy¹

osse³ \òs\ see oss¹

ossed \òst\ see ost³

osser \ò-sər\ Chaucer, crosser,
saucer
double-crosser

osset \äs-ət\ cosset, faucet, Osset,
posset
Samoset

ossible \äs-ə-bəl\ possible
cognoscible, embossable, impossible

ossic \äs-ik\ see ossick

ossick \äs-ik\ fossick
isoglossic

ossil \äs-əl\ see ossal

ossity \äs-ət-ē\ atrocity, callosity,
ferocity, gibbosity, monstrosity,
pomposity, porosity, precocity,
velocity, viscosity, zygosity
adiposity, animosity, bellicosity,
curiosity, generosity, grandiosity,
hideosity, luminosity, nebulosity,
preciosity, reciprocity, scrupulosity,
sensuosity, sinuosity, strenuosity,
tortuosity, tuberosity, varicosity,
virtuosity
impetuosity, religiosity, voluminosity
impecuniosity

ossly \òs-lē\ costly, crossly

osso \ō-sō\ see oso¹

ossos \äs-əs\ see ocess

ossular \äs-ə-lər\ grossular,
wassailer

ossum \äs-əm\ blossom, passim, possum
opossum

ossus \äs-əs\ see ocess

ossy¹ \äs-ē\ Aussie, bossy, dassie, drossy, flossy, glossy, posse, quasi
dalasi, Kumasi, Likasi, sannyasi

ossy² \ȯ-sē\ Aussie, bossy, lossy, mossy

ost¹ \äst\ sol-faist
Pentecost, teleost
—also -ed *forms of verbs listed at* os¹

ost² \ōst\ boast, coast, ghost, host, most, oast, post, roast, toast
almost, bedpost, compost, doorpost, endmost, foremost, gatepost, goalpost, Gold Coast, guidepost, headmost, hindmost, impost, inmost, midmost, milepost, Milquetoast, outmost, outpost, provost, rearmost, riposte, seacoast, signpost, sternmost, sternpost, topmost, upcoast, upmost, utmost
aftermost, ante-post, bottommost, coast-to-coast, easternmost, farthermost, fingerpost, furthermost, headforemost, hithermost, innermost, Ivory Coast, lowermost, nethermost, northernmost, outermost, rudderpost, southernmost, sternforemost, undermost, uppermost, uttermost, westernmost

ost³ \ȯst\ cost, frost, lost
accost, defrost, exhaust, hoarfrost, star-crossed
holocaust, Pentecost, permafrost
—also -ed *forms of verbs listed at* oss¹

ost⁴ \əst\ see ust¹

osta \äs-tə\ costa, pasta

ostal¹ \ōs-tᵊl\ coastal, postal
bicoastal
intercostal

ostal² \äs-tᵊl\ see ostel

ostasy \äs-tə-sē\ apostasy, isostasy

oste \ōst\ see ost²

ostel \äs-tᵊl\ hostel, hostile
Pentecostal

oster¹ \äs-tər\ coster, foster, Foster, roster
impostor, piaster
Double Gloucester, paternoster, snollygoster

oster² \ȯs-tər\ foster, Foster, roster
Double Gloucester

oster³ \ō-stər\ see oaster

ostic \äs-tik\ Gnostic
acrostic, agnostic, prognostic
diagnostic

ostile \äs-tᵊl\ see ostel

ostle \äs-əl\ see ossal

ostly¹ \ōst-lē\ ghostly, hostly, mostly

ostly² \ȯs-lē\ see ossly

ostomy \äs-tə-mē\ ostomy
colostomy
enterostomy

oston \ȯs-tən\ Austin, Boston
Godwin Austen

ostor \äs-tər\ see oster¹

ostral¹ \ȯs-trəl\ austral, rostral

ostral² \äs-trəl\ see ostrel

ostrel \äs-trəl\ austral, costrel, nostril, rostral, wastrel
colostral

ostril \äs-trəl\ see ostrel

ostrum \äs-trəm\ nostrum, rostrum
colostrum

osty \ō-stē\ ghosty, toasty

osure \ō-zhər\ closure, crosier, osier

composure, disclosure, disposure, enclosure, exclosure, exposure, foreclosure
discomposure
overexposure, underexposure

osy \ō-zē\ cozy, dozy, mosey, nosy, Osee, posy, prosy, rosy
ring-around-a-rosy

osyne \äs-ᵊn-ē\ Euphrosyne, Mnemosyne

osz \ȯsh\ see ash²

oszcz \ȯsh\ see ash²

ot¹ \ät\ aught, baht, blot, boite, bot, chott, clot, cot, dot, ghat, got, grot, hot, jat, jot, khat, knot, kyat, lot, Lot, lotte, motte, naught, not, plot, pot, rot, scot, Scot, Scott, shot, skat, slot, snot, sot, spot, squat, swat, swot, tot, trot, watt, Watt, what, wot, yacht
allot, ascot, begot, besot, big shot, bloodshot, bowknot, boycott, buckshot, bullshot, cachepot, calotte, cannot, Connacht, crackpot, Crockpot, culotte, dashpot, despot, dreadnought, earshot, ergot, escot, eyeshot, eyespot, feedlot, fiat, firepot, fleshpot, forgot, fox-trot, fusspot, fylfot, garrote, gavotte, grapeshot, gunshot, half-knot, have-not, highspot, hotchpot, hotshot, ikat, jackpot, Korat, kumquat, long shot, loquat, marplot, mascot, motmot, nightspot, one-shot, Pequot, potshot, Rabat, red-hot, robot, Sadat, sandlot, sexpot, Shabbat, shallot, Shebat, sheepcote, slingshot, slipknot, slungshot, snapshot, somewhat, stinkpot, stockpot, subplot, sunspot, teapot, tin-pot, topknot, tosspot, try-pot, upshot, wainscot, whatnot, white-hot, woodlot
aeronaut, aliquot, apparat, apricot, aquanaut, argonaut, astronaut, bergamot, cachalot, Camelot, caveat, carry-cot, coffeepot, cosmonaut, counterplot, diddley-squat, doodley-squat, flowerpot, gallipot, guillemot, Gujarat, Hottentot, Huguenot, kilowatt, Lancelot, megawatt,

microdot, Nouakchott, ocelot, overshot, paraquat, patriot, Penobscot, peridot, polka dot, polyglot, samizdat, sansculotte, scattershot, terawatt, tommyrot, touch-me-not, underplot, undershot, Willemstadt, Wyandot, wyandotte
compatriot, forget-me-not, immunoblot, Inupiat, requiescat
Johnny-on-the-spot

ot² \ō\ see ow¹

ot³ \ōt\ see oat

ot⁴ \ȯt\ see ought¹

ôt \ō\ see ow¹

ota \ōt-ə\ bota, flota, lota, quota, rota
biota, Dakota, iota, Lakota, pelota, Toyota
Minnesota, North Dakota, South Dakota

otable \ōt-ə-bəl\ notable, potable, quotable

otage \ōt-ij\ dotage, flotage
anecdotage

otal \ōt-ᵊl\ dotal, motile, scrotal, total
immotile, subtotal, teetotal
anecdotal, antidotal, sacerdotal

otalist \ōt-ᵊl-əst\ teetotalist
anecdotalist, sacerdotalist

otamus \ät-ə-məs\ see otomous

otany \ät-ᵊn-ē\ botany, cottony
monotony

otarist \ōt-ə-rəst\ motorist, votarist

otary \ōt-ə-rē\ coterie, rotary, votary
locomotory, prothonotary

otas \ō-təs\ see otus

otch \äch\ blotch, botch, crotch, hotch, notch, scotch, Scotch, splotch, swatch, watch
bird-watch, deathwatch, debauch, dogwatch, hopscotch, hotchpotch,

Sasquatch, stopwatch, top-notch,
wristwatch
butterscotch

otchet \äch-ət\ crotchet, rochet

otchman \äch-mən\ Scotchman,
watchman

otchy \äch-ē\ blotchy, boccie,
botchy, splotchy
hibachi, huarache, huisache,
Karachi, vivace
mariachi

ote¹ \ōt-ē\ dhoti, floaty, loti, roti,
throaty
cenote, coyote, chayote, peyote,
quixote

ote² \ōt\ see oat

ote³ \ät\ see ot¹

otea \ōt-ē-ə\ protea, scotia

oted \ōt-əd\ see oated

otem \ōt-əm\ see otum

oten \ōt-ᵊn\ see oton

oter \ōt-ər\ see oater

oterie \ōt-ə-rē\ see otary

oth¹ \äth\ broth, cloth, froth, Goth,
moth, sloth, swath, troth, wroth
betroth, breechcloth, broadcloth,
cheesecloth, dishcloth, facecloth,
floorcloth, loincloth, Naboth, oilcloth,
sackcloth, sailcloth, washcloth
Alioth, behemoth, tablecloth,
Ostrogoth, Visigoth

oth² \ōs\ see ose¹

oth³ \ōt\ see oat

oth⁴ \ōth\ see owth

othal \óth-əl\ see othel

othe \ōth\ clothe, loathe
betroth, unclothe

othel \óth-əl\ brothel
betrothal

other¹ \əth-ər\ brother, mother,
nother, other, rather, smother, tother
another, foremother, godmother,
grandmother, housemother,
stepbrother, stepmother

other² \äth-ər\ see ather¹

otherly \əth-ər-lē\ brotherly,
motherly, southerly
grandmotherly

othes \ōz\ see ose²

othesis \äth-ə-səs\ prothesis
hypothesis

othic \äth-ik\ gothic
neo-Gothic, Ostrogothic, Visigothic

othing \ō-thiŋ\ clothing, loathing
underclothing
—also -ing forms of verbs listed at
othe

otho \ō-tō\ see oto¹

oti¹ \ōt-ē\ see ote¹

oti² \ót-ē\ see aughty

otia¹ \ō-shə\ scotia, Scotia
agnosia, dystocia
Cappadocia, Nova Scotia

otia² \ōt-ē-ə\ see otea

otiable \ō-shə-bəl\ see ociable

otiant \ō-shənt\ see otient

otic¹ \ät-ik\ Scotic
aquatic, biotic, chaotic, demotic,
despotic, erotic, exotic, hypnotic,
narcotic, necrotic, neurotic, Nilotic,
osmotic, psychotic, quixotic, robotic,
sclerotic
abiotic, anecdotic, asymptotic,
bibliotic, embryotic, epiglottic,
homeotic, Huguenotic, idiotic,
melanotic, patriotic, posthypnotic,
sansculottic, semiotic, symbiotic
antibiotic, autoerotic, compatriotic,
homoerotic, macrobiotic

otic² \ōt-ik\ lotic, photic
aphotic, aprotic, dichotic, robotic

otic[3] \ȯt-ik\ see autic

otica \ät-i-kə\ erotica, exotica

otice \ōt-əs\ see otus

otics \ät-iks\ robotics
astronautics, bibliotics
—*also* -s, -'s, *and* -s' *forms of nouns listed at* otic[1]

otid \ät-əd\ see otted

otient \ō-shənt\ quotient
negotiant

otile \ōt-ᵊl\ see otal

oting[1] \ōt-iŋ\ see oating

oting[2] \ät-iŋ\ see otting

otinous[1] \ät-nəs\ see otness

otinous[2] \ät-ᵊn-əs\ see otonous[1]

otion \ō-shən\ Goshen, groschen,
lotion, motion, notion, ocean, potion
commotion, demotion, devotion,
emotion, Laotian, promotion, slow-motion
locomotion

otional \ō-shnəl\ motional, notional
devotional, emotional, promotional
unemotional

otis \ōt-əs\ see otus

otist \ōt-əst\ protist, Scotist
anecdotist

otive \ōt-iv\ motive, votive
emotive, promotive
automotive, locomotive

otl \ät-ᵊl\ see ottle

otle \ät-ᵊl\ see ottle

otley \ät-lē\ see otly

otly \ät-lē\ Atli, hotly, motley

otment \ät-mənt\ allotment,
ballottement

otness \ät-nəs\ hotness, squatness

oto \ō-tō\ koto, photo, roto, Sotho

Basotho, con moto, de Soto, ex-voto,
in toto, Kyoto, Lesotho, Mosotho,
Sesotho
Kumamoto, telephoto

otomous \ät-ə-məs\ dichotomous
hippopotamus

otomy \ät-ə-mē\ dichotomy,
lobotomy
tracheotomy
episiotomy

oton \ōt-ᵊn\ croton, Jotun, oaten
Lofoten, verboten

otonous[1] \ät-ᵊn-əs\ rottenness
monotonous, serotinous

otonous[2] \ät-nəs\ see otness

otor \ōt-ər\ see oater

otorist \ōt-ə-rəst\ see otarist

otory \ōt-ə-rē\ see otary

ots \äts\ Graz, hots, lots, Scots,
Spaatz, swats
ersatz, Galati
—*also* -s, -'s, *and* -s' *forms of nouns,
and* -s *forms of verbs, listed at* ot[1]

otsk \ätsk\ see atsk

otsman \ät-smən\ Scotsman,
yachtsman

ott \ät\ see ot[1]

otta \ät-ə\ see ata[1]

ottage \ät-ij\ cottage, plottage,
pottage, wattage

ottal \ät-ᵊl\ see ottle

otte[1] \ät\ see ot[1]

otte[2] \ȯt\ see ought[1]

otted \ät-əd\ knotted, potted, spotted
carotid, proglottid
polka-dotted
—*also* -ed *forms of verbs listed at*
ot[1]

ottement \ät-mənt\ see otment

otten \ät-ᵊn\ cotton, gotten, gratin, ratton, rotten, shotten
au gratin, begotten, forgotten, guncotton, ill-gotten
misbegotten, sauerbraten

ottenness \ät-ᵊn-əs\ see otonous¹

otter \ät-ər\ blotter, cotter, daughter, dotter, knotter, otter, plotter, potter, Potter, Qatar, rotter, spotter, squatter, swatter, Tatar, totter, trotter, water
alotter, backwater, bathwater, blackwater, boycotter, breakwater, cutwater, dewater, deepwater, dishwater, firewater, floodwater, flyswatter, freshwater, garroter, globetrotter, goddaughter, granddaughter, groundwater, headwater, jerkwater, limewater, meltwater, pinspotter, rainwater, rosewater, saltwater, sandlotter, sea otter, seawater, shearwater, springwater, tailwater, tidewater, wastewater
alma mater, imperator, milk-and-water, polywater, teeter-totter, underwater
—also -er forms of adjectives listed at ot¹

ottery \ät-ə-rē\ lottery, pottery, Tatary, tottery, watery

ottic \ät-ik\ see otic¹

ottid \ät-əd\ see otted

ottie \ät-ē\ see ati

otting \ät-iŋ\ jotting
wainscoting
—also -ing forms of verbs listed at ot¹

ottis \ät-əs\ glottis
clematis
epiglottis, literatus

ottische \ät-ish\ see ottish

ottish \ät-ish\ hottish, schottische, Scottish, sottish
sanculottish

ottle \ät-ᵊl\ bottle, dottle, glottal, mottle, pottle, ratel, rotl, throttle, wattle

atlatl, bluebottle, Nahuatl
Aristotle, epiglottal, monocotyl
Quetzalcoatl

otto¹ \ät-ō\ see ato¹

otto² \òt-ō\ see auto¹

ottom \ät-əm\ see atum¹

otty \ät-ē\ see ati

otum \ōt-əm\ notum, scrotum, totem
factotum, teetotum

otun \ōt-ᵊn\ see oton

oture \ō-chər\ see oacher

otus \ōt-əs\ lotus, notice, Otis
denotice, Pelotas

oty \òt-ē\ see aughty¹

otyl \ät-ᵊl\ see ottle

ou¹ \ō\ see ow¹

ou² \ü\ see ew¹

ou³ \aù\ see ow²

oubled \ə-bəld\ see ubbled

ouble \əb-əl\ see ubble

oubler \əb-lər\ bubbler, doubler, troubler

oubly \əb-lē\ see ubbly

oubt \aùt\ see out³

oubted \aùt-əd\ see outed

oubter \aùt-ər\ see outer²

ouc¹ \ü\ see ew¹

ouc² \ük\ see uke

ouc³ \ùk\ see ook¹

ouce \üs\ see use¹

oucester¹ \äs-tər\ see oster¹

oucester² \òs-tər\ see oster²

ouch¹ \üch\ see ooch¹

ouch² \üsh\ see ouche

ouch³ \əch\ see utch¹

ouch⁴ \aùch\ couch, crouch, grouch, ouch, pouch, slouch, vouch
avouch, debouch
retort pouch, scaramouch

ouche \üsh\ douche, louche, ruche, squoosh, swoosh, whoosh
barouche, capuche, cartouche, debouch, farouche, kurus, tarboosh
scaramouch

ouchy¹ \əch-ē\ see uchy

ouchy² \aù-chē\ grouchy, pouchy, slouchy

oud¹ \üd\ see ude

oud² \aùd\ boughed, bowed, cloud, crowd, loud, proud, shroud, stroud
aloud, becloud, enshroud, highbrowed, house-proud, purse-proud, Red Cloud, unbowed
overcrowd, thundercloud
—*also* -ed *forms of verbs listed at* ow²

ou'd \üd\ see ude

ouda \üd-ə\ see uda

oudy \aùd-ē\ see owdy

oue \ü\ see ew¹

ouf \üf\ see oof¹

ouffe \üf\ see oof¹

oug \əg\ see ug

ouge¹ \üj\ see uge¹

ouge² \üzh\ see uge²

ouge³ \aùj\ gouge, scrouge

ough¹ \ō\ see ow¹

ough² \ü\ see ew¹

ough³ \aù\ see ow²

ough⁴ \äk\ see ock¹

ough⁵ \əf\ see uff

ough⁶ \òf\ see off²

ougham¹ \ōm\ see ome¹

ougham² \üm\ see oom¹

oughed \aùd\ see oud²

oughen \əf-ən\ see uffin

ougher \əf-ər\ see uffer

oughie \əf-ē\ see uffy

oughish \əf-ish\ see uffish

oughly \əf-lē\ see uffly

oughs \ōz\ see ose²

ought¹ \òt\ aught, bought, brought, caught, dot, fought, fraught, ghat, lotte, naught, nought, ought, sought, taught, taut, thought, wrought
besought, distraught, dreadnought, forethought, handwrought, high-wrought, onslaught, self-taught, store-bought, unthought
aeronaut, aforethought, afterthought, aquanaut, argonaut, astronaut, cosmonaut, juggernaut, overbought, overwrought

ought² \aùt\ see out³

oughten \òt-ᵊn\ see auten

oughty \aùt-ē\ doughty, droughty, gouty, pouty, snouty, trouty

oughy¹ \ō-ē\ see owy

oughy² \ü-ē\ see ewy

ouie \ü-ē\ see ewy

ouille \ü-ē\ see ewy

ouis¹ \ü-ē\ see ewy

ouis² \ü-əs\ lewis, Lewis, Louis, Luis
Port Louis, Saint Louis

ouk \ük\ see uke

ouki \ü-kē\ see ooky¹

oul¹ \ōl\ see ole¹

oul² \ül\ see ool¹

oul³ \aùl\ see owl²

ould¹ \ōld\ see old¹

ould² \ùd\ see ood¹

oulder \ōl-dər\ see older¹

ouldered \ōl-dərd\ bouldered, shouldered
round-shouldered, square-shouldered
—*also* -ed *forms of verbs listed at* older¹

ouldest \ùd-əst\ couldest, shouldest, wouldest
Talmudist

ouldn't \ùd-ᵊnt\ shouldn't, wouldn't

oule¹ \ü-lē\ see uly

oule² \ül\ see ool¹

ouled \ōld\ see old¹

oulee \ü-lē\ see uly

ouleh¹ \ü-lə\ see ula

ouleh² \ü-lē\ see uly

ouli \ü-lē\ see uly

oulie \ü-lē\ see uly

ouling \aù-liŋ\ see owling²

oulish \ü-lish\ see oolish

ou'll¹ \ül\ see ool¹

ou'll² \ùl\ see ul¹

oulle \ül\ see ool¹

oulli \ü-lē\ see uly

oully \aù-lē\ see owly²

oult \ōlt\ see olt¹

oulter \ōl-tər\ see olter

oum \üm\ see oom¹

oumenal \ü-mən-ᵊl\ see uminal

oun¹ \aùn\ see own²

oun² \ün\ see oon¹

ounce \aùns\ bounce, flounce, jounce, ounce, pounce, trounce
announce, denounce, enounce, pronounce, renounce
mispronounce

ouncement \aùn-smənt\ announcement, denouncement, pronouncement

ouncer \aùn-sər\ bouncer announcer

ouncil \aùn-səl\ see ounsel

ouncy \aùn-sē\ bouncy, flouncy, jouncy
viscountcy

ound¹ \ünd\ stound, swound, wound
—*also* -ed *forms of verbs listed at* oon¹

ound² \aùnd\ bound, crowned, found, ground, hound, mound, pound, Pound, round, sound, stound, swound, wound
abound, aground, all-round, around, astound, background, black-crowned, bloodhound, campground, chowhound, compound, confound, coonhound, dachshund, deerhound, deskbound, earthbound, eastbound, elkhound, expound, fairground, fogbound, foot-pound, foreground, foxhound, go-round, greyhound, hardbound, hellhound, hidebound, homebound, horehound, housebound, icebound, impound, inbound, newfound, newshound, northbound, outbound, playground, pot-bound, profound, propound, rebound, redound, resound, rockbound, snowbound, softbound, southbound, spellbound, stone-ground, stormbound, strikebound, surround, unbound, well-found, westbound, white-crowned, wolfhound, year-round
aboveground, all-around, belowground, battleground, decompound, go-around, muscle-bound, outward-bound, paperbound, Puget Sound, runaround, turnaround, ultrasound, underground, weather-bound, wraparound
merry-go-round, superabound
—*also* -ed *forms of verbs listed at* own²

oundal \aún-d³l\ poundal, roundel

oundary \aún-drē\ see oundry

ounded \aún-dəd\ rounded
confounded, unbounded, unfounded,
well-founded, well-grounded

oundel \aún-d³l\ see oundal

ounder \aún-dər\ bounder, flounder,
founder, grounder, hounder, pounder,
rounder, sounder
all-rounder, backgrounder,
compounder, confounder,
dumbfounder, tenpounder

ounding \aún-diŋ\ grounding,
sounding
astounding, high-sounding,
rockhounding
—also -ing forms of verbs listed at
ound²

oundless¹ \ün-ləs\ see oonless

oundless² \aún-ləs\ groundless,
soundless

oundlet \aún-lət\ see ownlet

oundling \aún-liŋ\ foundling,
groundling

oundly \aúnd-lē\ roundly, soundly

oundness \aún-nəs\ roundness
unsoundness

oundry \aún-drē\ boundary,
foundry

ounds¹ \ünz\ see oons

ounds² \aúnz\ hounds, zounds
inbounds
Barren Grounds, out-of-bounds
—also -s, -'s, and -s' forms of nouns,
and -s forms of verbs, listed at ound²

oundsel \aún-səl\ see ounsel

oundsman \aúnz-mən\ see
ownsman

ounge \aúnj\ lounge, scrounge
chaise lounge

ounger¹ \aún-jər\ lounger,
scrounger

ounger² \əŋ-gər\ see onger¹

ounker \əŋ-kər\ see unker

ounsel \aún-səl\ council, counsel,
groundsel

ount¹ \änt\ see ant²

ount² \aúnt\ count, fount, mount
account, amount, demount, discount,
dismount, high-count, miscount,
recount, remount, seamount,
surmount, viscount
catamount, paramount, rediscount,
tantamount, undercount

ountable \aúnt-ə-bəl\ countable
accountable, demountable,
discountable, surmountable
insurmountable, unaccountable

ountain \aúnt-³n\ fountain,
mountain
transmountain
cat-a-mountain, Riding Mountain

ountcy \aún-sē\ see ouncy

ounter \aúnt-ər\ counter, mounter
discounter, encounter, recounter,
rencounter

ountess \aúnt-əs\ countess
viscountess

ountie \aúnt-ē\ see ounty

ounting \aúnt-iŋ\ mounting
accounting
—also -ing forms of verbs listed at
ount²

ounty \aúnt-ē\ bounty, county,
Mountie
viscounty

oup¹ \ōp\ see ope

oup² \ü\ see ew¹

oup³ \üp\ see oop¹

oupe¹ \ōp\ see ope

oupe² \üp\ see oop¹

ouper \ü-pər\ see ooper

oupie \ü-pē\ see oopy

ouping \ü-piŋ\ see ooping

ouple \əp-əl\ see uple¹

ouplet \əp-lət\ see uplet¹

oupous \ü-pəs\ see upus

oupy \ü-pē\ see oopy

our¹ \ȯr\ see or¹

our² \u̇r\ see ure¹

our³ \au̇r\ see ower²

our⁴ \är\ see ar³

our⁵ \ər\ see eur¹

oura \u̇r-ə\ see ura

ourable \ȯr-ə-bəl\ see orable

ourage \ər-ij\ courage
demurrage, discourage, encourage

ourbon¹ \ər-bən\ see urban¹

ourbon² \u̇r-bən\ see urban²

ource \ȯrs\ see orse¹

ourceful \ȯrs-fəl\ see orseful

ourcing \ȯr-siŋ\ outsourcing
—also -ing forms of verbs listed at orse¹

ourd \ȯrd\ see oard

ourde \u̇rd\ see ured¹

ou're¹ \ȯr\ see or¹

ou're² \ü-ər\ see ewer¹

ou're³ \u̇r\ see ure¹

ou're⁴ \ər\ see eur¹

oured \ȯrd\ see oard

ourer¹ \ȯr-ər\ see orer

ourer² \u̇r-ər\ see urer¹

ourer³ \au̇r-ər\ flowerer, scourer, showerer
deflowerer, devourer
—also -er forms of adjectives listed at ower²

ourg¹ \u̇r\ see ure¹

ourg² \ərg\ see erg

ourge¹ \ərj\ see urge

ourge² \ȯrj\ see orge

ourger \ər-jər\ see erger

ouri \u̇r-ē\ see ury¹

ourier¹ \u̇r-ē-ər\ courier
couturier, couturiere, vaunt-courier

ourier² \ər-ē-ər\ see urrier

ouring¹ \ȯr-iŋ\ see oring

ouring² \u̇r-iŋ\ see uring

ourish \ər-ish\ currish, flourish, nourish
amateurish

ourist \u̇r-əst\ see urist

ourly \au̇r-lē\ dourly, hourly, sourly

ourn¹ \ȯrn\ see orn¹

ourn² \ərn\ see urn

ournal \ərn-ᵊl\ see ernal

ournament \ȯr-nə-mənt\ see ornament

ourne \ȯrn\ see orn¹

ourney¹ \ər-nē\ Bernie, Ernie, ferny, gurney, journey, tourney
attorney

ourney² \ȯr-nē\ see orny

ourneyer \ər-nē-ər\ journeyer, vernier

ournful \ȯrn-fəl\ see ornful

ourning \ȯr-niŋ\ see orning

ournment \ərn-mənt\ see ernment

ours¹ \ȯrz\ see oors

ours² \ärz\ see ars

ours³ \aùrz\ ours
after-hours
—*also* -s, -'s, *and* -s' *forms of nouns,*
and -s *forms of verbs, listed at* ower²

ours⁴ \ùr\ see ure¹

ourse \ȯrs\ see orse¹

oursome \ȯr-səm\ see orsum

ourt¹ \ȯrt\ see ort¹

ourt² \ùrt\ see urt¹

ourtesy \ərt-ə-sē\ courtesy, curtesy
discourtesy

ourth \ȯrth\ see orth¹

ourtier \ȯr-chər\ see orcher

ourtly \ȯrt-lē\ see ortly

oury \aùr-ē\ see owery

ous¹ \ü\ see ew¹

ous² \üs\ see use¹

ousa¹ \ü-sə\ see usa¹

ousa² \ü-zə\ see usa²

ousal \aù-zəl\ housel, spousal,
tousle
arousal, carousal

ousand \aùz-ᵊn\ see owson

ouse¹ \üs\ see use¹

ouse² \aùs\ blouse, chiaus, chouse,
douse, Gauss, grouse, house, Klaus,
Laos, louse, mouse, scouse, souse,
spouse, Strauss
baghouse, bathhouse, Bauhaus,
birdhouse, blockhouse, bughouse,
bunkhouse, cathouse, chophouse,
clubhouse, cookhouse, courthouse,
deckhouse, degauss, delouse,
doghouse, dollhouse, dormouse,
espouse, farmhouse, firehouse,
flophouse, gashouse, gatehouse,

glasshouse, greenhouse, guardhouse,
henhouse, hothouse, icehouse, in-
house, jailhouse, lighthouse,
lobscouse, longhouse, madhouse,
Manaus, nuthouse, outhouse,
penthouse, playhouse, poorhouse,
roadhouse, roughhouse, roundhouse,
schoolhouse, smokehouse,
springhouse, statehouse, storehouse,
teahouse, titmouse, tollhouse,
warehouse, washhouse, wheelhouse,
White House, whorehouse, workhouse
boardinghouse, clearinghouse,
coffeehouse, countinghouse,
customhouse, house-to-house,
meetinghouse, Mickey Mouse,
overblouse, pilothouse, porterhouse,
powerhouse, slaughterhouse,
sugarhouse, summerhouse, treasure-
house, Westinghouse

ouse³ \aùz\ blouse, bouse, bowse,
browse, douse, dowse, drowse, house,
mouse, rouse, spouse, touse
arouse, carouse, delouse, doss-house,
espouse, rehouse, roughhouse,
warehouse
—*also* -s, -'s, *and* -s' *forms of nouns,*
and -s *forms of verbs, listed at* ow²

ouse⁴ \üz\ see use²

ousel \aù-zəl\ see ousal

ouser \aù-zər\ dowser, houser,
mouser, schnauzer, trouser, wowser
carouser, espouser, warehouser
rabble-rouser

ousin \əz-ᵊn\ see ozen¹

ousinage \əz-ᵊn-ij\ cousinage,
cozenage

ousing \aù-ziŋ\ housing, rousing
rabble-rousing
—*also* -ing *forms of verbs listed at*
ouse³

ousle¹ \ü-zəl\ see usal²

ousle² \aù-zəl\ see ousal

ousse \üs\ see use¹

ousseau \ü-sō\ see usoe

oust¹ \aùst\ Faust, joust, oust, roust
—*also* -ed *forms of verbs listed at* ouse²

oust² \üst\ see oost

ouste \üst\ see oost

ousy¹ \aù-zē\ see owsy

ousy² \aù-sē\ mousy
Firdawsi

out¹ \ü\ see ew¹

out² \üt\ see ute

out³ \aùt\ bout, clout, doubt, drought, flout, glout, gout, grout, knout, kraut, lout, out, pout, rout, route, scout, shout, snout, spout, sprout, stout, tout, trout
ablaut, about, all-out, bailout, blackout, blissed-out, blowout, breakout, breechclout, brownout, burned-out, burnout, checkout, clapped-out, closeout, cookout, cop-out, cutout, devout, dishclout, downspout, dropout, dugout, eelpout, fade-out, fallout, far-out, flameout, flat-out, foldout, force-out, freak-out, freeze out, full-out, gross-out, groundout, handout, hangout, hideout, holdout, ice-out, knockout, layout, lights-out, lockout, lookout, misdoubt, payout, phaseout, pitchout, printout, psych-out, pullout, punch-out, putout, rainspout, readout, redoubt, rollout, sellout, setout, shakeout, shoot-out, shutout, sick-out, sold-out, spaced-out, speak-out, spinout, stakeout, standout, straight-out, stressed-out, stretch-out, strikeout, takeout, thought-out, throughout, throw out, time-out, tryout, turnout, umlaut, veg out, walkout, washed-out, washout, way-out, whacked-out, whiteout, wigged-out, wipeout, without, workout, worn-out, zonked-out
all get-out, carryout, diner-out, down-and-out, falling-out, gadabout, hereabout, knockabout, layabout, out-and-out, roundabout, rouseabout, roustabout, runabout, sauerkraut, stirabout, thereabout, turnabout, walkabout, waterspout

oute¹ \üt\ see ute

oute² \aùt\ see out³

outed \aùt-əd\ snouted, spouted
undoubted
—*also* -ed *forms of verbs listed at* out³

outer¹ \üt-ər\ see uter

outer² \aùt-ər\ doubter, flouter, grouter, outer, pouter, router, scouter, shouter, spouter, touter
come-outer
down-and-outer, out-and-outer
—*also* -er *forms of adjectives listed at* out³

outh¹ \üth\ see ooth²

outh² \aùth\ mouth, routh, scouth, south
bad-mouth, goalmouth, loudmouth, poor-mouth
blabbermouth, cottonmouth, hand-to-mouth, motormouth, word-of-mouth

outherly \əth̲-ər-lē\ see otherly

outhey \aù-thē\ see outhy

outhful \üth-fəl\ see uthful

outhie \ü-thē\ see oothy

outhly \üth-lē\ see oothly

outhy \aù-thē\ mouthy, Southey

outi \üt-ē\ see ooty¹

outing \aùt-iŋ\ outing, scouting
—*also* -ing *forms of verbs listed at* out³

outish \aùt-ish\ loutish, snoutish

outre \üt-ər\ see uter

outrement \ü-trə-mənt\ see utriment

outs \aùts\ hereabouts, ins and outs, thereabouts, whereabouts

outy \aùt-ē\ see oughty

ou've \üv\ see ove³

ouver \ü-vər\ see over³

oux \ü\ see ew¹

ouy \ē\ see ee¹

ouyhnhnm \in-əm\ see inim

ouzel \ü-zəl\ see usal²

ov¹ \äf\ see off¹

ov² \òf\ see off²

ova \ō-və\ nova
Cralova, Jehovah, Moldova
bossa nova, Casanova, Czestochowa, Kemerovo, supernova

ovable \ü-və-bəl\ movable, provable
approvable, disprovable, immovable, improvable, removable
irremovable

ovah \ō-və\ see ova

oval \ü-vəl\ approval, removal
disapproval

ovat \əv-ət\ see ovet

ove¹ \əv\ dove, glove, love, of, shove
above, foxglove, hereof, kid-glove, ringdove, thereof, truelove, whereof
ladylove, light-o'-love, roman-fleuve, turtledove, unheard of, well-thought-of
hereinabove

ove² \ōv\ clove, cove, dove, drove, fauve, grove, hove, Jove, mauve, rove, stove, strove, throve, trove, wove
alcove, behove, cookstove, mangrove, woodstove
Garden Grove, interwove, treasure trove

ove³ \üv\ groove, move, prove, you've

approve, behoove, commove, disprove, improve, remove, reprove
disapprove

ovel¹ \äv-əl\ grovel, novel
antinovel, Yaroslavl

ovel² \əv-əl\ grovel, hovel, shovel

ovement \üv-mənt\ movement
improvement

oven¹ \əv-ən\ coven, oven, sloven

oven² \ō-vən\ cloven, coven, woven
Beethoven, handwoven
interwoven

over¹ \əv-ər\ cover, glover, hover, lover, plover
bedcover, discover, dustcover, hardcover, re-cover, recover, slipcover, softcover, uncover, windhover
undercover

over² \ō-vər\ clover, Dover, drover, Grover, over, plover, rover, stover, trover
allover, changeover, crossover, cutover, flashover, flopover, flyover, hangover, Hannover, Hanover, holdover, layover, leftover, makeover, moreover, once-over, Passover, popover, pullover, pushover, rollover, runover, slipover, spillover, stopover, strikeover, takeover, turnover, voice-over, walkover, warmed-over
carryover, crossing-over, going-over, Strait of Dover

over³ \ü-vər\ groover, Hoover, louver, mover, prover
earthmover, improver, maneuver, remover, reprover, Vancouver
disapprover

over⁴ \äv-ər\ see aver¹

overable \əv-rə-bəl\ discoverable, recoverable
irrecoverable

overly \əv-ər-lē\ loverly
Sir Roger de Coverley

overt \ō-vərt\ covert, overt

overy \əv-rē\ discovery, recovery

ovet \əv-ət\ covet, lovat

ovey \ə-vē\ covey
lovey-dovey

ovian \ō-vē-ən\ Jovian
Markovian, Pavlovian, Varsovian

ovie \ü-vē\ see oovy

ovo \ō-vō\ Provo
ab ovo, de novo
Porto Novo

ovost \äv-əst\ see avist

ovsk \ófsk\ Dnepropetrovsk,
Petropavlovsk

ow[1] \ō\ beau, blow, bow, bro, Chou,
crow, do, doe, dough, floe, flow, foe,
fro, froe, frow, glow, go, grow, ho,
hoe, jo, Jo, joe, Joe, know, lo, low,
mho, mot, mow, no, No, O, oh, owe,
Po, Poe, pow, pro, rho, roe, row,
schmo, sew, shew, show, sloe, slow,
snow, so, sow, stow, Stowe, strow,
though, throe, throw, toe, tow, trow,
whoa, woe, yo
aglow, ago, airflow, airglow, alow,
although, backflow, backhoe, bandeau,
Baotou, barlow, bateau, below, bestow,
bon mot, Bordeaux, bravo, by-blow,
cachepot, caló, Carlow, chapeau,
chateau, Chi-Rho, cockcrow, cornrow,
crossbow, Day-Glo, dayglow, Defoe,
de trop, deathblow, deco, down-bow,
elbow, escrow, fencerow, flambeau,
flyblow, fogbow, forego, foreknow,
forgo, Fuzhou, galop, gâteau, genro,
gigot, go-slow, Gounod, Guangzhou,
gung ho, hallo, Hangzhou, Hankow,
heave-ho, hedgerow, heigh-ho, hello,
hollo, hullo, inflow, jabot, Jane Doe,
jim crow, Jinzhou, John Doe,
Hounslow, kayo, KO, Kwangchow,
Lanzhou, longbow, low-low, macho,
mahoe, maillot, manteau, Marlowe,

matelot, merlot, Meursault, Miró,
misknow, Moho, mojo, Monroe,
morceau, Moscow, mucro, mudflow,
nightglow, no-no, no-show, nouveau,
outflow, outgo, outgrow, oxbow,
Paot'ou, Pernod, picot, Pinot, plateau,
pronto, Quanzhou, rainbow, reflow,
regrow, repo, reseau, rondeau, rondo,
Roseau, rouleau, Rousseau, sabot,
salchow, scarecrow, self-sow, serow,
shadblow, Shantou, sideshow, skid
row, Soho, so-so, sourdough, sunbow,
Suzhou, tableau, Taizhou, tiptoe,
Thoreau, tonneau, trousseau, Trudeau,
uh-oh, unsew, up-bow, upthrow, van
Gogh, Watteau, windrow, windthrow,
Xuzhou, Zhangzhou, Zhengzhou,
Zhuzhon, Zibo
afterglow, aikido, alpenglow,
Angelo, apropos, art deco, art
nouveau, audio, Baguio, Bamako,
barrio, Bergamo, bibelot, Bilbao,
bordereau, Borneo, buffalo, Buffalo,
bungalow, Bushido, buteo, calico,
cameo, cachalot, cembalo, centimo,
CEO, chassepot, cheerio, Cicero,
Clemenceau, cogito, comedo, comme
il faut, Comoro, counterflow, curaçao,
Curaçao, curassow, curio, daimyo,
danio, dataflow, Delano, Diderot, do-
si-do, domino, dynamo, embryo,
entrepôt, Erato, escargot, Eskimo,
extrados, fabliau, folio, fricandeau,
furbelow, gigolo, go-no-go, guacharo,
hammertoe, haricot, heel-and-toe,
hetero, HMO, Holy Joe, Idaho, indigo,
Jericho, kakapo, Kosciuszko, latigo,
long-ago, Maceió, Manchukuo, Mario,
massicot, medico, Mexico, mistletoe,
modulo, Monaco, Navaho, Navajo,
NCO, nuncio, oleo, olio, overflow,
overgrow, overthrow, ovolo, Pamlico,
Papago, patio, peridot, picaro, piccolo,
Pierrot, polio, pomelo, pompano,
portico, PPO, Prospero, proximo, quid
pro quo, radio, raree-show, ratio,
Richard Roe, Rochambeau, rococo,
rodeo, Romeo, saddlebow, Sapporo,
sapsago, Scorpio, semipro, sloppy joe,
so-and-so, SRO, standing O, status

quo, stereo, stop-and-go, studio,
subito, tallyho, tangelo, Taranto,
ticktacktoe, tic-tac-toe, tit-tat-toe,
TKO, to-and-fro, Tokyo, tombolo,
touch-and-go, touraco, tournedos,
tremolo, tuckahoe, tupelo, UFO,
ultimo, undergo, undertow, Veneto,
vertigo, vibrio, virago, vireo,
Zhangjiakou, zydeco
  Antonio, Arapaho, centesimo, con
spirito, continuo, DMSO, Etobicoke,
ex nihilo, fantastico, fellatio, Fernando
Póo, fortissimo, Geronimo, get-up-
and-go, Guantanamo, hereinbelow, in
utero, in vacuo, La Rochfoucauld,
lentissimo, lothario, magnifico,
malapropos, milesimo, New Mexico,
oregano, politico, portfolio, presidio,
prestissimo, punctilio, Querétaro,
Quintana Roo, Rosario, quo warranto,
Sarajevo, scenario, simpatico
  ab initio, archipelago, braggadocio,
duodecimo, ex officio, generalissimo,
impresario, internuncio, oratorio,
Paramaribo, pianissimo, rose of
Jericho

ow² \aủ\ bough, bow, brow, chiao,
chow, ciao, cow, dhow, Dou, dow,
Dow, Frau, hao, how, howe, Howe,
jow, Lao, mow, now, ow, plow, pow,
prau, prow, row, scow, slough, sough,
sow, Tao, tau, thou, vow, wow, Yao
  allow, avow, Belau, Bissau,
bowwow, cacao, cahow, Callao,
Davao, chowchow, chow chow,
Cracow, Donau, endow, enow, erenow,
eyebrow, gangplow, Haikou, Hankow,
hausfrau, haymow, highbrow,
hoosegow, Jungfrau, know-how,
kowtow, Krakow, landau, lowbrow,
luau, Lucknow, Macao, meow, miaow,
Moscow, Niihau, nohow, Pelau,
powwow, Qing-dao, snowplow,
somehow, Zwickau
  anyhow, curaçao, Curaçao, disallow,
disavow, disendow, middlebrow,
Mindanao
  Guinea-Bissau, Marianao
  holier-than-thou

ow³ \ȯv\ see off²

owa \ō-və\ see ova

owable¹ \ō-ə-bəl\ knowable,
sewable
  unknowable

owable² \aủ-ə-bəl\ plowable
allowable
  disavowable

owage \ō-ij\ flowage, stowage,
towage

owal¹ \ō-əl\ see oel

owal² \aủl\ see owl²

owan¹ \ō-ən\ see oan¹

owan² \aủ-ən\ Gawain, gowan,
rowan, rowen
  Bandar Seri Begawan

oward¹ \ȯrd\ see oard

oward² \aủrd\ see owered

owd¹ \üd\ see ude

owd² \aủd\ see oud²

owdah \aủd-ə\ see aude³

owder \aủd-ər\ chowder, powder
gunpowder
  five-spice powder
  —also -er forms of adjectives listed
at oud²

owdown \ō-daủn\ blowdown,
lowdown, showdown, slowdown

owdy \aủd-ē\ cloudy, dowdy,
howdy, rowdy
  cum laude, pandowdy
  magna cum laude, summa cum laude

owe \ō\ see ow¹

owed¹ \ōd\ see ode

owed² \aủd\ see oud²

owedly \aủ-əd-lē\ allowedly,
avowedly

owel \aủl\ see owl²

oweling \aủ-liŋ\ see owling²

owell¹ \aủl\ see owl²

owell² \ō-əl\ see oel

owen¹ \aù-ən\ see owan²

owen² \ō-ən\ see oan¹

ower¹ \ȯr\ see or¹

ower² \aùr\ bower, cower, dour, dower, flour, flower, gaur, giaour, glower, hour, lower, our, plower, power, scour, shower, sour, tour, tower, vower
avower, cornflower, deflower, devour, embower, empower, firepower, high-power, man-hour, mayflower, moonflower, off-hour, pasqueflower, Peshawar, repower, safflower, sunflower, wallflower, watchtower, wildflower, willpower
candlepower, cauliflower, disendower, Eisenhower, overpower, passionflower, person-hour, Schopenhauer, superpower, sweet-and-sour, thundershower, waterpower, womanpower

ower³ \ō-ər\ see oer⁴

owered \aùrd\ coward, flowered, powered, towered
high-powered
ivory-towered, superpowered, underpowered
—also -ed forms of verbs listed at ower²

owerer \aùr-ər\ see ourer³

owerful \aùr-fəl\ flowerful, powerful

owering \aù-riŋ\ lowering
nonflowering
—also -ing forms of verbs listed at ower²

owery \aùr-ē\ bowery, cauri, dowry, floury, flowery, kauri, Maori, showery

owff \aùf\ howff
langlauf

owhee \ō-ē\ see owy

owie \aù-ē\ Maui, zowie

owing \ō-iŋ\ see oing¹

owl¹ \ōl\ see ole¹

owl² \aùl\ bowel, cowl, dowel, foul, fowl, growl, Howell, howl, jowl, owl, prowl, rowel, scowl, towel, trowel, vowel, yowl
avowal, batfowl, befoul, embowel, peafowl, seafowl, wildfowl
disavowal, disembowel, waterfowl

owland \ō-lənd\ lowland, Poland, Roland

owledge \äl-ij\ college, knowledge
acknowledge, foreknowledge

owler¹ \ō-lər\ see oller

owler² \aù-lər\ growler, howler, prowler, scowler
waterfowler

owless \ō-ləs\ see olus

owline \ō-lən\ see olon

owling¹ \ō-liŋ\ see olling

owling² \aù-liŋ\ cowling, growling, howling, toweling
antifouling, biofouling, waterfowling
—also -ing forms of verbs listed at owl²

owlock \äl-ək\ see oloch

owly¹ \ō-lē\ see oly¹

owly² \aù-lē\ foully, growly, jowly

owman¹ \ō-mən\ see oman

owman² \aù-mən\ bowman, cowman, plowman

ow-me \ō-mē\ see oamy

own¹ \ōn\ see one¹

own² \aùn\ brown, Brown, clown, crown, down, Down, drown, frown, gown, lown, noun, town
blowdown, boomtown, breakdown, Bridgetown, bringdown, Capetown, clampdown, closedown, comedown, cooldown, countdown, crackdown, crosstown, downtown, drawdown, embrown, facedown, Freetown,

Georgetown, George Town, godown, hoedown, hometown, Jamestown, knockdown, letdown, lockdown, lookdown, lowdown, markdown, meltdown, nightgown, pastedown, phasedown, pronoun, pushdown, putdown, renown, rubdown, rundown, scale-down, shakedown, showdown, shutdown, sit-down, slowdown, Southdown, splashdown, stand-down, step-down, stripped-down, sundown, thumbs-down, tie-down, top-down, touchdown, turndown, uncrown, uptown, Von Braun, write-down, Youngstown
Allentown, broken-down, buttondown, Charlottetown, Chinatown, dressing-down, eiderdown, Germantown, hand-me-down, reach-me-down, shantytown, tumbledown, upside down, watered-down
man-about-town

ownded \aủn-dəd\ see ounded

ownding \aủn-diŋ\ see ounding

owned[1] \ōnd\ see oned[1]

owned[2] \aủnd\ see ound[2]

owner[1] \ō-nər\ see oner[1]

owner[2] \ü-nər\ see ooner

owner[3] \aủ-nər\ browner, crowner, downer, frowner
sundowner

owness \ō-nəs\ see onus[2]

ownia \ō-nē-ə\ see onia[1]

ownie \aủ-nē\ see owny

owning[1] \ō-niŋ\ see oning[2]

owning[2] \aủ-niŋ\ Browning
—*also* -ing *forms of verbs listed at* own[2]

ownish \aủ-nish\ brownish, clownish

ownlet \aủn-lət\ roundlet, townlet

ownsman \aủnz-mən\ gownsman, groundsman, roundsman, townsman

owny \aủ-nē\ brownie, browny, downy, townie

owper \ü-pər\ see ooper

owry \aủr-ē\ see owery

owse \aủz\ see ouse[2]

owser \aủ-zər\ see ouser

owson \aủz-ᵊn\ thousand advowson

owster \ō-stər\ see oaster

owsy \aủ-zē\ blousy, blowsy, drowsy, lousy

owth \ōth\ both, growth, loath, loth, oath, quoth, sloth, troth, wroth
betroth, outgrowth, upgrowth
Alioth, intergrowth, overgrowth, undergrowth

owy \ō-ē\ blowy, Chloe, doughy, joey, Joey, showy, snowy, towhee
echoey
kalanchoe

owys \ō-əs\ see ois[3]

ox \äks\ box, cox, fox, Fox, gox, Knox, lox, ox, pax, phlox, pox
aurochs, bandbox, boondocks, cowpox, detox, dreadlocks, firebox, Fort Knox, gearbox, gravlax, hatbox, hotbox, icebox, jukebox, lockbox, mailbox, matchbox, musk-ox, outfox, pillbox, postbox, redox, saltbox, sandbox, skybox, smallpox, snuffbox, soapbox, strongbox, sweatbox, toolbox, unbox, volvox, workbox, Xerox
chatterbox, equinox, orthodox, Orthodox, paradox, pillar-box, shadowbox, Skinner box, tinderbox, witness-box
econobox, Greek Orthodox, heterodox, homeobox, jack-in-the-box, unorthodox
neoorthodox

dementia praecox
—*also* -s, -'s, *and* -s' *forms of nouns,
and* -s *forms of verbs, listed at* ock¹

oxen \äk-sən\ oxen
Niedersachsen

oxer \äk-sər\ boxer, Boxer
bobby-soxer

oxie \äk-sē\ see oxy

oxin \äk-sən\ coxswain, tocsin,
toxin
dioxin
aflatoxin, mycotoxin

oxswain \äk-sən\ see oxin

oxy \äk-sē\ boxy, doxy, foxy, moxie,
oxy, proxy
epoxy
orthodoxy, Orthodoxy
heterodoxy
neoorthodoxy

oy \òi\ boy, buoy, cloy, coy, foy, goy,
hoy, joy, Joy, koi, ploy, poi, Roy, soy,
strawy, toy, troy, Troy
ahoy, alloy, Amoy, annoy, batboy,
bellboy, bok choy, borzoi, busboy,
callboy, carboy, charpoy, choirboy,
convoy, cowboy, decoy, deploy,
destroy, doughboy, employ, enjoy,
envoy, fly-boy, footboy, Hanoi,
hautbois, highboy, houseboy, killjoy,
Khoikhoi, Leroy, linkboy, lowboy,
McCoy, newsboy, pak choi, playboy,
plowboy, po'boy, postboy, potboy,
Quemoy, Rob Roy, Saint Croix,
Savoy, schoolboy, sepoy, tallboy,
teapoy, Tolstoy, tomboy, travois,
viceroy
Adonai, attaboy, bullyboy, copyboy,
corduroy, hoi polloi, Illinois, Iroquois,
maccaboy, Niterói, overjoy, paperboy,
redeploy, reemploy, Tinkertoy
Helen of Troy

oya \òi-ə\ see oia

oyable \òi-ə-bəl\ deployable,
employable

oyal¹ \īl\ see ile¹

oyal² \òil\ see oil

oyalist \òi-ə-ləst\ loyalist, royalist

oyalty \òil-tē\ loyalty, royalty
disloyalty, viceroyalty

oyance \òi-əns\ buoyance, joyance
annoyance, chatoyance,
clairvoyance, flamboyance

oyancy \òi-ən-sē\ buoyancy
chatoyancy, flamboyancy

oyant \òi-ənt\ buoyant
chatoyant, clairvoyant, flamboyant

oyce \òis\ see oice

oyd \òid\ see oid¹

oyden \òi-dᵊn\ Croydon, hoyden

oydon \òi-dᵊn\ see oyden

oyed \òid\ see oid¹

oyen \òi-ən\ doyen, Goyen
Iroquoian

oyer \òir\ coir, foyer, moire
caloyer, destroyer

oyes \òiz\ see oise²

oying \òiŋ\ see awing

oyle \òil\ see oil

oyless \òi-ləs\ joyless, Troilus

oyment \òi-mənt\ deployment,
employment, enjoyment
unemployment

oyne \òin\ see oin¹

oyo¹ \òi-ō\ boyo
arroyo

oyo² \òi-ə\ see oia

o-yo \ō-yō\ see ollo²

oyster \òi-stər\ see oister

oz¹ \əz\ see euse¹

oz² \òz\ see ause¹

oz³ \ōz\ see ose²

oza \ō-zə\ see osa[2]

oze \ōz\ see ose[2]

ozen[1] \əz-ᵊn\ cousin, cozen, dozen
cater-cousin

ozen[2] \ōz-ᵊn\ see osen

ozenage \əz-ᵊn-ij\ see ousinage

ozer \ō-zər\ see oser[1]

ozily \ō-zə-lē\ see osily

ozo[1] \ō-sō\ see oso[1]

ozo[2] \ō-zō\ see oso[2]

ozy \ō-zē\ see osy

ozzer \äz-ər\ rozzer
alcazar

ozzle \äz-əl\ Basel, Basil, nozzle,
schnozzle

U

u¹ \ü\ see ew¹

u² \ə\ Chang-de, Lao-tzu

ua¹ \ü-ə\ skua
Karlsruhe, lehua, Quechua
Timucua

ua² \ä\ see a¹

uable \ü-ə-bəl\ chewable, doable,
suable, viewable
accruable, construable, renewable

ual \ü-əl\ see uel¹

uan \ü-ən\ bruin, ruin, Siouan, yuan

uancy \ü-ən-sē\ see uency

uant \ü-ənt\ see uent

uart \ùrt\ see urt¹

ub \əb\ blub, chub, club, cub, drub,
dub, flub, grub, hub, nub, pub, rub,
scrub, shrub, slub, snub, stub, sub, tub
bathtub, flubdub, hubbub, nightclub,
washtub
overdub
Beelzebub

uba \ü-bə\ Cuba, juba, scuba, tuba
Aruba
Santiago de Cuba

ubal \ü-bəl\ Jubal, nubile, ruble,
tubal

uban \ü-bən\ see euben

ubbard \əb-ərd\ cupboard
Mother Hubbard

ubber \əb-ər\ blubber, clubber,
drubber, dubber, grubber, lubber,
rubber, scrubber, slubber, snubber,
tubber

landlubber, nightclubber
money-grubber

ubbery \əb-rē\ blubbery, rubbery,
shrubbery

ubbily \əb-ə-lē\ bubbly, chubbily,
grubbily

ubbin \əb-ən\ dubbin, nubbin

ubbing \əb-iŋ\ drubbing, rubbing,
slubbing
landlubbing
—*also* -ing *forms of verbs listed at*
ub

ubble \əb-əl\ bubble, double,
nubble, rubble, stubble, trouble
abubble, redouble, undouble
hubble-bubble

ubbled \əb-əld\ bubbled, doubled,
troubled
redoubled

ubbler \əb-lər\ see oubler

ubbly¹ \əb-lē\ bubbly, doubly,
nubbly, stubbly

ubbly² \əb-ə-lē\ see ubbily

ubby \əb-ē\ chubby, clubby, cubby,
grubby, hubby, nubby, Rabi, scrubby,
shrubby, snubby, stubby, tubby

ube \üb\ boob, cube, lube, rube,
tube
blowtube, Danube, flashcube,
haboob, jujube
hypercube

uben \ü-bən\ see euben

ubens \ü-bənz\ Rubens
—*also* -s, -'s, *and* -s' *forms of nouns*
listed at euben

uber \ü-bər\ Buber, cuber, goober, tuber

uberance \ü-brəns\ exuberance, protuberance

uberant \ü-brənt\ exuberant, protuberant

uberous \ü-brəs\ see ubris

ubic \ü-bik\ cubic, pubic cherubic

ubile \ü-bəl\ see ubal

ubious \ü-bē-əs\ dubious, rubious

ubis \ü-bəs\ pubis, rubus Anubis

uble \ü-bəl\ see ubal

ublic \əb-lik\ public republic

ublican \əb-li-kən\ publican republican

ubman \əb-mən\ clubman, Tubman

ubric \ü-brik\ lubric, rubric

ubrious \ü-brē-əs\ lugubrious, salubrious insalubrious

ubris \ü-brəs\ hubris tuberous

ubtile \ət-ᵊl\ see uttle

ubus \ü-bəs\ see ubis

uby \ü-bē\ see ooby

uca \ü-kə\ see ooka

ucal \ü-kəl\ ducal, nuchal archducal

ucan \ü-kən\ glucan, kuchen, Lucan interleukin

ucat \ək-ət\ see ucket

ucca¹ \ü-kə\ see ooka

ucca² \ək-ə\ see ukka

uccal \ək-əl\ see uckle

ucci \ü-chē\ see oochy

ucco \ək-ō\ see ucko

uccor \ək-ər\ see ucker

uccory \ək-rē\ see uckery

ucculence \ək-yə-ləns\ see uculence

uce \üs\ see use¹

uced \üst\ see oost

ucement \ü-smənt\ inducement, seducement

ucence \üs-ᵊns\ nuisance translucence

ucer \ü-sər\ juicer, looser adducer, Bull Mooser, inducer, lime-juicer, producer, transducer introducer, reproducer

uch¹ \ich\ see itch

uch² \ük\ see uke

uch³ \əch\ see utch¹

uchal \ü-kəl\ see ucal

uche¹ \ü-chē\ see oochy

uche² \üch\ see ooch¹

uche³ \üsh\ see ouche

uchen \ü-kən\ see ucan

ucher \ü-chər\ see uture

uchin \ü-shən\ see ution

uchsia \ü-shə\ see utia

uchy \əch-ē\ duchy, smutchy, touchy archduchy

ucia \ü-shə\ see utia

ucial \ü-shəl\ crucial fiducial

ucian \ü-shən\ see ution

ucible \ü-sə-bəl\ crucible deducible, educible, inducible, producible, protrusible

irreducible, reproducible
irreproducible

ucid \ü-səd\ deuced, lucid
pellucid, Seleucid

ucifer \ü-sə-fər\ crucifer, Lucifer

ucity \ü-sət-ē\ abstrusity, caducity

ucive \ü-siv\ see usive

uck¹ \ək\ buck, Buck, chuck, cluck,
cruck, duck, guck, huck, luck, muck,
pluck, puck, Puck, ruck, schmuck,
shuck, snuck, struck, stuck, suck,
truck, Truk, tuck, yech, yuck
amok, awestruck, bushbuck, Canuck,
dumbstruck, Kalmuck, lame-duck,
light-struck, moonstruck, mukluk,
muktuk, potluck, reedbuck, roebuck,
sawbuck, shelduck, stagestruck,
starstruck, sunstruck, unstuck,
upchuck, woodchuck
geoduck, Keokuk, Habakkuk,
megabuck, muckamuck, nip and tuck
high-muck-a-muck

uck² \ůk\ see ook¹

ukar \ək-ər\ see ucker

ucker \ək-ər\ bucker, chukar,
chukker, ducker, mucker, plucker,
pucker, shucker, succor, sucker,
trucker, tucker
bloodsucker, sapsucker, seersucker

uckery \ək-rē\ puckery, succory

ucket \ək-ət\ bucket, ducat, tucket
gutbucket, Nantucket

uckle \ək-əl\ buccal, buckle,
chuckle, knuckle, suckle, truckle
Arbuckle, bare-knuckle, parbuckle,
pinochle, swashbuckle, turnbuckle,
unbuckle
honeysuckle

uckled \ək-əld\ cuckold, knuckled
bare-knuckled
—also -ed forms of verbs listed at
uckle

uckler \ək-lər\ buckler, knuckler
swashbuckler

uckling \ək-liŋ\ duckling, suckling
swashbuckling
—also -ing forms of verbs listed at
uckle

ucko \ək-ō\ bucko, stucco

uckold \ək-əld\ see uckled

uckoo \ü-kü\ cuckoo
Maluku

ucks \əks\ see ux¹

uckus \ůk-əs\ ruckus, Sukkoth

ucky \ək-ē\ ducky, lucky, mucky,
plucky, yucky
Kentucky, unlucky
happy-go-lucky

uco \ü-kō\ pachuco
osso buco

ucre \ü-kər\ euchre, lucre

uct \əkt\ duct
abduct, adduct, conduct, construct,
deduct, destruct, eruct, induct,
instruct, obstruct
aqueduct, deconstruct, reconstruct,
usufruct, viaduct
—also -ed forms of verbs listed at
uck¹

uctable \ək-tə-bəl\ see uctible

uctal \ək-tᵊl\ ductal, ductile

uctance \ək-təns\ conductance,
inductance, reluctance

uctible \ək-tə-bəl\ conductible,
constructible, deductible, destructible
indestructible, ineluctable,
reconstructible

uctile \ək-tᵊl\ see uctal

ucting \ək-tiŋ\ ducting
semiconducting
—also -ing forms of verbs listed at
uct

uction \ək-shən\ fluxion, ruction, suction
  abduction, adduction, conduction, construction, deduction, destruction, eduction, effluxion, induction, instruction, obstruction, production, reduction, seduction
  deconstruction, introduction, reconstruction, reproduction
  photoreproduction

uctive \ək-tiv\ adductive, conductive, constructive, deductive, destructive, inductive, instructive, productive, reductive, seductive
  reconstructive, reproductive, self-destructive
  counterproductive

uctor \ək-tər\ abductor, adductor, conductor, constructor, destructor, eductor, inductor, instructor, obstructor
  deconstructor, reconstructor
  semiconductor, superconductor

uctress \ək-trəs\ conductress, instructress, seductress

uculence \ək-yə-ləns\ succulence, truculence

ucy \ü-sē\ see uicy

ud¹ \əd\ blood, bud, crud, cud, dud, flood, fud, Judd, mud, rudd, scud, spud, stud, sudd, thud
  coldblood, disbud, full-blood, half-blood, hotblood, lifeblood, oxblood, redbud, rosebud, warmblood
  stick-in-the-mud

ud² \üd\ see ude

ud³ \ùd\ see ood¹

uda \üd-ə\ Buddha, Gouda, Judah
  Barbuda, Bermuda, remuda
  barracuda, Buxtehude
  Gautama Buddha

udable \üd-ə-bəl\ excludable, extrudable, includable
  ineludible

udah \üd-ə\ see uda

udal \üd-ᵊl\ see oodle

udas \üd-əs\ Judas
  Santa Gertrudis

udd¹ \ùd\ see ood¹

udd² \əd\ see ud¹

udded \əd-əd\ see ooded¹

udder \əd-ər\ budder, flooder, judder, rudder, shudder, udder

uddha \üd-ə\ see uda

uddhist \üd-əst\ see udist¹

uddie \əd-ē\ see uddy¹

udding¹ \əd-iŋ\ budding, studding
  —also -ing forms of verbs listed at ud¹

udding² \ùd-iŋ\ see ooding

uddle \əd-ᵊl\ buddle, cuddle, fuddle, huddle, muddle, puddle, ruddle
  befuddle

uddly \əd-lē\ cuddly, Dudley, muddly, studly

uddy¹ \əd-ē\ bloody, buddy, Buddy, cruddy, cuddy, duddie, muddy, ruddy, study
  fuddy-duddy, understudy

uddy² \ùd-ē\ see oody²

ude¹ \üd\ brood, crowd, crude, dude, feud, food, hued, Jude, lewd, mood, nude, oud, pood, prude, pseud, rood, rude, shrewd, snood, stewed, who'd, wood, wud, you'd
  allude, collude, conclude, delude, denude, elude, etude, exclude, extrude, exude, fast-food, Gertrude, include, intrude, obtrude, occlude, postlude, preclude, prelude, protrude, quaalude, Quaalude, seafood, seclude, subdued, transude, unglued
  altitude, amplitude, aptitude, attitude, certitude, consuetude, crassitude, desuetude, finitude,

fortitude, gratitude, habitude,
hebetude, interlude, lassitude, latitude,
longitude, magnitude, mansuetude,
multitude, negritude, platitude,
plenitude, plentitude, promptitude,
pulchritude, quietude, rectitude,
seminude, servitude, solitude,
turpitude, vastitude
   beatitude, correctitude, decrepitude,
exactitude, inaptitude, incertitude,
ineptitude, infinitude, ingratitude,
inquietude, similitude, solicitude,
vicissitude
     dissimilitude, inexactitude
     verisimilitude

ude² \üd-ə\ see uda

udel \üd-ᵊl\ see oodle

udence \ü-dᵊn(t)s\ Prudence,
students
   imprudence
   jurisprudence

udeness \üd-nəs\ see udinous

udent \üd-ᵊnt\ prudent, student
   imprudent
   jurisprudent

udents \ü-dᵊn(t)s\ see udence

uder \üd-ər\ brooder, Tudor
   concluder, deluder, excluder,
extruder, intruder, obtruder, preluder
   —also -er forms of adjectives listed
at ude¹

udge¹ \əj\ budge, drudge, fudge,
grudge, judge, nudge, sludge, smudge,
trudge
   adjudge, begrudge, forejudge,
misjudge, prejudge

udge² \üj\ see uge¹

udgeon \əj-ən\ bludgeon, dudgeon,
gudgeon
   curmudgeon

udget \əj-ət\ budget
   fussbudget

udgie \əj-ē\ see udgy

udging \əj-iŋ\ drudging, grudging
   —also -ing forms of verbs listed at
udge¹

udgy \əj-ē\ budgie, pudgy, sludgy,
smudgy

udi \ü-dē\ see oody¹

udible \üd-ə-bəl\ see udable

udie \ü-dē\ see oody¹

udinal \üd-nəl\ altitudinal,
aptitudinal, attitudinal, latitudinal,
longitudinal, platitudinal

udinous \üd-nəs\ crudeness,
lewdness, rudeness, shrewdness
   altitudinous, multitudinous,
platitudinous, plenitudinous,
pulchritudinous

udis \üd-əs\ see udas

udish \üd-ish\ dudish, prudish

udist¹ \üd-əst\ Buddhist, feudist,
nudist
   —also -est forms of adjectives listed
at ude¹

udist² \ùd-əst\ see ouldest

udity \üd-ət-ē\ crudity, nudity

udley \əd-lē\ see uddly

udly \əd-lē\ see uddly

udo \üd-ō\ judo, kudo, pseudo,
scudo
   escudo, Matsudo, testudo

udor \üd-ər\ see uder

udsman \ùdz-mən\ see oodsman

udson \əd-sən\ Hudson, Judson

udu \üd-ü\ see oodoo

udy¹ \ü-dē\ see oody¹

udy² \əd-ē\ see uddy¹

ue¹ \ü\ see ew¹

ue² \ā\ see ay¹

ued \üd\ see **ude**

ueful \ü-fəl\ rueful
pantofle

ueghel \ü-gəl\ see **ugal**

ueil \əi\ Arauil
Argentueil

uel[1] \ü-əl\ crewel, cruel, dual, duel,
gruel, jewel, Jewel, Jewell, newel,
Newell
accrual, eschewal, refuel, renewal
Pantagruel

uel[2] \ül\ see **ool**[1]

uely \ü-lē\ see **uly**

uement \ü-mənt\ see **ewment**

uence \ü-əns\ affluence, confluence,
congruence, effluence, influence,
pursuance, refluence
incongruence

uency \ü-ən-sē\ fluency, truancy
affluency, congruency, nonfluency

ueness \ü-nəs\ see **ewness**

uenster \ən-stər\ see **unster**

uent \ü-ənt\ fluent, suint, truant
affluent, confluent, congruent,
effluent, influent
incongruent

uer \ü-ər\ see **ewer**[1]

uerdon \ərd-ᵊn\ see **urden**

uerile \ùr-əl\ see **ural**

ues \üz\ see **use**[2]

uesman \üz-mən\ see **ewsman**

uesome \ü-səm\ gruesome,
twosome

uesy \ü-zē\ see **oozy**

uet \ü-ət\ bluet, cruet, peewit, suet
conduit, intuit

uette \et\ see **et**[1]

uey \ü-ē\ see **ewy**

ufa \ü-fə\ loofah, tufa
opera buffa

uff \əf\ bluff, buff, chough, chuff,
cuff, duff, fluff, gruff, guff, huff, luff,
muff, puff, rough, ruff, scruff, scuff,
slough, snuff, sough, stuff, tough, tuff
dyestuff, earmuff, enough, foodstuff,
handcuff, rebuff
oeil-de-boeuf, overstuff

uffa \ü-fə\ see **ufa**

uffe[1] \üf\ see **oof**[1]

uffe[2] \ùf\ see **oof**[2]

uffed \əft\ chuffed, ruffed, tuft
candytuft
—also -ed *forms of verbs listed at* uff

uffel \əf-əl\ see **uffle**[1]

uffer \əf-ər\ bluffer, buffer, duffer,
puffer, rougher, snuffer, stuffer, suffer
candlesnuffer
—also -er *forms of adjectives listed
at* uff

uffet \əf-ət\ buffet, tuffet

uffin \əf-ən\ muffin, puffin, roughen,
toughen
ragamuffin

uffish \əf-ish\ huffish, roughish

uffle[1] \əf-əl\ duffel, muffle, ruffle,
scuffle, shuffle, snuffle, truffle
kerfuffle, reshuffle, unmuffle

uffle[2] \ü-fəl\ see **ueful**

uffled \əf-əld\ truffled
unruffled
—also -ed *forms of verbs listed at*
uffle[1]

uffler \əf-lər\ muffler, shuffler,
snuffler

uffly \əf-lē\ bluffly, gruffly, roughly,
ruffly

uffy \əf-ē\ chuffy, fluffy, huffy, puffy,
scruffy, snuffy, stuffy, toughie

ufi \ü-fē\ see **oofy**

ufous \ü-fəs\ rufous, Rufus

uft \əft\ see uffed

ufti \əf-tē\ mufti, tufty

ufty \əf-tē\ see ufti

ufus \ü-fəs\ see ufous

ug \əg\ bug, chug, Doug, drug, dug, fug, hug, jug, lug, mug, plug, pug, rug, shrug, slug, smug, snug, thug, trug, tug, ugh, vug
  bedbug, billbug, debug, earplug, firebug, fireplug, goldbug, humbug, lovebug, stinkbug, unplug
  antidrug, chugalug, doodlebug, jitterbug, ladybug, litterbug, mealybug, shutterbug

uga \ü-gə\ beluga, Cayuga, Kaluga, Sevruga, Tortuga
  Chattanooga

ugal \ü-gəl\ Brueghel, bugle, frugal, fugal, fugle, kugel
  conjugal

ugar \ug-ər\ see ugur

uge[1] \üj\ huge, kludge, Lodz, scrooge, scrouge, stooge
  deluge
  centrifuge, subterfuge

uge[2] \üzh\ Bruges, luge, rouge
  dcluge, gamboge, refuge
  Baton Rouge

ugel \ü-gəl\ see ugal

uges \üzh\ see uge[2]

uggaree \əg-rē\ see uggery[1]

ugger[1] \əg-ər\ bugger, chugger, lugger, mugger, plugger, rugger, slugger
  Bavagar, Jamnagar, Srinagar
  hugger-mugger, Navanagar

ugger[2] \ug-ər\ see ugur

uggery[1] \əg-rē\ buggery, puggaree, snuggery, thuggery
  skulduggery

uggery[2] \ug-rē\ see ugary

ugget \əg-ət\ drugget, nugget

uggie \əg-ē\ see uggy

uggish \əg-ish\ sluggish, thuggish

uggle \əg-əl\ guggle, juggle, smuggle, snuggle, struggle

uggler \əg-lər\ juggler, smuggler, struggler

uggy \əg-ē\ buggy, druggie, druggy, fuggy, luggie, muggy

ugh[1] \əg\ see ug

ugh[2] \ü\ see ew[1]

ughes \üz\ see use[2]

ugle \ü-gəl\ see ugal

ugli \ə-glē\ see ugly

uglia \ul-yə\ see ulia

ugly \əg-lē\ smugly, Ugli, ugly
  plug-ugly

ugn \ün\ see oon[1]

ugner \ü-nər\ see ooner

ugric \ü-grik\ tugrik, Ugric
  Finno-Ugric

ugrik \ü-grik\ see ugric

ugu \ü-gü\ fugu, goo-goo

ugur \ug-ər\ booger, bugger, sugar

uhe \ü-ə\ see ua

uhl \ül\ see ool[1]

uhr[1] \ər\ see eur[1]

uhr[2] \ur\ see ure[1]

ührer \ur-ər\ see urer[1]

ui[1] \ā\ see ay[1]

ui[2] \ē\ see ee[1]

uice \üs\ see use[1]

uiced \üst\ see oost

uiceless \ü-sləs\ see useless

uicer \ü-sər\ see ucer

uicy \ü-sē\ goosey, juicy, Lucy, sluicy, sprucy
 Brancusi, Watusi
 acey-deucey, Arginusae, loosey-goosey

uid \ü-id\ Clwyd, druid, fluid

uidable \īd-ə-bəl\ see idable[1]

uidance \īd-ᵊns\ see idance

uide \īd\ see ide[1]

uided \īd-əd\ see ided

uider \īd-ər\ see ider[1]

uidon \īd-ᵊn\ see iden

uiker \ī-kər\ see iker

uild \ild\ see illed

uilder \il-dər\ see ilder

uilding \il-diŋ\ see ilding

uile \īl\ see ile[1]

uileless \īl-ləs\ see ileless

uiler \ī-lər\ see ilar

uilleann \i-lən\ see illon

uilt \ilt\ see ilt

uimpe \amp\ see amp[3]

uin[1] \ü-ən\ see uan

uin[2] \ən\ see un

uin[3] \aⁿ\ see in[4]

uing \ü-iŋ\ see oing[2]

uint \ü-ənt\ see uent

uir \u̇r\ see ure[1]

uirdly \u̇r-lē\ see urely

uis \ü-əs\ see ouis[2]

uisance \üs-ᵊns\ see ucence

uisard \ī-zərd\ see isored

uise[1] \üz\ see use[2]

uise[2] \īz\ see ize

uiser \ü-zər\ see user

uish \ü-ish\ see ewish

uisne \ü-nē\ see oony

uiste \is-tē\ see icity[2]

uit[1] \ü-ət\ see uet

uit[2] \üt\ see ute

uitable \üt-ə-bəl\ see utable

uitage \üt-ij\ see ootage[1]

uite \üt\ see ute

uited \üt-əd\ see ooted[1]

uiter \üt-ər\ see uter

uiterer \üt-ər-ər\ fruiterer, pewterer

uiting \üt-iŋ\ see uting

uitless \üt-ləs\ see ootless

uitlet \üt-lət\ see ootlet

uitor \üt-ər\ see uter

uitous \ü-ət-əs\ circuitous, fortuitous, gratuitous

uits \üts\ see oots

uittle[1] \üt-ᵊl\ see utile

uittle[2] \ət-ᵊl\ see uttle

uity[1] \ü-ət-ē\ acuity, annuity, circuity, congruity, fatuity, fortuity, gratuity, vacuity
 ambiguity, assiduity, conspicuity, contiguity, continuity, incongruity, ingenuity, perpetuity, promiscuity, superfluity
 discontinuity

uity[2] \üt-ē\ see ooty[1]

uk[1] \ük\ see uke

uk[2] \u̇k\ see ook[1]

uk[3] \ək\ see uck

ukar \ə-kər\ see ucker

uke \ük\ cuke, duke, fluke, gook,
juke, kook, Luke, nuke, puke, snook,
souk, spook, suq, tuque, uke, yeuk
  archduke, Baruch, caoutchouc,
  Chinook, Kirkuk, Mamluk, rebuke
  Heptateuch, Hexateuch, Pentateuch

uki¹ \ü-kē\ see ooky¹

uki² \ù-kē\ see ookie

ukka \ǝk-ǝ\ chukka, pukka, yucca
  felucca

ukkah \ùk-ǝ\ see ookah

ukker \ǝk-ǝr\ see ucker

ukkoth \ùk-ǝs\ see uckus

uku \ü-kü\ see uckoo

ul¹ \ùl\ bull, Bull, full, pull, shul,
wool, you'll
  armful, bagful, bellpull, brimful,
  bulbul, canful, capful, carful, cheekful,
  chestful, chock-full, cupful, drawerful,
  earful, eyeful, fistful, forkful, glassful,
  handful, houseful, jarful, John Bull,
  jugful, leg-pull, mouthful, outpull,
  pailful, panful, pipeful, plateful,
  potful, push-pull, rackful, roomful,
  sackful, scoopful, shelfful, skinful,
  spoonful, stickful, tankful, tinful,
  topful, trainful, trayful, trunkful,
  tubful
    barrelful, basketful, bellyful,
    teaspoonful
    dyed-in-the-wool, tablespoonful

ul² \ül\ see ool¹

ul³ \ǝl\ see ull¹

ula \ü-lǝ\ Beulah, Fula, hula, moola,
pula, Tula
  ampulla, tabbouleh
  Ashtabula
  San Pedro Sula

ular \ü-lǝr\ see ooler

ulcent \ǝl-sǝnt\ see ulsant

ulcer \ǝl-sǝr\ see ulser

ulch \ǝlch\ cultch, gulch, mulch

ule¹ \ü-lē\ see uly

ule² \ül\ see ool¹

ulean \ü-lē-ǝn\ Boolean
  Acheulean, cerulean

uled \üld\ see ooled

ulep \ü-lǝp\ see ulip

uler \ü-lǝr\ see ooler

ules \ülz\ Jules
  —also -s, -'s, and -s' forms of nouns,
  and -s forms of verbs, listed at ool¹

ulet \ǝl-ǝt\ see ullet¹

uley¹ \ü-lē\ see uly

uley² \ùl-ē\ see ully²

ulf \ǝlf\ golf, gulf, Gulf
  engulf
  Beowulf
  Saronic Gulf

ulgar \ǝl-gǝr\ see ulgur

ulge \ǝlj\ bulge
  divulge, indulge
  overindulge

ulgence¹ \ǝl-jǝns\ divulgence,
indulgence, refulgence

ulgence² \ùl-jǝns\ effulgence,
refulgence

ulgent \ǝl-jǝnt\ fulgent
  indulgent

ulgur \ǝl-gǝr\ bulgur, vulgar

ulhas \ǝl-ǝs\ see ullus

uli \ùl-ē\ see ully²

ulia \ül-yǝ\ Julia, Puglia
  Apulia
  Friuli-Venezia Giulia

ulie \ü-lē\ see uly

ulip \ü-lǝp\ julep, tulip

ulish \ü-lish\ see oolish

ulity \ü-lǝt-ē\ credulity, garrulity,
sedulity
  incredulity

ulk \əlk\ bulk, hulk, skulk, sulk, yolk

ulky \əl-kē\ bulky, sulky

ull¹ \əl\ cull, dull, gull, hull, Hull,
lull, mull, null, scull, skull, stull, trull
annul, Choiseul, mogul, numskull,
pas seul
monohull, multihull, Sitting Bull,
Solihull
Kingston upon Hull

ull² \ul\ see ul¹

ulla¹ \ul-ə\ bulla, mullah, Sulla
ampulla

ulla² \ü-lə\ see ula

ulla³ \əl-ə\ see ullah¹

ullage \əl-ij\ sullage, ullage

ullah¹ \əl-ə\ Gullah, mullah, nullah
medulla
ayatollah

ullah² \ul-ə\ see ulla¹

ullan \əl-ən\ see ullen

ullard \əl-ərd\ see olored

ullate \əl-ət\ see ullet¹

ulle \ül\ see ool¹

ullein \əl-ən\ see ullen

ullen \əl-ən\ mullein, stollen, sullen
Lucullan

uller¹ \ul-ər\ fuller, puller

uller² \əl-ər\ see olor¹

ulles \əl-əs\ see ullus

ullet¹ \əl-ət\ culet, cullet, gullet,
mullet
cucullate

ullet² \ul-ət\ bullet, Bullitt, pullet

ulley \ul-ē\ see ully²

ullion \əl-yən\ cullion, mullion,
scullion
slumgullion

ullis \əl-əs\ see ullus

ullitt \ul-ət\ see ullet²

ullman \ul-mən\ fulmine, Pullman

ullus \əl-əs\ Dulles
Agulhas, Catullus, portcullis
Cape Agulhas

ully¹ \əl-ē\ cully, dully, gully, sully

ully² \ul-ē\ bully, fully, gully, muley,
puli, pulley, woolly

ulmine \ul-mən\ see ullman

ulp \əlp\ gulp, pulp
insculp

ulsant \əl-sənt\ pulsant
convulsant, demulcent

ulse \əls\ dulse, pulse
avulse, convulse, expulse, impulse,
repulse

ulser \əl-sər\ pulser, ulcer

ulsion \əl-shən\ pulsion
avulsion, compulsion, convulsion,
emulsion, evulsion, expulsion,
impulsion, propulsion, repulsion,
revulsion

ulsive \əl-siv\ compulsive,
convulsive, emulsive, expulsive,
impulsive, propulsive, repulsive

ult \əlt\ cult
adult, consult, exult, incult, indult,
insult, occult, penult, result, tumult
catapult
antepenult

ultancy \əlt-ᵊn-sē\ consultancy,
exultancy

ultant \əlt-ᵊnt\ consultant, exultant,
resultant

ultch \əlch\ see ulch

ulter \əl-tər\ consultor, insulter,
occulter

ultery \əl-trē\ see ultry

ultor \əl-tər\ see ulter

ultry \əl-trē\ sultry
adultery

ulture \əl-chər\ culture, multure,
vulture
  subculture
  agriculture, apiculture, aquaculture,
aviculture, counterculture, floriculture,
horticulture, mariculture,
monoculture, silviculture, viniculture
  arboriculture

ulty \əl-tē\ see alti[1]

ulu \ü-lü\ lulu, Sulu, Zulu
  Bangweulu, Honolulu

ulunder \əl-ən-dər\ see olander

ulva \əl-və\ ulva, vulva

ulvar \əl-vər\ see ulver

ulver \əl-vər\ culver, vulvar

uly \ü-lē\ bluely, boule, coolie,
coolly, coulee, duly, ghoulie, Julie,
muley, newly, puli, ruly, stoolie,
Thule, truly, tule
  Bernoulli, guayule, patchouli,
tabbouleh, unduly, unruly
  ultima Thule

um[1] \əm\ bum, chum, come, crumb,
cum, drum, dumb, from, glum, gum,
hum, lum, mum, numb, plum, plumb,
rhumb, rum, scrum, scum, slum,
some, strum, sum, swum, them,
thrum, thumb
  alum, aplomb, become, benumb,
degum, dim sum, dumdum, eardrum,
ho-hum, humdrum, income, outcome,
subgum, succumb, therefrom, Tom
Thumb, tom-tom, wherefrom, yum-
yum
  bubblegum, kettledrum, overcome,
sugarplum
  hop-o'my-thumb

um[2] \u̇m\ cum, groom, Qom
  Targum
  mare librum

um[3] \üm\ see oom[1]

uma \ü-mə\ duma, pneuma, puma
  satsuma
  Ancohuma, Montezuma

umable \ü-mə-bəl\ assumable,
consumable, presumable, subsumable
  inconsumable

umage \əm-ij\ see ummage

uman \ü-mən\ blooming, crewman,
human, lumen, Newman, numen,
Truman, Yuman
  acumen, albumen, albumin, bitumen,
ichneumon, illumine, inhuman,
panhuman, subhuman
  antihuman, catechumen,
protohuman, superhuman

umanist \ü-mə-nəst\ see umenist

umanous \ü-mə-nəs\ see uminous

umb \əm\ see um[1]

umbar \əm-bər\ see umber[1]

umbed \əmd\ green-thumbed,
unplumbed

umbel \əm-bəl\ see umble

umbency \əm-bən-sē\ incumbency,
recumbency

umbent \əm-bənt\ decumbent,
incumbent, procumbent, recumbent
  superincumbent

umber[1] \əm-bər\ cumber, Humber,
lumbar, lumber, number, slumber,
umber
  cucumber, encumber, outnumber,
renumber
  disencumber, Reynolds number
  Avogadro's number

umber[2] \əm-ər\ see ummer

umbered \əm-bərd\ unnumbered
  unencumbered
  —also -ed forms of verbs listed at
umber[1]

umberland \əm-bər-lənd\
  Cumberland
  Northumberland

umberous \əm-brəs\ see umbrous

umbery \əm-brē\ ombre, slumbery

umbing \əm-iŋ\ see oming

umble \əm-bəl\ bumble, crumble, fumble, grumble, humble, jumble, mumble, rumble, scumble, stumble, tumble, umbel
rough-and-tumble

umbler \əm-blər\ bumbler, fumbler, grumbler, humbler, mumbler, rumbler, stumbler, tumbler

umbling \əm-bliŋ\ rumbling, tumbling
—*also* -ing *forms of verbs listed at* umble

umbly¹ \əm-blē\ crumbly, grumbly, humbly, mumbly, rumbly

umbly² \əm-lē\ comely, dumbly, dumly, numbly

umbness \əm-nəs\ dumbness, glumness, numbness
alumnus

umbo \əm-bō\ gumbo, jumbo, umbo
Colombo
mumbo jumbo

umbra \əm-brə\ umbra
penumbra

umbral \əm-brəl\ see umbril

umbria \əm-brē-ə\ Cumbria, Umbria
Northumbria

umbril \əm-brəl\ tumbril, umbral
penumbral

umbrous \əm-brəs\ cumbrous, slumberous

ume \üm\ see oom¹

umed \ümd\ see oomed

umedly \ü-məd-lē\ consumedly, presumedly

umelet \üm-lət\ see oomlet

umely \ü-mə-lē\ see oomily

umen \ü-mən\ see uman

umenist \ü-mə-nəst\ humanist, luminist
ecumenist, illuminist, phillumenist

umer \ü-mər\ bloomer, Bloomer, groomer, humor, roomer, rumor, Sumer, tumor
consumer, costumer, exhumer, perfumer, presumer, schussboomer

umeral \üm-rəl\ humeral, humoral, numeral

umerous \üm-rəs\ see umorous

umerus \üm-rəs\ see umorous

umey \ü-mē\ see oomy

umf \əmf\ see umph

umi \ü-mē\ see oomy

umice \əm-əs\ see ummous

umid \ü-məd\ humid, tumid

umin¹ \əm-ən\ cumin, summon

umin² \ü-mən\ see uman

uminal \ü-mən-ᵊl\ luminal, noumenal

uminate \ü-mə-nət\ acuminate, illuminate

umine \ü-mən\ see uman

uming \ü-miŋ\ blooming
consuming
everblooming, time-consuming, unassuming
—*also* -ing *forms of verbs listed at* oom¹

uminist \ü-mə-nəst\ see umenist

uminous \ü-mə-nəs\ luminous, numinous
albuminous, aluminous, bituminous, leguminous, quadrumanous, voluminous

umma \əm-ə\ gumma, momma, summa

ummage \əm-ij\ rummage
West Brumage

ummary¹ \əm-rē\ see ummery²

ummary² \əm-ə-rē\ see ummery¹

ummate \əm-ət\ see ummet

ummel \əm-əl\ see ommel²

ummell \əm-əl\ see ommel²

ummer \əm-ər\ bummer, comer,
drummer, gummer, hummer, mummer,
plumber, rummer, slummer, strummer,
summer
latecomer, midsummer, newcomer
overcomer, up-and-comer
—*also* -er *forms of adjectives listed
at* um¹

ummery \əm-ə-rē\ flummery,
mummery, summary, summery
Montgomery

ummet \əm-ət\ grummet, plummet,
summit
consummate

ummie \əm-ē\ see ummy

ummit \əm-ət\ see ummet

ummock \əm-ək\ hummock,
stomach

ummon \əm-ən\ see umin¹

ummoner \əm-nər\ see umnar

ummous \əm-əs\ gummous,
hummus, pomace, pumice

ummox \əm-əks\ flummox,
hummocks, lummox, stomachs

ummus \əm-əs\ see ummous

ummy \əm-ē\ chummy, crummie,
crummy, dummy, gummy, mommy,
mummy, plummy, rummy, scummy,
slummy, tummy, yummy

umnar \əm-nər\ summoner, Sumner
columnar

umner \əm-nər\ see umnar

umness \əm-nəs\ see umbness

umnus \əm-nəs\ see umbness

umor \ü-mər\ see umer

umoral \üm-rəl\ see umeral

umorous \üm-rəs\ humerus,
humorous, numerous, tumorous
innumerous

umous \ü-məs\ brumous, humus,
spumous
posthumous

ump \əmp\ bump, chump, clomp,
clump, comp, crump, dump, flump,
frump, grump, hump, jump, lump,
mump, plump, pump, rump, slump,
stump, sump, thump, trump, tump,
ump, whump
mugwump, no-trump, tub-thump
callithump, overtrump

umper \əm-pər\ bumper, dumper,
jumper, lumper, plumper, pumper,
stumper, thumper
tub-thumper
Bible-thumper

umph \əmf\ bumf, humph
galumph, harrumph

umpish \əm-pish\ dumpish,
frumpish, lumpish, plumpish

umpkin \əŋ-kən\ see unken

umple \əm-pəl\ crumple, rumple

umply \əm-plē\ crumply, plumply,
rumply

umps \əms\ dumps, mumps
—*also* -s, -'s, *and* -s' *forms of nouns,
and* -s *forms of verbs, listed at* ump

umption \əm-shən\ gumption
assumption, consumption,
presumption, resumption,
subsumption

umptious \əm-shəs\ bumptious,
scrumptious
presumptuous

umptive \əm-tiv\ assumptive,
consumptive, presumptive

umptuous[1] \əm-chəs\ sumptuous
presumptuous

umptuous[2] \əm-shəs\ see umptious

umpus \əm-pəs\ see ompass[2]

umpy \əm-pē\ bumpy, clumpy,
dumpy, frumpy, grumpy, humpy,
jumpy, lumpy, stumpy

umulous \ü-myə-ləs\ see umulus

umulus \ü-myə-ləs\ cumulous,
cumulus, tumulus

umus \ü-məs\ see umous

umy \ü-mē\ see oomy

un[1] \ən\ bun, done, Donne, dun, fen,
foehn, fun, gun, hon, Hun, jun, maun,
none, nun, one, pun, run, shun, son,
spun, stun, sun, sunn, ton, tonne, tun,
won
  A-1, begun, blowgun, chaconne,
Chang-chun, Chaplin, finespun, first-
run, flashgun, forerun, godson,
grandson, handgun, hard-won,
homespun, long run, outdone, outgun,
outrun, popgun, pressrun, rerun, sea-
run, shotgun, six-gun, stepson,
undone, V-1, well-done, Xiamen
  Acheron, Algonquin, allemande, all-
or-none, Balzacian, hit-and-run,
kiloton, machine-gun, megaton, one-
on-one, one-to-one, overdone,
overrun, PL/1, Sally Lunn, scattergun,
tommy gun, twenty-one, underdone,
underrun
  alexandrine

un[2] \ün\ see oon[1]

un[3] \ün\ Fushun, Lushun, tabun

una \ü-nə\ Buna, Cunha, Luna,
Poona, puna, tuna
  Altoona, kahuna, lacuna, laguna,
vicuña
  Tristan da Cunha

uña[1] \ü-nə\ see una

uña[2] \ün-yə\ see unia

unal \ün-ᵊl\ communal, jejunal,
lagoonal, monsoonal, tribunal

unar \ü-nər\ see ooner

unary \ü-nə-rē\ unary
festoonery, sublunary
superlunary

unate \ü-nət\ unit
lacunate, tribunate

unc \ənk\ see unk

uncan \əŋ-kən\ see unken

unce \əns\ dunce, once
  —also -s, -'s, and -s' forms of nouns,
  and -s forms of verbs, listed at ont[1]

unch \ənch\ brunch, bunch, Bunche,
crunch, hunch, lunch, munch, punch,
scrunch
  keypunch
  ploughman's lunch

unche \ənch\ see unch

uncheon \ən-chən\ luncheon,
puncheon, truncheon

uncher \ən-chər\ cruncher, luncher,
muncher
  cowpuncher, keypuncher
  counterpuncher

unchy \ən-chē\ bunchy, crunchy,
punchy

uncial \ən-sē-əl\ uncial
internuncial

uncle \əŋ-kəl\ nuncle, uncle
  carbuncle, caruncle, furuncle,
  granduncle, peduncle

unco[1] \əŋ-kō\ bunco, junco, unco

unco[2] \əŋ-kə\ see unkah

unct \əŋt\ trunked
  adjunct, conjunct, defunct, disjunct
  —also -ed forms of verbs listed at
  unk

unction \əŋ-shən\ function,
junction, unction

compunction, conjunction,
disjunction, dysfunction, injunction,
malfunction
  extreme unction

unctional \əŋ-shnəl\ functional,
junctional
  dysfunctional

unctious \əŋ-shəs\ compunctious,
rambunctious

unctory \əŋ-trē\ emunctory,
perfunctory

uncture \əŋ-chər\ juncture,
puncture
  conjuncture, disjuncture
  acupuncture

uncular \əŋ-kyə-lər\ avuncular,
carbuncular, peduncular

unculus \əŋ-kyə-ləs\ homunculus,
ranunculus

und¹ \ənd\ bund, fund, gunned
defund, obtund, refund, rotund,
secund
cummerbund, orotund, pudibund,
rubicund, underfund
  —also -ed *forms of verbs listed at*
un¹

und² \u̇nd\ bund
dachshund

und³ \u̇nt\ see unt¹

und⁴ \au̇nd\ see ound²

unda \ən-də\ Munda, Sunda
osmunda, rotunda
barramunda, floribunda

undae \ən-dē\ see undi¹

undant \ən-dənt\ abundant,
redundant
superabundant

unday \ən-dē\ see undi¹

undays \ən-dēz\ Mondays,
Sundays, undies
  —also -s, -'s, *and* -s' *forms of nouns*
listed at undi¹

undem \ən-dəm\ see undum

under \ən-dər\ Bandar, blunder,
plunder, sunder, thunder, under,
wonder
asunder, hereunder, thereunder

underous \ən-drəs\ plunderous,
thunderous, wondrous

undi¹ \ən-dē\ Monday, sundae,
Sunday
Whitmonday, Whitsunday
barramundi, Bay of Fundy,
jaguarundi, Mrs. Grundy, salmagundi
coatimundi

undi² \ün-dē\ Burundi
Ruanda-Urundi

undies \ən-dēz\ see undays

undity \ən-dət-ē\ fecundity,
profundity, rotundity
moribundity, orotundity, rubicundity

undle \ən-dᵊl\ bundle, rundle,
trundle
unbundle

undness \ən-nəs\ see oneness

undum \ən-dəm\ corundum
ad eundem, Carborundum

undy \ən-dē\ see undi¹

une \ün\ see oon¹

uneau \ü-nō\ see uno

uneless \ün-ləs\ see oonless

uner \ü-nər\ see ooner

unes \ünz\ see oons

ung¹ \əŋ\ bung, clung, dung, flung,
hung, lung, pung, rung, slung, sprung,
strung, stung, sung, swung, tongue,
tung, wrung, young, Young
among, bee-stung, far-flung, high-
strung, Kaifeng, low-slung, unstrung,
unsung, well-hung
adder's-tongue, double-hung,
double-tongue, triple-tongue,
overhung, overstrung, underslung

ung² \ùŋ\ Jung, Kung, Sung
Antung, Bandung, Dandong,
Dadong, Hamhung, Kao-hsiung,
Tatung, Zigong
Nibelung
geländesprung
Götterdämmerung

ungal \ən-gəl\ see ungle

unge \ənj\ lunge, plunge, sponge
expunge

unged \əŋd\ see ongued

ungeon \ən-jən\ donjon, dungeon,
spongin

unger¹ \ən-jər\ lunger, plunger,
sponger
expunger

unger² \əŋ-gər\ see onger¹

ungible \ən-jə-bəl\ fungible
inexpungible

ungle \əŋ-gəl\ bungle, fungal,
jungle, pungle

ungo \əŋ-gō\ fungo, mungo

ungous \əŋ-gəs\ fungous, fungus
humongous

ungry \ən-grē\ see ongery

ungus \əŋ-gəs\ see ungous

ungy \ən-jē\ grungy, spongy

unha \ü-nə\ see una

uni \ü-nē\ see oony

unia \ün-yə\ petunia, vicuña

unic \ü-nik\ eunuch, Munich, Punic,
runic, tunic

unicate \ü-ni-kət\ tunicate
excommunicate

unich \ü-nik\ see unic

union \ən-yən\ bunion, grunion,
onion, ronyon, trunnion
Paul Bunyan

unis \ü-nəs\ see ewness

unish¹ \ən-ish\ Hunnish, punish

unish² \ü-nish\ see oonish

unit \ü-nət\ see unate

unitive \ü-nət-iv\ punitive, unitive

unity \ü-nət-ē\ unity
community, disunity, immunity,
impunity
importunity, opportunity
European Community

unk \əŋk\ bunk, chunk, clunk,
drunk, dunk, flunk, funk, gunk, hunk,
junk, monk, plunk, punk, shrunk,
skunk, slunk, spunk, stunk, sunk,
thunk, trunk
chipmunk, debunk, Podunk, punch-
drunk, quidnunc

unkah \əŋ-kə\ punkah, unco

unkard \əŋ-kərd\ bunkered,
drunkard, Dunkard, hunkered

unked \əŋt\ see unct

unken \əŋ-kən\ Duncan, drunken,
pumpkin, shrunken, sunken

unker \əŋ-kər\ bunker, Bunker,
clunker, Dunker, flunker, hunker,
junker, lunker, plunker, punker,
younker
debunker, spelunker

unkie \əŋ-kē\ see unky

unkin \əŋ-kəm\ see uncan

unks \əŋs\ hunks
quincunx
—also -s, -'s, and -s' forms of nouns,
and -s forms of verbs, listed at unk

unky \əŋ-kē\ chunky, clunky,
donkey, flunky, funky, gunky, hunky,
Hunky, junkie, junky, monkey, punkie,
punky, spunkie, spunky

unless \ən-ləs\ runless, sonless,
sunless

unn \ən\ see un

unnage \ən-ij\ dunnage, tonnage
megatonnage

unned \ənd\ see und[1]

unnel \ən-ᵊl\ funnel, gunnel,
gunwale, runnel, trunnel, tunnel

unner \ən-ər\ cunner, gunner,
runner, scunner, shunner, stunner,
tonner
forerunner, front-runner, gunrunner,
roadrunner, rumrunner

unnery \ən-rē\ gunnery, nunnery

unness \ən-nəs\ see oneness

unning \ən-iŋ\ cunning, running,
stunning
—also -ing forms of verbs listed at
un[1]

unnion \ən-yən\ see union

unnish \ən-ish\ see unish[1]

unny \ən-ē\ bunny, funny, gunny,
honey, money, runny, sonny, sunny,
tunny
Ballymoney

uno \ü-nō\ Bruno, Juneau, Juno
numero uno

unster \ən-stər\ Muenster, punster

unt[1] \ùnt\ dachshund, Dortmund
exeunt

unt[2] \ənt\ see ont[1]

untal \ənt-ᵊl\ see untle

unter \ənt-ər\ blunter, bunter,
chunter, grunter, hunter, punter,
shunter
confronter, foxhunter, headhunter,
pothunter, witch-hunter

unting \ənt-iŋ\ bunting
foxhunting, head-hunting, witch-
hunting
—also -ing forms of verbs listed at
ont[1]

untle \ənt-ᵊl\ frontal, gruntle
confrontal, disgruntle
contrapuntal

unty \ənt-ē\ punty, runty

unwale \ən-ᵊl\ see unnel

unx \əŋs\ see unks

uny \ü-nē\ see oony

unyan \ən-yən\ see union

uoth \ü-əs\ see ewess

uoy[1] \ü-ē\ see ewy

uoy[2] \ói\ see oy

uoyance \ü-əns\ see oyance

uoyancy \ói-ən-sē\ see oyancy

uoyant \ói-ənt\ see oyant

up \əp\ cup, dup, hup, pup, scup,
sup, tup, up, yup
backup, balls-up, bang-up, beat-up,
blowup, breakup, brush up, buildup,
built-up, call-up, catch-up, change-up,
checkup, chin-up, cleanup, close-up,
cock-up, crack-up, cutup, dial-up,
dried-up, dustup, eggcup, eyecup,
faceup, fill-up, flare-up, foul-up,
frame-up, fry-up, getup, giddap,
grown-up, hang-up, heads-up, hepped
up, het up, holdup, hookup, hopped-
up, jack-up, jam-up, kickup, kingcup,
lash-up, lay-up, lead-up, letup, line up,
linkup, lockup, lookup, louse up,
made-up, makeup, markup, matchup,
mix-up, mixed-up, mock-up, mop-up,
mug up, nip-up, one-up, pasteup,
pickup, pileup, pinup, pop-up, pull-up,
punch-up, push-up, put-up, re-up,
roundup, run-up, scaleup, screwup,
send-up, setup, shack up, shake-up,
shape-up, shook-up, shoot up, sign up,
sit-up, slap-up, slipup, smashup,
speedup, stand-up, start-up, step up,
stepped-up, stickup, stuck-up, sum-up,
sunup, take-up, teacup, thumbs-up,
tie-up, toss-up, touch-up, trumped-up,

tune-up, turnup, walk-up, warm-up,
washed-up, washup, windup, wised-
up, workup, wrap-up, write-up
belly up, buttercup, button-up, cover-
up, follow-up, higher-up, hurry-up,
pick-me-up, pony up, runner-up,
seven-up, shoot-em-up, summing-up,
up-and-up, wickiup, winding-up
Johnny-jump-up, sunny-side up

upa \ü-pə\ pupa, stupa

upas \ü-pəs\ see upus

upboard \əb-ərd\ see ubbard

upe \üp\ see oop[1]

upel \ü-pəl\ see uple[2]

upelet \ü-plət\ see uplet[2]

uper \ü-pər\ see ooper

upi \ü-pē\ see oopy

upid \ü-pəd\ Cupid, stupid

upil \ü-pəl\ see uple[2]

uple[1] \əp-əl\ couple, supple
decouple

uple[2] \ü-pəl\ cupel, duple, pupil,
scruple
quadruple, quintuple, sextuple

uple[3] \üp-ᵊl\ supple
quadruple, quintuple, sextuple

uplet[1] \əp-lət\ couplet
gradruplet, quintuplet, sextuplet

uplet[2] \ü-plət\ drupelet
quadruplet

uplicate \ü-pli-kət\ duplicate
quadruplicate, quintuplicate,
sextuplicate

upor \ü-pər\ see ooper

uppance \əp-əns\ threepence,
twopence
comeuppance

upper \əp-ər\ crupper, scupper,
supper, upper
stand-upper

uppie \əp-ē\ see uppy

upple[1] \üp-əl\ see uple[3]

upple[2] \əp-əl\ see uple[1]

uppy \əp-ē\ cuppy, guppy, puppy,
yuppie

upt \əpt\ abrupt, corrupt, disrupt,
erupt, irrupt
developed, incorrupt, interrupt
—also -ed forms of verbs listed at up

upter \əp-tər\ corrupter, disrupter
interrupter

uptible \əp-tə-bəl\ corruptible,
eruptible, irruptible
incorruptible, interruptible

uption \əp-shən\ abruption,
corruption, disruption, eruption,
irruption
interruption

uptive \əp-tiv\ corruptive,
disruptive, eruptive, irruptive
interruptive

upus \ü-pəs\ croupous, lupus, upas

uq \ük\ see uke

uque \ük\ see uke

ur[1] \ȯr\ see or[1]

ur[2] \u̇r\ see ure[1]

ur[3] \ər\ see eur[1]

ura \u̇r-ə\ dura, durra, Jura, sura,
surah
Agoura, bravura, caesura, datura,
Madura, tamboura, tempura
aqua pura, Arafura, Bujumbura
appoggiatura, Bonaventura,
coloratura, Telanaipura
Anuradhapura, camera obscura

urable \u̇r-ə-bəl\ curable, durable,
thurible
endurable, incurable, insurable,
perdurable

uracy \u̇r-ə-sē\ curacy
obduracy

urae \ùr-ē\ see ury[1]

urah \ür-ə\ see ura

ural \ùr-əl\ crural, jural, mural, neural, plural, puerile, rural, Ural
caesural
commissural, extramural, intramural

uralist \ùr-ə-ləst\ muralist, pluralist, ruralist

uran \ü-rən\ see urin[2]

urance \ùr-əns\ durance
assurance, endurance, insurance
coinsurance, reassurance, reinsurance

urate \ùr-ət\ curate, turret
obdurate
barbiturate

urative \ùr-ə-tiv\ curative, durative

urb \ərb\ see erb

urban[1] \ər-bən\ bourbon, Durban, rurban, turban, turbine, urban, Urban
exurban, suburban
interurban

urban[2] \ùr-bən\ bourbon, Bourbon, rurban

urber \ər-bər\ Berber, Ferber, Thurber
disturber

urbia \ər-bē-ə\ Serbia
exurbia, suburbia

urbid \ər-bəd\ turbid, verbid

urbine \ər-bən\ see urban[1]

urbit \ər-bət\ burbot, sherbet, turbit, turbot

urble \ər-bəl\ see erbal

urbot \ər-bət\ see urbit

urcate \ər-kət\ see ircuit

urch \ərch\ birch, church, Church, curch, lurch, perch, search, smirch
besmirch, Christchurch, research, unchurch

urchin \ər-chən\ birchen, urchin

urchly \ərch-lē\ churchly, virtually

urcia \ər-shə\ see ertia

urd[1] \ùrd\ see ured[1]

urd[2] \ərd\ see ird

urdane \ərd-ᵊn\ see urden

urden \ərd-ᵊn\ burden, guerdon, lurdane, verdin
disburden, unburden
overburden

urder \ərd-ər\ see erder

urderer \ərd-ər-ər\ murderer, verderer

urdle \ərd-ᵊl\ curdle, girdle, hurdle
engirdle

urdu \ər-dü\ see erdu

urdum \ərd-əm\ see irdum

urdy \ərd-ē\ birdie, sturdy, wordy
hurdy-gurdy, Mesa Verde, Monteverdi

ure[1] \ùr\ Boer, boor, bourg, cure, dour, ewer, fewer, lure, moor, Moor, Moore, Muir, poor, pure, Ruhr, sewer, skewer, spoor, stour, sure, tour, Tours, your, you're
abjure, adjure, Adour, allure, amour, Ashur, assure, brochure, ceinture, cocksure, coiffure, conjure, contour, couture, demure, detour, dirt-poor, endure, ensure, Exmoor, faubourg, Fraktur, grandeur, gravure, guipure, hachure, immure, impure, insure, inure, kultur, land-poor, langur, ligure, manure, mature, mohur, obscure, parure, perdure, procure, secure, siddur, tambour, tandoor, tenure, Uighur, unmoor, velour, velure
amateur, aperture, armature, blackamoor, carrefour, carte du jour, coinsure, commissure, confiture, connoisseur, coverture, cubature, curvature, cynosure, debouchure, embouchure, epicure, filature,

forfeiture, garniture, geniture, green-
manure, haute couture, immature,
insecure, ligature, manicure, overture,
paramour, pedicure, plat du jour,
portraiture, prelature, premature,
quadrature, reassure, Reaumur,
reinsure, saboteur, sepulture, sequitur,
signature, simon-pure, sinecure, soup
du jour, tablature, temperature,
troubadour, white amur, vavasour,
Yom Kippur
  candidature, caricature, discomfiture,
distemperature, divestiture,
entablature, entrepreneur, expenditure,
imprimatur, investiture, literature,
miniature, musculature, nomenclature,
nonsequitur
   primogeniture
   ultraminiature

ure² \ùr-ē\ see ury¹

urean \ùr-ē-ən\ see urian

ureau \ùr-ō\ see uro

ured¹ \ùrd\ gourde, Kurd, urd
  assured, steward
  underinsured
  —also -ed *forms of verbs listed at*
ure¹

ured² \ərd\ see ird

urely \ùr-lē\ buirdly, poorly, purely,
surely
  cocksurely, demurely, impurely,
maturely, obscurely
  immaturely, insecurely, prematurely

urement \ùr-mənt\ allurement,
immurement, inurement, procurement,
securement

uren \ùr-ən\ see urin²

ureous \ùr-ē-əs\ see urious

urer \ùr-ər\ curer, führer, furor,
furore, juror, lurer, tourer
  abjurer, assurer, insurer, manurer,
procurer, tambourer
  coinsurer, reinsurer
  —also -er *forms of adjectives listed*
at ure¹

urety¹ \ùr-ət-ē\ see urity

urety² \ùrt-ē\ see urti

urey \ùr-ē\ see ury¹

urf \ərf\ kerf, scurf, serf, surf, turf
  enserf
  bodysurf

urfy \ər-fē\ Murphy, scurfy, turfy

urg \ərg\ see erg

urgative \ər-gə-tiv\ see urgative

urge \ərj\ dirge, merge, purge,
scourge,serge, splurge, spurge, surge,
urge, verge
  converge, deterge, diverge, emerge,
immerge, resurge, submerge, upsurge
  dramaturge

urgence \ər-jəns\ see ergence

urgency \ər-jən-sē\ see ergency

urgent \ər-jənt\ urgent
  assurgent, convergent, detergent,
divergent, emergent, insurgent,
resurgent
  preemergent

urgeon \ər-jən\ burgeon, sturgeon,
surgeon, virgin

urger¹ \ər-gər\ burgher, turgor
  cheeseburger, hamburger, Limburger

urger² \ər-jər\ see erger

urgery \ərj-rē\ see erjury

urgh¹ \ər-ə\ see orough¹

urgh² \ər-ō\ see urrow¹

urgh³ \ərg\ see erg

urgher \ər-gər\ see urger¹

urgic \ər-jik\ see ergic

urgical \ər-ji-kəl\ surgical
  liturgical, theurgical
  dramaturgical

urgid \ər-jəd\ turgid
  synergid

urgle \ər-gəl\ burgle, gurgle

urgor \ər-gər\ see urger[1]

urgy \ər-jē\ clergy
dramaturgy, metallurgy

uri \u̇r-ē\ see ury[1]

urial[1] \u̇r-ē-əl\ curial, urial, Uriel
mercurial, seigneurial, tenurial
entrepreneurial

urial[2] \er-ē-əl\ see arial

urian \u̇r-ē-ən\ durian, Hurrian
Arthurian, centurion
epicurean

uriance \u̇r-ē-əns\ see urience

uriant \u̇r-ē-ənt\ see urient

urible[1] \u̇r-ə-bəl\ see urable

urible[2] \ər-ə-bəl\ see erable

uric \u̇r-ik\ uric
mercuric, sulfuric

urid \u̇r-əd\ lurid, murid

urie \u̇r-ē\ see ury[1]

uriel \u̇r-ē-əl\ see urial[1]

urience \u̇r-ē-əns\ prurience
luxuriance

urient \u̇r-ē-ənt\ esurient
luxuriant, parturient

urier[1] \er-ē-ər\ see errier

urier[2] \u̇r-ē-ər\ see ourier[1]

uriere \u̇r-ē-ər\ see ourier[1]

urin[1] \ər-ən\ burin, murrain

urin[2] \u̇r-ən\ burin, Huron, urine
Belgian Tervuren

urine \u̇r-ən\ see urin[2]

uring \u̇r-iŋ\ during, mooring,
touring
—also -ing forms of verbs listed at
ure[1]

urion \u̇r-ē-ən\ see urian

urious \u̇r-ē-əs\ curious, furious,
spurious
incurious, injurious, luxurious,
penurious, perjurious, sulfureous,
usurious

uris \u̇r-əs\ see urus

urist \u̇r-əst\ purist, tourist
manicurist, pedicurist
caricaturist, chiaroscurist, miniaturist
—also -est forms of adjectives listed
at ure[1]

urity \u̇r-ət-ē\ purity, surety
futurity, impurity, maturity,
obscurity, security
immaturity, insecurity, prematurity

urk \ərk\ see ork[1]

urka[1] \ər-kə\ charka, circa, Gurkha
mazurka

urka[2] \u̇r-kə\ Gurkha
mazurka

urke \ərk\ see ork[1]

urker \ər-kər\ see orker[1]

urkey \ər-kē\ see erky

urkha[1] \u̇r-kə\ see urka[2]

urkha[2] \ər-kə\ see urka[1]

urki \ər-kē\ see erky

urky \ər-kē\ see erky

url \ərl\ see irl[1]

urled \ərld\ see orld

urlew \ərl-ü\ curlew, purlieu

urlieu \ərl-ü\ see urlew

urlin \ər-lən\ see erlin

urling \ər-liŋ\ curling, hurling,
sterling
—also -ing forms of verbs listed at
irl[1]

urlish \ər-lish\ churlish, girlish

urly \ər-lē\ burley, burly, curly, early, girlie, hurly, knurly, pearly, squirrely, surly, swirly, twirly, whirly
hurly-burly

urman \ər-mən\ see erman

urmity \ər-mət-ē\ see irmity

urmur \ər-mər\ firmer, murmur, termer, wormer
infirmer

urn \ərn\ burn, churn, curn, earn, erne, fern, kern, learn, pirn, quern, spurn, stern, tern, terne, turn, urn, yearn
adjourn, astern, attorn, casern, concern, discern, downturn, epergne, eterne, extern, heartburn, intern, lucerne, nocturn, nocturne, outturn, return, sauternes, secern, sojourn, sunburn, unlearn, upturn, U-turn, windburn
Comintern, overturn, taciturn, unconcern

urnable \ər-nə-bəl\ burnable
discernible, returnable
indiscernible

urnal \ərn-ᵊl\ see ernal

urne \ərn\ see urn

urned \ərnd\ burned, durned
concerned, unearned, unlearned, well-turned, windburned
—also -ed forms of verbs listed at urn

urner \ər-nər\ burner, earner, turner
discerner, returner
afterburner

urnery \ər-nə-rē\ see ernary

urney \ər-nē\ see ourney[1]

urnian \ər-nē-ən\ see ernian

urnish \ər-nish\ burnish, furnish

urnt \ərnt\ see earnt

urnum \ər-nəm\ sternum
alburnum, laburnum, viburnum

uro \uṙ-ō\ bureau, duro, euro
enduro, maduro
politburo
chiaroscuro

uron \uṙ-ən\ see urin[2]

uror \uṙ-ər\ see urer[1]

urore \uṙ-ər\ see urer[1]

urous \uṙ-əs\ see urus

urp \ərp\ burp, chirp, slurp, stirp, twerp
usurp

urphy \ər-fē\ see urfy

urple \ər-pəl\ purple
empurple

urplice \ər-pləs\ see urplus

urplus \ər-pləs\ surplice, surplus

urps \ərps\ see irps

urr \ər\ see eur[1]

urra[1] \uṙ-ə\ see ura

urra[2] \ər-ə\ see orough[1]

urrage \ər-ij\ see ourage

urragh \ər-ə\ see orough[1]

urrain \ər-ən\ see urin[1]

urral \ər-əl\ see erral

urrant \ər-ənt\ see urrent

urray \ər-ē\ see urry

urre \ər\ see eur[1]

urred \ərd\ see ird

urrence \ər-əns\ concurrence, conference, deterrence, incurrence, occurrence, transference
countertransference

urrent \ər-ənt\ currant, current, weren't
concurrent, crosscurrent, decurrent, deterrent, occurrent, recurrent, susurrant

countercurrent, undercurrent, supercurrent

urrer \ər-ər\ see errer

urret \uṙ-ət\ see urate

urrey \ər-ē\ see urry

urrian \uṙ-ē-ən\ see urian

urrie \ər-ē\ see urry

urrier \ər-ē-ər\ courier, currier, furrier, hurrier, worrier
—*also* -er *forms of adjectives listed at* urry

urring \ər-iŋ\ furring, shirring, stirring
skiöring
—*also* -ing *forms of verbs listed at* eur[1]

urrish \ər-ish\ see ourish

urro[1] \ər-ə\ see orough[1]

urro[2] \ər-ō\ see urrow[1]

urrow[1] \ər-ō\ borough, burgh, burro, burrow, furrow, thorough

urrow[2] \ər-ə\ see orough[1]

urry \ər-ē\ blurry, burry, curry, flurry, furry, dhurrie, gurry, hurry, Moray, Murray, murrey, scurry, slurry, spurrey, surrey, Surrey, whirry, worry
hurry-scurry

ursa \ər-sə\ see ersa

ursal \ər-səl\ see ersal[1]

ursar \ər-sər\ see ursor

ursary \ərs-rē\ bursary, cursory, mercery, nursery
anniversary

urse \ərs\ see erse

ursed \ərst\ see urst

ursement \ər-smənt\ see ercement

urser \ər-sər\ see ursor

ursery \ərs-rē\ see ursary

ursion \ər-zhən\ see ersion[1]

ursionist \ərzh-nəst\ see ersionist

ursive \ər-siv\ see ersive

ursor \ər-sər\ bursar, cursor, mercer, nurser, purser, worser
disburser, disperser, precursor, rehearser, reverser, traverser

ursory \ərs-rē\ see ursary

urst \ərst\ burst, cursed, durst, erst, first, Hearst, thirst, verst, worst, wurst
accursed, airburst, Amherst, athirst, cloudburst, downburst, emersed, feetfirst, groundburst, headfirst, outburst, sunburst
liverwurst, microburst
—*also* -ed *forms of verbs listed at* erse

ursus \ər-səs\ see ersus

ursy[1] \ər-sē\ see ercy

ursy[2] \əs-ē\ see ussy

urt[1] \uṙt\ yurt
Erfurt, Frankfurt
Betancourt

urt[2] \ərt\ see ert[1]

urtain \ərt-ᵊn\ see ertain

urtal \ərt-ᵊl\ see ertile

urtenance \ərt-ᵊn-əns\ see ertinence

urtenant \ərt-nənt\ see irtinent

urter \ərt-ər\ see erter

urtesy \ərt-ə-sē\ see ourtesy

urthen \ər-thən\ burthen, earthen

urther \ər-thər\ further, murther

urti \uṙt-ē\ pretty, surety
Trimurti

urtium \ər-shəm\ nasturtium, sestertium

urtive \ərt-iv\ see ertive

urtle \ərt-ᵊl\ see ertile

urton \ərt-ᵊn\ see ertain

urture \ər-chər\ see ircher

uru \ùr-ü\ guru, kuru
Nauru

urus \ùr-əs\ urus, Arcturus,
mercurous, sulfurous
Epicurus, sui juris
tinea cruris

urve \ərv\ see erve

urved \ərvd\ see erved

urviness \ər-vē-nəs\ see erviness

urvy \ər-vē\ curvy, nervy, scurvy
topsy-turvy

ury¹ \ùr-ē\ curie, Curie, fleury, fury,
houri, Jewry, jury, Kure, Urey
Bhojpuri, de jure, Missouri, tandoori
lusus naturae

ury² \er-ē\ see ary¹

urze \ərz\ see ers

urzy \ər-zē\ see ersey

us¹ \əs\ bus, buss, crus, cuss, fuss,
Gus, Huss, muss, plus, pus, Russ,
suss, thus, truss, us
airbus, concuss, cost-plus, discuss,
nonplus, percuss, railbus, untruss
autobus, blunderbuss, microbus,
minibus

us² \ü\ see ew¹

us³ \üs\ see use¹

us⁴ \üsh\ see ouche

us⁵ \üz\ see use²

usa¹ \ü-sə\ Sousa
Azusa, Medusa
Appaloosa, Gebel Musa, Jebel Musa

usa² \ü-zə\ Sousa, Susa
Medusa
Arethusa

usable \ü-zə-bəl\ fusible, losable,
usable
abusable, diffusible, excusable,
infusible, reusable, transfusible
inexcusable, irrecusable

usae \ü-sē\ see uicy

usal¹ \ü-səl\ streusel
occlusal

usal² \ü-zəl\ foozle, fusil, ouzel,
snoozle, streusel
accusal, bamboozle, occlusal,
perusal, refusal

usc \əsk\ see usk

uscan \əs-kən\ buskin, Ruskin,
Tuscan
Etruscan, molluscan

uscat \əs-kət\ see usket

uscle \əs-əl\ see ustle

uscular \əs-kyə-lər\ muscular
corpuscular, crepuscular, majuscular

uscule \əs-kyül\ crepuscule,
opuscule

use¹ \üs\ Bruce, crouse, crus, cruse,
deuce, douce, goose, juice, loose,
moose, mousse, noose, nous, puce,
rhus, ruse, Russ, schuss, sluice,
spruce, truce, use, Zeus
Aarhus, abstruse, abuse, adduce,
Arhus, Atreus, burnoose, caboose,
Cayuse, Cepheus, ceruse, conduce,
couscous, deduce, diffuse, disuse,
educe, effuse, excuse, footloose,
induce, Lanús, misuse, mongoose,
Morpheus, negus, obtuse, Orpheus,
papoose, Peleus, Perseus, prepuce,
produce, profuse, Proteus, Purus,
recluse, reduce, refuse, retuse, reuse,
Sanctus, seduce, Tereus, Theseus,
traduce, transduce, unloose, vamoose
Belarus, Betelgeuse, calaboose,
charlotte russe, introduce, mass-
produce, Odysseus, Prometheus,
reproduce, self-abuse, Syracuse,
Typhoeus

hypotenuse
Sancti Spiritus

use² \üz\ blues, booze, bruise,
choose, cruise, cruse, Druze, flews,
fuse, Hughes, lose, Meuse, muse,
news, ooze, roose, ruse, schmooze,
snooze, trews, use, whose
abuse, accuse, amuse, Andrews,
bemuse, berceuse, chanteuse,
chartreuse, coiffeuse, confuse,
contuse, danseuse, defuse, diffuse,
diseuse, disuse, effuse, Elbrus,
enthuse, excuse, ill-use, infuse,
masseuse, misuse, perfuse, peruse,
recluse, recuse, refuse, reuse, suffuse,
Toulouse, transfuse, vendeuse
Betelgeuse, disabuse, interfuse,
mitrailleuse, Newport News, p's and
q's, Santa Cruz, Vera Cruz
Goody Two-shoes

used \üzd\ used
confused
underused
—*also* -ed *forms of verbs listed at*
use²

useless \ü-sləs\ juiceless, useless

user \ü-zər\ boozer, bruiser,
chooser, cruiser, doozer, loser,
snoozer, user
abuser, accuser, amuser, diffuser,
excuser, infuser, peruser
multiuser

ush¹ \əsh\ blush, brush, crush, Cush,
flush, gush, hush, lush, mush, plush,
rush, shush, slush, squush, thrush, tush
airbrush, bulrush, bum's rush,
hairbrush, hush-hush, inrush,
nailbrush, onrush, paintbrush,
sagebrush, toothbrush, uprush
bottlebrush, Hindu Kush, underbrush

ush² \ùsh\ bush, Bush, mush, push,
shush, squoosh, swoosh, tush, whoosh
ambush, rosebush, thornbush
Hindu Kush

ushabel \ə-shə-bəl\ crushable,
flushable

usher¹ \əsh-ər\ blusher, brusher,
crusher, gusher, musher, rusher, usher
four-flusher, goldrusher
—*also* -er *forms of adjectives listed*
at ush¹

usher² \ùsh-ər\ pusher
ambusher

ushi \ùsh-ē\ see ushy²

ushing \əsh-iŋ\ onrushing,
toothbrushing, unblushing
—*also* -ing *forms of verbs listed at*
ush¹

ushu \ü-shü\ Kyushu
Kitakyushu

ushy¹ \əsh-ē\ brushy, gushy, mushy,
plushy, rushy, slushy

ushy² \ùsh-ē\ bushy, cushy, mushy,
pushy, sushi

usi \ü-sē\ see uicy

usian \ü-zhən\ see usion

usible¹ \ü-sə-bəl\ see ucible

usible² \ü-zə-bəl\ see usable

usic \ü-zik\ music
Tungusic

usie \ü-zē\ see oozy

usil \ü-zəl\ see usal²

using \əs-iŋ\ busing, trussing
antibusing
—*also* -ing *forms of verbs listed at*
us¹

usion \ü-zhən\ fusion
affusion, allusion, Carthusian,
collusion, conclusion, confusion,
contusion, delusion, diffusion,
effusion, elusion, exclusion, extrusion,
illusion, inclusion, infusion, intrusion,
Malthusian, obtrusion, occlusion,
perfusion, prelusion, profusion,
prolusion, protrusion, reclusion,
seclusion, transfusion, Venusian
Andalusian, disillusion,
malocclusion
autotransfusion

usionist \üzh-nəst\ fusionist
diffusionist, exclusionist, illusionist,
perfusionist

usity \ü-sət-ē\ see ucity

usive \ü-siv\ abusive, allusive,
amusive, collusive, conclusive,
conducive, delusive, diffusive,
effusive, elusive, exclusive, extrusive,
illusive, inclusive, intrusive, obtrusive,
occlusive, prelusive, protrusive,
reclusive
inconclusive

usk \əsk\ brusque, cusk, dusk, husk,
musk, rusk, tusk
subfusc

usker \əs-kər\ busker, husker, tusker

usket \əs-kət\ muscat, musket

uskie \əs-kē\ see usky

uskin \əs-kən\ see uscan

usky \əs-kē\ dusky, husky, muskie,
musky

usly \əs-lē\ pussley, thusly

uso \ü-sō\ see usoe

usoe \ü-sō\ trousseau, whoso
Caruso
Robinson Crusoe

usory \üs-ə-rē\ delusory, illusory,
prolusory

usque \əsk\ see usk

uss¹ \us\ puss, Russ, schuss
chartreuse, sea puss, sourpuss
glamour-puss, octopus, platypus

uss² \üs\ see use¹

uss³ \əs\ see us¹

ussant \əs-ᵊnt\ mustn't
discussant

ussate \əs-ət\ see usset

usse \üs\ see use¹

ussel \əs-əl\ see ustle

ussell \əs-əl\ see ustle

usset \əs-ət\ gusset, russet
decussate

ussia \əsh-ə\ Prussia, Russia
Belorussia

ussian \əsh-ən\ see ussion

ussing \əs-iŋ\ see using

ussion \əsh-ən\ Prussian, Russian
concussion, discussion, percussion
Belorussian, repercussion

ussive \əs-iv\ jussive, tussive
concussive, percussive
repercussive

ussle \əs-əl\ see ustle

ussley \əs-lē\ see usly

ussy \əs-ē\ fussy, hussy, mussy,
pursy, pussy

ust¹ \əst\ bust, crust, dost, dust, gust,
just, lust, must, musth, rust, thrust,
trust, wast
adjust, adust, august, combust,
degust, disgust, distrust, encrust,
entrust, mistrust, moondust, piecrust,
robust, stardust, upthrust
antitrust, dryasdust, unitrust,
wanderlust
—also -ed *forms of verbs listed at*
us¹

ust² \əs\ see us¹

ust³ \üst\ see oost

ustable \əs-tə-bəl\ see ustible

ustard \əs-tərd\ bustard, custard,
mustard
—also -ed *forms of verbs listed at*
uster

usted \əs-təd\ busted
disgusted
maladjusted, well-adjusted
—also -ed *forms of verbs listed at*
ust¹

uster \əs-tər\ bluster, buster, cluster, Custer, duster, fluster, luster, muster, thruster
adjuster, blockbuster, combustor, deluster, gangbuster, lackluster, sodbuster, trustbuster
antitruster, filibuster

ustful \əst-fəl\ lustful, thrustful, trustful
distrustful

usth \əst\ see ust[1]

ustian \əs-chən\ see ustion

ustible \əs-tə-bəl\ adjustable, combustible
incombustible

ustin \əs-tən\ Justin
Augustine

ustine \əs-tən\ see ustin

ustic \əs-tik\ fustic, rustic

ustion \əs-chən\ fustian
combustion

ustious \əs-chəs\ robustious, rumbustious

ustive \əs-tiv\ adjustive, combustive
maladjustive

ustle \əs-əl\ bustle, hustle, muscle, mussel, Russell, rustle, trestle, tussle
corpuscle, crepuscle, Jack Russell

ustn't \əs-ᵊnt\ see ussant

ustom \əs-təm\ custom, frustum
accustom
disaccustom

ustor \əs-tər\ see uster

ustrious \əs-trē-əs\ illustrious, industrious

ustrous \əs-trəs\ blustrous, lustrous

ustule \əs-chül\ frustule, pustule

ustum \əs-təm\ see ustom

ustus \əs-təs\ Justus
Augustus

usty \əs-tē\ busty, crusty, dusty, fusty, gusty, lusty, musty, rusty, trusty

usy \iz-ē\ see izzy

ut[1] \ət\ but, butt, cut, glut, gut, hut, jut, mutt, nut, putt, rut, scut, shut, slut, smut, soot, strut, tut, ut, what
abut, beechnut, catgut, chestnut, clean-cut, clear-cut, cobnut, cockshut, crosscut, groundnut, haircut, locknut, offcut, peanut, pignut, rebut, recut, rotgut, shortcut, somewhat, tut-tut, uncut, walnut, woodcut
butternut, congregate, hazelnut, overcut, scuttlebutt, undercut, uppercut
open-and-shut

ut[2] \ü\ see ew[1]

ut[3] \üt\ see ute

ut[4] \u̇t\ see oot[1]

uta \üt-ə\ Baruta, likuta, valuta

utable \üt-ə-bəl\ mutable, scrutable, suitable
commutable, computable, disputable, immutable, inscrutable, permutable, statutable
executable, incommutable, incomputable, indisputable, irrefutable, prosecutable, substitutable

utage \üt-ij\ see ootage[1]

utal \üt-ᵊl\ see utile

utan \üt-ᵊn\ cutin, gluten, Luton, mutine, Newton, Teuton
Laputan, rambutan, Rasputin
highfalutin

utant \üt-ᵊnt\ mutant
disputant, pollutant

utative \üt-ət-iv\ putative
commutative, imputative

utch[1] \əch\ clutch, crutch, cutch, dutch, Dutch, grutch, hutch, much, scutch, smutch, such, touch
nonesuch, retouch
double-clutch, overmuch

utch² \ùch\ butch, putsch

utcher \əch-ər\ scutcher
retoucher

utchy \əch-ē\ see uchy

ute \üt\ boot, bruit, brut, brute, bute,
Bute, butte, chute, cloot, coot, cute,
flute, fruit, glout, hoot, jute, Jute, loot,
lute, moot, mute, newt, pood, root,
Root, rout, route, scoot, scute, shoot,
snoot, soot, suit, suite, toot, tout, ut,
Ute
  acute, astute, Asyût, beetroot, Beirut,
birthroot, bloodroot, breadfruit, butut,
cahoot, Canute, cheroot, clubroot,
commute, compute, confute,
crapshoot, deaf-mute, depute, dilute,
dispute, elute, en route, enroot,
folkmoot, freeboot, galoot, grapefruit,
hardboot, hirsute, imbrute, impute,
jackboot, jackfruit, jumpsuit, kashruth,
lawsuit, minute, nonsuit, offshoot,
outshoot, Paiute, pantsuit, permute,
playsuit, pollute, pursuit, recruit,
refute, repute, salute, seaboot,
snowsuit, solute, sunsuit, swimsuit,
taproot, tracksuit, transmute, uproot,
volute
  absolute, Aleut, arrowroot, Asyût,
attribute, autoroute, bandicoot,
bitterroot, bodysuit, boilersuit,
bumbershoot, constitute, convolute,
Denver boot, destitute, disrepute,
dissolute, evolute, execute, gingerroot,
institute, involute, kiwifruit,
malamute, overshoot, parachute,
persecute, prosecute, prostitute, qiviut,
resolute, restitute, revolute, subacute,
substitute, troubleshoot, undershoot
  electrocute, Hardecanute, Inuktitut,
irresolute, reconstitute

uted \üt-əd\ see ooted¹

utee \üt-ē\ see ooty¹

utely \üt-lē\ cutely, mutely
accutely, astutely, minutely
absolutely, dissolutely
irresolutely

uten \üt-ᵊn\ see utan

uteness \üt-nəs\ cuteness,
glutenous, glutinous, muteness,
mutinous
acuteness, diluteness, hirsuteness
absoluteness, destituteness,
dissoluteness
irresoluteness

utenist \üt-ᵊn-əst\ lutenist, Teutonist

utenous \üt-nəs\ see uteness

uteous \üt-ē-əs\ beauteous, duteous,
gluteus, luteous

uter \üt-ər\ cooter, neuter, fluter,
hooter, looter, pewter, rooter, router,
scooter, shooter, souter, suiter, suitor,
tooter, tutor
  accoutre, commuter, computer,
confuter, crapshooter, diluter, disputer,
freebooter, peashooter, recruiter,
saluter, sharpshooter, six-shooter,
trapshooter, two-suiter, zoot-suiter
  coadjutor, executor, instituter,
persecutor, prosecutor, prostitutor,
troubleshooter
  microcomputer, minicomputer
superminicomputer
  —also -er forms of adjectives listed
at ute

utes \üts\ see oots

uteus \üt-ē-əs\ see uteous

uth¹ \üt\ see ute

uth² \üth\ see ooth²

uther¹ \ü-thər\ Luther, Uther

uther² \ə-ther\ see other¹

uthful \üth-fəl\ ruthful, truthful,
youthful
untruthful

uthless \üth-ləs\ ruthless, toothless

uti \üt-ē\ see ooty¹

utia \ü-shə\ fuchsia
minutia, Saint Lucia

utian \ü-shən\ see ution

utic \üt-ik\ maieutic, scorbutic, toreutic
hermeneutic, parachutic, propaedeutic, therapeutic

utical \üt-i-kəl\ cuticle
hermeneutical, pharmaceutical

uticle \üt-i-kəl\ see utical

utie \üt-ē\ see ooty[1]

utiful \üt-i-fəl\ beautiful, dutiful

utile \üt-ᵊl\ brutal, cuittle, footle, futile, tootle, utile
inutile
Kwakiutl

utin \üt-ᵊn\ see utan

utine \üt-ᵊn\ see utan

uting \üt-iŋ\ fluting, luting, suiting
hip-shooting, sharpshooting, trapshooting
—also -ing forms of verbs listed at ute

utinous[1] \üt-ᵊn-əs\ glutinous, mutinous

utinous[2] \üt-nəs\ see uteness

utiny \üt-ᵊn-ē\ mutiny, scrutiny

ution \ü-shən\ Lucian
ablution, Aleutian, capuchin, Confucian, dilution, elution, locution, pollution, solution
absolution, allocution, attribution, comminution, consecution, constitution, contribution, convolution, destitution, devolution, diminution, dissolution, distribution, elocution, evolution, execution, exsolution, institution, involution, lilliputian, persecution, prosecution, prostitution, resolution, restitution, retribution, revolution, Rosicrucian, substitution
antipollution, circumlocution, electrocution, irresolution, maldistribution, reconstitution, redistribution

utionary \ü-shə-ner-ē\ illocutionary, revolutionary

utionist \ü-shnəst\ devolutionist, elocutionist, evolutionist, revolutionist
redistributionist

utish \üt-ish\ brutish, Vutish

utist \üt-əst\ chutist, flutist
absolutist, parachutist, therapeutist
—also -est forms of adjectives listed at ute

utive \üt-iv\ dilutive
constitutive, persecutive, substitutive

utl \ü-tᵊl\ see utile

utland \ət-lənd\ Jutland, Rutland

utlass \ət-ləs\ cutlass, gutless

utler \ət-lər\ butler, Butler, cutler, sutler

utless \ət-ləs\ see utlass

utlet \ət-lət\ cutlet, nutlet

utment \ət-mənt\ hutment
abutment

utney \ət-nē\ chutney, gluttony
Ascutney

uto \üt-ō\ Bhutto, Pluto, putto
Basuto, cornuto, Maputo, tenuto
sostenuto

uton \üt-ⁿ\ see utan

utor \üt-ər\ see uter

utriment \ü-trə-mənt\ nutriment
accoutrement

uts \əts\ see utz

utsch \u̇ch\ see utch[2]

utsi \üt-sē\ see uzzi[2]

utsk \ütsk\ Irkutsk, Yakutsk

utsy \ət-sē\ gutsy, klutzy

utt \ət\ see ut[1]

uttack \ət-ək\ see uttock

uttal \ət-ᵊl\ see uttle

utte \üt\ see ute

uttee \ət-ē\ see utty

utter¹ \ət-ər\ butter, clutter, cutter, flutter, gutter, mutter, nutter, putter, scutter, shutter, splutter, sputter, strutter, stutter, utter
   abutter, aflutter, haircutter, price-cutter, rebutter, stonecutter, unclutter, woodcutter

utter² \ùt-ər\ see ooter¹

uttery \ət-ə-rē\ buttery, fluttery, spluttery

utti¹ \üt-ē\ see ooty¹

utti² \ùt-ē\ see ooty²

utting \ùt-iŋ\ see ooting¹

uttish \ət-ish\ ruttish, sluttish

uttle \ət-ᵊl\ cuittle, scuttle, shuttle, subtile, subtle
   rebuttal

utto \üt-ō\ see uto

uttock \ət-ək\ buttock, Cuttack, futtock

utton \ət-ᵊn\ button, glutton, mutton, Sutton
   keybutton, unbutton
   leg-of-mutton

uttony \ət-nē\ see utney

utty \ət-ē\ butty, gutty, jutty, nutty, puttee, putty, rutty, smutty

utum \üt-əm\ scutum, sputum

uture \ü-chər\ blucher, future, moocher, suture

uty \üt-ē\ see ooty¹

utz \əts\ futz, klutz, lutz, nuts
   blood-and-guts
   —*also* -s, -'s, *and* -s' *forms of nouns, and* -s *forms of verbs, listed at* ut¹

utzy \ət-sē\ see utsy

uu \ü\ see ew¹

uvial \ü-vē-əl\ fluvial, pluvial
   alluvial, colluvial, diluvial, eluvial

uvian \ü-vē-ən\ alluvion, diluvian, Peruvian, vesuvian, Vesuvian
   postdiluvian
   antediluvian

uvion \ü-vē-ən\ see uvian

uvium \ü-vē-əm\ alluvium, colluvium, effluvium, eluvium

ux¹ \əks\ crux, flux, lux, tux
   afflux, aw-shucks, conflux, deluxe, efflux, influx, redux, reflux
   Benelux
   —*also* -s, -'s, *and* -s' *forms of nouns, and* -s *forms of verbs, listed at* uck¹

ux² \ùks\ see ooks²

uxe¹ \üks\ see ooks¹

uxe² \ùks\ see ooks²

uxe³ \əks\ see ux¹

uxion \ək-shən\ see uction

uy \ī\ see y¹

uygur \ē-gər\ see eager

uyot \ē-ō\ see io²

uyp \īp\ see ipe

uz¹ \üts\ see oots

uz² \ùz\ see use²

uze \üz\ see use²

uzz \əz\ see euse¹

uzzi¹ \ü-zē\ see oozy

uzzi² \üt-sē\ Tutsi
   Abruzzi

uzzle \əz-əl\ guzzle, muzzle, nuzzle, puzzle

uzzler \əz-lər\ guzzler, puzzler
   gas-guzzler

uzzy \əz-ē\ fuzzy, muzzy, scuzzy

Y

y^1 \ī\ ai, ay, aye, bi, buy, by, bye, chi, cry, die, dry, dye, eye, fie, fly, fry, guy, Guy, hi, hie, high, i, I, lie, lye, my, nigh, phi, pi, pie, ply, pry, psi, rye, scythe, sei, shy, sigh, sky, sly, spry, spy, sty, Tai, Thai, thigh, thy, tie, try, vie, why, wry, wye, xi, Y
  aby, agley, air-dry, ally, Altai, anti, apply, assai, awry, aye-aye, Bacchae, Baha'i, banzai, barfly, Belgae, belie, bigeye, birds-eye, blackfly, blow-dry, blowby, blowfly, blue-sky, Bottai, bone-dry, bonsai, botfly, Brunei, buckeye, bugeye, bulls-eye, bye-bye, canaille, catchfly, cat's-eye, cockeye, cockshy, comply, cross-eye, deadeye, decry, deep-fry, deep-sky, deerfly, defy, Delphi, deny, descry, drip-dry, Dubai, elhi, Eli, espy, firefly, fish-eye, flyby, forby, freeze-dry, frogeye, gadfly, gallfly, GI, good-bye, greenfly, grisaille, gun-shy, Haggai, Hawkeye, hereby, hi-fi, hog-tie, horsefly, housefly, imply, jai alai, July, Katmai, Kaui, Kenai, knee-high, lanai, Lanai, lay-by, Levi, magpie, mao-tai, Masai, medfly, Moirai, mooneye, nearby, necktie, nisi, outbye, outcry, oxeye, Panay, panfry, Parcae, piece-dye, pigsty, pinkeye, Po Hai, pop eye, potpie, Qinghai, quasi, rabbi, red-eye, rely, reply, re-try, rocaille, rough-dry, Sakai, sci-fi, semi, Sendai, serai, shanghai, Shanghai, shoofly, shut-eye, Sinai, sky-high, small-fry, sockeye, stand by, standby, stir-fry, supply, swing-by, terai, test-fly, thereby, tie-dye, titi, tongue-tie, two-ply, untie, Versailles, walleye, watcheye, well-nigh, whereby, whitefly, wise guy, worms-eye
  Adonai, alibi, alkali, amplify, apple-pie, argufy, basify, beautify, butterfly,

by-and-by, calcify, certify, Chou En-lai, citify, clarify, classify, cockneyfy, codify, crucify, cut-and-dry, DIY, damnify, damselfly, dandify, deify, densify, dignify, dobsonfly, do-or-die, dragonfly, edify, falsify, fancify, fortify, frenchify, fructify, gasify, Gemini, gentrify, glorify, goggle-eye, goldeneye, gratify, Haggai, hexerei, horrify, Iceni, justify, lignify, liquefy, lithify, Lorelei, lullaby, Madurai, magnify, Malachi, Maracay, modify, mollify, Molokai, Mordecai, mortify, multi-ply, multiply, mummify, mystify, nazify, nitrify, notify, nullify, occupy, Olduvai, ossify, overbuy, overfly, overlie, pacify, Paraguay, passerby, peccavi, petrify, PPI, preachify, prettify, prophesy, purify, putrefy, qualify, quantify, ramify, rarefy, ratify, RBI, rectify, reify, res gestae, resupply, Russify, samurai, sanctify, satisfy, scarify, semidry, signify, simplify, sine die, specify, speechify, stratify, stultify, stupefy, Tenebrae, terrify, testify, tigcreye, typify, uglify, ultrahigh, underlie, unify, Uruguay, Veneti, verify, versify, vilify, vinify, vitrify, vivify, zombify
  acetify, acidify, a priori, beatify, decertify, declassify, demystify, denazify, detoxify, Dioscuri, disqualify, dissatisfy, diversify, electrify, exemplify, facetiae, Helvetii, humidify, identify, indemnify, intensify, objectify, personify, preoccupy, reliquiae, reunify, revivify, rigidify, saponify, solemnify, solidify, syllabify, transmogrify, undersupply, vox populi
  a fortiori, caravanserai, corpus delicti, deacidify, dehumidify, ex

hypothesi, modus vivendi, nolle prosequi, oversimplify
  amicus curiae, curriculum vitae, modus operandi

y² \ē\ see ee[1]

ya \ē-ə\ see ia[1]

yable \ī-ə-bəl\ see iable[1]

yad \ī-əd\ dryad, dyad, naiad, sayyid, triad
  hamadryad, jeremiad

yan \ī-ən\ see ion[1]

yant \ī-ənt\ see iant

yatt \ī-ət\ see iet

ybe \īb\ see ibe[1]

ybele \ib-ə-lē\ Cybele
  ambiboly

yber \ī-bər\ see iber

ybia \i-bē-ə\ see ibia

ybris \ī-brəs\ see ibrous

ycad \ī-kəd\ cycad, spiked

ycan \ī-kən\ see ichen[1]

yce \īs\ see ice[1]

ych¹ \ik\ see ick

ych² \īk\ see ike[2]

yche \ī-kē\ see ike[1]

ychnis \ik-nəs\ see ickness

ycia \ish-ə\ see itia[1]

ycian \ish-ən\ see ition

ycin \īs-ᵊn\ see ison[1]

ycle¹ \ī-kəl\ cycle, Michael recycle
  Calvin cycle, epicycle, Exercycle, hemicycle, kilocycle, motorcycle, unicycle, Wanne-Eickel

ycle² \ik-əl\ see ickle

ycler \ik-lər\ see ickler

yd \ü-id\ see uid

yde \īd\ see ide[1]

ydia \i-dē-ə\ see idia

ydian \id-ē-ən\ see idian

ydice \id-ə-sē\ see idice

ydney \id-nē\ see idney

ye \ī\ see y[1]

yeable \ī-ə-bəl\ see iable[1]

yed \īd\ see ide[1]

yer \īr\ see ire[1]

yeth \ī-əth\ see iath[1]

yfe \īf\ see ife[1]

yfed \ər-əd\ see oved

yg \ig\ see ig

ygamous \ig-ə-məs\ see igamous

ygamy \ig-ə-mē\ see igamy

ygia \ī-jə\ see ijah

ygian \i-jən\ Phrygian, pidgin, pigeon, smidgen, stygian, wigeon religion
  callipygian, Cantabrigian, irreligion

ygiene \ī-jēn\ see aijin

ygma \ig-mə\ see igma

ygnet \ig-nət\ cygnet, signet

ygnus \ig-nəs\ see igness

ygos \ī-gəs\ see ygous

ygous \ī-gəs\ gigas azygos
  callipygous, hemizygous, homozygous steatopygous

ygrapher \ig-rə-fər\ see igrapher

ygraphist \ig-rə-fəst\ see igraphist

ygyny \ij-ə-nē\ see igine

ying \ī-iŋ\ crying, flying, lying, trying
high-flying, low-lying, outlying, undying
nitrifying, terrifying, underlying

yke \īk\ see ike²

yked \īkt\ see iked¹

yl \ēl\ see eal²

ylan \il-ən\ see illon

ylar \ī-lər\ see ilar

yle \īl\ see ile¹

ylem \ī-ləm\ see ilum

yler \ī-lər\ see ilar

ylet \ī-lət\ see ilot

yley \ī-lē\ see yly

yli \ē-lē\ see eely

ylic \il-ik\ see ilic

ylie \ī-lē\ see yly

yling \ī-liŋ\ see iling¹

yll \īl\ see ile¹

ylla \il-ə\ see illa²

yllable \il-ə-bəl\ see illable

yllary \il-ə-rē\ see illary

yllic \il-ik\ see ilic

yllis \il-əs\ see illus

yllium \il-ē-əm\ see ilium

yllo¹ \ē-lō\ see ilo²

yllo² \ī-lō\ see ilo¹

ylum \ī-ləm\ see ilum

ylus \ī-ləs\ see ilus

yly \ī-lē\ dryly, highly, maile, Philae, riley, shyly, slyly, smiley, Wiley, wily, Wyley, wryly
life of Riley

ym \im\ see im¹

yma \ī-mə\ Chaima, cyma

yman \ī-mən\ see imen

ymathy \im-ə-thē\ see imothy

ymbal \im-bəl\ see imble

ymbalist \im-bə-ləst\ cymbalist, symbolist

ymbol \im-bəl\ see imble

ymbolist \im-bə-ləst\ see ymbalist

yme \īm\ see ime¹

ymeless \īm-ləs\ see imeless

ymen \ī-mən\ see imen

ymer \ī-mər\ see imer¹

ymic¹ \ī-mik\ thymic
enzymic

ymic² \im-ik\ gimmick, mimic
bulimic
acronymic, antonymic, eponymic, homonymic, matronymic, metonymic, patronymic, synonymic, toponymic

ymical \im-i-kəl\ see imical

ymie \ī-mē\ see imy

ymion \im-ē-ən\ see imian

ymity \im-ət-ē\ see imity

ymmetry \im-ə-trē\ see imetry

ymn \im\ see im¹

ymp \imp\ see imp

ymph \imf\ lymph, nymph

ymric \im-rik\ Cymric, limerick

ymus \ī-məs\ see imis

ymy \ī-mē\ see imy

yn \in\ see in¹

ynah \ī-nə\ see ina¹

ynast \ī-nəst\ see inist¹

ynch¹ \inch\ see inch

ynch² \iŋk\ see ink

yncher \in-chər\ see incher

ynd \īnd\ see ind¹

yndic \in-dik\ see indic

yne \īn\ see ine¹

yness \ī-nəs\ see inus¹

ynia \in-ē-ə\ see inia

ynic \in-ik\ see inic²

ynical \in-i-kəl\ see inical

ynn \in\ see in¹

ynne \in\ see in¹

ynth \inth\ see inth

ynthia \in-thē-ə\ see inthia

ynx \iŋs\ see inx

yon \ī-ən\ see ion¹

yone \ī-ə-nē\ see yony

yony \ī-ə-nē\ bryony
Alcyone

yp \ip\ see ip

ypal \ī-pəl\ typal
disciple
archetypal, prototypal

ype \īp\ see ipe

yper \ī-pər\ see iper

ypey \ī-pē\ see ipy

yph \if\ see iff

yphen \ī-fən\ hyphen, siphon

yphic \if-ik\ see ific

yphony \if-ə-nē\ see iphony

ypic \ip-ik\ typic
philippic
genotypic, holotypic
stereotypic

yping \ī-piŋ\ see iping

ypo \ī-pō\ hypo, typo

ypress \ī-prəs\ cypress, Cyprus,
viperous

yprus \ī-prəs\ see ypress

ypse \ips\ see ips

ypso \ip-sō\ see ipso

ypsy \ip-sē\ gypsy, Gypsy, tipsy

ypt \ipt\ see ipt

yptian \ip-shən\ see iption

yptic \ip-tik\ cryptic, diptych,
styptic, triptych
ecliptic, elliptic
apocalyptic

ypy \ī-pē\ see ipy

yr \ir\ see eer²

yra \ī-rə\ Ira, Lyra, Myra, naira
bell-lyra, hegira, hetaira, palmyra
spirogyra

yral \ī-rəl\ see iral

yrant \ī-rənt\ see irant

yre \īr\ see ire¹

yreal \ir-ē-əl\ see erial

yria \ir-ē-ə\ see eria¹

yriad \ir-ē-əd\ see eriod

yrian \ir-ē-ən\ see erian¹

yric¹ \ī-rik\ pyric
oneiric
panegyric

yric² \ir-ik\ see eric²

yrical \ir-i-kəl\ see erical²

yrie¹ \ir-ē\ see eary

yrie² \ī-rē\ see iary¹

yril \ir-əl\ see eral¹

yrist \ir-əst\ see erist¹

yrium \ir-ē-əm\ see erium

yrna \ər-nə\ see erna

yro[1] \ī-rō\ biro, Cairo, gyro, Gyro, tyro

yro[2] \ir-ō\ see ero[3]

yron \īr-ən\ see iren

yros \ī-rəs\ see irus

yrrh \ər\ see eur[1]

yrrha \ir-ə\ see era[2]

yrrhic \ir-ik\ see eric[2]

yrrhus \ir-əs\ see erous

yrse \ərs\ see erse

yrsus \ər-səs\ see ersus

yrtle \ərt-ᵊl\ see ertile

yrup \ər-əp\ see irrup

yrupy \ər-ə-pē\ see irrupy

yrus \ī-rəs\ see irus

ysail \ī-səl\ see isal[1]

ysch \ish\ see ish[1]

yse \īs\ see ice[1]

ysh \ish\ see ish[1]

ysia[1] \ish-ə\ see itia

ysia[2] \izh-ə\ see isia

ysian[1] \is-ē-ən\ Piscean
Odyssean
Dionysian

ysian[2] \ish-ən\ see ition

ysian[3] \izh-ən\ see ision

ysian[4] \ī-sē-ən\ see iscean[1]

ysical \iz-i-kəl\ physical, quizzical
metaphysical

ysis \ī-səs\ see isis

ysm \iz-əm\ see ism

ysmal \iz-məl\ dismal
abysmal, baptismal
cataclysmal, catechismal

yson \īs-ᵊn\ see ison[1]

yss \is\ see iss[1]

yssal \is-əl\ see istle

yssean \is-ē-ən\ see ysian[1]

ysseus \ish-əs\ see icious[1]

yssum \is-əm\ see issome

yssus \is-əs\ see issus

yst \ist\ see ist[2]

ystal \is-tᵊl\ see istal

yster[1] \is-tər\ see ister

yster[2] \ī-stər\ see eister[1]

ystery \is-trē\ see istory

ystic \is-tik\ see istic

ystical \is-ti-kəl\ see istical

ystine \is-tən\ see iston

ysus[1] \ē-səs\ see esis

ysus[2] \ī-səs\ see isis

yta \īt-ə\ see ita[1]

yte \īt\ see ite[1]

yterate \it-ə-rət\ see iterate

ytes \īt-ēz\ see ites

ythe[1] \ī\ see y[1]

ythe[2] \īth\ see ithe[1]

ythia \ith-ē-ə\ lithia, Scythia
forsythia
stichomythia

ythian \ith-ē-ən\ Pythian, Scythian

ythmic \ith-mik\ rhythmic
arrhythmic, eurythmic
logarithmic

ythy \i-thē\ see ithy

ytic \it-ik\ see itic

ytical \it-i-kəl\ see itical

ytics \it-iks\ see itics

yting \īt-iŋ\ see iting

ytis \ī-təs\ see itis

ytton \it-ᵊn\ see itten

yve \īv\ see ive[1]

yx \iks\ see ix[1]

yxia \ik-sē-ə\ see ixia

yxie \ik-sē\ see ixie

yze \īz\ see ize